THE
POOR MAN'S
CONCORDANCE
&
DICTIONARY

by Robert Hawker

Solid Ground Christian Books
Birmingham, Alabama USA

Solid Ground Christian Books
2090 Columbiana Rd. Suite 2000
Birmingham AL 35216
205-443-0311
sgcb@charter.net
http://solid-ground-books.com

The Poor Man's Concordance and Dictionary
by Robert Hawker (1753-1827)

Taken from the 1828 edition by Ebenezer Palmer of London

ISBN – 1-932474-46-3

Acknowledgements

This reprint of Robert Hawker's *Poor Man's Old and New Testament Commentary and Concordance and Dictionary* has been accomplished, in God's good providence, by the assistance of many in the United States and England, who desire to see this excellent work made available to the public again. We wish to acknowledge and express thanks to them for their work and generosity. The following churches provided funds for the layout and printing costs.

Bethel Baptist Church
Spring Lake, North Carolina
Rupert Rivenbark, Pastor

Sovereign Grace Baptist Church
The Dalles, Oregon
Norm Wells, Pastor

Grace Baptist Church of Danville
Danville, Kentucky
Don Fortner, Pastor

The
Poor Man's Concordance

And

Dictionary To The Sacred Scriptures

Both Of The
Old And New Testament:
Arranged In Alphabetical Order,
And Containing, In Addition To The Usual Literal Explanation Of Words, Short
Doctrinal And Practical Essays Upon Certain Points Of The Truths Of God.

Designed For The General Use Of
All Pious Readers Of The Word Of God;
But More Especially For That Class
Who Read The

"Poor Man's Commentary On The Bible."

By

Robert Hawker, D.D.
Late Vicar Of Charles, Plymouth.

Ebenezer Palmer;
Is, Paternoster Row, London.
1828.

Acknowledgements

We wish to acknowledge and express our thanks to those who have assisted us greatly in making this reprint of Robert Hawker's **POOR MAN'S BIBLE DICTIONARY** available to the public.

Bro. Norm Wells, Pastor of the Sovereign Grace in The Dalles, Oregon and *Eld. Leroy Rhodes* of Mount Zion Primitive Baptist Church Crown Point, Indiana allowed us to use their old and very rare copies of this book to scan.

Mrs. Brenda Davis, member of Zebulon Baptist Church in Pikeville, Kentucky spent countless hours scanning the original work and correcting the text. Without her labor, you would not have this volume in your hand. We all owe Brenda a great debt of gratitude for her labor.

Mr. Larry Brown, member of Grace Baptist Church of Danville, Danville, Kentucky did the final typesetting and layout of the book.

Without the assistance of these friends, you would not hold this volume in your hands. We owe them a great debt of gratitude for their servce to us and to the cause of Christ.

Robert Hawker: Zion's Warrior (1753-1827)
By George Ella

Expository gems

Great Christian writers are often remembered more by their commentaries than their other works. This is the case with Matthew Henry, John Gill and Thomas Scott and perhaps reveals the Christian's greater longing to have the Word of God explained to him directly, verse by verse, rather than in essay, biography or story form. Food for the soul which is cut and served for immediate digestion is a delight indeed. Robert Hawker's commentaries provide such a delight. Though Hawker authored numerous theological works, school text books, readers and primers, it is to his commentaries that Christians today still turn. His *Poor Man's Commentary* and *Poor Man's Morning and Evening Portions* are still considered gems of exposition. Indeed, modern booksellers have noticed that Hawker is increasing in popularity and second-hand prices are growing with the demand.

Robert studies with a view to becoming a surgeon for his mother's and aunts' sake

Robert Hawker was born on April 13, 1753 in a house near Mary Steps Church, Exeter where his grandfather, an Alderman, had practised as a surgeon and where his father had now taken up that calling. In keeping with the covenant beliefs of his parents, he was baptised at Mary Steps on the following May 14. Hawker never knew his father who was carried off by a disease caught from a patient when his only surviving child was still a baby. This caused his mother and two aunts to take special care of little Robert and they made sure he grew up in the nurture and admonition of the Lord, teaching him to recite, read and write Scripture portions at a very early age.

Hawker attended the Free Grammar School, learning Greek, Latin and Hebrew. From his earliest years, he longed to become a clergyman, composed sermons and preached in secret but his mother, who had striven to keep up something of her husband's practice and worked as a midwife, begged Hawker to take up his father's profession. Hawker's aunts also felt that he could do the most good for his fellow creatures in the family profession. Having no heart to disappoint them, young Hawker was placed under the supervision of an Alderman White of Plymouth to be trained as a surgeon.

The young surgeon's apprentice developed into a most mischievous imp and did not leave his practical jokes outside of the church. One day, he smuggled himself into a service and set off a firework whilst Henry Tanner, the Evangelical minister, was preaching. Hawker never forgot this silly prank and when Tanner died, he supported his destitute widow and published Tanner's memoirs and works on her behalf.

A marriage made in Heaven

Though only nineteen years old, Hawker fell in love with Anne Rains, a girl of seventeen, whom he married at Charles parish church on January 6, 1772. Tongues wagged concerning their youth but the marriage proved of the Lord and the couple enjoyed over forty-five years of married life until Anne died in 1817, ten years before her husband. Robert and Anne had eight children, four boys and four girls. Three of the boys became ministers of the gospel and one a surgeon, three of the girls married well, Anna, the second eldest daughter, remained single, caring for her father until his death.

Hawker studied at St. Thomas's before obtaining a three-year post as surgeon in the Royal Marines. Stories are told how Hawker later went abroad with the army and was converted but John Williams, one of Hawker's biographers and a convert of his, claims that most of these stories are quite untrue and that Hawker never joined the army. He did become an army chaplain when Vicar of Charles and wrote a book called *The Zion's Warrior, or Christian Soldier's Manual* in which army life was compared to the spiritual life. These facts may have given rise to the supposition. There are no records of Hawker's conversion and it is probable that he entered the ministry without a deep awareness of God's grace in his life.

Hawker studies for the ministry

Nevertheless, Hawker's longing to become a minister never left him and, in May, 1778, feeling he had done his duty to his mother and though he had a wife and family, he entered Magdalen Hall, Oxford with a view to be trained for the ministry. His proficiency in the subjects studied was so great that the Bishop of Exeter ordained him as deacon in September that year. A few weeks later, Hawker was called to take over the curacy of his home church in Charles where he stayed forty-nine years until his death in 1827. The first sermon Hawker preached at Charles was on November 22, 1778, his text being 2 Corinthians 5:20, 'Now then we are ambassadors for Christ, as though God did beseech you by us: we pray you in Christ's stead, be ye reconciled to God.'

Hawker kept up his matriculation and occasionally visited Magdalen for lectures and examinations. He received priest's orders in 1779. He now began to publish his sermons but complained later that they contained no more knowledge of the truth than the bats and the moles could have supplied.

Becoming the Vicar of Charles

Two years later, Hawker's vicar, John Bedford, died. By one of the strange historical quirks of the Church of England, the living did not rest in the hands of the congregation but was under the patronage of the Mayor and corporation and Hawker, backed by his church, found that a stranger had put in a claim for the living. Mr White, Hawker's former employer was now Mayor and he quickly took Hawker's side so that when it came to the vote, there was only one 'nay' to all the 'ayes' and Hawker received the Bishop's seal to the vicarage of Charles on May 20, 1784.

A new note now appears in Hawker's preaching. The fine eloquence and language is still there but it is more suited to the ears of the ordinary man and there is far more Scripture in it. Hawker began to teach the children and, instead of spending his evenings with musical entertainment and card-playing, he visited the sick, the aged, the spiritual needy and the poor. He also set hours aside for social prayer and testimony. His teaching shows that he had obtained a deep understanding of the covenant of works and the covenant of grace. We note, too, that Hawker began to invite such people as William Romaine to preach. At first, Hawker felt he had to correct Romaine's 'unguarded expressions' but gradually came to realise that Romaine's words were pure gospel.. In his work *Visits to and from Jesus*, we find Hawker looking back on his previous thoughts concerning free grace and God's sovereign, electing love with dismay, saying:

> "How long and how daringly violent did I myself oppose this glorious
> truth, which now, through thy grace subduing my rebellion, and teaching

my soul its blessedness, is become my greatest joy and delight. Lord! thou knowest well, with what bitterness of a fallen nature, I contended against the sovereignty of thy grace, in thy free-will election; while in the very moment audaciously insisting upon my own power in a free-will ability of serving thee! Oh, what mercy hath been shewn me on the recovery of my soul from a delusion so awful!"

Opposition from the Establishment and Dissent alike

Hawker was opposed by Presbyterians, Anglicans and Baptists alike. The Presbyterian pastor in Charles was a man of ability who challenged Hawker's credentials as a man of God and his congregation as a true church. He, himself, preached Socinian notions enthusiastically so that in 1790 Hawker began to preach a series on Christ's divinity to protect and instruct his own flock. Hawker discovered that his preaching on the divine nature of Christ also angered many an Anglican minister so he decided to print his sermons for general distribution. So skilled was his reasoning and so successful was the spread of true Trinitarianism through the sales of the book that, two years later, the University of Edinburgh awarded Hawker a diploma as Doctor of Divinity. It is a tribute to the understanding of the university that a work that led to the conversion, edification and education of numerous souls received such formal acclamation. The Dissenting church intensified their efforts to de-throne Christ and, under the leadership of a Mr. Porter, declared themselves to be Arians and published a *Defence of Unitarianism* complaining that the writers of the New Testament were not inspired by God and had misunderstood Christ. This caused the *Evangelical Magazine* to write, "While a *Porter* disseminates the pernicious dogmas of Socinianism and infidelity, a *Hawker* opposes to him, and with success, the wholesome doctrines of grace and truth, which came by Jesus Christ."

Hawker takes on task after task

Next Hawker published a companion volume on the Holy Spirit and a *critique* of rationalism. He founded several charitable works for the poor and provided for the relief of the families of soldiers who had died in service or from a fever which had spread through the Plymouth area. By 1798, he was busy building an orphanage and a school. He now preached three times on Sundays besides holding numerous weekly teaching, prayer and testimony, meetings. He also preached two or three times a week for the soldiers and visited the military hospitals, never accepting a penny for his services. As the military buildings were miles apart, this witness consumed much of Hawker's time and energy in all weathers. Hawker also started a work amongst destitute women who had chosen a life of sin as a means of income.

Sadly, such evangelistic work drew protests from within the Church of England and a Cornish minister by the name of Polwhele campaigned to discredit Hawker. He felt his chance had come when Hawker journeyed to Falmouth to fetch his daughter home after a visit and accepted preaching invitations from three churches on the return journey. Polwhele complained to the Bishop of Exeter that Hawker was carrying out a 'Quixotic expedition' in his area, teaching blasphemy. Hawker's theme had been the imputation of Christ's righteousness and Polwhele had protested that if what Hawker preached were true, in the eyes of God the believer stood as righteous as Christ Himself because he had been clothed with God's own righteousness! Hawker had expounded Romans 3:22, 'Even the righteousness of God which is by faith of Jesus Christ unto all and upon all them that believe,' so Polwhele had faithfully reproduced Hawker's teaching. Yet Polwhele's knowledge of Scripture was so poor that on hearing this truth, he thought it was blasphemy! Polwhele also accused Hawker of itinerancy and neglecting his own flock. Actually Hawker had been absent from his pulpit only three Sundays in twenty years, twice due to illness and once when he preached for a friend. He was the only minister in the whole diocese with such a record! The good Bishop, the army and marine authorities and their chaplains all took Hawker's side and ignored Polwhele's protests.

Hawker's literary pilgrimage to Zion

In 1798 Hawker started writing for the *Zion's Trumpet*, a periodical founded by himself and Evangelical friends with a keen mission to spread the Word, record the work of the Holy Spirit in the lives of Christians and defend the *Thirty-Nine Articles*. The word 'Zion' was to be attached to a number of Hawker's works, such as his *Zion's Warrior* and *Zion's Pilgrim*. In the latter, a pilgrimage of meditations along the paths taken by John Bunyan's hero, Hawker gives us insight into his own spiritual history, lamenting that he only became a true pilgrim after he had 'passed a very considerable portion of time in the life of man.' On viewing the whirlpool of time that draws many a sinner into its vortex and drags them doomed out of a life which ought to have been lived in repentance, Hawker says, "Can I call to mind the past danger, and the present deliverance, unmoved with pity over the unthinking throng, and untouched with gratitude to thee the sole Author of every mercy? I feel (blessed be the grace that inspires it!) the rising hymn of thankfulness in my heart, while the tear drops from my eye: 'Lord, how is it that thou hast manifested thyself unto me, and not unto the world!'"

Hawker loved to muse on the pages of John Bunyan and John Milton. Like John Newton and Thomas Scott, he published notes on the *Pilgrim's Progress* and, like William Cowper, wrote a commentary on *Paradise Lost*. If we wish to find the heart of Hawker in his writings, it must be in *Zion's Warrior*, published in 1801. Here he defines the blessings of what it means to be a soldier of Christ, fighting the good fight with all his might, clothed in the armour of God. We also find him bemoaning the times spent as 'a deserter from the standard of Christ Jesus.' It is inspiring, when reading Hawker, to find him a man of flesh and blood as ourselves, yet one who was greatly used of Christ to proclaim His righteousness.

Hawker on missionary work

In 1802, we find Hawker distributing free Christian literature to the poor. He did this under the pompous title of *The Great Western Society for Dispersing Religious Tracts Among the Poor*, though he was the sum total of committee members, their chairman, treasurer, secretary and editor! During this year Hawker was invited to preach before the London Missionary Society and preached on *The Work of the Holy Ghost essential to give success to all missions for the Gospel* based on Romans 10:14-15. Hawker emphasised this need because the enormous fund-raising campaigns of the missionary societies were creating the impression that the more money raised, the more souls would be saved. He feared that the work of the Holy Spirit in the soul of a man, equipping him for the Great Commission was being reduced to a commercial enterprise that was doomed to waste money and neglect true soul-winning. Hawker also believed that true missionary work was church planting, each church having its own ministers and not to be ruled by an absentee committee thousands of miles away. Hawker withdrew his L.M.S. subscription but remained a praying and giving friend to a number of church-based missionary enterprises and supported missionaries such as W. B. Johnson at Sierra Leone, privately. Johnson's correspondence with Hawker reveals, contrary to the modern criticism that the doctrines of grace cripple evangelism, that preaching such doctrines is highly successful in converting sinners.

Hawker goes on his first preaching tour

In 1803, after twenty-five years at Charles, Hawker made his first preaching tour which lasted four weeks. Nowadays pastors seem happy to spend a month a year on holiday but Hawker never felt that such luxuries were necessary and preached twenty-five times on invitation during his month's leave of absence. The London ministers were glad to have Hawker at first as he filled all their pews and also the aisles. When, however, the doors were broken down by the sheer weight of the hundreds trying to get in and the masses outside caused a traffic chaos they began to fear Hawker was too much of a crowd-drawer for them. Notwithstanding, this Five-Point man whom many were calling an Antinomian and a Hyper-Calvinist received invitation after invitation to evangelise so that he had to plan a similar tour each year for the rest of his life. Yet modern critics of Hawker's doctrines invariably argue that such doctrines destroy evangelism! This is proof enough that such criticism is merely judgemental, and has no basis in true Christian experience. One tires nowadays of hearing the new, doctrinally wishy-washy, Reformed Establishment tell us that great preachers such as Tobias Crisp, Richard Davis, John Gill, John Ryland, James Hervey, William Romaine, Augustus Toplady, William Huntington, William Gadsby and, of course, Robert Hawker, believed doctrines that drive away the crowds, when history tells us that they were the very doctrines and the very people which drew them in their thousands.

Dealing with the 'righteous over-much'

Now Hawker worked hard on his penny commentaries for the poor. Dr Williams says concerning their teaching, "It was said of two celebrated commentators, Cocceius and Grotius, that the one found Christ everywhere, and the other nowhere. Dr. Hawker is of the former school." One well-bred lawyer, heartily disagreed with Hawker's testimony and in 1808 published an anonymous pamphlet to show that evangelical preaching encourages sin as it makes a man rely fully on Christ so that he does not strive to mend his own unrighteousness. Christian authors should therefore preach man-centred moral reformation. Needless to say, Hawker was soon telling the nameless man that in finding Christ he had also been taught the lesson of "denying ungodliness and worldly lusts, and living soberly, righteously, and godly in this present world." Seeing a man after his own heart in the nameless barrister, Polwhele rejoined the opposition, particularly after he had read Hawker's *A Prop Against All Despair* which even brings hope to those who feel they have sinned beyond all chance of pardon. It soon became obvious that these men's fight was not against Hawker but Christ Himself as they gradually revealed their Unitarian tendencies. Again, the church authorities and the Christian press stood fully behind the Vicar of Charles and we can thank God for such enlightened times.

Christ, our sole perfection

Now aged sixty-five and a widower, Hawker sent his last volume of his *Poor Man's Commentary* to the press. He professed that he had written the work "to hold up and hold forth the Lord Jesus Christ as God's Christ, and as the sole perfection of all his people." This endeavour met with mixed feelings in the churches. The perfectionist doctrine of progressive holiness was rampant owing to false teaching concerning the law and gospel. The believer's gaze was taken away from the Christ who had clothed him with righteousness. It was an effort to change fallen Adam into the New Adam by works of holiness. The folly of the view that the old man can become purer as the days go by, is well illustrated by Paul's testimony after many years serving the Lord, 'I know that in me, that is, in my flesh, dwelleth no good thing,' (Rom. 7:18). On the other hand, we read of the new man 'which after God is created in righteousness and true holiness.' The believer is created unto good works but even they do not sanctify him progressively, he is wholly such already by God's grace. Good works are the fruits of holiness and not their seed. If fruit occurs, then it is a sign that Christ has made the sinner whole. We are called to mortify the body but this is not progressive holiness but the testimony and effects of the sanctified new man in Christ.

The Biblical teaching of the sanctifying work of the Spirit in the soul of man revived

Hawker revived the Biblical teaching of the sanctifying work of the Spirit in the soul of man and spent much of his final years writing on the Person, Godhead and ministry of the Spirit. He wrote several works on the Spirit for the needs of the labouring class but did not neglect their physical needs. He bought bread in bulk and sold it to the poor at half price. The Vicar vainly thought that he could preach to the crowds as they came to buy bread but so great was the rush and commotion that even his powerful voice could not be heard. He thus hit on the idea of giving a tract of his composition with every loaf sold besides a short word of admonition.

Hawker's energies grew with his age as he published one work after another. The more he published, the more opposition grew alongside his great popularity. He had a penetrating effect on ministers who were orthodox on the outside but nurtured some secret error in their hearts. When debating with Hawker, their true selves invariably came out, displaying Socinianism, Sabellianism, Arianism or worse.

The Sonship controversy

The harshest criticism came from those who seemed doctrinally close to Hawker. He had, for instance, experienced sweet fellowship with the Old School Particular Baptists who were one with him on the doctrines of atonement, election, imputed righteousness, justification and sanctification. Unexpectedly, however, John Stevens of York Street Chapel, London, who had done tremendous work for the gospel, and was currently protecting his churches from the onslaught of Grotianism and New Divinity teaching, attacked Hawker furiously, not only for being a member of the Church of England but for not believing in the pre-existence of Christ before the incarnation. The accusation was ludicrous and the charge rebounded on Stevens who had to give a reason for his bizarre claim. It turned out, under scrutiny, that Stevens believed that Christ already possessed a human *soul* before His birth and merely took on Himself a human *body* at the incarnation. This hypothesis, of course, Hawker questioned and asked Stevens for Biblical proof. Stevens, arguing from Revelation 3:14, stepped full-scale into Arianism by stating that Christ was the first of God's creation, mistaking Christ's office as the origin and author of creation for his being a created person. Hawker had no difficulty in demonstrating that the idea that Christ was created as a soul before time and as a body in time was quite unscriptural.

Hastening with joy beyond the boundaries of time

Still writing and preaching powerfully at seventy-three, Hawker was obviously thinking more about leaving this world than the time spent in it. As two of his children and three of his grandchildren died shortly after one another, he longed for the Lord to speed on the chariot. The first signs that the chariot was ready came in 1826. On the first Sunday of the year, Hawker preached on Isaiah 3:10, 'Say ye to the righteous, it shall be well with him'. After the service, Hawker was stricken with inflammation of the lungs and spent twelve weeks as an invalid. He strove to preach on March 25 but realised that his strength was failing and was ill for a further eighteen weeks after which he stood before his congregation again to tell them that his last days were his best days. In his preface to a new work on the Holy Spirit, he confessed that he was "fast hastening towards the boundary of time . . . with more joy than they who watch for the morning.—For I know whom I have believed, and am persuaded that he is able to keep that which I have committed unto him against that day.' Like the church of old, I can and do say, 'make haste, my beloved, until the day break and the shadows flee away.'" Hawker's condition deteriorated and he continually vomited blood, so his daughter took him to Totness for a change of air. Though very weak, Hawker testified, "My soul is overfilled with joy; my spirit hath not room for its enjoyment; I am full of glory." As his condition worsened, Hawker asked to be taken home to die. Immediately on reaching home, he called his family together and gave them his departing blessing, expounding Ephesians 1:6-12. After this, Hawker laid his head on his eldest daughter's shoulder and his other children took his hands in theirs. He seemed to drop soundly to sleep. There were no physical signs of any kind that ushered in the silent hand of death. It took some time before the loving children realised that their father had fallen asleep in Jesus. As John Kent described the scene:

Death was to him as harmless as a dove,
While floods of glory overwhelm'd his soul.

A brief look at Hawker's works

Perhaps the reader will not be averse to reading a review I wrote shortly after the publication of the above in *New Focus* under the title *Hawker's Guidebooks to Zion: Genesis 33:12*. It was written as I was very conscious of the growing demand for Hawker's works and the fact that they were now available in an inexpensive edition:

Robert Hawker (1753-1827) combined sound Biblical doctrine with intense evangelistic fervour. Wherever he ministered, crowds longing to hear the Word of Life thronged to hear him. Hawker preached with great feeling and compassion because he knew that his labour was not in vain and God's Word never failed in its purpose. Some years ago, longing for more of Hawker's works, I approached an international 'Christian' bookseller who had a complete set for sale. His price would have rigged me out with a complete computer system so my fond idea was dropped. Then I heard from a friend who had actually been given a set. How envious I was! But the circumstances of the gift made me wonder what the Christian world is coming to. A certain denominational library had once treasured their set of Hawker's works but now they felt the books were an embarrassment to them; indeed dangerous for their modern-minded readers so they gave the gospel-bearing books away! The library's action is symptomatic of the present down-grading of sound gospel principles which once led thousands to Christ and were held in honour by eighteenth and nineteenth century Trinitarian denominations.

These thoughts led to my *New Focus* article on *Robert Hawker: Zion's Warrior*. When I received issue No. 05, I was overjoyed to see a Gospel Standard advertisement adjacent to my article listing Triangle Press reprints of Hawker at £2.75—£3.45 per volume. I immediately sent off my order and the books arrived speedily and what a blessing they proved to be!

This article is more a recommendation than a review as twelve volumes have now been published which hardly allows for a detailed analysis. First I delved into Hawker's *The Divinity of Christ* and the *Divinity and Operation of the Holy Ghost*, bearing in mind modern erroneous teaching featuring a Godhead halting between two opinions on salvation and the inane idea that the Spirit breathes contradiction and contention into the Scriptures.[1] In arguing for dissension within the Trinity concerning man's salvation and a breach in the logical harmony of Scripture in bringing this salvation home to the sinner, such writers are tearing the churches apart and actually boasting that such disunity fosters church growth! What has Hawker to say to these modern contenders for forked paths to heaven? His readers will find that his message is a God-given antidote to this modern plague.

Hawker was confronted with the very same heresy in his day. This prompted him to write on the Trinity. His opponents left the field with their tails between their legs, doing the only honest thing they could. They became Unitarians. This is why it is of the utmost importance that Hawker is read once more. As God's watchman and Zion's Warrior, he has proved his value in showing how gospel truths prevail. It will be sad to see modern tension and paradox preachers joining the Unitarians, but as their views of Christ and Scriptures are so low, they will feel more at home there and leave true religion to get on with its true work. Read Hawker on the unity of the Godhead as displayed in the salvation of His people. It will not only thrill your heart and soul but equip you for proclaiming the truth and combating error. If you are a child of God, it will certainly make a convinced Trinitarian of you.

Coefficient to the work of the triune Unity is the operation of the Holy Spirit in rendering the work of salvation effectual in the application of what the Father has wrought out in His Son, regenerating corrupt and fallen sinners. Indeed, Hawker argues that it is through the unity of the Spirit-breathed Word that the sinner sees the unity of God's nature in preparing salvation for him and the unity of the triune action in effectually redeeming him. Hawker argues that if such a work had been referred to in a Bible of irreconcilable, conflicting passages, and had not the unity of action been insisted on in every part of God's Word, then some apology might be made for the incredibility of mankind respecting it. However, as the Scriptures refer to the work of the Father Son and Holy Ghost in their joint and uniting enterprise of saving sinners and as thousands can testify to being born of God through this work, we see how trustworthy is the entire testimony of the revealed Word and the folly of men striving to find disharmony in the word via a reasoning which is in disharmony with God.

Union and Communion with Christ was written to prepare believers for the communion service and deals with the believer's standing in Christ. Christ is the Vine and we are its branches, He is the Head and we the body. Together we form a holy Temple and are members of one with another as the Bride of Christ and the family of God. I have rarely experienced the mysterious union we have with our Lord from eternity to eternity so sublimely taught as in this gem of a book. Hawker's advice on how to be assured of the unity one enjoys in Christ is pastoral care at its very best.

Hawker lays great stress on prayer and in his *Prop Against All Despair*, the writer coaches the believer lovingly through the most difficult of Christian exercises but perhaps the most rewarding. Hawker shows how prayer in the Spirit opens Heaven's doors. Few books have blessed their readers as Hawker's *Zion's Pilgrim*, *The Sailor Pilgrim* and *Zion's Warrior*.

---

[1] See especially David Gay's *Preaching the Gospel to Sinners: 2*, Banner of Truth, Issue 371-372 and his review of Iain Murray's *Spurgeon v. Hyper-Calvinism*, ET, August, 1996, p. 19. These articles laid bare the tendency to Socinianism in the British evangelical establishment and pioneered the negative re-evaluation of Spurgeon spreading through the churches which is doing nobody any good.

To believe that one is a stranger and pilgrim on earth but marching onwards to Zion is not just the theme of a revival hymn but the teaching of Scripture and the experience of every believer. Hawker shows in these works how the path upwards is strewn with grace, mercy and love from beginning to end. There is much personal testimony given here and I was left with the assurance that God had strengthened my weak faith by my following Hawker's advice on how to keep on Zion's true track. Hawker's testimony is so strong that, whilst reading, I actually imagined myself going on the way arm in arm with this great saint, feeling all the better for his company. Few books have such an effect on me.

Hawker was not only a parish pastor but a chaplain to the forces stationed at Plymouth and his book *Compassion for the Sick and Sorrowing* is based on a harrowing experience he had. Ship after ship entered the port full of troops dying of the fever and Hawker and his church did all they could to relieve them, converting barns into hospitals, but a thousand men died during the three months run of the epidemic. Though Hawker had a heavy schedule in his parish, he spent hours each day comforting the dying and burying the dead. Anyone terminally ill without knowing whether they are bound for Zion or anyone wishing to help the dying over the threshold of death should read this book as there is not a theoretical word in it but sheer practical experience and genuine comfort from cover to cover.

The above works show Hawker at his desk and in his pastoral work, his two volumes of *Village Sermons* and *Sermons on Important Subjects* reveal his faithfulness in the pulpit. The words contained in Hawker's memorial tablet sum up Hawker's prowess as a preacher: 'The elegancy yet simplicity of diction, the liveliness and brilliancy of imagination, the perspicuity and vigour of thought, the depth and compass of Christian knowledge and experience, with which he was talented and blest, are still extant in his sermons.'

Hawker was a didactically gifted man and improved the quality of Christian education greatly. As a school text-book author and curriculum writer, I approached *Hawker's Catechism for Children* with what we might call 'professional interest.' Though the *Heidelberg Catechism* is prescribed in our schools (North-Rhine Westphalia), it is little used because of its ancient language. Hawker's language should be no problem for modern English-speaking children over the age of eleven or so and the book would still make an excellent addition to Scripture lessons and family worship. Some Christians object to 'putting words into children's mouths' in catechetical work but have no objection to their children learning parts in plays and singing songs and hymns learnt off by heart. Hawker's questions and answers are Scriptural throughout and as Scripture is the language that tunes the heart to God, Christians should surely not cavil at this means of evangelising their children. Furthermore, Hawker's catechism provides pupils with a thorough knowledge of the history of the Jews as also a detailed knowledge of the two Testaments and the way of salvation. The Great Commission compels us to make this way known to all mankind, especially to children.

I cannot recommend these soul-saving and edifying works enough. The modern equivalent of a widow's mite is sufficient to purchase a single volume, but the spiritual value of each book is so enormous that it stretches from here to Heaven.

Taken from **MOUNTAIN MOVERS** *Champions of the Faith* (pp 347-362), George M. Ella, *GO Publications,* The Cairn, Hill Top, Eggleston, CO Durham, DL12OAU, England 1999

Preface

I have been prompted to the work proposed in the title page, from a humble hope, that under the blessing of GOD the HOLY GHOST, it may be rendered useful to the Christian world in general; and yet more particularly so, to that handful of the people; who read my **POOR MAN'S COMMENTARY** on the Bible, lately published in penny numbers. It struck me, that a work of this kind, might form a proper Appendix to it, and be found not a little helpful to serious readers. Under this impression I have engaged in this service; and for their accommodation, have directed the bookseller to publish an edition of it, upon the same plan and form as the Commentary. May the Lord commission both to his glory!

There can need no recommendation of the word of God, more than its own intrinsic excellency. In the Jewish Church, so infinitely important was it considered, that the prince of the people was enjoined, "To write a copy of the Law of the Lord with his own hand in a book; and to read in it all the days of his life: that he might learn to fear the Lord his God; and that his heart should not be lifted up above his brethren." (Deut. xvii. 18-20.)

How vastly increased is the obligation in the Christian church, which adds to the Old Testament Scripture, the whole confirmation of the New; and compriseth within its life-giving contents, every thing that can be called interesting, in reference to the Person, Work, Character, Offices, and Relations of the Lord Jesus Christ! which hath indeed, in the fullest sense of the word, "the promise of the life that now is, and that which is to come."

Here, the claim of the Word of Life is upon every soul! Here, both high and low, rich and poor, the king and the beggar, stand upon a level. And here, from hence must issue, the final decision of every man's everlasting state. "The word (saith Jesus)that I have spoken, the same shall judge him in the last day." (John xii. 48.) Many have reproached themselves in a dying hour, for having neglected the study of the word of life. But never was it known in the annals of mankind, that any in the close of life regretted that he had regarded the things of the world too little, and the Bible too much.

It will be highly proper that the reader should be informed in this place, and before he enters upon the work here presented to him, what is proposed in the contents of it: that he may not expect more from it than is intended, and in the end find himself disappointed. He should be told then, that the present CONCORDANCE, is meant to differ in a great measure, from all preceding Dictionaries of the kind. The author wishes to compress into as small a compass as possible, all that is useful in a way of explanation, so as to pass over nothing that is essential, and at the same time to notice nothing that is superfluous. Hence many words will be omitted, whose obvious meaning, in the present day of knowledge, is so well understood, as to render their insertion here unnecessary. While on the other hand, some, that perhaps are but just glanced at in former Concordances, (but which according to the author's view demand more attention) will have a larger discussion. In short, the present design aims rather to be useful than large; to suit the humble Christian more than the learned. The reader is requested to keep in remembrance, through the whole of the work, that it is the POOR MAN'S CONCORDANCE. And to all such it is hoped, that what is here offered, under the divine blessing, will prove helpful, in "making wise unto salvation, through the faith which is in CHRIST JESUS!"

One word more I would beg to offer, by way of Preface: namely, to observe, that with a view to greater usefulness, I have sometimes judged it might be profitable, when giving the names of persons, and of places, to direct the reader to the original word or root, from whence either hath been derived. It will not be unfrequently found that much meaning is veiled under it. And in doing this, I have only followed the plan of our old Bibles, whose marginal readings are truly valuable on this account. It is well known to all lovers of

Biblical truths, that it was the uniform custom with our fathers in the church of God, and from the earliest period, to own God in his providences, by giving names to persons and places, when at any time receiving some more than ordinary manifestation of divine favour. Thus Abraham called the mount of deliverance in a critical moment, JEHOVAH JIREH. Jacob styled the place where the visions of the Lord began with him, BETHEL; and Moses was so called by his mother, from being drawn out of the water. And Hannah, no less from the same view of the Lord, had her Samuel. And the margin of the Bible, at each of those histories, as well as in numberless other instances of a like nature, hath thrown great light upon the subject, in giving their explanation. (See Gen. xxii. 14. Gen. xxviii. 19. Exod. ii. 10. 1 Sam. i. 20.) It hath been my endeavour to render of the POOR MAN'S CONCORDANCE particularly useful, by adopting the same plan. And I venture to persuade myself, that I shall have thereby performed no unacceptable service to the truly pious reader.

Perhaps, with some readers, an apology may be thought necessary, that I have entered upon this service, in sending forth before the Public a CONCORDANCE before that I have finished my COMMENTARY. But the truth is, I have, through grace, concluded my writings on the Old Testament Scripture; and many months since set up my EBEN-EZER upon that occasion. What I propose therefore by this Concordance, is intended only by way of a parenthesis, between my finishing the Commentary on the Old Testament, and my entering on the New. I hope very shortly, if the Lord spares, (and long before my Printer is ready for me,) to re-assume that soul-refreshing service of the sacred word, and of going over the gospel of the ever blessed God; and sure I am, that when I have closed my Concordance, which furnisheth both profit and amusement for my leisure hours, I shall enter on the remaining engagement of the Commentary, with increasing earnestness and delight. In the meantime, I take occasion in this place, to beg an interest in the prayers of the faithful, for those, and indeed all my other poor labours in my honoured Lord's household; commending both myself and them to the Master's blessing.

I am well aware that I am proposing to myself great undertakings, with slender means; and marking out much to be done in the remainder of life, when but little of life itself remains to be filled up. Hastening now fast to the boundary of time, as it stands with me, it might be expected from my declining years, that I should rather retire from past labours than commence new ones. But I have long known that if "the pillar of the cloud" go before in the way, it matters not what year we count in the Arithmetic of human life. That sweet promise is sure, it hath never yet failed, "As thy day is, so shall thy strength be." If the Lord's glory be the end proposed, the Lord's grace will furnish means to the accomplishment. And if the Lord be pleased to appoint that I am to finish life, before that I have finished my proposed labours, it will he but to leave that imperfect, which forms a part in all the imperfections of human nature. And surely no man can propose to himself a sweeter close to the whole of his pilgrimage upon earth, than to depart with the Word of God in his hand, and Christ in his heart, the hope of glory.

Amen.

The Poor Man's Concordance To The Sacred Scriptures

A

A

In the very opening of this Concordance, I cannot pass over the first letter, which the Hebrews call Aleph, and which they pronounce A. And I do this the rather, because, as the Greeks call their first letter Alpha, and our adorable Redeemer graciously condescended to call himself by that name; so equally applicable is Aleph, to the person of Jesus. Indeed, as if to shew the infinite fulness and comprehensiveness of his nature and character, the Lord Jesus took the names, both of Alpha and Omega: the former, the first; and the latter, the last, in the letters of the Alphabet. There is no letter before Alpha, and none after Omega. Nothing can be more strikingly characteristic of Christ. For as Christ, he was, and is, and ever will be, the first letter in all JEHOVAH'S alphabet; and the last, in all the ultimate design of his glory. (See Rev. i. 8. Rev. xxi. 6. Rev. xxii. 13.) Now the word Aleph is expressive also of a first, a leader, or chief, and sovereign person. So that in this sense, Jesus is Aleph, as well as Alpha. And it is still worthy of farther remark, that as the sound of the Aleph, or A, in Hebrew, is only a soft breathing as it were, and needs nothing more to form it, than the mere motion of the lips; it may be supposed, to have a peculiar reference to Him, who first "breathed into man's nostrils the breath of life; and man became a living soul." (Gen. ii. 7.)

AARON

Son of Amram, and the elder brother of Moses. He was of the tribe of Levi. (Exod. vi. 19, 20.) His name is derived from Har, a Mountain: and consequently signifies somewhat great and lofty. And when we consider, to what an high honour Aaron was called; to be the type of Him, who, in the everlasting nature of his office, was, and is, JEHOVAH'S High Priest; both the altar, and the offering, the sacrifice, and the sacrificer, through whom alone, all offerings must be presented: surely, none taken from among men, could be more great and lofty in .office than Aaron. The history of Aaron, incorporated as it is with that of Moses, fills a large part in the books of Exodus, Leviticus, and Numbers. But the great eminency of his character is formed from his becoming so illustrious a type of the Lord Jesus Christ. Every thing in his priestly office ministered to this one point. Indeed the whole law, and consequently the priesthood, became "a shadow of good things to come; but the body, which formed that shadow, was Christ." (Col. ii. 17. Levit. xvi. 2. Numb. xvi. 46, 47.)

ABADDON

This word signifies a Destroyer. As such, it is given to the apostate angel of the bottomless pit, and very properly suits him. His whole pursuit, in scouring the earth, is, we are told, as "a roaring lion, seeking whom he may devour." (See Rev. ix. 11. 1 Pet. v. 8. See also Devil. Satan.)

ABAGTHA

One of the chamberlains of Persia. His name, if Hebrew, is compounded of Ab, father, and Gath, a press: probably, he was the "master of the wine-press." (Esther i. 10.)

ABANA

A river of Damascus, made memorable on account of Naaman's leprosy. Its name is compounded of Aben, a stone, and Bana, to build. The Syrian prided himself on the greatness of this river, and contemned the sacred streams of Jordan. His conduct was not unsimilar to modern Syrians in nature; who think high of their own moral excellency, and cannot brook the necessity of being washed from the leprosy of sin, in the blood of Christ. May we not say with the poor captive servant in the house of Naaman: Would God that sinners, conscious, like Naaman, of their disease, "were with the Lord God of the prophets, for he would recover them of their leprosy!" (See 2 Kings v.1-14.)

ABARIM

These were several smaller mountains, "Or hills, of rising ground, beyond Jordan, in the country of Moab; which went by the name of Abarim. Nebo, Pisgah, and Peor, were in the number. Nebo became ever-memorable, as being the sacred spot where Moses the man of God died. (Num. xxxiii. 48. Deut. xxxii. 49, 50. Deut. xxxiv. 1.)

ABBA

A Syriac word, signifying Father. It is thrice used in the New Testament. Once, by the Lord Jesus, (Mark xiv. 36.) and twice by his servant the apostle Paul. (Rom. viii. 15. and Gal. iv. 6.) It is a word of peculiar tenderness; and I could wish that the real and full meaning of it was strongly impressed on the mind of every regenerated believer. It would tend to give great confidence and comfort in a dark and trying hour. David, Levi, in his Lingua Sacra, derives it from a root, which signifies, desire, delight, complacency, satisfaction: and implying no less, special interest of relationship, as between the nearest of all connections. And agreeably to this account of the word, it is remarkable, that though the word, in its extensive sense, signifies the Ab, or Head, and Lord of a family; yet a slave, or menial servant, was never allowed to use it in addressing the Ab.

I very earnestly beg the reader not to lose sight of this view of the word Abba, but to let it possess a suitable place, equal to its importance, in his remembrance. For if it was so specially confined, among the people of the East, to the children of a family; and Jesus and his people in him, are enjoined to use it on this account; can any thing more strikingly prove their relationship? And I cannot but express my hope, that if the reader of this Poor Man's Concordance, is enabled, by grace, to see his own personal privilege herein, and can enter into a proper apprehension of the word, in this most endearing view, he will be led to discover the sweetness and blessedness of it, and from henceforth adopt it, in all his approaches to the throne of God in Christ. And how delightfully in this sense, doth it explain to us that passage of the apostle, in his epistle to the Galatians; where he saith, "Because ye are sons, [not because ye are to be made so, but because ye are already sons] God hath sent forth the Spirit of his Son into your hearts, crying Abba, Father." (Gal. iv. 6.)

While I am upon this word Abba, Father, I cannot forbear adding to those observations, though in a cursory manner, a remark upon the word Ammah, Mother. For it is from the same root, and is also of the like peculiarity of tenderness, in reference to the church of Jesus; which, as the apostle saith, (including both that in heaven and in earth, for they are but one and the same,) "is the mother of us all." (Gal. iv. 26.) We meet with the several branches of the same root in Scripture, according to the several relations arising out of it; but they are all one and the same family. (Ephes. iii. 14, 15.) Hence Zion is called, and by the Lord himself, the "Virgin daughter (the Almah) of Zion." (Isaiah xxxvii. 22.) So again she is spoken of as the sister (Ruhamah) (Hosea ii. 1.) And it is no uncommon thing for Christ to call his church by all these names. (See Song iv. 9, 10, 12.) And when Isaiah was commissioned to proclaim to the church, the subject of the miraculous conception, he used the same word as the Lord did of Zion. "Behold, a virgin, (Almah) shall conceive." (Isaiah vii. 14.) I venture to believe that if the recollection of these names, all springing as they do from one and the same source, were frequent in the believer's remembrance, they would much refresh the soul. And I think it worthy of yet farther remark, that there is a beautiful sameness between the first cry of nature, in the infancy of our being, and this language of grace when the souls of believers are first born to God. It was said by the prophet concerning Him, whom he predicted, that "before the child should know to refuse the evil and choose the good," the event leading to it should be accomplished. (Isaiah vii. 16.) And it must be truly said, that before the cry of the soul, in the new birth of grace, goes forth in Abba, or Ammah, the apprehending union, interest, and relationship in Christ with his church, had been settled long before, even from all eternity.

Though I have already far exceeded, under this article, the ordinary limits to be observed in a work of this kind, yet I must beg to trespass a little farther, by way of confirmation of the observations made upon it.

The special and personal interest of the word Abba, derives another authority, from the customs and manners of the East. It is well known, that the ancient nations of the Arabs, retain many of the usages we read of in sacred history. And although they know nothing of the true religion of the patriarchs, yet in provincial acts and habits, they are much the same people that they were, two or three thousand years ago. Hence, among many proofs in point, which might be given in confirmation of this sameness of manners, the mode of salutation is one, in which there is nothing changed. We find among the patriarchs, the general expression was, "Peace be to you." (Gen. xliii. 23.) In the days of the Judges, the salutation was the same. (Judges xix. 20.) So in the days of David, (1 Sam. xxv. 6.) and in the days of our Lord, and by Christ himself. (John xx. 19.) In like manner the limitation of the word Abba is still the same as ever, not being brought into common use, but wholly restricted to relations, and of the nearest and tenderest kind.

One proof more. In the common acts of respect observed in the East, when servants do reverence to their masters, or superiors, it is always done by kissing the feet, or the garment. Hence the poor woman we read of, Luke vii. 38. But when children meet their parents, and do reverence, they kiss the hand, or the head. Hence the father in the parable. (Luke xv. 20.) Moreover, the posture which is observed upon those occasions, differs materially according to the rank of the parties. From inferiors, in giving what is called the Asslem-mah, (Salutation) they always offer it, by laying their right hand upon their breast. Persons of equality, or relations, do it by kissing the hand, head, or shoulder of each other. So Dr. Shaw relates in his Travels to Aleppo, page 301. Let the reader connect this with Jacob kissing his son, and the church's call unto Christ. (Song i. 2.) How beautiful and striking both cases! How little the change made in those things, in a period of near four thousand years!

From the whole of these observations, I cannot but conclude, that the word Abba hath a peculiar sweetness in it, and is intended to intimate what a nearness and dearness of affinity there is, between Christ and his church. And I venture to believe, that our holy faith, not only warrants the use of it, but enjoins it, from the personal union, and oneness, of the Lord Jesus Christ with our nature. And under such high encouragement and authority, I confess, that I feel a disposition, upon every occasion, to adopt it, considering it the peculiar privilege of all true believers in Christ, to bring it into constant use, whenever they draw nigh to a throne of grace. See Ammi.

ABEDNEGO

This name was given to Azariah, by the Chaldeans. (See Daniel, i. 7.) I should not have thought it necessary, in a work of this kind, to have noticed the change of name; neither perhaps the name itself, more than many others, to be met with in Scripture, which I shall pass by; had it not been for the purpose of making an observation upon it; and which I hope will not be found improper or unprofitable. I humbly conceive, that the motive with the Chaldeans, for changing the names of the children of the captivity, was somewhat more than the naturalizing them. The Hebrew, and the Chaldee language were very similar. The Chaldeans perfectly understood the Hebrew names. And they no less knew, how tenacious Hebrew parents were to give names to their children, which bore some relation to the Lord God of their fathers. In changing their names therefore, they not only designed to make them forget their beloved Jerusalem, but the yet more beloved Lord God of Abraham, Isaac, and Jacob. And what a change they wrought here, in the instance of this man! Azariah, or more properly speaking, Azar-Jah, meant, as the words themselves indeed express, the Lord is my help; from Azar, assistance; and Jah, Lord. But Abed-nego means the servant of Nego; Abed or Obed being the Chaldee for servant. And Nego most probably was one of the dunghill idols of Babylon. So that from Azariah, to remind him, as often as he heard himself called, he might remember that JEHOVAH was his help; he is brought into remembrance whenever he now heard his name, that he was the servant of an idol, in whom there is no help. Lord! keep thy people from "mingling with the heathen, and learning their works." (Psalm cvi. 35.)

ABEL

The second son of Adam and Eve. His name is mentioned by the Holy Ghost with peculiar honour, in that illustrious list of Old Testament saints, who all died, as they had lived, by faith. (Heb. xi. 4.) "By faith, Abel offered unto God a more excellent sacrifice than Cain." By which we derive full authority to conclude, that Abel's faith in Christ, the promised seed, gave a blessedness in the acceptance of his sacrifice, which Cain's had not. Abel came to the Lord as a sinner; and, by the lamb he offered in sacrifice, testified the sense he had of sin, and his hopes of salvation by Christ. Cain came to the Lord, not under the apprehension of sin, but to present an offering of tribute. He therefore slighted the promised seed, and redemption by, Christ: and stands in the front of the Bible, the first desit the world ever knew. (Gen. iv. 3-5.) It may be not amiss to add, that the word Abel signifies vanity, a vapor, emptiness, and the like.

ABEL-BETH MAACHAH

We meet with this name, 2 Sam. xx. 15. And as Abel means vanity, mourning, and emptiness; so Beth, an house: and therefore the whole taken together implies; vanity or mourning to the house of Maachah.

ABEL-MAIM

The mourning of the waters. (2 Chron. xvi. 4)

ABEL-MEHOLAH

The mourning of sickness. (Judges vii. 13.)

ABEL-MIZRAIM

This name was given at the floor of Atad, on the occasion of the funeral of Jacob. The margin of the Bible renders it, "the mourning of the Egyptians." (Gen. i. 11.)

ABEL-SHITTIM

A place in the encampments of Israel; meaning the mourning in Shittim, in the plains of Moab. (Numb. xxxiii. 40.)

ABIB. See Month.

ABIDE

To abide, in the language of Scripture, means somewhat more than merely the remaining in one place. It implies an adherence to a thing; or an union with, and connection with it. Thus Jesus saith, (John xv. 4.) "Abide in me and I in you." So, speaking of the Holy Ghost, he saith, "He shall abide with you for ever." (John xiv. 16.) And his servants, the apostles, use similar expressions, in the same sense. The apostles, Paul and John, describe the indwelling residence of the Holy Ghost, and a vital union with Christ, under this character of abiding. (See 2 Tim. ii. 13. 1 John ii. 27, 9.8.) It is a blessed consideration, in the view of this doctrine, that when Jesus saith, "Abide in me, and I in you;" and a little after; "Continue ye in my love:" (John xv. 4, 9.) it is not a mere precept, without imparting with it ability. But it is, willing them into an ability, by virtue of a oneness with them, as the head of efficiency, to the members of his body. He directs the thing to be done and he enables them to do it; according to that blessed promise: "Thy people shall be willing in the day of thy power." (Psalm cx. 3.)

ABIEZER

We read of several of this name in the Scriptures. (Joshua xvii. 2. Judges vi. 34. 2 Sam. xxiii. 27.) The name is interesting, signifying my Father [God] is my help: from Ab, father; and Hazar, to help.

ABIGAIL

A memorable name in Scripture, whom the Lord, in his providence made instrumental to save David from blood-shedding. (See the history, 1 Sam. xxv. 2 to 35.) Her name is as remarkable, for the event the Lord enabled her to accomplish; for it means, the joy of the Father; from Gul, to rejoice, and Ab, father. I have often admired the sweet and gracious conclusion, which David made, on occasion of the sin-preventing providence, the Lord accomplished on the patriarch's mind, through the instrumentality of this woman. He saw the hand of the Lord in the appointment; and, first, he blessed God; and next, he blessed her advice; and next, he blessed her: for all come in for a blessing, since the Lord had wrought deliverance by such means from sin. "Blessed (said he) be the Lord; and blessed be thy advice; and blessed be thou that hast kept me this day from shedding blood." (1 Sam. xv. 32, 33.)

ABIHU

Son of Aaron, whose awful death, by the immediate judgment of the Lord, With his brother Nadab, is recorded Lev. x. 2. I refer the reader to that history, for the particulars of this visitation. Some have thought, that they were drunken, when they thus ministered in their priestly office; and so forgot to take the sacred fire in their censers. And they have formed this opinion, on the precept in the ninth verse: where it is said to Aaron, "Do not drink wine nor strong drink, thou, nor thy sons with thee, when ye go into the tabernacle of the congregation; lest ye die." But it should rather seem, that it was the act of taking

ABIJAH - ABRAM, and ABRAHAM

strange fire which was their offence, and for which the Lord smote them. Strange fire; not the fire which was appointed, and which was always durning upon the altar: and which typified Christ's fiery sufferings. And if so, what an awful view it affords, to shew the danger of all offerings, void of an eye by faith in Christ! (Isa. 1. 11.) The name of Abihu means, he is my father.

ABIJAH

We meet with many of this name in Scripture: and it is not to be wondered at; for it is a very blessed one, compounded of Ab, Father, JAH, Lord, and I, my. Sweet appellation, when a child of God can say, JEHOVAH is my Father! For this is what the Lord himself provided for his people. "But I said, (said the Lord) how shall I put thee among the children, and give thee a pleasant land, a goodly heritage of the hosts of nations? And I said, Thou shalt call me my Father! and shalt not turn away from me." (Jer. iii. 19.) For the several persons in Scripture, called Abijah, I refer to the several chapters (1 Kings xiv. 1. 1 Chron. xxiv. 10. 2 Chron. xxix.1. Nehem. x. 7.)

ABIMELECH

There are several of this name in the word of God: and it must be confessed, that a goodly name; compounded of Melech, king, my father; meaning, the king is my father were two kings of Gerar of this name, and son, in the days of Abraham and Isaac. (Gen. xx. 2.; xxvi. 1.) There was also an Abi-Cmeleeh the son of Gideon. (Judges ix.1). And also an Abimelech among the priests of the Lord, in the days of David. (1 Sam. xxi. 1.)

ABINADAB

There were several of this name in the Old Testament. Saul had a son of this name; and David a brother. (1 Chron. ii. 13.) And there was an Abinadab a Levite. The signification of the name is, my father is a prince.

ABNER

Captain of Saul's army. (1 Sam. xvii. 55.) The name means, father of light; from Ner, a lamp, and Ab, father.

ABOMINATION

In the language of Scripture, the word abomination for the most part means idolatry. Thus we read, (2 Kings xxiii. 13,) that Ashtoreth was the abomination (that is the idol) of the Zidonians; Chemosh, the abomination of the Moabites; and Milcom, the abomination of the Ammonites. Hence our Lord forewarned his disciples, that when they saw the abomination of desolation, spoken of by Daniel the prophet, in the holy place, namely, the temple, they should accept this, as a token, that Jerusalem would be destroyed, and should accordingly then take their flight. And this was done, when Titus Vespasian's army put up the image of idolatry in the temple. Compare (Dan. ix. 27. with Matt. xxiv. 15. and Mark xiii. 14.)

ABRAM, and ABRAHAM

The great father of the faithful, whose history is so dear to the church in all ages, and whose faith so illustrious, as to have procured for him this most honourable title. The memoirs of this friend of God, as he is called, (2 Chron. xx. 7. and James ii. 23.) begin at Gen. ix. 26, and run through the whole of Scripture, like a golden thread, from end to end. The distinguishing honour put upon this man, in depositing the covenant in his seed; and the change of name thereupon both in him and his wife, are most striking events, and on every account meriting the most particular attention. Concerning the cause of the former, we can form no certain conclusions upon it. There are indeed no grounds to form any data upon. All must be referred unto the eternal purposes of JEHOVAH, "who worketh all things after the counsel of his own will and pleasure." Concerning the latter, we can trace somewhat very sweet and interesting, of the Lord's approbation of his servants, both in the man and his wife, by the change of name. I shall beg to offer a short observation upon it.

The original name of Abram was truly honourable, meaning, in the compound of the word Ab, father, and Ram, exalted; a father of eminency or exaltation. But when the Lord added the Ha to it, and made it Abraham, this became still more honourable; for his name now, in the literal sense of it, was, a father of many nations. And all this became greatly increased in point of honour, on account of the covenant entailed on Abraham's seed, even Christ, (See Gal. iii. 16.) from whom, and in whom, all the nations of the earth were to be blessed.

But there is yet. another purpose which the Lord accomplished in the display of the riches of his grace, by this change of name: and which, if I mistake not, (the Lord pardon me if I err) seems to have been the Lord's great design, in this act of mercy and favour shewn both to the patriarch and his wife; namely, by this alteration, or rather addition given to each; by one of the letters which form the incommunicable name of JEHOVAH. By this express act of divine grace, Abraham and Sarah, both possessed in their name an everlasting symbol, or token of JEHOVAH'S glorious favour. And I am the more inclined to this belief, because, in the instance of Jeconiah, in an after age of the church, the Lord manifested his displeasure to this man, by taking from his name one of those distinguishing letters of JEHOVAH, and calling him Coniah, a "despised broken idol." (Compare Jer. xxiii. 24-30, with I Chron. iii. 16.) I beg the reader to observe, that I do not presume to speak decidedly on a point of so high a nature; I only propose the thought, and that with the most profound reverence.

May I not venture to suggest, that perhaps it was on this account, of the honour done to their father Abraham's name, by taking into it a part of JEHOVAH'S, that the children of Abraham, in every age of the church, have been so anxious to call their descendants by names, which either took in some of the letters of JEHOVAH'S name, or had an allusion to the Lord. This is so visible a feature, in almost all the Jewish names of the Old Testament, that we meet with very few among the pious Israelites where this respect is not had, in the choice of their children's names, through the whole Bible.

I cannot dismiss these observations on Abraham's name until that I have requested the reader to connect with the review, the sweet consideration, that all true believers in Jesus take part in the same. They have a new name given them, as well as Abraham their father, when, like him, they are by regeneration made "new creatures in Christ Jesus." They are interested in all the rich promises of God in Christ; and being Christ's children, by adoption and by grace: then are they "Abraham's seed, and heirs according to the promise." I pray the reader to turn to the following Scriptures by way of confirmation. Rev. ii. 17. 2 Cor. v. 17. Gal. iii. 7-29. Rom. iv. 16.

I know not how to turn away from this subject, concerning our great father Abraham, who in any, and in every view, opens a constant source for improvement, without offering a short observation more, in respect to that circumstance in his life, when compelled by famine to go down into Egypt, he begged Sarah to call herself his sister, and not his wife. We have the account of it in its own beautiful simplicity related to us, Gen. xii. 9. to the end. I beg the reader to turn to the Scripture and peruse it over. And when he hath so done I request him to attend to a short observation which I would offer upon Abraham's conduct, in this particular.

It certainly doth, in the first view of things, appear strange, that the great father of the faithful should have had upon this occasion his faith so slender, that he became alarmed for the safety of his wife's chastity, when he had before this, at the call of God, come out from his father's house, "not knowing whither he went." (Heb. xi. 8.) He had strength of faith to trust God for every thing respecting himself; yea afterwards, even to the offering up his only son: and yet he could not, when driven by famine into Egypt, trust to God's watchful care over Sarah. But we shall discover, that in this instance of danger respecting his beloved Sarah, humanly speaking, there was no possibility of her escaping with her chastity, unless the Lord accomplished her deliverance by a miracle. Sarah was exceedingly fair, we are told, and her beauty would soon be known (as we find it was) to the prince of the country, on their arrival at Egypt. Instantly she would be seized upon for Pharaoh's haram. And this was literally the case. In vain would be Abraham's remonstrances, or the humblest petitions. If he had said, She is my wife, his death would have immediately followed. But if he said, She is my sister, his life would be spared. And in this case, even then nothing short of the Lord's interposition could restore to him his beloved Sarah again. This therefore he hoped. And here Abraham's faith became as illustrious as before. The patriarch had grounds to hope it. Necessity, and not choice, had driven him down into Egypt, that he might not perish by the famine. And being in the path of duty, and no doubt, constantly in the path of faith and prayer; the whole terminated at length to the divine glory, and to his faithful servant's happiness. And when Sarah was taken, and separated from him: when no possibility of communication between Sarah and her husband was found: locked up in the haram of Pharaoh, from whence there could be no escape, (according to the custom of those Eastern courts, during the life of the prince, the women of the haram being confined there never to get out,) here was a season for the exercise of faith, and for the display of the Lord's favour to his servants. And the way the Lord wrought on the occasion, is as remarkable, in proof of his interposition, as the patriarch's faith in exercise. "The Lord plagued Pharaoh and his house with great plagues, because of Sarah Abraham's wife." (Gen. xii. 17.) And so the Lord overruled the visitation, as to give a voice to the rod, and cause the prince very gladly to give up Sarah, unviolated, to her husband. So that when the whole subject is properly considered and taken into one complete view, so far was the faith of the patriarch from being lessened by the exercise, as in the first blush of the history it seemed to appear, that by the means Abraham adopted, he still threw himself with confidence on the Lord, to save his beloved Sarah from ruin, and his life from danger; and without this trust in the Lord, and dependence on the Lord's interposition, Abraham could not but well know, that whether he had called Sarah, sister, or wife, the peril was the same.

If it be said, (as it has been said) but wherefore did the great father of the faithful make use of a falsehood in this instance? might he not have told the truth, and with more confidence still looked up to God for the issue? To which I answer. Certainly, truth at all times, and upon all occasions, is most closely and faithfully to be followed up, leaving it with the Lord to make all things minister to his own glory, and to his people's welfare. But it should be observed, that though upon this occasion, the patriarch did not tell the whole truth, he told no falsehood. Sarah was his sister, as well as his wife. If the reader will turn to the twentieth chapter of Genesis, and peruse a similar situation, into which Abraham and Sarah were afterwards brought at Gerar, he will there behold the patriarch's modest apology for calling his beloved Sarah his sister, rather than his wife. When Abimelech, the king of Gerar, remonstrated with Abraham for calling Sarah sister, and not wife, and said, "What sawest thou, that thou hast done this thing?" Abraham answered, "Because I thought, Surely the fear of God is not in this place; and they will slay me for my wife's sake. And yet indeed she is my sister; she is the daughter of my father, but not the daughter of my mother: and she became my wife." (Gen. xx. 10-12.)

But what I am more particularly earnest to impress upon the reader's mind, respecting this history of Abraham, (and indeed the sole purpose for which I have introduced the subject in this place) is, that the act itself was founded in faith and reliance upon the Lord. The patriarch had not recourse to mere human policy, without first throwing himself on divine aid. Abraham was well aware of his critical situation. He knew the danger to which both himself and Sarah would be exposed. He therefore used what he thought the best human means: but he certainly was all the while relying by ardent faith on the Lord. And let it be remembered, that in those journies the patriarch was prosecuting, they were by the Lord's command, and not Abraham's pleasure. So that the same faith which first prompted him, at the call of God, to leave his own country, and his father's house, and, as the Holy Ghost testifies of him, "by faith he went out, not knowing whither he went;" (Heb. xi. 8.) the same perfect reliance upon the Lord went with him all the way. How beautifully the patriarch accounts for this, as well as his whole conduct in calling Sarah his sister, and she calling him brother, in the close of his apology to Abimelech! "It came to pass, when God caused me to wander from my father's house, that I said unto her, This is the kindness which thou shalt shew unto me; At every place whither we shall come, say of me, He is my brother." (Gen. xx. 13.) What a sweet and interesting tale the whole forms! I beg the reader's pardon, for the length I have made of it; and shall now leave it to his own judgment, under the hope of divine teaching concerning it, from the Lord.

ABSALOM

Son of David. His history we have 2 Sam. 14th to the 18th chapter. His name was but ill suited to his character; for he was of a rebellious, turbulent spirit. Ab, the father, Shalom, of peace.

ABSTAIN, and ABSTINENCE

The Scripture sense of both these words hath a very extensive meaning, beyond the mere abstinence of the body. Fasting from food is easily done, and it is to be feared is often done by many, who give unrestrained indulgence to the lusts of the flesh and the mind. The Holy Ghost, by his servants the apostles, hath given them very blessed directions of "abstaining from fleshly lusts which war against the soul: and from the very appearance of evil." (1 Pet. ii. 11. 1 Thess. v. 22.)

ACCEPT or ACCEPTATION

There is nothing more opposed to each other, than the Scripture sense of acceptation, as it relates to the Lord, and as it relates to man. To accept any man's person, is the sinful act of a sinful man. And to accept a poor sinner in Christ, is the gracious act of a gracious God. And those different views of acceptation very fully explain the meaning of the apostle, in his sermon before Cornelius and his household. "Of a truth I perceive, (said Peter)that God is no respecter of persons." God hath no respect to the person of any, but as they are in Christ. It is to Jesus, that the Lord hath respect. And, therefore, "in every nation, he that feareth him and worketh righteousness, is accepted with Jesus." (Acts x. 34, 35.)

ACCESS

This, in Scripture language, means, the drawing nigh to a throne of grace, and having a nearness, and audience with God in Christ. The apostle Paul hath a short but comprehensive verse, (Ephes. ii. 18.) which explains this most fully; and at the same time shews, how each glorious person of the GODHEAD takes part, in the distinct office of each, on those sweet and blessed occasions. "For through him (that is the Lord Jesus) we both have access by one Spirit unto the Father." It is through the mediation of the Lord Jesus believers draw nigh, and have access unto the Father; and this, by the gracious leadings and influences of the Holy Ghost. And I beg the reader to note yet farther; the blessedness of this access to the throne. It is not simply as introduced by Christ, but beheld, and accepted also in Christ. He is our peace, our cause, both of access and acceptance: for it is "to the praise of the glory of JEHOVAH'S grace, wherein he hath made us accepted in the Beloved." (See Rom. v. 2. Ephes. i. 6.; ii. 18.; iii. 12. 1 Pet. iii. 18.) This seems to be the scriptural sense of access.

ACCUSED

In Scripture language, this means, being separated from, and under the curse of God. (Joshua vi. 17. Rom. ix. 13. I Cor. xvi. 22. Gal. i. 8, 9.) What a sweet relief to a poor burdened soul, when led to see that curse done away in Christ! (Gal. iii. 13.)

ACCUSER OF THE BRETHREN

One of the names of Satan. (Rev. xii. 9.) See Devil. Satan.

ACELDAMA

The field of blood. It was very properly called so, because it was purchased with the thirty pieces of silver, which the traitor Judas received of the chief priests for Christ's blood. (Matt. xxvii. 8. Acts i. 19.) It lay to the south of mount Zion, not far from the pool of Siloam. The name given it of Aceldama, is rather Syriac than Hebrew; and compounded of Achel, (from Chakel)field, and Damah, blood. This memorable ground is said to be shewn to travellers, even to the present day. Wherefore it was called the potter's field, is not so easy to say: unless, like our church-yards, some neighbouring potter dried his earthen pans there, as people now dry their clothes, after washing, in our church-yards. An old monk, called Drutmar, relates, that in his days, there was an hospital built in this charnel house for strangers, where the pilgrims, going to, and from, the Holy Land, used to lodge.

It is blessed to observe, how the Lord in his providence overruled events, at the crucifixion of Jesus, that his holy body should not have been thrown into this, or any other Aceldama, as a common malefactor. The Mishna reports, that it was not allowed, for any among the Jews who died by the common hands of justice, to be buried in the sepulchre of their fathers, except their flesh was first consumed. Now as the Lord Jesus, being considered by the law as a criminal, (John xvii. 30.) was thus liable to have been cast out with the common dead; what an overruling power must it have been, to prompt the minds of the honourable counsellor, Joseph of Arimathea, and Nicodemus a ruler of the Jews, to have begged the forfeited body from Pilate!

And there was another providence, directing all this to the accomplishment of the purpose intended; in that the request was so well timed before the chief priests could influence Pilate's mind to refuse; and Pilate's mind so guided by the Lord, to grant the request before that he had power to deliberate. Had the Sanhedrim foreseen such a thing, no doubt they would have been beforehand with Joseph and Nicodemus, and prevailed upon the governor to deny. But He that had predicted Jesus should make "his grave with the wicked, and with the rich in his death," (Isa. liii. 9.) took care not only that a new sepulchre, suited to the infinite dignity of his person, should be prepared; but all the steps leading to the accomplishment of placing his holy body there, should make way, so as to answer all the important purposes of that prophecy.

As the holy body of Jesus was not to see corruption, but to arise the third day from the dead; this new sepulchre, wherein never man had laid, not only corresponded to the dignity of his person, but served to identify that person, as an article of faith to the believer; that it was Jesus, the very Lord of life and glory, whom the disciples placed there, that arose the third day, as he had promised, from the dead. Thus confirming the faith by circumstances, which, considering the difficulties with which the thing itself was surrounded, and the little probability that one dying, as the Lord Jesus did, under the hands of the Roman government, as a common felon, should make "his grave with the wicked, and with the rich, in his death:" nothing but the over-ruling and determinate counsel and foreknowledge of JEHOVAH could have contrived; nor any less than the same sovereign power could have accomplished. Here, as in a thousand instances beside, we may well cry out, "O the depth of the riches, both of the wisdom, and knowledge of God! how unsearchable are his judgments, and his ways past finding out!" (Rom. xi. 33.)

ACHOR

A valley in Jericho: rendered memorable from the stoning of Achan, the son of Carmi, there. Indeed the valley seems to have borrowed its name from this man. See the history (Joshua vii. 17-26.) The margin of the Bible at the last verse so explains. Achor means trouble. It is somewhat remarkable, that one so injurious to Israel should have been born called Achan, as if from his birth ordained to this condemnation. (Jude iv.)

I know not whether I should have noticed this valley, or the history of Achan, to whom it refers, had it not been from the gracious use the Lord makes of it, in a way of figure, by allusion, in promising happier times to Israel. (Hosea ii. 15.) In this sweet chapter, the Lord is following up his rich promises of grace, in return for Israel's repeated ingratitude and rebellion. But grace shall triumph. For, saith the Lord, from trouble like that of Achan, I will raise up comfort to my people: when from the sorrows induced by sin, under the quickening convictions for sin, and the exercises wrought in the soul, by the power of the Holy Ghost, I will bring my people into the blessed consolations of deliverance by Christ. "And I will give her her vine-yards from thence; and the valley of Achor for a door of hope: and she shall sing there as in the days of her youth, and as in the day when she came up out of the land of Egypt." (Isaiah lxv. 10.)

ADAM

The first man. The name implies the earth, from whence he was formed, which signifies red. It is worthy remark, that Christ is also called Adam. (1 Cor. xv. 45.) And if we compare what the apostle saith of Christ, (Col. i. 15.) with what is said of Adam, at the creation of the world, (Gen. i. 26.) it serves to explain, in what sense we are to limit the expression concerning him, who was formed from the earth as the first man. In that Scripture of the apostle, when speaking of Christ, he is called, "the image of the invisible God, the first born of every creature." Hence we infer, that though the first Adam was indeed the first man, as manifested openly; yet the second Adam, so called, even the Lord from heaven, had a pre-existence in secret, and stood up the Great Head of his body the church, in the counsels of the divine mind, the Wisdom man, from all eternity. Indeed from this Wisdom man, this pattern, the first earthly man was formed. For so the charter of grace, at the creation, expressed it: "Let us make man in our image, after our likeness." (Gen. i. 26.) And if Christ was, and is, as

ADAR - ADMIRE.-ADMIRATION

the apostle was commissioned to tell the church, "the image of the invisible God, the first born of every creature," nothing can be plainer than that the first Adam, so called, because indeed he was the first man openly, was created in the image or likeness of Him, who alone can be said to be the image of the invisible God, and in his human nature, "the first born of every creature." (See Psalm lxxxix. 19. Prov. viii. 22-31. Micah v. 2.)

ADAR

The twelfth month among the Hebrews. See **MONTH**.

ADDER

One of the names figuratively given to the Devil. Hence, when the Lord Jesus Christ is said to bruise Satan, it is described under the similitude of "treading on the lion and the adder." (Psalm xci. 13.) Hence also, as sin is of the devil, the infusion of it into our nature, at the fall, is called in Scripture, adder's poison. (Psalm cxl. 3. See also Gen. xlix. 17. Prov. xxiii. 32.)

ADJURE

This word in Scripture language is much more striking and significant than is generally considered. It contains not only the nature of a command when used by a person in authority, that the adjured party shall answer to the question proposed, but it goes farther; to bind the person adjured under a fearful curse if aught be concealed, or kept back in his mind, whereby a discovery which is needed be hindered and prevented. Thus Joshua concerning Jericho, (Jos. vi. 26. Ahab to Micaiah, 1 Kings xxii. 16.) And still higher than both, when Christ was adjured by the high priest. (Matt. xxvi. 63.)

The law of adjuration appears to be founded in the divine authority. Thus we read, (Lev. v. 1.) "If a soul sin, and hear the voice of swearing, and is a witness, whether he hath seen or known of it, if he do not utter it, then he shall bear his iniquity." It should seem from hence, that the concealment of any iniquity, made the party concealing a joint partaker of it, in the sight of God. To the same purport, is that passage in the Proverbs, (chap. xxix. 24.) "Whoso is partner with a thief, hateth his own soul: he hearing cursing, and bewrayeth it not." Those views of concealment, according to the law of Moses, serve to explain to us the nature of adjuration, and throw a light upon the conduct of our Lord, in that unequalled moment of his meek and humble demeanour, when he stood before the high priest. "I adjure thee (said the high priest) by the living God, that thou tell us whether thou be the Christ the son of God." And while the reader thus observes the law of adjuration, so faithfully fulfilled by Christ, I hope he will never lose sight of the Lord Jesus Christ's answer: "Thou sayest that I am." Oh! precious testimony of Jesus, and from Jesus himself. Here was indeed a good confession. (1 Tim. vi. 13.)

ADMIRE.-ADMIRATION

In Scripture language, somewhat more is meant by those words than we annex to them, in our ordinary discourse. It is said, concerning the centurion's faith, (Matt. viii. 10.) that Jesus marvelled at it. But if this be supposed to imply any surprise wrought on the mind of Christ, this would be a mistake, and a perversion of language. We may apply the words of the Lord upon another occasion, and say," Because it is marvellous in the eyes of the remnant of the people, should it be also marvellous in mine eyes, saith the Lord of hosts?" (Zech. viii.6). The Hebrew word, in this instance, is the same as that given of Christ by the prophet, (Isaiah ix. 6.) when he calls him Wonderful. Hence in like manner, the Lord is said to shew his marvellous loving kindness. (Psalm xvii. 7.) So that it is marvellous, and it is to the admiration of his people and of all that look on, when the Lord by his grace distinguisheth them from others. They are men wondered at, (Zech. iii. 8.) In this sense, the Lord Jesus admired and praised, it may be said, by the notice he took of it, the faith of the centurion, and the faith of the woman of Canaan. (Matt. xv. 28.)

ADONAI

This is one of the names peculiarly applied to the person of the Lord Jesus Christ. By way of distinguishing it from JEHOVAH, it is rendered Lord in our English Bibles, in smaller letters, while JEHOVAH, which is also translated Lord, is in capitals. The reader will find a striking proof of it. (Psalm cx. 1.) The Lord said unto my Lord. The words in the original are, JEHOVAH said unto my Adonai. It is a sweet and interesting name of the Lord Jesus. It carries with it the idea of a stay, or helper, security, confidence.

ADONI-BEZEK

The lord of Bezel (Judges i. 4, 5.)

ADONI-JAH

The fourth son of David. His name forms a wonderful compound of two glorious names of the Lord. So very earnest were the children of Israel to preserve the constant remembrance of the Lord God of their fathers in their families, (1 Kings i. 5.)

ADONI-ZEDEK

The lord of Zedek: supposed to, have been one of the ancient names of Jerusalem; and which is said to have had four: Salem, Jebus, Zedek, (or Justice) and Jerusalem. (See Joshua x. 1.)

ADOPTION

This forms a most interesting word in Scripture, in the use that is made of it, in allusion to the state of adoption and grace, into which true believers are received by their union with Christ. They are said to be predestinated to the adoption of children. (Eph. i. 5.) And the purpose for which Christ is said to be made of a woman, made under the law, to redeem them that were under the law was, that they might receive the adoption of sons. (Gal. iv. 4, 5.)

The word adoption is borrowed from a custom well known among the Romans, under whose government Judea became a province, who adopted the children of strangers and acknowledged them for their own, when they themselves were childless. But though the term is applied to believers, from being openly adopted and acknowledged in the family of Christ, yet strictly and properly speaking, this is not done, because they were not of the family of Christ before; for in fact they always were; but it is done in a way of publickly confessing and acknowledging it. The Holy Ghost by the apostle is express to this purpose, when he saith, "And because ye are sons, God hath sent forth the Spirit of his Son into your hearts, where by ye cry Abba! Father!' (Gal. iv. 6.) And all the Scriptures are express to confirm this most unquestionable truth. (Isa. xliv. 3; lix. 21. Ezek. xxxvii. 5-14. Zech. xiv.) It is most blessed, when we consider the privileges of adoption, and know in ourselves that we are made, though grace, the happy partakers of it. By adoption, the children of God in Christ are brought out of the spirit of bondage into the glorious liberty of the sons of God. They are translated from the kingdom of darkness into the kingdom of God's dear Son. Hence they are regenerated, illuminated; justified, sanctified, and made partakers of grace here, to be made partakers of glory hereafter. Sweetly the Spirit witnesseth to their spirits, that they are the children of God. "And if children, saith the apostle, then heirs of God, and joint heirs with Christ: if be that we suffer with him, that we may be also glorified together." (Rom. viii. 16, 17.)

ADORE, ADORATION - ADVOCATE

ADORE, ADORATION

By the act of adoration is implied the full and most absolute acknowledgment of worship; and of consequence, such can only be suitable or proper to offer exclusively to Almighty God. JEHOVAH, in his threefold character of person, Father, Son, and Holy Ghost, can be the only object of adoration; and this, through the glorious mediator, the Lord Jesus Christ. "I am the way, and the truth, and the life; (saith Jesus) no man cometh unto the Father but by me." (John xiv. 6.) This, in the strictest sense of the word, is adoration. But in the Eastern world, the customs and methods observed in acts of reverence among men, from the humbler to the higher ranks, too nearly approach that homage, which is due only to the Lord. The prostration of the whole body, kissing the earth, and the like, savour much of idolatry. See Kiss.

ADVERSARY

This is a general name applied to all persons, in common, who have a controversy, or are at variance with each other. Thus the Lord saith to Israel, "I will be an adversary to thine adversaries." (Exod. xxiii. 22.) And the prophet describes the Lord as an adversary to his people, in the day of his displeasure. "He hath bent his bow (saith he) as an enemy; he stood with his right hand as an adversary." (Lam. ii. 4.) And the Lord Jesus describes God the Father, as a law adversary, when he saith, (Matt. v. 25.) "Agree with thine adversary quickly, whilst thou art in the way with him." The Scriptures represent also Satan, as an adversary to Christ and his church. Thus Jesus, by the spirit of prophecy, saith, "Who is mine adversary? let him come near to me." (Isa. l. 8.) And Zechariah (chap. iii. 1.) represents Satan as "an adversary standing at Joshua's right hand, to resist him." And the apostle Peter calls the devil an adversary going about to devour; and chargeth the church to resist him steadfast in faith. (1 Pet. v. 8.) From these different views of the word, it will be very easy to learn, that the name of adversary is indiscriminately given to all persons who are in a state of controversy with each other, whether good or evil.

ADVOCATE

-is one that pleads the cause of another.

In a very particular manner, the Scripture applies this to the Lord Jesus Christ. Indeed, it is so peculiarly and personally his, that it expressly forms one of his divine offices. Hence, the apostle saith, "If any man sin, we have an Advocate with the Father, Jesus Christ the righteous, and he is the propitiation for our sins." (1 John ii. 1, 2.)

It is very blessed to see the personal and peculiar fitness and suitability of the Lord Jesus Christ to this office, and in how endeared and affectionate a manner he is thereby recommended, and comes home with all the warmth of tenderness to our hearts. I persuade myself that I shall have the reader's pardon and indulgence, if I trespass for a moment, on dwelling a little more particularly, than the merely noticing it, on this sweet feature in the portrait of Our Lord.

That our poor nature, universally speaking, stands in need of an advocate, is unnecessary to insist, upon for "we have all sinned and comeshort of God's glory." And therefore, he who undertakes to plead the cause of the sinner, must himself be sinless. And he must not only possess sufficient abilities to the office of a special pleader, but,he must know every person, and every case, with all the disadvantages of all the causes for which he undertakes. Neither is it sufficient, that he hath all these qualifications, and more than these, unless that he be lawfully constituted to the office. It is not enough, in our common courts of justice, between man and man, that many an able and a feeling heart could stand up for poor guilty criminals, and plead their cause. He that advocates for them, must have a legal call to the office, and be sworn into it, according to the laws of the court. It is most blessed, therefore, to see that in the person of our Lord Jesus Christ all these different qualifications meet and centre, and shine forth in one full constellation.

An attention to a few leading particulars, will make this appear abundantly plain and obvious to every beholder. The Redeemer's claim to this office of an advocate, and the only advocate of our poor nature, is founded on the call of JEHOVAH. We are told by God the Holy Ghost, (Heb. v. 5, 6.) that Christ "glorified not himself to be made an High Priest, but was called of God, as was Aaron." And he was not only called to the office, but sworn into it, by the solemnity of an oath.-"The Lord sware, and will not repent; thou art a priest for ever after the order of Melchizedek." So then, it appears beyond all question and dispute, that JEHOVAH, who said unto him, "Thou art my Son, this day have I begotten thee;" said also, "Thou art a priest for ever;" and confirmed it by his oath. I beg the reader to keep the remembrance of this everlastingly in view. Your Jesus, your advocate with the Father, is your sworn advocate, and by JEHOVAH himself. And as by reason of the sin of our nature, God our Father is the law adversary of every poor sinner; (see Matt. v. 25.) so Christ is our law advocate, and fully and legally appointed to this office, by JEHOVAH himself. Sweet thought!

But we must not stop here, in examining into the right of Christ, for the exercise of this divine office, the advocate of his people. He is no less so, by virtue of his being the propitiation for our sins; and in a double sense in this particular, because, not only the infinite dignity of his person, and the infinite merit of his propitiation gives him this claim, but also he is the very propitiation which God "himself hath set forth, through faith in his blood." Let the reader consult those Scriptures for himself, which prove the certainty of these precious truths, and he will see how unanswerably conclusive they are. (Job xxxiii. 24. Isa. xlii. 21. Matt. xvii. 5. Rom. iii. 25.) Now, then, let me pause, and ask, Hath not this almighty advocate a right to plead for his own rights, and those of his people in him? Was it not an absolute promise, in the charter of grace, that "when he had made his soul an offering for sin, he should see of the travail of his soul, and be satisfied?" (Isa. liii. 10, 11.) And shall not the blessed Jesus stand up and plead for the fulfilment of those promises? Hath he, indeed, given himself as the sinner's surety "an offering and a sacrifice to God for a sweet smelling savour?" and can he rest satisfied, till he hath brought all his ransomed people around him in glory?

Moreover, there is one point more to be considered in this subject of Christ's advocacy, which we have not yet even glanced at, though it forms a principal object, for which the Lord Jesus carries on his high priestly office, in the court of heaven, namely, the destruction of all his enemies, and the enemies of his dear people. When the Lord Jesus, by the Spirit of prophecy, spake of the purposes of his coming, it was for the overthrow of the empire of Satan, as well as the establishment of his own kingdom. "The day of vengeance (said Jesus) is in my heart, and the year of my redeemed is come." (Isa. lxiii. 4.) So, then, it must follow, that unless we can suppose what is impossible, that when Jesus returned to heaven he ceased to take concern in the exercises and sorrows and temptations of his redeemed upon earth, and that the triumphs of the powers of darkness engaged not the attention of the Lord to destroy: surely he is now, as much as ever, carrying on, by his everlasting intercession, all the grand purposes of his victory over hell, until he come, in the fulness of the times appointed, finally to crush the foe, and to root out of his kingdom "all things that offend." I must not stay to describe what the

ADULTERY - ADULTERY

Scriptures of God so very largely and blessedly set forth, the numberless qualities of the Lord Jesus, in his abilities, and readiness, and grace, and a thousand endearing things beside, which render him so peculiarly suited to the office. The prophet sums up all in one, his character, in this department of it, when calling him the Wonderful Counsellor; and the Apostle no less, when declaring that "in Him are hid all the treasures of wisdom and knowledge." (Isa. ix. 6. Coloss. ii. 3.) And if it were not for swelling the pages of a work that I must rather study to abridge, I might easily shew, that such are the powerful recommendations the Lord Jesus brings with him, to induce any, and every poor sinner, that is conscious of the want of an advocate, to plead his cause before God, that not a soul, earnest for his everlasting welfare, would cease a moment from putting all his concerns in the hand of such a wise, tender, and successful High Priest as Jesus. Indeed, indeed, it is most blessed to behold the Lord Jesus in this endeared character. All he undertakes is altogether free, "without money and without price." No case of his people, however desperate, he refuseth; and none that he undertakes can fail. Other advocates may, and indeed must, ultimately bring forth disappointment, but no cause put into the hands of Jesus can. And the gracious manner in which the Lord carries it on, is most blessed; for he makes every case which he takes up his own. He enters into all their concerns, gives them to see how much he sympathizes with them, during their exercises, and supports their souls with an abiding assurance, that he is everlastingly attentive to them. Not all the hallelujahs of heaven can make him for a moment intermit his overlooking either the persons, or the causes, of all his redeemed upon earth. For it is not their deservings, but his love; not what they have done, or can do for themselves, but what he can do for them, that becomes the standard of his grace. What they are, and what they merit, comes not into the amount. That they are his, and that he hath purchased their redemption, and received them as the gift of his Father; these are the motives which operate in the heart of Christ. He saith himself, in his pleadings for them before the throne, (for the words are already given to us) "Father, I will that they whom thou hast given me, be with me where I am; that they may behold my glory which thou hast given me." (John xvii. 24.)

Ye sinners in Zion! here bring all your causes. Come to Jesus and put every concern in his almighty hand. Jesus waits to be gracious. He can, and will save to the uttermost, all that come to God by him, seeing he ever liveth to make intercession for them. (Heb. vii, 25.) Hail! thou glorious, gracious, lawful, and successful Advocate of my poor, soul!

ADULTERY

The law of Moses made this crime capital, both to the man and woman; and upon clear proof, they were both to be put to death. (Lev. xx. 10.) It is somewhat remarkable, however, that in the case of the adulteress brought to Christ, we hear nothing of the man. Was it the case then, as it is but too generally now, that both the sin and the shame are thrown, with fulness of every thing blameable, upon women, while the seducers and more worthless, pass off unrebuked? yea, to the disgrace of human nature, not unfrequently applauded! Not so in thine eye, blessed Lord Jesus! (See John viii. 1. 11.) It should be remarked under this article, that beside this natural adultery, noticed in the Scripture, there is a spiritual fornication of which the Lord complains, which is idolatry. (See Jer. iii. 9. Ezek. xxiii. 37. Hosea ii. 2.) Reader! if Jesus be the husband, that is, as the prophet calls him, the John of his people, who would forsake him for the idols of a dying world? (Hosea ii. 16. 17.)

AGES OF THE WORLD

There have been generally reckoned six ages from the creation of the world to the coming of the Lord Jesus Christ.
- The first, from the creation to the flood containing a period of
  1656
- The second, from Noah to Abraham
  425
- The third, from Abraham to the going forth of Israel from Egypt
  430
- The fourth, from the departure from Egypt to Solomon's temple
  479
- The fifth from Solomon's in the captivity in Babylon
  424
- The sixth, from the going into Babylon to the coming of Christ
  584

ALLEGORY

We meet with this word but once in the Bible, namely, (Gal. iv. 24.) where the apostle, speaking of the history of Sarah and Hagar, calls it an allegory; that is, a figure, or parable. The Old Testament writers were very partial to this way of teaching, in conveying divine truths through the medium of human illustrations; and sometimes by other objects from the world of nature and art. Our almighty Saviour was pleased to adopt a similar manner; and so much so at one time, that we are told, "without a parable spake he not unto the people." (Matt. xiii. 34.) This allegory of Sarah and Hagar, is not only uncommonly beautiful, but most highly interesting. We never can be sufficiently thankful to God the Holy Ghost, for bringing the church acquainted with the blessed truths which were folded up in this patriarchal history. Never would it have entered into the breast of any man alive, untaught of the church's almighty Teacher, that such glorious things were intended by the Lord to be shadowed forth in the children of the bond woman and the children of the free. Let the reader learn from it this most blessed truth, that the Lord hath been preaching all along, and from the first dawn of revelation, the covenant of redemption by his dear Son. Think reader, if it be possible, how JEHOVAH'S mind hath been occupied from all eternity, in bringing in, and revealing the Lord Jesus to his church and people. Well might it be said, as it is said, when Jesus, who had been secretly set up from everlasting the glorious Head of his body the church, was openly to be brought into the world,"Let all the angels of god worship him!" (Heb. i. 6.) It will be a blessed view of this sweet allegory, now so graciously explained to us as it is, by the Holy Ghost himself, if both he that writes and he that reads, when summing up the wonderful account, can say with the apostle, "We are not children of the bond-woman, but of the free." (Gal. iv. 31.)

ALLELUJAH or HALLELUJAH

This word which is become so general in use, in our churches and places of worship, is preserved to us in many parts of Scripture, as it is in the original Hebrew, compounded of Hallelu, Praise ye, and Jab, Lord. The beloved apostle John tells us, that in those visions he was favoured with, in seeing heaven opened, and beholding the glorified inhabitants of the New Jerusalem, he heard a great voice of much people in heaven, saying, Hallelujah. (Rev. xix. 1.-3.) And it is worthy remark, that the five last Psalms begin and end with this expressive word, Hallelujah; as if to teach the church, that the first and great end of man is the praise of God. And it is, and ought to be, a subject of sweet consolation and joy to every true believer in Jesus, to know that this will be, ere long, the everlasting employment of the Church in heaven. There the spirits of just men made perfect now are; many of whom we once knew upon earth, and with whom we shall know and be known, for ever in heaven. So that in the

ALMIGHTY

prospect of this never-ending eternity, we may now, by faith, mingle our Hallelujahs with theirs, until by sight we all surround together "the throne of God and the Lamb."

ALMIGHTY

I pause over the contemplation of this distinguishing name of JEHOVAH; desiring that the glories of it, and the fulness of it, may have their suitable impression upon my heart. This is the glorious name by which JEHOVAh in Christ chose to himself known to Abram. (See Gen. xvii. 1. with Exod.vi. 3.) I am El Shaddai, God all-sufficient. Some suppose it is derived from a word signifying many paps, or breasts, to suck from. (Isa. lxvi. 11.) The word Shaddai may be explained, both to bless his people, and to destroy their enemies. And certainly, both form a blessed security to the Lord's people. For when the Lord saith, I am God (all-sufficient) Almighty, it comprehends all in himself for them, and all to them. And oh! how blessedly are these explained, confirmed, and secured in Christ.

ALPHA

We meet with this word, Rev. i. 8.11. and in two other chapters of the Revelations. It is the first letter in the Greek alphabet. And the Lord Jesus, in having graciously condescended to call himself by this name, hath made it very precious to the believer. Jesus is, indeed, the Alpha and Omega, the first and the last, the Author and Finisher of salvation, It should seem that the Lord intended by this name, and adding to it Omega also, to imply the comprehensiveness of his nature, and being, both the first and the last, to intimate his eternity. (See Isa. xliii. 10.) See A. Aleph.

ALTAR

In the old church in the wilderness, there were three altars erected. One, called the altar of incense; another, the altar of burnt offerings; and the third, the altar, or table of shew-bread. These material altars were all typical of Christ. And so jealous was the Lord concerning the altar, on which all offerings were to be made, that the whole of the materials of which it was formed were to be of earth only; or, if of stone, it was not to be hewn stone. And wherefore were matters conducted with such caution? Surely it was to shew, that in all offerings the Lord was to be offered only what was his own. "If thou lift up thy tool upon it, thou hast polluted it."(Exod. xx. 24-26). For, as every altar represented Christ, it was lessening Christ's dignity and the infinite value of his sacrifice, to presume to mingle any thing with this. Now then, as Christ is our New Testament altar, let us see to it, that we bring nothing to offer upon this altar of our own. Let Jesus be all and in all; both the Sacrifice and the Sacrificer, the High Priest, the Offering, and the Altar. We have (saith Paul) an altar whereof they have no right to eat which serve the tabernacle. (Heb. xiii. 10.) I cannot forbear remarking, that seeing the holy jealousy of the Lord, as noted in these things, how very wrong must it be, not to say profane, to call the communion table the altar, and to talk of companions to the altar, in the books so called, as if such things could be companions to Christ. Surely it doth manifest great ignorance in divine things1

AM

I AM THAT I AM. One of the distinguishing names and characters of JEHOVAH. (See Exod. iii. 14.) and this solemn name demands our greater veneration and reverence, because it is the very name by which the Lord was pleased to reveal himself to Moses at the bush. The very expression carries with it its own explanation; that is, as far as creatures, such as we are, can enter into an apprehension of the meaning. When JEHOVAH saith, I AM THAT I AM, it is setting forth a right and power of existence, exclusive of every other. Of all others, some have been, some now are, and some may be. But then all these that have been, or are, or may be; all are what they are from Him, and by his appointment. But He that is I AM, is, and must be always, and eternally the same. His is a self-existence, underived, independent, subject to no change, and impossible to be any other; "the same yesterday, and to-day, and for ever." (Heb. xiii. 8.)

And what tends yet more to endear it to the heart of his people is, that this glorious name becomes the security of all his promises. I AM, gives being to all that he hath said, and becomes a most sure security for the fulfilment of all that he hath promised. Oh! for grace to bend with the lowest humbleness to the dust of the earth, in token of our nothingness before this great and almighty I AM. And no less to rest in holy faith and hope, in the most perfect confidence, that He will perform all his promises. And, reader! do not overlook by whom, and in whom, this and every other revelation is made. Always connect the I AM speaking from the bush to Moses, (Exod. iii. 14.) with the I AM speaking in the gospel, (John viii. 58.) And oh! that God the Holy Ghost, may give grace to discover that both are one and the same. (John x. 30.) See JEHOVAH.

AMALEK
See Mount Amalek.

AMEN

One of the distinguishing names of the Lord Jesus Christ, as Christ God-man Mediator. For so Jesus condescended to make use of it. (Rev. iii. 14.) And the meaning of it, in the original language, shews the great blessedness of it, as it concerns his people, in the Lord Jesus condescending to do so. For the word, in the original Greek, from whence it is taken, means verily, certain, sure, true, faithful. And surely, the Lord Jesus Christ is all these, and infinitely more, JEHOVAH'S Yea and Amen, as he saith himself; the Amen, the faithful and true witness, the beginning of the creation of God; that is in his mediatorial character.

And it is worthy our closest remark, that our Lord very frequently began his discourses with this word, and repeated it-"Verily, verily, I say unto you;" that is, in plain terms, (and indeed, it is the very word in the original) Amen, Amen. And it is yet worthy of farther remark, that none but the Lord Jesus ever did use such words, at the opening of the discourse, by way of confirmation. As if the use of it was particularly his, and belonged to him only, as his name. All the gospels, indeed, end with Amen. But then, this seems to be but as a farther proof that they are his, and he puts, therefore, his name as a seal at the end of them, by way of establishing their truth.

And I beg to remark yet farther, by way of shewing the sweetness and peculiar claim that the Lord Jesus hath to this name, that all the promises are said to be, Yea and Amen in Christ Jesus, (2 Cor. i. 20.) that is, strictly and properly speaking, they are His; for He himself is the One great promise of the Bible, and all are therefore, promises in and by Him. And the prophet Isaiah (chap. lxv. 16.) describes the believer in the gospel church, as saying, That he who blesseth himself in the earth shall bless himself in the God of truth; that is, the God Amen. It were devoutly to be wished, that whenever this sacred name is used, in our public worship, or private devotion, our minds were to recollect the person of the Lord Jesus. For certain it is, when we say Amen to the giving of thanks, (see 1 Cor. xiv. 16.) we do, to all intents and purposes, use the name of Christ, however inattentively it be said. And, therefore, if this were rightly considered, we should use it with an eye of love, and faith, and thankfulness to him.

I shall only beg to add, to what hath been offered on this precious name of our Lord Jesus, that as John is the only one of the Evangelists who hath recorded, so very particularly, our Lord's discourses with those double Amens, or Verilys, it is plain, that he considered them very highly important. And the apostle Paul, in desiring that no one should ignorantly say Amen in the church, at the assemblies of the faithful, seems to have same sentiment with John, that every one naming Christ should know Christ.

AMMI

That is, as the margin of the Bible renders it, my people; and Ruhamah, or perhaps, more properly Rachamah, having obtained mercy. (See Hosea ii. 1,) There is a great sweetness in these words, and the translators of our Bible, having retained them in their original language, as they have done, while at the same time giving the English of them in the margin, (as the reader will perceive if he consults his Bible) seem to show their view of the importance of the words themselves, and their wishes that the English reader should, in some measure, be acquainted with them, so as to have some apprehension of their importance.

I do not presume to decide positively upon the subject, yet I venture to believe, that the words themselves were meant to express somewhat of peculiar tenderness. Let the reader observe, that the Lord commands the prophet to call by this name, the brethren and sisters of the church. "Say ye to your brethren, Ammi, and to your sisters, Ruhamah: plead with your mother, plead." And whose brethren and sisters were those but of the Lord Jesus? And were they not the Ammi and Ruhamah of Christ from everlasting? Jesus had a people whom he was not ashamed to call brethren, and whom in the council of peace from the womb of the morning, the Lord JEHOVAH promised to make willing, in the day of Christ's power. (Ps. cx. 3.) Hence, therefore, as they had been always the Ammi, so had they been the Ruhamah; having obtained mercy, in their glorious and almighty Brother, from everlasting. And to such among them in the church, who in the days of the prophet, felt and rejoiced in their relationship to Christ, and their salvation by Christ, by the lively actings of their faith on Him that was to come; they were commanded to plead with their mother (the Ammah) the church, and to call her from her backsliding, that all her children might enjoy the same privileges. And the close of this same chapter, (if the reader will compare what is there said, with the sixth and ninth verses of the former chapter, he will find) becomes a blessed confirmation of the whole subject, for it explains wherefore it was, that the Lord thus remonstrated with his people. I will say to [to leave out the words,] them which were [for they are in Italics, and are not in the original, and have no business there] not my people, Thou my people, and they shall say, Thou my God; that is, I will put them in mind of the whole cause of my mercy towards them; namely, my covenant relation with them in Christ. And it is worthy the reader's closest consideration, in farther proof of these grand truths, that the putting them away, in consequence of their adulteries, had been done in strict justice, and by right. Such was the law of divorces. I beg the reader to see Deut. xxiv. 1-4. The prophet, therefore, had been commanded, by way of illustrating this doctrine, to take an adulterous woman, and to call the children born of her, Lo Ruhamah, and Lo Ammi; that is, not having obtained mercy, and not my people. And this was following up the law concerning the right of divorce. But though the law made no provision for recovery, the gospel, which was preached to Abraham four hundred and thirty years before the law, had done this; and the covenant which was confirmed before of God in Christ, the law could not disannul. And what was this covenant and promise? Turn to the apostle Paul's Epistle to the Galatians, chap. iii. 8. 17. and compare with Gen. xii. 3. where the charter of grace runs in those delightful words, In thee shall nations be blessed. Hence, though the law of divorce, among men, allowed not a return to each other after separation, yet, in the Lord's marriage with his church, the gospel not only allowed a return, but graciously appointed it. "They say (saith the Lord in one of the sweetest chapters of Jeremiah, and full of the sweetest promises, (Jer. iii.) they say, If a man put away his wife, and she go from him, and become another man's, shall he return unto her again? shall not that land be greatly polluted? But thou hast played the harlot with many lovers; yet return again to me, saith the Lord." (Jer. iii. 1.) What a full proof is here of the whole doctrine. Though put away by reason of her many adulteries, and though committing fornication with the idolatrous nations around, yet the everlasting provision made for her recovery in Christ, her lawful Husband, must take place; and she shall return to her rightful Lord. Plead, therefore, (saith the Lord) with her (Ammah) mother, plead; work upon her maternal feelings, give her to see, that though by adulteries she is by law justly liable to be divorced for ever, yet the right and interest of her (Ishi) husband, hath never been lost. He claims her as his own. Return again unto me, saith the Lord.

If the reader be led to consider the subject in this point of view, the expressions of Ammi and Ruhamah, with all the doctrine connected with both, become interesting and tender beyond all imagination. See Abba.

AMMI-NADIB

We meet with this word in Solomon's Song, chap. vi. 12. It is a compound word, consisting of Ammi, my people, and Nadib, willing, or generous, princely; some read the word, therefore, together, my princely people. And as all believers in Christ are made kings and priests to God and the Father, certainly, the expression is warrantable and just. But as the church is here speaking with grateful affection of her Lord, that so sudden and unexpected, as well as gracious, were the workings of his Holy Spirit upon her, it should seem that the word rather means in this place, a royal willingness wrought in her heart, by those impressions. It is therefore, as if she had said, Or ever I was aware of what my Lord, by his sweet influence, was working upon me, I found my whole soul going forth, in desires after him, as the swiftness of chariots. Blessed frame, and always to be desired.

AMMIEL

There were several of this name in Israel. Ammiel, the son of Gemal, (Num. xiii. 12.) Ammiel, the father of Machir, (2 Sam. ix. 4.) and Ammiel, the son of Obededom, (1 Chron. xxvi. 5.) And the name is, indeed, most desirable, meaning, the people of my God, from Arum and ll.

AMMIHUD

Several of the Israelites were called by this name. We find it, (Num. i. 10. Num. xxxiv. 20. 28.) It is a compound of Amm, people, and Hud, praise, and with the i, make it the people of my praise.

AMMISHADDAI

Ahiezer had a son of this name, (Num. i. 12.) and a very sweet and blessed compound it forms, meaning people of the Almighty, or the Almighty is with the people.

AMOS

A prophet of the Lord. See his prophecy. His name hath been sometimes spelt Omas, which signifies a burthen, or somewhat weighty. In allusion, perhaps, to the importance of his writings. But it is more generally spelt Amos, from Amatz, strong

ANATHEMA MARANATHA

We meet with this expression but once in the Scripture. (1 Cor. xvi. 22.) The apostle seems to have borrowed it from the Jews, whose custom was, when they could not find a punishment sufficiently great according to their apprehension of the crime, to devote the offender to the Lord's own punishment, in his own time and way. The apostle, therefore, in allusion to this custom, when speaking of those who love not the Lord Jesus Christ, as if no punishment he could think of would be equal to such horrible ingratitude and impiety, exclaims, Let him be Anathema Maranatha! The want of that love will be to him an everlasting source of bitterness. See Maranatha.

ANATHOTH
A beautiful village, in the tribe of Benjamin, about three miles from Jerusalem, remarkable for being the birthplace of the prophet Jeremiah. The name, if taken, as may be supposed, from Anath, signifies song.

ANCIENT OF DAYS
Three times, in the Prophecy of Daniel, and in the same chapter, we find the Lord distinguished by this name, and in no other part of Scripture. (Dan. vii. 9. 13. 22.) Some have thought that the person of God the Father is meant, and it should seem to be so, because it is also said, that One like the Son of man, (a well known character of the Lord Jesus Christ) came to him. See ver. 13. But others, considering the thrones spoken of in this chapter as the thrones of the house of David, and all judgment being committed to the Son, for the Father judgeth no man, (see John v. 22.) they have concluded, that it must be the Lord Jesus Christ which is spoken of under this glorious name. One thing however is certain, that this distinguishing name, and every other which marks the GODHEAD, may be and must be equally applied to each, and to all. The holy sacred Three, who bear record in heaven are One. (1 John v. 7.)

ANGEL
An order of beings with whom we are but little acquainted; and yet, in whose ministry the heirs of salvation are much concerned. (Heb. i. 14.) In Scripture we meet with many accounts of them. The Lord Jesus Christ himself is called the Angel or Messenger of the covenant. And his servants are called by the same name. But then, it should always be remembered, that these names, to both the Lord and his people, are wholly meant as messengers; for it is a sweet as well as an important truth, that Christ is no angel; "for verily he took not on him the nature of angels." (Heb. ii. 16.) So that as God, he is no angel; neither as man. I conceive, that it is highly important always to keep the remembrance of this alive in the mind. And that his people are no angels, they need not be told, for they are sinners; and they know themselves to be redeemed sinners, redeemed from among men. In the upper, brighter world, it is said that they shall be as the angels: that is, in glory and in happiness. But still men, and not angels, united to their glorious Head as the members of his mystical body to all eternity. (Exod. xxiii. 20. Zech. i. 12. Malachi iii. 1. Matt. xxii. 30. and xxv. 41. Rev. ii. 1.

ANGELS
Evil angels we read of, Psalm lxxviii. 49. And we read of "angels which kept not their first estate, but left their own habitation, that the Lord hath reserved in everlasting chains, under darkness, unto the judgment of the great day. (Jude 6.) And we read that Satan is sometimes - transformed into an angel of light." (2. Cor. ii. 14.) But the Scriptures are altogether silent respecting their nature, agency, and extent. The Holy Ghost hath been graciously pleased to give general precepts and warnings to the church, respecting the malignity of those evil angels, and to admonish the people of God to resist the devil, and that he shall flee from them. We are taught also, by the

several names given to the chief of those evil powers, to be always looking to the Lord Jesus for grace to resist the "fiery darts of this enemy," who is called, "the prince of this world." (John xii. 31.) "the prince of the power of the air; the spirit that now worketh in the children of disobedience," (Ephes. ii. 2.) But to numberless enquiries, which we feel highly disposed to put forth, concerning these things, there are no encouragements of any answers to be given in the word of God. It is very blessed, however, to be enabled by the promises of God, to take to ourselves those glorious and comprehensive assurances which belong to the whole church of Christ, and which ensure the present safety of every individual member, and the ultimate triumph in Christ, over Satan and all his angels. One Scripture tells the church, that " no temptation hath them taken, but such as is common to man: and that God is faithful, who will not suffer them to be tempted above that they are able; but will with the temptation also make a way to escape, that they may be able to bear it." (1. Cor. x. 13.) And another Scripture saith, that "the God of peace shall bruise Satan under their feet shortly." (Rom. xvi. 20.) Here then, is enough for every child of God to know and to rest in, until the whole comes to be explained in eternity. See Satan.

ANNUNCIATION
See Mary.

ANOINT
In the language of Scripture, this is a most important word. It means the consecrating, setting apart, and sanctifying, in a peculiar manner, persons or things to sacred purposes. Hence, in a very eminent and personal degree, the Lord Jesus Christ, as the Christ of God, is emphatically called the Messiah, or anointed of JEHOVAH. His name, Messiah, means this. It is, indeed, the same word in Hebrew, as Anointed in English. And what I particularly beg the reader to remark, under this article, as a proof of this dedication of

Christ, as Christ, to this office character, from everlasting, is, that he is all along in the Old Testament Scripture spoken of as such, the Messiah or Anointed, and shewn to be so in the New

A plain proof of his consecration by the Holy Ghost before his incarnation. I beg the reader not to pass on until that he hath turned to the following Scriptures, and read them all attentively. (Psal. lxxxix, 19, 20. 1 Sam. ii. 35. Psal. cx. 4.) Hence, Aaron as a type of Christ, (Exod. viii. 12; xxviii. 41. Psal. ii. 2; xlv. 7; cxxxii. 17.) Hence, the whole church is represented as calling upon God for acceptance and favour in Christ: "Behold, O God, our shield, and look upon the face of thine anointed!" (Psal. lxxxiv. 9.)

And as Christ is thus the Christ of God, so the church, by virtue of her union and oneness with him, is anointed with him, and that from the beginning. "Touch not mine anointed." (Ps. cv. 15; xxiii. 5. 1 John ii. 20. 27. 2 Cor. i. 21.) Reader! it is truly blessed to trace through both Testaments the testimonies of these things. What can be, indeed, more satisfactory to the soul than thus to discover, first, Christ, as the source and fountain and security of all our hopes; and then, secondly, to behold the church interested and made a rich partaker of the same in Him. (Acts iv. 27. Ps. cxxxiii. 3. Acts x. 38.)

APOSTLE
This is a word well known in the New Testament, It is peculiarly applied to the twelve men, whom the Lord Jesus called and commissioned to be his more immediate disciples and followers, to preach the gospel. But Christ himself condescended to be called by the same name. (Heb. iii. 1.) Indeed, he was the apostle of JEHOVAH. As it may be gratifying to have their names brought into one

APPAREL - ARCHANGEL

1 Peter.
Thomas.
2 Andrew.
3 John.
the Canaanite.
4 Philip.
brother of James.
5 James the Greater.
Less.
6 Bartholomew.
7
8 Matthew.
9 Simon
10 Jude, the
11 James the
12 Judas the Traitor.

Matthias was elected in the Traitor's room.

APPAREL

See Linen.

APPREHEND

In the language of Scripture, this word is peculiarly significant. Paul the apostle best explains it, when he saith, "I follow after, if that I may apprehend that, for which also I am apprehended of Christ Jesus." (Phil. iii. 12.) that is, if by faith, I may be enabled to lay hold of Christ Jesus, as the Lord by grace hath laid hold of me.

ARCHANGEL

I should not have thought it necessary, in a work of this kind, to have noticed this name, but for the purpose of noticing at the same time an error, into which, as I humbly conceive, not a few have fallen. I cannot find in all the Bible, the name archangel but twice; once in 1 Thess. iv. 16; and once in Jude 9. And as for archangels, as if there were more than one, or many, the very name itself implies that it is an error. For arch-angel signifies the first, or prince of the order of angels, consequently, there cannot be many firsts, without making it necessary to altar the term. So that, what is said of angels and archangels, together in hymns of praise, seems to be founded in a misapprehension of Scripture in relation to one arch-angel only, for the word of God speaks of no more, and the name is not plural.

The question is, who is this archangel, twice, and but twice only, noticed as such in Scripture? if the reader will consult both places, he will find that of whomsoever it be spoken of it is only spoken of him in office. And if the reader will compare the passage, particularly in Jude, with what the prophet Daniel saith, (chap. x. 13-21.) I conceive that both together will throw light upon the subject. "Lo!" saith the prophet, "Michael, one of the chief princes, came to help me." And again, he calls the same person, (ver. 21.) "Michael, your prince." In the passage of the apostle Jude's Epistle, he saith," Michael, the archangel, when contending with the devil, he disputed about the body of Moses." It should seem, therefore, pretty plain, that this Michael is one and the same person. In one he is called prince, in the other, archangel. But in both, it is evident, that the name is a name of office. For my own part, I do not hesitate to believe that it is Christ himself, which is meant by the name archangel in Scripture; and of whom it is said, in relation to his coming at the last day, that "he shall be revealed from heaven with his mighty angels." (2 Thess. i. 7.) And elsewhere, the Lord Jesus describes this advent in similar words. (Matt. xxv. 31; Zech. xiv. 5; Matt. xvi. 27.) And whether this appearing of Christ hath respect to his coming in his thousand years' reign upon earth, or to the universal judgment, the sense of the words (in reference to the subject of the archangel we are now considering) is the same. Some have thought that the archangel spoken of by Jude cannot mean Christ, because it is there said, that he durst not bring against Satan a railing accusation, but said, The Lord rebuke thee. But this is not an objection in the smallest degree. The Lord Jesus durst not do it; not because he dared not, or had not the power, but because it belonged not to the Redeemer's character, "who, when reviled, reviled not again, but committed himself judgeth righteously." (See Zech. iii.

1-4.) Here we have a similar contest. Now that he who spake was the Lord, appears by his saying, "Behold, I have caused thine iniquity to pass from thee, and I will clothe thee with a change of raiment." Hence, therefore, it is plain from this passage, that the angel before whom Joshua, as a type of the church, stood, was Christ, who is elsewhere called the angel of the covenant; (Mal. iii. 1.) the same as Jacob spake of. (Gen. xlviii. 16.) So that both the angel of the covenant and the archangel are one and the same; and both spoken of in the nature of the office and character of Christ, for Christ "took not on him the nature of angels, but the seed of Abraham." (Heb. ii. 16.)

From the whole view of this subject, I venture to believe, that, as Scripture speaks but of one arch-angel, and that officially, that archangel is Christ. For on the supposition, that it be not so, it becomes a matter of greater difficulty to say, who this arch-angel can be. If it be not Christ, it must be some created angel. And is there a created angel higher than Christ. If, while Jesus is called the angel of the covenant, is there an archangel also, above this angel of the covenant? I leave these questions with any one, not satisfied with my former observations, that the Lord Jesus Christ is the person spoken of twice in Scripture as the arch-angel. See Malachi and Michael.

ARK

We read in Scripture of the ark which the Lord directed Noah to make. (Gen. vi. 14.) And Moses in the wilderness was commanded to make an ark. (Exod. xxv. 10.) And we read of an ark seen by John in the temple in heaven; but then, this latter was visional. For the same apostle elsewhere saith, that he "saw no temple in heaven? (Rev. xi. 19. with Rev. xxi. 22.) The ark of Noah, as well as that of Moses, were types of the Lord Jesus Christ. Hence, Noah it is said by the Holy Ghost, (Heb. xi. 7.) "by faith being warned of God, "prepared an ark for the saving of his house." Faith in what? Surely, faith in the Lord Jesus Christ. And the ark in the wilderness is called the ark of the covenant, intimating Christ given of JEHOVAH to the people. (See Num. x. 33. Josh. iii. 11; vii. 6. with Isa. xlii. 6. 2 Chron. viii. 11.) We no where read of arks. Never is it said in the word of God of more than one ark; no more than one Lord Jesus Christ. They who talk of arks, like them who talk of archangels, do err, "not knowing the Scriptures, neither the power of God." And it were to be wished, that such men would call to mind the Lord's jealousy in the case of the men of Bethshemesh, (1 Sam. vi. 19.) and also the circumstance of Uzzah, (1 Chron. xiii. 10.) What was the sin of all those but overlooking Christ? And wherein do those differ, who talk of arks instead of one ark, and that expressly, and on no other account valuable, than as it represented the Lord Jesus? (1 Sam. iv. 3. 2 Sam. xv. 24.)

ARM OF THE LORD

In the language of Scripture, this is one of the names of Christ. Thus the prophet calls upon the Lord to arise for his people. (Isa. l. 9.) And thus the Lord promiseth, under this character, to make bare his holy arm; that is, to reveal Christ. (Isa. lii. 10. Luke i. 51.)

ARMIES

The church is called so, and said to be terrible. (Song vi. 10.) And in allusion to the same, the Lord himself is called the Lord of hosts. And hence, that expression in the hymn, Holy, holy, holy, Lord God of Sabaoth, or rather Zebaoth, which signifies, hosts or armies. Beautifully the Lord takes this title to himself; not only to indicate the greatness of his power, but the greatness of his security to his church and people, in his care and government over them. And it is a blessed thing to have this Lord God of Zebaoth for our stay. See Sabaoth.

ARMOUR - ASHES

ARMOUR

In Scripture terms, this word is for the most part used spiritually, meaning that divine strength is to be our armour against all opposition, and under all human weakness. (See Rom. xiii. 12. 2 Cor. vi. 7; x. 4. Eph. vi. 11-13.)

ARROW

This word is not unfrequently used in Scripture to denote divine judgments, and terrors in the soul from the arrow of the Lord. (See Zech. ix. 14. Job vi. 4. Ps. xxxviii. 7. Heb. iv. 12.)

ASCEND and ASCENSION

With peculiar reference to our Lord Jesus Christ, the Psalmist demands, "Who shall ascend into the hill of the Lord?" (Psal. xxiv. 3.) And in answer to the enquiry, we may truly say, that the glorious doctrine of the ascension is never cordially received, nor indeed properly understood, until that we are taught by the Lord the Spirit, to have both a just apprehension of his person who is ascended, and the blessed purposes included in that ascension for his church and people. The personal honour put upon Christ in our nature, and the oneness and interest all his redeemed have in that honour, are among the first and most important views we are called upon everlastingly to cherish in the heart, concerning our risen and exalted Saviour. It is our nature in the person of the man Christ Jesus that is thus exalted. And the purpose of that exaltation is, to receive gifts for men: or, as the margin of our Bibles renders the expression, it is to receive gifts in the man, even the human nature of Christ. Ps. lxvii. 18.) Oh! precious, precious in the GODHEAD of Christ's nature, no gifts could be received, all things being his in common with the Father and the Holy Ghost; so when received by Christ, as the Head of his body the church, it is as the Head of communication in "the fulness of Him that filleth all in all." (Eph. i. 22, 23.) And when this blessed doctrine is fully received, and lived upon, and enjoyed, what unknown blessings are contained in this one view, which the soul hath in this unceasing contemplation of our glorious and ascended Lord Jesus!

ASHER

One of the sons of Jacob, by Zilpah. (Gen. xxx. 12, 13.) His name means happy, or blessed; taken from the same word in the root which means blessed. Hence, Jacob, when adying, declared that "the bread of Asher should be fat." (Gen. xlix. 20.) And Moses, when blessing the children of Israel, with his last prophetical benediction, followed up the same in allusion to his name as blessed; "thy shoes (said Moses) shall be iron and brass; and as thy days, so shall thy strength be." (Deut. xxxiii. 24, 25.)

I cannot help remarking upon the name of Asher, that there is in it somewhat of peculiar gracefulness. The noun, which is taken from the root, is never used but in the plural number, blessedness instead of blessed, as in the first word of the first Psalm. And the Hebrews give a very decided reason for it. They say, that blessedness doth not depend upon a single blessing, but upon all. Hence, in allusion to the Lord Jesus Christ, he is the blessedness, the Asher of his people. So that the opening of that Psalm being plural, should be read with an eye to Christ; blessedness is the man, &c. And of none but Christ could this be said; neither to any other but Him, could the things spoken of in that Psalm refer.

ASHES

In the language of Scripture, ashes are sometimes spoken of to denote great humility and contrition of heart. Thus Abraham calls himself "dust and ashes." (Gen xviii. 27.) Job saith, that he "abhorred himself, and repented in dust and ashes." (Job xlii. 6. See Dan. ix, 3. Ps. cii. 9. Lam. iii. 16.)

ASP

The holy Scriptures, when speaking of the venom of asps, mean to convey by figure the awful nature of sin, which, like that deadly poison, hath infused itself into our whole nature. Hence Moses describes it, (Deut. xxxii. 33.) and Job, (xx. 14.) and Paul. (Rom iii. 13.) But how sweetly doth the prophet Isaiah describe, under the same figure, the application of Christ as a balsam, to cure the envenomed poison, and to render the serpent's bite as harmless. "The sucking child shall play on the hole of the asp, and the weaned child shall put his hand on the cockatrice den, They shall not hurt nor destroy in all my holy mountain." (Isa. xi. 8.)

ASS

I have thought it worth while, to stop the reader in this place, in order to make an observation or two on the condescension of the Lord Jesus, respecting his use of this animal, in the unequalled humility of our Lord's character. We read (Matt. xxi. 2, &c.) that the Lord Jesus, to fulfil the prophecy of one of his servants the prophets, made his entry into Jerusalem on an ass. But there seems to be a general mistake in respect to the humbleness of Christ, in what it consisted. Not, I apprehend, in riding on the ass, but in the person of the rider. White asses were among very noble animals in the estimation of the people of the East. Witness? what Deborah said of them in her song of triumph, (Judges v. 10.) "Speak ye that ride on white asses, ye that sit in judgment. (Judges xii. 14.) And Jacob, in his prophecy concerning Judah evidently had an eye to Christ: "Binding his foal (said Jacob) unto the vine, and his ass's colt unto the choice vine; he washed his garments in wine, and his clothes in the blood of grapes." (Gen. xlix. 11.) The humbleness of Christ, on this occasion, was the meekness and lowliness of his person, not from the noble beast he rode on.

But I will beg to detain the reader with another thought upon the subject, which hath not, as far as I have ever read or heard, been noticed; and yet may be after all, for aught I know, the chief circumstance for which the prophet predicted, and Jesus fulfilled, the prophecy. (Zech. ix. 9.) The ass, though a noble animal, was deemed by the Levitical law, unclean, for it chewed not the cud. (Lev. xi. 26.) And the same law declared, that whosoever touched such, should be deemed unclean. It was on this beast the Lord Jesus was pleased to make his entrance into Jerusalem. And was it not meant [I do not decide the point, but merely ask the question] to shew, that he came to take away the defilements and uncleanness of his people? If Christ became both a sin and a curse for his people, (2 Cor. v. 21. Gal. iii. 13.) might there not be somewhat significant and typical in thus riding upon a beast deemed by the law unclean? I leave the reader to his own determination on the point, under the grace of God.

AVENGER

Particular mention is made in Scripture of the avenger of blood, (Deut. xix. 6.) and cities of refugee were appointed for the manslayer. (Numb. xxxv. 12. Josh. xx. 5.) There is much of Christ as a refuge, represented under this appointment, and we shall do well at any time when reading those Scriptures, to be on the look out for discoveries of the Lord Jesus in the several features of the history. Every man, by sin, is a murderer, yea; a soul murderer, and that of himself. And the avenger, both in the law of God and the justice of God, is always, it may be said, in pursuit of the sinner, until he hath taken shelter in Christ. Jesus is the city of refuge. And Jesus is near to flee unto. (Heb. vi. 18.) It was not the stronghold of those places which secured the manslayer, but because it was the provision of divine mercy. "Salvation the Lord appointed for walls and bulwarks." (Isa. xxvi. 1.) And what endeared the city of refuge to the manslayer was, that it was wholly of God's own appointing. And the geneeral and extensive nature of its security was, that poor stranger, as well as the Israelite, found a sanctuary. (Num. xxxv. 15.) Such is the Lord in the greatness and extensiveness of his salvation. "For (saith the apostle) there is neither Jew nor Greek, neither bond nor free, male nor female, for they are all one in Christ Jesus." (Gal. 20.) Sweet type of Jesus, the city of refuge. See Bezer.

AWAKE

In scriptural language, this word is very frequently used to denote a spiritual recovery from death and deadness of sin. Hence, the apostle saith, (Ephes. v. 14.) "Awake, thou that and arise from the dead, and Christ shall give thee light." Hence, the church saith," I sleep, but mmy heart waketh." (Song v. 2.) Heace, the state my the unregenerate, who are never awakened, are described by the prophet under the image of a perpetual sleep. (Jer. li. 57.) Sometimes, the Lord himself is called upon by the church, under the image of awakening, to come to her deliverance, "Awake, awake, O arm of the Lord," &c. (Isa. li. 9.) And the church, in like manner, is called upon by the Lord, Isa. li. 17; lii. 1.

AZARIAH

There were many of this name among the Israelites. (See 1 Chron. vi. 9, 10. 2 Chron. xxvi. 17) The name means, assistance from the Lord, from Azar.

AZEL

One of the family of Kish. (1 Chron. viii. 37.) This name should seem to have been derived from Azazel, taken away, or separated, and by which the scape-goat in the wilderness was called. See Expiation.

B

BAAL

A name generally used for an idol. And when more than a single idol is spoken of, the word is made plural, Baalim. The children of Israel, from being surrounded with idolatrous neighbours, too often were led away by their allurements to the same idolatry. (See Num. xxii. 41. Judges ii. 13. 1 Kings xvi. 31. 2 Kings x. 19. Hosea ii. 8.)

I cannot take a more effectual method to shew the Lord's watchful care over his Israel, to preserve them from this contagion, than what the Lord himself hath manifested in that beautiful chapter, the second of the prophecy of Hosea. If the reader will turn to it, and peruse it from beginning to end, he will observe, that at that time the tribes of the Lord were much disposed to idolatry. The Lord sets himself therefore to bring them back, and in opening to them the prospects of salvation, shews how he will bring them under afflictions, in wilderness dispensations, and then having hedged their way up with thorns, compels them, by his grace, to return to him their first lover. And to keep them from revolting again, he will open to them a new name, whereby they shall know him and delight in him. "And it shall be in that day, saith the Lord, that thou shalt call me Ishi, and shalt call me no more Baali. For I will take away the names of Baalim out of her mouth." (Hosea ii. 16, 17.) In the margin of the Bible, Ishi is rendered my husband. The reader will have a full apprehension of the grace and loving kindness of the Lord in this ordination, when he is told, that as the word Baal, Lord; or Baali, my lord, was a general name to imply lordship, or sovereignty: the Lord JEHOVAH had been considered as Israel's Baal, to distinguish him from the nations' Baal around. But as there was not distinction enough in those general names, to preserve Israel in a proper sense of reverence between JEHOVAH, and those dunghill gods, being all alike called Baal, or Lord; the Lord graciously saith, in this sweet Scripture, that he will be no more called Baal, but will lose as it were, the name of Lord, in that of husband. Thou shalt call me Ishi; that is, my husband, my man. Was there ever an instance of such rich grace and condescension and love?

I beg the reader to pause over it, and ponder it well. And when he hath duly contemplated the unequalled subject, let him add to it the farther consideration, how the Lord Jesus Christ hath really, and indeed, fulfilled all he here promised, in becoming the Husband of his church and people. Hence the prophet sings, "For thy Maker is thine husband, the Lord of hosts is his name: and thy Redeemer the Holy One of Israel, the God of the whole earth shall he be called." (Isa. liv. 5.) Surely, nothing can be wanting to give the most finishing testimony to the grace that is in Christ Jesus. Blessed Husband of thy church; be thou my Ishi for ever!

BAAL-BERITH

(Judges viii. 33. and ix. 4.) This dunghill god was made the idol of the children of Israel, after the death of Gideon. The name Berith means the Lord of the covenant. But what covenant? Was Israel so far gone in idolatry, as not only to set up an idol, but to insult JEHOVAH in his gracious covenant? To what an awful state is our nature reduced by the fall! Into what an awful apostacy may, and will, every man sink, void of grace! Reader, turn to that sweet covenant promine, Jer. xxxii. 40.

BAAL-GAD

This was another of the heathen idols, and as we learn from the book of Joshua, (chap. xi, 17.) was set up in the valley of Lebanon.. Gad means fortune; so that Baal-gad means a lord of fortune.

BAAL-HAMON

I am inclined to think that this was not an idol, but a place; for the church, celebrating the glories of her Solomon, saith, that he had a vineyard at Baal-hamon (Song viii. 11.) Hamon, is people, multitudes, or riches. So that Baal-hamon may be rendered, lord or master of a troop, or people. We all apprehend, that "the vineyard of the Lord of hosts is the house, of Israel; and the men of Judah his pleasant plant." (Isa. v. 7.)

BAAL-MEON

This was the idol of Beth-jesimoth, and is rendered, "the Lord of the house." (Ezek. xxv. 9.)

BAAL-PEOR

This was the famous, or rather infamous dunghill idol of Moab; and which they tempted the Israelites worship. The Psalmist mournfully speaks of it, (Ps. cvi. 18.) "they joined themselves unto Baal-peor, and ate the offerings of the dead." (Num. xxv. 1-3. Hos. ix. 10.) From what this prophet saith of their shame; and from the impure name of this strumpet idol; there is reason to believe that the greatest indecency was joined with idolatry, in the, worship of this Baal-peor.

BAAL-PERAZIM

At this spot, the Philistines were put to flight by David, (2 Sam. v. 20. 1 Chron. xiv. 11.) The margin of the Bible hath rendered this name, the plain of breaches. And, consequently, David was the lord or master of it.

BAAL-SHALISHA

We meet with mention of this place, 2 Kings iv. 42, but whether there was an idol there, is not said. Shalesh is the Hebrew for three. So that it may be read the lord of three. But the cause for the name is difficult to explain.

BAAL-TAMAR

A place near Gibeah. (Judges xx. 33.) It might be famous for palm-trees; for so Tamar means.

BAAL-ZEBUB

So called from Baal, lord, and Zebub, a fly. And this was the ridiculous idol worshipped at Ekron, to whom Ahaziah, king of Israel, sent to enquire concerning his recovery from a fall he had from his terrace. (See 2 Kings i. 2, 3.) How very sadly this weak prince answered to his name! The man that was called Ahaziah should have had better views of the Lord, Achaz and Jah, meant, vision of the Lord. Whereas, his was a vision of folly!

The Egyptians, it should seem, as well as the being near neighbours, paid divine to this contemptible idol. It is possible, the folly of this idolatry might take its rise from the plague of the flies, which Egypt suffered on account of Israel. (See Exod. viii. 20, &c.) But it said also by historians, that the rivers of Egypt abound with flies whose sting is very painful. It is worthy remark, that the name of this idol changed only from Baal-zebub in Hebrew, to Beel-zebub in Greek, was given to the devil, in the days of our Lord's ministry upon earth. It doth not appear that was worshipped at that time; but it is evident so generally known and acknowledged by this name, that the Pharisees made use of it as a well known, and in a daring blasphemy, the miracles of the Lord Jesus to his power (See Matt. xii. 24.)

BAAL-ZEPHON

Some have thought that this was only the name of a place. And some have concluded that it was the name of an idol. The words together may be read, the lord of secret, meaning one that inspects, and discovers what is hidden. One thing however is certain concerning it, that it was over against Baal-zephon, the Lord directed

Israel to encamp, when the Egyptians were pursuing them after their departure from Egypt. I beg the reader to consult the Scripture concerning it, (Exod. xiv. 2.) Piha-hiroth it should seem was so called, because it formed the mouth or gullet of entrance to the sea. And Migdol, which means a tower, was a watch-place, where it is probable that this idol was placed to watch, or pretend to watch, at the extremity of the kingdom of Egypt, on this part to the sea, by way of deterring runaway servants, or slaves, like Israel, from attempting their escape. It was in this very spot, as if, at once, to shew Israel the folly of such ridiculous idols; and to shew Egypt of what little avail their dunghill deities were; Israel was commanded to encamp, from whence they should behold the arm of the Lord displayed for their deliverance, and at the same time Egypt's destruction. (See Exod. xii. 12, &c. Num. xxxii. 4.)

BABE

I should not have noticed this article, being so perfectly understood in its common sense and meaning, but for the peculiar use that is made of it, in reference to the person of the Lord Jesus Christ, and to his church in him. There is somewhat very sweet and interesting in it, considered in these views. To contemplate the Ancient of days as the Babe of Bethlehem; and to behold the church in every individual member, as babes in Christ, the imagination finds large scope for the indulgence of the most solemn meditation, when the subject is opened to the believer by God the Holy Ghost. We enter upon hallowed ground, when the Lord the Spirit leads us to behold by faith Him, whom the apostles called "the holy child Jesus." (Acts iv. 27.) And there is a most blessed and inexpressible sweetness in the soul's joy, when, at the same time, through the same almighty Teacher, we enter into an apprehension of our child-like union with him, and interest in him. (Luke ii. 12-18. Psal. viii. 2. Matt. xi. 25. I Pet. ii. 2.)

BABEL

This word is, what it is designed to be, babel, or confusion. And our English language; in the strong term of bablers, has very happily borrowed from the Scripture babel or babbel, to express confusion. It were unnecessary for me to add, that Babel was the name given to the tower which the impiety of men began to build after the deluge. (Gen. xi. 9.) And here also was the foundation of that city of Babylon laid, which in after ages became the confusion and sorrow of the church during the seventy years' desolation. (Gen. x. 10.) And to go farther still, mystical Babylon, in the error and follies by which it is distinguished, may well retain the name, as the Scriptures have given it, for nothing but confusion is in it, and in confusion must it end. (Rev. xvii. 5. and xviii. throughout.)

I cannot forbear adding one short, but I hope not unprofitable observation, by way of noting the wonderful grace and overruling power of God. By the confusion at Babel, in a diversity of tongues, and which ever since hath distinguished nations; the Lord rendered that miracle at Pentecost, of his poor servants speaking in every language then under heaven in a moment, and with the greatest fluency, a full proof of "the Lord speaking in them, and by them." But for this diversity of language the glory of this miracle would have been wanting; since, had all nations, as before the confusion at the tower of Babel they did, spoken but one language; the disciples of Jesus would have needed the use of no other. But by this punishment in the plains of Shinar, the Lord laid the foundation of his own glory and his servants' honour; and the wonderful conversion of souls, at that season of Pentecost, demonstrated both the power of God, and the wisdom of God, in confirmation of the faith.

BABYLON

This eminent city, which was once the most noble and magnificent in the whole earth, the capital of the Chaldean empire: and concerning which the Scriptures themselves speak so highly, (See Dan. iv. 30.) is now so totally overthrown, that not a vestige remains. By Isaiah the prophet, the Lord declared this ruin, (Isa. xiii. 19. to the end;) and every traveller that hath seen the ground it stood on confirms it. The approach to the ruins, on account of the venomous creatures which inhabit it, is so dangerous, that no man durst venture, and many parts for ages have not been explored. Who that considers this, and connects with it what the prophets declared concerning it, years before the event took place, but must be struck with wonder and praise! I beg the reader to look again at Isaiah's prophecy, chap. xiii. 19 to the end.

And when the reader hath duly pondered the subject, concerning the natural history of Babylon, thus desolated as the enemy of Christ and his church; he will do well to consider the subject in the spiritual sense of it, according to what the Scriptures have declared of mystical Babylon. Let him turn to the Revelations of John, and hear what the Spirit saith, concerning the awful close to all the enemies of Christ and his church. (See Rev. chap. xvii. and xviii.)

BACA, or BACHA

We meet with this word but once in Scripture, and that is in the book of Psalms, (Ps. lxxxiv. 6.) The meaning of it seems to be (weeping; though some consider it as referring to the mulberry tree.

BACKSLIDING

I humbly conceive that this word, and which we often meet with in Scripture, is not so well understood, by the generality of readers, as it were to be wished. The common received opinion concerning backsliding is, that it is turning back, or going away, from the Lord. Whereas the very word itself implies sliding backward, and not turning round, and going away. The Lord himself, by his servant the prophet Hosea, makes use of a simile, which seems to explain the meaning, "Israel (saith the Lord) slideth back as a backsliding heifer." (Hosea iv. 16.) Now, how doth an heifer slide back? I apprehend not by turning back, and going another path; but like one on slippery ground, whose steps, so far from gaining ground, rather lose ground. But all the while the heifer is still with her face and feet the same way, only sliding back, and not getting forward. And what follows, in the same verse, seems to confirm this sense of backsliding. "Now the Lord will feed them as a lamb in a large place." So that the Lord undertakes to preserve Israel from sliding back, by putting his people in a roomy place, where the ground shall not be slippery.

I do not presume to suppose, that I am right in this my conjecture concerning backsliding. I only venture to give my opinion upon it, as it strikes me. The Lord pardon me if I err. One thing, however, is certain, the recovery of all backsliding is of the Lord; and his promise to his people, on this subject, is most blessed. "I will heal their backslidings, I will love them freely." (Hos. xiv. 4, Jer. iii. 22.)

BALAAM

This was the famous, or rather infamous conjuror of the East, whose awful history is so fully recorded in the book of Numbers, and whose most awful end is given to us in the 31st chapter of the same book, and 8th verse. (See also Joshua xiii. 22.) His name, it should seem, is derived from Balel, and signifies old age. For his history, I refer the reader to Num. xx. and the two following chapters. In relation to the character of Balaam, it will be proper for me to beg the reader's attention to what the word of God hath left upon record concerning him, in order to have a clear apprehension of the subject; comparing Scripture with Scripture, as we are commanded to do, 1 Cor. ii. 13.

It appears from the accounts given of Balaam, in the opening of his history,

(Num. xxii. I, &c.) that Balak, prince of Moab, fearful of the growing power of Israel, invited this Balaam from the East, to come to Moab and to use enchantments against Israel. It should seem from the history of Egypt, in the magicians we read of in that history, that this custom of using enchantments among idolatrous nations, was very common. (Exod. vii. 11.) Prompted by the love of gain, Balaam readily listened to the messengers of Balak, and lodged them for the night, pretending that he would conconsult the Lord upon the subject, and go with them if permitted. But the Lord commanding him not to go, for that the people, the prince of Moab wished him to curse, were blessed; Balaam sent the messengers away, without going with them. We are not informed by what means the Lord communicated to Balaam his command: probably by a vision of the night; but, certainly, in such a way as left Balaam with full impressions on his mind, had he not heard the history of Israel before, that they were "a people blessed of the Lord."

Balak, not discouraged by Balaam's refusal, sent again to him: and the wretch, earnest to go, pretended again to ask the Lord's leave. And the sequel of this embassy from Balak was, that he arose and went. There seems to occur some little difficulty in the relation, as given in the Bible concerning Balaam's going; because it is said by the Lord, If the men come to call thee, arise and go. But the thing had been determined before by the Lord's telling Balaam, that the people were blessed. How then could he dare to tempt the Lord by any farther enquiry? and how could he presume to go forth, at the call of this idolatrous prince, to curse those whom the Lord had told him were blessed? We cannot but suppose that Balaam, coming out of the East, must have heard of Israel, and the Lord's care over them. Indeed his pretending to consult the Lord, at the first invitation of Balak, very fully proves, that he was no stranger to the history of Israel; and the Lord's bringing them out of Egypt, which all the people of the East had heard of with trembling. (Exod. xv. 14, &c.) So that Balaam could not be ignorant of the Lord's love for Israel.

But what decides the infamy of Balaam's character is this, that under all the impressions that the Lord had blessed Israel, and would bless them, Balaam was still so very earnest to oblige Balak, and get his promised reward, that he set off expressly the purpose of cursing Israel; neither, as the apostle saith, did "the dumb ass, speaking with man's voice, forbidding the madness of the prophet," keep back his feet from the evil of his journey; so much did he love" the wages of unrighteousness? (See 2 Pet. ii. 16.)

I need not go through with a comment on the several interesting particulars of Balaam's tampering with his conscience while with Balak, in seeking enchantments, and in using every effort to curse God's people, while all he said and did the Lord over-ruled to make him bless them. But there is one feature in the history and character of this man, which will serve to explain the whole; and to shew, that when disappointed of all the means he had used to gratify Balak, though compelled by a power he could not resist, to bless those he wished to curse; yet he gave Balak an advice concerning Israel, by way of accomplishing their ruin, which, but for the Lord's preventing and pardoning grace, would indeed have tended to the ruin of Israel more than all Balak's arms, or Balaam's enchantments; namely, in counseling Balak to tempt Israel to come to the sacrifices, and to open an intercourse of Israel's sons with the daughters of Moab. This plan, therefore, Balak adopted; and soon after we find Israel at the feast of their infamous sacrifices. The Psalmist, speaking of this sad history, (Ps. cvi. 28, 29.) saith, "they joined themselves unto Baal-peor, and did eat the sacrifices of the dead." This

BALAAM - BALAAM

Baal-peor was an obscene idol, before which image, the votaries offered the most horrid prostitution of their bodies, and wrought such abomination as would be shocking to the feelings of chastity to relate. (See Baal-peor. See Num. xxv. throughout.)

We should not have known that it was from the advice of Balaam, the Moabites enticed Israel to sin, in the matter of Baal-peor, had not the Holy Ghost graciously informed us of it, in his holy word. But, if the reader will turn to the second chapter of Revelations, and read the fourteenth verse, there the whole matter is explained. (See also Num. xxxi. 15, 16.)

The awful termination of the life of Balaam is just as might be expected. I refer the reader to the Scripture account of it." (Num. xxxi. 8.) How Balaam came to be amongst the Midianites when the Lord's judgments overtook them, is not said; for we are told, in the former history, (Num. xxiv. 25.) that he rose up and went unto his place. Probably, he returned afterwards to live with the Midianites, to see if he might be farther helpful to them by his enchantments. And, perhaps, as Balak had promised to reward him with very great honours, he might have quitted his home, in the east of Aram, to be made a prince among the Midianites. But be this as it may, here he was, by the overruling power and providence of God, when Moab and Midian were destroyed; and fell with, them, unpitied, and with infamy on his name for ever.

We must not close our view of Balaam, without a short observation of the awfulness of such a character. When we read the many blessed things which the Lord, as he had graciously said, compelled Balaam to utter concerning his Israel, "the word that I shall speak unto thee, (said the Lord) that thou shalt speak." (Num. xxii. 20-35.) When we hear this impious man's confession, that "he had heard the words of God, and knew the knowledge of the Most High; had seen the vision of the Almighty, falling into a trance, but having his eyes open." (Num. xxiv. 15, 16.) When we hear such things dropping from his lips, and in the same moment hiring himself out for the honours of this world, as an enchanter, to curse the people of God, whom God had told him were blessed; what an awful picture doth this afford of human depravity! Many of God's dear children, from mistaken views of such characters, have been frequently tempted to call in question their own sincerity, and to fear, lest like Balaam, they should be found apostates in the end. But all this from the misapprehension of things, and not from the smallest likeness between their circumstances and Balaam's. There may be, and indeed there often is, a natural apprehension which natural men often have, concerning divine things, where there is no one work of the Lord upon the heart. Men, by reading, or by hearing, may acquire great knowledge in the truths of God, so as to speak and discourse, as Balaam did very sweetly on the subject; but whose souls never felt any love of God, nor desire of salvation. This is head knowledge, not heart influence. This is all nature, not grace. Devils know more, in point of doctrine and the truths of Jesus, to their eternal sorrow, than many of God's dear children do, to their eternal joy, while here below. Witness what they said, Luke iv. 41. at a time when his people were, many of them, ignorant of him. How shall we mark the difference? The thing is very easy, under the blessed Spirits teaching; "when the Spirit witnesseth to our spirits that we are his children." There is a pleasure, a delight, an holy joy, in the soul of the regenerated, in the view of Christ and his salvation. Not all the riches of the earth would tempt such to curse the people of God, or even to hear the people of God cursed, but with the utmost indignation. In their darkest hours, and under the dullest of their frames, there is still a secret desire within to the love of Jesus, and the remembrance of his name, (Isa. xxvi. 9.)

And while such as Balaam write their own mittimus for everlasting misery, as in those soul-piercing words, when speaking of Christ, "I shall see him, but not now; I shall behold him, but not nigh;' (Num. xxiv. 17.) the hope and expectation of the poorest and humblest child of God is expressed in those sweet words, "As for me, I shall behold thy face in righteousness; I shall be satisfied when I awake with thy likeness." (Ps. xvii. 15.)

There is one thing more I wish to drop a word of observation upon, respecting the history of Balaam. The reader will, probably, anticipate the circumstance to which I refer; namely, the conversation which Balaam held with his ass. I do not hesitate to say, that I wholly agree with St. Austin, and accept the fact simply as it is related, and believe it to have been a miracle of the Lord's. I form my opinion on the authority of the Holy Ghost, who, by his servant the apostle Peter, expressly saith, that "the dumb ass, speaking with man's voice, forbad the madness of the prophet." (2 Pet. ii. 16.) The occasion was as extraordinary and interesting, as the event of the animal being so commissioned to reprove; and for such an occasion, as in numberless other instances in life, the ordinary appointments in the Lord's providences may be well supposed to be superseded. The only, or at least, the most striking circumstance in the whole relation is, the loss of the wonderful event on Balaam's mind, that he should have been so addressed, and give such an answer, and yet persist in his iniquitous journey. But even here again, similar effects on the minds of sinners, in every age, are continually produced, and the end is the same. What conviction was frequently wrought upon the minds of the Jews, when beholding the miracles of Christ. But yet, what lasting effect did that conviction ultimately produce! He who well knew the human heart, void of sovereign grace, hath left it upon record as an unerring conclusion, that where the word of God is despised and set at nought, no higher evidences, even of miracles, will succeed: "If they hear not Moses and the prophets, neither would they be persuaded, though one should rise from the dead." (Luke xvi. 31.)

BALADAN

A king of Babylon. (2 Kings xx. 12.) The name seems to be a compound of Baal and Adorn, both meaning lord.

BALAK

The Prince of Moab and Midian: the son of Zippor. We have his history, Num. xxii. and following chapters. His name signifies, wasting, from Lakak, to lick up, and the prefix Beth, with. See Balaam.

BAMAH

We meet with this name but once, namely in Ezek. xx. 29. It means an high place. Bamoth is the plural of it, and we meet with this several times, Num. xxi. 19, 20. Bamoth Baal, a city beyond Jordan. (Josh. xiii. 17.)

BANI

There are several of this name in Scripture, (See 2 Sam. xxiii. 36. 1 Chron. vi. 46. Ezra ii. 10.) Some render the word, from Ban, son. Hence, Rachel named her son, Benoni, in her dying moments, while Jacob called him Benjamin. The mother's name made him Ben, the son, oni, of my sorrow. The father's Ben, the son, jamin, the right hand, or the hand of strength.

BANNER

In a figurative language, Christ is said to be an ensign, or standard, to his people. (Isa. xi. 10, 12.) Hence, the Psalmist, in allusion to Christ, "Thou hast given a banner to them that feared thee, that it may be displayed because of the truth." (Ps. lx. 4.) And when Moses built an altar, after the victory obtained over Amalek, he called the name of it JEHOVAH Nissi; that is, the Lord is my banner. And what Lord but Christ? Were not both the altar and the banner tokens of the Lord Jesus Christ? (Exod. xvii. 15.) Hence, the church speaks, in allusion to Christ, "In the name of our God, we set up our banners." (Ps. xx. 5.) And hence also, the church, when beheld in her warlike appearance, fighting in the strength of her Lord, is said to be, "fair as the moon, clear as the sun, and terrible as an army with banners." (Song vi. 4. 10.) It is very blessed to eye Christ in this most glorious character, as JEHOVAH'S banner to his people, for their waging war with sin, death, and hell. He is lifted up from everlasting, in the glories of his person, as the church's Husband from all eternity. Hence, the Standard-bearer among ten thousand, under whose shadow all his redeemed are safe, and made more than conquerors through Him that loveth them. Reader! believer! friend! are we under this almighty Banner? Hath the Lord Jesus brought us to his banqueting house, and is his banner over us of love? Oh, then, let us sit down under his shadow, for, surely, all his fruit is sweet to our taste! Sure banner of peace with God, and good will towards men! See Jehovah Nissi.

BAPTISM

One of the ordinances which the Lord Jesus hath appointed in his church. An outward token, or sign, of an inward and spiritual grace. A dedication to the glorious, holy, undivided Three in One Father, Son, and Holy Ghost; in whose joint name baptism is performed, and from whose united blessings in Christ, it can alone be rendered effectual. (Matt. xxviii. 19.) Beside this ordinance, which Christ hath appointed as the introduction to his church, we are taught to be always on the watch, in prayer and supplication, for the continual baptisms of the Holy Ghost. Concerning the personal baptisms of the Lord Jesus Christ, we hear Jesus speaking of them during his ministry. (See Luke xii. 50.) Hence, to the sons of Zebedee, the Lord said, "Can ye drink of the cup that I shall drink of, and be baptized with the baptism that I am baptized with?" And Jesus added, "Ye shall drink of the cup that I drink of, and with the baptism that I am baptized withal shall ye be baptised." (Mark x. 38, 39.)

Some have thought, that these expressions are figurative of sufferings. But there doth not seem sufficient authority in the word of God to prove this. And, indeed, the subject is too much obscured by those expressions, to determine that sufferings were the baptisms to which the Lord had respect. Besides, had sufferings been meant by Christ, could he mean that the sons of Zebedee were to sustain agonies like himself in the garden and on the cross? This were impossible.

Others, by baptism, have taken the expression of John the Baptist literally, where he saith, "I indeed baptize you with water unto repentance; but he that cometh after me is mightier than I, whose shoes I am not worthy to bear, he shall baptize you with the Holy Ghost and with fire." (Matt. iii. 11.) Others, with more probability of truth, have considered the baptisms of the Holy Ghost, and with fire, to mean his manifold gifts and graces. The Old Testament spake of "the Spirit of judgment and the Spirit of burning." (Isa. iv. 4.) And the New Testament gives the record of the first descent of the Holy Ghost, after Christ's return to glory, in the shape of cloven tongues, like as of fire, which sat upon each of them. (Acts ii. 4.) It were devoutly to be prayed for, and sought for by faith, that all true believers in Christ were earnest for the continual influences of the Holy Ghost, as the only read and sure testimony of being baptized unto Christ, in having put on Christ. For if any man have not the Spirit of Christ, he is none of his? (Gal. iii. 27. Rom. viii. 9.)

BAPTIST

John the Baptist, the herald and fore-runner of our Lord, predicted by the prophets. (See Isa. xl. 1-8. Mal. iii. 1.) I must refer to the Gospels for the history of the Baptist. It would far go beyond the limits of this work, to enter upon the account of John's life. One feature in his history and character I would only beg to an observation upon, and that is, indeed, in view, a very important one; namely, on his to the person and glory of Christ. The reader will recollect, that concerning John the Baptist, Jesus himself declared, that "among them that were born of women, there had never arisen a greater prophet than John the Baptist." (Matt. xi. 11.) Now attend to what this greatest born of women saith, concerning his almighty Master: "The Jews sent priests and Levites to ask John who he was; and he confessed, and denied not; but confessed, I am not the Christ. And they said, Who art thou? And he said, I am the voice of one crying in the wilderness, Make straight the way of the Lord? (John i. 19-23. yea, to 31.) And what is a voice? Merely a sound, and no more. It is not so much as a person, but only ministers to a certain purpose, for which it is designed, and then dies away in the air, and is heard no more. Such, in comparison to the Lord Jesus Christ, was this greatest of all prophets, born among women. What a blessed testimony to the GODHEAD and glory of Oh! that Socinians and Deists would think of it!

BARABBAS

A well-known name, rendered memorable from being preferred by the Jews to the Lord Jesus Christ, though a murderer and a thief. His name signifies; son of the father, from Bar, son; and Ab, father.

BARACHEL

Father of Elihu. (Job xxxii. 2.) His name signifies, one who blesseth God; from Barach, to bless; and El, God.

BARACHIAS

Father of Zacharias, spoken of Matt. xxiii. 35. His name signifies, to bless the Lord; from Barach, to bless; and Jah, Lord. We meet with several of this name is Scripture. (1 Chron. iii. 20; vi. 39; and ix. 16.)

BARAK

The son of Abinoam. We have his history, Judges iv. and v. His name signifies, thunder.

BAR-JESUS

A false prophet, spoken of Acts xiii. 6. His name signifies, the son of Jesus.

BAR-JONA

The son of Jonah. (Matt. xvi. 17.) Sometimes Jonah means pigeon.

BARNABAS

The son of the prophet, from Nabi, a prophet. The writer of the Acts of the Apostles derives his name from Jabah, consolation. (Acts iv. 36,)

BARSABAS

The son of return; for so the word seems to be best explained. This man was so highly esteemed by the apostles, as to be put in nomination for the apostolic office, in the room of the traitor Judas. (Acts i. 23.)

BARTHOLOMEW

One of the apostles of Christ. His name signifies, a son of Tholomy, or, as some read, Ptolemy. Some are of opinion, that Bartholomew and Nathaniel are the same person. And in confirmation of this, it is remarkable, that where the one name is mentioned in Scripture the other is not.

BAR-TIMEUS

Son of Timeus: from Bar, son; and Thamam, finished. We have his history, and

BARUCH - BEER-LA-HAI-ROI

a very interesting history it is, Mark x. 46, &c.

BARUCH

Son of Neriah, An interesting character, as related to us in the prophecy of Jeremiah. (ch. xxxii. 36. 43. 45.) His name is derived from Barach, to bless.

BASHAN

A most rich and fruitful country. It lay beyond Jordan; and before Israel's conquest, it was possessed by Og. The sacred writers continually speak of the fertility of this land. The name seems expressive of it, Beth, in; Shen, the very mouth or tooth.

BATH

A measure among the Hebrews, of the same dimensions as the ephah, which contained seven gallons and four pints, liquid measure; and three pecks, three pints, dry measure. (Isa. v. 10. Ezek. xlv. 10, 11.)

BATH-SHEBA

The wife of Uriah. Her history we have 2 Sam. xi, &c. If from Shaboh, which is the number seven; probably as Bath, is daughter, means, the seventh daughter.

BEELZEBUB

See Baalzebub.

BEER-LA-HAI-ROI

The margin of our old English Bibles hath rendered this compound word by "The well of Him that liveth and seeth me." (Gen. xvi. 14.) The history which gave rise to this name being given to this well, is most beautiful and interesting. I entreat the reader to turn to it. His attention will be well rewarded. (Gen. xvi. 1 to 14.) It was Hagar, the handmaid of Sarai, which gave this name to the well, when she fled from her mistress, and was found by the angel of the Lord near a fountain of water in the wilderness of Shur. There is uncommonly striking in the history. I admire faith of this poor servant. And I beg to adore the Lord still more, in both giving her that faith, and affording so blessed an opportunity for the exercise of it

That Hagar should have her steps directed into the wilderness-that there she should find a well of water, already prepared to her hands, when we know how rare and precious wells were considered in the Eastern world; what pains men took to dig them; and what strife for possessing them they occasioned;--that there the Lord should manifest himself to her, and give her such gracious promises:--these are so many distinct tokens of divine love. And how blessedly did the Lord, that led Hagar there, and present before her such testimonies of his watchful care over all, give her grace also, to eye the Lord's hand in the Lord's appointment. Hagar perceived the Lord's grace in all. And she discovered his mercy towards her in all: so that, under the full impression of a full heart, she cried out, "Thou, God, seest me."

I cannot dismiss the subject before that I have first requested the reader to ask himself, whether, when at any time in the wilderness frames of his own heart, or under the wilderness dispensations the Lord hath brought him into, he hath not often found a well of seasonable and unexpected supplies, like that of Hagar, so that he could call it Beer-la-hai-roi? How very often hath it been found, yea, it may always be found, in the believer's exercises, that where we least expected, there most of Jesus hath been discovered. That precious Redeemer, always beforehand with his people, and going before them in all his providences, as well as in all his grace, hath been at length manifested to the soul, in the close of some trying dispensation, as having been all the while present, appointing all, regulating all, watching over all, and giving a sweet and precious finish in his sanctifying blessing on the providence to all; though to our timid and unwatchful hearts, he hath been supposed by us as absent, and inattentive to our distress. How truly blessed is it, like Hagar, when the seasoned relief, like the well at Shur, opens with such manifestations of the Lord's love, as to at the same time, the Lord's hand. The use of every blessing then calls forth the cry, as Sarah's handmaid, from the soul, "Thou, seest me. For she said, Have I also looked him that (first) looked after me?" (1 John 19.)

BEER-ELM

We meet with this name, Isa. xv. 8. But it is more than probable, that it is the name of well so sweetly spoken of Num. xxi. 16-18. I beg the reader to consult the Scripture, and let him judge for himself, whether it be not so. Beerelim means, the well of the princes. And the princes are said to have digged it. But when the reader hath satisfied his mind on this point, there is another object, and that of an higher nature, that I would request the reader to attend to. In those wells, I humbly conceive, we discover gospel lessons beautifully represented. Hence, the prophet sings, "Because God (saith he) is my salvation, therefore, with joy shall ye draw water out of those wells of salvation." (Isa. xii. 2, 3.) And hence, if, with an eye to the Lord Jesus Christ, who is himself, in the souls of all his redeemed, a well of water springing up unto everlasting life, (John iv. 14.) we accept those Beer-elim in the word, we then join the Lord's song, in the Lord's own words, as he directed Moses. This is the well whereof the Lord spake unto Moses, "Gather the people together, and I will give them water." Then Israel sang this song. "Spring up, O well! sing ye unto it. The princes digged the well; the nobles of the people digged it, by the direction of the lawgiver with their staves." (Num. xxi. 16-18.)

BEER-SHEBA

The well of an oath; So called, because here it was that Abraham made a covenant with Abimelech. (Gen. xxvi. 33.) The word is a compound of Beer, well; and Shabah, swearing.

BEGGING

I could not prevail upon myself to pass over this word, though it be perfectly well understood, and is not frequently found in Scripture: yet, it appears to me, that as the Word of God hath made ample provision, not only in precept, but in the very constitution and frame of the human heart, for beggars, it is our duty to attend to it. (Ps, xxxvii, 25. Mark x. 46.) It should seem, by the precept delivered by Moses, that the Lord thereby intimated that there should be no poor unrelieved among them, in that the Lord had so greatly blessed Israel, that Israel would prevent the necessity of begging; though, for the exercises of their brotherly love, the poor should never cease out of the land. (Deut. xv. 4. 7. 11.) I recommend the reader to consult this whole chapter, from whence he will form better ideas concerning the mind of the Lord on the character of the beggar, and his own gracious and all-wise appointments of the inequalities of life. And when he hath done this, I would recommend him yet farther to consider the whole subject spiritually, and with an eye to Christ. The brother waxen poor was to be relieved by the nearest of kin; and when he had sold his possession, this brother, born for adversity, was to redeem it. (Lev. xxv. 25.) Here Jesus, the nearest of kin, was plainly seen. And therefore, the beggar in Israel had always a claim upon every passer-by, who considered duly this relationship. And may I not ask was not this among the gracious designs of the Lord, in his providence, to afford luxuries to the minds of believers, in the true Israel of God, when, from the inequalities of life, the Lord afforded opportunity to follow the steps of Jesus, in relieving a poor brother? How little have those studied the Scriptures of God, and how little do they know of the mind of Jesus, who, to the numberless miseries of life, arising out of that sin which Christ hath put away, can, and do pass by, and behold, unpitied, and unrelieved, the wretchedness of the beggar, whether in soul or body!

BEGOTTEN

I detain the reader at this word, because of its importance. Not in respect to the real meaning of the word itself, either in a natural or spiritual sense, for both are generally understood, but for an higher purpose, It is easy to apprehend what is meant by the term begotten, in natural generation among men. (See Matt. i. 2, &c.) And we no less understand the scriptural meaning of spiritual generation, in application wholly to God. They who are new born in Christ, are expressly said to be born not of blood, nor of the will of the flesh, nor of the will of man, but of God. (John i. 13.) But the meaning of the word begotten, when applied to the person of Christ, differs wholly from both these and (according to my apprehension of the scriptural sense of the word) is perfectly another thing. I beg to explain myself upon it.

If we look at the several Scriptures which speak Christ being begotten, we find the word connected at different places with different terms. Sometimes, Christ is said to be the first begotten, and at other of the Father. (See Heb. i. 6. Rev. i. 5. John i. 14. 18; iii. 16. 18. I John iv. 9. Ps. ii. 7.) And some have supposed, that these expressions refer to the eternal generation of the Son of God as God. But with all possible respect to the judgement to those men, I venture to believe that those phrases have no reference whatever to that subject. The eternal generation of the Son of God as God, is declared in Scripture as a most blessed reality; and as such, forms an express article of our faith. But as God the Holy Ghost hath not thought to proper to explain it, in any part of his revealed word, it becomes an article of faith only, and here the subject rests. We are not called upon to say, how that eternal generation is formed, any more than we are to tell how Jehovah exists, or how that existence is carried on in an unity of substance, while distinct in a threefold character of person. Our capacities are, at present, incompetent to form any adequate conception, and perhaps, even in our future state, they never may be able.

But in relation to the Son of God, as the first begotten and the only begotten of the Father, full of grace and truth, if those terms are confined to the person of the Lord Jesus in his character and office as Mediator, here all difficulty vanisheth to the proper apprehension of our mind; and under divine teaching, we are not only brought to the full conviction of the glorious truth itself, but to the full enjoyment of it, in knowing the Lord Jesus Christ in his mediatorial character, God and man in one person, the Head of union with his people, and the Head of communication also to his people, for grace here and glory for ever.

In this sense, Christ is the first begotten and the only begotten of the Father before all worlds. In this sense, that sweet passage in the Psalms is explained, "Thou art my Son, this day have I begotten thee." (Ps. ii. 7.) Begotten; that is, when in the decree concerning redemption, the Father predestinated the Son unto the being and office of the God-man Mediator. And this day means, when in the covenant transactions, the Lord Jesus stood up the Head of his church, at the call of God the Father. Had this begetting referred to the eternal generation of the Son of God as God, how could it be called this day? Eternity is never spoken of as a day in Scripture. For when the Holy Ghost would describe the eternal nature of the Lord Jesus Christ, he speaks of him in the past, present, and future; "Jesus Christ, the same yesterday, and to-day, and for ever." (Heb.

xiii. 8.) And hence, when describing also the eternal and everlasting nature and essence of him, the high and holy One, who inhabiteth eternity, the Holy Ghost saith, "from everlasting to everlasting thou art God." (Ps xc. 2.) Everlasting, in the language of Scripture, is without beginning without ending. So that in the eternal generation of the Son of God, as the Father is eternal everlasting in his personal character as Father, must the Son be eternal and everlasting in his character as Son. If there had been a period in eternity when the Son of God was not in that same period the Father would not have been the Father; for both, in the very nature of things, in the constitution of each character, have been equally existing together. Hence, (according to my view of things) nothing plainer than that in those expressions of the begotten and only begotten of the Father, is not the least reference to the eternal generation of the Son of God; but those, and the like of Scripture, respect only the person of the Jesus in his character and office of Mediator. In farther confirmation of this doctrine, I beg the reader to turn to the forty-second chapter of Isaiah 1 to 9, compared with Matt. xii. 17, &c. the sixty-first chapter of Isaiah, 1 to 3, compared with Luke iv. 16 to 22; and yet as particularly as either, the Lord Jesus, under the Spirit of prophecy, describes his commission as Mediator both from the Father and the Holy Ghost, ages before his incarnation, and the consequent execution of his office as Redeemer to his church and people.

I hope that I have explained myself in the clearest manner, in order to render my meaning perfectly intelligible to the humblest capacity. And if so, and my view of this sublime subject is agreeable to the unerring word of the holy Scripture, and if the reader's apprehension of this doctrine corresponds with mine, he will find (what I bless the Lord I have found,) much sweetness in such precious views of the Lord Jesus Christ. The distinction is, in my apprehension, highly important in the exercises of faith, between the eternal generation of the Son of God as God, and the Son of God as Mediator, begotten to the office mid character of Mediator. The distinction is essential, that we may not confound things, and thereby lessen our proper conception of the Son of God, "one with the Father over all, God blessed for ever." And it is no less most blessed and interesting to behold the Son of God thus begotten of the Father, the God-man Mediator, when, for the gracious purposes of salvation, he stood up in his covenant character, that he might be both the head of union and of fulness for communication to his people in grace, and in glory, for ever.

I beg the reader to pause over a subject so infinitely sublime, and so infinitely consolatory. And I beg of him farther to pause and remark with me, the wonderful grace manifested to creatures, such as we are, in the Lord's giving such blessed manifestations of himself. Instead of being astonished that we know no more, the only astonishment is, that we know so much. Great must be the communicated influence of the Holy Ghost to our poor fallen nature, to enable us to grasp any thing relating to the GODHEAD, in his threefold character of person, in this our fallen state. By and by, we are promised that we shall know, even as we are known; that is, as far as our spiritual faculties, ripened into perfection, are capable of advancing. "But here below, we are only, in our highest attainments, in the twilight of knowledge, and our best discoveries are but as seeing "through a glass darkly." See Generation.

Before I depart from the contemplation of this sublime subject as it refers to the person of God's dear Son, I would beg to drop a short observation on what I humbly conceive to be a misapplication of the term begotten, as is sometimes made in reference to man, I mean, when ministers themselves, or others for them, are said to have begotten souls to

BEHOLD - BELIEVE or BELIEF

Christ by the instrumentality of their preaching. It is more than probable, that the first idea of such a thing took its rise from what the apostle Paul said to the Corinthians, (1 Cor. iv. 15.) I have begotten you through the gospel. And in like manner, concerning Onesimus, the apostle saith, Whom I have begotten in my bonds. (Epistle to Philemon, ver. 10.) But whatever the apostle meant by the expression, certain it is, that the act of the new creation, as the act of the old, is wholly of the Lord. And uniformly in Scripture, the act of begetting is altogether ascribed to the Lord. (See 1 Pet. i. 3. 1 John v. 1. 18.) And, perhaps it would be no difficult matter to shew, that the apostle did not mean what some have supposed, that when he used those expressions, he considered himself as their spiritual father. The very term sounds haughtily, and not scripturally; Paul himself would hardly have joined such words together: in application to one he thought the chief of sinners. But even admitting the contrary, supposing it be granted, that this inspired apostle used the term in relation to himself, what warrant would this be for the use of it among ordinary ministers? If it be said, that it is only meant to imply their instrumentality, I answer, that the term spiritual father is still unsuitable and unbecoming. There is no warrant in the word of God for such an appellation. And when it is farther considered, how much it tends to minister to spiritual pride, it is a very plain proof it cometh not of the Lord. I shudder to think to what lengths this misapplication of the words begetting souls to Christ, and spiritual fathers, have hurried men, when I have heard it hath been said from the pulpit, or committed to the press, that such preachers, at the last day, will have to say, "Behold I, and the children which the Lord hath given me!" Words which can belong to none but the Lord Jesus Christ, and never were intended to be used, or can with truth be used, by any other. (Isa. viii. 18. Heb. ii. 13.)

BEHOLD

This word is so often used in the word of God, that I do not think it unimportant to have a place in our Concordance. Sometimes, it is intended as a note of attention, by way of calling the notice of the reader in a more striking manner; and yet more eminently so, when the Lord himself is the speaker. Thus for example, the Lord JEHOVAH calls upon the church to regard with all possible attention, the person and character of his dear Son. "Behold, (saith JEHOVAH) my servant whom I uphold," &c. (Isa. xlii. 1. Zech. iii. 8. Mal. iii. 1.) Sometimes, the word is used as a note of admiration, as when Jesus speaks of the loveliness of his church, (Song i. 15.) or when the angels announced the birth of Christ. (Isa. vii. 14). It is sometimes used to express joy and gladness, as when Jesus calls upon his church to behold him, "Behold me! behold me!" (Isa. lxv. 1. Matt. xxi. 5. John xii. 15.) And sometimes the word is used by way of confirmation to the word spoken. Thus the Lord to Jacob at Bethel, "Behold, I am with thee, and I will keep thee," &c. (Gen. xxviii. 15.)

BELIAL

This is an Hebrew word, signifying somewhat evil. Hence, in Scripture, it is not unfrequently applied to wicked persons. Moses, when charging Israel not to follow vain and ungodly men, calls them sons of Belial. (Deut. xiii. 13.) The same by Hannah. (1 Sam. i. 16,) So Abigail to David. (1 Sam. xxv. 25.) In the language of the New Testament, Belial is another name for Satan. "What concord (saith Paul) hath Christ with Belial?" (2 Cor. vi. 15.)

BELIEVE or BELIEF

Perhaps, nothing is more simple than the act of believing; and yet, perhaps, nothing which hath created more mistakes and misapprehensions. In common life, we all perfectly understand what it is to believe one another: it is only in relation to our belief in God, that we find it difficult. If the servant of some kind and generous master was promised by him a favour, which he knew his master could perform, he would think it a base impeachment of his master's character for any one to call the promise in question. But when the same kind of reasoning is brought forward concerning God, we overlook the impeachment of the Lord's veracity, in doubting the assurance of what God hath promised. Now, to apply this to the case in point. God hath promised to the church eternal life; and this life is in his Son. To believe this on the simple word and authority of God, this is to give God the credit of God; and in doing this, we do in fact no more than the servant, as before stated, does to his kind master. The greatness of the promise,

and the undeservedness of our hearts; these things have nothing to do in the business. It is the greatness, and honour, and credit of the Promiser, which becomes the only consideration with faith. And to take God at his word, and to trust in his promise as God; this is the whole sum and substance of believing. So that the simple act of faith, after all, is the simplest thing upon earth; for it is only believing "the record which God hath given of his Son." (I John v. 10.)

BELOVED

We ought not to pass over this expression, though the word itself is so generally understood. There is somewhat in it so truly blessed, when we consider it in relation to Christ, as the Christ of God; and also, in relation to the church, considered from her union with Christ, and interest in Christ, that the word beloved, when spoken of either, comes home to the affection peculiarly sweet and endeared. To refer to all the passages of Scripture, in which Christ is declared beloved, would be very many indeed. It will be fully sufficient to all the present purposes intended, to remark, that in all the parts of the divine word, at every place, and upon every occasion, when God the Father is represented as speaking of his dear Son, or to him, he expresseth himself with the greatest rapture and delight. He calls him his elect, his chosen, his only beloved, his dear Son; as if he would have every individual member of his church, (and which is indeed the case) to fall in love with him. And what I would beg the reader particularly to remark with me on this occasion is, that this love of the Father to the Son is specially spoken of in Scripture, not with reference to his divine nature, but in his mediatorial character. It would have been of no profit to us, (for the subject is above our faculties of apprehension) to have been told of the love of the Father to the Son, in the nature and essence of the GODHEAD. How the divine persons love each other in the infinity and eternity of their nature, none but themselves in their eternal nature can have any conceptions concerning. But the love of God, yea, all the persons of the GODHEAD to the person of Christ, as God-man Mediator; this is a subject concerning which we find somewhat for the mind to lean upon; and, under divine teaching, can make discovery sufficient to create a joy from it, "unspeakable and full of glory." What a rapturous thought to the soul is it, that our Jesus is beloved of JEHOVAH, because he undertook our cause, became our Surety, lived for us as such, and died for us as such, and is now carrying on the one glorious design for which he became incarnate, in bringing "many sons unto glory." The Lord Jesus speaks of his Father's love to him on this very account. "Therefore, (saith Jesus) doth my Father love me, because I lay down my life that I might take it again. No man taketh it from me, but I lay it down of myself; I have power to lay it down, and I have power to take it again. This commandment have I received of my Father." (John x. 17, 18. See also Isa. xlii. 21.)

BELSHAZZAR - BENJAMIN

And as Christ is thus beloved on the account of his gracious office and undertaking as Mediator, so is the church on his account, and for his sake beloved also. He it is, indeed, that gives this loveliness to his church, for there is nothing in the church, or in the acts of the church, which can be lovely, but on the Lord's account, and as beheld and accepted in him. But as considered as one with Christ, and made comely, from the comeliness which Jesus hath imparted to her, and put upon her, she is lovely in God the Father's view, and beloved by JEHOVAH for ever. Yea, the Lord Jesus not only calls her his beloved, and tells her that she is all fair, and that there is no spot in her, but he saith, in that sweet prayer he put up to the Father, in the night before his sufferings and death, that "the Father loveth the church as the Father loved him." (See John xvii. 23.)

BELSHAZZAR

King of Babylon. His history, which is very awful, we have, (Dan. v.) His name is compounded of Baal, lord; and Otzer, treasure; intimating, no doubt, his great riches and power. See Mene.

BELTESHAZZAR

This name was given to Daniel by the Chaldeans in the time of the captivity. (Dan. i. 7.) And no doubt, the design was evil; that he might in it lose sight both of his own name, and with it the remembrance of the Lord God of his fathers. And what a change it was! Daniel, a compound of Dan, judgment; and I, El, my God: my judgment is with God, or God is my judge. Whereas, Belteshazzar was a compound of Bel, the idol which the Babylonians worshipped; and Shassar, from Etzar, to lay up. And as the idol's name was derived from Bulat, secret, they both together implied the laying up in secret. From Daniel's history, it should seem to convey the idea, as though the name Belteshazzar was given to him in compliment, on account of his great wisdom; but there can be but little question, that the great object was, that he might, in time, forget the Lord God of Israel, and be incorporated with the Chaldeans. See Abednego.

BENHADAD

King of Syria; the son of Hadad. (1 Kings xx. 1.)

BENJAMIN

The youngest son of Jacob, by Rachel. The mother of Benjamin had expressed her dissatisfaction in having no children. "Give me children (said she in her displeasure) or else I die." It is said in the after pages of her history, that God "remembered Rachel, and that God hearkened unto her and opened her womb; and she bare a son, and called his name Joseph;" that is, as the margin of the Bible renders it, adding; and said," the Lord shall add to me another son." (See the interesting history, Gen. xxx. throughout. See also Joseph.) After the birth of Joseph, Rachel conceived again, and bore Benjamin, on which occasion she died. Moses gives a very affecting account of it, Gen. xxxv. 15 to 20. As the soul of Rachel was departing from her body, she named her child Ben-oni; and the margin of our Bibles hath thought it proper to mark it with some degree of emphasis; the son of my sorrow, from Ben, son; and On, grief or burden; and the pronoun I, makes it personal, my sorrow. Poor Rachel! what a mistaken judgment she made! She earnestly desired children; but behold the event! God gave her a son; but he was, as she properly named him, a son of sorrow; a Benoni. How many Rachels have there been since, who in wrestling or wishing to take the government out of Lord's hands, have done it to their sorrow! Jacob, though his love to Rachel was unbounded, (see Gen. xxix. 18-20.) yet he would not suffer the child to retain the name of Benoni, but changed it to Benjamin, which is, the son of my right hand, from Ben, son; and jamin, the right hand. And his love to Benjamin is much recorded in the Scripture. Moses, the man of God, viewing, most probably, Benjamin typically in relation to the Lord Jesus Christ, makes a beautiful observation in his dying blessing, which he gave to the tribes of Israel; "And of Benjamin he said, the beloved of the Lord shall dwell in safety by him; and the Lord shall cover him all the day long, and he shall dwell between his shoulders." (Deut. xxxiii. 12.) See gold.

BETHANY

A place ever dear and memorable to the followers of the Lord Jesus, from being so sacred to the Lord's solemn moments of suffering. Perhaps the name is compounded of Beth, an house; and hanah, affliction. It lay about fifteen furlongs (nearly two of our miles) from Jerusalem, at the foot of the mount of Olives. See John, eleventh and twelfth chapters.

BETH-AVEN

It is the same place as Bethel. But after Jeroboam, the son of Nebat, who made Israel to sin, set up his golden calves there, the pious among the Israelites called it Beth-aven; meaning, the house of iniquity; for it was no longer proper to call it Beth-el, the house of God. (1 Kings xii. 26, to the end.)

BETHEL

This spot is rendered memorable, from being the place where the visions of God began with the patriarch Jacob. (Gen. xxviii. 19, &c.) The name is Beth, the house; El, of God. And this name hath ever since been applied, by the people of God, to the sacred ground where their first interviews opened with the Lord. Believers in Jesus have been accustomed to call the hallowed spot of their first manifestations of God in Christ, and indeed, all their after visits from the Lord, as Jacob's was, their Bethels; for Jacob there saw the gracious revelation of God in Christ, in the vision manifested to him. (See Gen. xxviii. 12 to 17.) And those are our first real views of God, when we discover the riches and fulness of God's glory as manifested to poor sinners, in the person, offices, and character of the Lord Jesus Christ. Thus the disciples, John i. 14. Thus Paul, Gal. i. 15, 16. And all the holy men of old, who saw the day of Christ afar off, rejoiced and were glad; made certain memorandums of the hallowed ground, where the Lord thus revealed himself, to bring to remembrance. Abraham's JEHOVAH Jireh, (Gen. xxii. 14.) and Gideon's JEHOVAH Shalom, in Ophrah, are sweet proofs in this way. (Judges vi. 11 to 24.) And may I not hope, that both the writer and reader of this short memorial do the same, through grace, and can speak of their Bethels also?

BETHER

We meet with this word only in the Songs of Solomon. In the second Song, 17th verse, the word is retained in its original, Berber; but in the eighth Song, 14th verse, it is translated "mountains of spices." In the margin of the Bible it is rendered division; as if separating from Christ. Some of the copies read the word Bethel; but it certainly is a different word, and of a different meaning. It hath been rendered very sweet and gracious, I believe at times, to the follower of the Lord, when feeling the desires of the soul going out in longings for the Lord Jesus. So Old Testament saints sought the coming of Christ, as upon the mountains of Bether, when in the dark shade of Jewish ordinances they saw the type and shadow of good things to come, and longed for the substance. And so New Testament believers, who have once seen and tasted that the Lord is gracious, are longing for renewed visits of Jesus, when in seasons of distance, and darkness, and unbelief, they feel as on the mountains of Berber, waiting his coming. And how do the best of saints, in the present day, and they who enjoy most of the Redeemer's presence and grace, still long for the full manifestation of his person, and the coming of that great day, when he will come "to be glorified in his saints, and to be admired in all that believe." (2 Thess. i. 10.) Say, reader, doth not your heart go forth, as the church of old did, (sure I am it must, if so be Christ is precious) crying out with the same rapture, "Make haste my beloved; and until that everlasting day, break upon my redeemed soul, be thou like to a roe, or a young hart, upon the mountains of Berber." (Song ii. 17. Song viii, 14.)

BETHESDA

The word signifies, the house of mercy; from Beth, an house; and Chesed, mercy. It was the pool which the evangelist John speaks of, John v. 2. I refer to the account. It is probable, that into this pool the waters from the temple emptied themselves: and if so, all the washings of the sacrifices. And some have been weak enough to fancy, that the efficacy of the pool arose from thence. And others, equally erroneous, have supposed that some mineral quality might be in the pool, from the waters imbibing it in passing over certain strata of the kind, as the mineral waters of Bath, and other places of the like nature. But had they attended to what the Holy Ghost hath recorded, by his servant John, in the history of the Bethesda, they would have observed, that the peculiar miraculous quality the pool possessed, was only at a certain season, and from the descent of an angel into the pool; and the miracle expressly limited also to one person.

Some have raised questions of doubt concerning the reality of the pool itself, because it is not noticed by any of the evangelists but John. But this, if admitted as an argument of doubt, would go farther than the objectors perhaps intend; since the same cause of objection would equally hold good against the pool of Siloam, the resurrection of Lazarus, several of the sweet and precious discourses of Christ, his miracle of Cana, at Galilee, and very many other blessed relations concerning the Lord Jesus, which are mentioned by none of the other evangelists. But these are childish objections, since we know that one among the many causes for which the gospel according to St. John was added to the other memoirs of the Lord Jesus Christ, was purposely to relate some circumstances, which Matthew, Mark, and Luke, had not done. (See John xx. 30, 31; xxi. 25.)

Some have expressed their surprise that Josephus, the Jewish historian, should have been altogether silent concerning the pool of Bethesda. But not to remark that Josephus was not born at the time the pool was in repute, the well-known hatred he bore to every thing that had respect to the person and glory of the Lord Jesus, might well account for his not even glancing at the Bethesda, which must have connected with it Christ's miracle there; rendered so memorable as it was, from the cure he wrought, by speaking a word, on the poor man, of a disease of thirty-eight years standing. And surely, no one who reads his history of Israel's Exodus, and their passage through the Red Sea, can be astonished that he should pass by all notice of the pool of Bethesda.

It is truly blessed to the believer in Christ, that his faith is not founded "in the wisdom of men, but in the power of God." The Holy Ghost hath given his, testimony to the many blessed truths in his servant John's writings, and of consequence, to the reality and certainty of this pool of Bethesda among the rest. And I humbly conceive, that the pool itself was specially intended, by the mercy of the Lord, to be a standing miracle among his people during their dark estate from the departure of the Spirit of prophecy, which ended with Malaichi to the coming of the Lord Jesus Christ; as is to shew, that the Lord "had not cast away his people whom he foreknew." Here, therefore, was a direction to wait for Christ. And as he was "the fountain to be opened in that day, to the house of David, and to the inhabitants of Jerusalem, for sin and for uncleanness," the pool of Bethesda might shadow forth his coming. So that when the Lord came and wrought the miracle on the poor man of long infirmity, without the ministry of the pool, this might shew that the intention for which this pool had been appointed was now answered, and the substance being come, the shadow ceased for ever. We hear no more of the pool of Bethesda, after this miracle of Christ in the cloisters of it; and, as is supposed, the efficacy of it was now no more.

I cannot take leave of the subject without first desiring the reader to remark with me, the improvement to be made of it. The Bethesdas of the gospel we still have, in the several ordinances and means of grace. But as then, it was the descent of an angel into the pool which gave efficacy to the waters, so now, it is by the coming of our Lord Jesus, the almighty angel of the covenant, into our midst, that any saving effect can be derived from the purest ordinances, or forms of worship. Where Jesus is not, there is no life-giving stream in any of the waters of ordinances. And it should be remarked, moreover, that our Bethesdas are not like this by the sheep market gate in Jerusalem. It is our mercy that the cure is not, as that was, limited to one poor sufferer, and him the first that came to it. But the gospel invitation in Jesus, is to every one that thirsteth. And the last is sometimes made first. And all that come, the Lord himself saith, "he will in no wise cast out." Yea, more than this still. Our Lord Jesus doth not limit his grace to our Bethesdas, or ordinances, but he worketh without them, (as in the instance of the poor man at the Jewish Bethesda) or with them, as seemeth best to his infinite wisdom, and for the display of his grace. Hail! thou glorious Healer! JEHOVAH Rophe of thy people! (Exod. xv. 26.)

BETHLEHEM

This was a city in Judah. (Josh. xvii. 7.) The name means, house of bread; from Beth, house; and lechem, or lehem bread. It was beautifully significant of Christ, who was from everlasting appointed to be born there, (Micah v. 2.) and was, and is, and ever will be, the bread of life, and the living bread to his people; of which whosoever eateth shall live for ever! Lord! I would say with the disciples, evermore give me this bread. There was another Bethlehem in Zebulun, though it is but rarely spoken of in Scripture. (Joshua xix. 15.) But this Bethlehem must be ever dear to every follower of Jesus. It was connected with and formed part of Ephratah. Here Jacob buried his beloved Rachel. (Gen. xxxv. 19, 20.) I would have the reader compare what Micah saith concerning this Bethlehem, with an eye to Christ, and look at what Matthew hath observed also on the subject. (Micah v. 2. Matt. ii. 1-6.) The Holy Ghost evidently had Jesus in view in that sweet history of Ruth, when the certain man, Eli-melech, representing our whole nature, left Bethlehem the land of bread, for the Moab of the world; and when with his children Mahlon and Chillon, sickness and disease overtook him and all his posterity. (Ruth i. 1.) David's cry for the waters of Bethlehem, (see 2 Sam. xxiii. 15-17.) hath always been considered as typical of the soul's thirst for Jesus, the bread of life.

BETH-PEOR

See Baal peor. It was a city of Moab. (Deut. iv. 46.) The house of opening; from Pahar, to open.

BETH-PHAGE

A well-known village, mentioned in the gospel, (see Matt. xxi. 1.) It should seem to be derived from Pep, opening; and Geeah, valley: the house of the valley. Probably, the opening of the valley at the foot of the mount of Olives. Here it was that Christ fulfilled that remarkable prophecy of Zechariah. (Zech. ix. 9. with Matt. xxi. 4, 5. Mark xi. 1. Luke xix. 28. John xii. 14.)

BETH-SHEMESH

A city belonging to the priests in the tribe of Judah. (Joshua xv. 10.) This place is rendered remarkable from the slaughter the Lord made on the men of Beth-shemesh for their curiosity in looking into the ark. (See 1 Sam. vi. 19.) An invasion by any into the priest's office hath been always punished. (See Numb. iv. 5, 15, 20.) How blessedly the Holy Ghost testifieth of Christ, that he took not upon him the office of High Priest uncalled of JEHOVAH A glorious consideration to all his people. (Heb. v. 4, 5.)

BETROTHING or BETROTHED

This engagement among the Hebrews was made very sacred; and it was in general made early. They considered it a breach of the divine command not to marry; and hence, the betrothing, or being betrothed, was a ceremony long used before the marriage was intended to be consummated: and, indeed, sometimes there was a great lapse of time between the one and the other.

I have thought it worth noticing, in a work of this kind, purposely to observe, upon the act itself, the gracious condescension of our God and Saviour in adopting the term with respect to his marriage with our nature. His was a long betrothing, even before all worlds. But the marriage was only consummated when, in the fulness of time, he took our nature upon him, and became the Husband and Head of his church. And what a beautiful and gracious manner doth the Lord Jesus make use of, in his usual way of unequalled condescension and love, when speaking of his union with our nature, the complacency and delight he took in it, and the everlasting duration of it, he saith, "And I will betroth thee unto me for ever, yea, I will betroth thee unto me in righteousness, and in judgment, and in loving kindness, and in mercies. I will even betroth thee unto me in faithfulness, and thou shalt know the Lord." (Hos. ii. 19, 20.)

BEULAH

We meet with this word but once in the Bible. (Isa. lxii. 4.) It should seem to be derived from Balak, or Baal-meon, lord of the house, or married.

BEZER

One of the cities of refuge appointed for the manslayer to flee unto, as provided. See (Deut. iv. 41, &c.) It lay in the country of the Reuhenites, but became somewhat like a frontier town, both to them, and to Edom and Moab; being near the borders of each. What makes it particularly meriting our attention is, that in the design and appointment of it we see clear traces of its being typical of the Lord Jesus Christ.

These cities of refuge were for the manslayer to flee to for shelter. Now Christ is the only refuge for the manslayer of the soul to flee unto; for every sinner is a soul-murderer: he hath slain his own soul. And if fleeing to Christ when the avenger of blood, that is, the law of God, and the justice of God, is pursuing him, he takes shelter in the Lord Jesus, the Bezer of his people, and the city of refuge for security, before he be overtaken, he is in safety for ever. All the days his High Priest liveth no condemnation can fall upon him; and that is for ever!

That the appointment of those cities (which were six in number, had an eye to Christ cannot be doubted, because a provision for the manslayer, if referring only to temporal things, might have been made in a much easier and more simple way. An express law for the magistrate or priest to have acted upon, in all cases of murder where there was no malice prepense, would have been equally easy in this case, as in every other. But when we see six cities expressly set apart for this one purpose only, and placed in certain situations convenient for the poor murderer to get most easily at; when we read so much as is said concerning it, and call to mind how much the Holy Ghost delighted in shadowing forth Christ, under the Old Testament Scripture, in type and figure; and when we observe, moreover, how very strikingly the things here marked down in the city of refuge point to the Lord Jesus Christ, we cannot hesitate to conclude, that it was thus, among a great variety of other ways, Christ was preached to the people. Christ, indeed, as a sanctuary, infinitely exceeds the type represented by the city of refuge. For though the manslayer, when entered within the suburbs, could not be taken from thence, yet neither could he go abroad; if he did, he died. But in Jesus we are both made safe and free; for "if the Son hath made us free, we shall be free indeed." (John viii. 36.) Moreover, the manslayer among the Jews had freedom only upon the death of the high priest, but our great High Priest giveth freedom both while we live on earth, and hereafter in heaven; and "he himself abideth a priest for ever."

I cannot forbear adding, what hath been always considered, by pious believers, as a farther testimony that these cities of refuge had an eye to Christ, and were plainly typical, namely, that the name given to each became expressive of somewhat significant in relation to the Lord Jesus Christ. Bezer means a strong hold. And such is Christ. Ramoth in Gilead, a place of eminency. And JEHOVAH'S testimony of Jesus is, that "he should be exalted, and extolled, and be very high? (Isa. lii. 13.) And Golan, in Bashan, carries with it the glory. And is there not joy and peace in believing when the soul abounds in hope, through the power of the Holy Ghost? Neither were the other three cities appointed beyond Jordan by Joshua, less striking, when considered in reference to Christ. (Josh. xx. 7.) Kedish, holy. And who is holy but Jesus? Shechem, the shoulder. And Christ's government is said to be upon his shoulder. (Isa. ix. 6.) And Kirjatharba, or Hebron, the city of fellowship. Into what sweet fellowship and communion doth Jesus bring all his people!

It is a very blessed addition to this merciful design of the Lord, that he so graciously appointed the whole six cities of refuge to suit the different situations of the people, that if they were central in the place where the manslaughter was committed, or at the remote end of their town, at each extremity there were avenues leading to the one or other of the city of refuge. And it was a law in Israel we are told, that one day in every year there were persons sent to repair the roads leading to them, and to remove all stumblingblocks or stones, which might by time have fallen in the way; and to see also, that the posts of direction, which were set up at every corner leading to the city, were carefully preserved, and the name Miklat, (that is, refuge) legible upon them. All these were so many express types of the Lord Jesus Christ. He is our Zoar, (Gen. xix. 20, &c.) our Bezer, (Ps. cxlv. 18.) our city of refuge to flee to. And he is always near at hand. He is also, (as the prophet described him) the repairer of the breach, the restorer of paths to dwell in. (Isa. lviii. 12.) And every ordinance and means of grace in the ministry of his word points, like the Miklat of the Jews, unto Jesus, saying, "This is the way, walk ye in it, when ye turn to the right hand, and when ye turn to the left," (Isa. xxx. 21.) Blessed Jesus, be thou indeed, "the way, and the truth, and the life!" and surely, the wayfaring men, though fools, shall not err therein." (Isa. xxxv. 8.)

BIBLE

This name is given to the Word of God; and no one is at a loss to know what is meant by it when we say, the Bible. But it is not, perhaps, so generally known wherefore the Sacred Scriptures are called the Bible. This is the reason.--The word Bible is taken from the Greek. Biblos, or book; and it is called

BIBLE - BIBLE

so by way of eminency and distinction, as if there were no other book (and which is, indeed, strictly and properly speaking, the ease) in the world. So then, by Bible is meant the Book, the Book of God, the only Book of God, including the holy Scriptures of the Old and New Testament, and no other; for these and these alone, are "able to make wise unto salvation, through the faith which is in Christ Jesus." The Hebrews call their Scriptures Mikra, which means, lesson, instruction, or Scripture.

When I said the Bible includes the holy Scriptures of the Old and New Testaments, and no other, I consider what is called Apocrypha as not included. The very name Apocrypha, (so called by those who first placed those writings in our Bibles) which means hidden, or doubtful, implies as much, for them is nothing which, can be called doubtful in the word of God.

Some pious minds, indeed, have gone farther, and have ceased to call those writings apocryphal, or doubtful, but have decidedly determined against them, and from their own testimony shewn that they are unscriptural and contrary to God's word. And, indeed, if what they have brought forward in proof be compared with the unalterable standard of God's own declarations in Scripture, without doubt, they ought not to have place in our Bibles.

It would by far exceed the limits I have laid down for myself in this work, to enter deeply into the subject by way of determining the matter. One or two observations is all I shall offer; leaving the reader to frame his own judgment.

The Book of Ecclesiastics, take it altogether, is by far the best of the whole apocryphal writings. In the prologue, or preface, the writer, or translator, begs pardon for any errors that he may have fallen into in this service; which at once implies his opinion that he had no idea the author wrote it under divine inspiration. In chap. iii. ver. 20. he speaks of giving alms as an "atonement for sins;" and chap. xxxv. ver. 3. he declares the forsaking unrighteousness to be a propitiation. Thus much may suffice without enlarging.

I cannot, however, take leave of the subject without first quoting the words of Tertullian, who lived in the second century. He speaks decidedly concerning the Apocrypha, and felt indignant that it should ever have had a place in our Bibles. "The prophet Malachi, (saith Tertullian) is the bound or skirt of Judaism and Christianity. A stake that tells us, that there promising ends, and performing begins; that prophecying concludes, and fulfilling takes place. There is not a span between those two plots of holy ground, the Old and New Testament, for they touch each other. To put the Apocrypha, therefore, between them, is to separate Malachi and Matthew; Law and Gospel. It is to remove the landmark of the Scriptures, and to be guilty of that breach in divorcing the marriage of the testaments, and what God hath joined together for man to put asunder."

Perhaps it may not be unacceptable to the reader to subjoin, under this article of the Bible, an account of the different copies of the sacred volume which have been handed down in the church through the several successive ages, for it will serve to manifest the Lord's watchful care over his own precious Word.

The first copy, called the Septuagint, in Greek, so called from the seventy pious men devoted to this service, was produced about two hundred and forty years before the coming of our Lord Jesus Christ, including all the sacred books, as we now have them, from Genesis to Malachi.

The second copy consisted of the Old Testament, from Hebrew into Greek by a Jew named Aquila, being converted to the Christian faith, in the time of the Emperor Adrian.

The third translation was about fifty-three years after the former. And to this succeeded a fourth, under the Emperor Severus. Eight years after this, another translation appeared by an unknown hand; and this was called the fifth translation. Afterwards Hieronymus translated it out of the Hebrew into the Latin tongue; this is what is called the sixth copy. And this is what is used in the Latin language to this day. Our first English translation was that of Myles Coverdale, Bishop of Exeter, bearing date 1535, and dedicated to King Henry the Eighth.

BLASPHEMY

I think it proper to stop at this word, as the sense and meaning of it is not so generally understood as it were to be wished; and many of God's dear children, it is to be apprehended, have their minds much exercised about it, fearing they have committed the unpardonable sin, in blasphemy against the Holy Ghost. It will not be amiss, therefore, to make an humble enquiry concerning it, looking up for the Lord the Spirit to be our Teacher.

The sin of blasphemy is peculiarly applied to those who sin against God by profaning his holy name, and speaking lightly and wantonly of his person, prefections, and attributes. The law under Moses's dispensation punished such crimes with death. (Lev. xxiv. 11.16.)

This is what may be called blasphemy in general. But added to this, our Lord speaks of a peculiar branch of blasphemy against the person and work of God the Holy Ghost, as being accompanied with aggravated malignity, and in its nature unpardonable. But as if that none of his children might make a mistake concerning it, with that tenderness and grace which distinguished his character, the Lord Jesus mercifully set forth in what the peculiar degree of the sin consisted. He had been casting out devils, and the Scribes and Pharisees, with their usaul malignity, ascribed those gracious acts to the agency of the Evil Spirit. Hence, our Lord thus expressed himself, "Verily, I say unto you, all sin shall be for given unto the sons of men, and blasphemies wherewith soever they should blaspheme. But he that should blaspheme against the Holy Ghost hath never forgiveness, but is in danger of eternal damnation." And then it is added, as an explanation of the whole, and to shew in what the unpardonable sin consisted, "because they said, he hath an unclean spirit." (Mark iii. 28, &c.) Here was the blasphemy, in ascribing the works of Jesus, wrought evidently the Spirit of JEHOVAH, to the agency of Satan; was blasphemy with a vengeance, and from its peculiar malignity unpardonable. And who are the persons that commit it? Surely, not they who desire to love Jesus, and to feel the gracious influences of the Holy Ghost. Their distresses and their fears are, lest they should come short of the grace of God. They are too well convinced that the Lord Jesus wrought all his miracles by his own almighty power, even to call it in question; so that in this sense, it is impossible for them to commit this unpardonable sin. They would shudder even to hear such blasphemy from the lips of others; and how then should it come from their own?

Who then were the persons to whom the Lord Jesus alluded when he thus expressed himself? Most evidently and plainly, the Scribes and Pharisees then before him. They had charged Christ with having an evil spirit, by whose influence he wrought miracles, and hence Jesus declared the sin, and shewed, at the same time, that it was totally unpardonable.

And what confirmed it more, and manifested that they were given up to a reprobate mind, was, that hardness and insensibility both of their sin and their danger. Here is another sweet and precious testimony to the timid and fearful child of God, if he would but attend to it as it really is. Your very softness of heart proves the reverse of those obdurate Pharisees. They had commited it, and were insensible and unconcerned. Your sorrow and apprehension most decidedly manifest that you have not so sinned, neither can have committed such an evil. The very different state of the different characters draws the line of distinction, and shews who are the blasphemers of the Holy Ghost, and who are not. The Lord be the teacher of his people.

BLESS

To bless in the language of Scripture, hath many different significations. When spoken of in reference to the Lord's blessing his people, it means bestowing upon them his loving kindness, and grace, and favour, as manifested in a way of temporal, spiritual, or eternal blessings. But when it is spoken of in respect to our blessing the Lord, or blessing one another, it is evident that the sense of it differs very widely. I cannot omit mentioning, under this article, a peculiarity concerning blessings in general, as they relate to the Lord's mercies in this way to his people, and because I do not believe that the subject is generally understood. All blessings are in Christ. This is the bottom of all our mercies; for Where Christ is not, there can be nothing truly blessed. "Men shall be blessed in him." (Psal. lxxii. 17.) But while the church are supposed to know this, and to look for no blessings but in him, believers do not so fully as they ought consider that Christ himself is their blessedness. There is a nice distinction in this view of the subject. It is not enough to see Christ's hand and Christ's blessing in the mercy he bestows upon me, in order to make that blessing sweet; but Christ himself must be the blessing to crown all. It is not enough that Jesus gives me life and salvation; but he himself must be my life and salvation. So the Psalmist, speaking in the person of Christ, saith of him, as the head of his church and people, Psal. xxvii. 1. And so the prophet also, speaking in the person of his Lord, for the same purpose, Isa. xii. 2. And so must all the church say concerning their glorious Head. And hence, the psalmist, when at any time speaking in the person of Christ, or of the person of Christ, doth not simply say, Blessed is the man (that is, the man Christ Jesus,) but, Blessedness is the man, using the word in the plural number, to intimate all blessings in him. For Christ is not a single blessing, but all; and the blessedness he gives, and is to his people, doth not consist in one thing, but in all. I hope the reader will understand my meaning. The first word of the first, thirty-second, and forty-first psalms (to mention no more,) which all speak of Christ, is on this account in the plural, and all ascribe blessedness to him for this express purpose.

BLINDNESS

The Scripture very frequently makes use of this word, by way of expressing the blindness of the soul while in an unawakened unregenerate state. Persons of this description are said to "have eyes, and see not;" and "ears, and hear not." And such, indeed, is the case of every man by nature. They see not their own corruption; they have no apprehension of their want of Christ; they see no beauty in Christ. So awful a state is this, that the Holy Ghost no less than seven times, in his blessed word, speaks of it in the same strong figures. (See Isa. vi. 9; Matt. xiii. 14; Mark iv. 12; Luke viii. 10; John xii. 40; Acts xxviii. 26; Rom. xi. 8.) It is a blessed testimony that Jesus hath opened our eyes to say, with the poor man at the pool of Siloam, "One thing I know, that whereas I was blind, now I see." (John ix. 25.)

BLOOD

Very important, in Scripture language, is the mention made of blood. So much so, indeed, that perhaps the perfect apprehension of it is not known. From the beginning of the creation of God, the Lord himself pointed to the blood as the life of the creature. And in a peculiar and special manner, the Lord intimated somewhat of an high nature in the blood, when speaking to

Cain concerning the blood of his brother Abel, which he had shed; the Lord said, "What hast thou done? the voice of thy brother's blood crieth unto me from the ground." In the margin of the Bible, the word is rendered bloods, in the plural number. (Gen. iv. 10.) In Deut. xii. 23, the prohibition of eating blood is mentioned with peculiar emphasis, and the reason assigned; "because it is the life." And it is again and again forbidden. There can be no question but that much of the Lord Jesus, and his precious blood-shedding, was veiled under it; though the subject is too mysterious to explain.

It is, no doubt, a wonderful dispensation from beginning to end, that of redemption by the blood of Christ. That blood should be an appointed laver for uncleanness, so that, "without shedding of blood there is no remission;" and that "the blood of Jesus Christ cleanseth from all sin," (1 John i. 7.) whereas according to all our natural ideas of blood, it defiles. Yea, the Lord himself, speaking of defilements in his people Israel, he expresseth their uncleanness under this figure: "Your hands are full of blood;" and instantly adds, "wash you, make you clean: put away the evil of your doings from before mine eyes." (Isa. i. 15, 16.) But here we stop; the subject is mysterious, and beyond our scanty line of knowledge to fathom. It is enough for us to know that that blood which Christ shed, as a sacrifice for sin, is, the only "fountain opened to the house of David, and the inhabitants of Jerusalem, for sin and for all uncleanness." In this the church on earth are beheld clean; and in this the church in heaven are accepted before God, having "washed their robes, and made them white in the blood of the Lamb." (Rev. vii. 14.) And hence, those strong expressions we every where meet with in the Scripture, "of the blood of the covenant, the blood of sprinkling, and the like." (Zech. ix. 11. Heb. xii. 24.)

BLOT OUT

This expression is used in Scripture both in a way of mercy and of judgment. The Lord saith, that he hath so completely blotted out the sins of his people, "that the iniquity of Israel should be sought for, and there should be none; and the sins of Judah, and they should not be found." (Jer. 1.20,) And elsewhere, the Lord describes the same thing, under the image of blotting out the sins of his people as a cloud, and as a thick cloud. (Isa. xlii. 25; xliv. 22.) In other parts of scripture, blotting out is spoken of as an awful judgment. (Deut. ix. 14; xxv. 19. Ps. lxix. 28.)

BOANERGES

The meaning of this name is explained to us, as given by Jesus himself, (Mark, iii. 17.) "the Sons of thunder." Perhaps the word is a compound, from Bini, son; Regem, thunder, or tempest; intimating, perhaps, that those sons of Zebedee would be powerful preachers under the Lord.

BOAZ

The son of Salmon and Rahab, and the father of Obed, by Ruth; of whom, by descent, after the flesh, sprung Christ. (See Matt. i. 5, 6.) I beg the reader not to overlook the grace of the Lord Jesus in this wonderful relation. Jesus will not only take our nature for the purpose of redemption, but he will take it from the lowest order of the people. Rahab was an harlot of the city of Jericho, cursed by Joshua, (chap vi. 26.) though famous for her faith in the Lord God of Israel; and Ruth a poor outcast of Moab. Both Gentiles, and yet brought into the genealogy of the Lord Jesus Christ. Was it to shew the astonishing condescension of Jesus? And was it not to shew also, that long before the great events of redemption were to be accomplished, the Jew and Gentile church were both in Christ? (Gal. iii 28, 29.) See Harlot.

BOAZ

One of the pillars in the porch of Solomon's temple, (1 Kings vii. 21.) It was on the left hand, as Jachin, the other pillar corresponding to it, was placed on the right. The names of both were significant. Jachin means, he that strengthens and makes steadfast. Boaz means, in it is strength and firmness. No doubt, they both were figurative of Him who condescends to call himself the Door; in whom, and by whom, unless an entrance be made into the temple, the same is "a thief and a robber." (John x. 1.9.)

We are told these pillars were eighteen cubits high each of them, and twelve in circumference, 1 Kings vii. 15. And from their magnificence, they formed no unapt resemblance of Him "who is the pillar and ground of the truth." (1 Tim. iii. 15.)

BOCHIM

We meet with this name, Judges ii. 1. 5. It was given in consequence of the message of an angel which caused the people to weep. Hence Bochim means a place of weeping, or the weepers. And so the margin of the Bible renders it. Some make the Word the plural of Baca, or Bocha, mulberry-tree; and so it might be a place of mulberries, and called Bochim, where the people received tidings from the angel, and wept. See Baca; see Mourning; see also Mulberry-tree.

BODY

In the language of Scripture, somewhat more is meant than the mere animal life, when speaking of the body. The whole church of Christ is his body. And the Holy Ghost, by his servant the apostle Paul, saith, "There is a natural body, and there is a spiritual body." (I Cor. xv. 44.) So that the term is variously used.

But I should not have thought it necessary on this account to have made any pause at the word body, it not been in reference to a subject of an infinitely higher nature; I mean, in relation to the body of our Lord Jesus Christ. The wonderful condescension of the Son of God in taking upon him our nature, and assuming a body, such as ours, in all points like as we are, yet without sin; makes it a most interesting subject, and comes home recommended to our tenderest affections, that it is impossible ever to pass by it, or to regard it with coolness and indifference. I would beg the reader's indulgence for a few moments on the occasion.

The Scripture account of this mysterious work is not more marvellous than it is endearing. It became necessary, it seems, in the accomplishment of redemption, that the great and almighty Author of it should be man, yea, perfect man, as well as perfect God. The relation which God the Holy Ghost hath given, concerning the Son of God becoming incarnate, is said to the church in so many sweet and blessed words, that the soul of the believer, methinks, would chime upon them for ever. "Wherefore (he saith) in all things it behoved him to be made like unto his brethren, that he might be a merciful and faithful High Priest in things pertaining to God, to make reconciliation for the sins of the people." Hence, therefore, the Son of God passed by the nature of angels, for an angel's nature would not have suited his purpose, nor ours. He was to be in all points like those he redeemed, sin only excepted; and, therefore, a body he assumes for the accomplishment of this great end. (See Heb. ii. throughout, but particularly xiv. to the end.)

This, therefore, being determined on in the council of peace, that He who undertook to redeem our nature, should partake of the same nature as those he redeemed; the next enquiry is, What saith the Scripture concerning the Son of God resuming our nature, and how was it wrought?

The Scriptures, with matchless grace and condescension, have shewn this, and in a way, considering the dulness of our faculties in apprehension, so plain and circumstantial, that under the blessed Spirit teaching, the humblest follower of the Lord, taught by the Holy Ghost, can clearly apprehend the wonderful subject. Under the spirit of prophecy, Jesus declared, ages before his incarnation, JEHOVAH had provided a body for his assumption. "Sacrifice and offering (said the Lord,) thou wouldst not, but a body hast thou prepared me." (See Ps. xl. 6. with Heb. x. 5, &c.) But how was the Son of God to assume this body? The Holy Ghost takes up the blessed subject, and by his servant the Evangelist Luke, records the whole particular's of a conference which took place between an angel and a Virgin Called Mary, whose womb, by his miraculous impregnation, and without the intervention of a human father, was to bring forth this glorious Holy One, as the great Saviour of his people. The Holy Ghost (said the angel to Mary,)" shall come upon thee, and the power of the Highest shall overshadow thee; therefore, also that Holy thing which shall be born of thee, shall be called the Son of God." I beg the reader to turn to the wonderful account, and read the whole. (Luke. i. 26-53.) And I would farther beg him to turn to the Scriptures of the prophets, who, with one voice, pointed to this great event in all their ministrations, (Isa. vii. 14; ix. 6. Micah. v. 2.) And when the reader hath gone over all these Scriptures of the Old Testament, I request him to finish the enquiry in reading the history of the facts themselves, as they are recorded in the New, and bless God for his grace and condescension in bringing the church acquainted with such an event, in the interest of which our present and everlasting happiness is so intimately concerned.

In speaking, therefore, or having a right conception of the body of the Lord Jesus Christ; this is the point of view in which the Scriptures of God teach us to regard that holy body. The Son of God as God, assuming this holy thing, so expressly called by the angel, underived from our fallen nature, and as to any shadow of imperfection, unconnected with it; becomes a suited Saviour for all the purposes of redemption, and being by this sacred and mysterious union, God and man in one person, formed one Christ: he, and he only, becomes the proper Redeemer and Mediator, the God-man Christ Jesus. And hence the plain and obvious meaning of all these Scriptures. God in Christ. "In him dwelleth all the fulness of the GODHEAD bodily." (2 Cor. v. 19. Col. ii. 9. 1 Tim. iii. 16. John i. 14; xvii. throughout.)

I must not enlarge. Neither ought I to dismiss the subject without first adding, to what I have said, one observation more; that by virtue of this union of our nature with the Son of God, his church is brought into an intimate union and oneness with him. And while we are taught to behold Christ as taking upon him our nature, we are no less taught, to consider every regenerated believer as a "member of his body, his flesh, and his bones." (Eph. v. 23 to the end.) And it is a matter of holy joy and rapture, never to be lost sight of by the humblest and poorest of his redeemed people, that the hand of God the Father is in all these glorious concerns, "who gave his dear Son to be the Head over all things to the church, which is his body, the fulness of Him that filleth all in all." (Eph. i. 22, 23.) See Mary.

BONDAGE

This is a word in Scripture of strong meaning. It is not unfrequently made use of for the whole of spiritual slavery, in those who are under a covenant of works. They are said to be in bondage to sin, to Satan, to their own consciences, to the law of God, to the justice of God, to the fear of death, and eternal judgment. Whereas, those that are brought into the liberty of the gospel, are said to be delivered "from the bondage of corruption, into the glorious liberty of the sons of God." Hence the Lord Jesus, in allusion to this blessed change, saith, (John viii. 36:) "If the Son shall make you free, ye shall be free indeed." The Holy Ghost by his servant the apostle Paul, (Gal. iv. 22. to the end,) hath exemplified both these doctrines in a beautiful allegory, in the instances of Sarah and Hagar.

BOOK

See Bible. And in addition to what is there said, I would beg to remark, that the Hebrews had several names for distinguishing their several books; such as "the book of the covenant," (Exod. xxiv. 7. 2 Kings xxiii. 21.) "the book of the law." (Deut. xxx. 10. and xxxi. 26.) Their general term for a book was Sepher. In the New Testament, we read of "the book of life." (Phil. iv. 3. Rev. xx. 12.) It is our happiness to have all that it behoves us to know, concerning the book of life, in the copy of it of the Bible, which becomes indeed, in the proclamation of grace it contains, "the book of life." Here we find the characters of those whose names are written in heaven fully drawn out, and they altogether correspond to those for whom JEHOVAH gave Christ as a covenant. (See Isa. xlii. 6, 7. Luke iv. 18. See also Dan. vii. 10. and xii. 1. Rev. v. 1-3. Psal. ii. 7.)

BORROW

We do not meet with this word very often in Scripture, nevertheless, seldom as it is used, it is not always used in the same sense. From that memorable passage in Scripture, Exod. iii. 22, where the Lord commanded Moses, that the people should borrow of their neighbours, on their departure from Egypt, jewels of gold and of silver, the idea hath arisen in many minds, that as the things then borrowed were never afterwards returned, there was intended, and committed, a real fraud. But it is to be observed, that the word borrow, from the same root, is differently rendered in the case of Hannah, when asking the Lord for a son. Had the root been regarded in her instance, from whence the word Hannah used it, and from whence it was taken, it would have been, she borrowed of the Lord a son. Whereas, there it is rendered she called his name Samuel, which (as the margin of the Bible renders it,) is asked of God; "for she said, I have asked him of God." (1 Sam. i. 20.) Now, here we find the word, though the same, from the same root is not to borrow, but to beg as a favour. And the subject is farther explained in the twenty-seventh and twenty-eighth verses of the same chapter. For when she brought Samuel to the temple, she tells Eli, for this child (said she) I prayed, and the Lord "hath given me my petition which I asked of him;" therefore also, I have lent him to the Lord; as long as he liveth he shall be lent to the Lord. In the margin it is, I have returned him, whom I have received by petition, to the Lord; or, he whom I have received by petition shall be returned. Hence, therefore, the original word is not, in the strict sense of it, to borrow as a loan; but may be rendered, to ask or request, or beg and crave. And so I find the verb, or root, rendered in Mr. Parkhurst's Lexicon, page 656.

I have thought it proper, in a work of this kind, to notice the above. But I beg that it may be considered, at the same time, that if the word be still accepted, as our translators have rendered it to borrow, Exod. iii. 22, there will not attach to it the least matter of fraud. Let it be remembered, that when the children of Israel, under the first Pharaoh, went down into Egypt, they were commanded by the king not "to regard their stuff; for the good of all the land of Egypt was to be theirs." (Gen. xlv. 16-20.) But it appears from their history, that when Jacob and his family went down to sojourn in "Egypt, they took their cattle and their goods with them." (Gen. xlvi. 1-7.) It becomes an important question in the subject, to ask, What became of this property, improved and increased, as we may reasonably suppose it to have been, when another king arose, who knew not Joseph? Moreover, we are told, that the children, when in bondage, built treasure cities for Pharaoh, Exod. i. 8. And what wages did the tyrant give them for those labours? We are told, indeed, that they made their lives bitter to them with their cruel bondage; "and that they cast out their children, to the end they might not live." (Acts vii. 19.) When, therefore, the Lord had turned their tables upon them, and by the plagues upon Pharaoh, and all his people, had made a way for the Exodus, of his chosen, no doubt, under the remorse of their minds, and their sorrow of heart, the Egyptians were glad to part with the Israelites at any rate, and therefore lent them, or gave them such things as they asked.

I only beg to add, under this view of the subject, that as the tabernacle in the wilderness was afterwards adorned with the gold and silver the Israelires brought with them from Egypt, it is plain that the Lord approved of the conduct of his servants in asking from their neighbours such things as they needed, and as the Lord himself had commanded. (Exod. iii. 21, 29,)

And might there not be somewhat typical in the thing itself, in reference to the future call (as was all along intended) of the Gentile church? I beg the reader to read that sweet passage of the prophet Isaiah, chap. xix. from 18th verse to the end; and see the rich promises of the call of Egypt with Assyria, when the Lord shall set up the New Testament altar, even the Lord Jesus Christ, in the midst of the land of Egypt; and five cities shall speak the language of Canaan, even the gospel language of salvation by the blood and righteousness of the Lord Jesus Christ. And I would ask, Is not that day, yea, that very day, at hand? Hath not the Lord, even now, been planting the gospel in Egypt? Hath not our God, when working by terrible things in righteousness, as he doth in the present awful war, caused even the Musselmen and inhabitants of Egypt to look on the congregations and prayer meetings of some of our pious soldiers who have been there? The writer of this hath himself received testimony to this striking providence of our God from a faithful soldier of the Lord Jesus Christ, as well as a faithful servant of his king and country, who was there, and an eye-witness to such characters looking in upon them, when he and a few of his devout comrades met together to read the Scriptures, and pray, and sing praises to the Lord. And who shall say what eventual blessed consequences may arise out of it? Who knows, but from this may spring up, as from a grain of mustard seed, a glorious harvest to our God? Oh! for that happy period when, according to this sweet prophecy, "the Lord of hosts himself shall bless, saying, Blessed be Egypt my people, and Assyria the work of my hand, and Israel mine inheritance."

BOTTLE

Before the invention of glass, bottles were made, for the most part, of skins. It is proper to keep this in remembrance when reading the Bible, both of the Old Testament and of the New; for the knowledge and use of glass is of modern date. Hence, when it is said, (Gen. xxi. 14.) that Abraham rose up early in the morning, and took bread and a bottle of water, and gave it unto Hagar, putting it on her shoulder, we may suppose, that this was not only a large skin for a bottle, but as it was put on her shoulder, it was somewhat cumbersome and heavy.

When the men of Gibeon acted wisely with Joshua, as if coming from afar country, we are told, that they not only produced their bread mouldy, but their bottles rent, and patched together, which they said, were new when they left their own country. Bottles rent would be useless if made of glass. (Josh. ix. 4, &c.) Modern travellers relate that, even now, large skins of oxen are made use of for containing liquor; though vessels made of earth are also known. But for large quantities, they tell us, that still the skins of beasts are in use.

In the days of our Lord, it is certain that stone, as well as earthen vessels, were known, for we read of such at the marriage in Cana of Galilee. (John ii. 6.) But skins were also used; for the Lord speaks of using caution, not to put new (fermenting) wine into old dried bottles. (Matt. ix. 17.) A beautiful figure this, of the precious wine of the gospel, which must not be put into the old skin of our dried nature, but into the new heart of grace. Both must be new, and both are then preserved. (Rev. xxi. 5. 2 Cor. v. 17.)

BOW

The bow, in Scripture language meaneth much more than the instrument called the bow, used in war. Hence, the dying patriarch, when blessing Joseph, speaks of "his bow abiding in strength, because his arms were made strong by the hands of the mighty God of Jacob. From thence (said the patriarch), is the shepherd the stone of Israel." (Gen. xlix. 24.) And the Redeemer himself is represented as having "a bow, when a crown was given unto him, and he went forth conquering and to conquer." (Rev. vi. 2.) And there can be no doubt, but that the bow mentioned by the dying patriarch referred to Christ. Hence, in allusion to the same, JEHOVAH saith, "I do set my bow in the cloud." (Gen. ix. 13.) And hence John, when he saw heaven opened, beheld "a rainbow round about the throne." (Rev. iv. 3.) And the mighty angel he saw "clothed with a cloud, had a rainbow upon his head." (Rev. x. 1.) It is blessed to view Jesus thus constantly typified.

BOWELS

I should not have thought it necessary to have offered a single observation on this word, considered in the general acceptation of it, for every one cannot but know its obvious meaning. But it may be proper, notwithstanding, to observe, that as in its literal sense, the bowels mean the entrails, so when used figuratively, it refers to the heart and the affections. Hence, it is said of the patriarch Joseph, that at beholding his brother, "his bowels did yearn upon him." (Gen. xliii. 30.) And the Lord himself is represented as expressing his tenderness for Ephraim raider the same similitude; "Is Ephraim my dear son? is he a pleasant child? for since I spake against him, I do earnestly remember him still; therefore, my bowels are troubled for him. I will surely have mercy upon him, saith the Lord." (Jer. xxxi. 20.)

But when the word is spoken in reference to the person of Christ in his human nature, here it is not figuratively used, but literally; and the meaning of it is uncommonly blessed and sweet. If the reader will turn to the fortieth Psalm, and eighth verse, he will find Jesus thus speaking by the spirit of prophecy, "I delight to do thy will, O my God! yea, thy law is within my heart." The margin of the Bible renders it, within my bowels, meaning, that so perfectly holy and pure was the human nature of Christ, that the law of his Father was incorporated in his very being; an inwrought holiness mixed up and becoming his person and his existence. What a precious blessed view doth it afford of the Lord Jesus!

And what I beg the reader also particularly to remark, this purity, this holiness of the Lord Jesus in our nature, is, to all intents and purposes, that holiness in which JEHOVAH beholds his church in Jesus. This, I believe, is not so generally understood nor considered by the faithful as it ought; but it is what the Scriptures of God, in every part, warrant. Jesus becoming our Surety is expressly said to have been made both sin and a curse for his redeemed, that "they might be made the righteousness God in him." (2 Cor. v. 21. Gal. iii. 13.)

And what a blessedness is there contained in this one view of the completeness of the church in Jesus? So that, in the very moment that the child of God feels the workings of corruption within him, and is groaning under a body of sin and death, which he carries about with him, though he sees nothing in himself but sin and imperfection, yea, sometimes, as it appears to him, growing imperfections, yet looking to the Lord Jesus as his Surety, and considering the Redeemers holiness, and not any thing in himself, as the standard of justification, here he rests his well-founded hope. This was blessedly set forth by the Holy Ghost: (Isa. xlv. 24.) "Surely, shall one say, In the Lord have I righteousness and strength; even to him shall men come, and all that are incensed against him shall be ashamed."

BRANCH

From the vast importance of this word in Scripture, as it refers to the Lord Jesus Christ, it is marked by the prophet Zechariah in capitals. It seems, therefore, to demand our more particular attention. We find Christ spoken of, under the spirit of prophecy, by the Lord JEHOVAH, in this character by three of the prophets, Isaiah, Jeremiah, and Zechariah. It will be profitable for the reader to consult the several passages. (Isa. iv. 2. and xi. 1. Jer. xxiii. 5. and xxxiii. 15. Zech. iii. 8. and vi. 12.) The word Branch in the original is Netzer, which signifies, a city of plants. And to shew the correspondence to Christ, the Netzer, or Nazareth, where Jesus dwelt, was named from the same root. (See Matt. ii. 23.) The parallel passage in Zechariah, chap. vi. 12. is to the same effect. Ezekiel, in allusion to the Lord Jesus, speaks of him under the similitude of the plants, like Nazareth, but describes him "as a plant of renown." (Ezek. xxxiv. 24-29.)

BRASS

This word is sometimes used figuratively, to express power, durableness, and hardness. Thus in relation to Christ, John saith, when he saw him in that glorious vision, (Rev. i. 15.) "his feet were like unto fine brass, as if burning in a furnace;" denoting the glory and everlasting nature of his person and kingdom. We read also of mountains of brass in reference to the everlasting establishment of JEHOVAH'S purposes, Zech. vi. 1. Sometimes the word brass is made use of to set forth the impudence of hardened sinners; "Thy neck is an iron sinew, and thy brow brass." (Isa. xlviii. 4.) And sometimes the Lord gives some sweet and precious promises to his people under this figure, "Arise, and thresh, O daughter of Zion! for I will make thine horn iron, and I will make thy hoofs brass." (Micah iv. 13.)

BREAD

Sometimes bread is spoken of in Scripture in the common acceptation of it, as the staff of natural life, but more frequently it is used in figure, by way of allusion to the Lord Jesus and the life in him. Jesus calls himself "the living bread, and the bread of God;" to intimate, that as the natural man is sustained day by day, life kept up and preserved by receiving the common bread for the body, so the spiritual life in Jesus is wholly supported by communications from Jesus, and life in Jesus. "Whosoever eateth of him shall live for ever." (John vi. 32-58.)

The shew bread of the Old Testament was of Christ. It consisted of twelve loaves made without leaven, to intimate that there is nothing leavened in Christ. The shew bread was placed new upon the golden altar. Christ is our New Testament altar; and all offerings must be offered upon the golden altar of his mediatorial nature. The shew bread was placed there every Sabbath. Christ is our Sabbath, and the rest the wherewith the Lord causeth "the weary to rest, and their refreshing." (See Exod. xxv. 30. Isa. xxviii. 12. Ps. cxvi. 7. Matt. xi. 28.) It may not be improper to add, that the term shew bread meant the bread of faces; and, probably, it was so called, because offered in the presence of the Lord, and placed before him on the table. The Israelites called all their loaves by the name of Huggath.

The unleavened bread of the passover, there is particular mention made of it, Exod. xii. 8. And concerning leavened bread, with which the blood of the sacrifice was never to be offered, what a beautiful type was this of the untainted, pure offering of the body of Jesus Christ, once for all. No altar but that of earth, (because the earth is the Lord's,) was to be made for offering. If but a tool was lifted up upon the altar of earth, or stone, the whole was polluted. (Exod. xxiii. 18. Exod. xx. 24, 25.) And is it not the same now in the believer's offerings in Jesus? When in commemoration of the Lord's supper we partake of the bread and wine, as tokens of the body and blood of Christ, would it not be a pollution to leaven this solemn service with any thing of ours? Is not Christ all and in all?

BREASTPLATE

This was a part of the high priest's dress, which he wore when performing his office in the temple service. On this breastplate were engraved the names of the twelve tribes of Israel, and it was called, "the breastplate of judgment." (Exod. xxviii. 15.) The design of it seems to have been to typify the Lord Jesus Christ, the great and almighty High Priest of his redeemed, who going in before JEHOVAH, bears the names, and persons, and concerns of all his people. Hence, the church so vehemently desired the Lord that she might be set "as a seal upon his heart, and a seal upon his arm." The former the tenderest, and the latter the strongest part in Jesus's affection. (Song viii, 6.) And hence, in allusion to the same, the apostle exhorts the church to put on "the breastplate of faith and love;" meaning, a steadfast looking unto Christ in the exercise of those graces, by relying wholly on him for mercy and salvation. (1 Thess. v. 8.)

BREATH

This word is sometimes made use of in Scripture in allusion to the Lord Jesus Christ. For as the breath of the body is the life of the body, so Christ is the breath or life of the soul. Hence, the prophet Jeremiah, in reference to Christ, saith, "the breath of our nostrils, the Anointed of the Lord was taken in their pits." (Lam. iv. 20.) And hence, when the Lord Jesus, after his resurrection, imparted to his disciples the gracious influences of his Spirit, it is said, that "he breathed on them, and said, Receive ye the Holy Ghost." (John xx. 22.)

BRETHREN and BROTHER

Holy Scripture hath several distinct meanings for this term, and of very different significations from each other. To be of the same nature, or disposition, to be of the same town, or country, or occupation in trade, is sometimes made the cause for calling men brethren. And in Scripture to be of the same stock, or family, though not of the same parents, constitutes a brother. Thus, as in the instance of our Lord Jesus Christ after the flesh, James and Joses were called the brethren of Christ, but in fact, were not so, but only relations of that tribe to which Jesus belonged. For Mary, the mother of James and Joses, was the wife of Cleophas, and not the Virgin Mary. (Matt. xxvii. 56. John xix. 25.) And sometimes the name of brother is used to describe men of like character, in idleness, or iniquity. Thus Solomon saith, "He that is slothful in his work, is brother to him that is a great waster." (Prov. xviii. 9.)

But when the reader hath carefully marked the application of the name brother to these and the like characters, there is a view of the subject perfectly foreign to every other, and above all, in which when the name of brother is considered as applied to the person of our Lord Jesus Christ, and our relationship in him, it forms the sweetest of all thoughts. Hence the church, before Christ's open manifestation in the flesh, so passionately longed for his coming. "O (said she) that thou wert as my brother that sucked the breasts of my mother! when I should find thee without I would kiss thee; yea, I should not be despised." (Song viii. 1.) And, indeed, Jesus in his human nature is the nearest and dearest of all brothers; and in his person is centered a comprehension of all relations. Brethren in Christ are all brethren by the Father's side, for they have all one father, "even the God and Father of our Lord Jesus Christ, of whom the whole family in heaven and earth is named." (Ephes. iii. 14, 15.) And they are all brethren by the mother's side, for they have all lain together in the same womb of the divine counsels and purposes of JEHOVAH, and that from all eternity. (Isa. xlix. 1. Tit. i. 2.) And they are all brethren by Jesus's side himself, for he is their elder brother, and the "first born among many brethren." (Rom. viii. 29.) And they are "bone of his bone, and flesh of his flesh." (Ephes. v. 20.)

I must beg the reader's attention a little farther to a subject so infinitely interesting. Evident it is, that from all eternity this relationship of Jesus with our nature began, even before that nature of ours was called into being. And hence, what we read in the Old Testament Scripture of the Jewish brother, and the precepts so frequently given of regarding him, had a special reference to Jesus. We lose the whole beauty of the Scripture if Christ be not first beheld in this subject. As for example.--When the law enjoined tenderness, and the relief to the brother waxen poor, here we behold the law of JEHOVAH, and Jesus the law fulfiller blessedly obeying it among his brethren, "If thy brother be waxen poor, and hath sold away some of his possession, and if any of his kin come to redeem it, then shall he redeem that which his brother sold." So again, "If thy brother be waxen poor, and fallen into decay with thee, then thou shalt relieve him; yea, though he be a stranger or a sojourner, that he may live with thee." (Lev. xxv. 25-35.)

Who is the brother waxen poor, having fallen into decay, and sold away some of his possession, but our poor ruined nature; ruined by the fall, and by sin, having sold away our possession? And who is the brother to whom the precept is given, and by whom it hath been fulfilled, and is fulfilling, but the Lord Jesus Christ? Who but him could redeem our mortgaged inheritance? Who but him had a right so to do, as the nearest of all kin, and the most compassionate of all relations? And do observe in those gracious precepts how blessedly provision is made, in this almighty Brother's obedience to this precept, for all the relations of Jesus, both Jew and Gentile; "Yea, (saith the command of JEHOVAH,) though he be a stranger, or a sojourner, that he may live with thee." Live with Jesus! what a precious consideration to my poor heart in the moment of writing, who am by nature a Gentile born, and at that time "an alien to the commonwealth of Israel." (Ephes, ii. 11, 12.) Blessed for ever be the almighty Lawgiver for enjoining those precepts! And, blessed for ever be the almighty Law fulfiller for his complete obedience to them! And blessed for ever be the almighty Author of Scripture for recording these things, and both bringing my soul acquainted with them, and causing me to believe them, to the divine glory and my soul's joy! And ought it not to be added, by way of rich consolation to every believer's heart, that Jesus our Brother is still carrying on the same blessed purposes, and fulfilling the precept even now in heaven? Jesus is still the Brother; for though his state is changed, yet not his nature. And amidst all the decays and poverty of his poor brethren on earth, Jesus is looking with the same compassion as ever on them; and they are authorized to look up for every needed relief unto him. He must redeem, yea, he hath in every individual instance of his people redeemed their lost possession. He must "open his hand wide to his poor and to his needy in the land." (Deut. xv. 7, 8.) He must bring every one of them home to live with him; for so the precept is. All the poor brethren of Jesus form one great body, of which Jesus is the Head. And surely, the Head and members being one, ought to be, and certainly will be, eternally united.

I cannot forego adding one sweet and interesting thought more, by way of finishing our present view of Jesus as our Brother; namely, that as Jesus hath thus condescended to become our brother, we ought to take great delight in looking up to him in this tender character. Is it said, that he is not ashamed to call us brethren; and shall we be ashamed of the relationship? Are the great ones of the earth in their carnal alliances, so proud to have their connections known, which are but for a day, and that a day of sin and vanity; and shall we, that are brethren to the Prince of the kings of the earth, and the almighty Lord of heaven, feel no joy in such an union, and which is to last for ever?

I do beg the reader to ponder well the soul-comforting subject, and to be more glad of it than of all the riches and grandeur of the world. And I mention this, the rather, because it is to be feared that some of the Lord's hidden ones are not sensible of their high birth, and relationship in Jesus; or at least, do not make that use of it which they ought. Would any man be shy of going to an earthly court if the king of that court was his brother? Nay, would he not be often going there; often telling of it to ever one around him; and delighting to have it known that he had access, at all times, to the person of the king his brother, and might have whatever he asked of him? But what are these privileges, or what great cause for taking pride and consequence in these transitory dignities, compared to that real unfading honour in a consciousness of not only coming to Jesus, the King of kings, and Lord of lords, as to a brother, but who hath made all his redeemed kings and priests to God and the Father, and "they shall reign with him for ever and ever!" (Rev. i. 6. xxii. 5.)

Suffer me yet farther to add, that the Scriptures of our God have made this subject of Christ's brotherhood, so peculiarly endearing to the church, that the gracious design of our Lord Jesus, in the assuming of our manhood, is not answered when his church "makes no use of it. Let the reader recollect that this astonishing condescension of Christ is altogether personal. It was the Son of God alone, and not either of the other persons of the GODHEAD which be came our Brother. For, although, all the glorious persons of JEHOVAH took part in our redemption, yet to neither can we look up as brother but to the Lord Jesus Christ. And is not this personal love and grace of Jesus intended to excite and call up personal affections towards him? Doth he not seem thereby as if to bid us approach him, in a peculiar manner, under this sweet character? Yea, doth he not say in language similar to his illustrious type, the patriarch "Joseph, to his brethren, when under a conscious sense of their crimes in having sold him for a slave they feared to approach him; doth not our Almighty Joseph say to us, under all our tremblings, and fears, and misgivings, in having nailed him to the cross by our sins: "Come near to me I pray you, I am Jesus your brother, whom ye sold into Egypt?" (Gen xlv. 3, 4.) Oh! thou glorious, gracious, all-lovely, and all-loving Brother! thou art a brother indeed, born for adversity; a friend that loveth at all times; one that sticketh closer than a brother. Thou art he whom thy brethren shall praise; thine hand shall be in the neck of thine enemies; and all thy

Father's children shall bow down before thee. (Gen. xlix. 8.)

BROOK
See Cedron.

BRIDE
This is a well known name in common life. It is very highly endeared to our affection when applied by Jesus himself to his church. If the reader wishes to see some beautiful instances, in which the whole church as one collective body is called the Lamb's wife, I refer him to the Songs of Solomon, and to the book of the Revelation at large. (Rev. xxi. 2-9. John iii. 29. Isa. lxii. 3. 45.) See Church, Spouse, Wife.

BRIDEGROOM
This, as a corresponding name to the former, is frequently in the Scriptures applied to Christ. John the Baptist beautifully describes Jesus under this character, John iii. 28, &c. And Christ himself, Matt. ix. 5. Mark ii. 19, 20. See Husband.

BURNT INCENSE
See Incense.

BURNT OFFERINGS
See Offerings.

BURIAL
We find the greatest attention paid by the Hebrews, from the earliest ages, to the depositing of the remains of their friends in sepulchres. Perhaps, in all the compass of language, and in all the refinements of courts, there is nothing to be found in history equal to the manners and address of the patriarch Abraham, when standing up before his people to ask a place for the burial of his beloved Sarah from the children of Heth.

Would men wish to behold a portrait of the most unaffected dignity with politeness, they must look for it in the twenty-third chapter of Genesis, where, I venture to say, is discovered every thing that can be truly called elegant, dignified, and venerable in the character of the great Father of the faithful. Surely, the patriarch here appears the most accomplished and finished gentleman the world ever beheld. In proof, I hope that I shall be pardoned if I recite a few words from that interesting chapter.

"And Sarah died in Kirjath-arba, the same is Hebron, in the land of Canaan. And Abraham came to mourn for Sarah, and to weep for her. And Abraham stood up from before his dead, and spake unto the sons of Heth, saying, I am a stranger and a sojourner with you; give me a possession of a burying-place with you, that I may bury my dead out of my sight.

And the children of Heth answered Abraham, saying unto him, Hear us, my lord: thou art a mighty prince among us: in the choice of our sepulchres bury thy dead. None of us shall withhold from thee his sepulchre, but that thou mightest bury thy dead. And Abraham stood up and bowed himself to the people of the land, even to the children of Heth."

What a very interesting view doth this afford of the conduct of Abraham on this occasion. And when in the after conversation, the children of Heth proposed giving the spot of ground the patriarch fixed on for a sepulchre for his beloved Sarah, with what grace and dignity did he decline it as a gift; but requested that he might have it by purchase. And during the transaction of this business, we are told, that Abraham again bowed down himself before the people of the land.

Last offices to the dead were among the first in the concern of the living. Probably, though it was reserved for the gospel dispensation to bring life and immortality to light, yet among those who,

BURIAL - BURIAL

like of Christ afar off, they were not wholly untaught concerning the doctrine of the resurrection in Jesus. But be this as it may, certain it is, that the greatest regard was had in the burial of the dead among the early followers of our Lord; and to be without a burial place, was considered among the severest calamities. Hence Jacob, when a-dying, charged his children to bury him with his fathers. "There (said he), they buried Abraham and Sarah his wife; there they buried Isaac and Rebekah his wife; and there I buried Leah." (Gen. xlix. 29.) And hence, Joseph also gave commandment "concerning his bones? (Gen. 1.25.) And it is spoken of in Scripture, by the Lord himself, as the marked punishment of Ithoiakim, that he should have no burial place, but be cast forth as an ass without the gates of Jerusalem. (Jer. xxii. 18, 19.) And what is it now? Believers in Jesus still feel some degree of concern, that the ashes of their friends may be deposited with decent solemnity in the grave. And when we consider what the blessed Scriptures have said, that the bodies of Christ's people are the temples of the Holy Ghost, there seems to be a manifest propriety, though void of all idle parade and ostentation, to commit the remains of those who die in the Lord to the bowels of the earth, in sure and certain hope of the resurrection to eternal life in him, and through him, and by him, who is himself the resurrection and the life. How blessedly the apostle Paul speaks on this subject, under the influence of the Holy Ghost, in his epistle to the church. "I would not (saith he) have you to he ignorant, brethren, concerning them which are asleep, that ye sorrow not even as others which have no hope. For if we believe, that Jesus died, and rose again, even so them also, which sleep in Jesus, will God bring with him. For this we say unto you by the word of the Lord, that we which are alive and remain unto the coming of the Lord, shall not prevent them which are asleep. For the Lord himself shall descend from heaven with a shout, with the voice of the archangel, and with the trump of God, and the dead in Christ shall rise first. Then we which are alive and remain, shall be caught up together with them in the clouds, to meet the Lord in the air; and so shall we be ever with the Lord. Wherefore, comfort one another with these words." (I Thess. iv. 13, &c.)

C

CAB

An Hebrew measure, containing about three pints in wine measure, and two pints of corn measure. This serves to explain the miseries of the famine in Samaria, when the fourth part of a cab of doves dung sold for five pieces of silver. (2 Kings, vi. 25)

CABUL

So Hiram called the twenty cities Solomon gave him for his aid, in the materials he furnished him with for the building of the temple. (1 Kings ix. 13.) The word signifies, unpleasant. Probably, it was one of those cities mentioned Josh. xix. 27.

CÆSAR

Perhaps the reader doth not know, or recollect, that this name was used by all the Roman Emperors, whatever their other name might be. Thus Tiberius was the Emperor in the days of our Lord. (See Luke iii. 1.) But our Lord only called him Cæsar. (See Matt. xxii. 21.) And Paul the apostle, when compelled to appeal against the injustice of Festus, said, I appeal unto Caesar; whereas, Nero was at that time the Emperor. (See Acts xxv. 10, 11.)

CÆSAREA

There are two places of this name spoken of in Scripture. Cæsasrea Philippi, supposed to have been built by Philip, no great distance from Zidon. This place is rendered memorable in the gospel, from Jesus passing near the coasts of it when Peter gave so blessed a testimony to the GODHEAD of his master. See Matt. xvi. 13, &c The other Cæsarea was in Palestine. Here lived Cornelius the Centurion. (Acts x.)

CAIN

The first born of Adam and Eve. His name is derived form Hanah, to possess. Hence Cain means, possession. And this agrees to Eve's name of her son, for she said, I have gotten a man from the Lord; or as it might be read, the man (that is the very one promised), from the Lord. (Gen. iv. 1.) Alas! how little did our poor mistaken mother know, what miseries among thousands and millions of her children would be induced, before He should arise to do away the evil of her transgression, by the sacrifice of himself! See Abel.

CAINAN or KEMAN

There were two of this name in the first ages of the world. Cainan, the son of Enos, Gen. v. 9. and Cainan, the son of Arphaxad, Luke iii. 36. His name is derived from Canah, to possess. Hence Cainan means, possessor.

CAIAPHAS

A name and person, memorable in Scripture from being overruled by God the Holy Ghost to deliver a prophecy the very reverse of his own wishes, and like another Balaam, to pronounce good when he intended evil. (See John xi. 49-52.)

CALEB

Son of Jephunneh, of whom honorable testimony is given, Num. xiii. 2. His name is somewhat singular; if it be derived, as it is supposed to be, from Keleb, dog. But some suppose it is a compound of Ke, and Lebab, the heart.

CALF

Golden calf, which it is said Aaron made, Exod. xxxii. 1-4, It is remarkable, that though it is expressly said, that this was but one idol, yet the children of Israel addressed it as in the plural, and said, "These are thy gods, O Israel!' Did the Israelites, in direct defiance of the divine law, make this idol to

CALVARY - CAPERNAUM

resemble, according to their gross conceptions, the true God? Wherefore, do they otherwise call it gods? Certainly, there is somewhat mysterious in it. Jeroboam, in his days, made two calves, (See I Kings xii. 26-28.)

CALVARY

Ever memorable and dear to the believer. It was near Jerusalem; and, probably, long before Christ, it was the place devoted, for the execution of criminals. Here the meditation of the follower of Jesus should frequently take wing, and view in faith that wonderful mount, from whence redemption came! See Gethsemane and Golgotha.

CANA

In Galilee. A small village near Nazareth. This place is rendered memorable in the gospel, being honoured with our Lord's presence at a marriage. and first miracle that he wrought of turning water into wine. (John ii.)

CANAAN

The son of Ham, Noah's son. From him sprang the Canaanites. (Gen. ix. 18.)

CANAAN

The land of promise; the glory of all lands. (Ezek. xx. 6.) So called, not only on account of its fertility and loveliness in point of situation, but more eminently, in having the special presence of the Lord and his ordinances. And as the temple, and all the services of the temple, were so many types of the Lord Jesus, Canaan might well be called the land of promise, with an eye to Him.

It is well worthy our observation, that while, among all the early writers, both sacred and profane, the very blessed state of Palestine, or Canaan, (for we name it by either, extending both the sacred river Jordan as a country, is continually described; later travellers speak of it as a dry, and inhospitable place. Moses, and all patriarchs, Ezekiel; and all the prophets, are praises of Canaan, and all describe it as a land "flowing with milk and honey. A land of wheat, and barley, and vines, and fig trees, and pomegranates. A land of oil, olive and honey; of brooks, and fountains, and depths, that spring out of valleys and hills. "A land (said Moses) whose very stones are iron, and out of whose hills thou mayest dig brass." (See Deut. viii. 7-9, &c. Ezek. xx. 6. 1 5.

And among profane historians of antiquity we find the like testimonies to those of Holy Writ. Hecatæus, who lived at the time of Alexander the Great, and who wrote in the reign of Ptolemy, describes Palestine as a most fruitful province.
And Pliny speaks of it in a degree of enthusiasm. Jordan was to his view a beautiful river, and the banks of it fruitful to an excess. He describes the palm trees, and the balm of Judah, and the city of Jerusalem, as most lovely indeed!

Modern travellers, however, have given a very different account. The provinces are said by most of them to be barren and unfruitful, and Jerusalem itself to be but a poor city. From these different statements the pious reader will, without my suggestion, feel his mind, I should hope, led to that beautiful observation of the Psalmist, and indeed, to the whole of the many blessed things to the same amount, as are said in that Psalm; "A fruitful land the Lord turneth into barrenness, for the wickedness of them that dwell therein." (Ps. cvii. 43.)

CANDLESTIC

See Golden Candlestics.

CAPERNAUM

A well known place in the gospel of Christ, where the Lord Jesus principally abode during his ministry. It was on the borders of Genesareth. The awful woe which Christ denounced upon the men of this city, in having seen his person, but despised his doctrine, still hangs in equal, or rather increased, terror, over all the Christ despisers of every generation. (Matt. xi. 23.)

CAPTAIN

We meet this title in one passage of the word of God, and but one, as far as my memory chargeth me, applied to the Lord Jesus Christ; and that is in the second chapter of Hebrews, and the tenth verse. And very sweetly and eminently so, must we consider the name in reference to him. For he it was, most probably, that Joshua saw in vision, long before his incarnation, before the walls of Jericho, as captain of the Lord's host, and before whom Joshua fell on his face. (Josh. v. 13-15.) It is very blessed to see and know the Lord Jesus under this character, and to fight under his banner.

CARMEL

There are two different places of this name in Scripture; Mount Carmel, near the brook Kishon; and Carmel, a city of Judah, where Nabal dwelt. Some read it Carmul, as if composed of Kar, lamb; and Mul, circumcised. But others, with more probability of being right, render it Carmel, vineyard, or harvest; as being full of vines and corn.

CEDAR TREE

The cedar tree of Lebanon, forms an interesting object in holy Scripture, and merits attention. The tree itself seems, for majesty and beauty, to take place of every other among the trees of the forest. Its branches are wide and spreading. They begin to form themselves nearly from the ground, and stretch forth on each side. The tree itself is an evergreen, and sheds forth a gummy substance, which is said to contain many salutary qualities. The wood of it formed a part in the service of the cleansing of the leper. (See Lev. xiv. 4.) One of the kings of Israel called himself by the name of the Cedar of Lebanon, 2 Kings xiv. 9.

The church, or Christ for the church, when celebrating the beauties and glories of their habitation, compares the beams of it to cedar. (Song, i. 17.) And the state of individual believers in the church is more than once spoken of, as resembled by the flourishing nature of the cedar of Lebanon. (Ps. xcii. 12-16; civ. 16.) The Hebrews called it Tashur, which the Septuagint rendered cedar. There is somewhat very interesting in such representations of the Lord's inheritance, when by figure and similitude we are sent, by God the Holy Ghost, to the loveliest objects in nature to form our views of the Lord's pleasure and delight, which he taketh in his people. Taught by such an infallible Teacher methinks I would never read of the Cedar of Lebanon, without connecting with it some sweet resemblance to be discovered in his people, which he saith himself are the branch of his planting, and which are so, that they might be called trees of righteousness, "the planting of the Lord, that he might be glorified." (Isa. lx. 21 lxi. 3.) And if Jesus himself, be in the view of JEHOVAH, and in his church's view, "the plant of renown," (Ezek. xxxiv. 29.) surely, it is blessed to know, that the church is in Jesus's view, the Cedar of Lebanon. And in how many ways do they bear resemblance to the glory of Lebanon, when made comely, from the comliness Jesus puts upon them! Is there any tree of the wood so graceful, or so lovely, as the Cedar of Lebanon? Neither is there any lily among the thorns so fair, and white, and fragrant, as Jesus's love is among the daughters. (Song ii. 2.) Do any trees out-top the Cedar of Lebanon, spread wider, or cast their branches with more luxuriancy farther than this fair one? Neither do any grow more upright, extend their usefulness in equal direction for general good, as the disciples of the Lord. For though they are poor and mean in man's opinion, yet do they stand high in the esteem of Christ Jesus; and in the grace of the Lord, like the branches of the cedar, they spread forth, by faith, in every direction, and by rich experience in the divine life, manifest forth the loveliness of their high calling all around. And as the Cedar of Lebanon is deep-rooted, evergreen, and ever-fragrant, so believers in Christ are deep-rooted in him, always flourishing in him, however unprofitable in themselves; and as the prophet describes the church, "their branches shall spread, and their beauty be as the olive tree, and their smell like Lebanon." (Hos. xiv. 6.) Such, and many more of the like nature, open to our view, while considering the church in Jesus's esteem, as the Cedar of Lebanon. (See a lovely account of this, Ps. xcii. 13-15.)

CEDRON or KIDRON

So called from Kedar, black, dark, gloomy. This was the memorable brook over which the great Redeemer passed, to enter the garden of Gethsemane, the night before his sufferings and death. Here, indeed, Jesus often walked, for he loved the sacred haunts of that hallowed ground, where he knew his last agony, in the conflicts with Satan, was to take place. (John xviii. 1, 2.) The brook itself lay in a valley to the east of the city, between Jerusalem and the mount of Olives; and it emptied itself in the dead Sea. Into this black and foul brook ran all the filth of the sacrifices from the temple; and most probably, like other sinks, for the most part, what was conveyed thither from the temple remained stagnant until the swelling rain carried off the contents. This was the ever to be remembered brook Cedron, concerning which it was prophesied of the Lord Jesus, a thousand years before his incarnation, that "he should drink of the brook in the way." (Ps. cx. 7.) Some, in reading that and connecting with it in the mind, the hot country of Palestine, might conceive it to have a pleasant thing to a dry thirsty traveller to drink of the brook in his way. And no doubt, of all earthly delights, the cooling streams in a sultry desert is the most grateful. But Cedron was no cooling, limpid, pure stream; but dark, and black, and filthy. When Jesus, therefore, is said to drink of it, the meaning is, that all our uncleanness was put on him. Here Jesus passed through all that torrent of divine wrath against sin, when "he that knew no sin, became sin and a curse for us, that we might be made the righteousness of God in him." (2 Cor. v. 21.) Here it was, that all the waves and billows of JEHOVAH'S just anger, for his broken law, went over the head of Christ, as the Surety and Representative of his people; and which brought forth those cries of the Glory-man, Christ Jesus, which, by the Spirit of prophecy, was recorded of him. (Ps. xxii. and lxix.) Such was Cedron. And this brook was rendered memorable in allusion to Christ, when David, as a type of Jesus, passed it in his ascent to the mount of Olives, when fleeing from his kingdom with his followers barefoot, his head covered, and weeping, and sorrowing, at the instance of Absalom, his unnatural son. (2 Sam. xv. 30.) Thus Jesus passed Cedron under the deepest of all possible sorrows, when, with his few faithful disciples, he entered the garden from the foul conspiracy of Judas, and the high priest, and elders of his people. And God the Holy Ghost was graciously pleased to make Cedron again memorable, as typical of the Lord Jesus Christ, when Asa, Hezekiah, and Josiah, burnt and destroyed the idols of the land, and cast the accursed things of the groves into this brook. As if to shew, by type, that the brook Jesus, in after ages, was to drink of, should be the common receiver of all our idols, and all our uncleanness, when, by his gracious undertaking, that blessed promise of a covenant God in Christ was to be fulfilled: "Then will I sprinkle clean water upon you, and ye shall be clean from all your filthiness, and from all your idols." (Ezek. xxxvi. 25. See also 2 Chron. xv. 16; xxx. 14. and 2 Kings xxiii. 4-6.) Such then was, and is, Cedron. Oh! the blessedness of beholding it thus explained to us by God the Holy Ghost, in reference to the Lord Jesus Christ! Here would my soul take frequent wing, and by faith, alight near the hallowed spot. And if Jesus oftimes resorted thither with his disciples, here, methinks, would my soul delight to roam, and see the place, and the memorable brook Jesus drank of by the way, See Gethsemane.

CENTURION

This is a word often met with in the gospel; and the meaning is, that the man who was a Centurion, commanded, or governed, an hundred soldiers.

CERTAIN

The word certain, when applied to man, hath a very special and particular meaning. It is not unlike, for importance, the phrase of a man of God, to distinguish from a man of the world; or the natural man, to distinguish from the spiritual and the inward man of the heart, to denote somewhat from that which is merely outward. So, in like manner, when in Scripture, at any time, it is said, a certain man, there is somewhat striking affixed to the expression; such as in that instance, when It is said, a certain man drew a bow at a venture, and smote the king, (1 Kings xxii. 34.) the meaning is the arrow was directed by the Lord. So again, when it is said in the gospel, a certain man had two sons, (Luke xv. 11.) a Certain man had a fig tree planted in his vineyard, (Luke xiii. 6.) a certain man made a great supper, and bade many, (Luke xiv. 6.) all these, and the like, directly refer to the Lord. So again, when it is said, (as in Ruth, chap. i.) a certain man of Bethlehem-judah went to sojourn in the country of Moab. And again, in the gospel, (Luke x. 30.) a certain man went down from Jerusalem to Jericho, and fell among thieves. Both these cases, as well as others of a similar kind, are designed to represent our nature universally. All men, from our first father, have left Bethlehem-judah, the land of bread, for so the name means; and Jerusalem, the holy city; and by going down to the Moabs and the Jerichos of the world, have fallen among thieves, and been left more than half dead by the great enemy of souls.

CHAFF

In the general sense of the word, chaff is the husk of wheat; in itself useless, and only intended to form a covering for the pure seed. But in Scripture language, it is used figuratively, to denote the uselessness and folly of a name to live, while virtually dead before God. Hence the Lord, speaking of the preciousness of his word to that of the invention of men, thus expresseth "What is the chaff to the wheat, saith the Lord?" (Jer. xxiii. 28.) And the sacred writers, under the same Almighty authority, describe the wicked as chaff, which the wind scattereth, and the storm carrieth away; and which the Lord will burn up in the end, with unquenchable fire. (See Job xxi. 18. Ps. i. 4. Hos. xiii. 3. Matt. iii. 12.)

CHAIN and CHAINS

In Scripture those expressions are frequently made use of to denote the constraining love of Christ. Thus Christ speaks of his church; (Song i. 10; iv. 9.) and again, by way of shewing Christ's property in his church, "I put bracelets upon thine hands, and a chain on thy neck." (Ezek. xvi. 11.) And Paul, the apostle, delighted to call himself the Lord's prisoner. "For the hope of Israel (said he,) I am bound with this chain." (Acts xxviii. 20.) "Be not thou, therefore, ashamed of the testimony of our Lord, of me his prisoner." (2 Tim. i. 8.)

CHALSEA

See Babylon.

CHAMBER and CHAMBERS

These words we meet in Scripture upon various occasions. We read of "the chambers of the south," in relation to the heavenly bodies. (Job ix. 9.) "The upper chambers" of Solomon's temple, respecting the services and ordinances; (2 Chron. iii. 9.) and inner chambers of the Old Testament; and the guest-chambers of the New. (2 Kings ix. 2. Mark 14.) But the sweetest sense of the word chambers, in Scripture language, is in reference to those endearing views of Jesus, when he brings his church into the chambers of his grace, to make himself known unto them, otherwise than he doeth unto the world. Thus the church saith, (Song i. 4.) "The King hath brought me into his chambers." probably, it might mean into the knowledge of covenant of redemption, the doctrines of his gospel, which Jesus calls "the mysteries of his kingdom," and of which he saith to his disciples, "It is given unto you to know, but to others in parables." (Matt. xiii. 10, 11.) But still more perhaps, chambers is meant, the sweet and intimate communion into which Jesus brings his people, and of which no eye sees, no heart is privy, but him to whom the Lord gives that bread in secret.

And it should seem, that this is the chief sense of the word, because it was the custom among Jews, to unfold the secrets of their religion in this way. Hence, the guest-chamber, where Christ held his last supper, was of this kind. And the same, where the disciples met after our Lord's resurrection, for fear of the Jews. Seen in this point of view, we can discover a great beauty in that lovely invitation by the prophet: "Come, my people, enter thou into thy chambers." (Isa. xxvi. 20, 21.) What a gracious acknowledgment is this, on the Lord's part, of being his people, when, from having taken our nature, Jesus claims the church for his own, and leads her, as the husband the wife, into his chambers, unveils all his glories to her, and gives her interest, and right, and possession, of himself, and all that belongs to him, as the great Head and Mediator of his body, the church, "the fulness of Him that filleth all in all."

CHARIOT and CHARIOTS

The word is used repeatedly in Scripture, both as a real representation of the thing itself, and also figuratively. Very terrible were the war chariots, with which men fought in battle. Jabin, king of Canaan, it is said, had nine hundred chariots of iron, and mightily oppressed the children of Israel. (Judges iv. 3.) But when the term of chariot is applied to express spiritual things, the matter becomes more interesting. Thus Elijah's chariot, by which he went up into heaven; is called, the chariots of Israel, and the horsemen thereof; by which is meant, the ascension of Elijah's fervent prayers for Israel, were more powerful and prevailing than all the chariots of Israel in their defence. And doubtless, as the prophet in this instance became a type of Christ, in his priestly and regal office, the whole is abundantly plain and evident. (2 Kings ii. 12.) So again, in the book of the Songs, (chap. iii. 9.) Solomon is said to have made a chariot of "the wood of Lebanon; the pillars silver, the bottom of gold, the covering purple, and the midst thereof paved with love, for the daughters of Jerusalem." There can be no doubt, but that this is designed to speak of the Lord Jesus Christ, whose chariot of love, founded in himself, both in his GODHEAD and manhood, whose acts of grace, are richer than gold and silver, and whose whole heart is full of love to his beloved Jerusalem. Hence, the church in return, feeling all her affections awakened by grace, to the love of Jesus, cries out in an holy rapture of joy and delight," Or ever I was aware, my soul made me like the chariots of Ammi-nadib?' (Song vi. 12.) See Am mi-nadib.

CHEBAR

A river of Assyria, made memorable by the church, when in the captivity of Babylon, being placed there. That beautiful, though pathetic poem (as it may well be called of Hebrew poetry), we have in the hundred and thirty-seventh Psalm, is supposed to have been written on the banks of Chebar. (See Ezek. i. 1.)

CHERUB and CHERUBIM

We meet with an account of these so frequently in the word of God, that it forms an important duty to seek, under the Spirit's teaching, for the clearest apprehension of their meaning. At the entrance of the garden of Eden, after the fall, we find the cherubim and a flaming sword placed. (Gen. iii. 24.) And during the church's continuance in the wilderness, several relations are made of the cherubim. (Exod. xxv. 18; xxvi. 1; xxxvii. 7, 8.) Solomon's temple also, was adorned with the representation of them. (1 Kings vi. 23, &c.) But more particularly, in the visional prophecy of Ezekiel. (See chapters nine and ten throughout.) The general representation of the cherubim was under the similitude of four living creatures: the face of a man; the face of a lion; the face of an ox, or calf; and the face of an eagle. That these figures were emblems of somewhat more important and higher than themselves, hath been the universal opinion, both in the Jewish and Christian church, through all ages. Some have considered them as representing angels. But there seems, in the first view of the subject, a total contradiction to this, because, no one reason upon earth can be shown, why angels should be represented with four faces. Neither could there be any necessity for any other representation of an angel, but as an angel. We meet with continued instances of angels appearing, in the word of God, to God's people without any danger of JEHOVAH himself only can it be said, "Thou canst not see my face and live." (Exod. xxxiii. 20.) Moreover, before the cherubim was sprinkled, on the great day of atonement, the blood of the sacrifice, which we all know was typical of Christ, and represented the one offering of the Redeemer. Now, to have this set forth before angels would have been contrary to the whole sense of Scripture. (See Exod. xxxvii. 9. Lev. xvi. 14. compared with Heb. ix. 7. 12.) Evidently, therefore, the cherubim could not be intended to prefigure angels.

The question is then, What, or whom, did they represent? I would very humbly say in answer, that I am inclined to think, with several who have gone before me in the study of this solemn and mysterious subject, that the cherubim were emblematical of the glorious persons of the GODHEAD, in their covenant engagements to redeem our fallen nature, as represented in those characters united with the manhood of Christ. And the foundation of this belief, I humbly beg to subjoin.

And first, to begin with the earliest representation at the gate of Paradise, we are told, (Gen, iii. 24.) that the Lord himself placed those cherubim there, which turned every way, to keep the way of the tree of life. By which I apprehend, the sense of the expression is, not to keep from, but to keep to, the way of the tree of life; meaning, that poor fallen man now had no access but by this way. And as we well know, from our Lord's own authority, that Jesus is "the way, and the truth, and the life; and no man cometh to the Father, but by him." (John xiv. 6.) Hence it should seem, that by these cherubic figures, among which the face of a man formed a part, immediately at the fall, redemption through Christ was set up by those emblems, as manifested to the church.

Secondly, Those cherubim were eminently displayed in the Holy of Holies, over and upon the mercy seat. (See Exod. xxv. 17-22, compared with Heb. xi. 1-24.) Now, as from the authority of those Scriptures, we have full licence to conclude, that the mercy-seat itself was an emblem of Christ, and the High Priest going into the Holy of Holies once in a year, with blood, a lively type of the Lord Jesus going in with his own blood into heaven itself, there to appear in the presence of God for us, we cannot for a moment suppose, but that these cherubim must have been designed to represent the holy and undivided Three persons in the one eternal JEHOVAH, before whom only, and to whom only, Christ, in his divine and nature united, made the one sacrifice of by which he hath prefected for ever them that are sanctified. The song of heaven declared, that the redemption by Christ was from God, as the first cause, and to God, as the final end. (Rev. v. 9.) To have set forth, therefore, these solemn representations, by type and figure, in the Jewish church, before any but JEHOVAH himself, would have been little short of blasphemy, and consequently cherubim, before which every great day of the same was regularly observed, could emblematical only of the glorious persons of the GODHEAD.

If it be objected, that in the vision of Isaiah, chap. so again, in the vision of John, Rev. viii. where in both Scriptures, we find the seraphim, or cherubim, (for they mean one and the same), are represented as worshipping God, and hence it be said, is there not a contradiction in supposing JEHOVAH worshipping JEHOVAH? I answer, certainly there would be, if this were in reality the case. But the fact is, that it is not so. Let it be remembered, that these cherubim are emblems, and not the very persons they represent. The representatives of another my join in any acts with others, to proclaim with them the worth, or praises, of those whom they represent. As the ambassador of an earthly king, though he represents his master, may, at the same time, join his fellow subjects in proclaiming with them his master's honour. This objection, therefore, falls to the ground. And though I do not presume, on a subject so mysterious and sublime, to speak decidedly, yet I cannot but think, that the cherubim of Scripture, are intended to represent the glorious persons of the GODHEAD, with the human nature united to the person of the Son of God, and by no means intended to represent angels.

CHILD, CHILDREN, SONS

These are variously used in Scripture, to denote one and the same. All the race of Israel are called the children of Israel. And in like manner, the children of God in Christ are called, children of the kingdom. But these things are so obvious and plain, that I should not have thought it necessary, in a work of this kind, purposely contracted into the narrowest compass, to have noticed the word Child, but for the introducing a short observation on the term itself, as applied to the Lord Jesus Christ. On his account I think it important, and the reader will, I hope, forgive me.

We meet with the word Child, in relation to Jesus, several times in Scripture; but there are two places where it occurs, with a peculiar emphasis of expression, and where the word holy is prefixed, as if to give it an endearedness to the believer's heart. The passages I refer to are in the prayer of the church, on that memorable occasion when the Lord answered, by an immediate shaking of the place where they were assembled. (Acts iv. 27-30.) "Of a truth, Lord, against thy holy child Jesus, both Herod and Pontius Pilate, with the Gentiles and the people of Israel were gathered together. And now, Lord, grant that signs and wonders may be done by the name of thy holy child Jesus." I know not whether the reader enters with me into an apprehension of the very great loveliness, as well as importance, of the expression, in respect to the holy child Jesus; but I cannot but think, that the church, in this prayer, laid the whole stress, for their prayers being answered, upon the person of Jesus, in the holiness of that nature; which nature the church considered as its own. And for the complete justification of the church, the Lord Jesus took that nature in its perfect holiness. So that as the church then did, so may, and so ought, all believers now to rest the whole hope and expectation of an answer to all their prayers before the throne, upon the sole ground of the same sweet and lovely expression, sent up to God Father, "by the name of thy holy child Jesus." Nothing, among the Hebrews was a more afflictive providence, than to no children; probably with an eye to the promised seed. Hence Abraham, the great father the faithful, when the Lord promised, that he himself would be his shield, and his exceeding reward, said, Lord God, "what wilt thou give me seeing I go childless?" (Gen. xv. 1, 2.) And the punishment the Lord appointed to unnatural alliances, was to bear their sins in dying childless. (Lev. xx. 20.) And in the case of Coniah, the Lord said, "Write this man childless," (Jer. xxii. 30.) It were well among Christians, if this was well understood. How many consider a large family the reverse, and overlook that Scripture, which declares the man "happy, that hath his quiver full of children!" (Ps. cxxvii. 5.)

CHILLON
See Mahlon.

CHOSEN OF GOD
We find this, act of special grace in JEHOVAH, as it concerns the person of Christ and his people in him, so often in the Scripture, and as it is so important, I have thought a reference to some of the more prominent texts would not be unacceptable, in a work of this kind. Concerning the person of the Lord Jesus Christ as chosen, and set apart from all eternity, the glorious Head and Mediator of his people, these portions are some among the many. Isa. xli. 8, 9; xliii. 10. compared with Matt. xii. 18. Neh. ix. 7. Num. xvi. 5. 7. Ps. xlvii. 4. Isa. xlix. 7. Ps. lxxxix. 3. 19. Isa. xlviii. 10. Luke xxiii. 35. 1 Pet. ii. 4. &c. And concerning the children of Christ chosen in him, and sanctified in him, the following are among the many with which the word of God abounds to the same doctrine. Ephes. i. 4. Isa. xiv. 1. Deut. vii. 6. Ps. cv. 5. 43. 1 Chron. xvi. 13. Ps. cvi. 5. Isa. xliii. 20; lxv. 15. Matt. xx. 16. Mark xiii. 20. John xiii. 18; xv. 16. 19. Acts. xxii. 14; ix. 15. 1 Cor. i. 27. Rom. xvi. 13. Jam. ii. 5. 1 Pet. ii. 9. Rev. xvii. 14, &c.

CHRIST
One of the adorable names of the Lord Jesus, and signifying the Anointed of JEHOVAH. It is precisely the same word as Messiah in the original Hebrew. The name Christ, specially and particularly, means the union of both natures in the person of the Lord Jesus, both divine and human; and as such becoming the Christ of God. The Scriptures are express and clear, in a great variety of instances, in proof of his eternal power and GODHEAD, being "one with the Father over all, God blessed for ever." (Rom. ix. 5. John i. 1. Matt. iii. 17.) And no less in testimony of his human nature. (John i. 14. Heb. ii. 9. to the end.) But when we speak of Christ, we neither mean Son of God only, nor Man only, but include both natures, constituting one person, the glorious Head of his body the church, "the fulness of Him that filleth all in all." (Eph. i. 22, 23.)

As the clear apprehension of the person of our Lord Jesus Christ is not only among the first things to be rightly impressed upon the mind, but the very first and most essential of all others, for the full enjoyment of our interest in him, I hope that I shall be forgiven, if I somewhat exceed the ordinary limits I have hitherto observed, under the several articles. Before I enter upon the subject, I beg first to remark, that the general errors we have run into concerning the forming of a proper apprehension of the person of Christ, hath arisen from misinterpreting Scripture on this point. Some parts of the word of God speak wholly of Christ's GODHEAD, and some of his manhood. And in those we cannot err. But the error ariseth from making application of those passages which

CHRIST - CHRIST

refer to Christ, under both as God-man Mediator, and concluding that they speak of him are holding him forth as Christ only, that is, God and man in one person. To this one cause must be ascribed the origin of all the Arian, Socinian, and Unitarian heresy. A small attention to the Scriptures, with this discrimination, will be sufficient to explain, and, I hope, set this important subject in a clear light.

Among many portions of God's word, which might be brought forward in proof, by way of illustration, I beg to refer to those two memorable passages in the first chapter of Paul's Epistle to the Colossians, and his Epistle to the Hebrews. When, as in the former, the apostle saith, "he is the Image of the invisible God, the first born of every creature; for by him were all things created that are in heaven, and that are in earth;" nothing can be more plain, than that this could never be said of the Son of God, as the Son of God only, for in his GODHEAD, he could never be said to be "the first born of every creature;" neither could it be of the Lord Jesus as man only, for then, how could "all things be created by him that are in heaven, and in earth?" But if we read the whole passage, as the apostle evidently meant it, with an eye to Christ, as the Christ of God, that is, God and man in one person, constituting God-man Mediator; in this sense every, difficulty vanisheth. For then Christ is, indeed, in his human nature, "the image of the invisible God," set up as the covenant Head of his church from everlasting. And though not openly manifested until the fulness of time, yet secretly, and as "the Lamb slain from the foundation of the world." (Rev. xiii. 8.) And no less Christ in his divine nature, he is here represented as testified in those acts of the GODHEAD; for creation can belong to none but God. And by the union of both God and man in one person he is the Christ of God, "by whom all things were created, and by whom all things consist." For as God only, there was nothing created that could stand in union with him. And as man only, neither of those acts could have been exercised and carried on, but in the union and junction of both; his GODHEAD gives power to the whole of what is here ascribed to him, and his manhood united to the GODHEAD, renders him the suited Head of all creation, and upholder of all, that "in all things he might have the pre-eminence."

Similar to the same plain and obvious truths, is that memorable passage also of Paul's first chapter to the Hebrews. "God (saith the apostle), who at sundry times, and in divers manners, spake in time past to the fathers by the prophets, hath, in these last days, spoken unto us by his Son. "Then follows the office-character of Christ, as Christ, in the Son of God assuming our nature, and taking it into union with the GODHEAD, thereby becoming Christ. "Whom he hath appointed heir of all things." How appointed? Not surely, as God only, for in this case the appointment was not only unnecessary, but impossible, for the Son of God, as God, possessed in common with the Father, and the Holy Ghost, the absolute inheritance of all things from all eternity. He could receive nothing in this sense, being "one with the Father over all, God blessed for ever." (Rom. ix. 5.) But if considered as Christ, that is, God-man Mediator, he then receives the appointment, as heir of all things, and Lord of all things, and in whom all things might be gathered. (Ephes. i. 10.-22,23.)

Read, in this point of view, the whole chapter is as plain and intelligible as words can render it: "Who being the brightness of his Father's glory, and the express image of his person, and upholding all things by the word of his power, when he had by himself purged our sins, sat down on the right hand of the Majesty on high," &c. Who was it purged our sins? Not the Son of God as God only. Not the Son of man as man only. But Christ as Christ; that is, God and man in one person. It was essential to salvation, that Christ should offer himself for a sacrifice, for "without shedding of blood there is no remission." (Heb. ix. 22.) Hence, the Son of God is introduced, under the spirit of prophecy, (Ps. xl. and explained by Heb. x.) as saying, "A body hast thou prepared me." But that that sacrifice might possess an infinite dignity and value, it must be united to the GODHEAD. And hence, in the union of both, there is an everlasting efficacy and glory in Christ's once offering of himself; once offered, not only to take away the sins of the whole world, but to bring in a redundancy of glory to JEHOVAH, which will continue for ever and ever. When, therefore, Christ, as Christ, had by himself purged our sins, He, the Christ of God, God-man in one person, "sat down on the right hand of the majesty on high." And who was it that the apostle saith, in this same chapter, was anointed with the oil of gladness above his fellows? Whom are the angels commanded to worship, when JEHOVAH brings in this first begotten into the world? Not surely, the Son of God as God only, neither the Son of man as man only; for of either, separately, these things could never be spoken. But it is of Christ, as Christ, the Christ of God, both natures united, and forming one glorious Mediator, suited to make up (and which, to the praise of the riches of his grace, he hath most completely done), the deadly breach which sin had made between God and man. And now having accomplished redemption by his blood, he is, and ever will be, the One glorious object of adoration, love, and praise, to all the creation of God, angels, and men, to all eternity. Such then is Christ.

It will be proper, for the better apprehension of Christ, as Christ, having thus explained the scriptural account of his person, to add to this account what the word of God hath revealed of his office, and character, and relation. In his office, we behold him undertaking and finishing the whole work of redemption. In his character, he stands forth as the great representative of his people. And in his relation to us, he comes home endeared to our warmest affection, not only in what he hath done for us, but for the nearness of affinity in which he is united to us; seeing that he fills all relations, for he is, in one and the same moment, our ever lasting Father, our Husband, Brother, Friend.

Moreover, to these views of Christ must be added, that He is the One great and glorious object of which the whole law, types, prophecies, and revelations point; and in whom they all, like rays of light converging to one centre, find their end and termination. He is the great sum and substance of all the promises of the Bible. Without him they are void of meaning, and never to be fulfilled; but in him they are all yea, and amen. In a word, Christ is the one glorious repository of all things in heaven and in earth, the fulness that filleth all in all. The church upon earth hath no resource for life and grace, but in him; neither hath the church in heaven to derive glory from, but the Lord Jesus.

It will form no improper conclusion to this account of Christ, if we add to it the names by which Christ is revealed in his sacred word, under the several views there given of him as God, as man, and as God-man Mediator. Distinct views of him under each, after what hath been said, will, it is hoped, be very acceptable to the gracious mind, and be owned and blessed of the Lord. — And first as God...

- He is the Alpha and Omega, Rev. i. 8. 11.
- He is the blessed and only Potentate, King of kings, and Lord of lords, 1 Tim. vi. 15. Rev. xvii.14.
- The brightness of his Father's glory, Heb. i. 3.
- The Creator of Israel, Isa. xliii. 15.
- Emmanuel, God with us, Isa. vii. 14. Matt. i. 23.
- Eternal life, 1 John v. 20.

CHRIST - CHRIST

- The Everlasting Father, Isa. ix. 6.
- The faithful witness, Rev. i. 5. 1 John v. 7.
- The first and the last, Rev. i. 17. Rev. ii. 8.
- God in common with the Father and the Holy Ghost, John i. 1. Rom. ix. 5. 1 Tim. iii. 16. 1 John v. 20. Jude 25.
- Heir of all things, Heb. i. 2.
- Most Highest, Ps. xviii. 13. Luke i. 32.
- Most high, Luke viii. 28.
- The Holy One of God, Mark i. 24.
- The Holy One of Israel, Isa. xli. 14.
- I AM, Exod. iii. 14. John. viii. 58.
- JAH, Ps. lxviii. 4. Deut. xxxiii. 26.
- JEHOVAH, Jer. xxiii. 6.
- The King, Eternal, Immortal, Invisible, the only wise God, 1 Tim i. 17.
- Lawgiver, Isa. xxxiii. 22. Jam. iv. 12.
- Light, John i. 9; viii. 12; xii. 46.
- Living God, I Tim. iii. 15.
- Life, John xiv. 6.
- Lord, and Lord of lords, Ps. cx. Rom. i. 3. Rev. xvii. 14.
- Son of God, Matt. iv. 13. &c.

Next let us attend to the names given to Christ, in Scripture, in testimony of his manhood. Christ is called…

- Adam, 1 Cor. xv. 45.
- Babe, Luke ii. 16.
- Child, Isa ix. 6. Acts iv. 30.
- David, Ps. lxxxix. 3. Jer. xxx. 9. Exek. xxxvii. 24, 25. Hos. iii. 5.
- Flesh, John i. 14.
- Friend of sinners, Matt. xi. 19.
- Husband, Isa. liv. 5. Jer. xxxi. 32.
- Brother, Heb. ii. 11.
- Jacob, and Israel, and Judah, Isa. xli. 8; xliv. 1.5. Rev. v. 5.
- Man, Acts, xvii. 31. 1Tim. ii. 5.
- Seed of the woman, Gen. iii. 15.
- Seed of Abraham, Gal. iii. 19.
- Seed of David, 2 Tim. ii. 8.
- Son of man, Matt. viii. 20.

Thirdly, Let us take a view of some of the names and characters by which Christ is known in the Holy Scripture, considered in the union of both God and man in one person, thus constituted as one Christ. I say some of the names, for to enumerate the whole would swell our Poor man's Concordance beyond the limits necessary to be observed, in a work of this kind. Christ in his twofold nature of God and man in one person, is known and distinguished in the sacred word, as…

- An Advocate with the Father, 1 John ii. 1.
- The Angel of the Covenant, Mal. iii. 1.
- The Ancient of days, Dan. vii. 22.
- The Anointed of the Father, Psal. ii. 2. Heb. i. 9. Ps. xlv. 7.
- The Apostle and High Priest of our profession, Heb. iii. 1.
- The Author and Finisher of faith, Heb. xii. 2.
- The Beginning of the creation of God, Rev. iii. 14. The Beloved in whom the church is accepted, Eph. I. 6.
- The Bishop of our souls. 1 Pet. ii. 25.
- The Bread of life and living Bread, John vi. 48. 51.
- The Branch of righteousness, Zech. iii. 8.
- The man whose name is the BRANCH, Zech. vi. 12.
- The Bridegroom of his church, John iii. 29.
- The Bright and Morning Star, Rev. xxii. 16.
- The Captain of our salvation, Heb. ii. 10.
- The One chosen of the people, Ps. lxxxix. 19.

CHRIST - CHRIST

- The Consolation of Israel, Luke ii. 25.
- The Corner Stone, and Foundation Stone which God hath laid in Zion, Isa. xxviii. 16. Eph. ii. 20. 1 Pet. iv. 6.
- The Covenant of the people, Isa. xlii. 6; xlix. 8.
- The Wonderful Councillor, Isa. ix. 6.
- The Hiding Place and Covert from the storm, Isa. xxxii. 2. Ps. xxxii. 7.
- The Day's man, Job ix. 33.
- The Day dawn, and Day Star in the heart, 2 Pet. i. 19.
- The Desire of all nations, Hag. ii. 7.
- The Deliverer that shall come out of Zion, Isa. lix. 20. Rom. xi. 26.
- He that promiseth to be as the Dew unto Israel, Hos. xiv. 5.
- The Diadem in JEHOVAH'S hand, Isa. lxii. 3.
- The Door of his sheepfold, John x. 7.
- The Elect in whom JEHOVAH'S soul delighteth, Isa. xlii. 1.
- The Ensign JEHOVAH hath set up to the people, Isa. xi. 10.
- The Express Image of the Father's person, Heb. i. 3.
- The first begotten of the dead, Rev. i. 5.
- The first-fruits, 1 Cor. xv. 23.
- The Fountain opened to the house of David, &c. Zech. xiii. 1.
- The Forerunner, Heb. vi. 20.
- The Unspeakable Gift of God, the Power of God, 2 Cor. ix. 15. 1 Cor. i. 24.
- The Wisdom of God, the Glory of God, the Sent of God, the Lamb of God, &c. Isa. xl. 5. 1 John iv. 14. John i. 29.
- The Head of his body the church, Ephes. i. 22, 23. Col. i. 18.
- The High Priest, the Prophet, and the King of his people, Heb. v. i. Luke iv. 24. Matt. xxi. 5.
- The Hope of Israel, and the Saviour thereof, Jer. xiv. 8. Acts xxviii. 20.
- Jesus, Matt. i. 21. 1 Thess. i. 10.
- Immanuel, Isa. vii. 14. Matt. i. 23.
- Judge, Isa. xxxiii. 22. Mic. v. 1. Acts x. 42.
- A Leader to the people, Isa. lv. 4.
- Christ is peculiarly called Master, Mat. xxiii. 8.10.
- The One Mediator, 1 Tim. ii. 5.
- Melchizedeck, Heb. vii. 1.
- Messiah, Dan. ix. 25. John i. 41.
- Michael, Dan. xii. 1. Rev. xii. 7.
- The Morning Star, Rev. ii. 28. Rev. xxii. 16.
- Christ our Passover, 1 Cor. v. 7.
- Prince, and Prince of peace, and of life, Isa. ix. 6. Acts v. 31; iii. 15.
- Redeemer, Isa. lix. 20; lx. 16.
- Resurrection, John xi. 25.
- Refiner, Mal. iii. 3.
- Rock, Deut. xxxii. 15. 1 Cor. x. 4.
- Root and Offspring of David, Rev. xxii. 16.
- Sacrifice, Ephes. v. 2
- Salvation, Isa. xlix. 6. Luke ii. 30.
- The Sanctification of his people, 1 Cor. i. 30.
- Sanctuary, Isa. viii. 14.
- The One Shepherd, the Good Shepherd, Ezek. xxxiv. 23. John x. 1.
- The Chief Shepherd, The Great Shepherd, 1 Pet. v. 4. Heb. xiii. 20.
- The Shiloh, Gen. xlix. 10,
- The Strength of Israel, 1 Sam. xv. 29.
- The Son of Righteousness, Mal. iv. 2.
- The Lord our Righteousness, Jer. xxiii. 6.

- The Surety of a better Testament, Heb. vii. 22.
- The True Tabernacle which the Lord pitched and not man, Heb. viii. 2.
- The Teacher come from God, John iii. 2.
- The Temple made without hands, Mark. xiv. 58 John ii. 19-21. Dan. ii. 45.
- The Testator, Heb. ix. 16, 17.
- The tree of life, Gen. iii. 24. Rev. xxii. 2.
- Truth itself, John xiv. 6. John xviii. 38.
- The Way, and only Way, John xiv. 6. with Isa. xxxv. 8.
- The water of life, and well of living water, John iv. 14. Song iv. 15. John vii. 37-39.
- The wisdom of God, and Wisdom, I Cor. i. 24. Prov. viii. 1, &c.
- The Witness, Rev. i. 5. Isa. xliii. 10. Rev. iii. 14.
- Wonderful, Isa. ix. 6.
- Jesus Christ, the same yesterday, to-day, and for ever, Heb. xiii. 8.

To these should be added, under a fourth division, the names which Christ hath, in Scripture, in common with his church; for these give a most endeared and interesting view of the loveliness and sweetness of his person; but as these will meet us under the next article, the church, which comes to be noticed in the Poor Man's Concordance, I refer the reader to it there. I only detain the reader one moment longer, just to remark, on what hath been already offered on this blessed name of our Lord, how gracious God the Holy Ghost hath been to the church, to give so many and such very precious names to the Lord Jesus in the word of God, for his church to know him by and to enjoy him in. Had it been the intention of the Eternal Spirit, merely to have revealed him to the people and no more, one name in this case, would have been sufficient to have identified his person. But no, God the Holy Ghost would not only identify his person, but endear Him to the heart of his redeemed, under all the sweet and gracious characters, and offices, and relations, into which the Son of God hath condescended to put himself for the salvation of his people; and therefore, all these, and numberless other names of the like nature, Christ shall be known by in his word of truth.

And what makes the love and wisdom of the Holy Ghost so blessed to the believer's heart in this particular is, that numerous and great as the names of Jesus are in his blessed word, there is not one by which Jesus is there called and known, but what becomes dear to their hearts, and which, at one time or other, they do not want, and which they would not have had left out in the Bible for a thousand worlds. Surely, the reader will never think of the subject, in which Christ appears thus lovely and endeared, without crying out with the apostle, "Thanks be unto God for his unspeakable gift!" (2 Cor. ix. 15.)

CHURCH

In the Old and New Testament language, by the church of God is uniformly meant, the whole body of the faithful, of which Christ is the Head. The apostle to the Hebrews defines the meaning of the church, when he calls it "the general assembly and church of the first-born, which are written in heaven." (Heb. xii. 23.) And the apostle John no less defines it, when he speaks of the names written in the Lamb's book of life. (Rev. xxi. 27.) Yea, our Lord himself fixeth the meaning, when bidding devils, being subject to them, in his name, but because their names were written in heaven. (Luke x. 20.) By the church therefore, is meant, the whole body of Christ both in heaven and earth, the elect of God in Christ, given by the Father to the Son, redeemed by the Son, and sanctified by God the Holy Ghost, and called. And, although we sometimes meet

CHURCH - CHURCH

with the expression of churches in the word of God, such as when it is said, the churches had rest throughout all Judea, (Acts ix. 31.) and again, all the churches of the Gentiles give thanks, (Rom. xvi. 4.) yet, the whole multitude of the people, of what kindred or nation forever, whether Jews or Gentiles, whether bond or free, from the beginning of the world to the consummation of all things, form but one and the same body, of which Christ is the glorious Head. Such is the church.

And it is blessed to see in the word of God how plainly and evidently this church, made up of Christ's members, and gathered out of the world's wide wilderness, is distinguished so as to prove whose she is, and to whom she belongs.

The Lord Jesus himself describes her union with himself under the similitude of branches in a vine, (John xv. 1, &c.) and shews, as plain as words can make if, that the vine and the branches are not more closely knit together, and forming one, than is Christ and his church. Yea, the figure doth not come up to the reality; for a branch may be, and sometimes is, separated from the vine, but not so can this take place between Christ and his church, for he saith, "Because I live, ye shall live also." (John xiv. 19.) And his servant, the apostle Paul, describes the intimate connection of Christ with his church, under the similitude of the marriage state. (Ephes. v. 25-32.) "This is a great mystery, (saith the apostle,) but I speak concerning Christ and the church." Nevertheless, even here again, this beautiful figure, tender and affectionate as it is, falls far short of the oneness and union between Christ and his church. For death puts an end to all the connections of man and wife upon earth. But in respect to Christ and his spouse, the church, the dying day of the believer is but the wedding day. It is but as an espousal, a betrothing before; but in that day the church is brought home by her all-lovely and all-loving Husband, to the marriage supper of the lamb in heaven. (See those Scriptures, Hos. ii. 19, 20. Rev. xix. 7-9.)

The best service, I apprehend, which I can render to the reader, under this article of the church, will be (to do what I should otherwise have done under the former, when speaking of Christ, but conceiving it might as well be noticed under this,) to bring into one view the several names which Christ and his church have, in common, in the word of God, which certainly form the highest evidence that can be desired, in proof of their union and oneness and interest in each other. Nothing, indeed, can be more lovely and delightful to the contemplation.

It will be proper to introduce this account, with first shewing some of the special and peculiar privileges the church possesseth, both in name and in interest, from her union and oneness with her Lord, and then follow this up with the view of those names and appellations Jesus and his church have in common together. The church is distinguished, by virtue of her interest in Christ, as...

- The body of Christ, Ephes. i. 23.
- Brethren of Christ, Rom. viii. 29. Heb. iii. 1.
- The bride, the Lamb's wife, Rev. xxi. 9.
- Children of the kingdom, Matt. Xiii. 38.
- They are called christians after Christ, Acts xi. 26.
- The church of God, 1 Cor. i. 2.
- Companions, Ps. xlv. 14. Song i. 7
- Complete in Christ, Col. ii. 10.
- Daughter of the King, Ps. xlv. 13.
- Comely in Christ's comeliness, Ezek. xvi. 14.
- Election, Rom. ix. 11.
- Family of God, Ephes. iii. 15.
- Flock of God, Acts xx. 28.
- Fold of Christ, John x. 16.
- Friends of God. James ii. 23.
- Glory of God, Isa. xlvi. 13.

CIRCUMCISION - CIRCUMCISION

- Habitation of God, Ephes. ii. 22.
- Heritage of God, Jer. xii. 7. Ps. cxxvii. 3. Joel iii. 2.
- The Israel of God, Gal. vi. 16
- The lot of God's inheritance, Deut. xxx ii. 9.
- Members of Christ, Ephes. v. 30.
- Peculiar people, 1 Pet. ii. 9.
- The portion of the Lord, Deut. xxxii. 9.
- The temple of God, 1 Cor. iii. 16.
- The treasure of God, Ps. cxxxv. 4.
- Vessels of mercy, Rom. ix. 23.
- The vineyard of the Lord, Isa . v. 1, &c.

These, with many others of the like nature, are among the distinguishing, names by which the church of Christ is known in Scripture, by reason of her oneness and union with Him.

But this view of the intimate and everlasting connection between Christ and his church will be abundantly heightened, if we add to it what was proposed to shew the sameness between them, from being known under the same names, as descriptive of this union. A few examples in point will be known by the name of Adam, as our first father: "As the first Adam was made a living soul, so the last Adam was made a quickening Spirit." (1 Cor xv. 45.) As Christ is called a Babe, so are they said to be babes in Christ. (Luke ii. 16. 1 Pet. ii. 2.) As Christ is declared to be the dearly beloved of the Father, (Jer. xii. 7.) so the church is said to be dearly beloved also, (1 Cor. x. 14. Phil. iv. 1. 2 Tim i. 2.) Is Christ the Elect, in whom JEHOVAH'S soul delighteth? so are they elect, according to the foreknowledge of God our Father, and the Lord Jesus Christ. (Isa. xlii. 1. 1 Pet. i. 2.) Is Jesus the heir of all things? (Heb. i. 2.) so are they heirs of God, and joint heirs with Christ, (Rom. viii. 17.) And when that Christ, by the spirit of prophecy, is called JEHOVAH our righteousness, the church as his wife, and entitled to every thing in him, is also called by the same name, JEHOVAH our righteousness. (See, compared together, Jer. xxiii. 6. with xxxiii. 16.) Yea, in one remarkable instance, the church not only bears Christ's name, but Christ bears hers. He is called Jacob, and Israel. (Isa. xli. 8. and xlix. 3.)

Without enlarging this point farther, for enough, I presume, hath been advanced in proof of the thing itself, nothing can be more plain, and nothing can be more highly satisfactory, than this oneness, from union and participation between Christ and his church. And I trust, the review will be always blessed to the believer's heart, and, under the Holy Ghost's teaching, be always leading out the affections to the full enjoyment of it, agreeably to the mind and will of God.

CIRCUMCISION

There is somewhat particularly interesting in this Jewish rite. And as the appointment is from God, it demands suitable attention for the proper apprehension of it. It evidently appears, from the first moment of its institution, that the ordination was with an eye to Christ, for the covenant of redemption by Jesus had this token or seal, and it is expressly said, "that Jesus Christ was a minister of the circumcision for the truth of God, to confirm the promise made unto the fathers." (Rom. xv. 8.) And by the ceasing of this Jewish rite, and the institution of Baptism to supersede it, it should seem, that it was understood by Christ's submitting to this act, he thereby became debtor to the whole law, and fulfilled it: and hence, all his redeemed not only are freed from it, but, in fact, they are prohibited the observance. Paul the apostle was so earnest on this point, that he declared to the Galatian church that an attention to circumcision virtually denied the covenant. "Behold, I Paul (said he) say unto you, that if ye be circumcised Christ shall profit you nothing." (Gal. v. 2.) And the reason seems to have been this: The seed of Abraham, by the act of circumcision, declared that they were looking for and waiting to the coming of the promised Seed, in whom all the families of the faithful were to be blessed. To be circumcised, therefore, after Christ was come, was in effect denying that Christ Was come, and by that act saying, We are looking for his coming. Hence, all the faithful posterity of Abraham were so tenacious of observing the rite of circumcision before Christ came, and so determined not to observe it after. And also, this other cause renders circumcision improper. The person circumcised, by that act, declared himself under obligations to fulfil the whole law. And hence Christ submitted to it with this view. But his redeemed are justified in Him, and therefore, to undergo circumcision would imply a defect in this justification. "I testify (said Paul,) again, to every man that is circumcised, that he is a debtor to do the whole law." (Gal. v. 3.) This, then, is the proper apprehension concerning the rite of circumcision.

CITY

Which hath foundations, whose builder and maker is God, (Heb. xi. 10.) I think it not improper to notice this, in a work of this kind, inasmuch as we meet with the expression frequently in Scripture, both in allusion to the church of God upon earth, and the church triumphant in heaven. (See Ps. xlvi 4; xlviii. 1.8; lxxxvii. 3. Song iii. 2, 3. and also Heb. xii. 22. Rev. iii. 12; xxi. 2-10; xxii. 19.) The city of God in his church upon earth, and in heaven, is one and the same. It is peculiarly called his, because he hath founded it and built it, and dwells in it, and is the governor of it, and grants to the citizens the privileges and immunities of it. It is the Lord's property both by purchase, and by conquest, and he hath the whole revenue of it. And hence, all the inhabitants of this city are, in heart and mind, one and the same. For though the church here below is in a militant state, and the church above, freed from this warfare, is triumphant, yet, equally dear are the citizens of both to the Lord of the country. They all speak the same language, all wear the same garment, Christ's righteousness, all love the same Lord, and his Zion, and prefer her interests above their chief joy. (Ps. cxxxvii. 6.) Reader, what saith your heart to those characters? (See that Scripture, Rev. xxii. 14, 15.)

CITIES OF REFUGE

See Refuge.

CLEAN

The Scripture sense of one clean deserves our particular notice. Solomon demands, (Prov. xx. 9.) "Who can say, I have made my heart clean, I am pure from my sin?" None among the sons of Adam can lay claim to this cleanness, much less, that any have made themselves so. But the apostle John, commissioned by God the Holy Ghost, tells the church in a sweetness and fulness of expression indescribably blessed, that the blood of Jesus Christ cleanseth from all sin." (1 John i. 7.) Here is the laver, the fountain, for sin and for all uncleanness, which JEHOVAH hath opened. (Zech. xiii. 1.) And hence, the Scripture sense of cleanness, is the sinner freed from the filth of sin, and the guilt of sin, and the dominion of sin, by the blood of Christ, and the sanctifying influences of the Holy Ghost. (Ezek. xxxvi. 25. John xiii. 10.)

CLOUD

Clouds in the air, I detain not the reader to notice, but the ministry of the cloud in the church of God, when the people went out of Egypt. I think the particularity of it, and the blessedness of it, demands the attention of the church in all ages. And more so, because the promise is still with the church, that "the Lord will create upon every dwelling place of mount Zion (let the reader not overlook the every dwelling place), and upon her assemblies, a cloud and smoke by day, and the shining of a flaming fire by night, for upon all the glory shall be a defence." (Isa. iv. 5.) When we consider the peculiarity of this cloud, when we read expressly who was in it, when we consider the wonderful progress of it in its ministry, then going before, and then shifting its station, as occasion required, and going behind, when we behold the striking account of its ministry, in the difference of its aspect of light to Israel, and darkness to the Egyptians, when we trace the history of it through all the wilderness dispensation of the church, and discover its blessed and beneficial influences to Israel, from Succoth even to Jordan, who but must exclaim, What hath God wrought! Surely, it is impossible for any reader, and every reader, to attend to the wonderful account without joining Moses, the man of God and saying, "Happy art thou, O Israel! who is like unto thee, O people saved of the Lord?" (Deut. xxxiii. 29.) Let the reader turn to those Scriptures, (Exod. xiii. 21, 22; xiv. 19, 20. 24; xvi. 10. Num. xii. 5. Deut. xxxi. 15. Neh. ix. 19. 1 Cor. x. 1.4.) But when the reader hath paused over these Scriptures, and duly pondered the wonderous subject, I entreat him to carry on the blessed consideration (for it is, indeed, most blessed), as it concerns the Exodus, or going forth of the church of Jesus now. For is not the church the same? Is not Jesus's love to it the same? And doth he not go before it now in the pillar of cloud by day, and follow it in the pillar of fire by night, to guide, to bless, to protect, yea, himself to be the very supply to it, through all the eventful journeys of its wilderness state, from the Succoth of the beginning of the spiritual life, even to Jordan, the river of natural death opening to glory? What though the cloud, in the miraculous movements of it as to Israel, is not seen, yet the Lord of the cloud, in his presence, grace, and love, is sensibly known and enjoyed. Surely, Old Testament saints had not advantages greater than New Testament believers. "We now with open face beholding, as in a glass, the glory of the Lord, are changed into the same image from glory to glory, even as by the Spirit of the Lord." (2 Cor. iii. 18.) We have the outer displays of the divine presence, in ordinances, and means of grace, and the blessed Scriptures of truth, like Israel's cloud. And we have the inward tokens, in the Lord himself in the midst, to bless and make himself known in his soul-comforting manifestations. This indeed, is the new creation the Lord promised upon every dwelling place of mount Zion, and upon all her assemblies. Here it may be truly said, "upon all the glory shall be a defence." Precious Lord Jesus! whilst thou art thus gracious, and thus blessed, to thy church and people, we still behold the cloud, yea, now look; through by faith, and behold thee in the cloud, a wall of fire round about, and the glory, as thou didst promise, in the midst of Zion! (See Zech. ii. 8.)

CLUSTER and CLUSTERS

We meet with this word upon many occasions in Scripture, but eminently so in two places. First, when the spies went up to search the promised land, and brought back the cluster of the rich fruit of Eshcol, (Num. xiii. 53.) And again, the church, in the book of the Songs, (chap. i. 14.) where she commends her beloved, under the sweet similitude of the same, "My beloved is unto me as a cluster of camphire in the vineyards of Engedi." I conceive, that the beauties of the comparison in both instances are well worth attending to, in a work of this kind, and, therefore, I take for granted, that the reader will not be displeased in my detaining him on the occasion.

Nothing could be more happily chosen in both instances, when intended, as in the first, to set forth the fulness, and sweetness, and blessedness of the promised land than a cluster of its fruits. Christ, who is himself the glorious object intended to be set forth, is, indeed, a rich cluster of all divine and human excellencies in one, full of grace for his people here, and full of glory to all above. An ancient author tells us, that the Jews were accustomed to call such men as excelled in good qualities, Eshcoloth; that is, clusters. And hence they had a saying, that after the death of Jose Ben Joezen, a man of Tzereda, and Jose Ben Jochanan, a man of Jerusalem, the clusters ceased.

In the other instance, in direct allusion to Christ, in the church's commendation of him, (Song, i. 14.) there in an uncommon degree of beauty in the similitude. The word camphire is in the original, copher, and in the Misnah is translated, cyprus. And Dr. Shaw, in his travels, describes the plant as being very beautiful and fragrant, advancing in height to ten or twelve feet, and full of clusters. Here also, as in the former instance, Christ is elegantly set forth. For as the grapes of Eshcol represented the fulness of Christ, and the blood of the grape became no unapt resemblance of Him who trod the wine press of the wrath of God, and whose blood, in cleansing the sinner, revives the soul in the assurance of pardon, mercy, and peace, by his cross, so the cypress, or the camphire, in the fragrancy of its clusters, becomes no less typical of His incense and merits, in whose righteousness alone the church is accepted. I must not dismiss this view of the subject before that I have farther remarked, that the word, translated camphire, is by some rendered (copher) atonement. The learned Bishop Patrick hath observed, that the Hebrew Doctors, by dividing the word Eshcol into two words, found out the mystery of the Messiah in the passage, and read them thus, my beloved is unto me the Esh, that is, the man; Col, copher; that is, a cluster of atonement. I leave the reader to his own observation upon the subject, with only remarking, that on the supposition the Hebrew Doctors were right, what a lovely Scripture this is in the Songs, (chap. i. 14.) when the church so sings of Christ. Surely, Jesus is all this, and infinitely more. Jesus calls himself the vine, (John xv. 1.) and the church saith that his growth is in the vineyards of Engedi, the richest soil of all the earth, where not only the finest grapes, but the loftiest palm trees abounded, even Hazazon-lamar. See 2 Chron. xx. 2.) In Jesus dwelleth "all the fulness of the GODHEAD bodily." He is, indeed, a cluster of all that is desirable "in the life that now is, and that which is to come."

COCK

Though this bird is too well known to need any account being given of him, yet being rendered so memorable in Scripture, from the circumstance of the apostle Peter's denial of Christ, I cannot pass it by without remarking, in allusion to that striking event, how slender the means which the Lord is pleased sometimes to make use of, to answer the most important purposes! The crowing of a cock is enough, in the Lord's hand, to accomplish the Lord's design. No one but Peter understood what the crowing of this cock meant; but to him it became more powerful than the sound of thunder. Such are the slenderest events in common life, when the Lord commissions them to be his messengers! Some of the Fathers have drawn a resemblance between the crowing of the cock, and the ministry of God's word. For as Peter heard the first crowing of the cock without the least emotion, so do men hear the word of God, when unaccompanied with grace, untouched and unconcerned. But when that word of God is sent home to the heart, by the powerful conviction of the Spirit of God, like the eye of Jesus which looked upon Peter, as the cock crew the second time, then the word is rendered effectual, and, like Peter, the sinner is led forth to weep bitterly. (Luke xxii. 61.)

COCKATRICE

See Asp.

CONCUBINE

The Scripture meaning of this name was not as opprobrious as it is in modern times. A concubine, indeed, in all ages, was not as highly ranked as a wife. She was ever considered as secondary and subordinate to the person to whom the husband and father of the family was married. But in those dark and ignorant times, when men were allowed (or rather allowed themselves), many wives, a concubine meant, one that he acknowledged for a wife, or a subordinate and inferior degree. And the children of this connection did not, by any right of their own, possess or claim the inheritance of their father. And there was this farther distinction between the lawful wife, and the concubine, there was no religious ceremony used at the taking of a concubine; whereas, the lawful wife was usually betrothed to her husband before marriage, and sometimes, from the very childhood of the respective parties. And when the time appointed for the consummation of the marriage arrived, this was always done with great order and solemnity: and all the friends of the respective parties were invited to the wedding. I hope the reader will not lose sight of the marriage of Jesus with our nature, in this view of the subject, and will remember, that the union of Christ with his church, is uniformly set forth in the most blessed similitudes and figures of this kind through the whole Bible. Jesus was set up, as the glorious Head and Husband of his church, from everlasting. And, in fact, the whole of the union, in the present state, is but a betrothing. (See Hos. ii. 19, 20.) At the final consummation of all things, Jesus will bring home his bride, and then will be the marriage-supper of the Lamb in heaven. (Rev. xix. 9.)

I beg to make a farther observation on this subject, while I am upon it, and to call the reader to remark with me, that even in those times of ignorance, when men gave loose to their corrupt affections, yet, the very law of usage concerning concubines carried with it a decided testimony, that even in the very moment they gavel way to their unbridled passions, yet, by the reverence shewn the lawful wife, they tacitly confessed the just and honourable appointment of the Lord. It was well known, and well understood, that at the beginning the Lord made our first parents, and united them together; teaching, that when thus formed in holy wedlock, they were no longer considered, in His eye, as separate, but one. The Lord himself said, "They shall be one flesh? And our Lord's own comment upon it decidedly determines the point. "What therefore (saith Jesus) God hath joined together, let not man put asunder." (Compare Gen. ii. 24. with Mark x. 9.) Now the introduction of a concubine, of how inferior a degree soever she may be, is, to all intents and purposes, a destroying this junction, and, by so much, a breach of the original appointment of the Lord.

And it were devoutly to be wished, that men would consider the subject in this point of view, for it is to be apprehended, by what passeth too often in common life, men have not accustomed themselves to this consideration of it. I am not now taking up the subject in respect to the sad immorality of it, though the awful consequences, in the instances of thousands, too loudly condemn daily the breach of the marriage vow on that score; but I am carrying the matter higher, in shewing the awfulness of it, as a defiance of the divine appointment. Hence, when the Pharisees came to our Lord to ask the question about putting away their wives, and pleaded Moses's permission in certain cases, our Lord expressly said, that Moses's permission was from the hardness of their heart, but from the beginning (saith Jesus), it was not so. The man and woman once united in wedlock, were no longer separable but by death. (Matt. xix. 3-9.) And his servant, the apostle, finished the matter from his Master's authority, when he saith, "Let every man have his own wife, and let every woman have her own husband." (1 Cor. vii. 2.)

I must not finish the subject without first desiring the reader to take with him that sweet thought, that in the marriage of the Lord Jesus with our nature (which the marriage-state in nature is a type of), both in the general purpose of it with his church at large, and with the person of every individual member of his mystical body in particular, there is no concubine to interrupt the present and everlasting happiness of our union with Christ Jesus. Though we have, indeed, proved unfaithful, yet hath not Jesus. Though, we have played the harlot with many lovers, yet still he saith, "I am married to you, saith the Lord." Oh! what unknown, what unspeakable glory is there in those words of our Lord--"I will betroth thee unto me for ever; yea, I will betroth thee unto me in righteousness, and in judgment, and in loving kindness, and in mercies; I will even betroth thee unto me in faithfulness, and thou shalt know the Lord." (Hos. ii. 19, 20. See the whole chapter.)

And think reader, what will it be in that day of final consummation, when the Lord shall bring home his church, and every individual of his mystical body shall be found one with the Lord, in an everlasting union never to be dissolved! Oh, the joy in Jesus's own declaration, "At that day ye shall know, that I am in my Father, and you in me, and I in you!" (John xiv. 20.)

CONSOLATION

The great work of God the Holy Ghost is consolation. And it is most blessed to the souls of the truly regenerate, in whose hearts the Lord graciously carrieth it on by his inward spiritual refreshments, to watch and observe how the tendencies of his grace are made towards them. "He takes of the things of Christ, and sheweth to them." And he it is that sheds abroad the love of God the Father in the heart, and directs the minds of the people into the patient waiting for Jesus Christ. So that all the actings of our faith upon either of the persons of the GODHEAD, are from his sweet influences; and all the manifestations the holy and sacred persons make to the believer, it is God the Holy Ghost teacheth the soul how to receive and enjoy. And by this continual process of grace, he doth what the apostle prayed he might do for the church, as "the apostle prayed he might do for the church, as "the God of hope, fill the soul with all joy and peace in believing, that they might abound in hope, through the power of the Holy Ghost." Rom. xv. 13.)

CONVERSION

This great work also is, like the former, the work of God the Holy Ghost. And the Lord Jesus, in his description of his person, describes also his office, work and character. "He shall reprove, saith Jesus, the world of sin, and of righteousness, and of judgment." (John xvi. 7-15.) And to remark the wonderful operations of his grace under those several branches of his almighty power, by which he gives the fullest discoveries of our worthlessness, and the glorious manifestations of Jesus's grace, and fulness, and suitability, these are among the highest instructions the souls of men can attain in the present life. Blessed and Sovereign Convincer! I would say, bring my soul under thy divine illuminations, that my whole heart may be savingly converted unto God.

CORBAN

We meet with this word but once in the Bible. (Mark vii. 11.) But it should seem, from the manner in which it is spoken of by our blessed Lord, that the Jews were much in the habit of using it. The word Corban applied by the Jews to all voluntary gifts. It should seem to have been taken from the word Karab, to give. And from a passage in the gospel by St. Matthew, it should appear that they not unfrequently swore by it. (Matt. xxiii. 18,

CORN - COVENANT

19.) As they used the word Corban upon certain occasions, so they, sometimes, used the word Mencha, which means offering, for all presentations to the temple. See Offering.

The manner in which our Lord hath condemned the Jews, for the use of the word Corban, plainly shews what a pretext, or covering, they made it to evade important duties. "Moses said, Honour thy father and thy mother; and whoso curseth father or mother, let him die the death. But ye say, If a man shall say to his father or mother, it is Corban; that is to say, a gift, by whatsoever thou mightest be profited by me; he shall be free. And ye suffer him no more to do ought for his father or his mother." (Mark vii. 10-12.) By which, it should seem, that those unfeeling men sheltered themselves, from affording relief to the necessities of their parents, under pretence, that they had made a Corban of what they had to the Lord. "It is Corban, said they; that is, it is the Lord's. I have devoted all I can spare to the service of the temple--I cannot help you."

Blessed Lord! how sweetly doth thy gospel explain and enforce that unceasing precept both of nature and of grace, and which needs no higher rewards to follow than a man's own uncorrupt feelings—"Honour thy father and thy mother, which (saith the Holy Ghost), is the first commandment with promise." (Ephes. vi. 2.) It is worthy observation, and deserves to be noticed under this subject, that this commandment is, indeed, the first to which a promise is given. For the first table of the law gives no promise. It is the first commandment in the second table that opens with a promise, and a blessed one it is, "that thy days may be long upon the land which the Lord thy God giveth thee." xx. 12.)

CORN

The corn of wheat is worthy notice in our Concordance, because Jesus is beautifully represented, and by himself, under this figure. (John xii. 24.) When the Son of God became incarnate, like a pure grain of corn, yea, and of the finest kind, he fell into the ground. And what an abundant harvest of redeemed souls hath he since produced to the glory of the Almighty Husbandman, his father! (John xv. 1.)

COVENANT

The Scripture sense of this word is the same as in the circumstances of common life; namely, an agreement between parties. Thus Abraham and Abimelech entered into covenant at Beersheba. (Gen. xxi. 32.) And in like manner, David and Jonathan. (1 Sam. xx. 42.) To the same amount, in point of explanation, must we accept what is related in Scripture of God's covenant concerning redemption, made between the sacred persons of the GODHEAD, when the holy undivided Three in One engaged to, and with, each other, for the salvation of the church of God in Christ. This is that everlasting covenant which was entered into, and formed in the council of peace before the word began. For so the apostle was commissioned by the Holy Ghost, to inform the church concerning that eternal life which was given us, he saith, in Christ Jesus, "before the world began? (Tit. i. 2. 2 Tim. i. 9.) So that this everlasting covenant becomes the bottom and foundation in JEHOVAH'S appointment, and security of all grace and mercy for the church here, and of all glory and happiness hereafter, through the alone person, work, blood-shedding, and obedience of the Lord Jesus Christ. It is on this account that his church is chosen in Christ before the foundation of the world. (Ephes. i. 4.) And from this appointment, before all worlds, result all the after mercies in time, by which the happy partakers of such unspeakable grace and mercy are regenerated, called, adopted, made willing in the day of God's power, and are justified, sanctified, and, at length, fully glorified, to the praise of JEHOVAH'S grace, who hath made them accepted in the Beloved.

Such are the outlines of this blessed covenant. And which hath all properties contained in it to make it blessed. It is, therefore, very properly called in Scripture everlasting; for it is sure, unchangeable, and liable to no possibility of error or misapplication. Hence, the patriarch David, with his dying breath, amidst all the untoward circumstances which took place in himself and his family, took refuge and consolation in this: "Although (said he,) my house be not so with God, yet hath he made with me an everlasting covenant, ordered in all things, and sure; for this is all my salvation and all my desire, although he make it not to grow." (2 Sam. xxxiii. 5.)

In the gospel, it is called the New Testament, or covenant, not in respect to any thing new in it or from any change or alteration in its substance or design, but from the promises of the great things engaged for in the Old Testament dispensation being now newly confirmed and finished. And as the glorious person by whom the whole conditions of the covenant on the part of man was to be performed, had now, according to the original settlements made in eternity, been manifested, and agreeably to the very period proposed, "in [what is called] the fulness of time, appeared to put away sin by the sacrifice of himself," it was, therefore, called Covenant, in his blood. But the whole purport, plan, design and grace, originating as it did in the purposes of JEHOVAH from all eternity, had all the properties in it of an everlasting covenant; and Christ always, and from all eternity, "was considered the Lamb slain from the foundation of the world." (Rev. xiii. 8.)

COUNSELLOR

One of the well known names of Christ, and most blessedly answering to his office, work and character in the hearts of his people. (See two beautiful proofs among a thousand. Isa. ix.6; xlviii. 16, 17.) This name at once sets forth the infinite dignity of his person, and the infinite suitableness of his salvation; "for in him are hid all the treasures of wisdom and knowledge." (Col. ii. 3.) In conjunction with the Father and the Holy Ghost, he was in the council of peace before all worlds, when the whole scheme of redemption was formed, and when it was determined upon, to be brought forth in time, and in its blessings to reach to all eternity. Wonderful Counsellor! give thy people grace to listen to thy gracious and divine teaching, "and to buy of thee gold tried in the fire." (Rev. iii. 18.)

COUNTENANCE

I cannot pass over this Scriptural term, because it contains in itself, and conveys to the people, so much in expression of the mind of Jesus. "The lifting up the light of God's countenance upon a soul," implies such an abundance of favour, that whenever we meet with the words, they ought to be treasured up as a renewed token of "the good-will of Him who dwelt in the bush." (Num. vi. 26. Ps. iv. 6. Deut. xxxiii. 16. Ps. xxi. 6. Song ii. 14. Acts ii. 28. Rev. i. 16.)

CREATOR

See Maker.

CROWN

In allusion to Christ, the Scripture meaning of crown is, that all the merit of redemption is his; and as such, he wears the crown. Hence in the book of the Revelations, he is said to have been seen with many crowns on his head, (Rev. x. 12.) meaning, from the different offices and characters which he sustained in accomplishing redemption, the crown of GODHEAD he wears in common with the Father and the Holy Ghost. But the crown of Mediator is peculiarly and personally his own. Hence, he is said to have "power over all flesh," as a Prince, and a Saviour, "for to give eternal life to as many as the Father hath given him." (John xvii. 2.) Hence, when JEHOVAH bringeth

CRUCIFIED - CRUCIFIED

in the first begotten into the world, he saith, "Let all the angels of God worship him." (Heb. i. 6.) And the crown of salvation put upon the sacred head of Christ by the church in one full body, and also by every individual of the church, multiplies the crowns of Jesus to an infinite extent, when any and every poor sinner is brought from darkness to light, and willingly and cheerfully ascribes the whole of his own personal salvation to the Lord Jesus Christ.

CRUCIFIED

When we consider how much the church of God owes to the cross of Christ, and that the everlasting joy of heaven springs from the crucifixion of the Lord Jesus, it may well merit a place in our Concordance, to dwell a few minutes on the astonishing subject.

The cross, as far as we can learn from history, on which criminals were executed, was a kind of gibbet, with timber across, on which the person condemned to suffer was nailed. The body was suspended from those nails, which were driven through the hands, and the arms stretched out to each extremity. In this manner the criminal remained until life, from the extremity of suffering, expired. Some have said, that the wretched sufferers were first nailed to the cross, and then the whole body lifted on high, and the bottom of the cross fixed in a socket prepared for that purpose. And as this was done by a jerk, some of the bones were generally broken by this act of violence. But this is not probable. Indeed, in respect to the person of our Lord Jesus Christ, it is very unlikely to have been done, for "a bone of Him was not to be broken."

As crucifixion was not only the most painful but the most disgraceful of all deaths, the Roman law never allowed a Roman, be his crime whatever it might, to be thus degraded. It was only inflicted on slaves and criminals, for some more atrocious transgressions. And in order to heighten the shame and pain, the poor victims, so condemned to death, were first scourged, and their backs lacerated with whips or leathern lashes; and not unfrequently led through the city naked with their blood streaming from their wounds, and carrying their cross to the proposed place of execution. The reader will not need to be told, that thus they treated the Lord of life and glory, whom none of the princes of this world knew, until that the holy Sufferer fainted from beneath the load and severity of his pain, when they compelled one that was passing by to bear the cross for the Lord Jesus.

It was an additional aggravation to the ignominy of crucifixion, that the sufferer was perfectly naked, and without the smallest covering. Thus all criminals suffered. And when we consider the personal cruelties all along shewn to the Lord Jesus, we cannot suppose, that the smallest respect was manifested in this particular to his sacred person. Such then was the death the Son of God in our nature endured, for the redemption of his church and people! But who shall describe the soul agonies of Jesus? Here I stop short. It is the crucifixion of the body that I am now limited to, when speaking of the cross of Jesus. Over this view only, let the reader and writer for a moment pause, while listening to the call of the Holy Ghost by his servant the Baptist, "Behold the Lamb of God which taketh away the sin of the world!" (John i. 29.)

Was there ever such an object proposed to the mind of contemplation as the Lord Jesus Christ on the cross? It should seem as if the Lord Jesus, thus stretched forth and thus lifted up, was inviting, with his arms extended and his heart bleeding, all his redeemed to come to him. Indeed, every part of his sacred body joined in giving the welcome. His arms spread to receive, his feet fixed to wait, and his head bowed down as if to kiss his people. Oh, for grace, with Paul, to determine "to know nothing among men, save Jesus Christ and him crucified!" And with the same holy indignation as he felt, against every thing that would check the ardour of his love, to cry out, "God forbid that I should glory, save in the cross of our Lord Jesus Christ, by whom the world is crucified unto me and I unto the world!" (Gal. vi. 14.)

CUBIT

The cubit was a measure used among the Eastern nations, containing about eighteen inches of our English measure. The Hebrews, by a very singular idea, called it Ammah; that is, mother: as if other measures were produced by this.

CUP

I need not make any observation, by way of explaining what is so very plain and well understood in common life, as that of a cup. Neither, indeed should I have thought it necessary to have detained the reader over the word, had that been all that I proposed from it. But as the word cup is sometimes, and indeed, not unfrequently in Scripture, used figuratively, I thought it proper to attend to what is implied in the term. Sometimes the cup is placed for sorrow, and sometimes for joy, and the lot or portion of a man is called his cup. Hence, the Psalmist speaking of the blessings of grace in the Lord Jesus, calls them, the cup of salvation. (Ps. cxvi. 13.) And Paul, when describing the blessedness of union with Christ, and communion in consequence thereof with God, calls the ordinance which resembles it, a cup. "The cup which we bless (saith he,) is it not the communion of the blood of Christ?" (1 Cor. x. 16.) Sometimes it is made use of to intimate a participation in suffering. "Awake, awake, stand up, O Jerusalem! which hast drunk at the hand of the Lord the cup of his fury; thou hast drunken the dregs of the cup of trembling, and wrung them out." (Isa. li. 17.) And as this, no doubt, under the language of prophecy, referred to Christ, so in open language the Lord Jesus himself, speaking of his soul-exercises, calls it a cup. (Matt. xxvi. 39-42. John xviii. 11.)

CURSE and CURSES

We cannot be too attentive to those terms, as they refer to the original curse pronounced on the fall of our first parents, and those curses again proclaimed at the giving of the law on mount Sinai, as the penalty of disobedience. For the proper apprehension of our whole nature being involved in the guilt and condemnation of them, and our total inability to help ourselves, will from a means, under divine teaching, to discover how Christ hath redeemed us from the curse of both, being made "a curse for us." (Gal. iii. 13.) The whole plan and purpose of redemption turns upon this hinge. Every thing that is blessed and consolatory in redemption is founded in this. Faith looks to Jesus for deliverance from all. And the apostle's hymn of praise becomes the hymn of every regenerated believer, that "as sin hath reigned unto death, even so doth grace reign through righteousness unto eternal life, by Jesus Christ our Lord." (Rom. v. 21.)

CYPRESS

See Clusters.

CYRUS

Prince of Persia. This man was an eminent instrument in the Lord's hand, for the deliverance of Israel from the Babylonish captivity. What is very remarkable and worthy the reader's attention concerning Cyrus is, that the Lord, by the spirit of prophecy, informed the church one hundred and fifty years, at least, before the captivity took place, that Cyrus was anointed to end that captivity and bring his people out of it. And that no mistake might arise, the Lord called him by his name Cyrus, then, so long before he was born. The reader will find much information on this subject by reading the forty-fifth chapter of Isaiah's prophecy, and comparing it with Ezra i. and Dan. vi. 28.

One circumstance I must beg to subjoin, because it is, in my view, very important and striking, concerning this prince of Persia, Cyrus. We plainly discover, that he was an instrument in the Lord's hand for good to the church. And we farther discover, that he was appointed to this long before he was born. And we also no less perceive, that the church was assured of this. by his name, for their comfort, under all their exercises, until the time should come. But all the while Cyrus himself felt no interest in the great event he was appointed to accomplish, and knew not the Lord. For so the Lord gives the awful account--I have surnamed thee, said the Lord to him, though thou hast not known me. And this is again repeated in the following verse. (See Isa. xlv. 3, 4.)

Depend upon it, reader, the case of Cyrus is not singular. Multitudes are appointed to minister to the Lord's people, who neither know the Lord, nor love his people. But they shall serve the Lord's purpose, however reluctantly, did they know all, they would go about it. For rather than the Lord's poor children shall want bread, Jesus will feed them at their very enemies' table. And when they have answered the Lord's purpose, they themselves are accounted as nothing. What an awful Scripture that is of our Lord's to this amount: (Matt. vii. 22.) "Many will say unto me in that day, Lord! Lord! Have we not prophesied in thy name, and in thy name cast out devils, and in thy name done many wonderful works? To whom Jesus will say, I never knew you; depart from me!"

D

DAGON

The dunghill god of the Philistines. We have the relation concerning this idol, Judges xvi. 23. and again, 1 Sam. v. 2, &c. The name seems well suited for such a purpose, being derived from Dag, fish. Some historians say, that the idol was formed like a fish.

DALMANUTHA

A place honoured with the presence of the Lord Jesus. Some make Magdala and Dalmanutha one and the same. (See Matt. xv. 39. and Mark viii. 10.)

DAMASCUS

The chief city of Syria; so called from Damashech, a place of blood, from Damah, blood. Here Paul was directing his course for the destruction of the church when the Lord converted him. (Acts ix. 2-6, &c.)

DAN

The fifth son of Jacob, and by Bilhah, the handmaid of Rachel. (Gen.. xxx. 4-6.) I notice this man more with a view to make an observation on his father's prophecy concerning his tribe, than from any thing particularly to be recorded relative to Dan himself. Jacob, when dying, prophesied concerning Dan in these remarkable words: (Gen. xlix. 16, 17.) "Dan shall judge his people as one of the tribes of Israel. Dan shall be a serpent by the way, an adder in the path, that biteth the horse's heels, so that his rider shall fall backward." This prophecy was accomplished in the person of Samson, who descended from Dan. It is worthy farther remark, that though in the first instance of Dan there were no very promising prospects of a numerous race, Dan himself having but one son, (Gen. xvi. 23.) yet, at the children of Israel's leaving Egypt, the tribe of Dan amounted to "threescore and two thousand, seven hundred men," all that were able to go forth to war. (Num. i. 38)

DANCE and DANCING

I think it not a little important, for every serious reader of the Bible, to have proper ideas of the Scripture meaning of dancing, and therefore it would have been wrong, in a work of this kind, to have passed it by.

It is very evident, that dancing formed, sometimes, a part in the religious duties of the Hebrews. Hence we read, (Ps. cxlix. 3.) "Let them praise his name in the dance." And David is said, (2 Sam. vi. 14.) to have danced before the Lord. Yea, the Lord himself is represented, (Jer. xxxi. 4.) as comforting his people with this assurance, "that they should again go forth in the dances of them that make merry." All which very evidently proves, that the dancing spoken of in Scripture totally differed from that vain, frivolous, and idle, not to say sinful, custom of dancing practised in modern times. It should seem to have been used among the people of God in a solemn manner, though, no doubt, accompanied with bursts of holy joy and praise. Hence, when "Miriam the prophetess, the sister of Aaron, took a timbrel in her hand, and all the women went after her with timbrels and with dances," at the triumph over the enemies of God and the church at the Red sea, we are told, that she answered them in holy song--"Sing ye to the Lord, for he hath triumphed gloriously; the horse and his rider hath he thrown into the sea." (Exod. xv. 20, 21.)

Some have thought, that the holy dances of the Scripture were by way of resembling the motions of the heavenly bodies, as if in the joy of the heart, in any renewed instances of God's grace and mercy manifested to the people, they looked up to heaven, and endeavoured by action of the body, as well as the going forth of the soul in praise, to testify their sense of the divine goodness. And certain it is, that when the heart is under very strong impressions of the Lord's special favour, there will be an involuntary motion of the whole frame. Even in modern times we have heard of whole congregations, such as the Jumpers in Wales, and the Shakers (so called) in America, whose devotions have been marked with action as well as voice. Yea, the Holy Ghost hath testified of certain instances where "smiting the thigh, and stamping the foot," have been observed as solemn tokens towards the Lord. (See Jer. xxxi. 19. Ezek. vi. 11.) But all these are so foreign to what is now known by the term dancing, that they differ in every point but the name.

I cannot dismiss this article without adding, that it were devoutly to be wished every parent of the rising generation would seriously consider to what danger of seduction they are preparing their little ones, when sending them forth to the dance. Who shall calculate the numberless instances of the kind, which dancing, by inflaming the passions, hath given birth to in modern life! (See a solemn account of such parents, and such children, with the issue of both, Job, xxi. 11-13.)

DANIEL

The prophet of the Lord. His name is very significant, meaning, the judgment Daniel was descended from the royal family of David, and was carried away captive to Babylon when quite a youth. The Chaldeans artfully gave him the name of Belteshazzar, which signifies, master or lord of the treasure; by way, it is most likely, of causing him to forget the Lord God of his fathers. (See Dan. i. 7.)

We have this man's history in his writings, and in the accounts given of him by Ezek. xiv. 14. for his great sanctity of life and manners. And his wisdom was so highly esteemed, that it became proverbial to denote a wise man by calling him Daniel. Hence, the prophet Ezekiel, (chap. xxviii.

3.) speaking, by the Lord's command, to the prince of Tyrus, speaks of his vanity and pride, as if he thought himself wiser than Daniel.

The prophecies of Daniel concerning the Messiah were so bright and clear, that the modern Jews endeavoured to call in question their authenticity, but without effect. In fact, the corresponding fulfilment of the prophecy with the prediction, becomes the best and most decided testimony to their truth; for this is the seal of God the Holy Ghost.

The death of this prophets in the place, and time, and manner, is not known. Some have thought, that he returned to Judea with the captives that returned with Ezra; but the word of God hath not noticed it, which renders it improbable. It is enough for us to be blessed with his ministry, in his inspired writings, while he lived, and to rest assured, that he died in the faith of that glorious Saviour, whose advent, and sufferings, and death, he was commissioned by the Lord so clearly to describe. This is enough for us to know. And the voice John heard from heaven concerning all such is conclusive and satisfactory. (See Rev. xiv. 13.)

DARKNESS

In Scripture language the word darkness is variously used. In the natural sense of the word, it means the obscurity, such as is described at the original state of things, when JEHOVAH went forth in acts of creation. It is said, "darkness was on the face of the deep." (Gen. i. 2.) In a spiritual sense, darkness is frequently made use of in Scripture to denote the blindness and ignorance of the mind, by reason of sin. Hence Paul, when speaking of the conversion of the church at Corinth, saith, "God, who commanded the light to shine out of darkness, hath shined into our hearts, to give the light of the knowledge of the glory of God in the face of Jesus Christ." (2 Cor. iv. 6.)

The darkness of the grave, and the darkness of hell, are both also spoken of in Scripture. (Job x. 21, 22. Matt. xxii. 13.) The darkness which took place at the death of Christ, and which lasted from the sixth to the ninth hour, differed from all these, and was among the miracles which marked that momentous event. Profane writers, as well as the sacred Scriptures, have it upon record. Dionysius the Areopagite, in his epistle to Polycarp, makes mention of it with decided convictions on his mind, that the event was supernatural. And another writer, Suidas, relates, that the same Dionysius said concerning it, that God either suffered, or took part with one that did.

But what are all the testimonies of profane writers to those which God the Holy Ghost gives of it? Some have thought, that this supernatural darkness was the Father's frown at the Jews' cruelty, in crucifying Christ. For my part, I believe it to have been the very reverse. For never was the Father more glorified than by those sufferings of the Lord Jesus. Never was Christ more glorified than by those sufferings. Then it was that Scripture was fulfilled, and Jesus set, as JEHOVAH'S King, "upon his holy hill of Zion." (Ps. ii. 6.)

What was it, this darkness then, under these views, meant to imply? Surely, that Jesus the Son of God, when becoming the sinner's Surety, shall do all, and suffer all, the sinner deserved, and must have borne for ever, had not Christ interposed. Darkness, yea, darkness to be felt, shall be in the Surety's lot. Christ is now lifted up a spectacle between heaven and earth. The sinner's Surety is now appearing as one forsaken of both, and meriting the favour of neither. He is now suspended on the cross in the air, to represent his territories, who is the "Prince of the power of the air." (Ephes. ii. 2.) The cataracts of divine wrath were now opened. Christ is beheld in the very character he had taken at the call of God the Father; first, made sin, and then, a curse, (see these Scriptures, 2 Cor. v. 21. Gal. iii. 13.) then follows, darkness, soul-trial, and death. It was not necessary the sinner's Surety should go down into hell, to suffer there the torments of the damned: it is not the place that constitutes the suffering, but the manner: and here the judgment due to the sinner seized him. He saith himself, "The sorrows of death compassed me, the pains of hell gat hold upon me." (Ps. cxvi. 3.) Surely, if ever the face of hell was seen on earth, or the darkness of hell known, it was on that day. Hence, when the whole was passed, and this eclipse gone by; and day-light brake in again upon Jesus, he cried with a loud voice," It is finished." (John xix. 30.) Reader! those cries of the Lord Jesus on the cross, during the dreadful darkness and desertion his soul endured, may serve to teach us somewhat of those eternal shrieks and cries of the damned, who are cast out of God's presence for ever!

DATHAN

Son of Eliab, one of the rebels with Korah. (Num. xvi. 1.) His name is derived from Dath, rites.

DAVID

The very important figure which David, king of Israel, makes in Scripture, demands, that in a work of this kind, he should not be overlooked. His services, as a prophet of the Lord, and his labours in the Scriptural writings which come to the church with his name, render it highly needful to notice him. But added to this, as a type of the Lord Jesus, and the great Mediator bearing his name, renders him still more endearing to our view. His very name from Dud, to love, means, dear and well-beloved; and as a type of the ever-dear and well-beloved Jesus, nothing could be more suited. I only beg the reader to observe concerning types in general, and of him in particular, that it is only in this very precise instance, in which the agreement runs, that the word of God considers them; and consequently, ought to be considered by the church. The Lord Jesus Christ after the flesh, is spoken of as the seed of David; and as such, the covenant runs in his name. (See Ps. lxxxix. 34, 35. 2 Tim. ii. 8.)

DAUGHTER

I should not think it necessary to offer any observation upon this name, if considered in natural alliances only. But there is a great sweetness in it, when read in Scripture in allusion to the church. It is very blessed to perceive, that as the Lord Jesus fills all relations to his church, and is, in one and the same moment, her everlasting Father, her Husband, and Brother, and Friend, so the church is to Jesus, his daughter, his sister, his spouse, his beloved, his fair-one, and the only one of her mother. (Ps. xlv. 9, 10. Song vi. 9.) How frequently do we find the Lord speaking of his church under the endeared character of daughter. "For the hurt of the daughter of my people, I am hurt." (Jer. viii. 21.) "Tell ye the daughter of Zion, Behold, thy King cometh unto thee!" (Zech. ix. 9. with Matt. xxi. 5.)

DEAD and DEATH

There is a threefold sense of death; natural, spiritual, and eternal. That which is natural, respects the separation of soul and body. "The body without the Spirit is dead." (Jam. ii. 16.) Spiritual death means, the soul unquickened by the Holy Ghost. "And you hath he quickened, who were dead in trespasses and sins." (Eph. ii. 1.) And eternal death implies the everlasting separation both of soul and body from God to all eternity. "I will forewarn you whom ye shall fear: Fear him, which after he hath killed, hath power to cast into hell; yea, I say unto you, Fear him." (Luke xii. 5.) See Hardness of heart.

DEBORAH

The eminent prophetess, whose history is recorded Judges iv. and v. She was the wife of Lapidoth. Her name is probably from Deborat, bee; perhaps, in allusion to the activity of her mind. The Holy Ghost hath endeared her memory, not only by the victory wrought by her instrumentality, in the deliverance of Israel, but by that divine hymn she sang, and is left upon re-record for the use of the church.

DEVIL

The accursed enemy of Christ and his church. He is known in Scripture under a great variety of names, all, more or less, expressive of his character. Abaddon, and the angel of the bottomless pit, (Rev. ix. 11.) Beelzebub, (Matt. xii. 24.) Belial, (2 Cor. vi. 15.) the Old Dragon, (Rev. xii. 3.) the father of liars, (John. viii. 44.) Lucifer, (Isa. xiv. 12.) a murderer from the beginning, (John viii. 44.) Serpent, (Isa. xxvii. 1.) Satan, (Job ii. 6.) the god of this world, (2 Cor. iv. 4.) a roaring lion. (1 Pet. v. 8.) See Satan.

DEW

The dew is a merciful provision the Lord hath ordained for moistening the plants and other productions of the earth in dry seasons, when there is no rain. And it is supposed, that the dew of the night is exactly in proportion to the heat of the day. But what I more particularly desire to notice respecting the dew is, the gracious condescension of the Lord, in resembling his blessings on his people to the figure of the dew. Hence, we read, by his servant the prophet Hosea, how the Lord saith, "I will be as the dew unto Israel." (Hos. xiv. 5.) And how is that? The Lord answereth in another Scripture. "It tarrieth not for man, nor waiteth for the sons of men." (Micah v. 7.) No predisposing cause in men, no, not even the wants or miseries of men, prompting the infinite mind of God to bestow his blessings. His love is before our misery, and his mercy makes no pause for our merit. Hence, we find numberless

DOVE - DREAMS

Scriptures speaking of the Lord's mercies under this figure. Jesus saith to the church, in a time when visiting her, "My head is filled with dew, and my locks with the drops of the night." (Song v. 2.) Hence, the resurrection of his people by grace, as hereafter to glory, is said to be "as the dew of herbs, and the earth shall cast out her dead." (Isa. xxvi. 19.) meaning that as from the rich dews which fall upon the earth, the dry, withered, and apparently dead plants of the winter shall again bud, and break forth in the spring, so the dead and dying state of Christ's redeemed shall, from the dew of his birth, "revive as the corn, and grow as the vine." Hence, the doctrines of grace are said to be of the same refreshing quality as the dew. "My doctrine (said Moses,) shall drop as the rain, my speech shall distil as the dew, as the small rain upon the tender herb, and as the showers upon the grass." (Deut. xxxii. 2. and xxxiii. 13.) See Rain.

DOVE

It would be unnecessary to offer any observations simply on this bird, as it is in itself, but as it is made use of by the Scriptures of God, as figurative of the Holy Ghost, and also by the Lord Jesus, to denote the loveliness of his church, it merits our attention.

It was in the form of a dove that the Holy Ghost descended upon the blessed Jesus at his baptism. (Matt. xiii. 6.) And it was the dove that brought the tidings of the waters being assuaged into the ark, by the olive branch in his mouth. (Gen. viii. 12.) And Christ compares his church to the beauty and gentleness of the dove. (Song. ii. 14.) And the comparison is certainly very just; for as the dove in nature is a very beautiful, and clean, and affectionate creature, so the church in grace, when washed in Christ's blood, and justified in Christ's righteousness, and made comely from the comeliness her Lord hath put upon her, is all-glorious within, and hath no spot, or blemish, but is without blame before Jesus in love. Hence, the Psalmist sweetly sings of the church--"Though she hath lain among the pots, yet shall she be like the wings of a dove, covered with silver, and her feathers with yellow gold." (Ps. lxviii. 13.)

DRAGON

One of the names of the devil. (Rev. xii. 9.) Hence, in allusion to the Lord Jesus Christ's victory over hell, the Psalmist saith, "Thou shalt tread upon the lion and adder, the young lion and the dragon shalt thou trample under feet."

DREAMS

The visions of the night are called dreams. And before the more open revelations by the Lord Jesus Christ, certain it is, that the Lord not unfrequently made use of their ministry in the church. Hence, the patriarchs Abraham and Jacob were thus exercised. (Gen. xv; xxviii.) And Joseph's dreams, when related to his father and brethren, were made instrumental to excite the envy of his brethren. (Gen. xxxvii. 5, 6, &c.) Yea, the Lord declared concerning dreams, while the church was in the wilderness, that he would make himself known to his servants the prophets in this way. (Num. xii. 6.) And even in the days of the New Testament dispensation, dreams were not in disuse for occasionally revealing the mind of the Lord. Concerning the safety of the child Jesus, by removing him into Egypt, this was directed by an angel appearing by night to Joseph in a dream. (Matt. ii. 13.)

But while the Lord was thus pleased, by the means of dreams, to make known to his people, as occasion might require, the purposes of his will, he was no less pleased to direct his servants the prophets, by open revelation, to guard against all imposition from lying dreams, and false visions of men's own forming. The prophet Jeremiah was taught thus to declare the Lord's mind concerning these things, "I have heard what the prophets said,

DREAMS - DREAMS

that prophecy lies in my name; saying, I have dreamed, I have dreamed. How long shall this be in the heart of the prophets, that prophecy lies? Yea, they are prophets of the deceit of their heart, which think to cause my people to forget my name by their dreams. (Jer. xxiii. 25-27.) In the open daylight of that full revelation the gospel hath brought, the greatest caution should be observed respecting attention to dreams. Upon every occasion of the sort, the faithful in Christ Jesus would do well to remember the Lord's direction upon another subject, in respect to them that sought after familiar spirits; "to the law and to the testimony, if they speak not according to this word, it is because there is no light in them." (Isa. viii. 19, 20.) Far be it from any one to limit the Holy One of Israel; but by this reference upon all exercises of the mind concerning dreams the children of the Lord will be preserved from error. To say that dreams are wholly done away under the gospel dispensation, and that the Lord never doth speak by them to his people, would be opposing a well known Scripture concerning them, which wholly related to the latter-day ministry. The prophet Joel was commissioned to declare, and the apostle Peter explained what he said, in direct reference to the days of the manifestation of the Holy Ghost, that the Lord would in the last days, "pour out of his Spirit upon all flesh; and that in consequence of his mercy, their sons and their daughters should prophecy, and their old men dream dreams, and their young men see visions." (Joel ii. 28. Acts ii. 17.) So that to say their entire use is done away, would be presuming to be wise above what is written. At the same time to suppose, that the common and ordinary dreams of the night are intended to direct the mind of the Lord's people, would be to lessen the divine authority of God's holy word, which, in all cases; is able to make us "wise unto salvation through the faith that is in Christ Jesus."

The exercise of the mind in dreams is certainly among the wonders we meet with in life, which are not the least surprising, though the least to be explained. We know that the whole body is perfectly conscious, and asleep; while there is a somewhat in us, or belonging to us, that is, at times, very busily engaged and employed. We talk apparently with others, and we hear them talk with us. We travel far and near; transact great concerns; not unfrequently converse with persons, whom in our waking hours we know to be dead; but yet in sleep sometimes forget this and sometimes not. We hear their voice and perfectly recollect it; their person, manner, and the like, are as familiar to us as when living. Yea, sometimes circumstances of a similar nature are brought before us in our sleep, both with the dead and living whom we never knew. These, with numberless other particularities, are among the dreams of the night, of which the body, asleep and torpid, is wholly unconscious; but of which the mind or thinking faculty, or the somewhat indescribable, be it what it may, is most earnestly engaged in, and highly interested about. Who shall say what this is? Who shall describe it? Who shall define its use? And there is another very striking particularity in dreams, that while it carries the fullest conviction to that thinking faculty, that somewhat indescribable being acted upon, in a way and manner no man can explain, serves to prove, that the whole is somewhat more than the effect of fancy, though not unfrequently the trifling nature of the thing itself is as trifling. I mean when persons far remote from each other, have one and the same dream, or are apparently engaged in one and the same concern in that dream, without any previous communication on the subject; yea, perhaps without any previous knowledge of each other.

And let me add another particularity as striking as any, concerning the exercise of the mind, or thinking faculty, in dreams, beyond the power of any man to account for; namely, when we receive instructions or help on any point, during our dreaming hours, from a person or persons, then supposed to be with us, which, without whose aid we could not in ourselves have accomplished. I will beg to illustrate this, by the relation of a plain matter of fact, which I had from a friend of mine, with whom I lived many years in the habits of great intimacy: indeed, the same, more or less, may be found perhaps in every man's experience, on one point or other.

My friend was a good classic, and conversant with the best Latin authors. In one of his dreams he fancied himself reading one of his favourite books, which he was in the habit of constant reading, when a passage occurred that he could not construe. He tried again and again to translate it, but all to no purpose. Mortified with himself, he was about to close the book and relinquish the attempt, when a person looking over his shoulder gently upbraided him on his dulness (Luke xxiv. 35.) and construed the passage to him. Now the question is, who was this looker-on, for he himself was asleep, and alone?

The reader will sadly mistake my meaning, from all that I have here said upon dreams, if he thinks I am bringing forward a justification of that farrago of unconnected, trifling, and impertinent stuff, which some make of dreams. Too many there are, whose waking hours are little better than the merest unmeaning dreams of the night. But making all due allowance for such things, certain it is, that in the early ages of the world, the Lord was pleased to make use of the ministry of dreams. And though under the gospel we have a more sure guide to take heed unto, yet it were to limit the Holy One of Israel to say, that they now are never used, and their ministry hath totally ceased. No doubt, the greatest jealousy maybe proper to exercise concerning them; and certainly, we must be safe in rejecting them in all points, where they are not in perfect agreement with the glorious gospel of the ever-blessed God.

DRINK

Is sometimes put figuratively in Scripture, to imply the thirst and desire of the soul after Christ. Hence, we find the Lord Jesus saying "If any man thirst, let him come to me and drink." (John vii. 37.) And again, "He that eateth my flesh, and drinketh my blood, dwelleth in me and I in him." (John vi. 56.) In like manner, at the close of Scripture, the coming of Christ is described under the similitude of drink. (Rev. xxii. 17.)

DWELL ALONE

This is a Scripture phrase of great beauty, concerning the Lord's heritage. The Lord compelled this declaration to be made out of the mouth of Balaam, when blessing the children of God while he wished to curse them. "The people shall dwell alone, and shall not be reckoned among the nations." (Num. xxiii. 9.) And I hardly know, in all the Scripture, a more blessed mark of divine discrimination. Very much it were to be wished, that the Lord's people would be always on the look out for it, as a token and badge of their high calling in Christ Jesus.

That the Lord's people have, from all eternity, been so appointed is certain. They have dwelt alone in God the Father's gracious purpose in giving them to his Son. They have dwelt alone in the mind of Jesus, when he stood forth as their Surety, and Head, and Husband, before all worlds. And they have dwelt alone in the view and love of God the Holy Ghost, when making them the objects of his grace. Hence therefore, as they dwell alone in the privileges of the everlasting covenant, and as the members of the mystical body of Christ, so are they supposed to dwell alone in their affections, pursuits, manners, habits, and daily delights. They may, and they do, hear that voice John heard from heaven concerning them, when calling them to dwell alone, and

DWELL ALONE - DWELL ALONE

to have no connection with the unfruitful works of darkness. "Come out of her, my people, that ye be not partakers of her sins, and that ye receive not of her plagues." (Rev. xviii. 4).

E

EAGLE

I cannot pass over this article in our Concordance, in as much as we find frequent mention made of the eagle in Scripture. And I do this the rather from the singularity of it, and especially in the way in which it is used. I mean, because it is declared in the Levitical law to be unclean; yea, all the different species of the eagle, including the vulture and the hawk, which are both of the eagle kind. (See Lev. xi. 13-16.) Now it is certain, that the Lord, (by which I apprehend is meant the Lord Jesus Christ in our nature,) condescends to make use of the similitude of an eagle, in describing his care over his people, when he saith, "I bare you on eagle's wings, and brought you unto myself." (Exod. xix. 4. Deut. xxxii. 11.) Is there not something of a most interesting nature implied in those affections of the Lord, beside the protection here set forth as shewn his people? As the eagle is among the creatures of uncleanness; is there not an allusion to the Lord's taking our uncleanness upon him, when he thus speaks of bearing his redeemed on eagle's wings? The reader will observe, I do but ask the question, and not determine the matter. But as we well know, and all redeemed souls rejoice in the glorious consolation, it was Jesus both "bare our sins, and carried our sorrows, when the Lord JEHOVAH laid on him the iniquity of us all," the Lord's making use of one of the unclean creatures, in a similitude to himself, may not be supposed unaptly to represent this unequalled mercy? Connect with this view, what the gospel saith, (2 Cor. v. 21. and Gal. iii. 13.) and let the reader judge the fitness of the observation. He, who in such infinite and unequalled love and grace, became both sin and a curse for his people, might go on in the humiliation, to compare himself to the eagle, when made sin for us; that we might be made the righteousness of God in him.

The beautiful comparison, made in allusion to this bird, in providing safety for her young, to that of the Lord Jesus carrying his people as on eagle's wings, is too striking hastily to pass it by. (Deut. xxxii. 11, 12.) The eagle's stirring up her nest, fluttering over her young, spreading abroad her wings; taking them and bearing them on her wings; are beautiful descriptions, and which it seems, in the case of the eagle's care over her brood, is literally the case. The young eagles are much disposed to sleep. The old bird therefore, rouseth them up, by disturbing them in their nest; when they are awakened, she fluttereth over them, spreading abroad her wings, to teach them how to use theirs, and how to fly. And until they are able to soar above all danger in the air, she carrieth them on her wings, that they may in due season use their own. Such, but in an infinitely higher degree of wisdom, love, and tenderness, doth Jesus, by his offspring. The Lord stirred them up from sleeping in the dangers of Egypt, and taught them how "to flee from the wrath to come." And the Lord is doing so now, in bringing up all his redeemed out of the Egypt of sin and death in this world.

But the most beautiful part of the representation remains yet to be noticed. The eagle is the only bird that carries her young upon her wings. All other birds use their talons for bearing up their little brood. Now, when the Lord Jesus useth this similitude, it teacheth us that it is impossible they can fall whom he bears; for they are on the wings and above, and not beneath, and like those birds, who catch up their young in their talons, and in their flight may drop them. Moreover, no weapon from beneath can reach the young, in the care of the eagle, without first piercing the old bird. So nothing can touch Christ's little ones without first destroying Christ. Was there ever a similitude more beautiful, lovely, and comfortable? Let me only add,

EAR and EARS - EAR and EARS

to this figure of the Old Testament church, that precious one also, of the Lord Jesus in the New. I mean, when to the strength of the eagle, Jesus subjoins the affection of the hen; "saying, How often would I have gathered you, even as an hen gathers her chickens under her wings!" (Matt. xxiii. 37.) There is another similitude made use of respecting the church, in allusion to the eagle. The prophet Micah, (chap. i. 16.) speaks of the boldness of the eagle. And some have asserted, that in old age, the eagle is renewed with youth. Whether this be so, or not; or whether the moulting time, common to other birds every year, is only once experienced by the eagle, and that in old age, I will not, for I cannot, determine; but certain it is, that the Lord himself makes use of the similitude, to describe his people by. In one of the sweetest promises, the Lord thus comforts them, "He giveth power to the faint, and to them that have no might, he increaseth strength. Even the youths shall faint and be weary, and the young men shall utterly fall; but they that wait upon the Lord shall renew their strength; they shall mount up with wings as eagles; they shall run and not be weary, and they shall walk and not faint." (Isa. xl. 27. to the end.) And while the Lord thus comforts his church with the assurance of the renewings of spiritual strength, like the eagle in nature, the church is described as praising God under the view of renewing grace, in the same figure: "Bless the Lord, O my soul, and all that is within me, bless his holy name: who forgiveth all thine iniquities, and healeth all thy diseases: who redeemeth thy life from destruction, and crowneth thee with loving kindness and tender mercies: who satisfieth thy mouth with good things, so that thy youth is renewed as the eagle's? (Ps. ciii. 1-5.)

EAR and EARS

In Scripture, such frequent mention is made of the hearing ear, and the uncircumcised in heart and ears, that it ought to be noticed in a work of this kind. In Scripture language, to uncover the ear, (1 Sam. xx. 2. 13.) as it is rendered in the margin of the Bibles, is to reveal somewhat particularly to a certain person, or persons, which, in general, to others, is not made known. And hence the Lord Jesus himself saith by the spirit of prophecy, (Ps. xi. 6.) Mine ears hast thou opened. So again, Isa. 1.5. "The Lord God hath opened mine ear, and I was not rebellious," In the Jewish church, it was the custom, and among the appointments of the Lord himself, when a servant, after six years' service, being freed by the law, so loved his master, that he would not leave him, he was to have his ear bored with an awl unto the door post, as a token of a free and voluntary service; and then to serve for ever. (Exod. xxi. 2. 5.) And in allusion to this, for this was a beautiful type of the Lord Jesus Christ), the Lord Jesus saith, Mine ears hast thou opened, or as the margin of the Bible hath, it, mine ears hast thou digged. (See Ps. xl. 6.) The apostle Paul commenting upon this passage, in quoting it, gives a free and full translation, and renders it, A body hast thou given me, or prepared me. (Heb. x. 5.) And certain it is, that the lesser, of boring the ear, implies the greater, of preparing the whole body. But how delightful is it to make interpretation, of what the Jewish servant said respecting the house of his servitude, in allusion to the Lord Jesus in the house of his! who, as the servant of JEHOVAH (for such he fully became, when he became our Surety), might be said thus to express himself, I love my master, I love my wife, my children; I will not go out free. Surely, it is blessed to eye Christ as our Surety, constantly represented by types in the Old Testament Scripture. As the uncovering the ear is a Scripture expression, to denote divine teaching, and the opening the heart and understanding, so the word of God abounds with figures and similitudes to represent the reverse. They are said to be uncircumcised in heart and ears, to whom the word of the Lord is unprofitable. Their ears are said to be heavy; to be waxed gross, and dull in hearing, and the like. (Jer. vi. 10.) Hence! no less than seven times in the Scripture; as, if to denote the awfulness of such a state) the dreadful condition of the ungodly is described under those characters. (See Isa. vi. 9, 10. Matt. xiii. 14, 15. Mark iv. 12. Luke viii, 10. John xii. 40, Acts xxviii. 26, 27. Rom. xi. 8.)

EARRING

We find that in the Old Testament scripture, the earring was a token and pledge of overtures to marriage. Thus Abraham's servant's first present, in his master's name, to Rebekah, was a golden earring. (Gen. xxiv, 22.) And hence Laban, her brother's, invitation, in consequence thereof. (ver, 30, 31.) In allusion to this, we find the Lord Jesus speaking of his church, "I put a jewel on thy forehead, and earrings in thine ears, and a beautiful crown upon thine head." (Ezek. xvi. 12.) And certain it is, that when the Lord Jesus is going forth in the graces of his Holy Spirit, to make his people willing in the day of his power; he doth all this and infinitely more. Yea, all the persons of the GODHEAD give of their golden blessings, the most precious jewels. "We will make thee borders of gold, with studs of silver." (Song i. 11.)

EARNEST

This word is of great importance in the Scripture tongue, applied as it is, with peculiar emphasis, to the work of the Holy Ghost upon the heart. The apostle, speaking of the wonderful gifts of God's grace, saith, "Now he that hath wrought us for the self same thing is God, who hath also given unto us the earnest of the Spirit." (2 Cor. v. 5.) And elsewhere, he calls it the earnest of our inheritance. (Ephes. i. 14.) It becomes the Lord's pledge, the Lord's token, and covenant of his love to the soul. Sweet evidence of divine faithfulness!

EARTH

There are many senses in which this word is used in holy Scripture. In general, it means the gross matter which forms a bed, and sustains the life of trees, and fruit, and of vegetable life. God called the dry land earth. (Gen. i. 10.) Sometimes it is put for the people, and sometimes for their property. The earth, it is said, was filled with violence. (Gen. vi. 13.) And respecting property, we are told, that while the heavens are the Lord's, the earth hath he given to the children of men. (Ps. cxv. 16.) I have somewhere read of the presumptuous gift of one of the princes of the earth, assuming to himself this grant, making a deed of gift to one of his favorites, of a certain portion of the land, the charter of which ran in words to this effect: "I give all that is from heaven to the centre of the earth, including the minerals in the bowels of it," &c. Poor vain man! when shortly after, all that he could embrace of the earth, or the earth him, was just his own breadth and length to lie down upon for corruption and to mingle with in the dust! The word earth is also spoken of by way of a natural and moral sense, Hence, in opposition to spirit, the Scripture describes the first man as of the earth, earthy; while the second man is declared to be, the Lord from heaven. And Jesus himself defines the essential difference, he that is of the earth, speaketh of the earth, he that cometh from heaven, is above all. (See I Cor xv. 47, 48. John iii. 31.)

EARTHQUAKE

The first account we have of an earthquake is in the book of Numbers, chap. xvi. 28-34. in the instance of God's judgments upon the rebellion of Korah, and his company. And it should seem from hence, but a manner of just conclusion, that earthquakes, notwithstanding that modern philosophers pretend to account for them by physical causes, are not so, but special indications of the Lord's displeasure. It is somewhat remarkable, that in the ten plagues of Egypt, this was not one. For of all alarming events, no doubt, the earthquake is the greatest. The Scripture relates another earthquake in the days Uzziah, king of Judah. (See Amos i. 1. Zech. xiv. 5.) And a third took place at the death of Christ. (Matt. xxvii. 51.) The Father in the church, St. Cyril, relates, that the rocks which were split on Mount Calvary on this occasion were visible in his days. Matthew tells us, that when the centurion saw this earthquake, it convinced him of the GODHEAD of Christ. (ver. 54.)

EATING, and TO EAT

The custom of eating in the Eastern world, totally differed from our customs and manners. It was always in a reclining posture. And there was great attention paid to the company, even in their ordinary meals. The patriarchs ate by themselves. And when our fathers were in Egypt, we are told, that it was an abomination for the Egyptians to sit at meat with the Hebrews. (Gen. lxiii. 32.) It is our happiness that these distinctions are done away. Jesus received sinners, and ate with them. Well it is for us he did. (Luke. xv. 2.) How blessedly the apostle speaks on the subject: "The kingdom of God is not meat and drink, but righteousness, and peace, and joy in the Holy Ghost." (Rom. xiv. 17.)

It may not be unacceptable to the readers, for whom I particularly intend this Concordance, to set before them an account of the extraordinary attention the ancient Jews observed in their seasons of meals, to a scrupulous exactness. It may be more than gratifying as an history, for it may be profitable in beholding what was unimportant among them, while we gather improvement from what was becoming. The view of both may be useful.

The Jews never sat down to the table until that they had first washed their hands. Hence, their surprise, at the freedom of Christ and his disciples on this occasion. (Matt. xv. 2. Mark vii. 2-4.) When they have finished their repast, they wash again. None of the company begin to eat until that the governor or master of the feast hath broken bread, and craved a blessing. One of the fathers gives us the usual words of this blessing. The words were "Blessed be thou, O Lord, our God, the King of the world, for it is thou who produceth the bread of the earth." All present say, Amen. And the master of the table generally helps the guests, however numerous they may be. When they have eaten, he takes the vessel of wine in his right hand, saying as before "Blessed be thou, O Lord our God, the King of the world, who hast produced the fruit of the vine." The Amen is, as before, repeated. Then is generally repeated the twenty-third Psalm. There is always reserved a portion of bread after their meals, which is suffered to remain on the table. Was not this with an eye to Christ, the bread of life? (John vi. 48.) A cup is usually washed at the close of the entertainment, and is filled with wine, when the governor or master of the feast saith, elevating it to the view of the whole company, "Let us bless him, of whose benefits we have been partaking." The company answer," Blessed be he who hath heaped his favours on us, and by his goodness hath now fed us." This is followed up with prayer, in which is generally expressed the Lord's goodness to Israel, beseeching him to pity Jerusalem and his temple, to restore the throne of David, and to send Elias and the Messiah, and to deliver them out of their long captivity: all answer Amen. A Psalm is again recited, and the cup of wine is given by the master of the table to every one. The table is then cleared, and the service finisheth. I have thought it worth rehearsing this custom of the ancient Jews, because it serves to shew how much devotion mingled even with their ordinary meals. I take shame and reproach to myself in the recollection, how such conduct puts to the blush modern Christians. At what table shall we go to find so much piety? They looked forward but to the Messiah to come. We profess to believe that he is come, and hath restored all things. Blessed Lord Jesus! How dost thou daily witness the graceless tables of thousands that call themselves after thee, Christians, but where not the vestige of the Christian is to be found.

EBAL

A mountain in the lot of Ephraim over against mount Gerizim. The name Ebal signifies, somewhat old and confused, from Balah, old. It was the famous spot from whence the curses were pronounced on the breaches of the law. And the place seemed to be well suited for this purpose, for it was a barren unfruitful spot. Whereas, Gerizim, which lay opposite to it, and from whence the blessings were delivered, was a beautiful and fruitful country. (Deut. xi. 29; xxvii. 4. Josh.viii. 30-32.)

EBED-MELECH

This man is spoken of with honourable testimony in Scripture, for his service to the prophet Jeremiah. His name shews who he was, Ebed, a servant, Melech, to the king. (See Jer. xxxviii. 7-13.)

EBENEZER

A well known name and I believe, often used by the Lord's people, after the example of Samuel, upon numberless occasions in life. If the reader will consult 1 Sam. vii. he will be enabled to enter into the Spirit of the expression, if so be the Lord be his teacher. And should the Lord give him also a right view of the subject, he will discover that the mercy was not confined to the days of Samuel, but in all ages of the church, the faithful can, and do, find causes daily to set up their Ebenezers, "to the praise of the glory of his grace, who maketh them accepted in the Beloved." Even in the moment of writing do I find cause to set up the Ebenezer of the morning, "hitherto hath the Lord helped!" And, reader, what a sweet additional thought is it, in the full assurance of faith, to refresh the soul, that he who hath hitherto helped, and doth help, will help, through grace, in life, and in glory, to all eternity. I only add, under this article, that there is a great strength of expression in the word Ebenezer. It is a compound meaning Eben, or Aben, a stone, JEHOVAH laid in Zion, "in whom whosoever believeth, shall never be confounded? (Compare Isa. xxviii. 16. with 1 Pet. ii. 6-8.)

ECCLESIASTES

One of the books of Solomon, and so called by the Septuagint. But it is worthy remark, that the first verse runs in this form, "The Words of Coheleth the son of David;" though the word is feminine, and is as if it is said, she who speaks. But that it is Solomon who is the writer, and who is describing in many parts of it himself, there can be no question, since we have in it so ample an account of his riches and treasure, and at the same time, of his discovery of the vanity of all.

EDEN

The garden of our first parents. Eden, means delights. (Gen. ii. 8.)

EGYPT

A well known kingdom in Scripture history, from whence the church, under the Lord, made their first Exodus. The believer in Christ knows also what it is to have been brought up in Egypt, and brought out of the Egypt of the soul.

ELDAD

See Medad.

ELDERS

In the church of the Old Testament, elders were the fathers of the tribes, and had the government in a great measure committed to them. Hence when the Lord appeared unto Moses at the bush, with a view to reveal himself in the deliverance of the

ELEAZOR - ELI

people; he said, "Go and gather the elders of Israel together." (Exod. iii. 16.) In the New Testament church, the term seems to be generally applied to fathers and governors of families. Peter called himself an elder. (1 Pet. v. 1.)

ELEAZOR

Son of Aaron, and his successor in the priestly office. His history commences from the death of his father Aaron. (See Num. xx. 23, to the end.) His name is very expressive, help of God,

ELECT

We meet with this word so very often in Scripture, that one might have been led to conclude, that it would have been received in the church with implicit faith, referring the act itself, as becometh sinful ignorant creatures to do, into the sovereignty and good pleasure of God. It is in the first and highest instance spoken of, and applied to, the Lord Jesus Christ, as the Christ of God. (Isa. xlii. 1. with Matt. xii. 17, 18. &c.) It is specially spoken of the church of Israel. (Isa. xlv. 4; lxix. 22.) It is also spoken of in relation to the Gentile church, gathered out of all nations. (Matt. xxiv. 31. Rom. xi. 5. Tit. i. 1.) And what endears this sovereign act of grace the more is, that it is all in, and for, Christ. (Eph. i. 4.) The Scriptures uniformly declaring while in the very moment of establishing the truth itself, that it is all of free grace, no merit, no pretensions of merit here or hereafter, becoming in the least instrumental to this distinguishing mercy, but wholly resulting from the sovereign will and purpose of the Lord. (Deut. vii. 1. Rom. ix. 11-16. 2 Tim. i. 9. Ephes. i. 6.) Hence the everlasting security of the church, and of the blessings of the church, are all sure, certain and irrevocable. (Rom. viii. 33.) Here also the interest the Lord takes in his church, and all her concerns. Do any afflict them? he saith, "Shall not God avenge his own elect who cry day and night unto him, though he bear long with them? I tell you that he will avenge them speedily. (Luke xviii. 7, 8.) Yea, the Lord declares, that he will "shorten the days of affliction for the elects' sake." (See Matt. xxiv. 22.) And these blessings are heightened in their personal nature. John speaks of an elect lady and her sister. (2 John i. 13.) And Peter speaks of the elect church at Babylon. (1 Pet. v. 13.) I must not overlook, under this article, what is said in Scripture of elect angels, also. (1 Tim.v. 21.) No doubt they owe their steadfastness to Christ, as their Head and Sovereign, in election and dominion; while Christ's seed, the church, are preserved by union. But without this preservation in Christ, by election, angels are no more secure from falling than men, who have fallen. For as some angels have fallen, so might all, if not upheld by a superior power to themselves. For as we read, (Job iv. 18.) "God putteth no trust in his servants, and his angels he chargeth with folly," that is, with weakness; so it is plain that their preservation is not in themselves, but in the Lord. And when we read of the elect angels, it implies their election, and upholding in Christ. Think what a glorious, blessed Almighty Lord the christian's Lord is! Well might the apostle Peter, under the deep impression of this sacred truth made upon his heart, cry out with holy rapture, "Elect according to the foreknowledge of God the Father, through the sanctification of the Spirit unto obedience, and sprinkling of the blood of Jesus Christ, grace unto you, and peace be multiplied." (1 Pet. i. 2.)

ELI

The High Priest, in the days of the judges. (1 Sam. 2-11.) His name is very significant, meaning, my God. The sin of Eli is remarkably striking. And it teaches most powerfully. We see in him a decided proof of the great danger of consulting the feelings of nature, rather than obeying the precepts of grace. His tenderness, as a father, tempted him to lose sight of his reverence for God. He therefore contented himself with reproving his sons for their vileness, when he should have publicly stript them of their office, and banished them from his presence. And though he was admonished of this evil conduct by the child Samuel, speaking to him in a vision from the Lord, yet we find no firmness to reform. And though the Lord deferred the threatened punishment of his two sons for near twenty and seven years, yet he allowed them still to minister in the service of the sanctuary. At length the judgment came, and a most tremendous judgment it was. (See Hophni, 1 Sam. iv. 12-22.) How different from him, of whom it is said, "He did not acknowledge his brethren, nor know his own children!" (Deut. xxxiii. 9.)

ELI ELI LAMA SABACHTHANI

The reader will not wish to pass over this well known cry of Jesus on the cross; but will be gratified with the continued attention of it. Those words of Christ are full of important signification; and every pious reader of his Bible ought to have a proper conception of their meaning. They are partly in the Hebrew, and partly in the Syriac tongue, and which, perhaps occasioned the perverse misconstruction in some, who supposed the Lord called Elias, when Jesus said Eli. The prophet had said, "That the Lord should roar out of Zion, and utter his voice from Jerusalem, and the heavens and the earth should shake." (Joel iii. 16.) And hence we find that prophecy fulfilled. The loud voice of Jesus was not like one whose strength was gone, but rather uttered in proof of what Jesus had said: "No man taketh my life from me, but I lay it down of myself, I have power to lay it down, and I have power to take it again. This commandment have I received of my Father." (John x. 18.) The words themselves seem to be a quotation from the xxiind Psalm, 1st verse, thereby intimating, that the prophet in that Psalm spake wholly of Christ. This was highly important for the church to know. And the meaning yet more important. The Holy Ghost hath caused his servants the Evangelists, to give the church the interpretation: Eli, Eli, lama, are Hebrew; Sabachthani, or Sabadetani, is Syriac. Astonishing words for the only beloved of the Father to utter! Jesus had uttered no cry of pain in the great tortures of his body; neither do we hear the meek Lamb of God complain of the insults of the rabble, in the unequalled repreaches cast upon him. These, and every other sorrow, seem to have been swallowed up and forgotten in the flood of divine wrath, which now opened like cataracts from heaven in the Father's desertion. Who shall say what this was? Who is competent to describe the horrors of it, when it induced such a cry in the soul agonies of Jesus? Well may every child of God pause over the renewed reading of it, and in the contemplation, consider the love and tenderness of Jesus to his people, who thus endured the being forsaken of his Father for a season, that they might not be forsaken for ever. (Heb. v. 7-9.)

ELIJAH

Though the history of this highly favoured servant of the Lord would afford much improvement to enlarge upon, according to the Scripture testimony concerning him, yet it would swell this work to a size much beyond the limits intended, for the writer to indulge himself in it. I have therefore noticed this prophet, only with a view to remark the greatness of his name. Elijah is a compound word, including two of the names of JEHOVAH. Eli, my God; and Jah, the Lord. It would be thought presumptuous to call our children in the present hour by such names, in the plain English of the words, but with the Hebrews it was done in honour of the Lord God of their fathers. And so particular do the pious fathers of the Old Testament seem to have been, in naming their children, that they studied to give them such as might have some allusion

ELIMELECH - ELISHA

to the Lord, or to retain one of the letters of JEHOVAH in them. If I venture to add another observation concerning this great man, it would be but just to remark, that in that memorable prophecy of Malachi, concerning the coming of Elijah before the day of Christ, (chap iv. 5.) though our Lord explained this to his disciples, in making reference to the spirit of Elias in the person of John the baptist, Matt. xvii. 11, 12.) yet our Lord did not limit the coming of Elijah to that season only. The Evangelists, in describing the transfiguration of the Lord Jesus, relate that Elijah and Moses were present at the solemn scene. (Matt. xvii. 3, 4,) And there doth not seem an objection, wherefore Elijah may not again appear before the Lord Jesus comes in glory, as is supposed, he will in his reign upon earth. The expression of Malachi seems to warrant this conclusion, for it is said, that this mission of Elijah will be "before the great and dreadful day of the Lord." The first coming of Christ, was indeed a great and glorious, but not a dreadful day. Whereas, the second coming is uniformly spoken of as the terrible day of the Lord. For while it will be "to be glorified in his saints, and to be admired in all them that believe," it is no less said to be "in flaming fire, taking vengeance on them that know not God, and that obey not the gospel of the Lord Jesus Christ." (2 Thess. i 8. 10.)

ELIMELECH

This man was the husband of Naomi, whom we read of with such honourable testimony for her faith in God, in the book of Ruth; and as so much is contained in that sweet fragment of sacred Scripture, in allusion to the Lord Jesus Christ, I thought it proper to notice in this place, this name. The whole of the book of Ruth is interesting, not only as a true history of events which took place in the church, but, like that of Joseph, is typical and figurative of higher things. The certain man, there spoken of, going down from Bethlehem-judah, the land of bread, to sojourn in Moab, the city of destruction, becomes no unapt representation of our first father, who, like the Samaritan our Lord describes, going down from Jerusalem, the holy city, to Jericho, the cursed city, fell among thieves. (Luke x. 30.) And as the persons of this certain man and his family were types of others, so their names were significant also of their history. Elimelech means, my God, a king; Naomi signifies, a pleasant one; and their sons, Mahlon and Chilion, sickness and consumption; for such will always be the fruits of leaving Jesus for the world. (See Ruth throughout.)

ELISHA

The successor, in the prophetical office, of Elijah. His name is also highly significant, meaning the salvation of my God. I must pass over many interesting circumstances in the history of this man of God, for the same reasons as in the former. But I beg to notice one event in Elisha's ministry, because it is not so generally regarded, and yet seems to lead to a profitable subject of meditation. The event I refer to, is that of his healing the waters of Jericho. (See 2 Kings ii. 19-22.) The reader will not forget, that Jericho is the city Jsohua cursed before the Lord. (See Josh. vi. 26, with 1 Kings xvi. 34.) There evidently appears from this history, the tokens of divine displeasure upon Jericho in the days of Elisha. For we read, that the men of the city said unto the prophet, "Behold, I pray thee, the situation of this city is pleasant, as my lord seeth, but the water is naught, and the ground barren." In the margin of our Bibles the barren ground is explained, in causing to miscarry. Hence it should seem that the divine displeasure was manifested in this way, in the rendering the climate unfavourable to the increase of children. I do not presume to decide upon the subject, neither do I say as much, when I ask in order to determine the point, as to enquire. But I humbly conceive, if by the naughtiness of the water of Jericho, barrenness was induced among the females, there was somewhat in this analogous to the Lord's appointment in Israel concerning the waters of Jealousy. In both cases, the matter is the same in relation to the cause. (See Num. v. 23. to the end.) That the barrenness mentioned of Jericho referred to the sterility of the women, or their miscarriages, which is the same thing in effect, I have no doubt. The same word Sheceleh, is made use of in this place, as in the instance of Jacob's expostulating with Laban: (Gen. xxxi. 38.) "Thy she-goats have not cast their young." And the Lord, when speaking in promises to his people, saith, (Exod. xxiii. 25, 26.) "He shall bless thy bread and thy water, and I will take sickness away from the midst of thee. There shall nothing cast their young, nor be barren, in thy land."

It appears then, that amidst all the pleasantness of Jericho, which abounded with palm trees (and, indeed, on that account was called the city of palm trees, (See 2 Chron. xxviii. 15.) there was still a certain somewhat, unfavourable to that which to the children of Israel (looking forward to the types that the promised seed would be in their lot), was among the most distressing of all calamities, the want of children. This was the state of Jericho. The prophet's cruse of salt cast into the waters, under the Lord's blessing, healed the land. Elisha cast the cruse into the spring, saying, "Thus saith the Lord, I have healed these waters; there shall not be from thence any more, death, or barren land. So the waters were healed unto this day, according to the saying of Elisha." I have thought it worthwhile to enter into the particulars of this interesting account, concerning the barrenness at Jericho healed by the cruse of salt cast into the spring of the waters, by way of introducing an infinitely more interesting observation on the subject itself. The cruse of salt, like the tree at Marah (Exod. xv. 25.) were both beautiful types of Jesus and his salvation. Both the cruse and the barrenness are effectually cured when Jesus takes them away. The waters of Marah lose their bitterness when his cross is put in them to sweeten and sanctify. The barrenness of Jericho is healed, and children are born, even in Jericho, when Christ's cruse of grace is applied. A Rahab and harlot is found in Jericho; and Æthiopia, and Seba, and the multitude of isles, shall stretch forth their hands unto God. Jesus hath taken out the curse when he was made a curse for us, that we might be made the righteousness of God in him." (Gal. iii. 13. 2 Cor. v. 21.) Hallelujah!

ELKANAH

His name signifies, to be zealous for God; from Kina, zealous; and El, God. See Hannah.

ELUL

The sixth month of the Israelites, corresponding to our August. The same signifies a cry.

ELYMAS

The sorcerer. His name answers to the character, for it means magician. (Acts xiii. 7.)

EMBALM

The embalming the bodies of the dead was a very ancient custom, both with the Hebrews and the Egyptians. Hence we read of Joseph giving directions to the physicians to embalm the body of his father. (Gen. i. 2.) This is the earliest account of embalming that we have in Scripture. And it should seem, therefore, to have taken its rise in Egypt. Some have said, that necessity first taught the Egyptians the art of embalming, for when the river Nile overflowed, sometimes the inundation continued for near two months; during which time the bodies of the dead not only remained unburied, but remained unavoidably in the tents. To avoid the dreadful effects arising from putrefaction, gave rise to the idea of embalming; which was done by taking away the entrails, and anointing the body with oil and a composition of spices, which formed a kind of transparent coating, preserving from corruption, and keeping the body entire. I beg the reader to remark, that the custom, thus probably borrowed from the Egyptians, became the custom also of the Hebrews, even to the days of our Saviour. For we read, that there was an intention of embalming the Lord of life and glory. But if the reader will consult all the evangelists, he will find that the thing was not done, but prevented by our Lord's resurrection. The pious women resting the Sabbath day became, by the Lord's providence, the overruling cause to this effect. The Almighty Redeemer could need no embalming. His holy body saw no corruption. Sweet thought to the believer! And the dust of his saints, in like manner, is embalmed in him. Infinitely more valuable than the golden dust of the goldsmith. Hence the Psalmist saith, "Precious in the sight of the Lord is the death of his saints." (Ps. cxvi. 15.)

EMMANUEL

We pause over this precious name, as well we may, before we presume to enter upon it, or to say what immense blessings are folded up in it. Who, indeed, can undertake to say? Nevertheless, if what we propose be wholly scriptural, and supported by Scripture authority, we can never err. And though our discoveries go but a little way, yet even that little way is blessed, when God the Holy Ghost goeth before us, and His voice is distinctly heard directing. (Isa. xxx. 21.) Concerning this blessed name of our adorable Lord, we find that it was given by the Lord himself, and that it was declared to be the Lord's sign to the house of David. (Isa. vii. 14.) "Therefore, the Lord himself shall give you a sign. Behold, a virgin shall conceive and bear a son, and shall call his name Immanuel." The Hebrew word Almah, virgin, strictly and properly speaking, a virgin, who hath never been seen by man. The word implies hidden, kept in, and secret. St. Jerome makes a nice distinction on this ground, between the ordinary word, Bethula, a young woman, and Almah, a virgin. In this memorable passage of Isa. vii. 14. the word is Almah.

But while I consider this distinction highly important, I beg the reader yet more particularly to consider the blessedness of the name itself of Emanuel, God with us. Sweet consideration to the heart of the believer! For as God, it is evident, that all he did when upon earth, and all that he is doing now in heaven, was, and is effectual to all the purposes of salvation. The infinite dignity of his person gives an infinite merit to his work, and cannot fail, both in his blood and righteousness, to justify his people, and render them truly acceptable in the sight of God their Father, and fully secure to them the everlasting blessedness and glory of heaven. And as He is man and God in our nature, so does his nearness and dearness give an interest to his people in all that belongs to him; yea, all the blessings come home with a tenfold sweetness to our hearts, because he is Emmanuel, God with us. God in our nature, and we the "members of his body, of his flesh, and of his bones."

EMMAUS

A village sixty furlongs (that is seven miles and a half,) north of Jerusalem, rendered memorable in being the place to which the two disciples walked on the day of our Lord's resurrection, and where he made himself known unto them, in breaking of bread, and blessing it. (See Luke xxiv. 13-32.)

END

This word would not have needed particular attention, but for that the Lord Jesus on the throne called himself by it. (Rev. xxi. 6.) And when we consider in how many ways the Lord is, both the beginning and the end, the Alpha and the Omega, surely it is very blessed to make him, what the Father hath made him, as the Mediator and head of his church and people, the first and the last in all our pursuits, affections, and designs: Jesus Christ, the same yesterday, today, and for ever.

ENGEDI

We read of the vineyards of Engedi Song i. 14. A place remarkable for palm trees and vines, and the church compares the Lord Jesus to both on account of his riches and sweetness and fulness. The word means, fountain of happiness.

ENOCH

The seventh from Adam. His name signifies dedicated, from Chanach. The Holy Ghost: hath given a blessed testimony to this man. (Heb. xi. 5.) Oh! for grace thus to walk, and thus to have communion with God in Christ!

ENON

The place where John baptized. (John iii. 22.) It lay south of Shalim and Jordan. The name signifies a cloud.

ENOS

The son of Seth. (Gen. v. 6.) The name signifies sickness, mortality, yea, the word itself, Enos, is sickness.

ENSHEMISH

A place toward the salt sea. (See Josh. xv. 7.) The name signifies the fountain of the sun, from Ain, fountain, and Shemesh, the sun.

ENSIGN

An ensign, as a banner, set up as a trophy of victory, or for a declaration of war. I should not have thought it necessary to have noticed it, but because Christ is said to be set up as an ensign to the people, and to call the nations from afar; alluding, perhaps, to both the Jewish and Gentile church. (See Isa. v. 26; xi. 10-12.) And the reader will forgive me when I add, that it is blessed to behold the Lord Jesus under, this figure. For He and He alone, is: the Standard-bearer among ten thousand. So hâth he been in JEHOVAH'S view, from all eternity. His victories mark him in the one point, and his warfare for his church mark him for the other. So that He is the signal of war to all his redeemed, for their contests with sin, death, and hell. Oh! may the Holy Ghost lift him up to my soul continually, that the Amaleks of the day may have no momentary success, until that my God hath put out, as he hath sworn, the name of Amalek from under heaven! (Exod. xvii. 10. to the end.) See Banner.

EPAPHRAS

It is supposed, that he was the first bishop of Colosse. (Col. i. 7.) His name is from the Greek, meaning covered with foam.

EPAPHRODITAS

An eminent servant of the church at Philippi. (Phil. iv. 8.)

EPENETUS

A convert to the gospel. (Rom. xvi. 5.)

EPHA

An Hebrew measure, containing about three pecks and three pints, like a Bath.!

EPHESUS

The celebrated city to which Paul sent his Epistle. And one of the seven churches to whom the Lord Jesus sent his message. (See Acts xix. 1. Ephes. i. and Rev. ii. 1.)

EPHOD

This formed part of the High Priest's dress, and no doubt, like the office itself, was intended as typical of Christ. It was a rich dress composed of different colours, blue, purple, and crimson, and adorned with gold. On that part of it which crossed the breast was a square ornament called the choschen, containing precious stones, with the names on them of the twelve tribes of Israel. Nothing could more aptly represent our great High Priest, the Lord Jesus Christ, going in before the presence of JEHOVAH with the names of his people on his breast. Hence the church, in allusion to it, vehemently urgeth Christ in that request, "Set me as a seal upon thine heart, as a seal upon thine arm;" (Song viii. 6.) meaning, that she might be always in his remembrance, to live in his heart, and to be always looked upon as a seal, or signet, on the arm. (See Exod. xxviii. 4-29. See Urim and Thummim.)

EPHPHATHA

This is more of Syriac than the Hebrew language. It comes from Pathach, to open. The Evangelist hath explained it, Mark vii. 34. Whenever we read this miracle of the Lord Jesus, shall we not beg the Lord to say to us, as to this poor man, that all our spiritual faculties may be opened at his sovereign voice, and all unite in his praises?

EPHRA

A city of Ephraim; perhaps the same as Ophrah. (Judges vi. 11.) It is derived from Epher, ashes. The prophet Isaiah hath a beautiful observation on this word, contrasted with Pheer, which is beauty. The Lord, he saith, will give them Pheer for Epher; that is, beauty for ashes; meaning the blessed change wrought by grace in the soul, when from sin they are brought to salvation in the Lord Jesus Christ. (See Isa. lxi. 3.)

EPHRAIM

One of the sons of Joseph. The name is derived from Pharah, fruitfulness. In the after ages of the church, the Lord frequently speaks of the whole church of Israel by the name of Ephraim.
(See Jer. xxxi. 20. Hos. vii. 1.-xii. 1.-xiii. 1.)
I do not presume to say the cause was, because the ten tribes had the chief city in Ephraim; but I think it probable. The Psalmist, when speaking of looking out a place for the ark, saith, we found it in Ephratah. (Ps. cxxxii. 6.)

EPHRAIM

A city. There were two of this name, one a city of Benjamin, several miles from Jerusalem; and the other belonging to Ephraim, near Jordan. Here it was the Lord Jesus went a few days before his crucifixion. (See John xi. 54.)

EPHRATH or EPHRATAH

This is the same as Bethlehem, where Christ was born. (See Micah v. 2. Matt. ii. 1.) The word is derived from Pharah, fruitfulness. See Bethlehem.

ESAU

The elder brother of Jacob, who despised the blessing, and was rejected. In the history of those two brothers, we have enough to answer and silence all cavils respecting distinguishing grace from God's own testimony. (See Gen. xxv. 21-23. Mal. i. 3. Rom. ix. throughout.)

But while this doctrine concerning distinguishing grace is fully displayed in the history of Jacob and Esau from those Scriptures, there is one point more relating to Esau which deserves to be particularly considered, and the more so, from the misapprehension of many respecting it. I mean what is said by the apostle of the rejection of Esau's repentance. (Heb. xii. 16, 17.) By a mistake both of the cause which gave birth to this man's repentance, and of the nature of that repentance itself, many erroneous opinions have been formed upon it. A short attention to the passage as given by the apostle, under the Holy Ghost's teaching, will put this subject in a clear light, and explain this seeming difficulty.

The passage is as follows: "Lest there be any fornicator or profane person, as Esau, who for one morsel of meat sold his birthright. For ye know how that afterward when he would have inherited the blessing, he was rejected, for he found no place of repentance, though he sought it carefully with tears." Now, if the reader will compare what is here said with the account given by the Holy Ghost, how he sold his birthright. (Gen. xxv. 29-34.) he will discover the contempt which he put upon his birthright, and the consequent resentment of God. This is the first thing to be observed in this transaction. The covenant blessing he still despised. This he wholly disregarded, and never repented that he had so done.

And if the reader looks attentively to what the Apostle hath said concerning his repentance, he will next discover, that Esau's repentance was not in respect to the promised blessing, in spiritual things conveyed to Jacob, but mere temporal possessions. Jacob was made Esau's lord, and Esau himself, by selling his birthright, had consented to it; of this he repented, and sought it carefully with tears, to prevail upon his father Isaac to call it back, hoping the known partiality of the father to him would prevail over his natural feelings. "And hence he cried with an exceeding bitter cry, and said, Hast thou but one blessing, my father, bless me, even me, also, O my father!" (Gen. xxvii. 34-38.)

The reader will perceive, that in this whole account here nothing but the natural feelings at work. The repentance of Esau is wholly concerning earthly possessions, and not a word spoken about the covenant blessing given to Abraham concerning the rejection of Esau's repentance is the rejection of his earthly father Isaac, and hath nothing to do with the rejection of the Lord. Esau offered no repentance to God. The blessing in Christ he regarded no more then, than he did when he sold his birthright. This was not in Esau's concern. Esau was still the same profane person as ever. So that, if men who read their Bibles would read them attentively on this point, and beg the great Author of his written word, even God the Holy Ghost, to instruct them, they would learn to make a proper distinction between what Paul calls the sorrow of the world, which worketh death, and that godly sorrow which worketh repentance to salvation not to be repented of. (2 Cor. vii. 10.) The former, like Esau's, is wholly from nature the latter, Paul describes, is from grace. The one is man's own creating, and wholly concerning, earthly things; the other is the Lord's creating, and wholly refers to heavenly things. The repentance that begins in a man's own heart from his own disappointments in worldly pursuits, ends as it began, and produceth death. The repentance which is from above and leads to true sorrow of soul, riseth to the source from whence it first came, and bringeth forth life. And this is confirmed by what the apostle declared; "Christ is exalted as a Prince and a Saviour, for to give repentance to Israel and forgiveness of sins." (Acts v. 31.)

ESHCOL

This was a valley or brook, so called, in the south of Judah, and perhaps took its name from the clusters of grapes there abounding. The name Eshcol, indeed, means bunch of grapes. It was in this place the spies sent by Moses to search the land cut down one bunch, which required two men to carry. (See Num. xiii. 23, 24.) See Cluster.

ESPOUSED, and ESPOUSALS

This term is well known among the Hebrews, in the ceremony of their marriages. The espousing each other, and the betrothing by promise to each other, from the time that this was done, was considered as sacred, though the marriage was not consummated sometimes for a considerable space after. Upon these occasions there was generally a pledge given from the man to the woman, as a token of this inviolable contract.

    This espousal, in the Jewish church, is frequently made use of, by way of figure, to represent the spiritual union and marriage of Christ with his people. Hence we find several striking Scriptures to this amount. (Isa. liv. 5. Hos. ii. 19, 20. Jer. ii. 2; iii. 14. Rev. xix. 7-9.) The Son of God married our nature when taking that holy portion of it, his body, into union with the GODHEAD. And he forms an union, as the Christ of God, with every individual of his mystical body, by betrothing each to himself. He also, like the Jewish husband, gives the pledge and token of his love, when he gives the influence of his Holy Spirit. From this time the contract is considered inviolable, and the Lord saith, "Thou shalt not play the harlot, and thou shalt not be for another man; so will I also be for thee." (Hos. iii. 3.) At length, when the Lord brings home his spouse, then it is called the marriage-supper of the Lamb in heaven. (Rev. xix. 9.) See Betrothing and Marriage.

ESTHER

Daughter of Abihail. See her history, Book of Esther. Her name means secret, from Sathar.

ETERNAL, and ETERNITY

The Scripture sense of these terms, in reference to the persons of the GODHEAD, and the events connected with them, are in the strictest sense of the word, for ever and ever. Very solemn, and yet very blessed, and full of the highest consolation, are those views of the eternity of JEHOVAH and his purposes in salvation. How infinitely sublime are those Scriptures! "Thus saith the high and lofty One that inhabiteth eternity, whose name is Holy." (Isa. lvii. 15.) "For I lift up my hand to heaven, and say, I live for ever." (Deut. xxxii. 40.) "The eternal God is thy refuge, and underneath are the everlasting arms." (Deut. xxxiii. 27.) And JEHOVAH, in a threefold character of persons, Father, Son, and Holy Ghost, is thus described in the eternity of his nature and essence, so Christ the Mediator, by virtue of the union of the manhood with the GODHEAD, is declared by JEHOVAH to be eternal. "Thy throne, O God, is for ever and ever." (Ps. xlv. 6. Heb. i. 8.) "The Lord sware, and will not repent; Thou art a Priest for ever, after the order of Melchizedec." (Ps. cx. 4.) And hence, in Christ and by Christ, and from an union with him, all that is connected in the blessed work of salvation is of eternal duration. The covenant is declared to be an everlasting covenant, ordered in all things and sure. (2 Sam. xxiii. 5. Jer. xxxii. 40.) The gospel is called an everlasting gospel. (Rev. xiv. 6.) Redemption is said to be an eternal redemption. (Heb. ix 12.). And the consequence certainly follows from these properties, that the glory purchased by an eternal redemption is an eternal weight of glory. So the apostle to the Corinthians calls it, 2 Cor. iv. 17. (See Heb. v. 9. 1 Pet. v. 10. 1 John v. 11.)

ETHIOPIA

One of the great kingdoms in Africa, sometimes called Cush in Scripture, from Cush, blackness. Blessed are the promises concerning the call of Ethiopia to the Lord, in the latter dispensations of the gospel. (Ps. lxviii. 31; lxxii. 10, 11. Isa. xlv. 14).

EVE

Our first mother. The name is taken from a Hebrew root, signifying life. The name woman seems to be a corruption of womb-man, because taken out of man; for the very reason thus assigned by our first father so explains it. (Gen. ii. 23.) There is a very great beauty and wisdom in the contrivance, as well as grace and favour in the Lord's ordination in peopling the earth. Both sexes shall have equal honour in the plan of creation and redemption. The man, saith the apostle, Adam was first formed, then Eve, (1 Tim. ii. 13.) Here the man hath the precedency. But in all the after circumstances the woman is to be the womb of creation. And yet to keep up this order, the rib of the man shall be, as it were, the womb for the women. And hence, she shall be called womb-man. But as both the man and the woman are equally involved in sin, in the redemption for both the Lord will make a new thing in the earth, and a woman shall compass a man. (Jer. xxxi, 22.) The man of the earth, therefore, Adam and all his race, shall have no hand in this generation; yea, the womb of the woman only shall be no more than but for the deposit of this Holy Thing. The body the Father prepared for his Son shall be produced by the miraculous overshadowing power of God the Holy Ghost. So that though Christ is of the seed of David, according to the flesh, and the seed of the woman, according to promise, and thus literally and truly belonging to both, yet indeed, and in truth, unconnected with either. So blessed and so wonderful are the ways of our wonder-working God! (Isa. xxvii. 29.)

EXPIATION

This was a solemn day among the Jews. It was observed on the tenth day of the month Tizri. The Hebrews called it Chippeen, meaning pardon. And they had a belief that the whole of the offences of the past year were then forgiven. What could be more striking in reference to "the blood of Christ which cleanseth from all sin?" (I John i. 7.) I refer the reader to Lev. xvi. for the relation of this day of expiation, where there is a circumstantial account of it.

The Rabbi had a high veneration for this day, and observed it with great strictness and solemnity. They make a point to have all breaches made up in families, or among the people on this day. And if one is conscious that he is the aggressor, he first makes overtures for a reconciliation with the person he hath offended. And if the other is averse to forgive or withhold it, the aggressor again and again sues for pardon. But if the offended will not be reconciled, the offender takes with him one or more witnesses, to testify what he hath done, and from hence the offended person, if he any longer refuseth, becomes the guilty party. The same is observed, if the party that was injured be dead. The offender goes to his grave and acknowledges his guilt, and this is considered as obtaining his pardon.

The day of Expiation was considered so solemn, and the office of the High Priest so sacred, that fearing he should commit an error when it was finished, and the day over, he changed his dress, blessed the people, and gave a great feast, blessing the Lord that he had come out unhurt from the sanctuary. See Goat.

EZEKIEL

The prophet. His name is very significant, meaning "the strength of God." The ministry of this man seems to have been carried on by signs and representations, more than by open preaching. The Lord indeed said that Ezekiel was for a sign unto his people. (Ezek. xxiv. 24-27.) And in nothing perhaps do the customs and manners of mankind differ more, than in the method of communication to each other. Language is rather an imperfection, notwithstanding all we boast of its beauty, than an accomplishment. It is most needful in numberless instances, suited to our present state. But in the world of perfection to which we are hastening, the communication of ideas will have a more complete and quick order. The word of God tells us as much, in saying, that in that blessed place, "whether there be tongues they shall cease? (1 Cor. xiii. 8.) In the eastern countries, and in the days of the prophets particularly, and even now, modern travellers say, that generally more than half the transactions of life are carried on by signs. The prophets delivered their messages by gesticulations and signs, similar to what was then in common use in common concerns, and thus made their message familiar and easy to be understood. Thus Ezekiel's removing into captivity, digging through the wall, not mourning for the dead, and the like, were declared to be tokens and signs respecting the Lord's dealings with his people. So Jeremiah's girdle hid by the river; the potter's earthen bottle, the wooden yoke he wore about his neck; these were all to the same amount, speaking by action, instead of words, and much better understood by the people. Isaiah speaks of the same signs. (Isa. viii. 18.) And Zechariah, of Christ and his fellows. (Zech. iii. 8.) In reading Ezekiel's prophecy, particular attention should be had to these things.

EZION-GEBER

A city of Arabia, meaning, the Wood of the strong. So called from Hets, wood; and Gaber, strong. (1 Kings ix. 26.)

EZRA

The Priest. See his Book. His name means help, from Ezer.

F

FACE

The face is frequently put for the whole body. It is meant for the person. Hence, when the church prayeth, "O Lord God, turn not away the face of thine Anointed;" that is, the person of thine Anointed. (2 Chron. vi. 42.) So again, when it is said, "The face of the Lord is against them that do evil," it means, that the Lord himself is so. (Ps. xxxiv. 16.) So again, the patriarch Jacob, speaking to his son Joseph, said, "I had not thought to see thy face;" that is, thy person; "and lo! God hath shewed me thy seed." (Gen. xlviii. 11.)

Concerning the face of the Lord, it is said by the Lord to Moses, "Thou canst not see my face; for there "shall no man see me and live." And yet in the same chapter we are told, that "the Lord spake to Moses face to face, as a man speaketh to his friend." (Exod. xxxiii. 20. See also Num. xiv. 14. Deut. v. 4.) But there is no difficulty in reconciling these Scriptures; in fact, they do not differ, when properly considered, from each other. The sight of JEHOVAH, in his own unveiled glory, is inadmissible to mortals. But the manifestation of JEHOVAH, so as to identify his person and reality as the speaker, is as plain in those discoveries as that of seeing him face to face.

Those Scriptures are best explained by each other. One part of the divine word throws a light upon another; and we are commanded thus to form our judgments, by "comparing spiritual things with spiritual." (1 Cor. ii. 13.)

But every difficulty is at once removed concerning seeing the face of JEHOVAH, by considering the person of the Lord Jesus in his mediatorial character and office, as the visible JEHOVAH. Thus for example;--when JEHOVAH promiseth to send his angel before the people, and commandeth them to obey his voice, he adds, "for my name is in him." (Exod xxiii. 2. 21.) In whom but Christ, as Christ, was ever the name of JEHOVAH? So again, when it is said. (1 Sam. iii. 21.) "And the Lord appeared again in Shiloh; for the Lord revealed himself to Samuel in Shiloh, by the word of the Lord." What word could this be but the uncreated Word, which was, in the after ages of the church, "made flesh, and dwelt among us?"' (John i. 1-4.) Surely, in these and numberless other instances, spoken of in the Old Testament Scripture, of JEHOVAH'S appearance, sometimes in the form of a man, and sometimes of an angel, the Lord Jesus is all along intended to be represented. In all those manifestations it is, as the apostle speaks, giving the church "the light of the knowledge of the glory of God in the face of Jesus Christ." (2 Cor. iv. 6.)

FAITH

This is the great and momentous word in Scripture, which hath given rise to endless disputes, and employed the minds of men in all ages to explain; and yet to thousands still remains as obscure as ever. But notwithstanding: all that the bewildered and erroneous mind of man may say on faith, the scriptural account of faith is the simplest and plainest thing in the world. Faith is no more than the sincere and hearty assent and consent of the mind to the belief of the being and promises of God, as especially revealed to the church in the person and redemption, work of the Lord Jesus Christ. JEHOVAH, in his threefold character of person, Father, Son, and Holy Ghost, hath mercifully been pleased to reveal himself as "forgiving iniquity, transgression, and sin," and giving eternal life to the church in Christ Jesus. And these blessings are all declared to be in the person, and procured to the church by the sole undertaking of the Lord Jesus Christ, as the glorious Head of his body the church, the fulness of him "that filleth all in all."

The hearty, cordial, and sincere belief in these blessed truths of God is called faith, because it is giving credit to the testimony of God, and relying upon his faithfulness for the fulfilment of them. The apostle John, in his first Epistle, fifth chapter, and ninth and following verses, puts this doctrine in so clear a point of view, that, under divine teaching, if attended to, it would be impossible to mistake it. "If we receive (saith John) the witness of men, the witness of God is greater; for this is the witness of God which he hath testified of his Son. He that believeth on the Son of God hath the witness in himself. He that believeth not God, hath made him a liar, because he believeth not the record that God gave of his Son. And this is the record that God hath given to us, eternal life; and this life is in his Son. He that hath the Son, hath life; and he that hath not the Son of God, hath not life."

No form of words could have been more happily chosen to state what is the act of faith, and to put it in a clear and full light. Immense and unspeakable blessings are promised by God. It is not the greatness of the blessings which demands our faith, but the greatness of the Being promising. Indeed, the greater the blessings are, the greater would be the difficulty of believing, unless some other warrant and authority become the foundation for belief. The bottom, therefore, of all faith is, that what we are called upon to is that cannot lie; JEHOVAH that will not lie. An Almighty Promiser that never can out-promise himself. Hence, when Moses at the bush desired a confirmation of the truth, the Lord gave him to deliver to Israel, by knowing his name, and having such assurances to make to them as might silence every doubt. "Behold, (said he,) when I come to the children of Israel, and shall say unto them, The God of your fathers hath sent me unto you, and they shall say unto me, What is his name? what shall I say unto them? And God said unto Moses, I AM THAT I AM." That is, I AM a being self-existing, and eternal; and which, therefore, gives a being to all my promises. So that this is the sure ground of faith. Not the greatness and blessedness of the promise; but the greatness, blessedness, and faithfulness of the Promiser. And to believe in the almighty Promiser in his assurances in Christ, is faith. I only add, however, under this article, that though faith is the simplest and plainest act of the mind, yet both the possession and the exercise of it is the gift of God. "Unto you, (saith an apostle,) it is given to believe." (Phil. i. 29.) And hence every truly awakened and regenerated believer finds daily reason, to cry out, as the apostle did to Christ, "Lord, increase our faith!" (Luke xvii. 5.)

FAITHFUL

After what hath been said under the foregoing article of faith, I shall not think it necessary to add much on the subject of faithfulness. The sense of it is very obvious. I only beg to observe, that it appears from Scripture the Lord delights to be known to his people, in his covenant engagements, by this distinguishing perfection. That sweet passage delivered to the church by Moses, is a most decided proof of it: "Know, therefore, that the Lord thy God, he is God; the faithful God, which keepeth covenant and mercy with the that love him and keep his commandments to a thousand generations." (Deut. vi. 9. See also 1 Sam. ii. 34. Ps. Lxxix.37. 1 Cor. i. 9. 1 Thess. v 24. Rev. i. 5; xix. 11.)

FALL

The fall of man is among the first of the portraits in the Bible on the great subject of redemption. When Adam came out of the hands of his gracious Creator, we are told, that he was created in the image of God. By which I apprehend, that he was formed in similitude to him who is "the image of the invisible God, the first born of every creature." "Let us make man in our image, after our likeness." (Gen. i. 26.) What image? Not the image of JEHOVAH as JEHOVAH, for JEHOVAH is invisible; but, according to what the apostle Paul hath delivered to the church, by the authority and instruction of the Holy Ghost, in the image of him who before all worlds stood up, at the call of God, as the glorious Head of his body the church secretly, though not openly, the "first-born of every creature." Let the reader read the whole passage. (Col. i. 15, &c.) "Who is the image of the invisible God, the first-born of every creature. For by him were all things created that are in heaven and that are in earth, visible and invisible; whether they be thrones, or dominions, or principalities, or powers, all things were created by him and for him: and he is before all things, and by him all things consist. And he is the Head of the body, the church; who is the beginning, the first-born from the dead, that in all things he might have the pre-eminence." Now from hence it plainly appears that Christ as Christ, that is, God and man in one person, had a priority of existence to every other, and was, and is, he image of the invisible JEHOVAH, in whose likeness Adam, the first man, was made. It appears also, that by him, that is, God and man in one person, all things were created. God created all things, we are told, by Jesus Christ. (Ephes. iii. 9.)

And it farther appears, that all things were not only created by him, but for him. The whole cause for which JEHOVAH went forth in acts of creation, as relating to our world, was for the glory of our Lord Jesus Christ. Yea, more than this; for the same Scripture saith, that he is not only before all things, but by him all things consist. As if this image of the invisible God became the only foundation for creation to rest upon, and the only power to preserve and keep the whole together. This image then of the invisible God was the Person in whose likeness, it should seem, Adam, the first man of the earth, was formed. And, therefore, in the holiness of that similitude, as well in mind as in body, our first parent came forth from the hands of his infinite and kind Creator.

By the fall he lost this resemblance, and all his faculties became ruined and defiled; yea, his whole nature virtually all sin. Hence the Scriptures, under the strongest expressions, speak of the mighty ruin. His understanding became darkened, so as to lose the knowledge of God. (Ephes. iv. 18, 19.) His affections became carnal, sensual, and devilish. (Ephes. ii. 1-3. James iii. 15.) His will stubborn, rebellious, proud, and disobedient. (1 Pet. iv. 3.). Yea, his whole mind enmity against God. (Rom. viii. 7.) The Psalmist, and after him the apostle Paul, hath given some of the more striking features of fallen man, when he saith, "The Lord looked down from heaven upon the children of men, to see if there were any that did understand and seek after God." But the result of the divine enquiry was, that "they were all gone aside, they were altogether become filthy, there was none that did good, no not one." (Ps. xiv. 2. 3. with Rom. iii. 10-19.) Such is the Scripture account of the fall.

Blessed be He that, by his great undertaking, hath restored our poor nature from the ruins of the fall, and by uniting his church, which is his body, to himself, hath given to us a better righteousness than man had before. The holiness of Adam was but the holiness of the creature, peaceable, capable of being lost; and was lost. The holiness of the Lord Jesus, in which all his redeemed are beheld and accepted before God, is the holiness of God-man, perfect, and incapable of being ever lost or lessened. How precious the thought! So then, our present fallen state is not the original state of man, neither is it the final state. In Jesus and his righteousness the injury sustained by the fall is more than repaired, and the everlasting welfare of the church, which is his body, eternally secured from all the possibility of loss from an union and oneness with him. Hail! thou glorious, gracious, holy one of God, "the Lord our righteousness." (Jer. xxiii. 6.)

FAMINE

Is one of God's four sore judgments which the Lord threatened to send upon Jerusalem; the sword, and the famine, the noisome beast, and the pestilence, to cut off from it man and beast. (See Ezek. xiv. 22.) And though it may be said by some, that famine may be induced by natural causes, yet it must be allowed by those who believe the Scripture, that natural causes are but the agents and instruments of divine appointment. Who can doubt but that the plenty in Egypt, which was succeeded by seven years famine, was to bring about the gracious purposes of the Lord concerning Joseph and his family, that Israel might be led out of Egypt? Who can question that the famine in the days of Elisha was the same, when we are told, that the Lord called for it seven years. (2 Kings viii. 1.) And who will put down to natural causes what the Lord accomplished lay instruments, in themselves so feeble, when in the days of Joel the Lord's great army ate up the whole produce of the land? (Joel 1, 2, etc.)

But reader! how dreadful soever a famine in a land may be, when for the wickedness of the people the Lord sends it, yet the word of God speaks of a famine yet more alarming. How very solemn are the words of the Lord, by the prophet, on this subject, Amos viii. 11, 12. "Behold, the days come, saith the Lord God, that I will send a famine in the land, not a famine of bread, nor a thirst for water, but of hearing the words of the Lord. And they shall wander from sea to sea, and from the north even unto the east; they shall run to and fro to seek the word of the Lord, and shall not find it." What an awful sentence is this! And by as much as the soul is infinitely more important in value than the body, by so much must be the famine of living bread here threatened. But to what period of the church are we to look for its accomplishment? Was it not eminently fulfilled in the instance of the house of Israel, when, after their rejecting the Lord of life and glory, the Lord scattered them over the face of the earth, and left the nation to a wandering state, "without a king, without a prince, without a sacrifice, without an image, without an ephod, and without teraphim?' Yea, are they not still in this awful state? Oh! that that sweet promise may be hastening for its accomplishment, which the prophet who related the famined state of Israel declared also, by the same authority, should be at length fulfilled. "Afterward (said he,) shall the children of Israel return, and seek the Lord their God, and David their king; and shall fear the Lord and his goodness many days." (Hos. iii. 4, 5.) But let not the reader close up his view of this spiritual famine as it relates to the Jews, without going farther, and enquiring whether the threatening may not belong equally to the Gentile church? yea, and whether it is not now in the present hour accomplishing in the earth? Is there not a famine of hearing the word of the Lord in numberless places which are called Christian countries, as well as idolatrous lands? Are there not multitudes who call themselves after Christ, but yet know no more of him than the name? Yea, to come nearer home, are there not villages and country places in this kingdom where the spiritual famine prevails, notwithstanding our land is called, a land of Bibles, and societies for disseminating the word of God are every where opening? Alas! while the grand and distinguishing principles of the faith of Christ are so openly and impudently denied; while God the Father's gracious purposes in the gift of salvation by his dear Son, is thought nothing of; while the GODHEAD of Christ, and redemption wholly by his blood, is daringly opposed; and while the person, work, and influence of God the Holy Ghost is not made the very foundation of a sinner's hope, in reading the sacred word to make wise unto salvation; while these things are kept in the back ground, and the object with many in teaching is but to introduce a flimsy system of morality to supply the place of vital godliness, is there not still a famine, yea, with many, with the Bible in their hand? Pious regenerated Christians see this, and find cause to mourn in secret over it; while they can only pray the Lord to take away the reproach of our land, and remove this spiritual famine from our people. Oh, for Jesus, the living bread, to feed his people with true understanding and knowledge!

FAST and FASTING

There seems to have been a disposition in all men, and from the earliest ages of antiquity, to testify a somewhat of sorrow in the mind in all abstinence, at certain times, and upon certain occasions, from food, by way of punishment for sin. Indeed, real and unfeigned sorrow of the heart will of itself naturally induce abstinence. For let a man be supposed to return from his labour with a keen appetite, and let it be supposed, that some one meets him at the door of his house with any evil tidings, his child or some beloved friend is dead, or himself threatened with some adversity; we know that the sudden relation of such, or the like calamities, will have an immediate effect to check the propensity of hunger. But whether the first observance of fasts had their origin in those feelings of nature, I would not presume to say; yet certain it is, the very mind of man since the fall hath always leaned to somewhat of doing, or suffering, by way of propitiation for the sins and transgressions of nature. We find this principle very general in the history of mankind. The Jews were very tenacious of their fast days; so were, and so are, the Musselmen of the Turks; and so are modern Christians, who observe the ritual of the form, more than regard the power of godliness. No one can doubt, who knows any thing of the human frame and character, that every individual by nature feels in himself a disposition to enter into a compromise or commutation with God; and if the Lord would but relax in certain demands which are enforced, he shall have offerings, of another kind by way of compensation or atonement. The cry of the heart in that sinner the prophet Micah speaks of, is the cry of every man's heart, more or less, however differently expressed in the various languages of the earth. "Wherewith shall I come before the Lord, and bow myself before the High God? shall I come before him with burnt offerings, with calves of a year old? Will the Lord be pleased with thousands of rams, or with ten thousands of rivers of oil? Shall I give my first-born for my transgression; the fruit of my body for the sin of my soul?" (Micah vi. 6, 7). But the grand question in relation to fasts is, What saith the word of God concerning them? We certainly do not read any thing in the divine appointment of fasts before the days of Moses, and in the patriarchal age. And under the law, excepting the solemn day of atonement, there are no express precepts on the subject. That the people of God set apart days and seasons for the affliction of the soul is most certain, and this by divine command, (Lev. xxiii. 27.29.) but the reader will be careful to observe, that there is a wide distinction between the sorrow of soul and the fasting of the body. It is concerning fasts we are now speaking; and the subject is, what authority do they derive for observance in Scripture? When holy men of old were, in their hallowed seasons, mourning over the sins of fallen nature, no doubt the bodies were neglected, in numberless instances, in refusing to take food. Indeed, when the soul is absorbed in grief, the body will feel but little inclination to meat. Joshua and the elders of Israel fell upon their faces before the ark, and put dust upon their heads, when the men of Ai had a momentary triumph over Israel. (Josh. vii. 6.) David fasted in the case of his child's sickness. (2 Sam. xii. 16.) And the apostle Paul, in the time of his conversion, was three days without sight, and neither did eat nor drink. (Acts ix. 9.) But all these, and many others of a similar kind, were effects from predisposing causes, in which fasting became involuntary, and not enjoined.

Our blessed Lord gives directions how fasts are to be observed, with an eye to the gracious improvement of them, but hath not appointed any particular seasons for their observance. (See Matt. vi. 16-18.) From whence arose the long ritual in the Romish church, and the special season of Ember Weeks, and the Wednesdays and Fridays in every week, and the vigil before every saint's day, and the whole of Lent, it is difficult to say. But while men of no religion, and strangers to vital godliness, may, and will take up with the outside of piety, and abstain from their ordinary food on fast days, and glut the appetite with dainties on feast days; the great question still again recurs, what can we gather from the word of God of instruction in relation to fasting? I answer in the words of the apostle, "The kingdom of God is not meat and drink, but righteousness and peace, and joy in the Holy Ghost." (Rom. iv. 17.)

The life of a truly regenerated believer in Christ, is at all times, and upon all occasions, a life of abstinence and self-denial. Every child of God well knows from his own experience, arising from a body of sin and death that he carries about him, that fleshly lusts of every kind war against the soul; that it is impossible to be too strict in abridging every species of indulgence in the body; and that pampering the flesh, is only causing that flesh to rebel. Hence, therefore, he desires to observe a perpetual fast in things pertaining to the body, that through grace he may put on the Lord Jesus Christ, "making no provision for the flesh, to fulfil the lust thereof." (Rom. xiii. 14.) But after the most rigid observance of humblings in the body, it is the distinguishing character of a truly regenerated believer in Christ, that neither by fastings, nor prayers, nor alms-deeds, nor offerings, no, nor the whole observance of outward or inward things, can poor fallen man recommend himself to God. Well is it for the faithful follower of Jesus, that He, the glorious High Priest of our profession, "beareth away the iniquity of our most holy things." (Exod. xxviii. 38.) Our fast sins, our prayer sins, our ordinance sins, all need the cleansing laver of his blood to take away, and but for this there could be no acceptation of our persons, but the holy jealousy of the Lord in the midst of fasting, prayer and humiliation, might consume us on our very knees.

FAT

In Scripture language there is something of great importance in this word. It is used upon many occasions to signify the best of the thing to whatsoever it is applied. Thus the fat of the earth is made use of to denote the whole of temporal blessings. Thus Isaac's prophetical blessings to Jacob. (Gen. xxvii. 28.) "God give thee of the dew of heaven and the fatness of the earth, and plenty of corn and wine." And as these temporal blessings were the consequence of spiritual mercies, and these all founded in Christ, nothing can be plainer than that the fatness had an eye to Him, in whom all nations of the earth were to be blessed. Hence, with reference to the same, the Psalmist saith, "My soul shall be satisfied as with marrow and fatness." (Ps. lxiii. 5.)

The soul cannot be satisfied with earthly things; but these are figurative expressions, to intimate the soul-enriching blessings in Jesus. Now from these explanations, we may discover what was all along alluded to in the fat of the Jewish offerings. If the reader will consult the Old Testament on the subject, he will find that in all the offerings made by fire, the fat was wholly the Lord's. (Lev. ii. 9. to the end.) And as it was uniformly connected with the blood of the altar, it should seem to have been intended all along to mean Christ. And hence it should seem also to have been meant in allusion to the wicked who despise Christ, that they setup their own righteousness in opposition to the righteousness of Jesus. Thus Jeshurun "waxed fat and kicked: thou art waxen fat, thou art grown thick; thou art covered with fatness. Then he forsook God which made him, and lightly esteemed the Rock (the Christ) of his salvation." (Deut. xxxii. 15.) Hence also, such characters are said to be "enclosed in their own fat." (Ps. xvii. 16.) If these views be well founded, it may serve also by way of additional testimony to the truth of Scripture, that the law in all points was but a shadow, the body is Christ. And JEHOVAH so strikingly saying, "all the fat is the Lord's," (Lev. iii, 16.) sets forth that Christ is the Christ of God. (1 Cor. iii. 23.)

FATHER

This name in Scripture hath many applications. Not only the father of a family and head of an house or tribe, but also it is frequently put for the inventor of any art or science. Thus Jubal is said to have been the father of such as dwell in tents; and "Tubal the father of all such as handle the harp or organ." (Gen. iv. 20.) And in a yet more interesting sense, the word of God calls them father, who stand distinguished in the church in a way of pre-eminency, such as Abraham, the father of the faithful, so called for the greatness of his faith. And so on the contrary, the wicked and ungodly are called evil. Hence Christ told the enemies of his gospel, "Ye are of your father the devil, and the lusts of your father ye will do." (John viii. 44.)

But while we carefully attend to these distinctions, respecting the application of the name of father in Scripture it should be always kept in remembrance that the name Father is in a peculiar and blessed sense had in special reference to God, as "the father of our Lord Jesus Christ, of whom the whole family in heaven and earth is named." (Eph. iii. 14, 15.)

Hence, in relation to him under this sweet appellation and character, the Lord Jesus himself said to Mary after he arose from the dead, "I ascend unto my Father and your Father, and to my God and your God." (John xx. 17.) Christ also is the everlasting Father of his church and people. (Isa. ix. 6.) I refer the reader to what was said under the article Abba, for the farther view of the blessedness of this relationship. Nothing can be more sweet or consolatory. (Let the reader consult also those Scriptures, Matt. xxiii. 9. Isa. lxiii. 16. Mal. ii. 10.)

FEAR

There are several ideas intended to be conveyed to the mind, by that passion which is called in Scripture fear. There is but one creature in the creation of God, that is said to be wholly void of fear, namely, the leviathan. (Job xli. 33.) The fear for the most part spoken of by the word of God, is what relates to our nature, of which there is a threefold description, natural fear, sinful fear and holy fear. Since the fall of man, the whole race of Adam have known the effects both of natural and sinful fear; none but the regenerated are acquainted with what is known in Scripture by a religious, or holy fear.

Natural and slavish fear, arising from a conscious sense of sin, manifested itself immediately upon the fall, when Adam sought to hide himself from the presence of the Lord amidst the trees of the garden. (See Gen. iii. 8.) But when a poor sinner is awakened from the sleep and death of sin, and brought forth to a new and spiritual life, "perfect love casteth out fear." Hence the apostle saith, "Ye have not received the Spirit of bondage again to fear; but ye have received the Spirit of adoption, whereby we cry, Abba, Father." (Rom. viii. 15.) It is very blessed when freed from slavish fear. And it is very blessed to have that child-like fear which marks the Lord's people. And it is very blessed to discover how the slavish fear which bringeth bondage is removed, and from whence the holy child-like fear is derived. The sweet promise of God by the prophet explains the whole. (Jer. xxxii. 40.) "I will make an everlasting covenant with them, that I will not turn away from them to do them good; but I will put my fear in their hearts, that they shall not depart from me."

I will only add, for the comfort and encouragement of the Lord's timid and tried ones, who, in the midst of strong faith, feel at times much natural fear, that it is sweetly accommodating to consider the Lord Jesus Christ, in the days of his flesh, was graciously pleased in this, as in all other points of grace, to be our example. Of Jesus it is said, that "though he were a Son, yet learned he obedience, by the things which he suffered. And in the days of his flesh he offered up prayers and supplications, with strong crying and tears, unto him that was able to save him from death, and was heard in that he feared." (Heb. v. 7, 8.) Sweet and precious thought! "Jesus who knew no sin, yet coming to us in the likeness of sinful flesh, and for sin condemned sin in the flesh, knew what it was to be sore amazed, to be sorrowful even unto death, to fear, and to be very heavy. Reader, think how Jesus sympathizes with his people under their fears, and heaviness, and sorrow of heart.

FEASTS

In the Jewish church we find much said concerning the festivals observed; and what makes the subject important is, that they were of the Lord's own appointment. They had the constant feast of the Sabbath every seventh day, in commemoration of the Lord's resting on the seventh day from the works of creation. And when the church was formed in the wilderness, they had the several feasts as appointed in regular order. The feast of the Passover, typical of the Lord Jesus Christ, on their going out of Egypt. The feast of Pentecost, the fifteenth day from the Passover, in commemoration of the giving of the Law on mount Sinai, fifty days after the people left Egypt. They had also the feast of Tabernacles, which formed the third great feast of the year, in which all the males were enjoined to appear before the Lord. (Deut. xvi. 16.) These were among the standing feasts appointed by the Lord in the church of Israel.

But beside these, they had others by the same appointment. The feast of Trumpets of the New Moon; the feasts of Expiation, or, as the Jews called it, Chippur; that is, pardon; because on this day it was considered, that an act of grace took place from heaven, for the cleansing the sins and infirmities of all the people through the year. What a striking allusion to that great day of the Lord Jesus, when "by the one offering of himself once offered, he perfected for ever them that were sanctified!" (Heb. x. 14.) And what a beautiful correspondence to the same, was the prophet Zechariah's account of this glorious event, when hosts: "I will remove the iniquity of that land in one day." (Zech. iii. 9.)

In this account of the Jewish feasts we must not overlook the feast of Jobel, or Jubilee Trumpets, in the forty-ninth year, called the Sabbatical year, or seven times seven. For surely, nothing could be more striking as typical of the Lord Jesus Christ. The Lord made a blessed provision, by this feast, for the freedom of every poor captive in the land. I refer the reader to the account of it in the Scriptures themselves, (Lev. xxv. throughout;) for it would not come within the limits of the present work, to go through the particulars. But of all the subjects in the Jewish church, which pointed in a direct allusion to the Lord Jesus Christ, there is not one more striking. And I venture to believe, that though this trumpet was never sounded but once in forty-nine years, and consequently few, if any, ever heard it before, or ever lived to hear it a second

Jubilee, yet there was not a soul in the camp but understood the joyful sound, and felt the meaning (if I may be allowed the expression,) like the archangel's trumpet, as it will be understood by all flesh, when Jesus comes to judgment. The rigorous master on the morning of the Jubilee, whose tyranny then expired, understood by it his sentence. And what were the feelings of the poor oppressed servant, whom the Lord hath then made free, when the mornirgshered in the sound of the blessed, though never before heard, trumpet!

I hope the reader will not overlook the sweetest and most interesting part of this feast of the Jubilee. It was the Lord Jesus in his great salvation who was thus proclaimed. Every poor sinner, captive to Satan, sin, and hell, who heard the sound, heard it in the sweet voice, "Ye have sold yourselves for nought, and ye shall be redeemed without money, saith the Lord." (Isa. lii. 3.)

I think it highly proper, before I dismiss this article concerning the Jewish feasts, to remark to the reader, the distinguishing privilege we enjoy in the Christian church, in having all in one the sum and substance of every feast in the person, work, grace, and glory of our Lord Jesus Christ. We have our Christian Sabbaths weekly, in which we commemorate all the blessings of creation, redemption, and sanctification at once. And all believers in Christ truly find their sabbaths to be all this and more.

Doth not every regenerated child of God in honouring the Lord's day, honour at the same time the Lord's work; and while he celebrates God the Father's resting from the works of the old creation, celebrate also God the Father's work in the new creation of his precious soul in Christ Jesus? (See Ephes. ii. 10.) And in the celebration of the sabbath in honour of God the Son, who by his triumph over death, hell, and the grave, when he arose on that day, and manifested himself to be the resurrection and the life; doth not every regenerated child of God thereby prove, "that he is risen with Christ from dead works, to serve the living and true God?" Yea, doth he not manifest his personal interest in that sweet promise, by those acts of giving honour to his Lord, where it said, "Blessed and holy is he that hath part in the first resurrection; on such the second death hath no power." (Rev. xx. 5.) And is not God the Holy Ghost glorified and honoured in the Christian sabbath, at the renewal of the sacred day, in that then is celebrated his first open and visible display of his love and mercy over the church, when at Pentecost he came down upon the people? Doth not every regenerated child of God here also, as in the other instances, testify, that it is by the sovereignty of his power and grace, he is quickened to a new and spiritual life, and now waits again on the Lord, in his holy ordinance of the sabbath, for the renewing of the Holy Ghost to be shed on him abundantly, through Jesus Christ our Lord? (Tit. iii. 5, 6.)

Surely, these are very clear and incontestible evidences of the true commemoration of the Christian sabbath, when, in the observance, special and distinct acts of praise and honour, are given to each glorious person of the GODHEAD, as they are represented to us in the Scriptures of truth, in the several character-offices of their divine agency. And thus while each and every one hath the special and distinct acts of praise given to them, for the special acts of grace and mercy shewn to the church in Christ, the whole form one and the same glorious object of adoration, love, and praise, as the eternal undivided JEHOVAH, Father, Son, and Holy Ghost, both to the church on earth, and in heaven, to all eternity.

Reader it is most blessed thus to see and enjoy our privileges. The believer's feast is a continual feast; yea, an increasing everlasting feast, a daily sabbath. Jesus himself is indeed the Jubilee; yea, the very sabbath of the soul. And when at his house,

FED and FEED - FELLOW

at his table, at his ordinances, in his word, in every promise, and by every providence, the soul is kept alive by grace in him, the feast is not at stated periods only, but continual. Jesus is the life of the soul; and the portion for ever.

FED and FEED

The expression of feeding in Scripture is, sometimes applied in a good sense, and sometimes in a bad one. When men are nourished with the word of life, they are said to be fed. Hence the Lord promised to give pastors to the church, "that should feed his people with understanding and knowledge? (Jer. iii. 15.) And on the contrary, in those who take up with false doctrines, they are said to feed on wind. (Hos. xii. 5.) to feed on ashes, and the like. (Isa. xliv. 20.)

But the general and principal use of the term in Scripture of feeding, is applied to the Lord Jesus Christ. "He shall feed his flock like a shepherd." (Isa. xliv. 11.) And as feeding is a comprehensive expression, to denote every thing relating to the office of a shepherd, so whenever this act of love and attention is spoken of in allusion to the Lord Jesus Christ, it means to convey the whole of his character, both in his relation as a shepherd to his people, and the tenderness of his care over them. The church is his flock, his property, his purchase, his glory. He hath a perfect knowledge of all his sheep. He provides pasture; yea, is himself their food and portion. He protects from beasts of prey, heals the diseased, gathers home the wanderer, leads the flock out to wholesome pastures, and, in short, doth the whole office of a shepherd; and doth it in such a way, and with so much love and tenderness, that they are most blessed who belong to his fold. Sweet thought of the Psalmist, and which equally may be taken up by every lamb of Christ's fold: "The Lord is my shepherd, I shall not want." (Ps. xxiii, throughout.)

FELLOW

I should not have thought it necessary to have called the reader's attention to this word, had it not been to remark to him, the great beauty of it in a double sense, when applied to the person of the Lord Jesus Christ in relation to his fellowship with his Father in the nature and essence of the GODHEAD, and in relation to his fellowship with his church in the human nature; under both which the Lord Jesus appears so lovely and so endeared to his people, as to render him most interesting indeed.

In the former sense of the word, as applied to Christ, or spoken of him, we have that very precious unequalled passage of the Lord, by the prophet Zechariah, thirteenth chapter, and seventh verse, where JEHOVAH calls him by this name, "The man that is my fellow, saith the Lord of hosts." Every one who knows any thing of the common terms made use of among men, knows also, that fellow means equal. The very name, indeed, would lose all its force and meaning, when spoken of persons in common, if there were supposed the least inequality between them. And this runs through all ranks and orders of the people, from the king to the beggar. The king's fellow, and the beggar's fellow, is perfectly understood as implying a common level. How truly blessed, therefore, is the word as applied by JEHOVAH himself to the person of the Lord Jesus Christ. Who but must rejoice, when he thus receives God the Father's own testimony to the oneness and fellowship in the divine nature between God the Father, and God the Son. "The man that is my fellow, saith the Lord of hosts."

In like manner, on the same ground, how very blessed is it to consider him who, in his divine nature, is fellow to the Lord of hosts; in his human nature, is fellow to his church and people. Here again, the Lord JEHOVAH, the Father, gives the like testimony; for speaking to Joshua, the type of Jesus, the Lord saith, "Here now, O

Joshua the high priest, thou and thy fellows that sit before thee, for they are men wondered at" (Zech. iii. 8.) Wondered at indeed, to be fellow to him in his human nature, who, in his divine nature, "is fellow to the Lord of hosts!" But so it is: for the truth is undeniable. Hence Jesus himself, by the spirit of prophecy, under the ministry of a prophet, is introduced as saying, "Behold, I and the children whom the Lord hath given me, are for signs and wonders in Israel; from the Lord of hosts, which dwelleth in mount Zion." (Isa. viii. 18.) See this more fully explained, Heb. ii. 11-13.) Hence also, the Holy Ghost bears testimony to the same in that glorious Scripture, when speaking of his mediatorial throne, and the covenanting of Christ for his people; "Thy throne, O God, is for ever and ever; the sceptre of thy kingdom is a right sceptre. Thou lovest righteousness, and hatest wickedness; therefore God, thy God, hath anointed thee with the oil of gladness above (or for) thy fellows:" for so the word may be rendered. And if I were writing a Concordance for the learned, and not for the poor man, I should say the original will justify that it should be, *non præ consortibus, sedpropter consortes*. (Compare Ps. xlv. 6, 7. with Heb. i. 8, 9.)

Now I beg the reader to ponder well the subject, and mark with me the blessedness and the preciousness of it. Here are all the persons in JEHOVAH testifying to this glorious character of the Lord Jesus, as the fellow of the Lord of hosts in his divine nature. And let me ask, what can be more blessed or precious? In the one, how glorious to consider the foundation and security of all that is interesting to our hopes for the life that now is, and that which is to come. And in the other, how very sweet and lovely it is, to know our nearness and fellow partnership in all that is in Christ Jesus as the Head and Husband of his body the church, "the fulness of him that filleth all in all." O! with what rapture ought every child of God to read what the Holy Ghost saith to this purport, in the close of the second chapter of the Hebrews. "For verily he took not on him the nature of angels; but he took on him the seed of Abraham. Wherefore in all things it behoved him to be made like unto his brethren, that he might be a merciful and faithful high priest in things pertaining to God, to make reconciliation for the sins of the people. For in that he himself hath suffered, being tempted, he is able to succour them that are tempted."

And now I hope from such unanswerable testimonies to this great truth as are found in all the persons of the GODHEAD witnessing to it, the reader will never be in danger of being led away from the uniform and unceasing belief, that he who in his infinite grace and mercy hath made himself our fellow, is, and hath been from all eternity, fellow to the Lord of hosts. If any would teach a contrary doctrine, let him first solemnly declare whether God the Holy Ghost hath taught it him. This question, if properly applied, would be a dreadful silencing to all such as pretend to be "wise above what is written." And I would solemnly recommend also, every one of this description, who, under the pretence of candour, is literally joining, however unintentionally, the Infidel's cause, to read the history of Nadab and Abihu, Lev. x. 2. and Uzzah, 2 Sam. vi. 6, 7. With such tremendous judgments in view, we should hear no more of such presumptuous reasonings.

And while the Lord Jesus himself bears testimony to the fellowship and equality between himself and his Father, saying, "I and my Father are one," (John x. 30.) none after this would fancy fellow meant neighbour. Neither would such venture to say, when our Lord quoted the passage of Zechariah, which he did in the hour of his sufferings, (see Zech. xiii. 7. compared with Matt. xxv. 31, 32.) he meant no more than a mere proverbial expression, and had not the most distinct relation to his sufferings and death.

FELLOWSHIP

The gospel sense of this, and especially in the Epistle of John, (chap. i. 1-3.) hath somewhat most endearing in it. The Greek word the apostle useth to express it, means partnership; and implies, that the church in and through Christ, hath an interest in all that belongs to Christ. (1 Cor. i. 9.)

FIG TREE

I should not think it necessary to notice this article in our Concordance, but for the occasion that offers thereby of making an observation on the fig tree which the Lord Jesus blighted near Bethany. It may be proper, for the better apprehension of the subject, to remark, that the fig tree grew, in Palestine, not unfrequently in the roads, and highways, and hedges, beside those that were cultivated in. the gardens. It is plain, that this fig tree which Christ withered was of this kind; a hedge fruit, and, consequently, it was no man's property. Matthew's account of this transaction is, that when Jesus "saw this fig tree in the way, he came to it, and found nothing but leaves only; and said unto it, Let no fruit grow on thee hence forward for ever: and presently the fig tree withered away." (Matt. xxi. 18.) And Mark adds to this relation, that "the time of figs was not yet." (Mark xi. 13.)

It is very evident from hence, that the Lord Jesus had an object of much higher moment to set forth by this action, than the mere blighting a hedge fig tree. For surely, the Lord did not expect fruit out of season; neither did he mean, as some have supposed, to shew anger, to a fig tree. It is well known, that in the eastern world almost all instruction was conveyed by parable and figure. And so much did the Lord Jesus, in his divine teaching, fall in with this popular way of conveying knowledge, that at one time we are told "without a parable spake he not unto them." (Matt. xiii. 34.) The question becomes exceedingly interesting to know, what particular instruction to his disciples the Lord meant to have impressed on their minds by this event.

Perhaps I may be singular in my view of the subject. But if I err, may the Lord pity and pardon my ignorance, and the reader find no injury from my statement of it. The whole stress of the subject, as it strikes me, is in the nature and quality of this fig tree. It was hedge fruit. It was in the highway; and no man's property. Now the church is expressly compared by the Lord himself to a fig tree of his own, and planted in his vineyard. (Luke xiii. 6.) And the prophet, in the Old Testament dispensation, celebrated the glories of God's grace to the church under a similar figure of his planting his vineyard with a choice vine. (Isa. v. 1. &c.) The fruitless fig tree of the hedge, and which at the command of Jesus withered away, according to my view of the subject, was intended by the Lord to represent the mere professors of the gospel, who to a traveller afford leaves, but no fruit. It is, indeed, without; not in the garden, the church. It cannot bring forth fruit unto God; for the Lord saith, when speaking of his church, "From me is thy fruit found." (Hos. xiv. 8.) Jesus hath a right and property in his people. They are his, both by the Father's gift, and by his own purchase. And he hath brought them in, and fenced them round, and they are "trees of his right hand planting." (Isa. lxi 3.)

The instant withering of the barren fig tree, at Christ's command, became the emblem of what must ultimately follow all the way-side productions in nature, void of grace, at the great day of the Lord. And our Lord's own comment upon the blasted tree, seems very fully to justify this view of the subject. For when the disciples remarked to Jesus how soon the fig tree was withered away, the Lord made this striking answer, "Have faith in God." As if he had said, all are but the mere leaves of profession where there is no vital union in me. As he said elsewhere, "I am the vine; ye are the branches." (John xv. 5.) If this be the right sense of the passage, and the Lord Jesus meant to teach his disciples thereby, that every hedge fig tree hath no part in the church, no owner in Christ by his Father's gift or purchase, no union with him, and, consequently, no communion in his graces, but must in the hour of decision instantly wither away; then will this parable of the barren fig tree form one testimony more to the numberless other testimonies with which the word of God abounds, that the children of the wicked one, and the children of the kingdom, are totally separate and dissimilar from everlasting, and so must continue to everlasting. Tares can never become wheat; neither can wheat become tares. Goats must remain goats; for their nature cannot admit in them the nature of sheep. The fig tree of the hedge, never planted in the vineyard of Jesus, hath no fruit in him; and, consequently, always barren. So infinitely important is it, to be found in Christ.

FINGER

The finger of God. This is a very common expression in Scripture, to denote the works of God. Thus the magicians in the court of Pharaoh were compelled to acknowledge the finger of God concerning several of the ten plagues of Egypt which the Lord brought upon the Egyptians. It appears, that the Lord permitted the magicians, in certain instances, to be led into the persuasion, that their arts produced similar effects to the works of Moses and Aaron. Such as in the case of the rods becoming serpents; but even here, is if to draw the striking difference, Aaron's rod swallowed up their rods. (Exod. vii. 10-12.) So in the turning the river into blood. (Exod. iii. 19. 21, 22.) But this permission was evidently intended to the better conviction of their minds in other instances; and accordingly we find the magicians themselves openly confessing, in the case of the lice on man and beast, "This is the finger of God." Exod. viii. 19. Our blessed Lord, in the days of his flesh, speaking of his miracles, made use of the same phrase. "If I (said Jesus) with the finger of God cast out devils, no doubt, the kingdom of God is come upon you." (Luke xi. 20. See Exod. xxxi. 18.)

The expression of the finger, for the whole action, is not to us in the western world a circumstance so generally understood; but it appears, that in the east the greater part of the transactions in common life were carried on by those means. The silence observed by them would to us be astonishing. Servants seldom spoke in the presence of their masters. They received, for the most part, all their commands by signs; and in their approach to their lord observed the most profound silence. By the gesticulation of the body, the motion of the eye, or the expression of the finger, directions were conveyed, and never misunderstood.

Some writer of ancient date hath interpreted one of the psalms of David (the hundred and twenty-third), under this view; and indeed, if read with an eye to this custom in the east, the beauty of it becomes abundantly more striking. Suppose David in that psalm had reference to the great humility and awe with which the lowest servants approach their lord, the expressions of his soul in that sweet psalm would strike the mind as if thus speaking: "Unto thee lift I up mine eyes, O thou that dwellest in the heavens. Behold, as the eyes of servants look unto the hand of their masters, and as the eyes of a maiden to the hand of her mistress, even so our eyes wait upon the Lord our God, until he have mercy upon us."

FINISH

This is a blessed word in Scripture language in application to the Lord Jesus Christ. The prophet Daniel, when proclaiming to the church the time of the Messiah's coming, added this also, as the distinguishing feature

FIRE - FIRE

of his mission. He was to be anointed as the Most Holy, to finish the transgression, and to make an end of sin. (Dan. ix 24.) And Zechariah no less, while describing him as the great Zerubbabel declared, that the same hands which laid the foundation of the spiritual temple should also finish it. (Zech. iv. 9.) And the Lord Jesus himself, speaking in his mediatorial character as the Sent and Servant of JEHOVAH, in the close of his ministry, lifted his eyes to heaven, and said, "Father, I have glorified thee on the earth; I have finished the work which thou gavest me to do." (John xvii. 4.) And in confirmation of the same, as the last act on the cross, he bowed his sacred head, and said, "It is finished!" (John xix. 30.) Think reader, what a blessed consideration this is to the mind of a poor self. condemned sinner, conscious that he can do nothing but sin; and cannot put forth a single act of his own to obtain salvation. Oh! how truly refreshing to the soul thus to behold Christ as the lawfulfiller, the sum and substance of all the types and sacrifices, and JEHOVAH'S salvation, to the ends of the earth. Jesus! I would say, add one blessing more to thy finished salvation; and "work in me both to will and to do of thy good pleasure."

FIRE

Is one of the great elements in nature by which the Lord is pleased to carry on the purposes of his holy will in the kingdoms of his government. But in Scripture language it is used upon many occasions. JEHOVAH himself is compared to a consuming fire. (Deut. iv. 24. Heb. xii. 29.) And agreeably to this, we find numberless appearances made of the divine presence in fire. To Moses at the bush, Exod. iii. 2. at the giving of the law on Mount Siani, Exod. xix. 18, 19. To Isaiah in the vision, Isa. vi. 4. To Ezekiel at the river Chebar, Ezek. i. 4. And to the beloved apostle John at Patmos, Rev. i. 14.

Add to these, the Lord is pleased to reveal himself under the similitude of fire, in several parts of Scripture. Thus the prophet Malachi describes Jesus in his priestly office as a refiner's fire. (Mal. iii. 2.) And John the Baptist, when drawing a comparison between the Lord and himself, in order to exalt his master, and set forth his own nothingness, saith, "I indeed baptize you with water unto repentance; but he that cometh after me is mightier than I, whose shoes I am not worthy to bear: he shall baptize you with the Holy Ghost, and with fire." (Matt. iii. 11.)

And it is worthy of farther remark, that many manifestations of the Lord's, under the Old Testament, were made by fire. In the covenant manifestations to Abraham, it was the representation of a "smoking furnace, and a burning lamp." (Gen. xv. 17, 18.) In the church in the wilderness, the going of the Lord before his people was under the form of a "pillar of fire." (Exod. xiii. 21.) Yea, the unceasing representation of the Lord on the altar, was by the "holy fire that never went out." (Lev. vi. 13.) And in short, the many manifestations made by fire of the Lord's presence and favour in the answers of the Lord to his servants, all shew the vast solemnity of the thing itself. (See Lev. ix. 24. Judg. xiii. 19, 20. 2 Chron. vii. 1. 1 Kings xviii. 38.)

It must not be omitted either to observe, that the ministering spirits and servants of the Lord from the upper and brighter world, are frequently spoken of under the same similitude. The Lord is said to make "his angels spirits; and his ministers a flaming fire." (Ps. civ. 4.) And the Psalmist elsewhere speaks of the chariots of God as chariots of fire, when at the Lord's brightness that "was before him, thick clouds passed, hail stones, and coals of fire." (Ps. xviii. 10-12.) And Daniel, in his lofty description, saith, that "a fiery stream issued, and came forth from before him." (Dan. vii. 10.) And Habakkuk also, "Before him (saith he,) went the pestilence, and burning coals went forth at his feet." (Habak. iii. 5.)

The word of God is compared also to fire. "Is not my word like a fire, saith the Lord, and like a hammer that breaketh the rock in pieces?" (Jer. xxiii. 29.) And hence, in allusion to the same, the Lord Jesus declares the purpose of his coming is to this effect. "I am come (saith Christ,) to send fire on the earth; and what will I, if it be already kindled?" (Luke xii. 49.) And one of the apostles declares that in the end of the dispensation of the gospel, "every man's work shall be tried by fire." (1 Cor. iii. 13.)

And lastly, to mention no more, the torments of the damned are uniformly described in Scripture under the image of fire. Some of the most sublime, and at the same time most awful passages in Scripture, are made use of in the description. Moses introduces the Lord as speaking in this language. "A fire is kindled in mine anger, and shall burn unto the lowest hell; and shall consume the earth with her increase, and set on fire the foundations of the nations." (Deut. xxxii. 22.) And Isaiah, as if in contemplation of the horrors of this eternal fire, exclaims: "The sinners in Zion are afraid; fearfulness hath surprised the hypocrites: who among us shall dwell with the devouring fire? who among us shall dwell with everlasting burnings?" (Isa. xxxiii. 14.) And our blessed Lord adopts the same language in allusion to the same awful destruction of the wicked. He speaks of a worm that never dieth, and a fire that never is quenched. And this Jesus repeats three times, following each other, in the same chapter. (Mark. ix. 44-48.) And in his solemn description of the last day, in the tremendous judgment of it, he hath already recorded the very words with which he will speak to the sinners. "Depart from me, ye cursed, into everlasting fire, prepared for the devil and all his angels." (Matt. xxv. 41.) John also, more largely dwells upon the subject in his book of the Revelations. (See chap. xx. throughout.)

Whether this fire is to be considered as the common, natural, and elementary fire, or whether the expressions are figurative, hath been the subject of much enquiry among persons whom the world hath been accustomed to call learned. But the world have sadly mistaken their name, in calling those learned who would fritter away the plain truths of Scripture into metaphor and figure. Indeed, nothing can more strongly mark the weakness of the human understanding, than the disputes which have been brought forward, in different ages of the church, by way of doing away the doctrine of the eternity of hell-torments. For unless men could persuade themselves, that God is not able to punish sin (of which the miseries and sorrows of the present life too plainly prove the contrary,) or that God will not make good his word in doing it (which his truth and veracity too awfully declare he will,) it matters not in what that punishment consists. Exactly suited to the deserts of sin, in every instance, we may be sure it will be. Too wise to err, too just to do wrong, becomes a decided answer to all the indecent and unbecoming objections of unbelievers.

Here, therefore, let the faithful rest. The plain, the sure, the unalterable language of the word of God on this momentous point, is summed up in a few words.--"The wicked shall be turned into hell, and all the nations that forget God." And at the same time it is said: "For the needy shall not always be forgotten; the expectation of the poor shall not perish for ever." (Ps. xix. 17, 18.) This is enough to ascertain the fact. The farther enquiry in what that hell for the wicked consists, or what will be the fulness of the Lord's remembrance to his poor and needy, both these points may be very safely left with him. The apostle Paul makes a full conclusion of the subject, for the exercise of faith to the church, and such as may be sufficient to answer all the cavils of men, until the whole comes to be realized.

FIRST and FIRST-BORN - FIRST and FIRST-BORN

Speaking to the church concerning the unjust sufferings the people of God endure from the ungodly, he saith, "Seeing it is a righteous thing with God to recompense tribulation to them that trouble you; and to you who are troubled rest with us, when the Lord Jesus should be revealed from heaven with his mighty angels, in flaming fire taking vengeance on them that know not God, and that obey not the gospel of our Lord Jesus Christ; who shall be punished with everlasting destruction from the presence of the Lord and from the glory of his power, when he shall come to be glorified in his saints, and to be admired in all them that believe." (2 Thess. i. 6-10.)

FIRST and FIRST-BORN

I should not think it necessary to detain the reader with any thing by way of explanation to these terms, being in themselves sufficiently obvious, but only when applied to the person of Christ, considered with an eye to him, they merit attention.

We are told by the apostle to the Colossians, first chapter, and eighteenth verse, that he who is the Head of his body the church, and who is the beginning, was also the first-born from the dead, that "in all things he might have the pre-eminence." It is astonishing to what minute circumstances every thing in the church of the Old Testament had a reference, by way of typifying the Lord Jesus Christ in this pre-eminency of character, as the first, and first-born, and first-fruits, and the firstlings of the flock, and of the herd. As if (and which in reality is the case), JEHOVAH would have every thing shadow forth and bring forward somewhat either by allusion, or by direct type, concerning him who is the Alpha and Omega, the first and the last, and sum and substance of all things, in the ordinance of God for salvation. We find this beginning even in the patriarchal age. So that Jacob, when a-dying, though he set aside Reuben from the right of primogeniture, for his particular offence against his father, yet still speaks of the dignity of it. "Reuben (saith he) thou art my firstborn, my might, and the beginning of my strength; the excellency of dignity, and the excellency of power." Then follows the sentence of degradation, "Thou shalt not excel;" that is, thou shalt not retain the right of heirship. (Gen. xlix. 4.) And at the formation of the church, at the Exodus by Moses, while the first-born of the Egyptians, both of man and beast, were all killed, the Lord declared, that all the first-born of Israel, both of man and beast, should be consecrated to him. (Exod. xii; 29; xiii. 2.)

I do not presume to speak with any confidence upon the subject; but I would very humbly ask, Is there not somewhat wonderfully striking in this appointment of the Lord? The Passover that was then observed, we have authority to say, was altogether typical of Christ; for God the Holy Ghost declared by Paul the apostle, that Christ, "our passover, was sacrificed for us." (1 Cor. v. 7.) And as this Passover, in the sprinkling of the blood of the lamb of the first year, without blemish, and without spot, on the houses of the Israelites, become the only cause of safety, to make all the difference between the first-born of Israel and the first-born of Egypt; are we not taught herefrom, that the year of Christ's redeemed is no less the day of Christ's vengance? (Isa. lxiii. 4.) God will have a sacrifice of judgment in the firstlings of his enemies, as well as of mercy in the firstlings of his people. So much will JEHOVAH in all things honour his dear Son, as the first, and first-born, and only begotten of his Father, that at the forming of the church there shall be a destruction in the first-born of those that hate him. I do not presume to speak decidedly on this point; but I cannot but conceive, that there is somewhat very striking on this ground is the difference here shewn between Israel and Egypt. (Exod. xi. 17.)

And if the reader will pursue the

subject through the Bible, in the several types by which Christ the first-born is set forth, he will, I am persuaded, be wonderfully struck, as he passeth through the sacred volume, with the vast attention manifested on the occasion.

The first-born among the children of Israel had a precedency and birthright, which certainly pointed to Jesus. The right of priesthood was with the elder son, and a double portion among his brethren. (Gen. xlix. 8.) And if a man had many wives, still the first-born of every one of them was to be consecrated to the Lord.

And under this view I must not forget to observe, that the offering appointed for every male that opened the womb, (see Exod. xiii. 2. with Exod. xxxiv. 19, 20. Lev. xii. 6. Luke ii. 21-24.) had a direct reference to Christ. Yea, some have thought (and it is a point worthy the most serious consideration,) whether this direction concerning the opening of the womb had respect to any other. For strictly and properly speaking, none but the Lord Jesus ever did open the womb. By the miraculous impregnation of the Virgin, from the overshadowing power of the Holy Ghost, the opening of womb was specially and peculiarly only effected at the birth of Christ; whereas, in every other instance, from the creation of the world, as anatomists well know, it is accomplished at the time of conception. And if this be the case in the instance of Christ, and this appointment of dedication to the Lord of the first-born, that openeth the womb had respect only to Christ; what an eye to this one birth, all along through the whole Levitical dispensation, was manifested by this right of the Lord, both in the first-born of men and of beast, to typify Christ!

I beg the reader on this occasion, as in many others, to observe, that I presume not to speak with any positiveness upon the subject; I only state it. Certain it is, that in all things, and by every way, it was and is JEHOVAH'S will, Jesus should have the pre-eminence. It is blessed, therefore, upon all occasions to discover it.

The redemption of the first-born among the children of Israel, was usually observed with great ceremony. The parents brought their son to the priest, together with the appointed offering for redemption, (See Num. xviii. 15, 16.) and the priest received the child from his mother's hands, with the solemn assurance, that it was her firstborn. The priest then claiming the child in right of the Lord, accepts at the parents' hands the appointed offering, and return the infant; and the day concludes in holy rejoicing.

It forms an additional testimony, that all this was with an eye to Christ, in that among the first-born of the Levites, the redemption of the first-born was not appointed. (Num. i. 47. iii. 12, 13.) And, wherefore, among the Levites this exemption, for it is evident our Lord sprang out of Judah? The whole of Israel is said to be unto JEHOVAH "a kingdom of priests." (Exod. xix. 6.) And therefore, in every thing, and by every way, both in a single tribe and in the whole people, as the Lord's chosen, as shall be typical of the Lord Jesus Christ. In a word, JEHOVAH'S great design all along, and from one eternity to another, is to glorify his dear Son. In all things and by all things, he shall have the pre-eminence. "Every knee shall bow before him, and every tongue confess, that Jesus Christ is Lord, to the glory of God the Father." Amen,

I will detain the reader no longer than just to remark, that the offering of the first fruits had an eye to the Lord Jesus, similar to what hath been shewn respecting the first-born. For the waving the first fruits towards heaven, and the lamb that was to be offered with it for a burnt offering, very plainly testified, that this also was typical. (See in confirmation Lev. xxiiii. 10-14.)

FISH

The Hebrews had no particular names, or very few, for the distinguishing of the

FLAME - FLIES

several species of fish. It is more probable, that as the law prohibited all that had no fins and scales, they were not very anxious to search the rivers in pursuit of them. (See Lev. xi. 9-12.) Our adorable Redeemer, when coming to deliver his people from a yoke that neither we nor our fathers were able to bear, both by his precept and example, taught, that what he had cleansed became no longer unclean. (Matt. xvii. 27. John xxi. 9. Luke xxiv. 42.)

FLAME

See Fire

FLESH

The word flesh hath different meanings in Scripture. It is a word of general acceptation in respect to animal life. Hence the apostle to the Corinthians, chapter the fifteenth, and thirty-ninth verse, saith, "All flesh is not the same flesh; but there is one kind of flesh of men, another flesh of beasts, another of fishes, and another of birds." And, hence, when the Lord determined the total destruction of the world, except the church preserved in the family of Noah, he said, "The end of all flesh is come before me." (Gen. vi. 13.) But beside this general acceptation of the word in relation to all animal life, the Scripture hath a more confined and special sense in reference to human nature.--"Hide not thyself from thine own flesh;" meaning, thine own nature. (Isa. lviii. 7.)

There is another and more endearing sense of the word flesh, when spoken of in Scripture in relation to the types and affinities of families. Thus in the instance of the sons of Jacob, when some were for killing Joseph, Judah restrained from the deed, saying, "What profit is it if we slay our brother, and conceal his blood? Let not our hand be upon him, for he is our brother and our flesh." (Gen. xxxvii. 26, 27.) And there is yet a far more endearing sense in which the word flesh is used in Scripture, when spoken of in the person of our Lord Jesus Christ; the nearest of all types, and the tenderest of all brothers. "For we are members (saith the apostle) of his body, of his flesh, and of his bones." (Eph. v. 30.) But the term flesh hath also another sense, when by of opposition to the spirit, it is taken as a comprehensive expression of our whole corrupt and carnal nature by the fall. "I know (saith Paul,) that in me, that is, in my flesh, dwelleth no good thing." (Rom. v. 18.) And "elsewhere the same apostle saith, The flesh lusteth against the spirit, and the spirit against the flesh; and these are contrary the one to the other, so that ye cannot do the things that ye would." (Gal. v. 17.) And hence when by the gracious work of regeneration wrought in the heart by the sovereign power of God the Holy Ghost, believers are then said "to be not in the flesh, but in the Spirit, it so be that the Spirit of God dwell in them." (Rom. viii. 9.) And hence this new life of God in the soul is called union with Christ, in living upon Christ, and walking with Christ. "As the living Father hath sent me, and I live by the Father, even so he that eateth me shall live by me." (John vi. 57.)

FLIES

By flies in Scripture are meant, not only those that have wings and fly in the open air, but also insects which creep upon the earth. They are reputed unclean by the law. (Lev. xi. 41. &c.) The plague of Egypt of the flies, (see Exod. viii. 20, &c.) may in some measure serve to explain, how pointed, as well as heavy, the Lord's punishments on the Egyptians were. The Egyptians had their Baalzebub, as well as the Philistines; and probably from the same cause. (See 2 Kings i. 2.) Hence this dunghill idol Baalzebub, that is, the god of the flies, they looked to to keep them from their destroying power. So then when the Lord made the very idol they worshipped thus contemptible before them, while under the smarting of his power, how strikingly did the Lord set forth the distinguishing mercy to his people, in the moment he thus visited their enemies. It is worthy of farther remark, that it was not until this plague that the Lord declared the separation he would put between his people and the Egyptians. I beg the reader to turn to the Scripture account of this. (Exod. viii. 20-26.)

I must not dismiss this article until that I have farther observed upon it, that in all probability it was a fly of the same species as infested Egypt, that the Lord, by the prophet Isaiah, called for, after that glorious prophecy concerning Christ; and which, it should seem, was to be among the plagues of those who received not Christ. "The Lord [saith the prophet,) shall hiss for the fly that is in the uttermost part of the rivers of Egypt, and for the bee that is in the land of Assyria." (Isa. vii. 17, 18.)

How strange soever the worship of a fly may appear to us, yet historians of modern times have given us an account of similar honours paid by the Hottentots to the fly; and perhaps to this very day the custom is not altered. Kolben in his history of the present state of the Cape of Good Hope relates, that there is an insect about the size of a child's little finger, that hath two wings and two horns, which is held in the highest veneration by this deluded people. They sacrifice two of the fattest sheep to this fly, whenever he appears in their kraal, or village. And the historian farther adds, that he thinks it impossible to drive the opinion out of their minds, but that the appearance of this insect in a kraal is an omen of great prosperity to the inhabitants.

Having said thus much, by way of shewing to what a degraded state our whole nature is reduced by the fall, I hope the reader will indulge me with making another observation, to point out the blessedness to which we are brought, in the recovery from such gross ignorance, by the glorious gospel of the ever-blessed God. Oh, what unspeakable mercy is it to be free from all dunghill deities and superstitious foolishness, in the knowledge of the true God and our Saviour Jesus Christ. "Thanks be unto God, for his unspeakable gift!" (2 Cor. ix. 15.)

FLOCK

The church of Jesus is so often spoken of in Scripture under the figure and similitude of a flock, that I could not think myself justified in passing it by unnoticed. That Jesus is himself called the Shepherd of Israel. (Ps. lxxx. 1.) and sometimes the good Shepherd. (John x. 11.) and chief Shepherd, (1 Pet. v. 4.) and the great Shepherd. (Heb. xiii. 20.) and the one Shepherd. (Ezek. xxxiv. 23.) These are familiar names, by which Christ is well known to his church in Scripture. And consequently, as every shepherd is supposed to have a flock, otherwise his very character of shepherd ceaseth; so the church hath various descriptions also as the flock of Christ by which she is known. The church is said by Jesus himself to be his sheep, which his Father hath given him, and which he hath also purchased by his blood, and made them his by the conquests of his grace. Hence he saith, he called them all by name. He knoweth all their persons, state, and circumstances; goeth before them, and them into wholesome pastures, and causeth them to lie down in safety. He undertakes for all their wants, heals the diseased among them, brings home wanderers, restores the misled, and is so watchful over the whole of his flock, that they must all pass again under the hand of him that telleth them. (Jer. xxxiii. 13.) and hence it is impossible that any of them should perish, but he giveth them eternal life. (John x. 1-16.)

And what tends, if possible, to endear yet more this view of Christ's church as his flock, is the several properties of it. The flock of Jesus is but one. (Song vi. 9.) though scattered in various parts of the earth, and divided into several folds. Both Jew and Gentile are brought into it, and hereafter will form "one in the general assembly and church of the first-born,

FLOOD - FLOUR

whose names are written in heaven." (Heb. xii. 23.) And this flock of Christ is not only one, but it forms a separate and distinct one. For separated by distinguishing grace and gathered out of the world's wide wilderness, Jesus hath pent it up, and hedged it in; so that it is for ever separated from the wolves and beasts of prey. Hence Jesus is represented as calling to his church in those sweet words: "Come with me from Lebanon, my spouse, with me from Lebanon; look from the top of Amana, from the top of Shenir, and Hermon, from the lions' dens, and from the mountains of the leopards." (Song iv. 8.)

There is another great feature of Jesus's flock, and this is, in the present life, compared to the world, they are but small and inconsiderable in number. Jesus himself calleth it a little flock. "Fear not, little flock, (said that gracious Shepherd), for it is your Father's good pleasure to give you the kingdom." (Luke xii. 32.) But overlooked and despised as the flock of Jesus is by the great ones of the earth, and low and humble as they are in their own view; yet when they are all brought home, and housed in his eternal kingdom, they will form a blessed company. John, the beloved apostle, in his days, when admitted in that glorious vision of the Lord to see heaven opened, related to the church, that he saw "a multitude, whom no man could number, of all nations, and kindreds, and people, and tongues." (Rev. vii. 9.) And who shall say what millions since, the Lord hath gathered and taken home to his everlasting sheepfold above? Oh! the blessedness of belonging to the flock of Christ! Well might the prophet in the contemplation, as if speaking to Jesus, the Israel of his people, cry out, "Where is the flock that was given thee, thy beautiful flock?" (Jer. xiii. 20.) And how beautiful, indeed, in the eyes of Jesus, must the flock appear, when made comely in his comeliness! How spotless like the whitest fleece, when washed in his blood, covered in the garment of his righteousness, and made all glorious within by the indwelling residence of the Holy Ghost! Hear what the Lord saith to his church: "Thou art beautiful as Tirzah, O my love! comely as Jerusalem, terrible as an army with banners. Thy teeth are like a flock of sheep that are even shorn, which come up from the washing, whereof every one bear twins, and none is barren among them." (Song vi. 4; iv. 2.)

FLOOD

This word is particularly and perhaps especially applicable only to the deluge, when the Lord by a flood of waters destroyed every thing that lived upon the earth of his creatures. But the word in Scripture is made use of to denote many things of an overwhelming nature. Thus, floods of sin, floods of sorrow, floods of ungodly men, and the like. So that there is one of the sweetest promises in the Bible, in allusion to the graces of the Lord the Spirit, made use of in a way of illustration, by the figure of a flood. "When the enemy shall come in like a flood, the Spirit of the Lord shall lift up a standard against him." (Isa. lix. 19.) Yea the Lord Jesus himself adopts the figure in reference to his own personal sufferings. "I am come, saith Christ, into deep waters, where the floods overflow me." (Ps. lxix. 2.) But the church takes comfort from hence, that no water spouts of divine wrath can cool the warm love of the heart of Jesus to his church and people. "Many waters cannot quench love, neither can the floods drown it." (Song viii 7.)

FLOUR

This word in Scripture is sometimes figuratively used, to express the Lord's gracious dealings with his people. Thus (Ps. lxxxi. 16.) JEHOVAH is said to have fed his people with the finest wheat; meaning, the spiritual and distinguishing blessings he poured out upon them. Hence the consecration of Aaron was with the finest wheat flour. (See Exod. xxix. 1, 2.) Hence the meat-offering was of the same. (Lev. ii.

1.) The Hebrews called all offerings made by grain, or flour, Mincha. Were not the whole of these offerings with an eye to Christ? Was not Jesus the first of the finest flour? And if the church, while presenting their offerings of the finest flour, with an eye to Christ, were in the appointments of the Lord, may we not, without violence to the original, suppose, that JEHOVAH feeding the people with the finest wheat had an eye to Christ?

FOOL

The term fool in Scripture language differs from what is understood in the general acceptation of the word among men. By fool we mean one that is weak in his intellect, and an idiot. But not so in the word of God. Thus in the psalms, "The fool hath said in his heart, There is no God." (Ps. xiv. 1). But the sense is, that the wicked and ungodly have by their action said this. So again, that pride and haughtiness of men, which prompts them to reject Christ, this in Scripture language is called folly. Hence the apostle saith, "The world by wisdom knew not God; and it pleased God by the foolishness of preaching to save them that believe." (1 Cor. i. 21.) By comparing two passages in Scripture together, the sense of the word is very strongly marked. Thus the prophet Isaiah saith, speaking of bad men, that "It is a people of no understanding; therefore, he that made them will not have mercy upon them, and he that formed them will shew them no favour." (Isa. xxvii. 11.) Now, that it might not be supposed, that this being void of understanding was the natural and unavoidable condition of idiotism, which brought upon them the displeasure of God, and for which the Lord would shew them no favour, the Holy Ghost, by his servant Job, hath very fully shewn in what that want of understanding consisted. "And unto man he said, Behold the fear of the Lord, that is wisdom; and to depart from evil is understanding." (Job xxviii. 28.)

FOOT or FEET

The Hebrews were so much accustomed to use parable and figure in their discourses, and gesture in their conversation, to convey to each other their meaning, rather than by words, that it is no wonder so many and various meanings should be conveyed by one and the same way. Thus by feet they meant to denote every thing that was humble, and conceal every thing immodest. "A wicked man, (saith Solomons) speaketh with his feet." (Prov. vi. 13.) The sense is, by motions of his feet he conveyed somewhat indecent and unbecoming "To leave off the sandals from the feet," was an indication of sorrow, and of great humility. Thus Ezekiel mourned for his wife. (Ezek. xxiv. 17.) And Moses was commanded at the bush to put off his shoes, in token that the ground where he then stood was holy ground. (Exod. iii. 5.) To sit at the feet of another, implied humility. (1 Sam. xxv. 24.) Mary sat at the feet of Jesus. (Luke. vii. 38.) To cover the feet, was a phrase used to imply attending to the wants of nature. Thus Ehud. (Judges. iii. 24.) "To open the feet to every one that passed by," was an expression of whoredom (Ezek. xvi. 25.) These phrases serve to throw a light upon the subject in general.

But if these things were so, and every action relative to the feet carried with it somewhat of a special nature, think what unequalled humbleness that was in the Lord Jesus Christ, the Lord of life and glory, when he condescended to wash the feet of poor fishermen. (See John. xiii. 3-8.) And what tends to endear this action of Christ the more is, that it was at a season, we are told, when all things were given into his sovereign hands. Never surely, was there an instance of equal humility. Poor vain man, that hath nothing, yea, is himself worse than nothing, is proud. But Jesus, who hath all things, and is himself infinitely superior to all things, is unequalled in humility. It were to be wished, that all his redeemed felt more of this spirit of their Lord. And it were to be wished, that every poor, tried, and humble believer, would never lose sight of this feature of character in the Lord Jesus Christ. And let any man, and every man, determine the point for himself: When is Jesus most lovely, most dear, and precious? Is it not when he is most condescending? Suppose the Lord Jesus were to wash my feet, as he did Peter's, would not such an act of grace overwhelm my poor heart with love? Yea, would not the Lord Jesus be the more exalted to my view and in my esteem when in his matchless grace he had been most condescending? How sweet are such views of Jesus!

FOREST
See Lebanon.

FOUNDATION
The word itself implies what it expresses, the basis and ground-work of a building. But in Scripture language it means Christ, the foundation God hath laid in Zion, and on which JEHOVAH hath built his church; and against which the gates of hell can never prevail. It is very blessed to see the ground and bottom on which this rests. It is founded in the purpose, counsel and will of JEHOVAH. The everlasting love, the everlasting wisdom, the everlasting power of God in which all the Persons of the GODHEAD are in the great design blended, all concur and all unite. And what endears it to the church, and gives a permanency and security to the whole is, that it is unchangeable, eternal, and for ever. And Christ in the united nature of God and man, becomes the sure foundation to give firmness and stability to it. He is the wonderful Person on whom it is built; the Rock of ages. So that he, and he alone, in the purposes of JEHOVAH, gives certainty to all that is included in redemption, for grace here and glory to all eternity. Well might the apostle in the contemplation of it say, "Other foundation can no man lay than that is laid, Jesus Christ." (1 Cor. iii. 11.)

And blessed is the corresponding experience and testimony of true believers in the heart, when built upon the foundations of apostles and prophets, "Jesus Christ being the chief corner-stone; they are in all the building fitly framed, and growing together unto an holy temple in the Lord." (Ephes. iii. 20,21.)

FOUNTAIN
This word is used in Scripture to denote the spring and source of divine life to the church; and what is worthy of remark, as if to confirm the fundamental truth of our holy faith, in that of JEHOVAH existing in a threefold character of persons, this word is equally applied to each and to all. To God the Father," as the fountain of living waters." (Jer. ii. 13.) To God the Son, who had opened a "fountain for sin and uncleanness to the house of David and inhabitants of Jerusalem." (Zech. xiii. 1.) And to God the Holy Ghost, as a "river of living water in the hearts of believers." (John vii. 38.) Hence the church sings so blessedly concerning her Beloved, calling him "a fountain of gardens; a well of living waters; and streams from Lebanon." (Song iv. 15.)

FOX and FOXES
From the well known subtilty of this creature, the sacred writers make use of his name, by way of describing craft, and hypocrisy, and guile. Hence false prophets are called in Scripture foxes. (Ezek. xiii. 4) And the church in the Canticles is forewarned against them. (Song ii. 15.) The Lord Jesus makes application of the name to Herod. (Luke xiii. 32.)

FREE and FREEDOM
The Scriptures considering our whole nature by the fall under the vassalage of sin and Satan, represent our deliverance from both by grace under the character of spiritual freedom. And Jesus, in a very

striking manner, represents the greatness of it by a contrast, drawn to a state of slavery. "Whosoever committeth sin (saith Jesus,) is the servant of sin; and the servant abideth not in the house for ever, but the son abideth ever. If the son, therefore, shall make you free, ye shall be free indeed." (John viii. 34-36.)

FRIEND

The word friend in the language of Scripture is very general; but eminently so when spoken of Christ. Abraham is called "the friend of God" (2 Chron. xx. 7.) And the friendship of David and Jonathan is proverbial. (1 Sam. xviii. 3.) But all friendship falls to the ground, when brought into any comparative statement with that of the friendship of the Lord Jesus. "Greater love hath no man than this, that a man lay down his life for his friends." So Speaks Jesus himself. (John xv. 13.) But though no man ever manifested greater love than this, yet the God-man himself far, very far, exceeded it; for he laid down his life for his enemies. (Rom. v. 8.) And what unceasing, what everlasting, what unexampled proofs did Jesus give of his friendship, before it came to this last finishing act of love in dying for his people. He engaged from everlasting as our Surety; he took our nature, married our persons, paid all our debts, cancelled all our insolvency, bore the whole weight and pressure both of our sins and his Father's wrath, endured the contradiction of sinners against himself, lest we should be weary and faint in our minds; and having died for us, he took up both the person and the causes of all his people. He is now carrying on the whole purposes of redemption, and never intermits one moment an unceasing attention to our present and everlasting interests; neither will he, until that he hath brought home all his redeemed to glory, that "where he is, there they may be also." Well might the spouse in the Canticles, in the contemplation of such unheard of unexampled love, exclaim, "This is my beloved, and this is my friend, O daughters of Jerusalem!" (Song v. 16.)

FRONTLETS

We find in the law of Moses a precept concerning frontlets. (Exod. xiii. 16. Deut. vi. 8.) And though we, under the glorious dispensation of the gospel, have no direction concerning them, yet it may not be improper, nor perhaps unprofitable, to notice them in a cursory way.

The religious world hath been divided in opinion concerning what was intended by frontlets. Some have contended that the precept was not meant in the literal sense of the word, but only figuratively. By frontiers between the eyes, they say, was shadowed, that all the Lord commanded should be continually before their eyes, that they might never lose sight of his precepts. And in confirmation of this opinion, it is said, that before the church was carried into Babylon, they were not known. And we do not find a word in any of the prophets in respect to their neglect, or the use of them. That they were in use in the days of our Lord seems more than probable; for Jesus, speaking of the Scribes and Pharisees, said, "that they made broad their phylacteries." (Matt. xxiii. 5.) It doth not appear, that our Lord condemned the use, but the abuse of them; and from the motive for which they wore them--to be seen of men. But those who accept the precept of Moses in the literal sense of the thing itself, not only believe, that the Hebrews wore frontlets, but have described the form and manner in which they were worn. The account is gathered from the thirteenth chapter of Exodus, and from portions of the book of Deuteronomy. If the reader will consult those chapters, he will find four distinct precepts; which four precepts they say, were marked on four pieces of a kind of skin or parchment, and wore on their foreheads. The first was, "Sanctify unto me all the first-born," &c. (Exod. xiii. 2-10.)

FRUIT and FRUITS - FULL and FULNESS

The second was, "When the Lord shall bring thee into the land of the Canaanites," &c. (Exod. xiii. 11-16.) The third was taken from the book of Deuteronomy, "Hear; O Israel! the Lord our God is one Lord." (Deut. vi. 4, 5.) And the fourth was taken from Deut. xi. 13-21. "If thou shalt hearken diligently unto my commandments," &c.

The frontlets of the head were called by the Jews Tephila. It is said, that even in modern times the most devout of the Jews wear them in their devotions. What a blessedness is it, in the holy faith the believer in Jesus is called to, that our great High Priest bears the names and persons of his people on his breast and on his arm, and is himself the sweet and holy frontlet for all the redeemed. How beautiful and expressive the prayer of the church on this point. (Song viii. 6.)

FRUIT and FRUITS

In addition to what hath been already offered under the title of First Fruits (which see,) it may not be amiss to observe, that the holy Scriptures are full of expressions to denote the blessedness of the fruits of the Spirit. The Lord in the Old Testament Scripture gave exceeding great and precious promises of blessings, which were to be expected in the fruits and effects under the New Testament dispensation; and in the gospel the Lord Jesus confirmed the whole, when promising to send the Holy Ghost, and testified of his manifold gifts which should follow. (Isa. xliv. 3-5; John xiv. xv. and xvi. chapters throughout; 1 Cor. xii. throughout.)

FULL and FULNESS

These expressions, when spoken in Scripture with an eye to the Lord Jesus Christ, imply more than language can convey, or the imagination conceive. Jesus Christ, as the glorious Head of his body the church, is the fulness that filleth all in all. So the apostle speaks, Ephes. i. 23. And in the same Epistle he saith, speaking of Christ," that he ascended up far above all heavens, that he might fill all things." (Ephes. iv. 10.) But when we have read those expressions, and pondered them to the utmost, What adequate conception have we of their meaning? So again, when it is said, that "in him dwelleth all the fulness of the GODHEAD bodily: (Col. ii. 9.) who shall undertake to say what that is? Not JEHOVAH dwelling in the God-man Christ Jesus, by filling that nature with grace and glory, as the Lord Jesus by his holy Spirit dwells in the saints, and fills their hearts, and unites himself to them, and they to him, by grace here, and glory above. Not thus; but the GODHEAD dwells in Christ Jesus, and fills that nature of Christ Jesus in a personal bodily union; as fire fills the iron substantially that is in it, so that it becomes itself fire from that union. Who shall go farther, and determine what this is?

And what endears all these precious views of our Lord in his fulness is, the interest his redeemed have in it. The apostle adds to this account of the GODHEAD in his fulness dwelling in Christ bodily, "and ye are complete in him." Here is the blessedness of the whole, as it concerns our happiness, and security, and glory in him. Hence the church is called "the glory of Christ." (2 Cor. viii. 23.) And so the church is; for it is, indeed, Christ, s glory, to give out of his fulness to his body the church, as the glorious Head of the church. And although his own personal glory is in himself, and to himself, in the GODHEAD, of his nature and essence, being "one with the Father, over all, God blessed for ever;" yet in his mediatorial glory, as the Head of his body the church, "of his fulness do all the members receive, and grace for grace." And it is the glory of the Lord Jesus to give out, and to make that body glorious like himself, and from himself, to be his glory for ever. Oh! the blessedness of thus beholding the fulness of the Lord Jesus. Oh! what encouragement to the faith of the Lord's poor, needy, empty people. In Jesus's fulness we are full; in

Jesus's glory we are glorified; yea, it is Jesus's glory to receive me, to give out to me, and to be more glorious in thus receiving and giving. Hallelujah!

FURLONG

See Mile.

G

GABBATHA

A memorable word in the believer's recollection, and rendered both solemn and sacred to the meditation, when frequently by faith the soul is looking over again the transactions at the hall of Pilate. The word Gabbatha our translators have thought proper to preserve, in our Testaments, in the original Hebrew; and yet have given the English of it, calling it Pavement. (John xix. 13.) It means an elevated spot; probably it formed a balustrade, or gallery, from whence to the court below, Pilate might more conveniently speak to the people. Let the reader figure to himself this gabbatha, with a seat for the Governor to sit above the people, and probably separated by railing. Let him fancy he sees the rabble below surrounding the sacred person of our Lord, and crying out, "Away with him, away with him; crucify him." Let him behold the meek and suffering Lamb of God, silent, patient, and submissive. And while with that contempt which marked Pilate's character, we hear him say, "Shall I crucify your king?" the chief priests, unconscious of what they said, answered, "We have no king but Caesar;" thereby fulfilling the dying patriarch Jacob's prophecy (that "the sceptre should not depart from Judah, nor a lawgiver from between his feet, until Shiloh come;" Gen. xlix. 10. and thus proving from their own testimony, that the Shiloh was come.) Let all these interesting views be but in the reader's contemplation when he reads of these transactions, and he will have a lively idea of the Gabbatha of Pilate's palace.

GABRIEL

The messenger sent to Daniel, and to Zacharias, and to the Virgin Mary. (Dan. ix. 21. Luke i. 11-26.) His name is compounded of Gaber, strength; and I-ei, my God.--Man of God, or God is my strength.

GAD

We meet with this name in the holy Scriptures, to denote three very different characters. The first is one of Jacob's sons, which he had by Zilpah, Leah's handmaid, (Gen. xxx. 11.) and she called his name Gad, which signifies armed; and, therefore, in the margin of our Bibles it is marked a troop, or company. The second Gad we meet with, is the prophet Gad, David's seer. (2 Sam. xxiv. 11.) The character of this man is well spoken of, by his conduct and faithfulness, in Scripture. He was much attached to David; (See I Sam. xxii. 5.) yet faithful to the Lord at the time of David's transgression. (See 2 Sam. xxiv. 10-19.) We read also, that Gad compiled a history of the acts of David. (See I Chron. xxix. 29, 30.) The third mention of Gad is as an idol. There was a Baal-Gad in the valley of Lebanon. (Josh. xi. 17.) And the prophet Isaiah speaks of some "who prepared a table for that troop [Gad,] and that furnished a drink offering for that number." [meni] (Isa. lxv. 11.) The dying patriarch Jacob blessing his sons, made a memorable prophecy concerning Gad: "A troop (said Jacob) shall overcome him, but he shall overcome at the last." (Gen. xlix. 19.) Considered in a temporal sense, this was literally true. For the Gadites were a numerous tribe, and a warlike tribe. We find no less than forty-five thousand six hundred and fifty, came out of Egypt, (Num. ii. 15.) "men both of might, and men of war, fit for the battle, that could handle shield and buckler; whose faces were like the faces of lions, and were as swift as the roes upon the mountains." (1 Chron. xii. 8.) And considered in a spiritual sense, the seed of Israel, though frequently overcome by troops of foes, yet though conquered, still they are a conquering people. Troops of lusts, troops of corruptions, troops from hell, and troops from the world, may, and will, bring the poor exercised soul too often under: yet the victory is still on the side of Jacob's seed. The praying seed of Jacob, at length come off as the prevailing Israel; for they must overcome "by the blood of the Lamb," and be more than conquerors through his grace making them so.

GADARA and GADARENES

A place and people made memorable by the visit of the Lord Jesus. It was a city of Palestine, so called, perhaps, from being walled, from Cedar, surrounded or trooped in. Here it was, that Jesus met the man with an unclean spirit, who had his dwelling among the tombs, whom no fetters nor chains could bind, and whom Jesus healed. It forms a most interesting miracle, in the account of Christ's ministry, (See Mark v. 1-30.) Who can say, but that the Lord Jesus directed his steps to this very spot, purposely for the salvation of this poor man, and him only? For we are told, that while he sat at the feet of Jesus, (after that the Lord had dispossessed the evil spirit) clothed, and in his right mind: the Gadarenes began to pray Jesus to depart out of their coasts. What higher proofs can be needed to mark distinguishing grace! What an act of mercy had Jesus wrought, not only to the poor demoniac, but to the whole country, in delivering them from his violence and outrage, while under possession of the devil. And yet, though thus freed from all apprehension in future; the presence of Him, that by his sovereign and Almighty power, had wrought the gracious act, is painful to them. "Depart from us, for we desire not the knowledge of thy ways!" (Job xxi. 14.) And awful to say, but too true to be questioned, such is the language of every man's heart by nature.

GALATIA

A province in Asia Minor. Here the apostle Paul preached, and it should seem that the apostle Peter had done the same, for he directs his first Epistle to the Jews scattered there. Here there were several churches, for Paul expressly sends his Epistle to the churches of Galatia. It should seem by the account which we have, (Acts xvi. 6. and again, Acts xviii. 23.) that Paul laboured personally with the Galatians, at two different periods, if not oftener. The church of Christ finds cause to bless God for having directed Paul's mind to this people, which gave rise to this most blessed Epistle. The plan of justification by Christ is so plainly and beautifully set forth in that Epistle, that we have daily reason to adore the riches of grace for the mercy. Neither is it probable, that the church would have known the history of Sarah and Hagar, to have been a type and allegory of the covenants, had not that Scripture said so.

GALILEE

A province in Palestine. Nazareth was a city of Galilee. And as the Lord Jesus was brought up in this city, he was called, by way of reproach, the Galilean. Isaiah, speaking of the gospel, ages before Christ came, pointed to this memorable spot, as comprehensive of all blessings in the advent of Jesus; and Matthew made application of the prophet's words to Christ. "The land of Zebulon, and the land of Naphtali, by the way of the sea beyond Jordan, in Galilee of the nations. The people that walked in darkness have seen a great light: they that dwell in the land of the shadow of death, upon them hath the light shined." (Isa. ix. 1, 2. Matt. iv. 15, 16.)

GALL

This word is used in Scripture, variously, but in all it means to convey an idea of great bitterness. The drink of bitter sorrow, is called, "the water of gall." (Jer. viii. 14.) And sin is sometimes described under the figure of "the gall of bitterness, and bond of iniquity." (Acts viii. 23.) Moses, describing the apostacy of any man or woman, or family, or tribe in Israel, calls it, "the root that beareth gall and wormwood." (Deut.

xxix. 18.) And elsewhere, speaking of Israel's enemies, and their sad prospects, strongly marks the bitterness even of their comforts under this figure. "For their vine is of the vine of Sodom, and of the fields of Gomorrah; their grapes are grapes of gall, their clusters are bitter." (Deut. xxxii. 32.) The Lord Jesus, speaking of his sufferings on the cross, noticeth "the gall the Jews gave him to eat, and the vinegar to drink." We are told, that in his thirst they gave the Lord "wine mingled with myrrh." It was a custom with the Romans in their execution of criminals, to blunt their pains in this way. Bitter myrrh, with wine or vinegar, had a tendency, it was thought, to accomplish this purpose. And thus they treated "the Lord of life and glory." But how little did they know, what thirst of soul Jesus felt in that earnestness and vehemeney he endured for the salvation of his people. Solomon had before said, "Give strong drink unto him that is ready to perish, and wine to those that be of heavy hearts; let him drink and forget his poverty, and remember his misery no more." (Prov. xxxi. 6, 7.) The strong drink of Jesus was the cup of salvation for his redeemed. To Jesus "a cup of trembling;" to them the cup of rejoicing. Here he was to see "the travail of his soul, and be satisfied." In drinking of this draught, bitter as it was, and to the dregs, Jesus forgot all his sorrows, and remembered his misery no more. Oh! that the drunkards of Ephraim would seriously lay this to heart. Oh! that every follower of the Lord Jesus would now take "the cup of salvation, and call upon the name of the Lord."

GALLERY and GALLERIES

I should not have paused at this word, but for the better apprehension of what the church saith of "holding the king in the galleries." (Song vii. 5.) The proper idea of the gallery in the eastern buildings is necessary, in order to enter into the sense of this passage. Dr. Shaw in his Travels, page 274-5, tell us, that the court in the summer-season, among persons of rank, is sheltered from the heat, or inclemency of the weather, by a *velum umbrella*, or veil; which being expanded upon ropes from one side of the parapet wall to the other, may be folded or unfolded at pleasure. The Psalmist seems to have an allusion to this, when speaking of the covering above, he describes the Lord as "spreading out the heavens like a curtain." (Ps. civ.) This court is, for the most part, surrounded with a cloister or colonnade, over which there is a gallery erected of the same dimensions with the cloister, having a balustrade of carved or latticed work. From the cloister and gallery, there is a passage into large and spacious chambers. It should seem, therefore, that by the act of "holding the king in the galleries" is meant, that here the church detained Jesus for sweet communion and fellowship. And here they had frequent meetings, unnoticed and unknown to others; in which the Lord opened to his church the secrets of his love, in leading her into the chambers of his covenant mercy and grace; and the church held him fast in those galleries, not suffering him to depart until "that she had brought him whom her soul loved, as she saith elsewhere, into her mother's house, and into the chamber of her that conceived her." (Song iii. 4.)

That this is the sense of the expression of "holding the king in the galleries" seems plain, from another consideration; namely, that the word held signifies being bound as a prisoner with chains and fetters. And this corresponds to the whole passage; yea, to the whole song. For while the church is made blessed in Christ, as her Head, which is said to be upon her "like Carmel, and the hair of her head like purple;" meaning, that Christ being the Head of his body the church, high, like the lofty mount Carmel, all the innumerable members on him beautiful as the purple coloured hair, the most lovely and valued among eastern women, the Lord praises his church with saying, "How fair and how pleasant art thou, O love, for delights! Thou hast ravished my heart, my sister, my spouse! thou hast ravished my heart with one of thine eyes, with one chain of thy neck." (Song iv. 9.)

The reader will indulge me, I hope, with barely adding, that if such was the sweet result of Jesus being held by the church in the galleries of old, surely, believers now ought to take confidence and delight to detain the Lord in the galleries of ordinances; from whence, while they hold him fast by the lively actings of faith and prayer, like the wrestlings of their father Jacob of old, (See Gen. xxxii. 26.) they may be led by him into the chambers of rich communion, in the high privilege of near and familiar enjoyment of all covenant blessings. It is by these gracious acts the Lord acknowledgeth the church, and, consequently, every individual of the church to be his bribe, when as the church elsewhere saith, "The king hath brought me into his chambers." (Song i. 4.) "For there Jesus manifesteth himself to his people otherwise than he doeth to the world. (John xiv. 21, 22.) And until that he brings them home to the marriage-supper of the Lamb in heaven, while upon earth, having espoused them to himself, he brings them by faith into his chambers, opens to them more and more of his unsearchable riches, gives a foretaste of the glory hereafter to be revealed, and by the gracious influences of his Holy Spirit, induceth all those blessed effects in the soul which the apostle Peter so delightfully describes: "Whom having not seen, ye love; in whom, though now you see him not, yet believing, ye rejoice with joy unspeakable, and full of glory; receiving the end of your faith, even the salvation of your souls." (1 Pet. i. 8.)

GALLEY

The name of a ship used in the early days for annoyance, and not trade. Mention is made of it by Isaiah, chap. xxxiii. 21. Since navigation hath in modern times been carried to such an extent, the idea of a galley with oars is not calculated to make much alarm. But in the remote age of the church in which the prophet ministered, a galley with oars was as formidable as now a fleet of ships of war. Who could have thought, that in the first attempt of joining a few rafters together to float around the creeks and shores of the sea, an idea would ever have been started in the human mind, to venture into the open ocean; yea, and to cross the great Atlantic by means of any vessel constructed by human art? And even when long experience had found the measure practicable, and commerce opened her rich invitations to men of different countries and climates to barter with each other their traffic by means of shipping, what imagination was vast enough to have conceived the possibility of making such floating machines instruments for human destruction? Could it ever have entered into the heart of any man to conceive, that the time would arrive when nations would construct vessels of the magnitude we now behold them, stored with implements for war, and that they should meet on the mighty waters purposely for battle? The storms and tempests of the great deep are in themselves at times so tremendous, that the stoutest and strongest built ships are upon these occasions as nothing, when "men are carried up to the heavens, and down again to the depths; and the souls of the mariners are melted because of the trouble." (Ps. cvii. 23-31.) Indeed, in the calmest seasons at sea, it may be truly said, that there is but a step between the whole ship's company and death. (1 Sam. xx. 3.)

It is said of Anacharsis, that when he was demanded where the majority of mankind was to be numbered, among the dead, or the living? He said, You must first tell me in which class I am to rank seamen. Intimating by the answer, as if he thought they were in the midway, and belonged to neither. But in vessels of war fitted for destruction, we behold to what a state of presumption and evil sin hath hardened the mind.

There is a beautiful thought suggested in the passage of Isaiah, where he speaks of the galley with oars, which may be in some measure a relief from the distressing views before noticed; and for the introduction of which, indeed, I have mentioned this article, and that is, the peculiar security of the Lord's presence over his people upon such, and upon every other occasion of alarm. The prophet, when speaking of this galley with oars, was speaking also of Jerusalem, the holy city, as a quiet habitation, a tabernacle not to be taken down. "But there (said he) the glorious Lord will be unto us a place of broad rivers and streams, wherein shall go no galley with oars, neither shall gallant ship pass thereby." (Isa. xxxiii. 20, 21.) The great beauty of the figure lies in this, that Jerusalem had no rivers of any extent. The brook Kidron, which emptied itself into the Dead Sea, was the only one near it. So that having no sea to keep off an enemy, and no frontiers or garrison-walls to keep and secure it by land, Jerusalem lay open on all sides. But, saith the Lord by the prophet, "the glorious Lord will be, instead of all these to us, a place both of broad rivers and streams." No galley with oars can come into that river, which is God himself. No gallant ship can pass by him, who is purposely there to prevent it. Sweet thought! The tacklings of the enemy may be loosed, but they can neither strengthen their mast, nor spread their sail. "The Lord is our judge; the Lord is our law-giver; the Lord is our king: he will serve us." (See the whole passage, Isa. xxxiii. 20. to the end.)

GAMALIEL

Paul's teacher of the law. His name is probably derived from Gamal, gift; and I-el, my God.

GARDEN

It would be wholly unnecessary to notice the name of garden (taken from the Hebrew word Gan), being so generally understood, were it not that the church of Christ is so frequently represented under the similitude. Indeed, the church is sometimes called gardens, to denote both their number and variety; by which is meant, the particular names of the churches of Jesus, such as the apostles of Christ; yea, Christ himself directed Epistles to the churches at "Rome, Corinth, Galatia, Philippi," and the like, and the seven churches in Asia. But though these were diversified, and scattered abroad in the earth, yet still, after all, the church of Christ is but one and the same. So said Christ himself. "My dove, my undefiled, is but one; she is the only one of her mother: she is the choice one of her that bare her." (Song vi. 9.) The Jerusalem which is above, and which is the mother of us all, knows but of one church, of which Jesus is the Head; for both Jew and Gentile will ultimately be brought into one fold. And in the meantime all true believers in Christ have one faith, one hope, one spirit, one heart and affections; all united to their glorious Head, and all united to each other, as "members of his body, his flesh, and his bones." (Gal. iv. 26. John x. 16. Ephes. iv. 4, 5; v. 30.) And what endears the whole, and renders it most blessed is, that Christ the glorious Head, to whom the whole body is united, supplies all, justifies all, sanctifies all, and is himself the all of life and strength, and the portion to his people, in grace here, and glory hereafter. So sung the church, and so all the redeemed know. "A fountain of gardens is my beloved, said the church, a well of living water, and streams from Lebanon." (Song iv. 15.)

And while we eye Jesus as the source of life and fruitfulness to his garden the church, it is blessed to see how very lovely the similitude of a garden, corresponds to the state of Christ's church. As first a garden is an enclosure, separated and fenced round; so the church stands in the midst of the world's wide wilderness, gathered from it by sovereign grace. (Song iv. 12. Isa. v. 1, 2.) Secondly, a garden is the property of some owner; it is not alike common or open to all: so is the church. Jesus hath bought it with his blood; the Father hath given it to Christ by grace; and the Holy Ghost hath made it Christ's, by the sealing act of covenant faithfulness. Thirdly, a garden is distinguished from the common fields or hedges of the highway, by having nothing growing there but what has been planted; exactly thus with the church. Every thing in it is of the Lord's right hand planting; for Jesus saith himself, "Every plant which my heavenly Father hath not planted shall be rooted up." (Matt. xv. 13.) Fourthly, in a garden there are great varieties of plants and shrubs, and fruit-trees and flowers; so in Christ's church the fruits of the Spirit appear in a beautiful and regular order, some by the exercise of one grace, and others by another, but "all these worketh that one and the self-same Spirit, dividing to every man severally as he will." (1 Cor. xii, 11.) Fifthly, a garden is under the eye and inspection of its owner, and very frequently visited by him; and the Lord Jesus is said to have his eyes upon his Judea from the one end of the year even to the other end of the year. Yea, the Lord Jesus walks in his garden the church, and makes this his sacred haunt, where he delights to come and visit his people. The church speaks of her Lord to this effect: "My beloved is gone down into his garden, to the beds of spices, to feed in the gardens and to gather lilies." (Song vi. 2.) And elsewhere she invites Jesus to come into his garden, and to eat of his pleasant fruits. And Jesus as instantly accepts the invitation, and saith, "I am come into my garden, my sister, my spouse! I have gathered my myrrh with my spice." (Song iv. 16; v. 1.) Sixthly, a garden requires much care in dressing, and pruning, and weeding, and the like; so the church of Jesus hath the constant care of her Lord. He saith himself, "I the Lord do keep it; I will water it every moment, lest any hurt it; I will keep it night and day." (Isa. xxvii. 3.) And how, through pruning dispensations weeding out the remains of indwelling corruption in the heart, and by the digging round and nourishing the graces of her Lord's own planting, doth Jesus keep alive and cause to flourish the several circumstances of his church and people. And lastly, to mention no more, as in gardens the owners gather for their use the several productions of their gardens, so Jesus for his own glory gathers the fruits of his own Holy Spirit, planted in the hearts of his redeemed while on earth, gathers their persons at death, and transplants them into his garden above, to flourish under his almighty hand in glory for ever. So very beautiful is the similitude of a garden to the church; and, no doubt, under several other particulars the allusion might be found to correspond. Jesus! I would say, let thy garden thy church be always blessed with thy presence!

GAREB

The word means a pitcher. It was a hill near Jerusalem. (See Jer. xxxi. 39.) If this hill was, as it is said to have been, three miles distant from Jerusalem, it serves to give a beautiful idea of the future extensiveness of the holy city. (See Ezek. xl. &c. Zech. ii. &c. Rev. xxi. 10. to the end.)

GARMENT

The wedding garment of Scripture, particularly spoken of, (Matt. xxii. 11.) hath been a subject of so much anxiety to many precious souls, that the matter itself ought to be put in the clearest light possible. The general belief is, that by it is meant Christ's person, work, and righteousness. And hence the church is represented as singing, "I will greatly rejoice in the Lord: my soul shall be joyful in my God, for he hath clothed me with the garments of salvation, he hath covered me with the robe of righteousness, as a bridegroom decketh himself with ornaments, and as a bride adorneth herself with her jewels." (Isa. lxi. 10.) And this corresponds to what the Lord Jesus counselled the church of Laodicea to buy of him "white raiment, that she might be clothed." (Rev. iii. 18.) Hence, therefore, what is the garment, but Christ's righteousness, in which all the faithful are clothed, when justified in the perfect salvation of the Lord?

GATE and GATES

In Scripture these expressions are not limited to the doors, or entrances, into an house, or city; but the term is figuratively made use of to denote place, or person, or people. Thus the gates of hell means hell itself; gates of judgment, the place where justice was awarded. "Salvation will God appoint for walls and bulwarks;" meaning, that all rests upon this bottom, in a way of grace, mercy, and salvation. (Isa. xxvi. 1.)

GATH

A city in the land of the Philistines, from Gath, a press. Hence Gath-opher, to dig at the wine press, from Chaphar, to dig; and Gath, a press. So Gathrimmon, the press of the pomegranate, from Garb, a press; and Rimmon, a pomegranate tree.

GAZA

Another city in the land of the Philistines. This was given by Joshua to Judah. (Josh. xv. 47.)

GENEALOGY

This record of families which we call genealogy, is termed in Hebrew Sepher Toledoth; or the book of generations. The Jews were particular to an excess, to record their families; no doubt, with an eye to Christ.

GENERATION

This word derived from the same root is much the same as the preceding word genealogy. As it relates to the common act of man in the circumstances of descent from father to son, I should not have though it needful to have detained the reader with a single observation; but in relation to the Son of God, as God, it becomes of infinite importance as an article of faith, that we should have the clearest apprehension which the subject will admit. Here, therefore, I beg the reader's close attention to it.

The Scriptures in many places have said so much in defining the person of the Father and of the Son, as distinctions in the GODHEAD, that there can be nothing rendered more certain and as an article of faith to the believer, and none is more important. But while this is held forth to us in this view as a point most fully to be believed, God the Holy Ghost hath in no one passage, as far as I can recollect, pointed out to the church the mode of existence, or explained how the Son of God is the Son, and the Father is the Father, in the eternity of their essence and nature. Perhaps it is impossible to explain the vast subject to creatures of our capacities. Perhaps nothing finite can comprehend what is infinite. The doctrine of the eternal generation of the Son of God is therefore proposed as an article demanding our implicit faith and obedience; and here the subject rests.

But while this doctrine of the eternity of the Son of God in common with the Father, is held faith to us in the Scripture as a most certain truth, though unexplained, because our faculties are not competent to the explanation of it, the Holy Ghost hath been very explicit in teaching the church how to understand the phrases in his sacred word, where the Son of God, when standing up as the Mediator and Head of his church before all worlds, is called the "first begotten Son, and the only begotten of the Father," full of grace and truth. All these and the like phrases wholly refer to the Son of God, in his humbling himself as our Redeemer and Mediator, the God-man in one person, Christ Jesus; then begotten to this great design; the first in all JEHOVAH'S purposes for salvation. Here we cannot be at a loss to have the clearest apprehension; because they refer to his office-character. Hence all those titles are very plain. "He is the head of his body the church." (Ephes. i. 22.) The Head of Christ is God. (1 Cor. xi. 3.) He is JEHOVAH'S servant. (Isa. xlii. 1.) and his Father is greater than he. (John xiv. 28.) And God is the God and Father of our Lord Jesus Christ. (Ephes. i. 17.) All these and numberless expressions of the like nature, wholly refer to the Son of God as Christ; and have no respect to his eternal nature and GODHEAD abstracted from his office-character as Mediator. See Begotten.

And I cannot in this place help expressing my wish that the writers of commentaries on the word of God had kept this proper distinction, when speaking of the Lord Jesus, between his eternal nature and essence, as Son of God, which is every where asserted, but no where explained, and his office-character as God-man Mediator, the Christ of God, which is fully revealed. The Scriptures have done it. And it would have been a proof of divine teaching, if all writers upon the Scriptures had done the same. Our almighty Saviour, in a single verse, hath shewn it, when he saith, (Matt. xi. 27.) "No man knoweth the Son but the Father;" that is, knoweth him as Son of God, knoweth him in his Sonship as God, one with the Father, and impossible to be so known but by God himself. And it is in this sense also, that it is said, "No man hath seen God at any time; the only begotten Son, which lay in the bosom of the Father, he hath declared him;" (John i. 18.) that is, no man hath seen God, as God, in his threefold character of person, Father, Son, and Holy Ghost. But when he who lay in the bosom of the Father came forth in our nature, and revealed him as the Father and himself as the Son, equal in the eternity of their nature as God; then the glorious truth was explained. Then was it understood, that the Father, as Father, and the Son, as Son, were from all eternity the same; their existence the same, their nature the same; the Father not being Father but in the same instant as the Son the Son; for the very name of the one in the relationship implies the other, and the eternity of the one including the eternity of the other also. So that both, in union with the Holy Ghost, form the one eternal undivided JEHOVAH, which was, and is, and is to come.

GENESIS

The first book of Moses; so called because it contains the genealogy of the patriarchs. The original name in Hebrew is Berescheth, beginning. It includes a period of near two thousand four hundred years, from the beginning of the world to the death of Joseph.

GENTILE

The Hebrews called the Gentiles, Goyim; that is, the nations who did not receive and acknowledge the law: all such were called Goyim. And in case of the conversion of any to Judaism, they were then called Proselytes of the Gate.

GEBA Benjamite, (2 Sam

xvi. 5.) from Gera, pilgrimage.

GERGESENES

A place rendered memorable by our Lord's having visited it, and working a miracle there upon a poor creature under possession of an evil spirit. (See Matt. viii. 28.) It is more than probable, that this was the same nation as is called in the Old Testament Girgashites; one of the cities of Canaan beyond the sea of Tiberias.

GERIZIM

This in the mount from whence the Lord

commanded Joshua to bless the people; while mount Ebal was the mount appointed for the proclamation of the curses. (See Deut. xxvii, throughout; Josh. viii. 30. to the end.) Both those mountains were near Shechem in Ephraim, a province of Samaria. It should seem, that Gerizim was very near to Shechem; for Jotham, the son of Gideon, addressed the people of that city from it. (See Judg. ix 7.) The Samaritans had a high veneration for this mountain; witness the words of the adulteress at Jacob's well to Christ. "Our fathers (said she) worshipped in this mountain; and ye say, that in Jerusalem is the place where men ought to worship." (John iv. 20.)

GETHSEMANE

This name derives its origin from Ge, or Ghie, a valley; and Shemin, oil. It adjoined the foul book of Kedron, into which all the filth and uncleanness of the temple emptied itself. Here it was also, into this black brook, that the accursed things which the king of Israel destroyed were cast. (See 2 Kings xxiii. 12.) A striking type of the defilement and guilt emptied upon the person of Christ, as the Representative and Surety of his people, when passing over this brook Kedron, to enter the garden of Gethsemane, when the things typified were all to be fulfilled. Gethsemane was itself a village, at the foot of the mount of Olives; and the garden Jesus of times resorted to, saw part of this village. Gethsemane will always be memorable, and always sacred, to the mind of the true lover of the Lord Jesus Christ. It is impossible to have the very idea of this hallowed spot cross the recollection, without awakening the tenderest emotions. The Jews, unconscious of the cause, called it Gehennon, the valley of hell. It is the same word as Tophet. Here the sorrows of hell compassed the Redeemer. And as in a garden it was, that the powers of hell ruined our nature in the corruption of our first parents; so in a garden Jesus conquered hell. But not so, as without, blood. Witness his soul-agony, and those great drops of blood which fell from his sacred body. I would desire grace, that by faith I might often visit Gethsemane; and while traversing the hallowed ground, call to mind, that here it was Jesus entered upon that soul-conflict with the powers of darkness, which, when finished, completed the salvation of his people. Hail, sacred Gethsemane! (See Golgotha.--Cedron.)

GIANT and GIANTS

The Scripture speaks of such characters in the old world, Gen. vi. 4. And in the days of the church going though the wilderness, the king of Bashan, which opposed Israel, is described as having a bedstead of iron of nine cubits long, and four wide; so that the length was fifteen feet and four inches. And yet of later times, even in our own days, Mr. O'Brien, the Irish giant so called, was said to have been nine feet high. (See 2 Sam. xxi. 16. to the end.) The term for giant in Hebrew is very singular; it is Nophel: meaning, a monster.

GIBEON, GIBEONITES

Gibeon was the chief city; so called from Gabah, an hill. The Gibeonites form a very interesting subject in the Scripture history, and lead to an enquiry not less interesting. They were descendants, it is probable, from the Hivites; that is, of the nations of Canaan whom the Lord would drive out before Israel. And yet we find the fear of God was upon them, so as to act wisely to get interest with Israel. (See their history, Josh. ix. 3. throughout.) And we find in their farther history, (2 Sam. xxi. 1-6.) that the Lord took part with them when Saul would have destroyed them, and even sent a judgment upon Israel on their account. Were the Gibeonites in those instances a type of the salvation of the Gentile church, brought in by sovereign grace into the privileges of Christ Jesus? Was this nation set apart in those early ages of the church, by way of shewing Christ's interest in his people, in

GIDEON

See Jerubbaal.

GIFT

I should not have noticed this word, but with a view to speak of God's highest and best gift. The sweetest feature in the gospel is, that Christ, the great Author of it, is a gift of God; yea, the greatest and most important of all gifts, and including every other. For where Jesus is, there all blessings abound. Where he is not, it matters not what else there is. Hence Paul exclaims, "Now thanks be unto God for his unspeakable gift!" (2 Cor. ix. 15.)

GILBOA

See mount Gilboa.

GILEAD

There were several mountains of this name lying eastward of Jordan. The term itself is evidently taken from the word Gal, an heap; and Houd, testimony. The balm of Gilead is used in Scripture as typical of Christ. Hence the prophet exclaims, "Is there no balm in Gilead, no physician there?" Yes! both were there. Jesus's blood is a never-failing balm; and he himself a physician which never failed of a cure. "Why then is not the health of the daughter of my people recovered?" The answer is direct. If this balm be never used, and this physician never known or regarded, how shall the blessings of either be experienced? (Jer. viii. 22.)

I must not dismiss this article of Gilead without first taking notice of a beautiful similitude of our Lord's in Scripture, when comparing his church to this mount, on account of its loveliness. "Behold, (saith Jesus,) thou art fair, my love, thou art fair; thou hast dove's eyes within thy locks; thy hair is as a flock of goats, that appear from mount Gilead." (Song iv. 1.) Perhaps the fairness so often repeated by the Lord concerning the spouse, is to shew how lovely she is in his eyes, from "the comeliness he hath put upon her and the high value he hath for her. And the quickness of sight in the dove, shews how much knowledge Jesus imparts by his regenerating grace. The hair, it should seem, is commended for its beauty by the Lord, because of its nearness to the head, and immediately having its root there. So the saints of God are all beautiful in their order, from being united to, and deriving all their life and nourishment from, Jesus their glorious Head. And as the flocks on mount Gilead, high and lifted up, live securely, feed luxuriously, and are lovely in their numbers and good order; so the fold of Christ have their Gilead, that glorious mountain which was once "a stone cut out without hands;" but now filling the earth, where they live and dwell securely. Jesus himself is their food and their pasture, "their munition of rocks, where their bread is given and their water sure; where they lie down in safety, and none shall make them afraid." (Isa. xxxiii. 16.)

GIRDLE

There are several sorts of girdles spoken of in Scripture. The Jews, in general, wore girdles. Soldiers wore belts for their swords; (Neh. iv. 18.) and the priests had their girdles also. (Exod. xx. 4-8.) The holy Scriptures, by a beautiful allusion to this strengthener of a man's loins by the girdle, conveys to the church a most lively and striking idea of God's strengthening himself in his faithfulness to his people. "Righteousness shall be the girdle of his loins, and faithfulness the girdle of his reins." (Isa. xi. 5.) The meaning is, that as the labourer goeth forth in the morning of the day to his labour, and strengthens himself for the work by bracing up his loins with his girdle; so the Lord, speaking after

GITTITH - GLORIFY

the manner of men, takes his righteousness for the girdle of his administration, which cleaves to him as the girdle to the loins of a man; and his faithfulness becomes the bandage of his word and truth to all his covenant promises, as the rectitude of his reins. And to carry on the figure--As the Lord is thus clad with both, and they surround him like a girdle, so his people are called upon to take hold of both, or either, as occasion requires, whether before or behind, and hang upon the gracious assurances of a gracious faithful covenant God in Christ. "Wherefore (saith one of the apostles,) gird up the loins of your mind; be sober, and hope to the end; for the grace that is to be brought unto you at the revelation of Jesus Christ. (1 Pet. i. 13.)

GITTITH

This word is found in Scripture only at the head, or title page, of several Psalms; namely, the eighth, eighty-first and eighty-fourth. Various have been the opinions of the learned concerning it, and for the most part different. Some contend, that it means the wine-presses. Others will insist, that it refers to some musical instruments used in the temple-service. Some derive it from the word Gath; and, therefore, conclude it refers to that city. And another class suppose it means Goliah, the Gittite. But be it what it may, certain it is, that the knowledge of it in the present hour cannot be very important, as God the Holy Ghost hath not thought it essential to be known by the church. The Psalms which bear this name in the title, are not less blessed for our ignorance on this point; though if it be, as it is possible it may have, a reference to the Lord Jesus Christ, it would be gratifying to know it. See Musician.

GLORIFY

We meet with this word very often in Scripture, and we cannot be too particular in our proper apprehension of its meaning. It is not very difficult to understand how JEHOVAH is glorified actively, when we give to him the glory that is due to his holy name. God is said to be glorified, when we honour him in his word, his attributes, his perfections, and in all his dispensations, both in nature, providence and grace. "Whoso offereth me praise, saith JEHOVAH, he glorifieth me." (Ps. li. 23.) We may be said to glorify God, when we give him the credit due to God in believing him, and especially in that record he hath given of his dear Son. In this view of giving glory to God is included all that self-abasement becoming poor lost creatures, and ascribing the whole of redemption to sovereign, free, and unmerited grace. In short, in every way, and by every means, we may be said to glorify JEHOVAH when Christ, as the Christ of God, is exalted as the only Saviour of a lost world; and the soul lies low at the footstool of the throne of grace, ascribing "salvation only to God and the Lamb." This is to glorify God actively.

But then it should be carefully remembered at the same time, and never lost sight of, that all this, and ten thousand times more, in giving glory to JEHOVAH, doth not in fact add an atom to his glory. God is all-glorious in himself, whether his creatures praise him, or do not. Resting in his own eternal glory and all-sufficiency, nothing can add to, or take from that glory. Sooner might light be added to the sun by a faint taper of the night, or sound to the thunder by the human voice, than that JEHOVAH can receive additional glory from any act, or from all the acts of his creatures, put them all together in one. No! the giving glory to God is spoken of in accommodation to human apprehension, and after the manner of men, to intimate the suitable and becoming frame in man towards God, and his sense of divine goodness.

But beside this glorifying God actively, there is another method by which the Lord is said to be glorified by his creatures passively; namely, when under suited impressions of his goodness the soul lies passive, and comes to receive, and not to give; and from the Lord's grace thereby to minister to the Lord's glory. And this is as blessed a way as the former, and in which the Lord is truly glorified.

When God in Christ gives out of his fulness mercy, pardon, grace, yea, imparts of himself the suited supply to the wants of the millions of his people, this is to his glory. He doth, indeed, get himself a glorious name, and is glorified in all the gracious acts by which his love and rich mercy is thus made known. And if poor needy creatures had but such views of the clemency of heaven, they would see what encouragement it gives to faith, to be always looking up to God's free bounty in Christ, to receive from his fulness, and grace for grace. When a poor believing soul can say, it is the glory and perfection of a God in Christ to be laying out upon his redeemed of his infinite and inexhaustible fulness; and Christ in God is as much glorified by my poor heart, when passively receiving from his grace bestowed upon me, as when I actively praise him with joyful lips, when by his Holy Spirit he enables me to bring my poor boon of love and thankfulness. This is to glorify God.

The reader will be pleased to observe, that in all I have here noticed of glorifying JEHOVAH, I have hitherto confined the subject to that part of the divine glory given to him by his church and people, under those two branches of it, actively and passively. But a yet far higher view of glorifying the Lord remains to be considered. The transcendent glory of JEHOVAH is in the person of Christ, as God-man Mediator. Here the whole glory of JEHOVAH, Father, Son and Holy Ghost, centres. In Christ that glory shines out in one full constellation. The Holy Ghost, by the apostle, describes it in a short verse, when speaking of Christ's person. "In him dwelleth all the fulness of the GODHEAD bodily." (Col. ii. 9.) But what angels or men can describe this? And in Christ's ministry, offices, character, work, and relations in the accomplishment, who shall undertake to set forth the glory of the Father in the Son, and the glory of the Son by the Father, through the efficient operation of God the Holy Ghost?

I will only add, that it forms a part of that glory which all the persons of the GODHEAD are concerned in, and will be loved, and praised, and adored for, to all eternity by the church, when the church is glorified and made everlastingly happy, from her union with her glorious Head Christ Jesus, and brought home through a life of grace here, to a life of unspeakable nearness, felicity, and glory in Christ Jesus hereafter, and to rest in the uninterrupted enjoyment of it for evermore. This also is to the divine glory.

GLORY

This word in the abstract, properly speaking belongs only to God; for there can be glory in no other. Hence the prophet speaks to the church, "Thy God thy glory." (Isa. ix. 19.) So that JEHOVAH, in his threefold character of person, is truly and strictly glory. Hence, when the Lord is speaking of the great works of creation, in creating the heavens and stretching them out, and spreading forth the earth; and also of the wonders of redemption by his Son; he confirms the oneness in nature, work, and design of Christ, and the adoration due to him as one with himself; and saith, "I am the Lord, that is my name, and my glory will I not give to another, neither my praise to graven images." (Isa. xlii, 5-8.) Where by the way, it may be observed, here is the highest confirmation of the GODHEAD of Christ. For in the same moment that JEHOVAH declares his jealousy of his name and glory, and that he will not give his glory to another, neither his praise to graven images, he commands both praise and glory to be given to his dear Son, whom he gives as a covenant to the people, that he

GLORIOUS - GLORIOUS

may have all the praise and glory of redemption. A plain proof that in JEHOVAH'S esteem Christ is one with the Father, "over all, God blessed for ever." Amen. (Rom. ix. 5.) The glory of JEHOVAH, though, no doubt, existing personally in the essence of the GODHEAD, can only be known by his creatures in the manifestation of it. "He dwells in that light, or glory, which no man can approach unto." So that all we can know or conceive of his glory, must result from such manifestations as he hath been pleased to make of himself in his works. Thus when Moses desired, that the Lord would shew him his glory, the Lord said, "I will make all my goodness pass before thee; and I will proclaim the name of the Lord." (Exod. xxxiii. 18, 19.) His name, which is his person, therefore is, in the abstract; glory; and the manifestation of it is in his ways and winks. Hence the church is said to be his glory, inasmuch as the Lord is glorified in her salvation. For as the glorious Head of his body the church in his mediatorial character, "is the brightness of his Father's glory, and the express image of his person;" so the brethren, the messengers of the churches, are said to be the glory of Christ, 2 Cor. viii. 23. And the Lord promiseth to be to the church, not only "a wall of fire to defend round about, but the glory in the midst." (Zech. ii, 5.)

Names are sometimes given by the vanity of men to creatures concerning glory, but the holy Scriptures express their total disapprobation of it. Thus the Lord, speaking of the pride of the king of Assyria, (Isa. viii. 7.) declares, that all his glory shall come to nought. And the Lord Jesus speaking of Solomon's glory, describes it as nothing compared to the humblest lilies of the field. (Matt. vi. 28. 29.) And hence that gracious precept of the Lord by the prophet: "Thus saith the Lord, Let not the wise man glory in his wisdom, neither let the mighty man glory in his might; let not the rich man glory in his riches; but let him that glorieth, glory in this, that he understandeth and knoweth me, that I am the Lord which exercise loving kindness, judgment, and righteousness in the earth; for in these things I delight, saith the Lord." (Jer ix. 23, 24.)

I cannot forbear requesting the reader's attention, under this article, to a sweet and interesting feature of Christ, as the Glory-man Christ Jesus. I say, as the Glory-man; for I would beg to be understood, that this name is peculiarly belonging to our Jesus, and to him only. His people in him, and through him, will hereafter be brought to glory, and will be, we are told, in point of glory as the angels. (Matt. xxii. 30.) But though glorious from a derived glory from Christ, yet not glory, in the abstract, in themselves. This is peculiarly and personally his; so that Jesus is the Glory-man, as the God-man Mediator. If the reader would wish to see the Scripture authority for this name, he will find it John xvii. 5. where the glory Jesus then speaks of as Mediator, was unquestionably the glory in which he stood up at the call of God when "the Lord possessed him in the beginning of his ways before his works of old, and when his delights were with the sons of men." (See Prov. viii. 22-31.)

I would only beg to add one thought more upon this subject, and to observe to the true believer in Jesus the blessedness the heart of that man feels, who, to such views of the divine glory, can set to his seal the truth of it in his own personal experience, when with the apostle he can say, "God, who commanded the light to shine out of darkness, hath shined in our hearts, to give the light of the knowledge of the glory of God in the face of Jesus Christ." (2 Cor. iv. 6.)

GLORIOUS

This is a term we meet with in Scripture, taken from the former, and is applied to the Lord as solely his. But the church, considered from her union with Christ as part of himself, is also spoken of as glorious in him. Moses's song celebrates the Lord's glory in relation to his perfections. "Thy right hand. O, Lord, is become glorious: who is like unto thee, O Lord, among the gods? who is like thee, glorious in holiness, fearful in praises, doing wonders." (Exod. xv. 6. 11.) So the church, in consequence of her union with Christ, is said to be all-glorious within. (Ps. xlv. 13.) And the great object of redemption is said to be, that Jesus might present to himself a glorious church. (Ephes. v. 27.) But it should ever be remembered, that all the glory of the church is with an eye to Christ. If she be without spot, or wrinkle, or any such thing, and made comely, it is only "from the comeliness Jesus hath put upon her." (Ezek. xvi. 14.)

GOAT

This animal was one of the clean beasts, and used in the Jewish church both for food and sacrifice. (Lev. xvi. 5.) and the veil of the tabernacle was made of the hair of the goat. (Exod. xxv. 4.) But in the after ages of the church, the goat became figurative of the ungodly. And, perhaps, this arose from the calves and devils (literally goats), which Jeroboam set up for idol worship. (See 2 Cor. xi 14, 15.) Hence the Lord is represented by the prophet, as punishing the goats; that is, the worshippers of those dunghill idols. (Zech. x. 3.) Hence also another prophet exclaims, "Hell from beneath is moved for thee, to meet thee at thy coming; it stirreth up the dead for thee, even all the chief ones of the earth;" The margin of the Bible hath it, even all the great goats of the earth; meaning the princes and great men. (Isa. xiv. 9.) Hence our blessed Lord, in describing the solemn events of the last day, describes the wicked and ungodly as goats on his left hand, destined for destruction. (Matt. xxv. 33.)

I have been more particular on this subject, in order to explain wherefore it is, that as the goat was by the Lord's own appointment of the clean beasts both for good and sacrifice, that the Lord Jesus and his servant should make the goat a figure, or emblem, of the reprobate, and as distinguished from the sheep of his fold. And this the account of the goat set up as an idol by Jeroboam, and sacrificed to by the people in direct opposition to the God of Israel, very fully explains.

While I am upon this subject of the goat, it may not be unacceptable to the pious reader, to say a few words on the very striking ceremony appointed by the Lord of the scape goat on the great day of atonement. I need not describe the ceremony itself, for the reader will find a full account thereof, Lev. xvi. There is somewhat most wonderfully interesting when this service of the scape goat is considered with an eye to Christ. The high priest laying both his hands on the head of the beast, and making a confession over him of all the iniquities of the children of Israel, with all their transgressions in all their sins, as if transferring both the sin and guilt from themselves to another; certainly this had no meaning but in reference to the Lord Jesus Christ; and certainly, beheld in allusion to him, the whole service becomes plain and obvious. The Suretyship of Christ is hereby most blessedly shadowed forth; and both the law of God and the justice of God in that Suretyship evidently satisfied. Indeed, the type falls short of the thing itself in one point; for the scape goat was altogether passive in the act, but Christ, in his voluntary surrender of himself, manifested a willing offering. On the part of God the Father, the type, and the thing signified by the type, became one and the same. For though it is out of any creature's power, to make a transfer of sin to another, yet it is not beyond the sovereignty and prerogative of God. And when the Lord Jesus, at the call of God, stood up from everlasting as the covenant Head of his people, his voluntary offering gave efficacy to the whole. In this he undertook to answer for all

GOD - GOD

their sins, and to do away the whole of their guilt and pollution by the sacrifice of himself. Hence JEHOVAH is represented by the prophet, as "laying upon him the iniquity of us all." (Isa. liii. 6.) And Jesus is no less represented as saying, "Lo, I come to do thy will, O God." (Ps. xl. 7, 8.)

I would just ask the reader, whether such a view doth not bring comfort to the soul, in thus beholding the transfer of sin, with all its defilement, taken from our poor nature, and put upon the person of Christ. How blessed must it have been in God the Holy Ghost, to have had the representation made of it in an age so distant from the thing itself, as if to testify the Lord's approbation of it in the people's safety. Though the Scriptures are silent upon it, yet the history of the scape goat among the Jews, has handed down by tradition the account, which is not uninteresting. It is said, that when the two goats were led into the inner court of the temple and presented to the high priest, according to the Lord's appointment of casting lots, (Lev. xvi. 8.) the scape goat, or as the margin of the Bible expresseth it, the Azazel, had then a fillet, or a narrow piece of scarlet, fastened to its head, which soon became white. And hence the prophet is supposed to allude when saying, "though your sins be as scarlet, they shall be white as snow; though they be red like crimson, they shall be as wool." (Isa. i. 18.) The scape goat was then sent away, by the hand of some fit man, or as the margin of the Bible hath it, by a man of opportunity, into the wilderness. Some of the Jews say, that the edge of the wilderness had a precipice where the Azazel fell over, and was dashed to pieces. But the "wilderness which no man went through, and none inhabited," carried with it the same idea, that "the iniquity of Israel when, sought for, there should be none; and the sins of Judah, and they should not be found." (Jer. l. 20.) When the Lord puts away sin, in Scripture language it is said, "that he remembers it no more." (Heb. viii. 15. with Jer. xxxi. 34.)

GOD

We enter with profound veneration and holy awe upon any attempt to explain what is in itself beyond the grasp of men or angles to apprehend. When we pronounce the glorious name of God, we desire to imply all that is great, gracious, and glorious in that holy name; and having said this, we have said all that we can say. The Scriptures have given several names, by way of expressing all that can be expressed of him; that he is the First and the Last, and the Author and Creator of all things. It is worthy observation, that the Lord speaking of himself to Moses, (Exod. vi. 2, 3.) saith, "I am JEHOVAH: And I appeared unto Abraham, unto Isaac, and unto Jacob, by the name of God Almighty (El Shaddai,) but by my name JEHOVAH was I not known to them." By which we are not to imagine, that the Lord was not known to the patriarchs as their Creator, and as self-existing; but the meaning is, that he had not so openly revealed himself. They know him in his adorable perfections, but not so clearly in his covenant relations. So that the name itself was not so different, as the great things implied in the name. For certain it is, that very early in the church men began to call upon the name of JEHOVAH, (Gen. iv. 26.) And Abram told the king of Sodom, that he had lifted up his hand unto the Lord, the most High God. Here we have both the names expressly used by Abram, Gen. xiv. 22. But certain it is, that never until this revelation by Moses, did the church understand how the incommunicable name of JEHOVAH became the security of fulfilling all the promises.

And this seems to be more fully revealed from the very manner in which the Lord communicated it to Moses. I AM that I AM; that is, I have a being in myself, and, consequently, I give being to all my promises. And it is worthy farther of remark, that the very name JEHOVAH carries this with it; for it is an Hemantick noun, formed from Hayah, he was; as expressing his eternity. The Jews had so high a veneration for this sacred name, that they never used it but upon memorable occasions. We are told by Eusebius, that in his days the Jews wrote the holy name in Samaritan characters, when they had occasion to mention the name of the Lord, lest that strangers, and not of the stock of Israel, should profane it. And in modern times it is generally observed by the seed of Abraham, when marking the number fifteen (which in the ordinary way of doing it by letters would take the Yod (10,) and the He (5.) forming the incommunicable name of Jah,) they always take the Teth and the Vau, that is the 9 and the 6, instead of it, to make the number fifteen by. A plain proof in what high veneration the sacred name was held by them. It were devoutly to be wished, that men calling themselves Christians were always to give so lively an evidence of their reverence to that "glorious and fearful name, **THE LORD THY GOD.**" (Deut. xxviii. 58.)

It is said in the history of the Jews, that after their return from Babylon, they lost the true pronunciation of this glorious name JEHOVAH. And certain it is, that none know the real and correct manner in which it should be pronounced. But what a precious thought is it to the believer in Jesus that "if any man love God, the same is known by him." (I Cor. viii.3.) I only add, that in confirmation of the blessed doctrine of our holy faith, it is our happiness to know, that this glorious name is equally applied to each and to all the persons of the GODHEAD. To God the Father, Eph. i. 3; to God the Son, John i. 1; and to God the Holy Ghost, Acts v. 3, 4. And to the whole Three glorious persons in the unity of the divine essence, 1 John v. 7. (See JEHOVAH.)

GOG and MAGOG

Gog, whose name signifies roof, or covering, it should seem, was some prince; and Magog not a person, but the kingdom. So that it is Gog, and prince of Magog. Some have thought, that these names are general names for the enemies of the church, because they are spoken of both in Ezekiel's prophecy, and the book of Revelation by St. John. (Ezek. xxxviii, and Rev. xx.) It will well reward the reader to turn to the prophecy of Ezekiel, at the thirty-eighth chapter, in confirmation of this latter opinion.

The land of unwalled villages, and the people that dwell in the midst of the land, or as the margin of the Bible hath it, the navel of the land, can mean no other than Jerusalem, supposed to be the centre of the earth; and, therefore, the sea that bounds the borders in these parts very properly called the Mediterranean. And let the reader judge for himself how suitable it was, and proper, that when the Lord Jesus came on earth to do away the sin and guilt of all nations, the solemn transaction of his "one all-sufficient sacrifice and obedience unto death" should be set forth in the center of the earth, that like the sun in the midway of the heavens which illumines both east and west; so Christ, the sun of righteousness, might extend the efficacy of his light, and life, and warmth in every direction to his people; and his blood, as from the high altar of his own divine nature, flowing down, might wash away, from the morning of creation to the end of time, the whole of human transgression.

GOLD

I should not have paused over this word, had I not recollected in the moment of reading it, that the Holy Ghost is graciously pleased to make use of it as a figure to represent the Lord Jesus by, in several parts of the divine word; and also the church is spoken of, from her union with her Lord, by the same similitude. "His head (said the church, when commending the beauties of her Lord,) is as the most fine gold." (Song

GOLD - GOLD

v. 11.) "His hands are as gold rings set with the beryl." (Song v. 14.) And the Lord Jesus, speaking of his church, made comely in his comeliness, saith, "Thy cheeks are comely with rows of jewels; thy neck with Chains of gold. We will make thee borders of gold, with studs of silver." (Song i. 10, 11.) As gold is the richest and most valued of all metals, so by this figure is meant to say, that the Headship of Christ is every thing that is rich, valuable and glorious to his body the church. Yea, as the Scripture saith, when referring to the Lord Jesus as God-man Mediator, "the head of Christ is God." (1 Cor. xi. 3.) It is probable, that an eye to God the Father, under this similitude, might also be meant. For though in respect to the divine nature, Christ is "one with the Father, over all, God blessed for ever." (Rom. ix. 5.) Yet in respect to his human nature, the Father may truly be said to be the head of Christ; for he saith himself, "A body hast thou given me, or prepared me." (Ps. xl. 6. with Heb. x. 5.)

But it is very blessed to eye the Lord Jesus under this figure. As the Head of his body the well be compared to the most fine gold; for the Psalmist saith, in allusion to his royal dignity and power, JEHOVAH put "a crown of pure gold upon his head, When he made him most blessed for ever." (Ps. xxi. 1-7.) And as all this, and infinitely more to the same effect, is spoken of Christ in allusion to his mediatorial character, the Head of his church and people, so this endears Jesus the more, inasmuch as all his people are so highly interested in all that belongs to him. Gold is a proper figure to represent the glories of his person, the excellency of his kingdom, the purity and spiritual nature of it, the durableness of it and the splendour and everlasting glory of it; for all his people are made kings and priests, by virtue of his riches and glory to God and the Father. (Rev. i. 6.) And as Christ's head is compared on all these, and the like accounts to gold: so his hands to rings of gold set with beryl, from the liberal manner in which he bestows gifts and graces to his redeemed. "In his right hand, saith Solomon, is length of days, and in his left hand riches and honour." (Prov. iii. 16.) The beryl was one of the precious stones in the breastplate of the High Priest. (Exod. xxviii. 20.) And John tells the church, that the beryl was among the foundation-stones of the new Jerusalem. (Rev. xxi. 20.) What those precious stones implied cannot need inquiry, since elsewhere we are told, that Christ is the foundation-stone JEHOVAH hath laid in Zion; and the church, both in heaven and earth, rests wholly upon him, the chief corner stone, "in whom all the building fitly framed together, groweth unto an holy temple in the Lord." (Ephes. ii. 20, 21.)

It is blessed to behold also the church spoken of under the same similitude, from her union and oneness with her Lord. The neck and cheeks of the church, the parts connected with the head, made comely with jewels and chains of gold, may be supposed to mean those graces, with which her Lord hath adorned her, "more to be desired than gold, yea, than much fine gold." And when a soul is blessed in the everlasting covenant with all spiritual blessings in Christ Jesus, there is a loveliness indeed, which is as an "ornament of grace unto the head, and as chains about the neck." (Prov. i. 9.) And what tends to endear the whole is, that all the persons of the GODHEAD concur in this vast work of adorning the church with blessings, more valuable than the "golden wedge of Ophir." It is said, "We will make thee borders of gold, with studs of silver;" meaning, surely, the joint work and grace of Father, Son, and Holy Ghost, in whose joint names all true believers in Christ are baptized, and blessed upon earth, and everlastingly made happy and glorious in heaven. (Matt. xxviii. 19. 2 Cor. xiii. 14. Rev. vii. 9-12.)

GOLDEN CANDLESTICKS

The view which the beloved apostle had of the Lord Jesus as related to the church. (Rev. i. 10. to the end,) makes it proper to notice something of what seems to have been highly emblematical in our Lord's appearing in the midst of the golden candlesticks. I detain the reader, therefore, in this place, to take a short notice of it. Of the Jewish church we read of one candlestick of gold, with six branches, in the tabernacle, (Exod. xxv. 31, 32.) But here we read of seven candlesticks, and the Lord Jesus in the midst. We can easily conceive concerning the one, that it was intended to prefigure the church, which until Christ came and gave light to it, like a candlestick which is a receiver only, and hath no light in itself, is as nothing. And when in the gospel church we behold seven candlesticks and the Lord Jesus in the discover that from the coming of Christ, when having finished redemption-work he returned to glory, he sent down the Holy Ghost in his seven-fold gifts to illumine the whole church of God with the revelation of his grace: so that the gracious office of the Holy Ghost in his unceasing agency is very blessedly set forth. And I do not think, that the Lord Jesus, in his high priestly office, could have been more strongly represented than by appearing thus in the midst of the candlesticks, his churches. For as it was the office of the Jewish high priest to trim the wicks and supply the oil, so Jesus, our great High Priest, supplies the whole by his blessed Spirit both to his ministers and people.

GOLGOTHA

Or perhaps better read Gulgultha, a skull. This was the memorable spot where the Lord Jesus was crucified; a mountain northwest of Jerusalem. The Romans called it Calvarea, which we translate Calvary. And the tradition in the eastern world concerning it was, that this name was given to it from Adam having been buried there. So that the men of Syria called it Cranium, the skull. But be this as it may, here it was the Lord of life and glory offered up that holy sacred oblation of himself, for the sin and transgression of his redeemed, by which he obtained eternal redemption for all them that are sanctified. Sweet and solemn the meditation, when from Gethsemane to Golgotha the believer by faith traverses the sacred ground. If Moses with such earnestness desired to see the goodly mountain, and Lebanon, as he tells us he did, (Deut. iii. 24. 25.) because, that there he knew He whose "good will he had begun to enjoy at the bush," would go through the whole of redemption work, and finish it; what may be supposed the favoured contemplations of the faithful now at Gethsemane and Golgotha where they know Jesus did, indeed, according to the most sure prophecies concerning him, complete the salvation of his people! Here would my soul delight to wander, and often review the sacred ground. From hence it was, that clear and distinct views were first taken of the city of the living God. Golgotha's mount opened the perspective of the New Jerusalem, and gave to the eye of faith not only clear and distinct prospects of the certainty of the place, but also as clear and distinct assurances of the believer's right and interest by Jesus to the possession of it. And from that period to the present hour, and so on to the end of time, these views have never since been darkened. The song of faith is still the same, and the triumphs in the cross furnish out the same soul-reviving notes. "Blessed be the God and Father of our Lord Jesus Christ, which according to his abundant mercy hath begotten us again unto a lively hope, by the resurrection of Jesus Christ from the dead, to an inheritance, incorruptible, and undefiled, and that fadeth not away." (1 Pet. i. 3, 4.) See Gethsemane.

GOLIATH

The gaint of Gall, one of the sons of Amak.

GOMER - GOMORRHA

(See Josh. xi. 22.) His name signifies an heap, from Galah. The size of this man was enormous. "Six cubits and a span." So that supposing what is the common allowed measure of the cubit to have been, "one and twenty inches," and that a span was half a cubit, this man was eleven feet and four inches high. The armour he wore bore a correspondence to the greatness of his stature. His coat is said to have weighed five thousand shekels. A shekel was half an ounce. And if all the other parts of his armour carried a proportion to this, in his "helmet of brass, and the greaves of brass, and the target, and his spear's head, six hundred skels of iron," what an astonishing man must he have been in such an astonishing ponderous armour, in carrying that for exercise and slaughter which few strong men could lift from the ground! (See 1 Sam. xvii. throughout.) But how soon David the stripling conquered him, when armed and lead on to victory by the Lord. But in reading the history of this battle we stop short of the chief glory of it, if we do not eye the Lord Jesus Christ, the almighty David of his Israel, conquering hell, death, and the grave, in all his Goliahs which come forth to defy the army of the living God. Oh! how blessed it is in all to behold Christ going forth "for the salvation of his people!"

GOMER

The purchased wife of the prophet Hosea. She is said to have been the daughter of Diblaim--whether Father or mother--for it might the either. Her name signifies to finish or complete. (See Hos. i. 2, 3. and Hos. iii. 1-3.) The history as it is given to us in the Bible, both of the prophet and this adulteress, appears very singular and surprising. But some light is thrown upon it from the account given us by writers concerning the customs of the east. Contracts for marriages, it is said, were never formed without giving with the woman a certain measure of corn, as well as money, for a marriage portion. The corn intimated the hope of fruitfulness in children. But it should seem in the case of Hosea, that the portion here was not given by the parents, but by the prophet; and that this was of the Lord. The Lord said unto Hosea, "Go take unto thee a wife of whoredoms." And hence the prophet saith, "So I bought her to me for fifteen pieces of silver, and for an homer of barley, and an half homer of barley." (Hos. iii. 2.)

The spiritual sense of it is more plain than the literal. For the marrying an adulteress, and by the Lord's command, and the union of a prophet of the Lord with such a character, seems a measure not easily explained. But as typical of the Lord's being married to his adulteress Israel, the subject is not only clear, but highly instructive. We see in it God's grace amidst all our undeservings; and that "where sin hath abounded grace doth much more abound." To what a degree of spiritual adultery and fornication was our nature gone, when Christ betrothed that nature to himself! Here surely the prophet typified Christ, when he said, "Go yet, love a woman (beloved of her friend, yet an adulteress) according to the love of the Lord toward the children of, Israel." (Hos. iii. 1.)

GOMORRHA

The city of the plain destroyed by fire. (Gen. xix. 24.) The name seems suited to the place. Om, or Am, a people; Morah, or Marah, of bitterness. We have the awful relation of the event of Sodom and Gomorrha's overthrow in the chapter before referred to. And certain it is, that it was intended as a standing monument in the church of divine judgments. Israel is reminded of it Deut. xxix. throughout. And in allusion to the fire of Gomorrha, the apostle Jude describes the sad ruin of sinners under the image of suffering eternal fire. (Jude 7.) And Peter to the same effect. (2 Pet. ii. 6.) And in the Revelations the everlasting torments of the damned are described by the same image, in reference to Sodom and Gomorrha--"in a lake that burneth with fire and brimstone." (Rev. xxi. 8.)

Had there been ten righteous men in Sodom and Gomorrha, the Lord's grace would have been manifested in the salvation of the place. Blessed be our God, there is one in the Gomorrha of our world whose name is Wonderful, and for whose sake it stands to the present hour, and who will be the cause of his people's salvation to all eternity!

GOSHEN

Perhaps so called from Goshen, rain, or the dew of heaven in blessings. For this place being nearer to the Mediterranean sea than Upper Egypt, had plentiful showers to make it fertile. Here it was Jacob and his children dwelt, when brought down into Egypt. (Gen. xlvii. 1-6.) Perhaps there might have been even in those days, a remote idea to the times of the gospel in the name of Goshen; for even now in the present hour, that is truly a land of Goshen where Christ is truly known, and where heaven hath shed and is shedding its blessed influences, in the showers of his Holy Spirit; while all the earth is as Egypt in the dryness, where no rains are known, and where the gospel of Christ is not.

GOSPEL

Or God's spell. This is a Saxon word, meaning good tidings. The Greeks called the gospel evangelical; hence the writers of it are called Evangelists. The word itself, as used in modern language, means the proclamation of pardon, mercy, and peace, in and through Jesus Christ our Lord. And so infinitely important and interesting is it in the eyes of all men that are made partakers of its saving grace, that the very feet of them that are commissioned to preach it are said to be beautiful. "How beautiful upon the mountains are the feet of him that bringeth good tidings, that publisheth peace, that bringeth good tidings of good, that publisheth salvation, that saith unto Zion, Thy God reigneth!" (Isa. lii. 7.) And, indeed, the gospel is, without exception, the best news JEHOVAH ever proclaimed to man, or man ever heard. Angels thought so, when at the command of God they posted down from heaven, at the birth of Christ, as if ambitious to be the first preachers of it to a lost world, and in a multitude of the heavenly host met together, to proclaim the blessed tidings to the Jewish shepherds, saying, "Glory to God in the highest, and on earth, peace, good will towards men." (Luke ii. 13, 14.)

GOURD

Jonah's gourd makes the thing itself memorable, which without the circumstance referring to him, would have formed nothing more important in the church than any other plant. The Hebrews called it Kikajon. The wild gourd is of another genus, and called Pekaah. It is said to be so bitter, that it is called "the gall of the earth." (2 Kings iv. 89.) Some have thought, that Jonah's gourd is the same as the Palma Christi. See Palm tree. I would only observe under this article of Jonah's gourd, how beautiful a lesson was the prophet taught (and, consequently, we ought to learn from it,) had he been wise to have improved it, how little to be valued are all earthly comforts, which even a poor worm of the earth may destroy. A night brings forth our worldly enjoyments; and a night is more than enough to destroy them. Oh! how blessed to live upon an unchangeable God in Christ, "the same yesterday, and to-day, and for ever!"

GOZAN

The name of a river. (2 Kings xvii. 6.)

GRACE

This word hath a variety of meanings in the word of God, as it relates to the divine power, and as it relates to man. When we speak of grace in relation to God, it hath a vast comprehension of meaning. The whole gospel is called the grace of God. And the application of it, in any individual instance of its saving power, is called "the grace of God. By grace ye are saved (saith the apostle,) through faith; and that not of yourselves, it is the gift of God." (Eph. ii. 8.) The grace of God is free, like the light, or the dew of heaven. Grace acts from itself to itself; nothing of human power, Or merit, disposing to it, nor of unworthiness keeping from it. So that every thing by Christ is grace; and to suppose any one pre-disposing act in the creature, or any merit in the creature, would altogether alter and destroy the very property of grace. (See Rom. xi. 6.) What is meant by grace in man, means altogether favour and affection. Thus Joseph found grace; that is, favour in the sight of his master. (Gen. xxxix. 4. So Abraham, Gen. xviii. 1-3. The case is similar in the case of Lydia, Acts xvi. 15.)

GRAPES

The Scripture speak of two sorts of grapes, the true, and the wild. And while the former is both good for food and delight, the other is poisonous and destructive. The blood of the grape is spoken of by the dying patriarch Jacob, (Gen. xlix. 11.) perhaps not without reference to the sacramental ordinance of the Lord's Supper. Moses beautifully contrasts the vineyards of the wicked with the vineyards of the Lord of hosts. "Their vine (saith he,) is of the vine of Sodom, and of the fields of Gomorrha; their grapes are grapes of gall, their clusters are bitter." (Deut. xxxii. 32,) Whereas the vineyard of the Lord of hosts is compared to the "rich clusters of Engedi." (Song i. 14.) We are told by an ancient writer, that so luxurious were the branches and clusters of grapes in the eastern world, that there have been seen some of ten and twelve pounds. Indeed, in our own country in hot houses, clusters of many pounds have been gathered. I cannot, under this article, forbear remarking the kindness of that precept in Israel concerning the vineyard, that when the Israelites gathered in their vintage, the gleanings should be for those that had no vineyard (Lev. xix. 9, 10.) And it should seem, that in the gleaning season the vineyards were thrown open, for the traveller passing by to have the benefit of it. I leave the reader to make his own comment; but I cannot but think, that there was much of gospel veiled under this precept. The gleaning season in Christ's church is all the year. Thousands going by have found gleaning seasons to their souls daily; and the invitation, indeed, is to the highways, and lanes, and hedges of the city, to call in "the poor, and the maimed, and the halt, and the blind." And even when these are come, and their souls have been filled, "still there is room." So infinitely full and so infinitely gracious is the great Lord of the vineyard, that all application ceases before that any diminishing is found in him and his vineyard, to supply. (Luke xiv. 21, 22.) See Cluster.

H

HABAKKUK

The prophet. His name is derived from Chabak, signifying, one that embraceth. Of his descent and family the Holy Ghost is silent. His prophetical writings are truly scriptural, and are contained in three chapters, which we have in our Bibles. They carry evident marks with them of divine inspiration. The apostle Paul makes a quotation from the second chapter, and fourth verse. (See Heb. x. 38.) The story related of Habakkuk carrying a dinner to Daniel in the lions' den, as it is stated in the fabulous tale of Bel and the Dragon, is like the story itself, altogether a fiction, and is as disgraceful as it is untrue. The time of Habakkuk's ministry is, in itself, enough to confute it; for this prophet lived long before the Babylonish captivity, as appears from his predicting that event. (See Habak. i. 6.) Some have endeavoured to soften the story, by supposing the dinner Habakkuk is said to have carried Daniel was his writings, particularly that passage in them where it is said, "The just shall live by his faith." But this is rather giving countenance to a story that ought to be refuted, and by no means admissible. The very Jews themselves deny the tale.

HABITATION

This word is of gracious import. In reference to the sweet promises of God, as indwelling in his people, and they living by faith upon the gracious truth, nothing can be more delightful. "Lo, I come; and I will dwell in the midst of thee, saith the Lord." (Zech. ii. 10.) And in one of the richest promises of the Bible, our blessed Lord Jesus speaks to the same effect: "If a man love me (saith Jesus,) he will keep my words; and my Father will love him, and we will come unto him, and make our abode with him." (John. xiv. 23.) And the apostle Paul following the gracious words of his divine master, saith, that the whole spiritual building the church, is for "an habitation of God through the Spirit." (Ephes. ii. 22.)

HACHALIAH

The father of Nehemiah the Tirshatha. His name is compounded of Chakah and Jab, signifying a waiter upon the Lord. (See Neh. i. 1.)

HAGAR

Sarah's handmaid: she was an Egyptian. Her name Hagar signifies a stranger. We have her history at large, in the sixteenth and twenty-first chapters of Genesis; and a very interesting history it is. But we never should have known the spiritual import of it, had not God the Holy Ghost graciously taught the church, by the ministry of his servant the apostle Paul in his Epistle to the Galatians. From thence we learn, that the whole of those transactions respecting Sarah and Hagar was an allegory, or figure, of the covenants; the one of bondage in nature, the other of freedom by grace. Without this divine illustration the mind of man never could have conceived such an idea, neither have entered into a proper apprehension of the subject. Indeed, from the tendency of every man's mind by nature, to take part with flesh and blood rather than spiritual objects, we should have felt disposed to consider Hagar hardly dealt with, and Sarah unkind and cruel. But taught by divine instruction, from this beautiful allegory we learn the vast importance of being found belonging to a covenant of grace, and not with the bond-woman under the law of works. As the subject is so very highly interesting, I venture to persuade myself, that it will not be tedious to the reader, neither, under grace, will it be unprofitable to consider it yet a little more particularly.

The apostle was commissioned to tell the church, that this allegory represented the two covenants. Hagar and her son Ishmael, the law-covenant, gendering to bondage; Sarah and her son Isaac, the gospel-covenant, leading to freedom. And agreeably to this statement of the apostle, all the features of both correspond.

Ishmael, Hagar's son, was born in the ordinary course of nature; Isaac, Sarah's son, was born out of it, and contrary to the general laws of nature. Ishmael was the natural result of things; Isaac the child of promise. The one born without an eye to the covenant; the other wholly on account of the covenant. Had Ishmael never been born, no interruption would have taken place in respect of the promised seed; but had Isaac never been born, the promise itself could not have been fulfilled; for so the terms of the charter ran, "in Isaac shall thy seed be called." (Gen. xxi. 12.) And though a period of somewhat more than twenty years had elapsed between the promise given to Abraham and the fulfilment of it, yet the thing itself was as sure and certain as the promise concerning the coming of Christ himself. "To Abraham and his seed was the promise made. He saith not unto seeds, as of many, but as of one, and to thy seed, which is Christ." (Gal. iii. 16.) And how striking was the difference in the gift of these two sorts to Abraham! Ishmael was the product of lust; Isaac a child of prayer. "Lord God, said Abraham, what wilt thou give me, seeing I go childless? Look now (said God,) towards heaven, and tell the stars, if thou be able to number them. And he said unto him, So shall thy seed be. And he believed in the Lord; and he counted it to him for righteousness." (Gen. xv. 2-6.) It may not be improper to add, that as in the two covenants the one is in direct opposition to the other, so in the allegory the same is manifested. "He that was born after the flesh, persecuted him that was born after the Spirit; even so it is now." The everlasting hatred of nature to grace was then strikingly set forth, by the mocking of the bond-woman's son. And as Ishmael, as well as Isaac, was circumcised, the allegory hereby manifested, (what hath not been so much noticed as it deserves,) that the persecution of the true seed doth not arise only from the world, but from those who profess the same faith. A faith, like Ishmael's, of nature, but not, like Isaac's, of grace. But what a blessed thing it is, when by a true saving grace we are led to know our birthright, and as sweetly to enjoy it. When we can say with the apostle, "Now we, brethren, as Isaac was, are the children of promise." And surely, the bond-woman and her son cannot be heir with the son of the free-woman; for all of the Hagar, the mount Sinai covenant, are in bondage. They are under the precept of a broken law; they are subject to the condemning power of that law; and they are exposed to the penalty due to the breaches of that law. Oh! the blessedness of being for ever freed both from the guilt and condemnation of it in Christ. Well might the apostle comfort the church with that sweet assurance, "so then, brethren, we are not children of the bond-woman, but of the free., (Gal. iv. 31.)

HAGARENES

The descendants of Hagar. They dwelt chiefly in Arabia.

HAGGAI

The prophet, who lived after the Babylonish captivity, and at the time of building the second temple. His name signifies a feast of the Lord, from Chagag, a feast; and Jah, the Lord. His prophecy is but short, yet most blessed in pointing to Christ.

HAGIOGRAPHY

This word is not used in the Bible, but, nevertheless, as it hath been used by the Jews in a way of distinction concerning certain parts of the word of God in the Old Testament Scripture, it may not be improper to notice it in a work of this kind. The word Hagiography, which means holy writings, is generally applied, by the Jews to all the books of the Old Testament, excepting the Law and the Prophets. For though, as Maimonides saith, it is the general consent of their nation, that several of the sacred writings, such as Daniel; and the Book of the Psalms, were written by the influence of the Holy Spirit, yet they say, not by prophecy; thus making a distinction between the works of the Spirit, than which nothing can be more absurd. The reason of denying that those writings were prophetical is easily seen, because they are so pointed to the person of the Lord Jesus, that when fulfilled in him, as they evidently were, and in such a way as they never could be fulfilled in any other, must have left the Jews without the least excuse, if they confessed them to have been prophetical. And yet what a poor and flimsy covering they find in denying the Spirit of prophecy to be in them, and yet allowing them, to have been written by the influence of the Spirit. The prophecy of Daniel in particular, was so exact in pointing to the time of the Messiah's coming and the object of his sufferings, that one of the Rabbins who lived about fifty years before the coming of Christ, asserted, that the time of the Messiah, as signified by Daniel, could not be deferred longer than those fifty years. Maimonides himself owns, that Daniel, and the other writers of the Hagiography, may be called prophets. Aben Ezra saith much to the same amount. And Josephus doth not scruple to say that Daniel was one of the greatest prophets. But enough hath been said on this subject. The reader will, I hope, clearly understand what is meant by Hagiography in the Scripture, and wherefore the Jews so distinguished them from the five books of Moses and the prophets.

HALLELUJAH
See Allelnjah.

HAM
The Son of Noah, brother to Shem and Japheth. Of these three sons of Noah was the whole earth overspread; for it doth not appear, that Noah had any other children. (Gen. ix. 18, 19.) The prophecy of Noah concerning his three sons is very remarkable, and was literally fulfilled. Ham is called Canaan in the prediction, and declared to be a servant of servants. When Joshua conquered Canaan this was literally accomplished. (Josh. ix. 23.) The blessing of Shem is striking, and the manner of it. God is blessed on Shem's account, and is called the Lord God of Shem. And as Christ after the flesh sprang from Shem, it is truly interesting to behold this preacher of righteousness, for so Noah is called, thus preaching and predicting Christ. (2 Pet. ii. 5. Heb. xi. 7.) And the blessing of Japheth is not less to be noticed. The prophesying father declared, that God would enlarge Japheth, or, as the margin of the Bible expresseth it, would persuade him to dwell in the tents of Shem; meaning, that the race of Japheth, in the Gentiles, should come into the fold of the Lord Jesus. For none but the Lord can persuade, and none but him, by his Holy Spirit, can render all persuasions successful. So that we see, from the ark in this man's family, how effectually the Lord provided for the eventful circumstances that were to follow the new world. Ham and his posterity are declared to be cursed. Shem hath the deposit of all the promises; and Japheth, the father of the Gentiles, it was said, should be brought over to the knowledge of salvation, and to take part in the blessings of it. God will enlarge. (See Isa. xlix. 1-6.)

HANANIAH
A false prophet, in the days of Jeremiah, whose history, though short, is so very striking and awful, that the Holy Ghost hath been pleased to appoint a whole chapter in the writings of Jeremiah to record it; as if the Lord the Spirit intended it to be

HANNANEAH - HANNAH

frequently read in the church. Indeed, it cannot be read too often, and especially by all that minister in holy things. The chapter is the twenty-eighth of Jeremiah's prophecy. I make no farther comment in this place upon it, unless it be to observe, that Hananiah's name but ill corresponded to this character. The word signifies the grace or gift of the Lord, from Chen or Chanan, grace; and Jah, the Lord. Hanan-Jah.

HANNANEAH

See Shadrach.

HAND

It was so much the custom in the eastern world to do great and interesting actions by the motions and signs of the hand, that we find in Scripture continued expressions to this amount. The "giving of the hand," as in the instance of Jehu and Jehonadab. (2 Kings x. 15.) The "washing of the hands," as in the case of Pilate. (Matt. xxvii. 24.) The "stretching out of the hands," by way of entreaty, as mentioned Prov. i. 24. and again Isa. lxv. 2. All these, and much more to the like import, plainly shew, that the manners of the east were such as to carry on important concerns by the ministry of the hand. Indeed, in the western world, and in our own country, the action of the hand is not unfrequently made use of to testify the consent of the mind. The ceremony of putting the fight hand on the New Testament in the administration of oaths, and the ordinary salutation of friends, by the shaking of the hand, are proofs in point. But what I would yet more particularly remark on this subject, is the sacredness of the action in reference to the Lord Jesus Christ. The right hand of JEHOVAH is well known to be one of the names by which the Mediator, as Mediator, is mentioned in Scripture. (Exod. xv. 6.) And his return to glory is spoken of under this expression of "sitting down on the right hand of God." (Ps. cx, 1. Heb. i. 3.) Hence, therefore, with an eye to Christ, the church is represented as looking to Jesus, and stretching forth the hand to Jesus, in all those expressions of the word of God where the ministry of the hand is used, in all the earnest actions of faith. "I have set the Lord always before me; for he is on my right hand, that I shall not be moved." (Ps. xvi. 8.) So again it is said, "The Lord shall stand at the right hand of the poor, to save him from those that condemn his soul." (Ps. clx. 31.) I only detain the reader yet farther to remark, what a peculiar blessedness is in the subject, considered with reference to the hand of Jesus over his people. All that we read in the word of God of the hands, and eyes, and ears of the Lord, as continually engaged for his church and redeemed, is spoken of Christ in his human nature; and most blessed are those things in relation to Christ. By thus representing the Lord Jesus in those familiar acts of our own nature, it implies, what the church never should lose sight of, that sympathy of Jesus to our nature, whose hands are unceasingly stretched forth to lead, guide, and defend, and whose ears are always open to the cries of his redeemed, and whose eyes are upon them for good, for his delight, and their happiness. How sweet to this purpose are those Scriptures: "I know the thoughts I think towards you, saith the Lord; thoughts of peace, and not of evil, to give you an expected end." (Jer. xxix. 11. So again, Jer. xxxii. 41.) "Yea, I will rejoice over them to do them good, and I will plant them in this land assuredly, with my whole heart, and with my whole soul."

HANES

A town on the frontiers of Ethiopia. Some have thought it the same as Tahapanes. (See Isa. xxx. 4. Jer. ii. 16.)

HANNAH

The wife of Elkanah. Her name signifies gracious; and she was, indeed, a very gracious woman. We have her history in the first book of Samuel, chapter first and second. Her hymn is truly spiritual, and forms a blessed song concerning redemption. It is worthy remark, that though the patriarchs, and other holy men of old, before the days of Hannah, spoke of the Lord Jesus under various characters belonging to him, yet Hannah is the first that was commissioned by the Holy Ghost to speak of him as the Messiah, the Anointed. (See 1 Sam. ii. 10.) This was her honour. It is worthy remark, that the Lord so distinguished this Old Testament saint: to be the first preacher of Jesus as the Anointed, and Mary Magdalen, in the New Testament, to be the first preacher of Jesus in his resurrection. (Mark xvi. 9.)

And while I remark it in her history, I beg to call the reader's attention to an infinitely more important consideration on the subject. If the Lord Jesus was thus anointed, and called as such the Messiah (which is, in fact, the Anointed), so many ages before his incarnation, as the glorious Head of his body the church, was not the church, the body of that glorious Head, anointed also in him? Could the Head, in this instance, be considered detached and separated from the members? Surely Christ, as Christ, that is, Anointed, could not have been thus called, had not the Holy Ghost virtually and truly, in the secret councils of JEHOVAH, anointed him as much as God the Father called him. (See Isa. xlii. 6.). And as such the church was as much called and anointed in him as his body, and that from everlasting; and in the everlasting love of God, the Holy Ghost presented to the Father the object of his everlasting love thus anointed, sanctified, and set apart, for his glory, and the spouse of the Lord Jesus. "A body hast thou prepared me." (Heb. x. 5.) Oh! what a sweet and precious thought, or rather numberless thoughts of rapture and delight arise out of this one view of the church's oneness and connection with her glorious Head and Husband before all worlds! Eyeing Jesus thus, as the Anointed, in his secret name and character, before the open display of it in time, was, without all doubt, in relation to his spouse, the church. Had not the Father given his dear Son a church, Jesus had not given himself to the church, and for the church, neither would the Holy Ghost named him as the Messiah, the Anointed, before his incarnation; neither after would he have anointed him and given him without measure of his influence. But as we find the same name given of the Anointed before, as after, he became man, and tabernacled in the substance of our flesh, nothing can be more plain, in confirmation of this blessed truth, than that God the Holy Ghost had an everlasting love to the church, as the body of the Lord Jesus, before the world began, and anointed the glorious Head, and the church in her glorious Head, watched over her, protected her, blessed her, and set her apart, in all and every member of her, as "the church which is his body, the fulness of him that filleth all in all." (Eph. i. 22, 23.)

HARDNESS OF HEART

We meet with this expression very often in the word of God, and for the most part connected with the blindness of the heart. Thus, it is said, (Mark iii. 5.) the Redeemer was grieved for the hardness of their hearts; the margin of the Bible renders it the blindness of their hearts. So again, in Paul's Epistle to the Romans, (chap. xi. 25.) it is said, that "blindness in part is happened to Israel." In the margin, blindness is rendered hardness. And in the second Epistle to the Corinthians, third chapter, fourteenth verse, there the expression is, that "their minds were blinded." From these, and the like passages, it is plain, that the terms are one and the same, and both mean hardness of heart unfavourable to the reception of divine impressions. But what I beg the reader yet more particularly to mark in the phrase that not unfrequently in Scripture this blindness and hardness of the heart is ascribed to the Lord's act. Thus in Isaiah the church in her prayer saith, "O Lord! why hast thou made us to err from thy ways, and hardened our heart from thy fear!" (Isa. lxiii. 17.) And in John xii. 39, 40. it is said, that "they could not believe, because that Esaias had said, He hath blinded their eyes, and hardened their hearts." This memorable passage of the prophet Isaiah, which is in chap. vi. 9, 10, hath been considered so very important by God the Holy Ghost, that he caused it to be quoted by all the four Evangelists, once in the Acts of the Apostles, and once in the Epistle to the Romans. (Matt. xiii. 14, 15. Mark iv. 12. Luke viii. 10. John xii. 39, 40. Acts xxviii. 25-27. Rom. xi. 8.) But it is remarkable, at the same time, in those quotations, how the hardening the heart by the Lord is blended with the hardening of the heart by themselves. In the passage as quoted by Matthew, it is expressly said, that their eyes they have closed. And the same expression is used by Paul in his quotation. (Acts xxviii. 27.) And is there the least contradiction in the account? Most certainly not; the very original passage in the prophet explains itself. "Make the heart of this people fat, and make their ears heavy, and shut their eyes." And may not the Lord be said to do this, when in a fulness of blessings of his providence the tables of such men are so flowing over, that the bountiful hand which spreads the whole is lost and hidden from their view in a cloud of his own gifts? And when men become intoxicated, and over fed, and their eyes bloated with fatness, so that they neither discern the Lord's hand, yea, sometimes they see not one another, may not the Lord be said to make their heart fat, and their eyes heavy, by thus furnishing the means, while the beasts themselves, by abusing the bounties of the Lord (which, if rightly used, would have made them his blessed instruments in disposing of them to feed the hungry bellies of the poor), may be truly said no less to close their own eyes, and to harden their own hearts?

I must not dismiss this article without taking with it the observation, how suited the Lord. Jesus is to remedy all the evils of a hardened heart, and the blinded eye, in that lovely commission of his, "to heal the broken in heart, and to give sight to them that were blind." A broken heart, in the full sense of the word, is a dead heart, and the blind in Scripture is where the eyes are put out, as in the instance of Zedekiah. (See Jer. lii. 11.) And in the similar case of Samson, whose eyes were bored out, for so the expression hath it in the margin of the Bible. (Judg. xvi. 21.) And where the Lord Jesus exerciseth his grace, his almighty work is described under the strong term of making a new heart, taking away "the heart of stone, and giving an heart of flesh; making all things new." Hence the apostle saith, "If any man be in Christ, he is a new creature." (2 Cor. v. 17.) Thus without Christ the heart of all men is for ever hardened. And with Christ's sovereign grace, he, and he alone, can make every faculty "willing in the day of his power." (Ps. cx. 3.)

HARLOT

We cannot be at a loss for the Scriptural meaning of this word, for the word of God, in this instance, corresponds with the general sentiments and customs of mankind in all ages. A harlot is the same name as a prostitute, a woman of ill fame, or as we say, a woman of the town. (Prov. xxix. 3.) The Lord makes use of the name by way of shewing the spiritual fornication of Israel. "Thou hast played the harlot with many lovers, yet return again to me, said the Lord." (Jer. iii. 1.) It hath supposed by some, that in the case of Rahab the harlot, it was not intended to imply the character of a woman of ill fame. But certainly there is no authority for supposing any other. The original Hebrew Zona, (Josh. ii. 1.) means a harlot. And Septuagint, in the Greek Porne, can admit no translation. Both Paul and James use this and our translators have most faithfully rendered it, by the word harlot. (Heb. xi. 31. James ii. 25.) The objection respecting Salmon, a prince Israel, marrying her, is so far from an objection to her being a prostitute, that it should seem rather confirmation. We find the Lord commanding Hosea the prophet to marry an adulteress. (See Hos. iii. 1.) And as a figurative representation, by type, of Jesus marrying our adulterous nature, nothing could be more striking. Strange, indeed, to our view, are all the ways and works of God! But it is not more marvellous that Christ, after the flesh, should spring from Rahab, than from Thamar by Judah. (Gen. xxxviii. 12. to the end.) The former was by an harlot: in the instance of the latter it was incestuous. But certain it is, that both, after the flesh, were in the genealogy of the Lord of life and glory, how strange soever it appears to us.

HATE

This word is so very plain in its simple meaning, and so universally understood, that there would have needed no observation upon it, but for an expression of our Lord's concerning it, which appears to me, according to all the commentators I have seen or read upon it, to have been totally mistaken. The passage in which our Lord hath spoken concerning hatred is Luke. xiv. 26. Where Jesus hath said, "If any man come to me, and hate not his father, and mother, and wife, and children, and brethren, and sisters, yea, and his own life also, he cannot be my disciple." The hatred of father, and mother, and the like, they say, is in contradiction to the divine command, and, therefore, they have conceived, that the expression means no more than by a comparative statement, to say, that none can be the disciple of Jesus who loves his earthly friends equal to this heavenly one. But certainly this is not our Lord's meaning; for here is nothing said in the whole passage by way of comparison. And every one that knows the original word here made use of to express the verb hate, knows that Misei can mean no other than to hate. Neither is the doctrine, when duly considered, contradictory to the whole design of the gospel. All the claims of nature are, for the most part, unfavourable to the pursuits of grace. And the love of our near and dear connections in nature, every one knows that is brought acquainted with the feelings of his own heart, is but too often leading us on the confines of sin and corruption, Hence, to hate whatever opposeth the best and purest desires of the soul, is among the clearest evidences of a follower of the Lord Jesus Christ. And the latter clause in this expression of our Lord serves to explain the whole; "yea, and his own life also." Self-loathing, and self-abhorring, mark the true believer's character. And wherefore doth a child of God loathe his own flesh, but because that flesh is always rising up in rebellion against the Spirit. Hence, therefore, if my own body becomes a rebel, and an enemy to my own soul, so that I cannot do the things I would, certainly I hate it; and if I hate my own flesh, from the opposition it is continually making to a life of grace, in the same sense, and upon the same account, I must, and do hate all the opposers of the divine life, be they who they may, or what they may. Nothing is to come into competition with Christ in our affection. I believe I may venture to affirm, that many of God's dear children look forward to the humiliation of the grave with holy joy on this very account, as knowing that then, and not before, they shall drop this body of sin and death, which now so often makes them groan. It is blessedly said of Levi, that in his zeal and love to JEHOVAH'S Holy One he said, "of his father, and his mother, I have not seen him, neither did he acknowledge his brethren, nor knew his own children." (Deut. xxxiii. 9.) I venture, therefore, upon the whole, to accept the words of the Lord Jesus in this Scripture by the Evangelist. (Luke. xiv. 26.) precisely as the words themselves express this solemn truth. And since every thing in nature is hostile to a life of grace, so that my own corrupt heart is a much greater enemy to my soul's enjoyment in Christ, than either the world, or the powers of darkness, I do hate all, and every tie of nature, yea, and my own life also, in every degree, and by every way in which they are found to oppose, or run counter, to the pursuit of the soul in her desires after the Lord Jesus Christ.

HAVOTH-JAIR

The villages of Jair, so called from being in the lot of Jair the son of Manasseh. (Num. xxxii. 41.)

HAZAEL

His name is derived from Chazah, to see; and the El joined to it means to see God. We have his history, and the effect wrought upon the mind of the prophet Elisha in beholding him with his prophetic spirit, foreseeing the cruelties of Hazael on the children of Israel. (2 Kings 8-15.) The circumstance of Hazael's spreading a cloth dipped in water over the face of Benhadad, hath been thought by some to have been done not with the design to kill him. Historians tell us, that it is the custom in the east, in those violent fevers called Nedad, to make use of chilling methods for their recovery. The patients drink cold water, and a quantity of water is thrown upon them. So that whether Hazael wished the death of his master, or not, the dipping the cloth in water and covering his face with it, was among the methods used on those occasions for recovery. Be this, however, as it may, Hazael stands on record for a very awful character, and his name was highly unsuitable to his conduct. All that the prophet Elisha foretold literally came to pass; and he, that, while the servant of the king his master, stood astonished at the bare mention only of the cruelties Elisha admonished him of, actually perpetrated the very murders which he had shuddered at, when he became clothed with the royal purple. (See 2 Kings xiii. 3-7.) Oh, what an awful representation doth his history afford of the sin and iniquity lurking in the human heart! In the whole nature of man it must be the same, for the seeds of sin are alike in all; and that they do not ripen and bear the like deadly fruit in all, is wholly owing to the preventing and restraining grace of God. The heart that is not conscious of this, is not conscious of the preciousness of the Lord Jesus Christ.

HAZEROTH

The place where Israel, in their journey through the wilderness, encamped. (Num. xi. 35.) This name, like some others, Hazerim, Hazar-addar, (Num. xxxiv. 4.) Hazah-gadda, (Josh. xv. 27.) mean one and the same thing. Hazer signifies the entry to the place, or village. Thus Hazezom-Tamar, the entrance to the city of palm trees, the same as Engedi. (See Gen. xiv. 7.)

HEAD

It would have been unnecessary to have noticed this article in the general acceptation of the word, since every one cannot but know, that as the head of the body, in every thing that liveth, is the prime mover of the body; and, indeed, is sometimes put for the whole of the body, so is it in common conversation considered as the first and pre-disposing cause of all life and action, whether considered individually, or in a community at large. But the term Head when applied to the Lord Jesus Christ, as "the Head of his body the "church," opens so sweet a subject for contemplation, that in a work of this kind it would be unpardonable to pass it by. Indeed, the subject even looks farther than this, and directs the mind of the truly regenerated believer to behold JEHOVAH, in his threefold character of person, as being the Head of Christ, considered in his mediatorial office, and giving truth to all the glorious purposes of salvation in him. It was the Lord JEHOVAH, in the great scheme of redemption, before the earth was formed, that set up Christ as the Head of his church. All the persons of the GODHEAD engaged in this plan of grace, and set the wheels agoing from all eternity; and hence God the Father is called the God and Father" of our Lord Jesus Christ, of whom the whole family, in heaven and earth, is named." (Eph. iii. 14, 15.) And as to God the Father is peculiarly ascribed the calling, of Christ, as the Head of his body the church, (Isa. xlii. 6.) so to God the Holy Ghost is peculiarly ascribed no less the anointing of Christ to the special office of Mediator. (Isa. xlviii. 16, 17.) And hence, in conformity to this order of things, the apostle tells the church, when speaking of this subject, "I would have you know, that the head of every man is Christ, and the head of the woman is the man, and the head of Christ is God." (1 Cor. xi. 3.)

Next, in the order of things, we may view the Headship of Christ to his church, and a most blessed and interesting subject it becomes to our view. The Scriptures are full of this most delightful truth. Jesus, as Mediator, is the Head the Surety, the husband, the all in all, of his people. He is the source of life, of light, of salvation, of grace here, and glory forever. So that in this view of the Lord Jesus, and the church in him, it is incalculable in how many ways, and by what a variety of communications, this Headship of Christ becomes a source of continual joy and comfort to all his redeemed. They have an unceasing, communion with him whether they are conscious of it or not; and it should be among the highest felicities of the soul to go every day, and all the day, in the perpetual actings of faith upon the glorious person of the Lord Jesus, as the Head of his body the church, "the fulness of him that filleth all in all." (Eph. i. 22, 23.)

HEART

The heart in all languages is considered as the leading principle of action and of character.

A good man, (saith the Lord Jesus) out of the good treasure of his heart, bringeth forth that which is good; and an evil man, out of the evil treasure of his heart, bringeth forth that which is evil; for out of the abundance of the heart the mouth speaketh." (Luke vi. 45.) Hence a change of circumstances in spiritual concerns, from darkness to light, is called "the taking away the heart of stone, and giving an heart of flesh, turning the heart of the fathers to the children, and the children to the fathers." Hence the Lord saith, in reference to his whole church, "I will give them one heart, and one way, that they may fear me for ever." (Jer. xxxii. 39.)

HEAVEN

And the heaven of heavens, are expressions generally made use of to denote the more immediate place where JEHOVAH hath fixed his throne. For thus it is expressed in Scripture. "Thus saith the Lord, The heaen is my throne, and the earth is my footstool: where is the house that ye build unto me? and where is the place of my rest?" (Isa. lxvi. 1.) But Solomon breaks out in an expression, as one overwhelmed with surprise and wonder in the contemplation: "But will God indeed (said he) dwell on the earth? behold, the heaven, and the heaven of heavens cannot contain thee!" (I Kings viii. 27.) But what would this mighty monarch have said, had he lived to have seen the Lord of heaven and earth tabernacling in the substance of our flesh?

But, though, according to the language of Scripture, we call that place heaven which John saw opened, and where the more immediate presence of the Lord is gloriously displayed, yet it were to limit the Holy One of Israel to suppose, that JEHOVAH dwelleth in any place, to the exclusion of his presence or glory elsewhere. In the immensity of his GODHEAD, and the ubiquity of his nature and essence, he is every where; and, consequently, that place is heaven where

HEBRON - HERITAGE

JEHOVAH'S presence, in grace, and favour, and glory, is manifested. How little do they know of heaven, or of the divine love and favour, that conceive, if they could get to heaven in the crowd, though they know not how, and I had almost said, they care not how, provided they could get there, how little do they know in what consists the felicity of the place! Alas! an unsanctified, unrenewed, unregenerated heart would be miserable even in heaven. Sweetly doth David speak of the blessed work of assurance and grace in the soul respecting heaven, and in that assurance describes the suited preparation for it. "I shall behold (said he) thy face in righteousness; I shall be satisfied, when I awake; with thy likeness." (Ps. xvii. 15.)

HEBRON

See Mount Hebron.

HELL

The Hebrews called it School. Some apply it to the grave; but the most general acceptation of it, according to Scripture language, is a place of torment. Thus the Psalmist saith, "The wicked shall be turned into hell, and all the nations that forget God." (Ps. ix. 17.) And our blessed Lord, three times in one chapter, speaks of it in alarming terms. "If thine hand offend thee, cut it off: it is better for thee to enter into life maimed, than having two hands, to go into hell, into the fire that never shall be quenched: where their worm dieth not, and the fire is not quenched." (Mark ix. 43-48.)

Some, however, have ventured to call in question the reality of hell torments, and the very existence of the place itself. But there is nothing so weak and so impious as disputes on these points; for unless men could satisfy their minds, that God cannot punish sin, or that he will not, it becomes a matter more presumptuous than becoming, to enquire the very particulars in which that punishment shall consist. The Lord hath declared, that the "wicked, and those that obey not the gospel of our Lord Jesus Christ, shall be punished with everlasting destruction from the presence of the Lord, and the glory of his power." (2 Thess. i. 8, 9.) Here is sufficient account to certify every one of the reality of the thing itself. And the fact itself being once admitted, the method may surely be well supposed, that it will be such as infinite wisdom, joined with infinite power, shall appoint and accomplish. Here let us rest--only following up the conviction with a prayer to Him that hath the keys of hell and death, that he will keep our souls from going down into hell, and preserve us to his everlasting kingdom. Amen.

HEPHZIBAH

The mother of Manasseh was called by his name. (2 Kings xxi. 1.) But it is infinitely more interesting to consider, that the Lord calls his church by this name, and the cause for which he did, namely, because the Lord delighted in her. The name itself conveys as much, from Chaphatz, to will: as if the Lord had said by Hephzibah,. My will is in her.

HERESY

The church of Christ hath, in all ages, been persecuted and divided by heresies. Indeed, the apostle Paul saith, that "there must be heresies among you, that they which are approved may be made manifest among you." (I Cor. xi. 19.) Our Lord himself speaks of the Nicolaitanes, Rev. ii. 15. The Scriptures do not tell us in what their heresy consisted, but evidently in a departure from the truth, and probably in practices unsuitable to the purity of the gospel of Christ. But the last days' dispensation, we are told, will be distinguished by great departures from the faith; and, we may truly say, already do they appear. (1 Tim. iv. 1, &c.)

HERITAGE

We find the Lord frequently speaking, in his

holy word, concerning the heritage of his people. Canaan is all along described as the heritage the Lord had designed for Israel. (Exod. vi, 8.) And we find also the people not unfrequently delighting themselves in it. "The lines are fallen unto me (said one of old) in pleasant places; yea, I have a goodly heritage." (Ps. xvi. 6.) But the Lord himself, over and above these things, is spoken of as the heritage of his redeemed. In the same sweet psalm, the sacred writer takes comfort in this assurance, and saith (ver. 5.) "The Lord himself is the portion of mine inheritance, and of my cup: thou maintainest my lot." So again the Lord, as the security of his people, saith himself, that "this is the heritage of the servants of the Lord, and their righteousness is of me, saith the Lord." (Isa. liv. 17.) And as the Lord is the heritage of his people, so his people are said to be his; hence in times of trouble, the church is heard to say, "They break in pieces thy people, O Lord, and afflict thine heritage." (Ps. xciv. 5.) See some other sweet Scriptures to this amount: (Joel ii. 17. Micah vii. 14-18. Isa. lviii. 14.)

But when the reader hath duly pondered the blessed thought of beholding the Lord and his fulness as the heritage of his people, and his people as his heritage of delight, both in nature, providence, and grace, there is one thought more the subject of heritage proposeth to the meditation that ought not to be forgotten, The customs and manners of the eastern world differ so widely in many points from ours, that unless due attention be had to them we lose much of the sense and spirit of the things spoken of. Thus on the subject of heritages or inheritance. By virtue of alliance and relationship, these things were unalienable, and not liable to be lost to the right heirs of them. A child had an undoubted right, whether by natural birth or adoption, when once lawfully acknowledged as such, to the heritage of his birthright; neither could he be dispossessed by the caprice, or will, of his father. And there was another distinguishing property in the rights of heritage among the customs and laws of the eastern world, namely, that a son needed not to wait the death of the father for the possession of his heritage. He might at any time, when of age, claim it. And this throws a light upon the subject of the younger son in the parable. (Luke xv. 11, 12.) And although, as in that instance, the father foresaw the abuse and misapplication of his heritage, yet by the laws of the east, the father could not withhold his portion from him.

Now, if we make application of these customs of the eastern world to the phrases and expressions we meet with in Scripture, which of course, as they were written there, had an eye to them in those writings, what beauties do we find they frequently give to the sense of Scripture on many points, which we should otherwise overlook and be ignorant of. Thus for instance, on the subject of heritage now before us. The heritage of Christ's children cannot by those laws be ever lost, or become alienable. Jesus hath adopted them as his, both by his Father's gift, and by his own purchase, and by the conquests of his grace; nothing therefore, can dispossess their undoubted right in Jesus and his fulness as their heritage for ever. Hence David saith, (Ps. cxix. 111.) "Thy testimonies have I claimed, as mine heritage for ever; for they are the rejoicing of mine heart."

Neither is this all: the heirs of God in Christ do not wait to a distant period for the possession of their heritage. Their God and Father never dies to render their rightful enjoyment necessary. He lives to put them into possession: and this they have not by reversion, but by present inheritance, here by grace through faith, and hereafter in glory. And though too often, like the prodigal in the parable, we waste and abuse the bounties of our heritage, yet, like him, the eye of our God and Father is always on the look-out for our return, and when by grace brought back, as he was, we are graciously received, and made happy in the pardoning mercy and love of our Father.

And as our person, so our mortgaged inheritance; both are secured from the same cause and fullness of salvation. As we have sold ourselves for nought, so are we redeemed without money. (Isa. lii. 3.) Jesus our elder brother, our nearest of kin, hath ransomed both person and property. Our inheritance was not alienable for ever, but only to the year of jubilee. God our Father commanded him to open his hand wide to his poor brother, and he hath done it; so that we are brought into the full liberty wherewith he makes his redeemed free, and brought home also, at length, into the possession of an inheritance infinitely surpassing the one we originally forfeited, even "an inheritance incorruptible, and undefiled, and that fadeth not away." "Oh, the depth of the riches both of the wisdom and the goodness of God!" See those Scriptures, (Lev. xxv. 25. Deut. xv. 7, 8. 1 Pet. i. 3-5. Rom. xi. 33.)

HERMON

The sacred hill of Hermon is often spoken of in Scripture, and furnisheth out sweet subject to the Hebrew poetry. David describes the love and unity of brethren as like the dew of Hermon. (Ps. cxxxiii. 3.) The falling of the dew of Hermon upon the hill of Zion was very natural, for Zion joined to it. And travellers describe the dew of this place as falling plentifully like showers.

HEROD

It may be proper, for the better apprehension of the name of Herod. to state some short account of the several we meet with in the New Testament. There are several mentioned, but they are different men. Indeed, but for their history being incorporated with the history of our Lord and his apostle, their names would not be worth recording, but their memory might have perished with them.

The first Herod made mention of in holy Scripture, was called Herod the Great. He reigned in Judea at the time of our Lord's birth. (Matt. ii. 1) His name, according to the Greek language, signified the glory of the skin. But it became a very unsuitable name for the miserable end he made, according to the historians of his time, for he died of an universal rottenness. He reigned more than thirty years, and by his death, as we read Matt. ii. 19, gave opportunity for the return of the Lord Jesus, to depart from Egypt about the third year before we begin the *date of Anno Domino*. I mention this the more particularly, to guard the reader against the mistake into which some have fallen, in confounding this Herod with the Herod mentioned Acts. xii. which was his grandson.

The second Herod we meet with in the Bible, is Herod called Philip. (See Mark vi. 17. and Luke iii. 1.) This Herod, as history informs us, was son to the former. And the third Herod went by the name of Antipas. This man was also son of Herod the Great, and brother to Philip. And this was he who, during the life of his brother, had married Herodias, his brother's wife; and John the Baptist faithfully reproving him for the shameful deed, Herod, at the instance of her daughter, whom she had by Philip her first husband, caused John to be beheaded. (See Matt. xiv. 1-12. Mark. vi. 14-29.)

The fourth Herod we meet with in Scripture, is the one mentioned with such everlasting infamy in the twelfth chapter of the Acts of the Apostles. His name was Agrippa, but surnamed Herod; the son of Aristobulus and Mariamne, and grandson to Herod, the Great. So much for the Herods! An awful though short account of such awful characters; while living, a terror to all around them, and when dead, lamented by none!

HERODIANS

Were a sect of Jews, so called, perhaps, from appearing at the time of Herod the Great, and not before; though some have thought, that by way of complimenting Herod they assumed the name of Herodians. Certain it is, that Herod affected to be thought of the seed of David, though there could be but little doubt, that he was, by nation, an Idumean. But as the general expectation of the Jewish nation, at that time, was on the tiptoe for their king the Messiah to appear, to deliver them from the Roman yoke, and to raise an empire that should conquer the world, Herod was glad to fall in with this popular idea, not doubting but that they would regard him as the person. His disappointment at the birth of Christ, and the account the wise men who came from the east to Jerusalem, to seek for the new-born Prince, explains what we read of him, and his infamous cruelty. (Matt. ii. 1-18.) This sect was evidently the creatures of Herod, and as such bore his name. Their endeavours to entangle Jesus in his talk, and to accuse him before the Roman government, very plainly prove how inimical they were to the doctrines of Christ. (Matt. xxii. 15, 16.)

HEZEKIAH

King of Judah, the son of Ahaz and Abi. His name is striking, Hezek and Jah, signifying the strength of the Lord. We have his history 2 Kings xviii. xix. xx. And so very important was the life of this prince considered, to form a part in the records of the church, that the Holy Ghost directed the prophet Isaiah to give it again in his prophetical writings. (See Isa. xxxvi. xxxvii, xxxviii, xxxix.) The miraculous effect wrought on the sun dial, in confirmation of the Lord's promise to Hezekiah, is an evident testimony of the Lord's favour to this prince. Hezekiah's hymn is beautiful, Isa. xxxviii. 10-20.

HID and HIDDEN

I pause over these words merely to remark, that in Scripture they express a great deal. It was the custom very generally through the eastern world, to secrete and bury their treasures and valuables. We are told by a certain author, that there are a set of men who make it their business to go about in search of treasure supposed to have been hidden; and so general is the idea, that vast treasures are concealed in the earth, by men who died without making discovery of them to their friends, that this employment of digging in pursuit of wealth is a common thing. This will throw a great light upon those expressions in the word of God, which enjoin an earnest pursuit after the knowledge and love of the Lord. "If thou seekest after wisdom (saith Solomon,) as silver, and searchest for her as for hid treasures, then shalt thou understand the fear of the Lord, and find the knowledge of God." (Prov. ii. 4, 5.) Nothing could be more happily chosen to intimate that earnest unwearied pursuit after Jesus, as men seeking for what lay buried out of sight. And when that life, which the apostle saith, is hid with Christ in God, (Col. iii. 3.) is discovered, yea, in the smallest degree, this is like what the Lord said to Cyrus: "I will give thee the treasure of darkness, and hidden riches of secret places." (Isa. xlv, 3.) Views of Jesus, to the discovery by God the Holy Ghost, lead the soul to the enjoyment of him, "in whom are hid all the treasures of wisdom and knowledge." (Coloss. ii. 3.)

HIEL

The Bethelite of Jericho. His name implies, the life of God; from Chajak, to live; and El, God. I refer the reader to those two passages in Scripture, for the short but striking account of this man, whose boldness, in face of the curse Joshua pronounced, led him to so daring an act as that of building Jericho, and whose rashness the Lord so fully punished, in conformity to his servant's prediction. (See Josh. vi. 26.

with I Kings xvi. 34. See also Elisha.)

HIGH PLACES

We meet with frequent mention in the Bible of high places. Perhaps in the original design of them, they had been made sacred spots, and hallowed to the service of the true God of Israel; but, in process of time, they were used for idol-worship. The people called them Bamah, or, perhaps more properly, Bamoth, (See Ezek. xx. 29.) Those places were continued to the days of Christ, and called Proseuchy, or prayer-houses. Some of the kings of Israel, though going a good way in a spirit of reform, had not courage enough, or wanted the grace, to abolish those places of idol-worship. See (1 Kings xxii. 43.) Of good king Josiah, much praise was due to him on this account. See (2 Kings xxiii. 15.)

MOST HIGH and MOST HIGHEST

We find frequent mention made, in holy Scripture, of the Lord JEHOVAH under these appellations; and very blessed and proper they are, when speaking of him. The latter of them, except with an eye to him, would be a breach of grammar, but becomes beautiful, in compounding two superlatives, in reference to the Lord JEHOVAH, of whom it must be truly said, without exceeding the bounds of language, as one of the sacred writers expresseth it, "There is no end of his greatness." (Ps. cxlv. 3.)

HILKIAH

The father of Eliakim, (2 Kings xviii. 18.) His name signifies, the Lord is my portion, from Cheleath, a portion; and Jah, the Lord. So also the father of Jeremiah was called by this name, (Jer. i. 1.) and the son of Amaziah. (1 Chron. vi. 45.)

HIND

We meet this name, with peculiar emphasis of expression, in the title of the twenty-second Psalm; and whoever reads that psalm, as it is evidently written, prophetically of Christ, will not hesitate to conclude, that he is the hind of the morning, to which the whole psalm refers. Hunted as a hind, or a roe upon the mountains, from the morning of his incarnation to the close of his life on the cross. "Dogs (as he said) compassed him about, the assembly of the wicked enclosed him; they pierced my hands and my feet," said the meek Redeemer.

And if we consider the quality and character of the hind, we discover strong features of resemblance whereby Jesus might be pictured. The hind is up with the first of the morning, at break of day. So was our Jesus first in the morning councils of eternity, when, at the call of God, he stood forth the Surety for all his people. Moreover, the sweetness of the hind is almost proverbial." Be thou (saith the church to Jesus), "be thou as a roe, or a young hart, upon the mountains of Bether." (Song ii. 17.) And who shall speak of the earnestness of the Lord Jesus to come over the mountains of sin, and hills of corruption, in our nature, when he came to seek and save that which was lost? Who shall describe those numberless anticipations which we find in the Old Testament of Jesus, in appearing sometimes as an angel, and sometimes in an human from? as if to say, how much he longed for the time to come, when he should openly appear, in the substance of our flesh, as "the hind of the morning!"

And there is another beautiful resemblance in the hind, or roe, to Christ, in the loveliness as well as swiftness of this beautiful creature. Nothing can be more lovely than the young roe, or hart. And what equally so to Christ, who is altogether lovely, and the "fairest among ten thousand?" He is lovely in his form and usefulness; hated indeed, by serpents, but to all the creation of God excellent. His flesh the most delicious food--"whose flesh is meat indeed, and his blood is drink indeed."

"Be thou, (said the church,) like to the roe, or to the "young hart, upon the mountains of spices." (Song viii. 14.)

HINNOM

The valley Gehennon, called also the valley of Tophet. Gehennon is the Syriac word for hell. The same is meant by Tophet. These several names it should seem, were all equally applied to the same place. The prophets Isaiah and Jeremiah both speak of this awful spot. (Isa. xxx. 33. Jer. vii. 31.) And it is said, that Josiah, the good king, "defiled the place;" that is, he destroyed it for the purpose for which it had been used, by those wretched parents who had been deluded to sacrifice their children to the idol-god Molech, in this spot. (See 2 Kings xxiii. 10.) For by destroying it, that cruel, unnatural, and impious practice could no more be done there. Some have thought, that the name Tophet took its rise from Thoph, a drum; for it is supposed, that this, and perhaps other musical instruments, were loudly sounded upon those occasions, to drown the piercing cries of the poor children. The name of Hinnom is derived from the sons of Hinnom. (Joshua xv. 8.) See Molech.

HIRAM

King of Tyre. A name rendered memorable from his friendship with Solomon. His name, according to the Hebrew phraseology, Huram, signifies a lifting up. (See I Kings v. 1.)

HIRELING

In Scripture language, our nature is frequently spoken of as an hireling. "Is there not an appointed time to man upon earth? are not his days also like the days of an hireling?" (Job vii. 1.) By the law, the Lord made a gracious provision for the hireling, commanding that his wages should not abide all night, until the morning. (Lev. xix. 13.) Under the gospel, the term of hireling is and also as a mark of worthlessness. Thus faithful servants of the Lord, in the ministry of his word and ordinances, are described as labourers sent into the vineyard by the "Almighty Householder, and who, after the labour of the day, are called home to receive their hire; beginning from the last to the first. So that solemnly engaged in Christ's service, and hired to the work, they are supposed to labour in the word and doctrine with a single eye to the Lord's glory. They are, as instruments in the Lord's hand to break up the fallow ground of the hearts of their people, and to water the garden of Jesus. (Matt. xx. 1-16.) Whereas the mere hirelings, who enter the service of the Lord Jesus, not for love to the Lord, nor affection to his people, are represented as engaged only for filthy lucre's sake. These seek the fleece, not to serve the flock. They look for gain, every one to his own quarter; for so the prophet describes them. (Isa. lvi. 11.) Our Lord, in his unequalled manner, hath strikingly defined their character. (John x. 12, 13.)

HISS

In the general acceptation of this word, as we now use it, it is universally, I believe, considered as a mark of reproach or contempt. And we find, that it was so used from the earliest ages. The patriarch Job, (Chap. xxvii. 23.) saith, that the hypocrite shall be so confounded, that men shall clap their hands at him, and shall hiss him out of his place. And the Lord declared, that if the people departed from following him, he would cause the house which Solomon had built for the Lord to become a proverb and a bye-word, and men should hiss at it as they passed by. (1 Kings ix. 7, 8.) But, beside this acceptation of the word, certain it is, that it is also used in a favourable point of view, and sometimes means the call of the Lord to his ministers and messengers, for the performing his sovereign will and pleasure. Thus the Lord saith, that he will

HOBAB - HOLY, HOLINESS, most HOLY

"lift up an ensign to the nations from far, and will hiss unto them, that is, will call them from the end of the earth." (Isa. v. 26.) So again the bee of Egypt, and the bee of Assyria, meaning the armies of those nations, the Lord saith, he will hiss for: that is, will call them. (Isa. vii. 18.) But the ultimate object of this hissing of the Lord, in his sovereign command, is, to bring on the perpetual reproach of the ungodly. "I will make this city desolate, and an hissing: every one that passeth thereby shall be astonished, and hiss because of the plagues thereof." (Jer. xix. 8.)

HOBAB

Son of Jethro, and brother-in-law to Moses, His name signifies, beloved, from Chabab, to love.

HODAVIAH

Of the tribe of Manasseh. (1 Chron. v. 24.) His name is compounded of Hod, praise, and Jah, the Lord.

HOLY, HOLINESS, most HOLY

In Scripture language, strictly and properly speaking, these terms are only applicable to the Lord. In short, the very term means JEHOVAH himself, for he, and and he only, is holy in the abstract. Hence it is, that we so often meet with those expressions descriptive of his person and character. "Thus saith the Lord, the Holy One of Israel. Thus saith the High and Lofty One that inhabiteth eternity, I dwell in the high and holy place." (Isa. lvii, 15.) Hence the term is applied to all the persons of the GODHEAD distinctly and separately, and to all in common; the Father speaks of it with peculiar emphasis, yea, confirms his promises by the solemnity of an oath, and does this, by pledging his holiness as the fullest assurance of the truth: "Once have I sworn by my holiness, that I will not lie unto David." (Ps. lxxxix. 35.) The Son of God is also spoken of with peculiar emphasis, as essentially holly in himself, in his divine nature, "being One with the Father, over all God blessed for ever, Amen." (Rom. ix. 5.) Thus in special reference to the Lord Jesus, as the Son of God, when the prophet is speaking both of the Father and the Son, he joins in one verse the person of each, and gives to each the distinguishing character of the GODHEAD. "Fear not, thou worm, Jacob, and ye men of Israel: I will help, saith the Lord, and thy Redeemer the Holy One of Israel. (Isa. xli. 14.) In like manner, God the Holy Ghost is peculiarly and personally considered under this Almightiness of character, his Holiness; and the same divine perfection declared to be essentially his, in common with the Father and the Son. Indeed, as if to define the glory of his person, Holy is the essential and incommunicable name by which the Eternal Spirit is known and distinguished throughout his sacred word. Hence, in his offices it is said of him, that by his overshadowing power acting on the body of the Virgin, at the conception of Christ, that Holy Thing, so called, should be born. (See Luke i. 35.) So again, at the baptism of Christ, the blessed Spirit seen by Christ, decending like the hovering of a dove, and lighting upon the person of Christ, and thus distinguished in point of personality from God the Father, whose voice from heaven, in the same moment, declared Jesus to be his beloved Son, in whom he was well pleased. (Matt. iii. 16, 17.) And holiness is essentially and personally ascribed to God the Holy Ghost, in that gracious office of his, when it is said of the Lord Jesus, that God the Father anointed Jesus of Nazareth with the Holy Ghost, and with power. (Acts x. 38.)

But what I beg the reader particularly to observe with me, under this glorious distinction of character, belonging to each and to all the persons of the GODHEAD, is the very peculiar manner in which the holiness of JEHOVAH is spoken of in Scripture. While each person of the

HOLY, HOLINESS, most HOLY - HOLY, HOLINESS, most HOLY

GODHEAD is thus plainly said to be holy, in the abstract of the word, and in a way of holiness that can be ascribed to no other; the worship and adoration of the Holy Three in One is peculiarly offered up in this very character. When Isaiah saw Christ's glory, (see Isaiah vi. compared with John xii. 41.) the acclamations of the heavenly host resounded to the praises of JEHOVAH, under thrice ascriptions of the same, to the holiness of the Lord. So in like manner in John's vision. (See Rev. iv. 8.) Certainly (this Trisagium,) this peculiar adoration of JEHOVAH in the holiness of his nature, rather than to any of the other perfections of the Lord, must have a meaning. Wherefore this divine attribute should be singled out, rather than the faithfulness of JEHOVAH, which we know the Lord delights in, (see Deut. vii. 9.) or the eternity of JEHOVAH, which the Lord describes himself by, (see Isa. lvii 15.) I dare not venture even to conjecture. We are commanded to worship the Lord, indeed, in the beauty of holiness. (Ps. xcvi. 9.) And Moses's song celebrates the Lord's praise, in being glorious in holiness. (Exod. xv. 11.) And no doubt, as in the portrait of a man, to behold it in its most complete form, we should take all the prominent features of beauty, so the holy Scriptures of God, when sketching the divine representation, do it in all that loveliness of character, so as to endear the Lord to every heart, Hence David made this the "one great desire of his soul, "to dwell in the house of the Lord all the days of his life, to behold the beauty of the Lord, and to enquire in his temple." (Ps. xxvii. 4.) I must not forget, under this article yet farther to observe, that the thrice ascribing holiness to JEHOVAH in the song of heaven, hath been uniformly and invariably considered by the church, as the suited adoration to each person of the GODHEAD, and, at the same time, to all, collectively considered, in the one glorious and eternal JEHOVAH, existing in a threefold character of persons, "Father, Son, and Holy Ghost. (I John v. 7.)

Having thus briefly considered the subject, as referring to the holiness of JEHOVAH in his own eternal power and GODHEAD, the subject must now be considered in reference to the person of the God-man Christ Jesus, and then to the church in him.

As strictly and properly speaking, the term "holy can belong to none but JEHOVAH, and so the song of Hannah beautifully set forth, (1 Sam. ii. 2.) so none but the person of the Lord Jesus Christ, as the Christ of God, can be holy. The highest order of created beings, angels of the first magnitude, have only a derived holiness from the Lord, as the moon's brightest light is only borrowed from the sun. The holiness of creatures can be no other than as the shadow to the substance. Hence we are told, that in the very moment of adoration "angels veil their faces," as if to testify their nothingness in the presence of the Lord. (Isa. vi. 2.) But, by the union of that pure holy portion of our nature which the Son of God hath united to himself in the GODHEAD of his nature, he hath communicated an infinite dignity to that nature, and made it holy as himself. In fact, it is truly and properly himself; for in Christ, God and man in one person, dwelleth "all the fulness of the GODHEAD bodily." (Col. ii. 9.) And hence, in proof, we have these blessed Scriptures. Daniel, when speaking of Christ as coming "to finish transgression, and to make an end of sin," saith, that this is "to anoint the Most Holy." (Dan. Ix. 24.) And another prophet calls Christ, as Christ, the Holy One. "Thou shalt not suffer thine Holy One to see corruption." (Ps. xvi. 10.) And the Lord Jesus had this name specifically given him before his incarnation, the Holy Thing. (Luke i. 35.) And Peter, in his sermon, peculiarly denominates the Lord Jesus Christ, in his mediatorial character, the Holy One, and the Just. (Acts iii. 14.) All which, and more to the same amount, are expressly spoken of the Lord Jesus Christ,

HOLY, HOLINESS, most HOLY - HOLY, HOLINESS, most HOLY

in his person and character as the Head of his body the Church, God and man in one person. "For such an high priest became us, who is holy, harmless, undefiled, separate from sinners, and made higher than the heavens." (Heb. vii. 26.) Such, then, is the personal holiness of the Lord Jesus Christ-- an holiness higher than the angels, be cause the infinite holiness of the GODHEAD in him is underived. Hence of angels, it is said, the Lord "chargeth them with folly;" (Job iv. 18.) that is, with weakness, and the possibility of sinning. But of the Son, he saith, "Thy throne, O God, is for ever and ever;" that is, his mediatorial throne, as is plain by what follows: "Thou hast loved righteousness, and hated iniquity; therefore, God, even thy God, hath anointed thee with the oil of gladness above thy fellows." (Heb. i, 8, 9.) Here is a double proof that this is said to Christ, as Christ; for in the first place, the anointing of the Lord Jesus could not have been as God only, but as God and man in one person. And, secondly, this anointing with the oil of gladness is expressly said to have been, "for, or above his fellows," that is, his body the Church; evidently proving hereby, that he is considered, and here spoken of, as "the glorious Head of his body the church, the fulness of him that filleth all in all." (Ephes. i. 22, 23.)

Next, we must take a view of the term holy and holiness; as relating to Christ's church, made so only by virtue of her union with him. And this becomes a most interesting part to be considered, because without an eye to the Lord Jesus, nothing in the creation of God can be farther from holiness, than poor, fallen, ruined, undone man. I beg the reader's particular attention to this, as forming one of the sweetest features of the gospel. The whole Scriptures of God declare, that the great purpose for which the Son of God became incarnate, was to destroy the works of the devil, and to raise up the tabernacles of David that were fallen down, and to purify to himself "a peculiar people, zealous of good works." One of the apostles, in a very interesting and beautiful manner, describes the Lord Jesus in this endearing character, as engaged in the great work of salvation. "Christ (saith he) loved the church, and gave himself for it: that he might sanctify and cleanse it with the washing of water, by the word, that he might present it to himself a glorious church, not having spot or wrinkle, or any such thing; but that it should be holy and without blemish." (Eph. v. 25-27.) And hence, in conformity to this gracious design of the Lord Jesus, we find the church of God, beheld as in oneness and union with her glorious Husband, spoken of, in all ages of the church, under this precious character. "Ye shall be (saith Moses to the true Israel of God) a peculiar treasure unto me above all people; and ye shall be unto me a kingdom of priests, and an holy nation." (Exod. xix. 5, 6.) And hence the gospel-charter, corresponding to the same as the law by Moses had typically represented, makes the same proclamation. "Ye are (saith Peter) a chosen generation, a royal priesthood, an holy nation, a peculiar people, that ye should shew forth the praises of Him who hath called you out of darkness into his marvellous light." (1 Pet. ii. 9.) And if it be asked, as well it may, how is it that the church of the Lord Jesus, which in every individual member of it is continually complaining of a body of sin and death, believers carry about with them from day to day, how is it that such can be called holy before the Lord? The answer is at hand, and perfectly satisfactory: They are so, from their union with, and their right and interest in their glorious Head; for if he was made sin for them, who knew no sin," it is but just that they, who in themselves have no righteousness, should be made" the righteousness of God in him." (2 Cor. v. 21.) And if the church be commanded, as that the church is, and by God the Father himself; to call Christ "the Lord our righteousness," equally proper is it, and by the same authority also, that the church should be called the Lord our righteousness, as the lawful wife bearing her husband's name. (Compare Jer. xxiii. 6. with xxxiii. 16.) And all this because the Lord Jesus hath married his church, hath made her holy in his holiness and is become to her, by God the father's own covenant-engagements, "wisdom, righteousness, sanctification, and redemption; that, according as it is written, he that glorieth, let him glory in the Lord." (1 Cor. i. 30.) Such, then, are the beautiful Scripture views of holy and of holiness, in the lovely order of it. First, as beheld in the persons of the GODHEAD, in the very being of JEHOVAH. Secondly, as the same in the personal holiness of the Lord Jesus Christ, as the Christ of God, and the glorious Head of his body the church. And thirdly, as making holy the whole body of the church in Jesus, and from Jesus, and by Jesus, united to him. And hence, from this union, every thing that is called holy in Scripture, derives that sanctity. The temple, the holy of holies, the vessels of the sanctuary, the ordinances, sacrifices, and all that belonged to the Jewish church. And, under the Christian dispensation, every thing found in the simple services of Christ's church is no otherwise holy, than as it derives that purity from Christ's person; Christ is all, and in all. Yea, heaven itself, into which Jesus is gone as the forerunner of his people, hath all its holiness and blessedness from him. John tells the church, that "he saw no temple there, for the Lord God Almighty, and the Lamb, are the temple of it." (Rev. xxi. 22.)

HOLY GHOST

Besides referring back to the former article concerning this almighty Lord, it may be proper to subjoin some of the names and offices by which God the Holy Ghost is known in Scripture. I say some, for to bring forward all is perhaps beyond the power or the province of man. Our blessed Lord, over and above the sacred names the Holy Ghost hath in common with the Father and the Son in the essence of the GODHEAD, hath graciously taught his church the special titles and appellations by which the Lord the Spirit is known. He is called the "Spirit of truth, by Jesus that leads his church into all truth." (John xiv. 17.) Jesus speaks of him as a "Witness to testify of him." (John xvi 26.) And his servant, the apostle Paul, following the steps of his divine Master, calls the Holy Ghost by the same name. See a beautiful account of the almighty Spirit to this amount. (Rom. viii. 1-16.) As the Holy Ghost the Comforter, the Lord Jesus most blessedly describes him. (John xiv. 16-26.) Indeed, this is his great work; for under whatever divine operations the Lord the Spirit brings the people of God, the first and ultimate design of the whole, is for consolation. Hence Paul prays for the communion and fellowship of the Holy Ghost to be with the church. (2 Cor. xiii. 14.) And it is most blessed to every child of God, when brought into the fellowship and communion of the Holy Ghost, to discover how that almighty Comforter opens a communication between Christ and the soul, and keeps it open by the exercises of his grace; so that, while the person of the Father, or the Son, is coming forth to bless the soul, he draws forth and leads out the actings of the soul's faith and love upon the glorious persons of the GODHEAD, and gives "a joy unspeakable and full of glory."

The Lord Jesus also points to the person and office of the Holy Ghost, as a Leader and Guide to his chosen, John xvi. 13; as a Glorifier of Jesus, John xvi. 14; as the Remembrancer also of Jesus, John xiv. 26. And as the prophet Isaiah had been commanded to tell the church of this sovereign Lord, under his almighty offices, as acting with "a spirit of judgment and a spirit of burning," (Isa. iv. 4.) the Lord Jesus more fully opens the nature of these heart-searching works of the Holy Ghost, in shewing that it consists in "convincing of sin, of righteousness, and of judgment." (John xvi. 8-11.) In short, so many, so diversified, so constant, and so unremitting are the operations of the Holy Ghost on the hearts and minds of the Lord's people, that it must with truth be said, that he, and he only, is the almighty minister in the church of Christ, and to him alone the who efficiency of the gospel, both in work and blessing, is committed.

And, indeed, the beautiful order in the covenant of grace, and the economy of redemption, makes it necessary so to be. For, as the whole Three persons of the GODHEAD all concurred in the vast design, and all guaranteed to each other concerning the several offices in the departments of grace, so it became essential, that in the carrying "on and completing the work, each almighty person should be engaged in it in his own specific office and character. The Father gave the church; the Son redeemed the church; and God the Holy Ghost sanctifies the church. God the Father appears in the Old, Testament dispensation, holding forth the promised Saviour with all his blessings, as coming for salvation; God the Son takes up the wonderful subject under the New Testament dispensation, as thus coming and finishing all that was promised in the Old; and now that the Son of God hath finished transgression, made an end of sin, and is returned unto glory, God the Holy Ghost is come down, agreeably to Jesus's and his Father's most sure promise, to render effectual the whole purpose of redemption, by his divine offices in the hearts of the redeemed. And thus the church is taught to give equal and undivided praise and glory to the united source of all her mercies, in the Father's love, the Son's grace, and the Spirit's fellowship.

It would be little less than the brief recapitulation of the Bible, to go over all that might be brought forward concerning the agency of God the Holy Ghost in the church. From the first awakenings of grace in the heart, until grace is consummated in glory, believers are taught to look to that Holy and eternal Spirit, for his leadings and influences in and through all. The regeneration by the Holy Ghost, in the first motions of the spiritual life, John iii. 3; the baptisms of the Spirit, so essential in the spiritual life, 1 Cor. xii. 13; the illuminations of the Spirit, 2 Cor. iv. 6; the "indwelling residence of the Spirit," John xiv. 16 17; the "receiving of the Holy Ghost," Acts viii. 15-17; the "walking in the Spirit," Acts ix. 31; the "renewing of the Holy Ghost," Tit. iii. 5; the sealings and earnest of the Spirit, Ephes. i. 13. 2 Cor. v. 5. All these, and infinitely more to the same effect, prove his sovereign and unceasing agency. But having already swollen this article beyond the usual limits, I must close these observations with only praying that holy and eternal Teacher in the church of the Lord Jesus, to grant some sweet and precious token of his grace and power, by setting his seal in the heart both of the writer and reader, that the truth of his ministry may be known, and felt, and adored, to his glory, and to our comfort and joy. "May the God of hope fill you with all joy and peace in believing, that ye may abound in hope, through the power of the Holy Ghost." (Rom. xv. 13.)

HONEY

There is frequent mention made in Scripture concerning honey. It is made, indeed, by the Lord himself, a type of the promised land. And the manna from heaven, that the Lord fed the church with in the wilderness forty years, is said in taste, to have been "like wafers made with honey." (Exod. xvi. 31.) Notwithstanding this, it is somewhat remarkable, that the Lord forbade the offering of it upon the altar. (Lev. ii. 11.) The Lord Jesus, in commending the loveliness and sweetness of his church, compares her lips to the "droppings of the honeycomb." (Song iv. 11.) We may well suppose the figure is just, as well as beautiful, because Christ himself useth it. And when the church is in public prayer, or a believer is in private devotion, and the Holy Ghost is leading the soul in those sacred exercises, it is indeed "sweet as the honeycomb to the soul, and health to the bones." (Prov. xvi. 24.) And when Jesus's name and salvation are the gracious themes of the believer's exercise; whether in prayer or praise or reading the word, or religious conversation; every act, like the sweetness of honey, is grateful. The prophet describes the blessed effect in a very lively manner. (Mal. iii. 16, 17.) "Then they that feared the Lord, spake often one to another, and the Lord hearkened and heard it; and a book of remembrance was written before him, for them that feared the Lord, and that thought upon his name. And they shall be mine, saith the Lord of hosts, in that day when I make up my jewels; and I will spare them, as a man spareth his own son that serveth him." See Milk.

HOPE

In the strict and proper sense of the word, this is Christ; for He, and He only, as the prophet hath described him, "is the Hope of Israel, and the Saviour thereof? (Jer. xiv. 8.) And, indeed, this view must be uniformly preserved and kept up, because, without an eye to Christ, there can be no such thing as hope, for all our whole nature is, in its universal circumstances, "without God, and without hope in the world." (Eph. ii. 12.) And it is very blessed to turn over the Scriptures of God, and behold the Lord Jesus Christ set forth under this endeared character, in a great variety of figures and representations, throughout the whole Bible.

Jesus was the grand hope of all the Old Testament believers before his incarnation. They all, like Abraham, saw "his day afar off," rejoiced and were glad; and, like him, amongst all the discouraging circumstances they had to encounter" against hope, they believed in hope." Hence, though the longing expectation of the church, as Solomon expressed it, was like "hope deferred, which maketh the heart sick;" (Prov. xiii. 12.) yet, as Jeremiah was commissioned to tell the church, there was still "hope in the end, saith the Lord, that the children of Christ should come to their own border." (Jer. xxxi. 17.)

Christ, therefore, being held up to the church's view as the hope of his redeemed, is set forth under various similitudes corresponding to this character. His people are called "prisoners of hope." (Zech. ix. 12.) And the apostle Paul, under the same figure, calls himself the Lord's prisoner, and saith, it is for "the hope of Israel, I am bound with this chain." (Acts xxviii. 20. Eph. iv. 1.) And elsewhere, he described it under the strong metaphor of "an anchor to the soul, both sure and steadfast." (Heb. vi. 19.) In short, Christ is the only hope of eternal life, to which we are "begotten by his resurrection from the dead. In him our flesh is said to rest in hope," when returning to the dust; and all our high expectations of life and immortality are expressed, in "looking for that blessed hope, and the glorious appearing of the Great God, and our Saviour, Jesus Christ." (See those Scriptures, Titus ii. 13. 1 Pet. i. 3. Ps. xvi. 9.)

As Christ then is the only true hope the Scriptures speak of, it is very evident, that every other hope, not founded in Christ, is and must be deceitful. The world is full of hope, and the life of carnal and ungodly men is made up of it. But what saith the Scripture, of all such. "The hope of the hypocrite, saith Job, shall be cut off, and his trust shall be as a spider's web." (Job vii. 14.) So that the hope of the faithful, which is Christ himself, affords the only well-grounded confidence for the life that now is, and that which is to come. And this "hope maketh not ashamed, because the love of God is shed abroad in the heart by the Holy Ghost." It is founded in Christ, and is, in. need, Christ formed in the heart, "the hope of glory." (Rom. v. 5. Col. i. 27.)

HOPHNI

One of the sons of Eli. His name signifies to cover, from the Hebrew Chaphah. This man's history is a very awful one, as we read it, 1 Sam. ii. iii. iv. His brother Phinehas, or Pinehai more properly, and which signifies a countenance or face, from Panah, to behold, was another such a character as himself. Both lived in the commission of the same sins, and both died under the same judgment of God. The infamy of these men while ministering before the Lord, the Holy Ghost hath faithfully recorded; and their history presents itself as a monument in the church, to be read by all that minister in holy things. Oh, that the Lord may cause it to operate as an alarm in the Lord's holy mountain!

The sin of those priests respecting the sacrifice is not, at first view, so generally understood. The peace-offerings, as prescribed by the law, (Lev. iii. 1, &c.) give directions for the fat of the beasts offered in sacrifice, and also for the parts to be taken away. The portion allotted to the priests Moses directed. (Lev. vii. 31-34.) For the servants, therefore, to demand the portion for his master before the Lord's portion, was irreverent and unbecoming. Add to this, they were not content with the priest's portion, it should seem, but took more, and that, if not immediately given, by violence. They were what the prophet called "greedy dogs, that never could have enough." (Isa. lvi. 11.) The irreverence of the priests brought contempt, as might well be supposed, upon the offerings of the Lord. Alas! what accumulated evils follow the commission of sin in the service of the sanctuary! See Eli.

HOR

The mountain where Aaron died, the fortieth year of Israel's departure from Egypt. The name of Hor means, who conceives.

HOREB

The memorable place where the visions of God began with Moses. Here it was, that this great leader of the armies of Israel had his first view of God in Christ. That this was Christ, the Angel of the Covenant, who manifested himself to the man of God, there can be no question, by comparing the account of this solemn interview, as it is related in Exodus, chap. iii. and as it is explained by Stephen, Acts vii. 30-32. Horeb, and mount Sinai, were so close to each other, that they both, at a distance, appeared but as one mountain. Here it was, that Moses struck the rock at the foot of Horeb. (Exod. xvii. 6-8.) And Rephidim was near at hand. From hence the progress of the rock that followed Israel took its rise, and which the apostle to the Corinthians plainly declares was Christ. (1 Cor. x. 4.) So that Horeb, which in its original sense signifies a desert and dryness, was admirably suited both to Moses and Israel, to teach them that from the dry and desert state of our fallen nature ariseth the very cause of finding springs in Christ. It is from our misery Christ takes occasion to magnify the glory of his mercy; and from the drought of Horeb, the rock that follows Israel, even Christ, furnished a fulness of living water to the soul. The name of Rephidim, which is in the plural number, and signifies places of rest, from Raphab, rest, is esentation of our nature resting in itself, without any thing in our own power to give satisfaction to the dry soul. Here will be always "Massah and Meribah, that is, temptation and chiding," till Christ, the rock of living water, is discovered and enjoyed. See Sinai.

HORITES

An ancient people, who dwelt in mount Seir. (Gen. xiv. 6.) Perhaps, in latter days, they were mingled with, and lost their name in the Edomites, or children of Esau. (Deut. ii. 1, &c.)

HORN and HORNS

This word in Scripture doth not seem to be very generally understood. Certainly it is more than once spoken of in reference to the Lord Jesus Christ. Thus JEHOVAH saith, "I will make the horn of David to flourish," meaning Christ. (See Ps. cxxxii. 17.) And Zacharias celebrates Christ to the same amount in his song, when saying, "the Lord hath raised up an horn for salvation for us, in the house of his servant David." (Luke i. 69.) But when it is said, that the Lord "will cut off the horns of the wicked, and the horns of the righteous shall be exalted," (Ps. lxxv. 10.) here it appears, that the expression is in allusion to somewhat of a man's own, and not simply with an eye to Christ. Perhaps the word may be considered as referring in general to strength. Thus the son of "Chenaanah made him horns of iron, and said, with these shalt thou push the Syrians." (1 Kings xxii. 11.) And, indeed, the prophet describes the Lord as having "horns coming out of his hand, when before him went the pestilence." (Habak. iii. 4.) Hence also we read of the horns of the altar." (Jer. xvii. 1. Rev. ix. 13.) But whether these had reference to any thing ornamental, or to objects more important, when "the sacrifice was bound with cords even to the horns of the altar," I cannot determine. (Ps. cxvii. 27.)

HORNET

We read of this insect a particularly commissioned by the Lord, to punish and drive out the enemies of Israel. In hot countries, it may easily be conceived, how formidable a swarm of such creatures armed with stings must become to any people, and especially when sent, like the flies of Egypt, in judgment by the Lord. (See Deut vii. 20 Josh. xxiv. 12.) But some, beside the history of the fact itself, in the hornets the Lord literally and truly sent to drive out before Israel their enemies, take the expression also in a figurative sense, and consider hornets from the Lord as the buzzing and stinging effects of a guilty conscience. And these age still more formidable and alarming. "I will send my fear before thee, saith the Lord." (Exod. xxiii. 27, 28.) And where the Lord sends his fear, a man's own feelings will make him flee. See Flies.

HOSANNA

The Hebrews read it Hoshiah-na. The meaning is, "Save me, I beseech you;" from Jahash, to save; and Na, I pray you. It is hardly necessary to tell the reader, that it was with this salutation the multitude hailed Christ, in his public entrance into Jerusalem, five days before his death. The prophet Zechariah had predicted of the Messiah, that he should so come; and none but Christ ever did so. (Compare Zech. ix. 9. with Matt. xxi. 1-11.) It was prohesied also by David, that "prayer should be made for him continually." (Ps. lxxv. 15.) And here we find the unceasing cry Hosanna, which is a form of blessing and prayer included; as if they had said, "Preserve, Lord, this son of David!" And the spreading of their garments in the way, and strewing the road with branches of trees, were all figurative of laying every thing at the feet of Jesus. The feats of Tabernacles was so celebrated, to denote holy joy in the gathering in all the Lord's blessings; and some have thought, that this feast was particularly typical of this entry of the Lord Jesus; for it is somewhat remarkable, that at this feast they carried branches, which they called Hosannas. I cannot dismiss the consideration of this article, without subjoining one thought more, to remark the conduct of the Jewish children upon this occasion. For what but a divine overruling power could have produced such an effect, that in the moment their fathers, and the scribes and pharisee's were moved with indignation, those little children should join the Redeemer's train, and mingle their infant voices in the Hosanna of the multitude! And the reader will not overlook in this account, I hope, how thereby that

HOSEA--the Prophet

blessed prophecy was fulfilled, and which Jesus himself explained and applied. "Have ye never read, Out of the mouths of babes and sucklings thou hast perfected praise?" (Matt. xxi. 16. Ps. viii. 2.)

HOSEA--the Prophet

His name is the same as that of Joshua, and signifies a Saviour. He was the son of Beevi. He is placed the first of what is called the minor prophets; not so called as if the writings of those holy men of old were considered less important than others--not so--but the reason of their being called minor prophets, was on account of the bulk of their prophetical writings being less. Very highly indebted hath the church been, in all ages, for their ministry; and believers in the present hour, find daily cause to bless God the Holy Ghost, for the instrumentality of those men. Hosea began to prophecy very early in the church, prehaps, as some think, the first of all the prophets whose writings have been preserved in the canon of Scripture; and he continued through several reigns, as the preface in his first chapter shews. On the subject of his marriage with Gomer, (see Gomer) some have thought, that this was a parable, and only intended by the Lord in a figurative way, to shew the Lord's grace to his adulterous Israel and Judah. But certainly the thing itself is real. And wherefore should it be more improbable, in the case of Hosea's marrying an adulteress, than in Jeremiah's instance, and in the case of Ezekiel also, being continued types of the doctrines they were directed to deliver to the people.

I cannot take leave of the history of Hosea without first desiring the reader to remark with me, what numberless things we discover in this man's writings, pointing to the person, offices, relation, and ministry of the Lord Jesus Christ. What grace, mercy, love, and condescension in the Lord marrying our adulterous nature! What blessedness is set forth in that betrothing nature, for ever! What sweet views of Jesus doth this man's writings give concerning his recoveries of his people under all their backslidings, and departures, and rebellions, and ingratitude! Surely, it is impossible for any enlightened eye to read the records of the prophet, and not perceive the Saviour in almost every chapter and verse, from beginning to end, And how blessed was it and gracious in God the Holy Ghost, in those distant ages from Christ, when the prophecy of Hosed was delivered; and how blessed and gracious now in our day, upon whom "the ends of the world are come;" that this man's ministry should be made instrumental to comfort and refresh both, concerning the glorious person, love, grace, and mercy of our Lord Jesus Christ. Oh, what a sweet proof of the constant and unceasing love watching over and blessing the church of Jesus, by God the Holy Ghost, (See Isa. xxvii. 3.)

There was another Hosea in the church, who was last king of Israel. (See 2 Kings xvii. 1.)

HOSHAIAH

The tother of Jezaniah. His name is a compound of Hosha and Jah, from Jasha, Saviour; and Jah, Lord, (See Neb. xii. 32.)

HOSPITALITY

The apostles strongly recommended this virtue to the church. "Use hospitality one to another without grudging," saith Peter, (1 Pet. iv. 9.) And Paul begged the Hebrews, (chap, xiii. 2.) not to be forgetful "to entertain strangers, for thereby, he said, some had entertained angels unawares? alluding very probably, to the case of Abraham and Lot, as related Gen. xviii. 3. and Gen. xix. 2. And Moses commanded the same gracious conduct, upon another account: "Love ye the stranger, for ye were strangers in the land of Egypt." (Deut. x. 19.) But how infinitely higher are the motives enforced in the consideration, that Jesus, the heavenly stranger, came to visit us in our ruined state, and so journeyed among us as a wayfaring man for a little space, that we might dwell with him for ever! And how blessed also, on the other hand, is the consideration, that when this divine Samaritan, as a stranger, passed by, and saw our whole nature robbed and plundered by the great enemy of souls, he took us up, and brought us to the inn of his church and ordinances, and hath there commanded us to be well taken care of until his second coming, when he will recompense every minute act of kindness shewn us for his sake! Such views of Jesus enforce hospitality indeed, in the highest extent, and compel by a motive of the most persuasive nature. The "cup of cold water" given in the name and for the sake of a disciple, cannot be given unnoticed, neither pass unrewarded. Jesus hath already left it upon record, what he will say in that day when he cometh to be glorified in his saints, and to be admired in all that believe me in; naked, and ye clothed me; I was sick, and ye visited me; I was in prison, and ye came unto me." And when the conscious sense of the littleness of services, and the unworthiness of the doer, shall make the souls of Christ's people exclaim, "Lord, when saw we thee a stranger, and took thee in; or naked, and clothed thee; or when saw we thee sick, or in prison, and came unto thee? The Lord Jesus will graciously explain the seeming impossibility in manifesting, before a congregated world, the oneness between himself and his redeemed. "Verily I say unto you, Inasmuch as ye have done it unto one of the least of these my brethren, ye have done it unto me." (Matt. xxv. 34-40.)

HOUR and HOURS

We do not find any particular method made use of in the Old Testament Scripture, for dividing the hours of the day in one regular plan. The Hebrews made four parts in each day--morning, noon, the first evening, and the last evening. And the night was again formed into three parts--the night watch, the midnight watch, and what was called the morning watch, to the break of day. Hence David beautifully speaks of the waiting of his soul on the Lord, "more than they that watch for the morning;" yea, said he, repeating it with earnestness, "yea, I say, more than they that watcheth for the morning." (Ps. cxxx. 6.) The dial of Ahas is the first account we have in Scripture of the method the Hebrews had to mark down the progress of time; and this it should seem, was by marks or lines of degrees, and not of hours. In the New Testament we find our fathers then arrived at some method of calculating hours; and certainly then they did, as we do now, divide the day into twelve hours. Hence Jesus said, "Are there not twelve hours in the day?" (John xi. 9. see also Matt. xx. 3-5). But the time of reckoning always began at six in the morning; and the seventh was the first hour. The reader of the New Testament should always keep this in remembrance. Hence when we read, (Acts iii 1.) that Peter and John went up together into the temple at the hour of prayer, being the ninth hour, that was three in what we call the afternoon; and, consequently, the twelfth hour was six in the evening.

While I am upon this subject of the Jewish hours, I cannot forbear calling the reader's attention to one circumstance, which I think, now in the present day of the church, still equally interesting as it was of old always regarded, I mean the time of the evening sacrifice. If the reader will turn to the first account of any appointed sacrifice, even the lamb of the Passover, (Exod. xii. 5.) he will find, that the whole assembly of the people were to kill this lamb of the first year without blemish in the evening, or, as the margin of the Bible hath it, between the two evenings, that was what we should call three o'clock in the afternoon; and to this precise time all the sacrifices of the evening corresponded. Hence, we are told, (1 Kings xviii. 29.) they prophesied till the evening sacrifice. Ezra saith, "I sat astonied until the evening sacrifice, and at the evening sacrifice I arose up from my heaviness." (Ezra. ix. 4, 5.) Hence David also prays, "Let my prayer be set forth before thee as incense, and the lifting up of my hands as the evening sacrifice," (Ps. cxli. 2.) And Daniel tells the church, that the man Gabriel touched him about "the time of the evening oblation,"' (Dan. ix. 21.)

Now what I beg the reader particularly to notice in all these instances, is the uniformity as to the time of the hour; and then let him turn his attention, and look at the cross of Christ, and behold the Lord Jesus at that very hour fulfilling the whole in the sacrifice of himself. The Evangelists are all particular to remark, that there was darkness over all the earth, from the sixth hour (twelve at noon) until the ninth hour, (three in the afternoon.) And then it was Jesus, cried with a loud voice, and gave up the ghost. Now let the reader pause, and consider the subject attentively. Who was it but God the Holy Ghost, that caused the evening sacrifice, from the first moment of appointed sacrifices in the church to the glorious finishing of all sacrifices in the death of the Lord Jesus, thus minutely to correspond? And what a sacred hour that was all along considered in the divine mind, when not the sacrifice only, but the very hour of offering it was so scruptulously regarded! Think then reader, how infinitely momentous must be the thing itself, when the mere shadow of the substance was so solemnly attended to; when through a period of more than fifteen hundred years the evening lamb was regularly sacrificed in the very hour which, in after ages, Christ, the Lamb of God, should offer himself in a sacrifice to God, to take away the sins of the world! Lord, I would say, for myself and reader, cause this hour of the afternoon, which was so sacred in the Jewish church, to be sacred to my soul also; and wherever I am, or however engaged, at the sounding bell at three in the afternoon, call my forgetful wandering thoughts to the hill of Calvary. Let me as often as the circumstances of my poor, empty, and unsatisfying life will allow, by faith, do as Peter and John did, indeed, go up to the Lord's house at the hour of prayer, the three o'clock hour; and there may my soul meet the Lord of Peter and John, and like the cripple healed in Christ's name at the gate of the temple, may my feet and ankle bones receive strength in the name of Jesus; and while the Lord himself takes me by the hand, may I, as he did, leap up and stand, and with Jesus enter into his temple walking, and leaping, and praising God. (Acts iii. 1-26.)

HOUSE

The word house, in Scripture, means somewhat more than the mere residence of a family; indeed, it hath various significations. Heaven is called the house of God, "an house not made with hands, eternal in the heavens." The grave is called "the house appointed for all living." (Job xxx. 23.) The church is called "the house of the living God." Ye also, saith Peter, speaking to the faithful, "are built up a spiritual house." (1 Pet. ii. 5. Heb. iii. 6.) But in a more general way, a family is called an house, such as the house of the Rechabites, (Jer. xxxv. 2.) the house of David, (Zech. xiii. 1.) But amidst all these, and more to the like import, that undoubtedly is the highest and the best sense of the word which considers the Lord Jesus Christ himself as the High Priest and Head of his body the church, and the bodies of his people the temple of his indwelling residence by his Spirit. And the conscious sense of his presence, in upholding, acting upon, comforting, refreshing, stengthening, and witnessing to the soul, and for the Lord in the soul, these are among the most blessed evidences in the enjoyment of the household of faith. Here, in the fullest sense of the expression, the church, and every individual believer forming a part in that church, may and is called the house of the living God. "Lo! I come, said JEHOVAH, and I will dwell in the midst of thee;" (Zech. ii. 11.) and this scriptural sense of the word may serve to shew why it was the patriarchs, and holy men of old, were so anxious concerning their households and brailles. Thus the faithful Abraham, after that the Lord had revealed himself unto him in vision, and said, "Fear not, Abraham, I am thy shield, and thine exceeding great reward;" the patriarch felt a boldness to ask of God concerning his household. Abram said, "Lord God! what wilt thou give me, seeing I go childless, and the steward of ray house is this Eliezer of Damascus?" (Gen. xv. l, 2.) meaning, that he was not born of his bowels, but Damascus born, probably a black. Now as it is well known, that every black slave when freed by his master, was always after known by the name of the child" of the house, (for so the phrase steward of my house means,) it is likely, that Abram felt some jealousy concerning this freed slave being his heir. And the very name Eliezer was not a little in countenancing this idea, which signified the help of my God. But I leave the reader to his own views of this subject, only remarking farther, that the Lord's gracious answer concerning Isaac seems a confirmation, that it was in this, or some such like sense, the house or family was regarded. See Gen. xv. 4-6.

HUKKOK

A city in the tribe of Asher. (Josh. xix. 31. probably Chakak, so called, meaning statutes, writings.

HUL or CHUL

The son of Abram. (Gen. x. 23.) The name means infirmity.

HULDAH

The prophetess, the wife of Shallum. Her name is the same as the Hebrew name for the world. Josiah consulted her on account of the book found in the house of the Lord. (2 Kings xxii. 14.) We cannot sufficiently admire the firmness of this woman, in the answer she returned to king Josiah. Tell the man that sent you, thus saith the Lord, "Behold, I will bring evil upon this place; but because thine heart was tender, and thou hast humbled thyself before the Lord, thine eyes shall not see all the evil which I will bring upon this place." It is a blessed thing to be found faithful both to God and man!

HUMTAH

This was a city of Judah. (Josh. xv. 54.) Humtah is the Hebrew word for snail.

HUNTING

One of the old Lexicons for the Bible speaks of hunting as the apprenticeship of war; and certain it is, that the transition from hunting beasts is easily made to that of hunting men. It seems to be no unfair inference, that he who can take pleasure in tearing poor timid hares to pieces by dogs, would not melt into tears in beholding men torn to pieces by horses, Nimrod is the first hunter we read of in history, and of him it is said to a proverb, that he was a mighty hunter before the Lord. (Gen. x. 9.) And as the beginning of his kingdom was Babel and Erech, and other places, it is very probable, that be was a mighty conqueror also of men, It is worthy remark, that when the Lord speaks: of sending a scourge upon the earth, he speaks of his instrument to punish under the character of hunters. (Jer. xvi. 16.) And it is still worthy of farther remark, that at a time when the Lord delivered David from his enemies, he describes the deliverance under the name of "the snare of the fowler? (Ps. xci. 3.)

HUR

He that went up with Moses and Aaron to the Mount when Amalek fought with Israel. (Exod. xvii. 10.) His name signifies a cavern, from Chur.

HUSBAND

I should not have made the pause of a moment over this word, neither have deemed it necessary to have said aught by way of explaining a name so familar, had it not been for the special relationship of this character, when considered in reference to the Lord Jesus Christ, But looking up to him as the Husband of his people, in the union of our nature, it becomes a most interesting subject, and demands the clearest apprehension by every true believer in Christ. Now the Scriptures with one voice concur in the relation of the fact itself. "Thy maker is thine husband, the Lord of hosts is his name; and thy Redeemer, the Holy. One of Israel, the God of the whole earth shall he be called." (Isa. liv. 5.) And to the same amount do all the Scriptures declare. (See Jer. iii. 14. Hos. ii. 19, 20.) And the New Testament writers follow up the same blessed doctrine, telling us, that Christ "took not on him the nature of angels, but he took on him the seed of Abraham." (Heb. ii. 16.) Indeed as the Surety and Sponsor of his church and people, it became essentially necessary that he should take our nature," and be in all things tike to his brethren, sin only excepted." Agreeably to all this, as settled in the council of peace before all worlds, he stood up as the covenant-head and husband of his people. As the husband of his church he under took to pay all our debts to God which by sin we had incurred; he engaged to disannul all our former contracts, and to divorce our poor hearts, which sin, Satan, and the world had captivated, and by his Holy Spirit to win over our affections, and make us willing in the day of his power. He engaged both for our debt and for our duty, and promised, as the husband of his church, that he would beat down all our foes before our face, and at length bring his bride home to "the marriage-supper of the Lamb in heaven."

These were among the obligations into which the Son of God put himself, when at the call of his Father he came forth the bridegroom of his church. And when the fulness of time was come, Jesus came, full of grace and truth, and in his holy gospel proclaimed the wonderful proposal, that the Son of God, desired to woo our nature and unite it to himself, in grace here, and glory hereafter. He sent all his servants also with his royal decree, that God the Father had made a marriage for his Son, and now expected that the bride should make herself ready. A thousand, and ten thousand love tokens, the Lord Jesus accompanied his offer of marriage with to his spouse the church. And when, at any time, in a single instance, he hath by his Holy Spirit espoused and united a soul to himself, he gives a dower, and an interest in all that belongs to him; and after continued manifestation of his unalterable love and affection to his fair one, made fair in his comliness, he at a length brings home, to his house in heaven, his bride, where she lives with him forever. Happy and blessed is it, in any and in every single instance, when the church can look up to Jesus and call him Husband, and say as of old: "This is my beloved, and this is my friend, O ye daughters of Jerusalem!" (Song v. 16.)

HUSHAI

The Archite, David's friend, (2 Sam. xvi. 16.) The name signifies one hastening, from Chush.

HYMN

It is somewhat remarkable, that the Hebrews have no peculiar or specific name for an hymn. A Canticle, or Song, or Psalm, they have words for. Perhaps those which are called Hal-lah might mean as much, for the Hallelu-Jah of David's psalms imply as much.

HYPOCRITE

The general acceptation of this word, and the character of the person under the influence of hypocrisy, is not well understood. We perfectly well apprehend, that an hypocrite, and especially in religion, means one that wishes to be thought what he is not, and takes pains to impose upon others a seeming sanctity of character, which, in fact, his heart is a stranger to. This is the supposed meaning of an hypocrite, and this, as far as it goes, is right; but this is not all. For the full arid complete description of the character is, when he imposeth upon himself also: this is the finishing of the term hypocrisy. And very awful is it to say, that the deception is but too possible. Our Lord's expression is solemn to this amount. (Luke xii. 1, 2.) "Beware ye of the leaven of the pharisees, which is hypocrisy: for there is nothing covered, that shall not be revealed; neither hid, that shall not be known." Hence that most interesting desire of the soul as expressed by David, "cleanse thou me from secret faults." (Ps. xix. 12.)

HYSSOP

From Esob, an herb. The Lord pointed to the use of this shrub for sprinkling at the Passover. (Exod. xii. 22.) The shrub itself is a very humble, not to say uninviting plant; like him to outward appearance "who had no beauty that we should desire him;" but like him, the fragrancy of it is sweet, though mingled with bitter. Christ and his cross are two that cannot be separated, but must be received together. Reader! depend upon it, both are blessed guests worth receiving; and however painful to flesh and blood the cross may be, yet, like the waters of Marah to Israel, Jesus's presence sweetens and sanctifies.

I

I

IS but a letter, yet as expressive of person is as important a one as can be, and when used with peculiar and special respect to JEHOVAH, and spoken by himself, is infinitely dignified indeed. JEHOVAH in his threefold character of person graciously proclaims himself in his holy word by it, and in many instances repeats it both in identifying his person and being, and to express the glorious, incommunicable, and distinguishing nature of his existence. "I, even I, am the Lord, and beside me there is no Saviour." (Isa. xliii. 11.) So again, (Deut. xxxii. 39.) "See now that I, even I, am he, and there is no God with me: I kill, and I make alive, I wound, and I heal; neither is there any that can deliver out of my hand." And this distinguishing feature in identifying JEHOVAH, is equally made use of by all the persons of the GODHEAD. See (Exod. iii. 14. with John viii. 58. Mark xiv. 62. See also in reference to the identity of God the Holy Ghost, Acts x. 19; xiii. 2. 4.) In a subordinate sense, and by way of distinguishing both persons and things, all the creatures of God may be supposed to speak. Thus Moses, speaking of himself, saith "Who am I, and I should go unto Pharoah, and that I should bring forth the children of Israel out of Egypt?" (Exod. iii. 11.) And thus inferior creatures (Num. xxiii. 30.) yea, even inanimate things, (Judg. ix. 9, 11, 13.)

ICHABOD

This name was given by a dying mother, in the moment of her departure, to her new-born-son. The sense is, "the glory is departed, or alas! the glory; from Kabod, glory. (1 Sam. iv. 19. &c.) What a solemn question ariseth out of the subject--On how many places may the word Ichabod be written?

ICONIUM

A place rendered memorable from Paul's preaching. (See Acts xiii. and xiv.)

IDOL and IDOLATRY

These things have been generally confined to the idea of the worshipping of creatures or images, but, in fact, may be properly applied to every thing which men set up in their hearts to regard, and which tend to the lessening their reverence for the Lord. (Exod. xx. 3, 4. Ezek. xiv. 1.5.)

IMAGE

I should not have thought it necessary to have noticed this word, being in the general acception of it so very plain and obvious, had it not been so peculiarly made use of in relation to the person of our Lord Jesus Christ, as "the Image of the invisible God." He and he only, is the image of the invisible God, "the first born of every creature;" and though not openly revealed, yet secretly, and in reality set up from everlasting. Hence, as Christ, thus the glory-man, is declared to "be the brightness of his Father's glory, and the express image of his person." (Heb. i. 3.) So this is the very person in whose likeness, Adam the first open man, was created and made; "Let us make man in our image, after our likeness." (Gen. i. 26.)

IMMANUEL

See Emmanuel.

IMMORTAL and IMMORTALITY

Strictly and properly speaking, this can only be applied to JEHOVAH in his threefold character of person; for of Him, it is justly said, "who only hath immortality." (1 Tim. vi. 16.) But in Him, and by Him, and from Him, the church is said to have rendered to it "glory and honour and immortality, eternal life." (Rom. ii. 7.) But then, the striking and essential difference is here; JEHOVAH hath immortality in himself. It is His very Being--The church hath it by gift, and enjoys it only from her union with Christ. Of what nature or kind that immortality is, which distinguisheth the state or existence of the miserable in hell, Scripture hath not said. It is said, indeed, "their worm dieth not, and the fire is not quenched." (Mark ix. 44. 46. 48.) How ought true believers in Jesus to rejoice in the consciousness of their interest in him, to join the hymn of the apostle; "Now unto the King eternal, immortal, invisible, the only wise God, be honour and glory for ever and ever, Amen." (1 Tim. i. 17.)

IMPOSITION OF HANDS

We find this a very ancient custom among the Jews, and it should seem to have its use, founded in somewhat of a divine authority. The dying patriarch blessed the sons of Joseph, putting his hands significantly upon the head of each. (Gen. xliii. 13-20.) But in the striking act of laying on of hands on the day of atonement, and which was done by the express appointment of the Lord, we discover yet more of its importance. (See Lev. xvi. 21, 22.) So again, by the same express command of the Lord, Joshua was ordained by the laying on of the hand of Moses, his successor. The ceremony must have been most solemn and affecting, as related Num. xxvii. 15. to the end. But what endears this service to the church most is those instances in which our adorable Redeemer used it. How lovely Jesus appears in receiving little children, and putting his hands on them, and blessing them! (Mark x. 13-16.) We find the apostles in Jesus's name, using the imposition of hands, and the Lord confirming this act, by his accompanying it with the blessing of the Holy Ghost. (Acts viii. 17; xix. 6.) But how far the Lord hath honoured it in the after ages of the church, I presume not to speak.

IMPURE and IMPURITY

Under the law of Moses, we find many circumstances spoken of respecting legal impurity. Thus touching a dead body, or any creature deemed unclean by the law: touching a living person when under uncleanness; a leper, or one with a running sore, and the like; or garments unclean, &c. And this impurity attached itself to the person so touching any thing of uncleanness, though it was done involuntarily, and himself unconscious of it. And the law which pointed to these acts of impurity, prescribed the modes of cleansing; some by bathing, others by sacrifice. No doubt many of these things had a gospel signification, and preached Christ the only laver and fountain for sin and for uncleanness. But what blessed views ought all true believers in Christ to have of these things, when reading at any time the law of Moses, in beholding the whole done away in the person, work, and finished salvation of Jesus. Think how dear, and endeared in every way, and by every means, is the Lord Jesus Christ when brought home to the heart, and formed "in the heart the hope of glory."

IMPUTE and IMPUTED

This word, and the sense of it, according to the gospel, forming so important an article in the faith of a believer, I have thought it highly proper that it should have a distinct place of attention in a work of this kind. To impute is to charge a thing upon a person whether guilty or not, as the circumstances hereafter are proved, or not. Thus Shimei intreated David, that he would not "impute iniquity to him" for some former transaction. (2 Sam. xix. 19.) And the apostle Paul (Rom. iv. 8.) declares them blessed to whom the Lord "will not impute sin." This is the general sense of imputation. But in the case of the imputed righteousness of the Lord Jesus Christ to his people, and their sins imputed to him; the sense of imputation goes farther, and ascribes to Christ, and to the sinner, that which each hath not, but by the very act of imputing it to them. Hence the apostle Paul explains it in the clearest manner in two Scriptures: the first, in 2 Cor. v. 21, where speaking of this imputation of our sins to Christ, and his righteousness to us, he refers it into the sovereignty and good pleasure of God the Father. For speaking of Christ, it is used, "God hath made him to be sin for us who knew no sin; that we might be made the righteousness of God in him." Here the doctrine of imputation is most plainly and fully stated. Christ is the imputed sinner, or rather sin itself in the total abstract, and in the very moment when he knew no sin. And the sinner is said to be righteous; yea, the righteousness of God in Christ; when in the same time he hath not a single portion of righteousness in himself, or in any of his doings. This is, therefore, to impute Christ's righteousness to his people, and their sins to him. The other Scripture that explains the doctrine is but in part, namely, respecting the imputation of sin. (Gal. iii. 13.) "Christ hath redeemed us from the curse of the law, being made a curse for us." Here Christ stands with all the curse of a broken law charged upon him, as the sinner's Surety; yea, as the curse itself. And consequently, as in the doing of this, he takes it from his people; they are redeemed from it. The original debtor, and the Surety, who pays for that debtor, cannot both have the debt at the same time charged, upon them. This, therefore, is the blessed doctrine of imputation. Our sins are imputed to Christ. His righteousness is imputed to us. And this by the authority and appointment of JEHOVAH; for without this authority and appointment of JEHOVAH, the transfer could not have taken place. For it would have been totally beyond our power to have made it. But surely not beyond the right and prerogative of God. And if God accepts such a ransom; yea, he himself appoints it: and if the sinner by Christ's righteousness be made holy: and if the sins of the sinner be all done away by Christ's voluntary sufferings and death: if the law of God be thus honoured; the justice of God thus satisfied; all the divine perfections glorified by an equivalent; yea, more than an equivalent, inasmuch as Christ's obedience and death infinitely transcend in dignity and value the everlasting obedience of men and angels; surely, here is the fullest assurance of the truth of the doctrine of Christ's imputed righteousness, and the perfect approbation of JEHOVAH to the blessed plan of redemption. Well, therefore, might the apostle, when speaking of the faith of Abraham on this point, declare the cause of it: "Abraham believed God, and it was imputed unto him for righteousness. Now (saith the apostle) it was not written for his sake that it was imputed to him: but for us also, to whom it shall be imputed, if we believe on him that raised up Jesus our Lord from the dead; who was delivered for our offences, and raised again for our justification." (Rom. iv. throughout.)

If I have succeeded in thus stating the gospel sense of imputation, in the transfer of our sins unto the Lord Jesus, and the imputation of his righteousness to us: nothing can be more blessed than the doctrine itself, and nothing more important than the cordial belief of it, to bring consolation and joy to the heart of every believer.

IMRI

Son of Omri. (1 Chron. ix. 4.) There was another of this name in the church. (See Neh. iii, 2.) The name is from Marah, bitter.

INCENSE

In the old church we find great attention paid respecting the offerings of incense in the holy place. Aaron was enjoined to burn incense perpetually before the Lord. (Exod. xxx. 7, 8.) An awful judgment followed the sons of Aaron for offering strange fire before the Lord. (Lev. x. 1.) And the instance of Korah, Dathan, and Abiram, is another proof of the Lord's jealousy concerning offerings made by fire and incense. (Num. xvi. throughout.) Through many parts of the Bible, we find the great regard had to the sacred nature of incense. And as the prophet Malachi was commissioned to tell the church, that in the days of the Lord Jesus, "incense should be offered unto the Lord from the rising of the sun, unto the going down of the same, with a pure offering;" it appears, that the whole appointment of incense was intended as typical of Christ. Hence, the beloved apostle John, when he saw heaven opened, beheld the Lord Jesus beside the golden altar, with his golden censer, "to whom was given much incense, to offer with the prayers of all saints." (Rev. viii. 3, 4.) It is very blessed to consider how the intercession of the Lord Jesus, in his everlasting priesthood, was thus shadowed forth from the earliest ages of the church; and it is doubly blessed, when through the sweet influences of the Holy Ghost, the Lord's people are brought to live and act in all their approaches to the throne, under the censer of Christ's incense and righteousness.

INHERITANCE
See Heritage

INSTRUMENTS
See Music.

INTERCESSOR and INTERCESSION

We meet with but one passage in the Bible where the word Intercessor is used, namely, Isa. lix. 16. though by virtue of the office of interceding as our great high priest, it is a well known character of Christ. But though the name and title is but once mentioned, being implied in that of his priestly office, yet the Lord Jesus, in his sweet employment as our Advocate with the Father, is held up to the view of the church in this most endearing character every where throughout the word of God. He is said "to make intercession for the transgressors when he was numbered with them and bare their sins." (Isa. liii. 12.) And the apostle Paul as blessedly points to Jesus in his priestly office, when he encourageth the poor sinner to come to him, because "he ever liveth to make intercession for them, and is able to save to the uttermost all that come to God by him." (Heb. vii. 25.) And God the Holy Ghost is careful to shew the church how the Lord Jesus carrieth on this gracious office. First by personally appearing, "in the presence of God for us." (Heb. ix. 24.) John saith, that he saw him in the midst of a throne as "a lamb that had been slain." (Rev. v. 6.) intimating, that his wounds still appeared fresh and flowing, to denote the everlasting efficacy of it. And secondly, the Lord Jesus carrieth on this high office not only by a naked appearance in the presence of JEHOVAH for his people, but by pleading the merits and worth of his sacrifice and righteousness. Paul the apostle calls Christ's blood a speaking blood, (see Heb. xii. 24.) and so it certainly is; for if, as the Lord said to Cain, "The voice of thy brother's blood crieth unto me from the ground," (Gen. iv. 10.) what a voice must there be in Christ's blood, crying as it doth for mercy and salvation! Surely it speaks to God of God's faithfulness to his promises, and Christ's claim to his merits; and it speaks from God for our sure pardon, and all the blessings of redemption to JEHOVAH'S glory and Christ's and his church's triumph and happiness. Such are the blessed views of Christ in his intercessional character.

I would beg yet farther to observe, that this blessedness is abundantly heightened when we consider that he who intercedes, and he with whom intercession is made, are one in the same design and end. The divine glory is the first cause, and the final issue of all. The church, made up of redeemed sinners, is originally the Father's gift to the Son. (John xvii. 6.) The son hath purchased the Church with his blood. (Acts xx. 28.) Hence, therefore, all the persons of the GODHEAD are engaged and interested in the same concern. And as Christ is God the Father's dear Son, so is the

INTERPRETER - INTERPRETER

church the dear children of God in Christ: so that what our blessed Lord Jesus saith, when speaking of this very subject, comes home to the heart of the believer with the strongest and sweetest recommendation of tenderness. "At that day ye shall ask in my name, and I say not unto you, that I will pray the Father for you; for the Father himself loveth you, because you have loved me, and have believed that I came out from God." (John xvi. 26, 27.) These are blessed views both of the Father's everlasting love, and Christ's unceasing intercession. And it is highly important to remark, and a point that should never be lost sight of, that Christ in all his intercessions never once prayeth for the Father's love to the church, but for the fruits and effects of that love and his own merits and death. Yea, Christ himself, with all his fulness, blessedness, and glory, is the gift of the Father; for the express doctrine of the gospel in its first and leading point is, "that God so loved the world, that he gave his only begotten Son, that whosoever believeth in him should not perish, but have everlasting life. (John. iii. 16.) For a farther illustration of Christ's office of Intercessor, see Advocate.

INTERPRETER

We meet with this word twice in the history of Joseph. (Gen. xl. 8; xlii. 23.) and once in the history of Job, (chap. xxxiii. 23.) The office of an interpreter, in the general acceptation of the word, is not difficult to apprehend. It means, in our present use of the term, merely a person who explains to each party between whom he acts what each saith, because they do not understand one another's language, and this interpreter understands both. But in the Scripture sense of the word, the character of an interpreter riseth much higher. The original word, translated interpreter, (Gen. xlii. 23.) which is Malats, means something that is persuasive, smooth, or to soften, like our English word mollify. And the person that did this office between Joseph and his brethren is supposed, by the expression and the name of Malats, by which he is so called, to be a softener of Jacob's sons' speeches, by way of conciliating the favour of Joseph. And it would have been no violence to the passage if, instead of reading it as it is in our Bibles, it had been read, "and they knew not that Joseph heard them, for the Advocate was between them." The character of an interpreter in this sense, is truly interesting, and throws a great beauty upon this oriental history; and no less upon the similar passage in Job, for the word is the same in both. Indeed, some have not scrupled, in this last passage, to translate Malats, mediator, as conveying much nearer the sense of the passage, than that of an interpreter, unless it be remembered that in the eastern world a Malats, or interpreter, advocated the cause he interpreted.

And this view appears still more striking from Joseph's history as related to us in our own translation. For beside this interpretation given by the Malats to Joseph, it is plain, that Joseph and his brethren conversed together without the medium of an interpreter, as we read in the twenty-fourth verse: for there it is said, "that he turned himself about from them and wept; and returned to them again and communed with them." Hence, therefore, it should seem, that in the eastern countries this office of interpreter was, as the very name implies, a very affectionate, tender, and interesting office. And though I would not go so far as to say, that the glorious Mediator of his people was prefigured in every use of it, yet I do venture to think it was peculiarly significant on this occasion amidst the brethren of Joseph. The church of Christ now, which those sons of Israel then represented, when standing before our governor, do not always know, that our Almighty Joseph knows, hears, and regards all; and yet, while carrying on his many offices, how often doth he commune with his people, both with and without mediums! Well might John behold him with his many crowns upon his head; for surely every office of his, in every individual sinner saved by him, demands a new crown of glory. (Rev. xix. 12.)

INVISIBLE
One of the distinguishing attributes of JEHOVAH. (1 Tim. i. 17.)

IRIJAH
He who arrested Jermemiah. (Jer. xxxvii. 13.) His name means, the fear of the Lord; from Jarah, to fear; and Jah, the Lord.

ISAAC
Abraham's son, the child of promise. See Hagar.

ISAIAH
The prophet, the son of Amos. Highly, under God the Holy Ghost, is the church indebted to the ministry of this man. Amidst many events in this man's life, was that of this walking three years barefoot and naked. (See Isa. xx. 2.) Was not this also typical of Christ's three years ministry? His name signifies salvation of the Lord; from Jashah, salvation; and Jah, the Lord. I cannot forbear mentioning the commonly-received opinion, that Isaiah was sawn asunder, in the beginning of the reign of Manasseh, and that his body was buried near Jerusalem, under the fuller's oak near Siloam. And the tradition concerning this event is, that it was brought upon him by the event of his publishing his vision, (chapt. vi.) in which he saith, "he saw the Lord sitting on a throne high and lifted up." Manasseh said, that this was blasphemy, as Moses had recorded the Lord's words, Exod. xxii. 20. "No man shall see me and live."

Isaiah prophesied many years, not less than threescore, though some make his ministry to have extended to four-score. Who can read the prophecy of Isaiah without the most profound admiration! It is not only unequalled in point of language, but it contains so much of Christ, that it looks more like an history than a prophecy. It is more like the writings of a person who was present at Pilate's hall, and Herod's judgment-seat, when describing the sufferings of Jesus, than of one who wrote those events, by the spirit of prediction, more than seven hundred years before the things there spoken of came to pass. St. Jerom calls Isaiah's prophecy, an abridgment of the holy Scriptures. And Grotius prefers Isaiah to all the writers of Greece and Rome. But how truly blessed are the predictions of Isaiah to the believer who hath lived to see the whole fulfilled in the Lord Jesus Christ, and by the Holy Ghost is led to discover not only the correspondence between them, but his own personal interest therein.

ISCARIOT
A name peculiarly suited to the traitor Judas: for the word means, a man of murder; from Ish, a man; and Corath, he that cuts off.

ISHBIBENOB
The son of Ob, (2 Sam. xxi. 16, 17.) The meaning of the name is, he that sits in the word, or prophccy, from Isheba, to sit; beth, in; neba, the prophecy.

ISHBOSHETH
The son of Saul (2 Sam. ii. 8.); a man of shame; from Ish, a man; and bosh, shame.

ISHI
We meet with this word Hos. ii. 16. Our translators have thought proper to preserve the word in its original, giving the meaning of it in the margin, my husband. And it becomes a subject of no small concern to ask the cause wherefore the translators have thought proper to do so? I do not presume to speak decidedly to the point, and to determine what their designs were; yet I venture to conjecture, and shall give the

ISHMAEL - ISSACHAR

reader my opinion.

Let the reader first observe, that the prophet was commissioned to tell the church, that in the gospel-day, when the glorious Messiah, whom the church had been all along expecting, should come, the church should know the Lord by this name Ishi, my husband, or my man; and should drop the common name of Baali, my Lord: as if this was not sufficiently expressive of the nearness and dearness between them. The church was then to know here Lord in his human nature, as well as his GODHEAD, and in the union of both as her Lord her Righteousness. Now then, saith the Lord Jesus, (for observe it is Jesus himself that is the speaker in this chapter) now then, thou shalt call me by that tender and endearing name, in the nature that I shall then openly appear in among you, my man. I have been from everlasting the Husband and Head of my church, in the secret transactions of covenant redemption; but in that day when I shall openly manifest myself in that character I will be called Ishi: "for my people shall know my name, therefore they shall in that day know that I am he that doth speak, behold, it is I!" (Isa. lii. 6.) Reader think if of the love and tenderness of thy Jesus! Was there ever such grace manifested as by him? Who but must love him? Who but must delight in him? Yes, Lord, I will do as thou hast said, and call thee Ishi, my Husband, my man, and also the Lord my Righteousness! See Ammi.

ISHMAEL

The son of Abraham and Hagar. His name is derived from Shamah, to bear; and El, God. (Gen. xvi. 1.)

ISHTOB

An inhabitant of man of Tob, a country north of mount Gilead, where Jephtha resided. (See Judg. xi. 3.) The name is a compound of Ish, a man; and Tob, good: so that to say, an inhabitant of Tob, seems to have been proverbial for a good man.

ISMACHIAH

A person in the days of Hezekiah, to whom the king intrusted the offerings of the temple. (2 Chron. xxxi. 13.) The name signifies, one joined to the Lord; for Samach, to unite; and Jah, the Lord.

ISRAEL

—Or more properly, as it is rendered, Ishrael, the name given to Jacob by the Lord himself, on his wrestling with God in prayer and prevailing, (See Gen. xxxii. 21-28.) from Sharah, to subdue or govern; and El, God. The whole people of God are frequently in Scripture called by this name. (Exod. iii. 6,7. So again, chap. vi. 6,7.) But what endears this name yet infinitely more is, that the Lord Jesus himself, as the glorious Head of his church and people, including both Jew and Gentile, calls himself by this name; and JEHOVAH doth the same by Christ. (See Isa. xlix. 1-6. and Isa. xliv. 1-5.) And hence the whole church of the Lord Jesus are called Israelites. (Rom. ix. 4.) and the Lord Jesus, when speaking of his sheep under one view, saith, that they shall be brought into "one fold under one shepherd." (John x. 16).

ISSACHAR

The son of Jacob, by Leah. (Gen. xxx. 14-18.) His name signifies a price of hire; and so it is rendered in the margin of our Bibles, derived from Shachar, a price. The most remarkable circumstance in the history of Issachar, is his father's prophetical blessing of him. (Gen. xlix. 14-15.) "Issachar (said the dying patriarch) is a strong ass, couching down between two burthens; and he saw that rest was good, and the land that it was pleasant; and bowed his shoulder to bear, and become a servant into tribute." If the sense of this passage (as most of the other blessings Jacob when a-dying bequeathed to his children are) be spiritual, there is much of Jesus, and his person and salvation in it. Issachar, like all true Israelites, bends between the two burthens of sin and sorrow, for they are inseparable; and no rest but Jesus can be found, to deliver from the dreadful pressure. He is, indeed, "the rest wherewith he causeth the weary to rest" from the burden. Easy will be the tribe of a redeemed heart to the Lord, to bless him for his mercy. We find similar beauties in the blessing of Moses, the man of God, over Issachar, if explained in the same gospel-sense. (See Deut. xxxiii. 18-19.)

ITHAMAR

The fourth son of Aaron. (Exod. vi. 23.) His name signifies, island of the palm tree, from Tamar, a palm tree, on Ai, an island. We have nothing particularly interesting in the Bible concerning this man.

ITHIEL

The son of Jessaiah. (Neh. xi. 7.) The name signifies, with God; from Eth, with—and El, God.

ITHMAH

One of David's worthies, (I Chron. xi. 46.) Perhaps the name means admiration; from Thamah, to admire.

ITUREA

A province of Syria. (See Luke iii. 1.) The meaning is, what is guarded; from Thur, to keep.

IZHAR

The son of Kohath and father of Korah, (Num. Iii. 19; xvi. 1.) The name signifies light, from Itzar.

JAAKAN - JAEL

J

JAAKAN

This is spoken of in Israel's journey when they went from Beeroth. (Deut. x. 6.) If it be a place, perhaps it was so called from the meaning of the word Canan, rest; otherwise, if referring to the children of Jaakon, we might have expected the name would have been Bene Jaakan, the sons of Jaakan.

JAAZINIAH

We meet with this name several times in the Bible, (2 Kings xxv. 23. Jer. xxxv. 3. Ezek. viii. 11. and xi. 1.) The name itself is a compound of Jazen and Jah, the Lord will hear.

JABAL and JUBAL

The sons of Lamech and Adah. (See Gen. xx. 21.) The former was the father of those who lodge in tents, and the latter of those who handle the pipe or organ; by which is meant, that these men were the first inventors of those things. The name of both is one and the same meaning, like the Jobel or trumpet, somewhat that like sound glides away, and is lost in the air.

JABESH GILEAD

A city beyond Jordan, in the half tribe of Manasseh. (1 Sam. xi. 1.)

JABIN

King of Caanan. A mighty oppressor of Israel, (Judg. iv. 2, 3.) His name signifies to understand, from Binah.

JABBOCK

A brook on the other side Jordan, rendered memorable from being near the spot where Jacob wrestled with the angel, (Gen. xxxii. 22-24.) The name signifies to make empty.

JACHIN

The name of a pillar in Solomon's temple. See Boaz.

JACOB

The ever-memorable name of the ever-memorable person, concerning whom it hath pleased God the Holy Ghost to say so much throughout the whole Scripture. His name signifies a supplanter; but after the memorable scene at Jabbock, when Jacob wrestled with the angel and pevailed, the Lord himself changed his name to Israel, a prince. (See Gen. xxxii. 27, 28.) For his history I refer to the book of Genesis, from Gen. xxv. to the end.

JAEL

The wife of Heber the Kenite

Her name is a compound of Jah and El. Her history is but short, yet truly blessed. We have it Judg. iv. 17 to the end. And the Holy Ghost hath recorded her heroic act of faith, Judg. v. 24-27. Some have wantonly "traduced the character of Jael, and charged her with a breach of hospitality in slaughtering one who fled to her for protection, and especially as she had taken Sisera into her haram. And it hath been farther said, that the refreshment Jael gave him was, according to the custom of eastern nations, a pledge of friendship. But to both of these I answer, it becomes no breach of hospitality to destroy the known foes of God. Besides, Sisera asked for refreshment, and requested her to tell a lie. It was not Jael's offer, neither did she give him a promise of security. The tyranny of this man, and zeal for God's glory and his people's safety, prompted her generous mind to deliver Israel from his oppression. Add to these, the Lord's hand must have been in this transaction, as Deborah the prophetess foretold the event, Judg. iv. 9. But let men say what they may, God the Holy Ghost hath honoured her memory for ever, and declared it blessed. And I cannot but conclude, that she is one of those worthies, of whom the Holy Ghost hath again spoken so hononrably in the New Testament, "who through faith subdued kingdoms." &c. (Heb. xi. 33.)

JAH

One of the glorious incommunicable names of JEHOVAH. We find it joined with many Hebrew names in the Scripture. The grand Anthem hymn is called Hallel-Jah, praise the Lord, which we pronounce Hallelujah. So again, when speaking of JEHOVAH in his covenant-relation in Christ, we say Adon Jah, or Adoni, my Adoni Jah. And hence the Hebrews were so fond of calling their children by some name that took in and comprehended somewhat of this name. Thus Isaiah, Jeremiah, Zephaniah, Zechariah, &c. See JEHOVAH.

JAMES

One of the apostles of Christ. There were two of this name, and both apostles; one the son of Salome, the other of Mary. Hence by way, of distinction, they are called James the Elder, and James the Less. The former was the brother of John, (Matt. iv. 21.) the latter is called by Paul the Lord's brother, (Gal. i. 19.) not so in reality, as we now mean by the term brother, but as the custom then was, from tribes and families, Mary, James's mother, was sister to the blessed Virgin. James the Elder was the son of Zebedee; James the Less the son of Alpheus, (Matt. x. 2, 3.) The former was killed by Herod, (Acts xii. 1); the latter we have no scriptural relation of his death. It is to this man, under God the Holy Ghost, that we are indebted for that gracious Epistle which bears his name.

JANNES and JAMBRES

There is but once mention made of these persons in holy writ, namely, (2 Tim. iii. 8.) and the apostle when recording their names gives this short but awful history of their characters--they withstood Moses. Some have supposed, that they were the magicians who for a while confronted Moses, when, at the command and in the name of the Lord, he wrought miracles before Pharaoh and his court. But if it be so, certain it is, the Holy Ghost thought it not of importance to tell the church, or it would have been noticed. The most important circumstance to the believer to remark is, that the magicians were permitted to resemble somewhat of what Moses wrought to a certain point purposely, that when this permission was withdrawn, they might the more readily be compelled to see and acknowledge the finger of the Lord. This they did; and thereby became the unwilling witnesses for God, and to their own confusion. Oh, that the opposers of God's truth and God's Christ, in all ages, would tremble in the recollection of James and Jambres!

JAPHETH

The son of Noah; not, as some have supposed, the younger of his sons, because placed last, (see Gen. ix. 18, 19.) for Moses expressly calls Ham the younger. (Gen. ix. 24.) The prophecy of his father Noah concerning Japheth is very striking: "God shall enlarge Japheth, and shall dwell in the tents of Shem." (Gen. ix. 27.) Yes! it is none but God that can enlarge or persuade. And as from Shem, after the flesh, sprung Christ; so Japheth, who is supposed to be the father of the Gentiles, and as such, in this prophecy, may be supposed to represent the whole body of the Gentile church given to the Lord Jesus Christ, could only be brought into Christ's fold by Christ's power. (See Isa. xlix. 6. Ps. cx.3.)

JAPHIA

There was a city of this name, (Josh. xix. 12.) and there was a king of this name, Japhia king of Lachish, (Josh. x. 3.) And David had a son named Japhia. (2 Sam. v. 15.) The name perhaps is derived from

JARMUTH or JARAMOTH

This was one of the cities of Judah, which lay in the way to Jerusalem. Joshua, in his battles, killed the king of Jarmuth. (Josh. x. 5.)

JESUS

See Jerusalem.

JEDIDIAH

The name the Lord gave to Solomon; meaning beloved of the Lord. (2 Sam. xii. 24 25.)

JEGAR SAHADUTHA

The heap of witness; so rendered in the margins of our Bibles. (See Gen. xxxi. 47. to the end.) Jacob called it Galeed and Mizpah; as if he had said, let the Galeed be witness, and this Mizpah be witness, There is something very tender and interesting in this parting of natural ties never to meet again. Such will be the everlasting separation in every instance of nature, where our affinities are not new-formed in grace.

JEHOAHAZ

There are two sons of kings of this name in Scripture--Jehoahaz, son of Jehu. (2 Kings xiii. 1.) and Jehoahaz, or Shallum; son of Josiah, king of Judah, (Jer. xxii. 11.) The name is a compound, signifying, from Achaz, a possession of the Lord.

JEHOIACHIN

The son of Jehoiachim. This is the man whom the prophet had it in commission from the Lord to write childless. (Jer. xxii. 24. to the end.) His name is also a compound, signifying from the root to prepare, that the Lord would prepare. But how seldom do we find, notwithstanding the striking names given by the Hebrews to their children, that they answered to them. In what sense Jehoiachiu was written childless, I cannot determine; somewhat different from natural things it must have been, for certain it is, that he had several sons. (See 1 Chron. iii. 17, 18.) But what the sentence referred to besides, I know not. I should have thought it had respect to the promised seed, and that the writing this man childless might have been in other words to say, the Messiah shall not be in his family. For this was the great desire of all the tribes of Israel; and for the accomplishment of which they all earnestly longed for a numerous progeny of children. But this was so far from being the case, that in the generations of the Lord Jesus Christ after the flesh, we find his son Salathiel enumerated. (See Matt. i. 12.) Some have thought, that the expression childless meant in relation to his kingdom, that he should have no successor in his family to sit upon the throne. And if this be the meaning, it was literally fulfilled; for Salathiel was born in Babylon, and so was his son Zorobabel. (See Matt. i. 13.) But here I leave the subject.

JEHORAM

Son of Jehoshaphat. (2 Kings iii. 2, 3.) The meaning of the name is, exaltation of the Lord; from Ram, exaltation; and Jah, the Lord.

JEHOSHAPHAT

King of Judah. (1 Kings: xxii. 42.) His name meaneth, the Lord judgeth; from Shephat, to judge; and Jab, the Lord. There was a valley of this name, but it is undetermined where situated. Some have thought, near the mount of Olives. (See Joel iii. 2. 12.)

JEHOVAH

The glorious incommunicable name of the I AM THAT I AM. In addition to what was offered under the article God, (which see) I would beg to observe, that this ineffable and mysterious name belongs to each glorious person of the GODHEAD, Father, Son, and Holy Ghost, and is used in common by each and by all. It implies every perfection of the divine nature, in the eternity, immensity, sovereignty, omnipotency, invisibility, &c. of the Lord. We find it sometimes joined with certain leading characters of the GODHEAD, all descriptive of the divine glory, as for example:

JEHOVAH JIREH

The margin of our Bible renders it very properly, "the Lord will see or provide." (Gen. xxii. 14.) And the general acceptation of the words in the esteem of believers is, that the Lord will do by all of that character as he did by Abraham, and in every critical moment manifest his grace towards them, in proof that he doth both see and provide for them. This is certainly one sense of the titles, and a blessed one it is: but this is not all. Abraham saith, "to this day in the mount of the Lord shall it be seen;" by which it appears, that the mount of the Lord was to be the place where this provision and sight of JEHOVAH was to be seen. Surely there was a prophecy in these words relating to the very spot of Abraham's mercy, as well as the mercy itself. And was not this with an eye to the Lamb of God, in after-ages to be provided for the whole church, as well as the ram the Lord had then provided for Abraham's burnt offering? Recollect that this mount Moriah was near the spot, if not the very spot itself, afterwards called mount Calvary. And as Abraham's offering was wholly typical, surely nothing could be more suited to the expression in calling the place JEHOVAH Jireh. As if Abraham had said, Here shall be one day seen the wonders of redemption! Here God will, indeed, provide himself a lamb for a burnt offering!

JEHOVAH NISSI

(Exod. xvii. 15.) The margin of our Bible renders it, "This is the Lord my banner." There is somewhat uncommonly beautiful and striking in this blessed name of our covenant God in Christ. No doubt, Christ himself is his people's banner; for so the Lord described him, (Isa. xiii. 2.) and as a leader and commander to the people. (Isa. lv. 4.) Now in every point of view this is most blessed; for as a banner displayed is a signal of war, so when the believer takes Christ for his banner, he declares war with sin, death, hell, and the grave, and takes to him the whole armour of God; moreover, he fights in sure and certain hope of victory, because Jesus hath already gotten to himself the victory, and his own arm hath brought to him salvation. So that when JEHOVAH Nissi is the banner under which we fight, we are "more than conquerors through him that loveth us." Never may I go forth against the Amaleks of the present day, without JEHOVAH Nissi as my banner; but with him, and under him, wage an everlasting war against the enemies of God and his Christ.

JEHOVAH OUR RIGHTEOUSNESS

The margin of our Bible hath preserved the original Hebrew, JEHOVAH Tzidkenu, in both places where meet with this glorious name of the Lord Jesus, (Jer. xxiii. 6; xxxiii. 16.) and a most blessed and soul-comforting name it is for the present and everlasting joy of a poor sinner, conscious that in himself he is void of all righteousness. For doth any one ask the question--Wherefore we call Jesus JEHOVAH? The answer is direct; Jesus is not only JEHOVAH by reason of his own personal GODHEAD, but JEHOVAH the Father hath commanded his people to call him and to know him by that name. And if it be farther asked--Wherefore do you call him your righteousness? The answer is, Because he is so, and is the very righteousness in which all his people become justified before God; and in confirmation of it JEHOVAH hath commanded the people so to call him, and

JEHOVAH SHALOM - JEHOVAH SHAMMAH

so to apprehend and know him. And reader, do but attend to the several blessed causes by which it is confirmed and assured to the heart and conscience, and very fully will it appear to you, in all its glory, if so be God the Holy Ghost be your teacher. That Jesus is JEHOVAH in common with the Father and the Holy Ghost, the whole Bible confirms. (See in proof if but a single passage, Isa. xlv. 22-25.) And that he is our righteousness, the Holy Ghost hath asserted in numberless places of his blessed word. (See but two passages among many that might be brought forward, 1 Cor. i. 30. 2 Cor. v. 21.)

But what I more particularly beg the reader to observe with me on this glorious name of our Redeemer, is, that JEHOVAH Jesus our righteousness is the very righteousness of his people. Let the reader remember that Jesus is not said to be a righteous person, but righteousness itself. Angels may be, and sometimes are, called righteous, and so are the servants of God; but none of them can be called righteousness. This belongs only to God our Saviour: all other righteousness is derived, and is from him; but the righteousness of the Lord Jesus is essentially and necessarily his own. He is righteousness itself; and his GODHEAD both proves his righteousness, and his righteousness demonstrates his GODHEAD. This is one sweet feature of this name of our Lord; and there is another included in it, namely, that this righteousness is ours. For by virtue of union and oneness with him, all that he is as the Head of his body the church, he is for and in his people. Hence he is said to have been made sin for them when he knew no sin that they might be made the righteousness of God in him. (2 Cor. v. 21.) "And he is made of God to them wisdom and righteousness, sanctification and redemption." (1 Cor. i. 30.) And what crowns the whole is, that Christ and his righteousness being so for ever, so must his people be in him. His person being infinite, so must be his righteousness; and therefore, he is said to have saved his people with an everlasting righteousness, by reason of which they shall not be ashamed nor confounded, world without end. Well might the Holy Ghost command the church to exclaim, "Surely shall one say, In the Lord have I righteousness and strength." (Isa. xlv. 24.) I would only add, as a farther confirmation of the interest the church hath in Christ and the oneness there is between them, the church also is called the Lord our righteousness, because her glorious Husband is so; thus proving her marriage by taking the name of her husband. (See Jer. xxxiii. 16.) Oh, the blessedness in that one title, JEHOVAH our righteousness!

JEHOVAH SHALOM

The margin of the Bible renders this title of a covenant God, "The Lord send peace." It was ascribed to the Lord by Gideon, in the prospect of conquering Midian. (Judg. vi.24.) It proved so then, and it has proved so in numberless instances ever since. But seen with an eye to Christ, it is eminently blessed; here, indeed, JEHOVAH, in the covenant of peace founded in Christ before all worlds, may, and must be called, in the strongest emphasis, JEHOVAH SHALOM.

JEHOVAH SHAMMAH

"The Lord is there." Such is the name of the church in consequence of the presence of her glorious husband. (See Ezek. xlviii. 35.) The prophet is speaking by the Spirit of prophecy, and looking into the days of the gospel; so that here is a mark to know the church by now, and which will be the character of Christ's church for ever. Without the Lord's presence there is no church: unless he be in the midst of us, we may go lean all our days. Lord! write JEHOVAH Shammah in our churches, in our hearts, in our houses, in our families!

JEHU

A well-known king in Israel, raised up in this office to punish the house of Ahab. His name is emphatical, signifing, himself: from pronoun Hua, and this also seems to be from Havah, to be. (See 2 Kings ix. 1. to the end. See also 1 Kings xix. 15-18.)

It is a remarkable feature concerning Jehu, that the appointment of Jehu, and his becoming king, occupied a period of more than twenty-two years; which will be seen by comparing the dates of those two Scriptures. There was another Jehu a prophet, the son of Hanani, who flourished in the reign of Baasha king of Israel. (See 1 Kings xv. 1.7. See also 2 Chron. xix. 1-3.) It should seem, that this Jehu, was a faithful servant of the Lord, in thus reproving both the kings of Judah and Israel. In the second chapter of the Second Book of Chronicles, thirty-fourth verse, it is said, that this prophet wrote the records of Jehoshaphat, king of Judah. There are two other Jehus mentioned in Scripture, Jehu the fourth son of Rehoboam, king of Judah, (2 Chron. xi. 19.) and Jehu the son of Obed. (1 Chron. ii. 38.)

JEHUDI

The servant of Jehoiakim, king of Judah, (Jer. xxxvi. 14.) His name signifies, the Lord is my praise.

JEHUDIJAH

The wife of Ezra. (See 1 Chron. iv. 18.) The name is very striking in the Jah twice-- to the praise of the Lord.

JEMIMA

One of Job's daughters. (Job xlii. 14.) The meaning of the name implies, beautiful as the day.

JEPHTHA

One of the judges who judged Israel. (See Judges xi. 1. to the end.) His name signifies, one that will open. The vow of Jephtha concerning his daughter, hath exercised the learning of the studious in all ages of the church. Some have decidedly been of opinion, that Jephta did actually sacrifice his daughter; and others have as flatly denied it. The Chaldee Paraphrase, St. Ambrose, and St. Chrisostom, were of the former opinion; but by far the greater part of the old commentators, as well as modern ones, are in the latter judgment. I shall beg to offer an observation or two upon the subject, and then leave the reader, under grace, to think for himself on this point.

The first thing I beg to observe, is concerning the character of Jephta. The Holy Ghost, by his servant Paul, hath recorded his name among those worthies who "by faith subdued kingdoms, and wrought righteousness." (Heb. xi. 32.) And in the first account of Jephta's valour we are told, that the "Spirit of the Lord came upon Jephtha." (Judg. xi. 29.) Hence, therefore, we may safely conclude, that he was a child of God.

The next thing to be observed in his history, is that the vow he made was a solemn engagement between the Lord and his own soul. It was personal; it was himself concerned only to fulfil it; neither could it be supposed to imply, the disposing of what was not his to dispose of. "All souls are mine, (saith JEHOVAH,) as the soul of the father, so also the soul of the son is mine." (Ezek. xviii. 4.) It could not be, therefore, implied in Jephtha's vow, that he would engage to offer to the Lord what was not his own. The disposal of his daughter's person in marriage was, indeed, a parent's right, and frequently done; but this right never extended to the offering a child in sacrifice.

Thirdly, Human sacrifices were prohibited by the law, neither would the priest have offered the daughter of Jephta; so that, unless it be supposed, that Jephta invaded the priestly office, and offered his daughter himself, there should seem even hence to have arisen a great difficulty to the belief, that the daughter of Jephtha was

JEPHTHA - JEPHTHA

really sacrificed.

Add to these considerations, it is well known, that the law had made provision for the redemption of persons by purchase. Thus the Lord enjoined, (Lev. xxvii. 1, &c.) "And the Lord spake unto Moses, saying, Speak unto the children of Israel, and say unto them, When a man shall make a singular vow, the persons shall be for the Lord by thy estimation. A male from twenty years to sixty, shall be fifty shekels of silver; and if it be a female, then thy estimation shall be thirty shekels." Hence, therefore, here was at once a provision, and made by the Lord himself, to prevent every human sacrifice by redemption.

Let us suppose, that instead of Jephtha's daughter, some unclean bird or beast, forbidden by the law in sacrifice, had come forth to meet him--what would he have done in this case? Surely, he could not have offered it: then must it have been destroyed, since it could not have been consecrated to the Lord. The expression in Jephtha's vow, according to some readers of the Bible, seems to have made a provision for this uncertainty, what or whom he should first meet. "And Jephtha vowed a vow unto the Lord, and said, If thou shalt without fail deliver the children of Ammon into mine hand, then it shall be, that whatsoever cometh forth of the doors of my house to meet me, when I return in peace from the children of Ammon, shall surely be the Lord's, and I will offer it up for a burnt offering." (Judges xi. 30, 31.) In the margin of the Bible it is rendered, or I will offer it up; that is certainly by redemption, according to the law concerning redemptions. And it may be farther asked, Is not the expression in the vow," shall surely be the Lord's," similar to that of Hannah's, in dedicating the child she asked of God in prayer. (1 Sam. i. 11.) "And she vowed a vow, and said, O Lord of hosts, if thou wilt indeed look on the affliction of thine handmaid, and remember me, and not forget thine handmaid, but will give unto thine handmaid a man child, then will I give him unto the Lord all the days of his life. And when she had weaned him, she brought him into the house of the Lord in Shiloh, and brought the child to Eli: and she said, For this child I prayed, and the Lord hath given me my petition; therefore also I have lent him to the Lord: as long as he liveth he shall be lent unto the Lord." (See 1 Sam. i. 11. to the end.)

These are amongst the reasons wherefore it seems probable, that Jephtha's daughter was not offered in sacrifice. It hath been said, however, by those who suppose she was, that the distress of the father in meeting her at his return home, the expression he made use of, and the request she made him of a given space to be allowed her for lamentation, and his doing with her according to his vow after that time was expired, are proofs in point. But to these suggestions it might be said, that supposing the former opinions right, and that she was not offered in sacrifice, it becomes very easy to explain both her lamentations on the mountains, and the daughters of Israel going to lament yearly on the occasion. For it is one of the most notorious truths, that among the Hebrews no lamentations was equal to that of being doomed to a single unmarried state. For every daughter of Israel had an eye to the promised seed the Messiah; to be devoted, therefore, to an unmarried life totally precluded that hope; and the daughters of Israel going yearly to lament the daughter of Jephtha being so, is a proof of it. Besides, where did they go? It should seem, to visit the daughter of Jephtha, for the margin of the Bible renders it, that the daughters of Israel went yearly "to talk with her:" that is, in her nunnery. (See Judges xi. 34-40.) But having now stated all I think necessary to state on the subject, I leave the reader to his own opinion, taught, as I pray he may be, by the grace of God, only adding one short observation: how blessed is the condition of God's Israel now, freed from vows and sacrifices, while looking to, and wholly depending upon that glorious, all-sufficient, all effectual offering of the body of Jesus Christ once for all, "whereby he has perfected for ever them that are sanctified." (Heb. x. 14.)

JEPHUNNEH

The father of Caleb. (Num. xiii. 6.) His name means one that beholds--from Phanah, to behold.

JERAH

The son of Joktan. (Gen. x. 26.) His name is borrowed perhaps from Jerah, the moon.

JERAHMEEL

The son of Kish. (1 Chron. xxiv. 29.) His name is a compound of Racham, mercy; El, God. There were others of this name. (See 1 Chron. ii. 25, &c. Jer. xxxvi. 26. And there was a prince so called. 1 Sam. xxvii. 10. 1 Sam. xxx. 29.)

JEREMIAH

The mournful prophet so called. A man famous in his day and generation as the Lord's servant, and his memory ever blessed in the church through all ages. His name, it should seem, is a compound--from Ram, exaltation; and Jah, the Lord. The pronoun prefixed makes it, my exalted in the Lord." And exalted indeed he was in the Lord's strength, though continually buffeted and ill-treated by men. It is blessed to read his prophecy, and under the Holy Ghost's teachings to enter into the spirit of this man's writings.

I beg the reader to behold, with suited attention, the account given of him in the first chapter. We find him ordained to the ministry before his birth. And who that reads this account of the servant, but must be struck with full conviction of what is said of his Master, called from the womb of eternity, and set up from everlasting to be JEHOVAH'S servant, to bring Jacob again to him. (See Isa. xlix. throughout, and Prov. viii. 12. to the end.) What a decided proof and conviction by the way doth this afford, that if Jeremiah was ordained a prophet to the church before he was formed in the belly, surely the glorious Head of that church, and that church in him, was set up, and Christ in all his offices and characters ordained the Lord God of the prophets before all worlds. (Col. i. 15-18.) It should seem from the date of the prophet's commission, when the word of the Lord first came to him, namely, in the thirtieth year of Josiah's reign, that Jeremiah could not be above fourteen years of age when he preached his first sermon. And what a sermon it is! (See chap. ii. iii. and iv. &c.) But what may not a child preach when God the Holy Ghost hath ordained him? Oh, that more of that blessed voice was heard in this our day, which was heard by the church in Paul's day! (See Acts xiii. 1-4.) It was the lot of Jeremiah to live in an age when the nation was given up to daring impiety, and rebellion against God. Faithfulness at such a time, could not fail of bringing upon the poor preacher the hatred and indignation of all of a contrary way of thinking to himself. We have the relation of the persecution frequently raised against him, in several parts of his writings. The opposition made to him by the false prophet Hananiah, and the sequel of that awful event is recorded at large, chap. xxviii. (See Hananiah.) Blessed is the memory of Jeremiah, and will be in the churches to the latest generation. The Lord ordain many such, if it be his holy will, from the womb! There are several of this name in Scripture. (See 2 Kings xxiv. 18. See also 1 Chron. v. 24. Two of the name of Jeremiah in David's army. 1 Chron. xii. 4. 10. 13.)

JERICHO

The name means, his moon--from Jareac. This is the famous city before whose walls the Lord manifested such a miracle of grace to Israel, in causing them to fall to the ground at the blasting of the rams' horns. (See Josh. vi.) It was situated about seven leagues from Jerusalem, and about two from the river Jordan, (Josh. xviii. 20, 21.) and was called by Moses the city of palm trees; and, no doubt, in point of pleasantness, must have been a lovely place. (See Deut. xxxiv. 3.) But we find, in the after days of Israel's history, the barrenness of Jericho spoken of, (2 Kings ii. 18-22.) See Elisha. There is somewhat particularly striking concerning Jericho being cursed by Joshua before the Lord, and yet that Rahab the harlot should be of this city, concerning whom such blessed things are spoken of in Scripture. (See on the one hand, Josh. vi. 26. compared with 1 Kings xvi. 34; and on the other, see Josh. ii. with Heb. xi. 31.) If the reader will be at the trouble to count the period between Joshua's curse on Jericho, and the rebuilding of Jericho by Hiel the Bethelite, he will find that near five hundred and thirty-seven years had passed between the one and the other. The Hebrews paid great respect to the Cherem, that is, the curse of Joshua. This anathema was carefully remembered by them; and, no doubt, when Hiel in defiance of it began to build Jericho, the pious believers among the Hebrews felt indignant at the daring attempt, and marked the issue in the event that followed on Hiel's two sons.

JEROBOAM

This man's name is proverbial.--Jeroboam, the son of Nebat, who made Israel to sin. Such is the awful account given of him by God the Holy Ghost. His name seems to be in some measure characteristic of the man-- he that rejects--from Jarah to reject; and his history awfully proves, how he rejected the counsel of God against his own soul. His history we have in 1 Kings, from xi. 28. to xiv. 20. There was another Jeroboam, the son of Jehoash. (See 2 Kings xiv. 23.) During this man's reign, the prophets Hosea, Amos and, Jonah exercised their ministry.

JERUBBAAL

One of the names of Gideon: he was so called for destroying the grove of that idol Baal-Jerub, meaning, that he destroys. (See Judg. vi. to the end.) This man was evidently led on by the Spirit of the Lord; and his history affords very striking testimonies in the Scripture referred to, and also in the following chapter. Alas! what is the best of men, if for a moment acting without the influence of grace!

JERUSALEM

The holy city: and so generally known was Jerusalem by this name, that the eastern part of the world never called it by any other name than the Elkuds, the holy. Not that this would have made it so, but it proves the general consent of nations to the title: no doubt, the thing was from the Lord. That the Lord Jesus distinguished it in a very peculiar manner with his love, his lamentation over it proves. (Matt. xxiii. 37.) And Matthew twice calls it by this name. (Matt. iv. 5. and xxvii. 53.)

Jerusalem was anciently Jebus. Some called it Solyma, or Jerosolyma; but the general name by the Hebrews was Jeruschalem, meaning, the vision of peace; from Rahe, to see; and Shalom, peace. Joshua first conquered it, (see Josh. xviii. 28.) but the Jebusites were not totally drawn out of it until the days of David, (See 2 Sam. v. 5.) The history of Jerusalem is truly interesting; but it would form more the subject of a volume than a short notice in a work of this kind, to enter into particulars. If we were to go back to the first account of it in Scripture, we must being with Gen. xiv. where we find Melchisedeck king of it, and then called Salem. The church, perhaps on this account, speaks of it as the Lord's tabernacle, (Ps. lxxvi. 2.) and when we consider, that all the great events of the church were carried on here, no doubt, it riseth in importance to every believer's view. Here it was the Lord Jesus made his public appearance, when he came into our world for the salvation of his people; here he finished redemption-work; here he made that one offering of himself once offered, by which he perfected for ever them that are sanctified; and here all the great events of salvation were wrought. No wonder, therefore, that Jerusalem hath been called the holy city, and is rendered so dear to all his redeemed. Hence Jerusalem, now in the present moment, means the church on earth, and is prayed for under that name. (Isa. lxii. 1. Ps. cxxxvii. 5, 6.) And hence the church in heaven is called the New Jerusalem. (Rev. iii. 12. and xxi. 2.) Jerusalem is said to be the centre of the earth; and the prophet Ezekiel, (chap. xxxviii. 11, 12.) describing the insolent threats of Gog concerning his proposed destruction of Jerusalem, calls the people of it, those who dwell in the midst of the land, or as the margin of the Bible renders it, in the navel of the earth.

The tears of Jesus over Jerusalem having been misconstrued, and as such made use of to support an opinion foreign to the general scope of the gospel, I cannot dismiss the article without offering a short observation upon it.

We are told by the Evangelists, that "when Jesus was come near to Jerusalem, he beheld the city, and wept over it, saying, If thou hadst known, even thou, at least in this thy day, the things which belong unto thy peace: but now they are hid from thine eyes. For the days shall come upon thee, that thine enemies shall cast a trench about thee, and compass thee round, and keep thee in on every side, and shall lay thee even with the ground, and thy children within thee; and they shall not leave in thee one stone upon another, because thou knowest not the time of thy visitation." Whoever attends with any degree of diligence to those several expressions of our Lord, will plainly discover that all that is here spoken refers to the destruction of Jerusalem as a city and nation, and wholly in temporal things. It hath nothing to do with grace, as some have improperly concluded, as if Jerusalem had outlived her day of grace, and, therefore, could find no mercy from the Lord; and all sinners, in like manner, might outlive their day also. There is not a word of the kind in it. Jesus, in that tenderness of heart which distinguished his character, wept over the beautiful and beloved city, in contemplating the overthrow of it by the Roman power, that he knew would sack and destroy it. And knowing that their rejection of him as the Lord of life and glory was the cause; he expresseth himself in tears with this compassionate apostrophe. But what have those expressions to do with the doctrine that some men raise out of it, as if Jesus had limited a day of grace to individuals, and that men might outlive that day, and then the saving means of grace would be hidden from their eyes! Surely, there is not a syllable in the whole passage to justify or give countenance to such a doctrine. The Lord is speaking wholly of Jerusalem in temporal things. Hadst thou known (said Jesus), in this thy day the things which belong to thy peace. It is Jerusalem's day, not the Lord's day of grace. It is thy peace, not God's peace. The promise to all the Lord's people is absolute--"Thy people shall be willing in the day of thy power." (Ps. cx. 3.) And this secures the day of grace to all whom the Father hath given to the Son; for Jesus saith, "of all thou hast given me I have lost none." (John xvii. 12.) So that this holds good respecting the gift of grace to all generations of the church; but in temporals, like Jerusalem, the Lord's judgments may, and the Lord's judgments will follow and overthrow nations, where the gospel is preached and rejected. And while the Lord knoweth them that are his, and will save them by his grace, the nations who reject Christ, nationally considered, must perish.

JERUSHA

The mother of Jotham, son of Uzziah king of Judah. The name signifies, one that possesseth the inheritance--from Jarash, to possess. (2 Kings. xv. 33,)

JESAIAH

Son of Palatiah, meaning, salvation of the Lord, compounded of Jashah, to save; and Jab, the Lord. (1 Chron. iii. 21.)

JESHIMOM

A city in the wilderness. The name means solitude. (1 Sam. xxiii. 24.)

JESSE

The son of Obed, and father of David--derived from Jesh, to be. (Ruth iv. 17.) He is memorable in the genealogies of the Lord Jesus Christ. (See Matt. i, 5.)

JESUS

See Jerusalem.

JESUS CHRIST

One of the glorious names of him which is, and, which was, and which' is to come. (Rev. i. 8. 11.) The name of Jesus, which is originally so called in the Greek tongue, signifies a Saviour. Hence the Hebrews call him, Jehoshuah, or Joshua, or Joshuah, he who shall save; and as Christ means, anointed of JEHOVAH, the Sent, the Sealed of the Father; full of grace and truth; both names together carry this blessed meaning with them, Jesus Christ the Saviour of the world by the anointing of JEHOVAH to all the purposes, of salvation. See Christ. I only detain the reader just to remark on the blessed name, that all that bore it in the Old Testament church became types, more or less, of the Lord Jesus. Joshua the successor of Moses, and Joshua the high priest in the church, after the church was brought back from Babylon. (See Zech. iii. l.).

JETHRO

The father-in-law of Moses. This man is rendered memorable in Scripture history from his connection with Moses; but for this, it is more than probable he would never have been known even by name in the christian church. His name signifies excellence. His being a priest in Midian, doth not explain what his religion was. Some have thought, that he had a knowledge of the God of Israel, else Moses would not have been allied to him; and they that are of that opinion say, that he was descended from Midian, the son of Abraham, and Keturah. (See Gen. xxv. 1, 2.) There is some little difficulty in explaining one Scripture by another respecting this man. Exod. iii. 1. he is called Jethro; Num. x. 29. he is called Raguel; and some have thought, that Hobab was a third name by which he was known: but this, it should rather seem, was the brother of Moses's wife, Zipporah.

JEWS

So called from Judah. The account of this most singular people would form a wonderful history, could it be gathered into one mass of particulars. Mingled, as they now are, with all the known nations of the earth, and yet incorporated with none; carrying with them in their very countenance, customs and manners, one uniform singularity, so as to be known by all, and yet connected with none; despised, hated, persecuted, attached to their own religion, supporting it in spite of all opposition, and pertinacious still to preserve what the most learned of them do not understand; surely they are, as the Lord hath marked them, and as they are designated to be, living evidences of the truth of the gospel. Blessed be God, there is a promise concerning them, which all the faithful in Christ Jesus long to see fulfilled: "The Redeemer shall come to Zion, and unto them that turn from transgression in Jacob, saith the Lord." (Isa. lix. 20.)

JEZEBOL

The wife of Ahab, king of Israel. (1 Kings xvi. 31.) Her name is very singular,

JEZREEL - JOEL

meaning an island of the habitation--from Ai, island; and Zebal, habitation. The horrid character of this woman is strongly marked in the Scriptures, from 1 Kings xvi. to 2 Kings ix. Indeed, the very name in the church, hath been always considered odious. Hence our Lord, in his message to the churches, calls some worthless person by the name. (See Rev. ii. 20.) The awful termination of her life is strongly given. (2 Kings ix. 33.) And the events which followed her being eaten by dogs, which the prophet had foretold in the same chapter, ver. 10. were literally fulfilled.

It may appear somewhat marvellous, that such a circumstance should take place as that of dogs being allowed to eat human flesh, and in the very open streets of the city. But modern historians confirm the fact, and speak of it as no uncommon thing. They say that at Gordar, it is usual to hew in pieces the unhappy prisoners, which fall into their hands; and that when this is done, their scattered fragments are suffered to lie in the streets, being denied burial. And the stench would be intolerable, did not the beasts of prey in the neighbouring mountains visit the streets by night, and carry off as carrion the bodies of those so murdered. None of the inhabitants on account of these beasts, ever venture out of their houses after it is dark, without a guard and fire-arms. And this may serve to explain also that passage in the prophet: "I will appoint over them four kinds, saith the Lord, the sword to slay, and the dogs to tear, and the fowls of the heaven, and the beast of the earth, to devour and destroy." (Jer. xv. 3.)

JEZREEL

A city of Judah. (Joshua xv. 56. Hos. ii. 22.) The name means, seed of God; from Zeruah, seed, and El, God. Children were called by this name. (1 Chron. iv. 3. Hos. i. 4.) The Jezreel, where Ahab's palace was, lay distant from the city of Judah. (2 Kings ix. 10.)

JIAR

The second month among the Hebrews, answering to our April.

JOAB

One of the captains in David's army. His name is expressive of genealogy--from Ab, a father. His history begins 2 Sam. ii. and runs through the greater part of the life of David.

JOAKIM

The same as Eliakim. (Luke iii. 23).

JOANNA

Wife of Cuza. (Luke viii. 3.) Her name signifies, the gift or grace of God.

JOB

The man of Uz. His name signifies, what he himself was, one that weeps. His name is quoted with great honour by the Lord himself. (Ezek. xiv. 14.) and his patience recommended very forcibly by an Apostle. (James v. 11.)

JOCHEBED

The mother of Miriam, Aaron, and Moses. (Exod. vi, 20.) The name is of Cabad, glory; and Jah, the Lord.

JOEL

The prophet, whose writings form part of the sacred canon of Scripture, and are quoted by Peter in his sermon on the day of Pentecost. (See Joel ii. 28, 29, &c. Acts ii. 16, &c.) There were several Joels beside the prophet, whose names are recorded in Scripture.

- Joel, son of Samuel, 1 Sam. viii. 1, 2.
- Joel, son of Josebiah, 1 Chron. iv. 35.
- Joel, son of Jorabiah, 1 Chron. vii. 3.
- Joel, one of David's army, 1

Chron. xi. 38.
- Joel, a Levite, 1 Chron, xv. 7.
- Joel, son of Pedaiah, 1 Chron. xxvii. 20.

JOHANAN

Son of Careah. (2 Kings xxv. 23.) His name is compounded of Chanan, grace; and Jah, the Lord.

JOHN

Is an abbreviation of Johannan, and of much the same meaning. We need not dwell much upon this name, neither the persons so eminently distinguished by it. Their histories and worth are graciously preserved in the New Testament by God the Holy Ghost, and their names are in the book of life.

John the Baptist hath the priority in point of time, being born six months before the birth of the Lord Jesus Christ. John, the beloved apostle, was the youngest of all the disciples, and is not unfrequently distinguished by the title of the disciple whom Jesus loved. We have abundant cause to bless God for the ministry of this man, on account of the precious gospel which bears his name, and also for those three Epistles, as well as the Book of the Revelations, with which the sacred canon of Scripture closeth.

There is another John surnamed Mark, spoken of with honourable testimony in the New Testament. (Acts xii. 12.) This man, though called John, and surnamed Mark, was neither the apostle John nor the evangelist Mark, but another person. Paul speaks of him. Coloss iv. 10.

JONADAB

The son of Rechab, (Jer. xxxv. 6; derived from Nadab, a prince.

JONAH

The son of Amittai the prophet. His history we have incorporated with his writings. If there were no other cause to recommend Jonah to the attention of the church, than his being declared by Christ himself to have been his type, this were enough. And how striking a one it is, the most inattentive reader can hardly fail to observe. On the subject of the Gourd, I believe that the general opinion of all travellers hath been, that it was the same as is called at Aleppo, the Polma Christi. Its growth is said to have been so rapid, that the Kekajon, for so it is called, will send out shoots, in the compass of a night, near four inches. In the margin of our Bibles it is called, "the son of the night," to intimate its quick progress, and consequently its short duration.

JONATHAN

Saul's son, David's dear friend, (1 Sam. xviii. 1.) His death, with that of Saul, gave birth to one of the most poetical as well as devout elegies the world ever knew (2 Sam. i. 17. His name is compounded of Nathan, a gift; and Jab, the Lord. There are many of this name in Scripture.

- Jonathan, a Levite, the son of Gershom, Judg. xviii. 20.
- Jonathan, the son of Abiather the priest, 1 Kings i. 42.
- Jonathan, the son of Shage the Hararite, I Chron. xi. 34.
- Jonathan, the son of Shimeah, 1 Chron. xx. 7.
- Jonathan, or Jehonathan, the son of Uzziah, 1 Chron. xxvii. 25.
- Jonathan, the son of Ashel, Ezra x. 15.
- Jonathan, the High Priest, Neh. xii. 10.
- Jonathan, the Scribe, Jer. xxxvii. 14, 15.

JOPPA

The sea-port in Palestine in the Mediterranean. The name signifies beauty--from Japhah, Here it was that Jonah went to flee from the presence of the Lord. (Jonah i. 3.). Here Peter dwelt when sent for by

Cornelius And Tabitha also lived here, whom Peter by the Lord raised from the dead. (See Acts ix. 36. and x. 5, 6.)

JORDAN

That sacred river where the Lord Jesus Christ was baptized. It takes its name from Jor, a spring, and Dan, a small town near the source of Jor. Some have called it Jordan: and they say it means the river of judgment, from Dun, judgment. Every thing tends to endear this river to the believer. Numberless are the meditations it affords to the regenerate, in the many sacred events which have taken place at and on the banks of Jordan. (See Gen. xiii. 11. Num. xxxiv. 12. Josh. iii. 8. 11. 15. and iv. 3.17. 23. 1 Kings xvii. 3. 2 Kings ii. 6, 7. 2 Kings v. 10. 14. Matt. iii. 6, 17. &c.)

JOSEPH

The well known son of Jacob, whose history we have in Genesis from the thirtieth chapter to the end of the book. This made, in the margin of the Bible, is Adding--from Jasaph, to increase. It were needless to enter particulars of Joseph's history, when the Bible hath given it so beautifully. But perhaps it may not be an unacceptable service to observe on the history of this patriarch, what a remarkable character he is, and in what numberless instances he appears as a type of Christ: taken altogether, perhaps the greatest in the whole Scriptures. I shall particularize in a few leading features.

As Joseph was the beloved son of Jacob, and distinguished by his father with special tokens, of his affection, and which excited the envy of his brethren; so Christ, the beloved and only begotten son of God, by means of that distinguishing token of JEHOVAH, in setting him up, the Head of his body the church, and giving him a kingdom, in his glorious character of Mediator, called forth, as is most generally believed, that war we read of in heaven in the original rebellion of angels. (See Rev. xii.) The coat of many colours Joseph wore might not unaptly be said to represent the several offices of the Lord Jesus when on earth--his prophetical, priestly, and kingly character. The dreams of Joseph, implying his superiority over his brethren and his father's house, interpreted with an eye to Christ, are very striking circumstances of the preeminency of his character. Of him, indeed, might the prophecy of Jacob respecting Judah be fully applied: "Thou art he whom thy brethren shall praise: thy hand shall be in the neck of thine enemies, and thy father's children shall bow down be fore thee." (Gen. xlix. 8.) The mission of Joseph to his brethren, by the father, to see if they were well, and how they fared, (Gen. xxxvii. 14.) is a striking representation of the mission of God's dear Son to this our world. He came indeed, not only to seek, but to save that which was lost; but like another Joseph, the treatment he received corresponded in all points, only in an infinitely higher degree of baseness and cruelty. They sold Joseph for a slave, for twenty pieces of silver, and he was carried down into Egypt, and from the pit and the prison he arose, by divine favour, to be Governor over the whole land. But our Joseph was not only sold for thirty pieces of silver, but at length crucified and slain, and from the grave which he made with the wicked and with the rich in his death, by his resurrection and ascension, at the right hand of power, he is become the universal and eternal Governor both of heaven and earth.

The temptations of Joseph, by the wife of Potiphar, bear no very distant resemblance to the temptations of the Lord Jesus by Satan. The trial to the one, was the lusts of the flesh; the trial to the other, was the pride of life. But the grace imparted to Joseph, to repel the temptation, and the punishment he suffered by a false imputation, very beautifully set forth the innocency of Christ triumphing over the Devil's temptation in the wilderness, and the imputation of our sin to Jesus, who himself bore our sins in his own body on the tree, though himself without sin, neither was guile found in his mouth. In the exaltation of Joseph at the right hand of Pharaoh, and all the famished country coming to him for bread, we behold a lovely type, indeed, of our Almighty Joseph exalted at the right hand of God, and dispensing blessings of grace and mercy in the living bread, which is himself, to a famished world. And as then the Zapnathpaaneah of Egypt revealed secrets, and the cry was, Go unto Joseph, what he saith unto you do: so now, in the person of the Lord Jesus Christ, we do, indeed, behold our Wonderful Counsellor, who hath made known to us his and his Father's will, and the one desire of every soul is, to go unto Jesus, whatsoever he saith unto us is blessed, and our duty to obey.

In the going down of Israel into Egypt with all his house, constrained by famine to seek bread—what a striking portrait is here also drawn of the true Israel of God, constrained by the famine of soul to seek to Jesus for supply. And though like the brethren of Joseph, little do we at first know, that the Lord of the country is our brother, though in the first awakenings of spiritual want the Governor may seem with us, as Joseph did to them, to speak roughly; yet when the whole comes to be opened tour view, and Jesus is indeed discovered to be Lord of all the land, how, like Joseph's brethren, are we immediately made glad, and eat and drink at his table with him, forgetting all past sorrow in present joy, and partaking of that "bread of life, of which whosoever eateth shall live forever!"

Such, among many other striking particularities, are the incidents in the history of the patriarch Joseph, which are highly typical of Christ.

Under the article of Joseph we must not forget to observe, that there are several more of the name mentioned in Scripture, and of some importance.

- Joseph the husband of Mary, the mother of the Lord Jesus Christ, Matt. i. 15.18.
- Joseph, or Joses, son of Mary and Cleophas, supposed to be one of those who did not at first believe on Christ, but was afterwards converted, John vii. 5.
- Joseph, called Barsabas, a candidate for the apostleship with Matthias. See Acts i. 23.
- Joseph of Arimathea, John xix. 38.
- Joseph, husband to Salome.

JOSHUA

The son of Nun, whose name and history we have very fully related in the church of the wilderness, and afterward in his victories, as set forth in the book which bears his name. His name in Hebrew is the same as Jesus in Greek, signifying a Saviour; from Jashah, to save; and Jah, the Lord. This man was an evident type of Christ. See his history in the Book of Joshua.

JOSIAH

Son of Amon, king of Judah, (2 Kings xxii. 1, &c.) The name signifies, the fire of the Lord; from Esh, fire; and Jah, the Lord.

JUBAL

The son of Lamech, (Gen. iv. 21.) He invented instruments of music. His name is from Jobel, he that produceth. See Father.

JUBILEE

—Or Jobel more properly, which signifies a ram's horn

The day of Jubilee was a high feast in the Jewish church, and appointed by the Lord for the great year of release, every forty-ninth year, or seven times seven. In the twenty-fifth of Leviticus, we have the whole account of the appointment. Some have taken for granted, that the name itself was taken from Jubal, or Jobel, the son of Lamech, because he was the father or inventor of music; but others, more probably, derived it from the verb Hebiel, to bring back; because it was the year of general restoration, or bringing back. The imagination cannot conceive the effect of the morning of the day which commenced the Jubilee, which must have been wrought upon the different orders, of the people among the Jews. It began we are told on the first day of the month Tizri, the first month of the civil year, and the seventh of the ecclesiastical year, and corresponded to our month of September; and on the ninth day of Tizri, when the trumpets sounded, at that instant, every poor captive among the Jews was freed; and every mortgaged inheritance returned to its original owner. I leave the reader to his own reflections, what feelings must have been wrought on the different minds of all concerned; both of the master and of the servant, both of the man with whom was vested bonded land, and the one who received back his mortgaged inheritance. But while I pass over the Jewish camp on these particulars, I cannot help observing how infinitely surpassing must be the effect of the Jobel trumpet in the Christian church; when the captive sinner, and the poor soul who hath mortgaged his; inherited, inheritance, first hears the joyful sound of redemption by the blood of Christ, and is brought "to walk in the light of the Lord's countenance." (Ps. lxxxix, 15.) And this is not limited, to every forty-ninth year, but is every year and every day, yea, every hour of the day since Christ wrought salvation for his people, and the type of the Jubilee trumpet done away by the thing signified being come. Concerning this blessed event the Lord hath said, "the year of vengeance is in mine heart, and the year of my redeemed is come." (Isa. lxiii. 4.) See Feastes. It is said, that after the Jews returned from Babylon the Jubileee was discontinued, but they observed the Sabbatical year. See Sabbatical.

JUDAH

The fourth son of Jacob, by Leah. The name more properly is Jehudah. And Leah his mother made this remarkable observation on his birth, she said: "Now I praise the Lord:" therefore, that is, on that account, she called his name Jehudah, that is, (as the margin of the Bible renders it) praise. (Gen. xxix. 35). And this name is a plain compound (as Mr. Parkhurst observes) of Jah, the Lord; and hudah, to convess. Now then, if we turn to the prophetical expressions of the dying partiarach Jacob, (Gen. xlix. 8.) concerning Judah, we shall arrive at the full sense of both passages, Leah's, and her husband's. "Judah, thou art he whom thy brethren shall praise." This reading doth not convey to us the expression as strongly though the sense is the same, as by reading it thus: Thou, Judah, thy brethren shall (confessor,) or praise, (as Jehudah;) "thy father's children shall bow down to thee:" that is, they shall acknowledge thee to be the Jeehudah, and as such shall bow down to thee.

And this forms a beautiful correspondence to what the apostle, in the gospel-church, in after ages, was commissioned, by the same Holy Spirit that moved the patriarch, (2. Pet. I. 21.) to tell the people of the Lord Jesus, who sprang out of Judah after the flesh, and was, and is the Jehudah of his people—"who being (saith the apostle) in the form of God, thought it not robbery to be equal with God; but made himself of no reputation, and took upon him the form of a servant, and was made in the likeness of men: and being found in fashion as a man, he humbled himself, and became obedient unto death, even the death of the cross: wherefore God also hath highly exalted him, and given him a name which is above every name: that at the name of Jesus every knee should bow, of things in heaven, and things in earth, and things under the earth; and that every tongue should confess, that Jesus Christ is Lord to the glory of God the Father." (Phil.

JUDAH - JUDAH

ii. 6-11.)

While I am speaking, of Judah, under this one view of him in this memorable prophecy, it may not be amiss to consider him also in another. The same prophetic spirit that was in Jacob, leading him to the acknowledgment of Judah under one character typical of the Messiah, prompted him to speak of him under another. "The sceptre shall not depart from Judah, nor a lawgiver from between his feet, until Shiloh come." (Gen. xlix. 10.) The Jews themselves, however unintentionally and unconsciously, confirmed the certainty that this Scripture referred to the Lord Jesus Christ under a double evidence. For when in the hall of Pilate Jesus stood before the Governor, and the Governor asked him, saying, "Art thou the king of the Jews?" Jesus acknowledged it, and said unto him, Thou sayest. (Matt. xvii. 11.) But soon after, when to the cry of the Jews for Christ's crucifixion, Pilate said, "Shall I crucify your king?" the chief priests answered, "We have no king but Cæsar." Here was a confirmation to the one part of Jacob's dying prophecy, that the Shiloh should not come until the sceptre was departed from Judah—the chief priests confessed that that sceptre was departed, for they acknowledged that they had then no king but Cæsar; and, therefore, the Shiloh was come. The other testimony, and from their own lips, also became equally strong. Jacob said, that a lawgiver should not depart from between his feet until Shiloh came; and this law they proved did remain, for they contended with Pilate to enforce that law, for supposed blasphemy in the person of Christ. Take ye him, and crucify him said Pilate, for I find no fault in him. They then made this memorable answer: "We have a law, and by our law he ought to die, because he made himself the Son of God." Thus confirming the other prediction of the patriarch, that the lawgiver was not gone from between the feet of Judah until the Shiloh was come, to whom the whole referred. Two such striking evidences, and from the Jews themselves, on this important subject, never surely could have been expected; and now obtained, could only have been brought to pass by the overruling power and ordination of the Lord.

The reader will, I hope, indulge me with one observation more concerning Judah, in respect to this memorable prophecy of his father Jacob; because I humbly conceive it is important, and every thing connected with our Lord Jesus cannot fail of being interesting to his people. It is well known that the word Shebeth, which is translated, (Gen. xlix. 10.) sceptre, and signifies a powerful kingly office, is the same word which, (Judges v. 14.) is translated pen. "Out of Machir came down governors, and out of Zebulon they that handle the Shebeth of the Scribes. Now it is evident, from the use of the Shebeth upon both occasions, (Gen. xlix. 10. and Judges v. 14.) the one speaking of the office of a king, and the other of the scribe, that without violence to the expressions in either case, and in reference to the glorious person typified, his ruling the sceptre, or writing with his pen, conveys the idea of equal offices. The governors of Machir, and the pen of the writer of Zebulon, are put in parallel rank of equal dignity and importance. Hence, therefore, why may not the Shebeth of our Almighty Jehudah be supposed to convey an idea of his taking down the names of his people, whose names we know are "written in the Lamb's book of life?" (Rev. xxi. 27.) Who but him wrote those names in the book of life? Is not Jesus described, and by himself under the spirit of prophecy, as having "a tongue as the pen of a ready writer?" (Ps. xlv. 1.) And if a tongue to speak, why not the hand to write of the things touching himself? Moreover, if none but Jesus was found worthy "to open the book, and to loose the seals thereof," which was seen by John in the hand of him that sat on the throne, who but him could be worthy to write the records in it? (Rev. 1-

10.)

I beg the reader to observe, that I desire to deliver these sentiments, on a subject so necessarily sublime and mysterious, with the most profound awe and reverence. I would be always understood on these deep things as rather inquiring than deciding, rather desiring to be taught than to teach; but I cannot but think, that such views of the Lord Jesus are very sweet and interesting, and tend, under the Holy Ghost's guidings, to endear Christ to the heart, when we behold him thus typically represented in so many engaging services for his people. And surely, as it is said of Christ in one blessed Scripture, that the names of his people are all "written in the book of life," (Rev. xx. 15.) and in another he bids his people to "rejoice that their names are written there," (Luke x. 20.) as when considering himself the shepherd of his flock, and his people the sheep of his fold, he saith that "he calleth them all by name, and leadeth them out," (John x. 3.) and as the whole flocks of the mountains and of the vale, and of the cities of Benjamin, Jerusalem, and Judah, shall all pass again under the hands of him that telleth them, (Jer. xxxiii. 13.) surely it is not stretching the Scripture to say, that the Shebeth of Jehudah is as eminently descriptive of the greatness of his character, when speaking of this use of it, in writing, as in ruling, for sovereignty is implied in both, And the poor feeble hand that is now writing these lines, (earnestly begging forgiveness if he errs in the matter) cannot conclude this article without first saying, (and will not the reader for himself also join the petition?) Oh, that the almighty Jehudah may have graciously exercised the Shebeth of his power, and written my poor name, worthless as it is, among the millions he hath marked down in the book of life! Amen.

JUDAH

The land of Judah. When this is named in Scripture, as distinguished from Israel, it is meant thereby to denote that the kingdoms were divided. The kingdom of the ten tribes, or Samaria, was distinct from Judah. It formed a divided character concerning Judah, that this kingdom retained a reverence for the true religion, and the priesthood, and the law, at a time when the ten tribes were following idolatry. It were needless to remark after what was said before concerning Judah, that the name means, the praise of the Lord.

JUDE or JUDAS

There were two of this name well known in the Scriptures of the New Testament, the one an apostle of Christ, called in Matthew's gospel, (chap. x. 3.) Lebbeus, whose surname was Thaddeus, and by Luke, the brother of James; and he is again noticed by the persons who thought slight of our Lord and his doctrine, as his brother, Matt. xiii, 55. This was the Judas which spake to Christ in the midst of our Lord's sermon, and said, "Lord, how is it that thou wilt manifest thyself unto us, and not unto the world?" (John xiv. 22.) He is the Jude to whom, under the Holy Ghost, we are indebted for that precious morsel of gospel truth which is contained in the Epistle that bears his name. The other Jude or Judas is he who was surnamed Barsabas, (see Acts xv. 22.) and who was commissioned by the apostles to go to the church at Antioch. We have the account of his journey in the same chapter, ver. 30, &c. There is another Judas different from both the former, mentioned Acts ix. 11. Lastly, Judas Iscariot, the traitor. Some read it "Ish-cariot, the man of cariot; but certainly more properly Ish and corath, the man of murder. See Iscariot. The awful character of this man is related to us so fully in the gospels, that there can need nothing more than a reference to those sacred records to obtain the most complete account of him, together with his tremendous doom: for what can more fully decide the everlasting ruin of the traitor

JUDE or JUDAS - JUDE or JUDAS

than the Lord Jesus's account of him, when summing up all in one the most finished picture of misery, Jesus saith "good were it for that man, if he had never been born!" (Mark xiv. 11.)

It hath been a subject of some debate in the early church respecting Judas Iscariot, whether he did or did not receive the Lord's Supper. Some have insisted upon it that he did, and others, equally positive, have asserted that he did not. The best way to determine the point, will be to regard what the Evangelists have said upon the subject; for it must be from their testimony alone a right judgment can be formed. I shall therefore, bring each of them in their relation concerning this matter before the reader, and then leave it to his own determination which opinion to take. Matthew gives a particular account of the whole proceedings of the Supper from first to last, chap. xxvi. 20-30, and expressly states that when the twelve:" consequently Judas was included. And so unconscious were the rest of the disciples who the traitor was, when the Lord at the table intimated that one of them should betray him, that they were exceeding sorrowful, and began to say unto him every one, Lord, is it I? And when the Lord to the enquiry of Judas declared that he was the person, there is nothing said of his departure, but that the Lord proceeded to bless the bread and the cup, and said, "Drink ye all of it." After the supper, when they had sung a hymn, they went out into the mount of Olives. This is the whole relation as given by Matthew. Mark states the circumstances very nearly to the same amount; the fourteenth chapter, from the twelfth to the twenty-sixth verse. This evangelist observes, that prior to the supper Judas had been with the chief priests, and covenanted with them to betray Christ unto them. This however did not prevent him from mingling with the other disciples at the table, for Mark saith, that in the evening Jesus "came with the twelve;" and he adds, that "as they sat and did eat" Jesus intimated the circumstance of one of them betraying him. But from this evangelist's account it doth not appear that any discovery was then made of the traitor, neither is there the least idea afforded as if Judas was not present at the whole supper.

Luke is yet more particular in his account of the supper. (See Luke xxii. 14-39.) He saith, that when the hour was come, Jesus sat down, and "the twelve apostles with him." And what is much to the point in respect to the question now under consideration, this evangelist, in his statement of this memorable transaction, represents the Lord as proceeding to the supper, and giving both the bread and the cup to them before he intimated the presence of the traitor. So that, according to this relation of the subject, the Supper was finished when Jesus declared concerning the act of betraying him. John hath said nothing of the Supper itself, except he had respect to it in the opening of the thirteenth chapter of his Gospel. The reason, no doubt, of his silence was, that as the other evangelists had related the circumstances so particularly, and his gospel being principally intended as supplementary, to record those things of the Lord Jesus which they had omitted, there needed not again the account of the transactions of the Supper. But if the evangelist meant the Lord's Supper in the Passover, when he said, (chap. xiii. 2.) "And supper being ended, the devil having now put into the heart of Judas Iscariot, Simon's son, to betray him"—if this was the sacramental supper, then it will follow that all that is subsequent in this chapter was also subsequent to the service. And as the evangelist John saith also in this same chapter, that it was after the sop which Jesus gave him, as a token of the traitor, that "Satan entered into him," then must it have been after the supper. Such are the several relations given by the several evangelists on this memorable point. The reader will now judge for himself, when he hath duly considered the whole taken together. But I cannot see the very great importance of the question, whether Judas Iscariot did or did not receive the Lord's Supper. Put the case that he did—what did he receive? Nothing, surely, more than the mere outward sign. He had no part or lot in the matter. He had no union with Christ, and consequently no communion with him in the ordinance. For as the apostle justly and decidedly states it, "what concord hath Christ with Belial?" (2 Cor. vi. 15.) Judas being present at the table, and partaking of the elements of the table, became neither benefited himself, nor was it injurious to others. We read in earlier periods of the church, that "when the sons of God came to present themselves before the Lord, Satan came also among them." (Job i. 6.) But was the meeting unhallowed to the sons of God because the devil came in the midst? Were the apostles of Christ less apostles because Judas was "numbered with them, and had obtained part of this ministry?" (Acts i. 17.) And surely if the Lord Jesus, well knowing as he did whom he had chosen, was pleased to number him for a time with the apostles, might he not for a time also allow him to sit down with the apostles at the same table? Yea, did not the Lord Jesus expressly tell the church, that these things were his own appointment, and perfectly known in all their consequences by his divine mind, when he said, "Have I not chosen you twelve, and one of you is a devil?" (John vi. 70.) If choosing Judas to be an apostle, at the time Christ knew that he was a devil, did not in the least contaminate the rest of the apostles, neither injure the cause of Jesus, it must undeniably follow, that his being present at the supper could not pollute the supper, nor the faithful partakers of the supper. These things can never be injured by outward causes. The "precious and the vile" must necessarily in this world be often brought together, but the ordinance can receive no taint from the worthlessness of partakers. Ordinances of every kind, like the gospel itself, will prove "a savour of life unto life" unto some, whilst "a savour of death unto death" unto others. Here lies the grand discriminating mark, "the Lord knoweth them that are his." (2 Tim. li. 19.) And while the Lord knoweth them that are his, he no less knoweth them that are not. And we have already left upon record, the awful sentence which will be read to all such in the great day of God. "Then shall ye begin to say, We have eaten and drunk in thy presence, and thou hast taught in our streets. But he shall say, I tell you I know ye not whence ye are; depart from me, all ye workers of iniquity." (Luke xiii. 26, 27.) Indeed, may we not go farther, and suppose, that from this very appointment the Lord intended special good to his people? Was it not in effect saying, that if in the instance of the Lord Jesus himself a Judas is permitted, yea, appointed to attend his person, can it be wondered at in the minglings up of life, that his people should be so exercised? If in the college of apostles, out of twelve persons one should be a devil, can his people complain that they are sometimes called "to dwell with Mesech, and to have their habitation among the tents of Kedar?" Did Jesus, the Lord of life and glory, who might have commanded twelve legions of angels to attend him, permit, yea, even appoint a known devil to be his servant, to be with him in his miracles and his ministry, yea, to be one of the party at his farewell super—and what doth the meek and gentle Saviour teach thereby all his tried ones upon earth but this, that in their intercourse with the graceless they are to call to mind the unequalled humblings of Jesus in such instances. If he endured such a contradiction of sinners against himself, they are not to be wearied nor faint in their mind. The most blessed purposes are in the design. It hath been so in the church of God from the beginning, and will continue so unto the end. In the family of Adam there was a Cain; in Noah's house there was a Ham; Isaac had his Esau as well as Jacob;

and, above all, the Lord Jesus had Judas. Tares are in the church as well as the pure wheat; and it is Jesus himself that saith, "Let both grow together unto the harvest." But then when the harvest comes, the final and everlasting separation takes place; then it will be no longer needful that characters so very opposite should dwell together. "Then will I say (saith the Lord Jesus) to the reapers, Gather ye together first the tares, and bind them in bundles to burn them: but gather the wheat into my barn." (Matt. xiii. 30.)

I cannot dismiss the view we have taken of this subject without making one short observation more on the occasion, namely, to remark how ill-judged it is in our reading the Scriptures hastily to leap to conclusions, and to frame our opinions according to our supposed fitness of things, and not by the standard of the divine word. Assuming it for granted that Jesus, who knew the hearts of all men, neither needed that nay should shew him, would not have permitted Judas to partake of his supper, they instantly leap to a conclusion, that it could not be, and decide upon it accordingly. We are told by Chrysostom, that a similar offence was taken in his days, by some weak and injudicious Christians, at that sweet passage in St. John's Gospel, (chap. xi. 35.) where it is said, that Jesus wept. Concluding, that it was unsuitable and unbecoming the person and dignity of the Lord Jesus to be affected with human passions, they struck it out of their Bibles. But it was happy for us, and the Christian world at large, that when striking it out of their Bibles they could not strike it out of ours. Blessed be the Lord for presiding over his word, and preserving to us the sweet passage; for surely, to all true believers in Jesus, such views of Jesus are among the loveliest and most endearing parts in his divine character. Nothing can be more soothing and consolatory to a poor, sorrowful, afflicted follower of the Lord Jesus in his hours of suffering, than the consideration that he who is now exalted at the right hand of the majesty on high, was once, when on earth, "a man of sorrows and acquainted with grief." And the highest possible relief to the anguish of the soul under temptation, is the consciousness of the sympathy and compassion of Christ. He who wept when upon earth in beholding the tears of his people, cannot be unfeeling of them now though in heaven. And we have authority to conclude, that this sweet feature in the character of Jesus is as much his as ever; "in that he hath suffered, being tempted, he knoweth how to succour them that are tempted."

Let me only beg to add one observation more in relation to the traitor Judas, and then take a final farewell of his history forever; namely, concerning the awful death of the man, and the judgments that followed in his bowels gushing out. One of the evangelists saith, that he hanged himself. (Matt. xxvii. 3-5.) And another adds, "that falling headlong, he burst asunder, and all his bowels gushed out." (Acts i. 18, 19.) both events, no doubt, took place: and as by the suffocation induced by hanging, a great swelling might most probably take place, when he fell, the rupture of the lower part of the belly, called the abdomen, gave way, and the bowels gushed out. Think, what a spectacle! How justly the object of detestation both to God and man! And think if possible what followed.—To all the tremendous miseries of eternity he had to add, the special and peculiar aggravation in the everlasting and unceasing thought—that he, of all the creation of God, had this worm of conscience that never dieth, to prey upon him to all eternity, that he it was that betrayed the Lord of life and glory.

JUDGE and JUDGMENT

Every one perfectly understands what is meant both by judge and judgment. I should not have thought it necessary, therefore, to have swollen the bulk of The Poor Man's

Concordance by noticing the terms, had the mere explanation been the only thing intended. I have higher objects in view. I wish, while directing the reader both to the judgment that is to follow the present life, and the Judge who is to preside at the grand tribunal, to offer a short remark with an eye to the Lord Jesus Christ upon those subjects which under grace will not fail, I hope, to be profitable. In respect to the Judge, the Scriptures with one voice concur to assure us, that Christ is to be the Judge both of quick and dead. This, among other characters of our Lord, is one which he is to exercise as his own personal and peculiar right. "For the Father judgeth no man, (it is said,) but hath committed all judgment to the Son: that all men should honour the Son, even as they honour the Father." (John v. 22, 23.) Jesus, and Jesus only, could be the proper person to possess this honour. He who undertook and accomplished man's redemption, hath by right a power to be the Judge of man; and, indeed, it is expressly said, that the Father hath given him authority to execute judgment also, "because he is the Son of man." (John v. 27.) Observe the expression—because he is the Son of man! Not because he is the Son of God; for in that case no authority could be given to him, for he possesseth in common with the Father and the Holy Ghost all supreme and eternal power. But as the Son of man he receives this power, and it becomes the suited reward of his labours, and sufferings, and death. And what a beautiful order and harmony there is in this appointment as well as grace and mercy to his people. He who once came to save, will one day come to be our Judge; he who then acted as our Redeemer, will then appear as our Sovereign and our King. And what tends infinitely to endear the Lord Jesus under all these characters is, that while he carries on the authority of the one he never forgets the tenderness of the other. In him is most blessedly blended the judge and the brother. See those Scriptures. (Gen. xviii. 25. Deut. xxxii. 36. Dan. vii. 9-14. Matt. xxv. 31-46. Acts x. 42. Rev. xx. 11. to the end.)

And while we thus contemplate Jesus as our Judge, and the judgment seat his, wee find another sweet consolation arising out of it, in that when he comes to "judge the world in righteousness, and to minister true judgment unto the people," he comes to confirm what hath already passed respecting his redeemed, and not to try, but to declare his justification of their persons and state before God. All true believers in Christ are in a justified state now before God, in his blood and righteousness; and therefore they cannot come then into any condemnation. The solemn events of that great day of God, as they concern the believer, are not left to the smallest state of suspense. They have already found pardon in the blood of the cross; they have passed from death to life. "There is therefore, now (saith the apostle) no condemnation to them that are in Christ Jesus." (Rom. viii. 1.) And if there be no possibility of condemnation, there can be no issue of trial. Washed in the blood of Christ while upon the earth, they will be found without spot and blameless then at the court of heaven: clothed in the robe of Jesus's righteousness now, it is impossible to be found naked then. Awful, therefore, as the process of that day may be, (and most tremendously awful it will be to the unregenerate and unredeemed) yet to the saints of God it is called, and must be found, "the glorious appearing of the great God and our Savior Jesus Christ." (Tit. ii. 13.) Jesus comes "to be glorified in his saints, and to be admired in all them that believe." (Thess. i. 8, 9, 10.) Sweet, consoling, and soul-reviving thought to the believer! Some of the blessed words Jesus will speak to his people are already upon record, and should often comfort them now, as they will ravish them then. "Then will the king say unto them on his right hand, Come ye blessed of my father, inherit the kingdom prepared for you from the foundation of the world." (See Matt. xxv. 34. Luke xxii. 28-30.)

JUDGES

The judges which governed in Israel were, from the death of Joshua until the Israelites demanded a king over them, and Saul was appointed, a period of about three hundred and thirty-nine years. They were called in Hebrew Shophatim. The Book of Judges is supposed to have been written by Samuel. Some have thought that the Sanhedrim, which was a council consisting of seventy elders, always presided beside those judges, and regularly continued from the time of the Lord's appointment (see Num. xi. 16, 17.) until the days of the Lord Jesus Christ. But there doth not seem to be sufficient foundation for this belief. During the Babylonish captivity such a thing was hardly possible; neither during the reign of the kings before the captivity, do we meet with any account of the Sanhedrim. That such a court subsisted in the time of our Lord is certain, and continued until the destruction of the temple.

We have but little account in Scripture concerning this Sanhedrim. That this court, composed of seventy persons, possessed great power, even in the days when the Jews were under tribute to the Romans, is certain But thought they contended with Pilate, in their wishes for the death of Christ, that they had a law, yet we do not find, excepting upon this occasion, any mention made of its exercise. It seemed to have been but the mere shadow of authority; for the whole substance was taken into possession by the Roman Governor.

JUST ONE

A well-known name and character of the Lord Jesus Christ: (Acts iii. 24; vii. 52.) See Christ.

JUSTIFIER

A well-known name and character of God the Father. (Rom. iii. 36.) See Father.

JUSTIFY

The act of God's free grace, whereby he freely pardons the sinner, and justifies him in Christ notwithstanding all his own unworthiness and transgressions; delivering him both from the guilt of sin, the dominion of sin, and the punishment due to sin; accepting him in Christ, and thus blessing him in and through the finished salvation of Jesus Christ our Lord. (Gal. iii. 8.) See Impute.

JUSTUS

One of Paul's acquaintance. (Col. iv. 11.)

JUTTAH

A city of Judah. (Josh. xv. 55.) The name means perhaps, to spread; from Natah.

K

KABZEEL
There was a city in the south of Judah called by this name. (Josh. xv. 21.) The word is compounded of Kabatz, to assemble--and El, God.

KADESH
A place in the desert of Zin. (Num. xx. 1.). The name means, holy or holiness.

KADESH-BARNEA
Travellers are at a loss to determine whether the original Kabesh we read of Gen. xiv. 7. is the same with the Kadesh, Num. xiii. 26. And it is not clearly accounted for, wherefore Barnea was added to it. The term Kadesh means holy. Barnea is a compound of Bar, a son--and Nuah, one who is moving about. Perhaps Barnea might have been given to Kadesh, from the frequent movings about of Israel while in the wilderness state. And in this sense the name was well-termed, and may be said of the church always on earth. Oh! that our journeyings might be ever to Kadesh, and always as Kadesh; for surely Moses said, so in Jesus it may be said of the church now, "ye are an holy people unto the Lord thy God." (Deut. vii. 6.) It was at Kadesh Miriam died. Here also was the memorable rebellion of Israel concerning water; and here the Lord's grace notwithstanding that rebellion. (See Num. xx. 1 13. Ps. cvi. 32, 33.)

KADMIEL
The name of one of the captives returned from Babylon. (Ezra ii. 40.) If the word be derived, as it should seem likely to be, from Kadem, ancient, then is meant by Kadmiel, the ancient of God. Hence the Kadmonites, or ancient inhabitants of the east.

KEDAR
The son of Ishmael. (Gen. xxv. 13.) His name signifies, blackness. The posterity of Kedar dwelt in the deserts called Arabia-deserta, (Isa. xlii. 11.) and their employment was chiefly that of keeping cattle. They dwelt in tents made of hair cloth, which from the alternate heat of the scorching sun, and heavy rains beating on them, gave a dirty blackness rather forbidding to the eye of the traveller. And this may serve to explain to us, in some measure, those passages in Holy Writ in which the church complains of her sorry appearance. "Woe is me, that I am constrained to dwell with Mesech, and to have my habitation among the tents of Kedar." (Ps. cxx. 5.) The expression is figurative, meaning, that in this world a child of God finds himself not at home, nor those with whom he sojourns favourable to the promotion of the work of grace in the heart; and hence the soul goes lean from day to day, and to her own view appears wretched and black, like the tents of Kedar.

The spouse in the Canticles makes use of a similar expression in relation to herself, while taking comfort from the consciousness how differently she appeared in the eyes of her Lord from his beauty put upon her. "I am black, but comely, O ye daughters of Jerusalem, as the tents of Kedar, as the curtains of Solomon." (Song i. 5.) And the whole doctrine is blessedly explained Ezek. xvi. 1 to 14. Indeed, the spouse's figure of the black tents of Kedar, and the golden curtains of Solomon, that is, the wretchedness of a desert, and the rich tapestry of a palace, is very obvious. Believers, considered in themselves, and carrying about with them, as they do, a body of sin and death, are always black. Hence mount Sinai covenant is represented as a dispensation, like the mount itself, of blackness and darkness and terror; because it set forth that dread of conscience which filled the mind when under a conscious sense of having broken it. On the other hand, the covenant of promise full of grace and mercy, giving as it doth, a joy and peace in believing to the soul, lightens the countenance, and makes the child of God comely. The apostle Paul hath beautifully set these things forth in his allegory. (Gal. iv. 22 to the end.) I only add, how blessed it is to have such views as the church had, in one and the same moment, of ourselves. Considered in nature, we are black as the tents of Kedar; viewed in grace, comely as the curtains of Solomon; and still going humble and softly all our days, from the consciousness of the remains of indwelling corruption; still taking comfort in the assurance, that we are "beautiful as Tirzah, comely as Jerusalem, and terrible as an army of banners." (Song vi. 4.)

KEDEMAH

One of the sons of Ishmael: he was the last of the twelve princes which the Lord promised to give to Ishmael. (See Abraham's prayer, and the Lord's answer, Gen. xvii. 18-20. compared with Gen. xxv. 13-16.) The name of Kademah, it should seem, is taken from Kedem, or the east. And in confirmation of it, it is remarkable that the account given of the journeying after the flood is expressed by this term, "they journeyed from Kadem," or as the margin of the Bible renders it, "they journeyed eastward." (Gen. xi, 2.)

KEDESH NAPHTALI

So called from being given to that tribe. (Josh. xix. 37.) See Kadesh-barnea.

KEEPER

One of the gracious offices of the Lord. All the persons of the GODHEAD have this blessed name and character applied to them in the Scriptures of truth; but it should seem to have a peculiar reference to the person of God the Father. Hence the Lord Jesus, with inexpressible sweetness, consigns the case of his church to his Father in the night before his sufferings and death. "Keep, Holy Father, (saith Jesus) through thine own name, those whom thou hast given me." (John xvii. 12.) So again the same or a similar request is made, ver. 15. so also Ps. cxxi. 5. And the Holy Ghost, by Moses the man of God, when giving directions to Aaron to bless the people, appointed this form in reference to the Father. (See Num. vi. 24. see also Isa. xxvii. 3.) And certainly there is a blessedness in the thought, that the church in Jesus is the continued object of the Father's love and care. And what an asylum do believers find in the view, that all the attributes of JEHOVAH are engaged for the security and comfort of his people. What the Lord said to Abraham is in effect said, and from the same cause, to all his seed: "Fear not, Abraham, I am thy shield, and thine exceeding great reward." (Gen. xv. 1.)

KEILAH

A town of Judah. (Josh. xv. 44,) The word is compounded of Kol, a voice; and Jah, the Lord.--The voice of the Lord.

KEMUEL

Son of Nahor. (Gen. xxii. 21.) If it be derived from Kum, to arise; and El, God, the sense is, God hath raised.

KENITES

A people that dwelt with the Amalekites: so called from Kanah, a possession. Jethro, the father-in-law of Moses, was of this people. (1 Sam. xv. 6.)

KETURAH

Abraham's handmaid. (Gen. xxv. 1.) The name means, to burn, from Kather.

KEZIAH

One of Job's daughters, (Job xlii. 14.) from Katza, or bassia, meaning, a sweet-scented plant.

KEY

I should not think it necessary to notice this, the thing is so familiar, were it not that the Lord Jesus hath condescended to use the figure with reference to his grace and power. He calls himself the "Key of David, who openeth and none shutteth; who shutteth and none openeth." (Rev. iii. 7. Isa. xxii. 22) It is blessed to see in how many ways the Lord manifests the supremacy of his power, He hath the key of heaven, to admit whom he pleaseth: he hath the key of hell, to shut up all his foes; he hath the key of his word, to unfold the mysteries of his kingdom; he hath the key of the heart, to open it, and to render that word effectual. Hence, in all things, from the highest heaven to the lowest hell, Jesus governs. What a sweet thought for all his redeemed to cherish! He it is that opens his church, opens the mouth of his ministers and the souls of his saints, opens the opportunities of ordinances, and gives blessings to ordinances, and the several means of grace upon earth, and finally; fully, and completely opens an entrance for all his redeemed into his everlasting kingdom in heaven. Gracious Lord Jesus, "open thou mine eyes, that I may see the wondrous things of thy law!"

KIBROTH-HATTAAVAH

(Num. xi. 34, 35.) The margin of our Bibles very properly renders this name by the graves of lust; perhaps from Kerab, turning up, or ploughing. The readers of the Bible may find much spiritual profit from contemplating the graves of lust. Here, we may say, as we tread the ground idea, and tread over the ashes of those lusters, here are the sad records and monuments of those whose examples teach us the effect of dying martyrs to the indulgence of corrupt passions. It is to find death in the pot, when we seek that from the creature which the Creator only can supply, Oh, how many Kebroth-hattaavahs doth the present world afford, as well as the wilderness to Israel!

KIDRON

See Cedron.

KING

There is somewhat very blessed in eyeing the Lord Jesus in this character, His church must always find in this view of their Lord a very high satisfaction. His is the blessed: office, in this royal character, to govern, rule, maintain, support, to pardon, reward, countenance, favour, and bless all his kingdom. He hath indeed made all his kings and priests to God and the Father. And what a rapturous thought is it to recollect, that his kingdom is for ever, and his dominion that which shall have no end! While we behold the Lord Jesus in this exalted point of view, it becomes an interesting enquiry of the soul, whether we are subjects of his kingdom. (See Rom. vi. 16.)

KINGDOM OF CHRIST

By the kingdom of Christ is meant, his mediatorial kingdom, as the head of his body the church; and though this supreme power and glory of the Lord Jesus hath undoubtedly its foundation in his eternal power and GODHEAD, inasmuch that had, he not been one with the Father over all, God blessed for ever, he never could have formed this kingdom as Mediator, yet his sovereignty, as the glorious Head of his church is distinct from that kingdom of his oneness in the GODHEAD with the Father and the Holy Ghost. His kingdom of Mediator is a kingdom given to Christ. As God he had a natural right to it, and it could not be given to him; but as Christ, God-man in one person, he hath a gifted right, and an acquired right, by virtue of which it becomes his. And most blessed it is to eye the Lord Jesus in this his kingdom, and to behold the furniture of this kingdom, when brought to see our interest in it. All the blessings that belong to a kingdom constitute Christ's kingdom: all temporal, all spiritual, all eternal blessings. Every thing in grace here, and glory to all eternity, are his to bestow upon his people. Blessedly Jesus spake of this to the Father, in that comprehensive manner: (John xvii. 2.) "As thou hast given him power over all flesh, that he should give eternal life to as many as thou hast given him." So that to speak of this kingdom of the Lord Jesus Christ in a comprehensive manner, he hath universal, unceasing, unchanging, and everlasting supremacy, in the kingdom of grace here, and glory to all eternity. How beautifully doth the apostle speak of the privilege of all the happy subjects of this kingdom, when he saith, "wherefore, we receiving a kingdom which cannot be moved, let us have grace whereby we may serve God acceptably, with reverence and godly fear." (Heb. xii. 28. See Exod. xix. 6. John xviii. 36. Luke i. 33.)

KINSMAN

This is a sweet and precious name when applied to the person of the Lord Jesus, and full of very blessed signification as relating to the church of God in him. In order to enter into a proper apprehension of its delightful meaning, it will be necessary to remark, that sometimes the same word which we translate kinsman is also translated Redeemer. Thus Ruth iv. 14. "Naomi saith, Blessed be the Lord, which hath not left thee this day without a kinsman. (Goel.)" In the margin of the Bible the same word Goel is translated Redeemer; therefore, the sense is, hath not left thee this day without a Redeemer. So again Job xix. 25. "For I know that my Redeemer liveth," In the original it is the same word Goel, meaning kinsman, Redeemer. So once more, (Isa. xliv. 6.) the same word Goel, which is rendered kinsman in Ruth, is rendered Redeemer here.--" Thus saith the Lord, king of Israel, and his Redeemer, the Lord of hosts." Hence, therefore, from these and the like passages, it is blessed to see that one and the same person is all along spoken of under both characters, our kinsman, Redeemer. Having premised these things by way of illustration, it will be proper next to enquire, what was the special relation and duty of the kinsman in the church of God, and how was the office to be performed. To answer this enquiry it should be observed, that the right of redemption belonged to this kinsman, for thus the law enjoined: "If thy brother be waxen poor, and hath sold away some of his possession, and if any of his kin come to redeem it, then shall he redeem that which his brother sold." (Lev. xxv. 25.) And hence we find in the case of Ruth the Moabitess, the right of redemption founded upon this law was first proposed to the kinsman that was nearest of kin, and upon his refusal Boaz claimed the privilege as the next of kin. The reader may see this stated at large very particularly Ruth. iv. 1-12.

Now then we come to the marrow of the whole subject, as it relates to the person of the Lord Jesus Christ in the redemption, of our nature. Jesus, by virtue of taking our nature, becomes the nearest of kin to our nature, and is, to all intents and purposes, our Goel, our kinsman, Redeemer. He is the brother born for adversity, and is not ashamed to call us brethren. Now as Jesus's poor brother, our whole nature was waxen poor, and had by sin and rebellion sold away some of our possession, and had both brought our souls into captivity and mortgaged our inheritance, to him alone belonged the right of redemption for both; and Jesus hath fully and completely redeemed both. Hence he hath proved himself to be our Goel in the full sense of the word, our kinsman, and our Redeemer, and our kinsman-Redeemer; and very blessed it is to know the Lord Jesus Christ in those united characters. Job found it so in an eminent degree; and so ought all the faithful. "I know (said he) that my (Goel, my kinsman) Redeemer liveth, and that he shall stand at the latter day upon the earth: and though after my skin worms destroy this body, yet in my flesh shall I see

God; whom I shall see for myself, and mine eyes shall behold for myself, and not another for me.' (Job xix. 25, 26.) Reader! if you can join the man of Uz in this precious testimony, and his creed and your creed on this great point are the same, you will enter into the beauty and blessedness of this relationship of kinsman as belonging to the Lord Jesus Christ, and enjoy the privilege of it in your heart. See Brother.

KIRHARASETH

A city of Moab. It is supposed to mean, a place of heat. We know that Kir is city; and Haresh is sometimes put for brick or baked. The prophet Isaiah saith, that his bowels "sounded like an harp for Moab, and his inward parts for Kei-haresh," which was the chief city of Moab. (Isa. xvi. 11.) Whether the prophet's lamentation for Moab was from the ruin of it as a city, (see 2 Kings iii. throughout,) or whether spiritually considered, I know not. The city itself was certainly fertile, and the whole country of Moab delightful for fruits and vineyards, which historians tell us extended even to the borders of the Dead Sea. Such was our nature originally, like the garden of Eden; and who but must lament to behold the ruin by the fall. Oh, the blessedness of that recovery by the Lord Jesus Christ!

KIRJATH

A city, Josh. xviii. 28.

KIRJATHAIM

Two cities so called, Josh. xiii. 19.

KIRJATH-ARBA

The city of four; Arba, four, being joined to it, Josh. xv. 13. See Cities of Refuge.

KIRJATH-ARIM

The city of cities, Ezra. ii. 24.

KIRJATH-BAAL

The city of Baal, Josh. xv. 60.

KIRJATH-JEARIM

The city of woods, Josh. xv. 9. so called from Jahar, a forest.

KIRJATH-SANNAH

The city of the bush, from Senah, a bush, Josh. xv. 49.

KIRJATH, SEPHER

The city of the book or letters. This was the portion which Joshua assigned to Caleb, and it was called Debir before. See Josh. xiv. 6, 7. and Judg. i. 10-13. What the ancient inhabitants meant by the name of Debir, meaning words, is not so generally understood. Some have thought it had relation to certain records deposited there, but there is not the smallest authority for this opinion.

KISH

There were several of this name in Scripture. (See 1 Sam. ix. 1. 1 Chron. viii. 30. 2 Chron. xxix. 12.) The word itself simply means somewhat hard.

KISHON

The river so beautifully spoken of in Deborah's song, Judg. v. 21. Perhaps the name is derived from Kish. This river was but small: it arose in the valley of Jezreel, and passed on to the south of mount Tabor, emptying itself the Mediterranean Sea.

KISS

In the eastern world so much was implied by this action of the kiss, that we lose many beauties of the Holy Scriptures for want of our knowledge of their customs and manners concerning it. There were the kiss of love, the kiss of reverence, the kiss of adoration and homage, the kiss of peace and reconciliation, the kiss of holy joy and delight; and, on the other hand, we read of the kiss of idolatry, the kiss of hypocrisy, of deceit, of the traitor, and the like.

It may not be amiss, for the better apprehension of the subject, to look over the Scripture a little for particular instances of this ceremony, that we may remark the diversity. I need not particularize the kisses of natural affection, so common in the word of God, between near and dear relations; for those are well understood, and require no illustration. Such, I mean, as the tender kiss of Isaac with Jacob, when receiving his son's venison, Gen. xxvii. 26. Joseph kissing his brethren, Gen. xlv. 14, 15. Jonathan with David, I Sam. xx. 41. and numberless other instances of the like nature. But the kisses spoken of in Scripture implying different significations, it may not be improper to be somewhat more particular in defining. Thus the kiss of reverence or adoration, whether in religious veneration of JEHOVAH, or whether used in idolatrous worship, was meant to convey every thing that was dutiful, obedient, and affectionate. Thus the direction given in the second Psalm to kiss the Son, the Lord Jesus Christ, evidently conveys the acknowledgment due to his person and government, with the most cordial acceptation of him in his glorious mediatorial character as the Christ of God. (Ps. ii. 12.) On the other hand, the prophet represents the worshippers of Baal as commanding this service, in token of absolute submission to this idolatrous worship as expressed in this single act of kissing. "Let the men that sacrifice (say they) kiss the calves." (Hos. xiii. 2.)

Besides the actions of kissing to imply the most complete adoration, we find among the orientals the act of kissing the hand, together with the corresponding action of bending the knee, smiting on the thigh, and the like, intended as expressive altogether of the most implicit subjection and reverence. (See Isa. xlv. 23. Jer. xxxi. 19.) Thus we find Pharaoh giving commands concerning the homage to be paid Joseph. "Thou shalt be over my house, (said Pharaoh) and according to thy word shall all my people be ruled." In the margin it is, be armed or kiss: that is, shall all my people kiss thy word, thy command. (Gen. xli. 40.) So Job, "If I (said Job) beheld the sun when it shined, or the moon walking in brightness, and my heart hath been secretly enticed, or my mouth hath kissed my hand, this also were an iniquity to be punished by the judge, for I should have denied the God that is above." (Job xxxi. 26-28.) A similar passage we meet with in 1 Kings xix. 18. where the Lord, in telling his servant the prophet Elijah, that the idolaters in Israel, many as they were, did not yet come up to the fears of his mind, saith, "Yet I have left me seven thousand in Israel, all the knees which have not bowed unto Baal, and every mouth which hath not kissed him." Both which passages are to the same amount, that the kiss was a token of the most perfect adoration.

We may notice the usage of the kiss also in token of peace and friendship, and of the greatest cordiality subsisting between persons joining in the same sentiments of civil and religious communion. Hence Paul directs the churches to this amount, when he saith, "Salute one another with an holy kiss." (Rom. xvi. 16.) "Greet all the brethren with an holy kiss." (1 Thess. v. 26. 1 Pet. v. 14.)

This was supposed (however treachery lurked under the garb), to have been the case when Joab took Amasa by the beard with the right hand to kiss him. (see 2 Sam. xx. 9.) And yet more, in an infinitely greater degree, when Judas hailed Christ with the awful salutation, "Joy to thee Rabbi, (for so hail means) and kissed him? (Matt. xxvi. 49.) In the former instance, Joab took Amasa by the beard, we are told, which was an action betokening the highest regard of affection: for as the beard was always considered the chief honour and ornament of a man, so to touch it or kiss it was considered the highest proof of respect. On the contrary, to shave it, or to do any thing to it reproachfully, was counted the highest token of contempt. In the eastern world, many would have preferred death to the loss of the beard: and hence when David changed his behaviour before Achish, king of Gath, and feigned himself mad, and scrabbled on the doors of the gate, and "let his spittle Pall down upon his beard," (see 1 Sam. xxi. 13.) Achish considered this disgrace done to his beard as the most confirmed proof of his madness, for no man in his right senses, he concluded, would have done so. For if by accident only, in walking the streets, one touched another's beard, nothing could atone for the injury and affront but by kissing it, to show the utmost respect. So tenacious were the orientals on these points.

I have not yet mentioned the kisses of grace in spiritual tokens, and yet these form by much the most interesting part of the subject. Hence the spouse in the Canticles, speaking of her soul's desire for the coming and manifestation of Christ in the flesh, with all the blessings connected with that manifestation, sums up her very ardent request in that comprehensive expression, "Let him kiss me with the kisses of his mouth, for his love is better than wine." (Song i. 2.) And as those kisses of Jesus are meant to imply every thing in Christ, and with Christ, Jesus in his person, and Jesus in his fulness, suitableness, and all-sufficiency, so on our part the kiss of grace implies every thing that can denote love, adoration, faith, dependance, homage, subjection, and praise. Poor Mary at the feet of Jesus meant to express all these and more, when she washed his feet with her tears, and wiped them with the hairs of her head, when she kissed his feet, and anointed them with the ointment. (See Luke vii. 38.) In these kisses she expressed all that a broken heart could testify of her soul's hope, love, faith, contrition, sorrow, and the like. It was in effect saying, I cast my-self on thee, as a poor, perishing, dying sinner, and venture all on thy blood and righteousness!

KNIFE and KNIVES

In the early ages of the world, before that instruments of metal were formed, the eastern inhabitants used sharp stones for the purpose of cutting. Thus Zipporah took a sharp stone for the circumcision of her son. (Exod. iv. 25.) And Joshua, at the command of the Lord, made sharp knives for the same purpose. The margin of the Bible saith, that they were "knives of flints." (See Josh. v. 2, 3.) And as knives of stones were then in use, it is more than probable that the earlier ages had none formed of better materials. (Gen. xxii. 6.)

KOHATH

Son of Levi, Gen. xlvi. 11. signifies congregation, from Karah.

KORAH

Son of Izhar, (Exod. vi. 21.) meaning cold, from Karak. There were two others of this name in Scripture, (Gen. xxxvi. 15.) and the famous, or rather infamous Korah, son of Izhar. (Num. xvi. 1.)

KUSHAJAH or KISHI

The son of Abdi. (1 Chron. xv. 17.) The name means, hardness, from Cashar, chan; and Jah, the Lord.

L

LAADAH
The son of Shelah, 1 Chron. iv. 21. The signification of the name is ornament, from Hadah.

LAADAN
Son of Gershon, 1 Chron. xxiii. 7, 8. It seems to be derived from Hadan, pleasure.

LABAN
The Syrian, son of Bethuel, brother to Rebekah, and father to Rachel, whose history forms so interesting a page in Scripture from his connection with Jacob. (See Gen. xxviii. to xxxi.) His name means, white.

LACHISH
A city south of Judah, Josh. x.23. The word signifies, she walks, from Jalac.

LAISH
Father of Phalti, 1 Sam. xxv. 44. There is a city of this name, Isa. x. 30.

LAKE
There are three lakes spoken of in Judea, namely, the Asphaltites, Tiberias, and Semechon. In the original we should read Bor as a lake, or pit, or cistern. In Palestine, we are told, they make lakes for their wines. That passage in the Revelations concerning the wine-press means a take. (Rev. xiv. 19, 20.)

LAMA
Matt. xxvii. 40. (See Eli Eli.)

LAMB
It would have been needless to have paused over this word, or inserted it in this place, but from the very earnest and special use made of it in reference to the Lord Jesus Christ, as typical of his person and nature; but considered with an eye to him, nothing can be more interesting than to behold how unceasingly the Holy Ghost is glorifying our Lord under this beautiful figure through the whole word of God.

Every one knows the character of a lamb: among all the creatures of God there are none so harmless, inoffensive, meek, and gentle as the lamb. A lamb will receive injuries, but will offer none. There is a loveliness in the tender lamb of the fold which interests every beholder. In every point the lamb is useful: its fleece affords covering, and its flesh food; both in life and death the lamb is eminently profitable. Nothing could be more happily chosen to depicture Christ Jesus in his immaculate holiness and purity; his meekness, gentleness, and patience, is indeed as the Lamb of God, "for in his mouth was found no guile; who when he was reviled, reviled not again, when he suffered, he threatened not." He was "holy, harmless, undefiled, separate from sinners, and made higher than the heavens." Well might it be said of him, that "he was led as a lamb to the slaughter, and as a sheep before her shearers is dumb, so opened he not his mouth." (Isa. liii. 7.) And what endears Christ in this lovely character, and which the typical representation of the lamb eminently sets forth, he is both the covering for his people, and their sustenance; for his righteousness is their garment of salvation, and "his flesh is meat indeed, and his blood drink indeed., In every and all points of view, in his designation as a sacrifice, he is "the Lamb slain from the foundation of the world." (Rev. xiii. 8.) In his manifestation to Israel in the days of his flesh, his humiliation unto death, and his exaltation to glory, still is he the Lamb of God, and the Lamb in the midst of the throne, the Christ of God, and the salvation of God to every one that believeth. The song of heaven is one and the same with the hymn of earth: "Worthy is the Lamb that was slain to receive power, and riches, and wisdom, and strength, and honour, and glory, and blessing; for thou wast slain, and hast redeemed us to God by thy blood." (Rev. v. 9-12.)

LAMECH

The son of Methuselah, and father of Noah, (See Gen. v. 25-31.) His name means somewhat poor, or made low, from Macac. His observation at the birth of Noah was remarkable. "This same, said he, shall comfort us concerning our work and toil of our hands." (Gen. v. 29.) The Holy Ghost hath not given us authority to say it was prophetical, but when we consider the eminency of Noah, a preacher of Jesus, by faith, (see Heb. xi. 7.) we may well suppose, that his father's hopes concerning him sprang from somewhat more than nature. Creature-hopes and creature-prospects are for the most part deceitful, and the more we lean upon them the feebler they prove. I should hope, therefore, that Lamech's hopes of his son Noah were on the church's account, and had an eye to the covenant of grace.

There was another Lamech of the descendants of Cain. (See Gen iv. 17, 18.) He appears to have been the first who broke the divine commandment, by taking more wives than one. (See Gen. ii. 24.)

See the Lord's displeasure at this, Mai. ii. 14-16. And yet more particularly hear what the Lord Jesus Christ saith upon this subject, Matt. xix. 3-10. The names of his two wives are in some measure descriptive of his sin and folly, for Adah and Zillah compounded, would imply an assembly, a shadow. It were well if the favourers of polygamy would consider these things. The Lord Jesus declares, that from the beginning it was not so; and perhaps in no one instance hath it been free from sorrow. And as from an authority which becomes unquestionable, the married state is declared to be sacred, as typical of Christ's union with his church, the abettors of double marriages would farther do well to consider, what a running counter this is to this blessed doctrine, as well as to the original appointment of heaven. (See Ephes. v. 23. to the end, 1 Cor. vii. 2.) See Concubine.

LAMENTATIONS

I only just notice in a cursory way, the sweet Book of Jeremiah which bears this name. The Jews called it Echa, or Kinnoth, which is Lamentations. It is the mournful prophet's elegy over the calamities of the beloved Jerusalem. And in after-ages how tenderly the Lord Jesus wept over the same city, (Matt. xxiii. 37-39.) But besides this, there is much of Christ discoverable in it, indeed, though in the first face of the book it refers to history, yet the chief beauty of it is as prophetical of Christ and his church.

LAMP

Much is said in the holy Scripture concerning the lamps of the temple. And when the Lord Jesus appeared to John, he was seen in the midst of the golden candlesticks (Rev. i. 12, 13.) And John saw before the throne, at another vision, seven lamps of fire burning before the throne, (Rev iv. 5.) See also Exod. xxv. 37; xxxvii. 23. Num. viii. 2. Zech. iv. 2.) No doubt, that besides the general use of lighting the temple, they had a reference to spiritual things, and were meant as emblems of the illuminating and brightening offices of God the Holy Ghost to the churches and people. We know that this almighty Minister in the church of Jesus, acts as "a spirit of judgment, and a spirit of burning." (Isa. iv. 4.) And how blessedly he manifests the sovereignty of is power in both "convincing of sin, and of righteousness, and of judgment," the church of God in all ages hath borne witness. Precious are his sevenfold gifts, when by his gracious influence he penetrates the heart of the redeemed, melting by his burning the frozen affections, softening and subduing the stubborn mind, and making it willing in the day of his power. Oh, what unknown influence doth the Holy Ghost manifest in the hearts of those he makes his temple! (I Cor. vi. 19.) what light, what grace, what information, what comfort, the Lord the Spirit imparts! Oh, ye ransomed of the Lord, who know the infinite preciousness his grace, see that ye "grieve not the Holy Spirit of God, whereby ye are sealed unto the day of redemption!" (Ephes. iv. 30.)

I cannot dismiss the subject of the sacred lamps of the temple, emblems as they were of the light of the Spirit, without one observation more, namely, that it should seem, the perpetual, use of them was designed to keep alive the remembrance of his unceasing, presence, who is the light of his people. It is said in the history of Samuel, "that ere the lamp of God went out in the temple of the Lord where the ark of God was, and Samuel was laid down to sleep, that the Lord called Samuel." (1 Sam. iii. 3, 4.) Was not this emblematical of the Spirit of prophecy, that before one lamp of the Lord went out another should be lighted, before Eli was quite extinguished Samuel should be kindred? Do we not find it so through the church's history in all ages? Did not the spirit of Elijah rest on Elisha? Did not all the prophets succeed one another in their ministry, as might best promote and carry on the Lord's cause in the earth? I do not presume to speak decidely upon the subject, but if the thought be right, is there not great sweetness in that Scripture explained in reference to this view, and with an eye to the Lord Jesus? "I have ordained a lamp for mine anointed." (Ps. cxxxii. 17.)

That lamps are constantly used figuratively in Scripture, I need not insist upon. The Lord is said to be the light of his people, (Ps. xxvii. 1. Job xxix, 3.) and even his servants, shining by his brightness, are spoken of by the same figure. Thus David was called "the lamp of Israel," 2 Sam. xxi. 17. and John the Baptist said to be "a burning and a shining light." (John v. 35.)

LANGUAGE

It is plain from Scripture, that in the early ages of the world, "the whole earth was of one language and of one speech." (Gen. xi. 1.) The diversity arose as a punishment for the building of Babel. It hath been a subject of more curiosity than profit to enquirers from whence arose the first communication of thought by speech, and who taught men the use of language, or the power to diversify sound for conveying ideas. Some have gone so far, in order to ascertain what would be the first articulation of a child untaught by hearing others so as to express his own thoughts, that infants have been kept from all hearing of conversation, purposely to discover what the first sounds of speech would be. But while men have thus employed their time and attention to the discovery of what, even if it could have been attained, would not have profited, the word of God teaches the cause of speech in the great Giver of all good, and the diversity of speech when the entrance of sin into the world had made man rebellious. But what a decided proof is this, among may, of the overruling power of God to cause good to spring out of evil, that as sin induced a confusion of languages, grace rendered this very confusion a means for the greater display of the riches of mercy in the confirmation of the truth of the gospel; for by the confusion at Babel, and the diversity of languages that followed, what a blessed opportunity was thereby afforded, when at the day of Pentecost, the poor, ignorant, and unlearned disciples of Jesus gave testimony of the truth by conversing with the greatest fluency in no less than fifteen different languages to the different nations of the earth then assembled at Jerusalem. So the Lord overruled the sin of Babel to his own glory. (See Acts ii. 1-11.)

LAODICEA

A city rendered famous from its connection with Scripture history. (See Col. ii. 1. and iv. 16. See also Rev. i. 11. and iii. 14-22.)

What an awful consideration, that not a vestige of this church remains, but the place where it stood is now inhabited by infidels!

LAPIDOTH

The husband of Deborah, (Judg. iv. 4.) The name, it should seem, means light, or enlightened, from Leppad.

LAST

One of the characters of the Lord Jesus Christ. He who is the Alpha is also the Omega, the first and the last, meaning that he is the first cause and final end of all things. See Christ.

LATTICE

The manner of building in the east differs so totally from the custom of other countries, that it renders many parts of the word of God less intelligible on this account. Dr. Shaw, in his travels, hath given upon several occasions many circumstantial particulars of the construction of their houses in Palestine, and, among the many, of their plan of the lattices used in the terrace, and in the other parts of their buildings. For the most part, the windows open into their own courts, except a latticed window, or balcony, that for conveniency is formed to look into the street. And this retirement and secrecy forms a lively representation, suited to the natural jealousy of the people. But the latticed window, or balcony, formed the only opening for communication (except the entrance) with the public street, It was at this lattice-work window, most probably, that Jezebel looked out at the time that Jehu entered into Jezreel. (2 Kings ix. 30.) Now, from this account, it is easy to apprehend the beauty of that expression of the church concerning the Lord Jesus, and the extent of that indulgence he shewed her upon the occasion. "My beloved (said she) standeth behind our wall, he looketh forth at the windows, shewing himself through the lattice." (Song ii. 9.) The manner in which the church introduceth her observation, with a note of admiration, behold! speaks the high sense. She had of the condescending goodness of her Lord. There was but this one opening from the house; and such is the retired privacy of all the inhabitants, that it is only on special occasions the lattice window is made use of. But such was my Lord's grace towards me, (saith the church) that from hence, as the most open place of communication, he shewed himself to me. Though Jesus might be said to stand behind our wall; that is, perhaps, through a vail of flesh, to manifest himself to his people while on earth, and to look forth at the windows of his grace; that is, when in the ordinances of his word he doth distinguish himself to them otherwise than he doeth to the world; yet, through those lattices, he makes known what he is, and what his love to his people is, and ever will be, until the shadows flee away, and the day break of the everlasting morning shineth in upon the soul, and the sun of his redeemed ariseth no more to go down, neither the moon to withdraw his shining, but the Lord himself becometh their everlasting light, and their God their glory. (Isa. lx. 19.)

LAW

See Testimony.

LAZARUS

It is to be supposed, that the Lazarus of the New Testament, is a corresponding name to the Eleazar of the Old. The name itself is a compound of Hazar, help--and El, God. Lazar-houses and Lazarettos, seem to have taken their name from the Lazarus of the parable. (Luke xvi. 20.) Lepers, and persons under diseases of a pestilential or epidemic nature, were sent to them

LEAH

The wife of Jacob. (Gen. xxix. 23.) Her name, it should, seem, meant weary.

LEAVEN

The leaven among the Jews, became an object of much religious concern. They were cautious that no leaven should be found in their houses. (See Exod. xii. 15-19.) No doubt this had a gospel signification, and was intended to teach, that nothing would be permitted to leaven or mingle with the blood and righteousness of the Lord Jesus Christ, for acceptance before God.

LEBANON

A mountain famous in Scripture, and highly celebrated: it separates Syria from Palestine. The name in Hebrew is Leban, and signifies white,--probably so called from the everlasting snow covering the summit or it. The cedars of Lebanon, and the streams from Lebanon, are spoken of in highly figurative language, to intimate the blessings in Christ. Hence the spouse in the Canticles speaks of Jesus as "a fountain of gardens, a well of living waters, and streams from Lebanon." (Song iv. 15.) And the idea is as beautiful as the figure is just and correct: for as the cold flowing waters which descend from the mountain of Lebanon refresh the earth, and cool the hot climate, and are very copious, and run with rapidity; so the grace of God in Christ Jesus, like the water of life, runs freely, graciously, and abundantly, to make "glad the city of God." So Christ himself is said to be "as rivers of water in a dry place, and as the shadow of a great rock in a weary land." (Isa. xxxii. 2.) Hence the prophet, exclaiming against the folly of Israel's leaving the Lord, saith, "Will a man leave the snow of Lebanon which cometh from the rock of the field; or shall the cold flowing waters that come from another place be forgotten?" (Jer. xviii. 14.)

LEBBEUS

One of the apostles of Christ. (Matt. x. 3.)

LEGION

A Roman legion, of six thousand men. If the poor man possessed of a legion of devils was thus numbered, what a state to contemplate! (See Mark v. 9.) I rather think the expression is of the figurative kind, or, as the poor man himself saith, a legion meant many. Our Lord meant the expression, no doubt, exactly as it is, when he said "twelve legions of angels." (Matt. xxvi. 53.)

LEPER and LEPROSY

I do not take upon me to decide, whether the leprosy among the Jews differed from the Elephantiasis of other nations; but I venture to believe that it had somewhat of peculiarity, from the account given of it in Scripture. It was, without doubt, among the Hebrews, not only a loathsome disease in itself, but was intended to denote in the strongest characters the nature of sin both original and actual. And this, I think, is plain, from this one striking circumstance; namely that it was deemed an impious presumption of the prerogative of God, to attempt by any human means to cure it. I refer the reader to the word of God for the account of it, (Lev. xiii. and xiv.) both for the nature of the disease, and the rites and sacrifices appointed for the cleansing; all which very fully prove the sad state of the leper, shut out of all civil and religious communion, to testify, perhaps, the odious nature of sin in the sight of God, and to set forth, by the shadowy representations of washing and sacrifice, that nothing but the blood of Christ and the regenerating power of the Holy Ghost can effect the cure of the leprosy of sin. What a beautiful and endearing view have the evangelists given of the tender mercy of the Lord Jesus, manifested to that poor leper which came to Christ at the foot of the mountain. (See Matt. viii. 2, 3. Mark i. 40. Luke v. 12.) The poor man could have had no conception, that Jesus in the cure would have done what was never done before, put his hand upon him: but, as it was sweetly said of Jesus, "himself took our infirmities, and bare our sicknesses;" so Christ, as if to shew the love of his heart and sympathy to our poor nature, not only healed the leper, but put forth his hand and touched him, (Matt. viii. 17. Isa. liii. 4.) There is somewhat in such views of Christ as tends to endear him in the highest possible degree of endearedness, and which ought never to be lost sight of in the mind of his people.

LEVI

The third son of Jacob and Leah--from whence sprung the Levites. The name of Levi, it should seem to have meant, one that is tied, perhaps in reference to the office afterwards to be attached to the Levites. The personal character of Jacob's son Levi, occasioned the dying patriarch to speak with displeasure concerning him. (See Gen. xlix. 5-7.) And the prediction of this tribe being divided in Jacob, and scattered in Israel, was literally fulfilled; for we find in the settlement in Canaan, the sons of Levi had no share in the division of the land, but only certain cities among the other tribes. Yet the Lord was graciously pleased to choose this tribe for his own more immediate service, and placed this, highly honourable and distinguished mark upon it: "At that time the Lord separated the tribe of Levi, to bear the ark of the covenant of the Lord to stand before the Lord to minister unto him, and to bless in his name unto this day: wherefore Levi hath no part nor inheritance with his brethren; the Lord is his inheritance, according as the Lord thy God promised him. (Deut. x. 8, 9.)

The services of the Levites, seem to have been a constant, ministration in the temple. We have the account, Num. iii. They were subordinate to the priests, and their consecration to their offices was not with so much ceremony, (see Num. vii. 5-7.) nevertheless they were all of one tribe, (see 2 Chron. xxix. 34.) Their provision was noble. (Num. xxxv.)

I cannot close this article without desiring the reader to take notice with me of the blessing of Moses, the man of God, wherewith, amidst the blessings he pronounced in the Lord's name on the children of Israel before his death, he distinguished Levi. (See Deut. xxxiii. 8.) "And of Levi he said, let thy Thummim and thy Urim be with thy Holy One, whom thou didst prove at Massah, and with whom thou didst strive at the waters of Meribah; who said unto his father and unto his mother, I have not seen him, neither did he acknowledge his brethren, nor knew his own children; for they have observed thy word, and kept thy covenant. They shall teach Jacob thy judgments, and Israel thy law; they shall put incense before thee, and whole burnt sacrifice upon thine altar. Bless, Lord, his substance, and accept the work of his hands: smite through the loins of them that rise against him, and of them that hate him, that they rise not again."

Surely with an eye to Christ (though our Lord sprang out of Judah, and not Levi, Heb. vii. 14.) did Moses here, by the spirit of prophecy, declare, that the Urim and the Thummim, that is, lights and perfections, should be with JEHOVAH'S Holy One. The waters of Meribah was that memorable spot where the people, soon after the children of Israel came out of Egypt, did chide with Moses and Aaron for want of water. (See Exod. xvii. 1-7.) Here Moses and Aaron stemmed the torrent of the people's anger; and it should seem to have been in allusion to this, that the man of God, speaking of Levi, said, "whom thou didst prove, and didst find faithful," who did not acknowledge the feelings of nature when those calls of grace demanded faithfulness. See another instance, (Exod. xxxii. 25-28.) The other instance at Meribah, sets forth the frailty both of Moses and Aaron: (see Num. xx. 1-13.) But by taking into one view both instances at Meribah, we are certainly constrained to look farther than to the Aarons, or to all the sons of Levi, under the Old Testament dispensation, for the accomplishment of Moses's dying prediction that the Urim and Thummim of JEHOVAH might be with the Lord's Holy One; and to none can we make the smallest application, but to the Almighty Aaron of "a better covenant, established upon better promises." Levi and his sons were all types of our Lord Jesus, JEHOVAH'S Holy One. With him are hid all the treasures of wisdom and knowledge; and with him only could the Urim and Thummim be said to be, and with him to be for ever; for though the high priest wore on his breast the representations of the Urim and the Thummim, yet during the Babylonish captivity all this was done away, and never after was it restored under the second temple. Hence, therefore, in Christ alone could this be found, and him alone could Moses mean. The prophecy therefore, had a blessed fulfilment in Jesus, and in him for ever. Here, reader, is brought the pure incense, and that whole burnt sacrifice, Christ Jesus upon JEHOVAH'S altar; even Christ himself, who is both the New Testament altar of JEHOVAH, the high priest, and the sacrifice. O Lord! may we well say, in making our responses to the prayer of Moses, Bless, Lord, our Lord Jesus, the sum and substance of all salvation: accept the work of his hands the infinite merit of his whole redemption work! Let sin, Satan, death, and hell, be smitten all of them through the centre, the very loins of their rebellion, and let all that hate our Jesus flee before him! Amen.

LEVIATHAN

In the book of Job we meet with the mention of this huge creature, Job xli. Some have supposed it the whale, and others the crocodile. The word itself is probably compounded of Leviath, what is joined together---and Than, a great fish. It should seem to be a specific word, in allusion to this sea-monster, as if they said, there is the leviathan, that is, the great fish, whose parts are so closed together that nothing scarce can pierce them. The sacred writers, in more than one instance, make use of this name figuratively, to describe the devil and his ministers. Thus (Isa. xxvii. 1.) "In that day the Lord, with his sore and great and strong sword, shall punish the leviathan, the piereing serpent, even leviathan, that crooked, serpents and he shall slay the dragon that is in the sea." The great enemy of souls will be reckoned with in the great day of God, and he shall be punished in due time; and subordinately to him, all the enemies of the church of Christ, the leviathans, and dragons, and serpents which act in the devil's name, and fight in his cause, will come in also for the doom. So again the Psalmist, speaking figuratively, saith, (Ps. lxxiv. 14.) "Thou brakest the head of leviathan in pieces, and gavest him to be meat to thy people inhabiting the wilderness:" meaning, that as in the Red Sea the Lord overthrew and destroyed that type of the devil, Pharaoh, so in the after-journies of the people during their wilderness state, whenever they were put to wilderness straits, the recollection of the Lord's deliverance of them in that memorable instance, became meat for their faith to feed upon. He that had delivered them from so great a death, they were taught to believe, did and would still deliver them. It is blessed thus to feast upon past mercies; when new ones are only coming on, and not fully come. Every enemy subdued, every affliction past, then becomes sanctified, when the Holy Ghost as the Remembrancer of Christ Jesus, brings them forth again to our recollection. Oh, how many leviathans, and serpents, and scorpions, have the Lord's people, in the Lord's strength, contended with and conquered during their short pilgrimage state. Surely it may be said of the church now, as well as of the church of old, "the Lord thy God led thee through that great and terrible wilderness, wherein were fiery serpents, and scorpions and drought, where there was no water." And what was the result? "The Lord thy God brought thee forth water out of the rock of flint; he fed thee in the wilderness with manna, which thy fathers knew not, that he might humble thee, and that he might prove thee, to do thee good at thy latter end." (Deut. viii. 15, 16.)

LEVITICUS

The third book of Moses bears this name; and it appears to derive its name from the Septuagint, who called it the book of Leviticus, from containing the laws of the Levitical priesthood.

LIFE

This is one of the characters of the Lord Jesus Christ. In him, saith the apostle John, "was life, and the life was the light of men." (John i. 4.) And elsewhere Jesus saith himself, "I am the life and the light of men. I am the resurrection and the life. I am come that they might have life, and that they might have it more abundantly." It is most essential to our happiness, that we should have clear conceptions of this most blessed truth, so as to see and know from whence and in whom all the springs of life are. It is not, in my view of things, sufficient to understand that Christ gives life to his people, but that he is himself the life of his people. He saith himself, "Because I live, ye shall live also." So that Jesus is, to the soul of his redeemed, the very life of the soul, as our soul is the life of the body. When the soul departs from the body, the body dies; and could it be supposed that Christ was to depart from the souls of his redeemed, the soul would die also. But this is impossible; for it is said, that he hath quickened them, who were by nature dead in trespasses and sins. And the apostle to the church of the Colossians saith, "Your life is hid with Christ in God; so that when Christ, who is your life, shall appear, then shall ye also appear with him in glory." What a world of blessedness there is in this one consideration of the Lord Jesus as the life of his people! Precious Lord, I would say, thou art indeed both the life and the light of men! Thou art in thyself the whole of their spiritual and eternal life. Keep alive, I beseech thee, the renewed life thou hast given me in thyself; and cause me to enter into the full apprehension and enjoyment of that most glorious proclamation of thine in which thou hast, said, "I am the resurrection and the life; he that believeth in me, though he were deadly, yet shall he live, and he that liveth and believeth in, me shall never die."

LIGHT

This is another of the characters of the Lord Jesus Christ; for as Jesus is the life, so is he the light of men. Coming up from all eternity in the councils of peace, for the salvation of his people, he is the everlasting light and glory of his people. He it is that first caused the light to shine out of darkness in the original creation of nature. In like manner, he is the first to cause light to shine out of darkness in the new creation, when the day spring from on high first shines in upon the soul, to give the light of the knowledge of the glory of God in the face of Jesus Christ. (2 Cor. iv. 6.) Oh! rise, thou Son of righteousness, on the souls of thy redeemed with healing in thy wings that they may go forth and grow up as calves of the stall, (Mal. iv. 2. Luke ii. 32. Ps. iv. 6. John viii. 12, &c.)

LILY and LILY OF THE VALLIES

Song ii. 1-2.) Those are fragrant flowers, well known by name in this our climate; but there is reason to suppose, that what are distinguished by those names in Scripture very far excel in beauty, fragrancy, and medicinal use, the lilies of those colder countries like ours. However, even with all those disadvantages, the lily, and the lily of the valley with which we are acquainted, may merit a place in our Concordance, in that Christ and his church are spoken of under the similitude. The original name in

LILY and LILY OF THE VALLIES - LILY and LILY OF THE VALLIES

the Jewish Scriptures, is Susan or Schuschan. Some have said, that this is the Persian lily, or the crown imperial; but it is evident, that what the church saith of Christ, Song v. 13. (that his lips are like lilies,) must prove, that this was a red flower. But be this as it may, one thing I beg to observe, that all historians agree in this, that this lily was common in Judea, and grew in fields. Hence Jesus saith, (Matt. vi. 28-29.) "Consider the lilies of the field how they grow; they toil not, neither do the spin; and yet I say unto you, that even Solomon in all his glory was not arrayed like one of these."

There is a great beauty in the similitude of this flower to Jesus. Jesus is the flower of the field; Jesus is also imperial; Jesus is open to the traveller by the way. And as the flower of the field is not of man's planting, neither cultivating, so this plant of renown is wholly raised up by the Lord JEHOVAH himself. (See Ezek. xxxiv. 29.) And if we consider the lily of the vallies also, (as Jesus speaks of himself, Song ii. 1.) There is no less the same striking resemblance in every view. Nothing surely could be more suited, to denote the unequalled humility of the Son of God, than the figure of the lily, which loves the retired, low, and obscure spot of the valley. It was in the valley of this our lower world the Son of God came, when he came "to seek and save that which was lost." And when we consider the modesty, the whiteness, the fragrancy, the fruitfulness, in short, the whole loveliness of this beautiful flower, what can more pointedly set forth the Lord Jesus, under all these endearednesses of character, than the lily of the vallies? Oh, thou holy, harmless, undefiled Lamb of God, without blemish, and without spot!

But we must not stop here. It is a sweet and interesting part of this subject to consider, that while Jesus compares himself to the lily of the vallies, so doth he no less compare his church to the same lovely flower. "As the lily among thorns, saith Jesus, so is my love among the daughters."

There is this difference indeed between the comparison; for while Jesus saith, that he is the lily of the vallies, he only saith of his church, that she is as the lily. And the reason is very plain: what Jesus is, he is in himself, underived, and of himself; whereas, what the church is, she is wholly in him, and from him. But while this distinction is never to be lost sight of, but thankfully preserved in the recollection, it is very blessed to see, that from our union with him, and interest in him, such as Jesus is so are we in this world. Is Christ the lily of the vallies? so, saith Jesus, is my love among the daughters. Is Jesus JEHOVAH our righteousness? then shall his spouse the church be called by the same name. (Jer. xxiii. 6. and xxxiii. 16.) Is Jesus fair and lovely, sweet and fragrant as the lily of the vallies? so shall the church be in his sight, from the comeliness that he hath put upon her, (Ezek. xvi. 14.) In a word, all that Jesus is as the glorious Head of his body the church, such shall be his body, glorious in his glory, and lovely in his loveliness, because in him, and from him all is derived, for "we are members of his body, of his flesh, and of his bones." There is one thought more the subject suggests concerning the church, and that is, that as a lily the church is said to be among thorns; meaning, that in this world Jesus's church is in a wilderness. Corruptions within, and persecutions without, the cares of the world, and the deceitfulness of the heart, the lusts of the flesh, and the pride of life, the reproaches of some, and the heresies of others,

These make the situations of the godly but too strikingly resembled by the lily in the midst of thorns. For, as the prophet speaks, "the good man is perished out of the earth, and there is none upright among men; the best of them is a brier, the most upright is sharper than a thorn hedge." (Micah. vii. 2.4.) How truly blessed is it thus to prove the doctrine of Christ by testimony, and yet more when a child of

God discovers, through the Holy Ghost, his own personal interest in it.

LINEN

The linen of the Hebrews seems to have been originally made from flax, called by them Phistah. (Exod. ix. 31.) And it should seem also, that they had another sort of a kind of cotton, which they called Schesch. We meet with precepts in the Old Testament Scripture respecting apparel, that, taken in the literal sense, do not appear altogether accountable. That of restoring the poor man's pledge of raiment before the sun set, is plain enough, because the poor man might want it for covering. (See Exod. xxii. 26, 27.) And perhaps of that precept, that the "woman should not wear the dress pertaining to a man, neither the man put on the woman's garment;'" (see Deut. xxii. 5.) the reason doth not seem difficult to discover, For in this change of garments, in the first face of it, there is implied somewhat of deception; and when we consider the retirement of woman in those eastern nations, no man ever. Presuming to appear in the apartments of the women, there seems an evident propriety in this prohibition, lest men, under the garb of a woman's dress, might get in unperceived among them. But when a law of this kind is found, "thou shalt not let a garment mingled of linen and woollen come upon thee." (Lev. xix. 19.) there is somewhat certainly mysterious in this, if considered only with an eye to the mere wearing of apparel. We might be prompted humbly to ask, why is it that the Lord hath so prohibited the wearing of linen and woollen together? Can it be an object of moment in itself? Since the fall our poor sinful bodies requires: covering, which in innocency, it should seem, was unnecessary either for warmth or decency; and as the fleecy garment is for warmth, and, the linen for cleanliness can it be offensive to our God, that his poor creatures should use both? Nay, it is, well known that we do use both, and do not consider it as any breach of this command. Have we not reason therefore to believe, that somewhat of an higher nature is implied than the mere dress of the body? May it not be intended as figurative respecting the covering, of the soul? Certain it is, that under the law almost every thing became a shadowy representation of the gospel; and not only sacrifices and washings, but numberless other appointments preached the Lord Jesus Christ. Under this view it hath been thought by some, that this precept of not mingling linen and woollen for covering, the body represented the still higher concern of not mingling the covering, for the soul, but that one garment, and one only, and that one found in Christ's perfect robe of righteousness, was the great object referred to: and if so, the precept is beautiful and interesting. The fine linen, we are told in Scripture (see Rev. xix. 8.) "is the righteousness of the saints;" and this righteousness, the prophet saith, (Isa. liv. 17.) is of the Lord. Hence, therefore, if the conjecture be well founded, we not only behold a blessed appointment in the thing itself, but it may serve moreover to teach the church in what an exalted point of view the Lord considered, the righteousness of his dear Son as the alone covering of his people, since he caused it thus to be preached in type and figure so many ages before the Lord's coming. See the church's song of joy in the conscious covering of her Lord. (Isa. lxi. 10.)

LINUS

One of Paul's companions. (2 Tim. iv. 21.)

LION

We meet with many passages in Scripture concerning the lion. This beast was very common in Palestine, and hence, in the sacred writings, frequent allusion is made to the lion by way of similitude and figure. It would have been unnecessary, in a work of this kind, to have noticed the lion, had it not been that the Lord Jesus Christ is spoken of under this title, as "the Lion of the tribe of Judah." The comparative view of Gen. xlix. 9. with Rev. v. 5. will serve to explain. The dying patriarch blessing the tribe of Judah, and holding forth his prophetic sayings with an eye to Christ, describes our glorious Judah, or Jehudah, under this strong figure--his hand was to be "in the neck of his enemies;" meaning that he would totally destroy them from the head to the feet. And all his father's children were "to bow down before him." It is the distinguishing feature of Jesus, that while bringing hell and all his foes under his feet, his redeemed bend in holy adoration, and love, and praise before him. "He is the praise of all his saints." (Ps. cxlvii. 14.) There is a great beauty in the figures Jacob makes use of concerning Christ. Not content with simply speaking of him as a lion, which includes every thing in the similitude, that is royal, courageous, terrible, and full of dignity and majesty, Jacob particularizes the figure under the several characters of the lion, and the lion's whelp, and the old lion. "Judah (said he) is a lion's whelp; from the prey, my son, thou art gone up; he stooped down, he couched as a lion, and as an old lion, who shall rouse, him up?" It is said of the lion, that both in his rampant state, when couching, he is equally formidable; when seizing his prey, or when consuming it, none dare to follow or oppose.

We should not have understood the beauty of those similitudes in reference to Christ, had not the sacred writers been so very particular: But it is remarkable, how many and various the names the Hebrews adopted to describe the different characters of the lion by. We find, as here by Jacob, they had names for the lion's whelp, and the young lion, and the old, and the lion from "the swellings of Jordan," (Jer. 1:44.) and the lion like men of Moab. (2 Sam. xxiii. 20.) Frequent expressions we find of the kind by say of allusion in the Scriptures. What a sweet consoling thought to the believer travelling through this waste and howling wilderness, that our Jesus is the sovereign of all, and the ruler over all. "The Lion of the tribe of Judah" is gone up from the prey, and he alone hath power to kill and to save.

The Scriptures speak of the old serpent the devil under this character, as "a roaring lion going about seeking whom he may devour." (1 Pet. v. 8.) But while we behold the almighty Lord Jesus in his victories having subdued our foe, we have nothing to fear, but to resist him stedfast in the faith, and sure we are "to overcome by the blood of the Lamb," as all have done before. (See Rev. xii. 10, 11.)

If I might be permitted under this article to offer one observation more, it should be to say, what a mercy it is for us that this apostate Spirit which scours through the earth, and the Prince of the power of the air, and now worketh, as we are told he doth, in the children of disobedience, is invisible. The sight of such an enemy would freeze our very nature. The common lions and beasts of the forest, would shrink with terror from the view. How happy ought the people of God to consider themselves, that though so near them in his devilish devices, yet he dare not become visible; and though he is so busy in the cruelties of his temptations, yet his power is limited. When I hear or see some awful effects of his devices, on the minds of my fellow creatures and fellow sinners; oh! how powerfully doth it teach me the blessed consequences of distinguishing grace! Doth he work his devilish purposes on others, and am I preserved from his snare? Doth he accomplish their destruction, and do I escape? Reader! think of this precious subject! How doth it exalt my Lord in the consciousness of preserving grace! And how doth it tend to humble my soul!'

LIP and LIPS

The fruit of the lips is sometimes spoken of in Scripture, for the whole of the life and conversation. Thus JEHOVAH takes to himself the sovereignty of this work, when he saith, (Isa. lvii. 19.) "I create the fruit of the lips." Hence the church is represented as speaking the effusions of the heart, when she saith; "So will we render thee the claves of our lips." (Hos. xiv. 2.) And hence, when commending the beauties of Jesus, she saith; "his lips are like lilies, dropping sweet smelling myrrh:" (Song v. 13.) meaning, that so sweet and fragrant are Christ's words, his gospel of salvation, and his tokens of grace, so refreshing to the soul of a poor sinner conscious of the want of it; that as lilies, they charm and afford a sweet smelling savour, by which all the spiritual senses are ravished and made glad.

LOAMMI
See Ammi.

LOCUSTS

The Scripture account of the locusts is to be closely attended to, in order to aright apprehension. The locusts of Egypt, it is more than probable, differed widely from the locusts which John the Baptist ate for food in the wilderness. The former appear to have been instruments of God for man's punishment. The latter, the gracious gift of God for man's food. Joel, the prophet, speaks of the same destructive creature, as the Lord's army. It should seem to have been an innumerable host of little insects, so little that a man might tread at one time many of them under his feet; but yet from the vast swarms, the destruction of thousands brought no relief, for the millions remaining were enough for the accomplishment of ruin wherever they came. What a solemn lesson this taught, when a creature so contemptible had power from the Lord to humble the haughtiness of man! If the reader will compare what Joel hath said chap. i. 6.7. and ii. 3-11. with Rev. ix. 1-12, he will find large scope for meditation. Whether the latter is figurative of some great and awful events yet remaining to be fulfilled in the earth; or whether the locusts, described by the beloved apostle John in this chapter, be altogether different from the locusts of Egypt, or those mentioned by the prophet Joel, I stay not to enquire. It will be sufficient for the great purposes of improvement from such Scripture, to consider how terrible the Lord's judgments are, who can, from causes so apparently trifling and insignificant, throw down the props of all human comforts. The reflection of the prophet on the subject is uncommonly striking and impressive. "Therefore also now saith the Lord, Turn ye even to me with all your heart, and with fasting, and with weeping, and with mourning: and rend your heart, and not your garments, and turn unto the Lord your God: for he is gracious and merciful; slow to anger, and of great kindness, and repenteth him of the evil. Who knoweth, if he will return and repent, and leave a blessing behind him, even a meat offering, and a drink offering, unto the Lord your God!" (Joel ii. 12-14.)

I cannot dismiss this article, without making a farther observation on the different relations of the sacred writers on the subject of locusts; that they should seem to justify the opinion, that they differed very widely from each other. The locusts of Egypt, formidable as they were, and so numerous as to cover the face of the whole earth, and to darken the land, it should seem, must have been of the caterpillar kind; for their destruction, we are told, was directed to the herbs and trees, and every thing green in the land. (See Exod. x. 14, 15.) Such, in like manner, were the locusts which Joel describes, in their destruction of food; but from certain peculiarities with which he describes them also, it should seem that they very probably were a species of much larger kind than the locusts of Egypt. Indeed, in relation to the locusts of Egypt, we are told, that "before them there were no such locusts as they, neither after them should be such." (Exod. x. 14.) The locusts, described by Joel, are said to be as "the appearance of horses, and as horsemen, shall they run. Like the noise of Chariots, on tops of mountains; like the noise of a flame of fire that devoureth the stubble." They are said, moreover, to march in such a regular way, that they shall not break their ranks, nor thrust one another in their path. Whereas the multitude of the smaller species of insects are in clusters, for the most part, and their movements in the most irregular manner. And if we turn to the account in the Book of the Revelations, we are informed of another kind of locusts, apparently still more formidable. These are said to be of the scorpion kind. Their shapes are said to be like unto horses prepared for battle. In the Book of the Proverbs, chap. xxx. 27, the locusts are said to have no king. But the locusts John describes, are said to have a king over them, which is "the angel of the bottomless pit." (Rev. ix. 11) So that upon the whole, it should seem the Scripture relates, under the general name of locusts, different species of them, but all ministers and instruments of the Lord for destruction; and most awful each and all of them are. Profane writers describe the locusts of Africa and some parts of Asia, as sometimes swarming to such a degree, as to darken the face of the sun. The locusts of Palestine certainly differed from those, in that they were not unfrequently used for food. And such it was, most probably, John the Baptist made his sustenance, with the wild honey of the desert. (Matt. iii. 4.)

LORD

This glorious name is peculiarly and properly the distinguishing name of JEHOVAH, and ought to have been so hallowed and sacred, as never upon any occasion whatever to have been applied to any other, For we read that JEHOVAH is very jealous of His name, and will not allow the very mention of it, unless in a way of reverence to himself, without attaching guilt to the person that doth it. Thus we read, "Thou shalt riot take the name of the Lord thy God in vain: for the Lord will not hold him guiltless that taketh his name in vain." (Exod. xx. 7.) So again (Isa. xlii. 8.) "I am the Lord; that is my name, and my glory will I not give to another, neither my praise to graven images." With what reverence and sanctity, therefore, ought the glorious name of JEHOVAH, Lord, to be held? Indeed, though among men, master and lord are sometimes used from servants to their superiors, yet the incommunicable name of JEHOVAH, is never used in this way by any. It is impossible to preserve it too sacred.

JEHOVAH, or Lord, is equally adapted and made use of in common to teach us all the persons of the GODHEAD, Father, Son, and Holy Ghost. We find, it, every part of the word of God, JEHOVAH the Father, so called, (see Zech. ii. 10.) where JEHOVAH the Father is represented as sending JEHOVAH the Son. So again we find JEHOVAH the Father speaking to JEHOVAH the Son, (Ps. cx. 1. Isa. xlii. 5-8.) and numberless other instances occur throughout the Bible. In like manner, God the Son is called by this glorious name, (Jer. xxiii. 6.) with express designation of character, and this also by JEHOVAH the Father, And throughout both Testaments of Scripture, God the Son possesseth in common with the Father and the Holy Ghost, the distinguishing name of Lord. And no less God the Holy Ghost, (Num. vi. 24-26.) where each glorious person is severally and distinctly called JEHOVAH. (2 Cor. iii. 17. 1 John v. 7.) See God JEHOVAH.

LO RUHAMAH

See Ammi.

LOT

Son of Haran, and nephew to Abraham. His name signifies wrapped up, or hidden. His history we have interspersed with that of Abraham, from Gen. xi. 27. to xix. 36.

LOTS

To cast lots.--A common practice among the Hebrews: they called it Goral. Nay, we find the Lord himself appointing the casting lots for the scape goat, Lev. xvi. 8. What was called the feast of Put, or Purim, was founded upon the same custom. The word Pur, or Phur, is not Hebrew, but Persian, taken from the Persians, among whom at that time the children of Israel were, and under their government. The feast of Pur, in honour of the destruction of Haman the Aggagite, was so great a festival among the Jews, that even to this day it hath been handed down, and is kept. And the reason assigned wherefore they called this festival Pur, or Purim, casting lots, was, because when Haman planned the destruction of the Jews, he had lots cast before him from day to day. (See Esther iii. 7. to the end.) The Jews, therefore, when through God's mercy they had caused the ruin of Haman, appointed this feast on the same month in every year, and called it Pur. (See Esther ix. 18. to the end.)

LUCIFER

We meet with this name Isa. xiv. 12. Various have been the opinions of commentators, who is meant by it. Some have supposed it refered to the morning star, because to the name Lucifer is added "son of the morning;" and in confirmation they refer to that passage, (Job xxxviii. 7.) where at the creation, the morning stars are said "to have sung together, and all the sons of God shouted for joy." But it should seem, that this is a total perversion of the passage, for Lucifer is said to be fallen; and moreover, Jesus is, in a special and personal manner, called "the morning star." (Rev. xxii. 16.)

Other commentators, with much greater probability of truth, have supposed, that by Lucifer is meant the Devil, who once was among the bright ornaments of heaven, but by apostacy is fallen; and this agrees with the whole context. Hell from beneath is said to have moved; at his coming. (Isa. xiv 9.) And agreeably to this opinion) we find that the general name of Lucifer hath been assigned to the devil in all the christian church,

But there are others, who in their comments on this part of Isaiah's prophecy, accept the whole passage as referring literally to the king of Babylon, with which the subject opens at the fourth verse. If read in this light, the whole passage is solemn, magnificent; and striking. The greatness and power of the king of Babylon is described in very lofty characters: his city is called the golden city. He is said to have made the earth to tremble, and to have shaken kingdoms. The prophet next describes his tyranny, despotism, and cruelty. He smote the people in wrath, and that not occasionally, but continually; and so irresistible was his power, that none could hinder. At length he falls. The earth gains instant rest, and by a beautiful figure of rhetoric, is said to break forth into singing. Then comes in the awful account of the succeeding state to the present life. "Hell from beneath is moved at his coming." The territories of the damned are represented as opening to receive a more than ordinary guest, now come to take up his eternal dwelling there; and the dead, and the chief ones of the earth, who when alive trembled at his power, now all brought together into one common level of horror and misery, are represented as insulting over his calamity. "Art thou also become weak as we? art thou become like unto us? Thy pomp is brought down to the grave, and the noise of thy viols: the worm is spread under thee, and the worms cover thee. How art thou fallen from heaven, O Lucifer, son of the morning!"

Perhaps there never was a finer piece of imagery in any description ever given. The movement of hell to meet this stranger, this great one, is beyond all conception sublime, as if those infernal regions of horror felt convulsed at his approach, and thus testified their welcome. And the taunting compliments from the kings and great men of the earth, whom the monarch of Babylon had hastened and sent there before their time, is wonderfully conceived, to shew what deep and bitter malignity the conversation of hell is made up of, to aggravate the torments of the damned, and to fill up the full-heaped measure of corrosive and everlasting misery. But when the reader hath done with his observation on this awful prospect, I beg yet more earnestly to call his attention to another, by way of finishing the subject, which comes home to every breast, or ought at least so to do, and which is not confined to person or character, but universally concerns all mankind.

Whether this Lucifer, son of the morning, be or be not either of the characters before mentioned, yet for every character and for every person, the entrance into the world of spirits is opened at death. Whether, hell from beneath is moved at the unawakened sinner's coming, or heaven from above opens her golden gates to receive the redeemed regenerated saint in Jesus, this Scripture, with others to the same amount, plainly testify that that thinking faculty, that immortal incorporeal part, which at death separates from the body, hastens into the world of spirits like its own, and exists in a state perfectly distinct from and unconnected with the body, and will so continue until the general resurrection. What a solemn thought, if properly attended to, and yet increasingly more solemn to every inhabitant of the earth when considered also, that the time of this separation may be the next moment for ought we know, when the disembodied soul shall receive the summons for departure.

And there is another thought connected with it, which gives solemnity to the former, and which this Scripture tends to prove, namely, that in that world of spirits they think and speak, have conversation and fellowship, with each other, as familiarly as we have with each other that are yet in the body. How remote from hence is not said. It may be immensely distant; it may be very near. One thing is certain, as this Scripture shews, namely, that they are intimately acquainted with the past circumstances of their own lives, and the lives of others with whom they dwelt. And hence, though they cease for ever from us, and we from them, in respect to farther communion; though as the Scripture saith, "Abraham be ignorant of us, and Israel acknowledge us not," (Isa. lxiii. 16.) yet the existence is made up of identity, consciousness, and unceasing thinking, and acting, and the most lively perception. Hence, in either state, and in both states, the happiness of the blessed, and the misery of the damned, infinitely surpasseth the utmost conception our present faculties can form. Oh, the multitude, the unnumbered, unknown, unanswerable arguments which the Scriptures hold forth "to seek the things which make for our everlasting peace, and to flee from the wrath to come."

LUCIUS

One of the prophets of the Christian church at Antioch. (See Acts xiii. 1.) His name signifies, light. There is another of this name, styled Paul's kinsman. (See Rom. xvi. 21.)

LUHITH

A city of Moab. (Isa. xv. 5.) The name signifies, a table, or floor.

LUKE

The beloved physician, whose praise is in the gospel. His name is borrowed from a Latin word signifying light. He was Paul's companion in several journies, as appears from Col. iv. 14. 2 Tim. iv. 11. Phil. xxiii. 24. The church is highly indebted to this man, under the Holy Ghost, for the blessed gospel which bears his name, and the Acts of the Apostles. (See, in confirmation, Acts

i. 1.)

LUNATIC

It may not be improper, in a work of this kind, to take notice of the lunacies of Scripture, because, in all probability, they differed from the common supposed lunacy, or moon-sick-disease, common in life. The lunatics we read of in the gospel, certainly were those which were possessed by the evil spirit. And in the days of our Lord, those maladies were more than ordinarily common; for as the Son of God was manifested, that he might destroy the works of the devil, so the possession by the evil spirit was then permitted, for the purpose of the display of Christ's power. No doubt, the mystery in relation to spiritual mercies in Christ had much signification, teaching us that Jesus alone had power for the accomplishment of so much good. And one feature in respect to the disease of lunacy was very prominent and striking, namely, that the poor creature, under possession of Satan had no desire in himself for a cure. Such became a lively emblem of every sinner; for the language of every man by nature is the same as we find the lunatic used: "What have we to do with thee, Jesus, thou Son of God? I beseech thee torment me not." (Mark v. 7.) What a sweet and endearing view it gives of Christ! Jesus is the first in every act of mercy: we cannot make our application to Jesus, however early, before that Jesus hath first applied to us by his blessed Spirit, Did the Lord withhold his blessings till we asked them, or until we had prepared ourselves for them, they would never be received at all. The lunacy in this sense, like all other diseases of our fallen state, is sough after by Jesus to heal. "Himself bare our sins, and carried our sorrows."

LUST

Graves of lust. See Kibroth Hattaavah.

LUZ

The original spot called afterwards "Bethel, the house of God." (Gen. xxviii. 19.) Luz seems to have meant separation.

LIBYA

A province in Egypt: (see Acts ii. 10.) so called from Libin, the heart of the sea.

LYCAONIA

So called from the Greek, meaning a she wolf Here Paul preached. (See Acts xiv. 6-10.)

LYCIA

A province of Asia Minor. Paul landed here in his way to Rome. (Acts xxvii. 5.)

LYDDA

Here Peter came and healed Æneas. (Acts ix. 33, 34.)

LYDIA

A woman of Thyatira, for whose conversion Paul was called by a vision to preach at Philippi. (See Acts xvi. 14-40.) Her name, it should seem, was taken from Ludim, births.

LYSANIAS

Tetrarch of Abilene. (Luke iii. 1.) The name is formed from the Greek, signifying to destroy.

LYSTRA

The birth place of Timothy. Here Paul and Barnabas preached, and wrought a miracle on a man lame from his birth. We have the history, Acts xiv. 6, &c.

M

MAACHA or MAACAH
A province of Syria, so called from Maacah, pressure. (See 2 Sam. x. 26.) There are several persons called by this name in Scripture. (See Gen. xii. 24. 2 Sam. ii. 3. 1 Kings xv. 2. 1 Chron. ii. 48, &c.)

MAASEIAH
There are several of this name in Scripture. (1 Chron. xv. 18. 2 Chron. xxviii. 7.) The signification, it should seem, is the hope of the Lord; from Chasah, hope, and Jab, Lord.

MACEDONIA
A kindom of Greece. (See Acts xvi. 9.)

MACHBANIA
A man of valour in David's army, 1 Chron. xii. 13. The word is compounded of Machae, poverty--and Ben, a son; and the pronoun I renders it, my son.

MACHIR
The son of Manasseh, Gen. i. 23. The name signifies, he that sells. There was another of the same name, 2 Sam. ix. 5.

MACHPELAH
The cave that Abraham bought for a burying place, Gen. xxiii. 9. The word means double. See Burial.

MAGDALENE
See Mary Magdalene.

MAGICIANS
In Scripture language, the word means a pretender to curious arts. Such as have familiar spirits and wizards. Such were the magicians in the court of Pharaoh, Exod. vii. 11, &c. Balaam, the son of Bozor, was of the same class. (Numb. xxii. 5, &c. Dan. i. 20.) See Balaam.

MAGOG
See Gog.

MAHALALEEL
Son of Cainan, in the line of Seth, the chosen seed, Gen. v. 15. The word means, he that praises God. The word is a compound, from Hillel, to praise--and El, God.

MAHALATH
The title of the liii. and lxxxviii. Psalms. The design is wholly conjectural, what the meaning of the phrase is. If the word be derived, as some have said, from Machol, it hath respect to singing. Some derive it from Chalah, signifying infirmity. See Musician.

MAHANAIM
It should seem to be a place of some importance when the Israelites were in possession of Canaan, for lsh-Bosheth, Saul's *son,* made it the metropolis of his kingdom, (see Sam. ii. 8, 9.) Here David retreated from the rebellion of Absalom, (2 Sam. xvii. 24.) Jacob gave the name to this spot, from the angels he met there. (See Gen. xxii. 2.) The margin of the Bible renders it, two hosts or camps.

MAHER-SHALAL-HASH-BAZ
In the margin of some of our Bibles, the translators have given the English of this name, as it is of several words, and they render it, making speed to the spoil; or he hasteneth to the prey.

And when we consider that the prophet was commanded to mark the roll of the prophecy then delivered by this name, and also called the child he had by the prophetess by the same name, no doubt the matter became very significant.

I would only detain the reader for one short observation upon it, just to remark, how very earnest the Lord's people were to carry, in the names of their children, continual records of the Lord's providences and dispensation. The prophet's son never heard himself called by this name, but it served to remind every faithful Israelite that heard it, of the Lord's hastening his purposes of redemption. And though the captivity of Babylon lay between, yet the glorious redemption from sin, death, hell, and the grave, by the Lord Jesus Christ, was seen beyond it. Hence faithful men were taken by the prophet to witness the record. (See Isa. viii. 1.4. Ps. lxxvi. 4.)

MAHLON

One of the sons of Elimelech, Ruth i. 2. His name is derived from Mahol, infirmity. Perhaps the father's name, and the whole family were figurative. In the history of this house, we read that in the days when the Judges ruled, there was a famine in the land. The Book of the Judges, at the close, saith, that in those days, "there was no king in Israel, every man did that which was right in his own eyes." (Judg. xxi. 25.) And this we may be sure, was bad enough. In such seasons there is always a famine, not perhaps of bread and water, but a famine to the soul in not hearing the word of the Lord. (Amos viii. 11.) In this state this house in Israel left Bethlehem-Judah, the land of bread, and the bread of JEHUDAH, (for so Bethlehem-Judah means) and went to sojourn in Moab. In other words, left the Lord to seek the world in Moab. To this history correspond the names. Elimelech signifies, my God, a king. Naomi, my pleasant one; now called Marah, bitterness; and Mahlon and Chillon, sickness and consumption.

MAKAZ

A city of Dan. (1 Kings iv. 9.) Some have thought, that it was the same as Makteosh, which Samson called Enak kore, the jaw tooth; from the supply of water the Lord gave him for his thirst, from the jaw bone of the ass. (see Judg. xv. 15 -19.)

MAKKEDAH

A place rendered memorable by Joshua's victory over it. (See Josh. x. 29.) The word means adoration.

MAKER

One of the glorious characters of JEHOVAH. Hence, in reference to this perfection, the Psalmist invites the whole creation of God to "worship and bow down and kneel, before the Lord our Maker." (Ps. xcv. 6.) So again the prophet Isaiah, (chap. lii. 12, 13.) "Who art thou that thou shouldest be afraid of a man that shall die and of the son of man which shall be made as grass; and forgettest the Lord thy Maker, that hath stretched forth the heavens, and laid the foundations of the earth!" It is not a little interesting, but highly important to be kept in view, that the act itself is connected with the glorious and fearful name of JEHOVAH-ALEHIM, (see Deut. xxviii. 58.) to intimate the plurality of persons in the GODHEAD. As for example, (Gen. i. 26.) it is there expressed; "And God said, Let us make man after our image, after our likeness." And accordingly in the following verse it is said, "So God created man in his own image." And elsewhere, the church is called upon to remember the Lord under this threefold character of persons in the plural of the word. Remember thy Creators. (Eccles. xii. 1.) So again in Job, (chap. xxxv. 10.) the word is plural, where is God my Makers? And yet that the church might never lose sight of the unity of the divine Essence, while thus believing in the existence of a threefold character of person in the GODHEAD, the Lord, by Moses, delivered this glorious fundamental truth in the plainest and strongest terms; "Hear, O Israel, the Lord our God is one Lord!" (Deut. vi. 4.) Oh! that these sacred, hallowed truths, were both duly and reverently considered and pondered over, agreeably to their immense sublimity, in these days of Arian and Socinian blasphemy!

MALACHI

The last of the prophet, in closing the sacred canon of the Old Testament Scripture. So little is known of this man, either of his person or connections, and tribe, or family, that some have doubted whether his name means any more than what the word itself expresses, my angel or messenger, from Malach, angel, or messenger. The point cannot be determined, for it is well known, that the Lord Jesus Christ himself, as well as his messenger, is spoken of by this same word in the third chapter and first verse. This is striking, and highly proper to be regarded. The name of the person writing is called Malachi; in the first verse of the first chapter, John the Baptist is called my messenger by the same word Malachi, in the first part of the third chapter. And Christ is called the messenger of the covenant, by the same word Malachi, in the middle part of the same verse of the same chapter. So that Malach, a messenger or angel, is the common term made use of in reference to all under this character. And such views of the name tend, in my humble opinion, to confirm what I have before remarked in the former part of this Concordance, under the word Archangel, (which see) that Christ, the glorious angel of the covenant, is the only archangel of Scripture. For to admit the supposition of any other as archangel, while Christ is expressly called the Angel of the covenant, must imply some inferiority in Christ: a thing impossible. And as we well know that Jesus Christ is the all in all of the covenant, both the angel or messenger of it; the fulfiller of it; the sum and substance of it; the administrator of it; in all present and everlasting concerns; we do no violence to the expression, when we express Christ's personal offices in the great work of redemption, by all and every term of character that can tend to bring home the Lord Jesus to our affections, in the most endeared and endearing manner. See Archangel.

It may not be improper to observe respecting Malachi, the prophet, that his services were exercised about three hundred and fifty years before the coming of the Lord Jesus Christ. And with this man's ministry, the Holy Ghost closeth the sacred volume of the Old Testament Scripture.

MALCHIAH

We meet with many of this name in Scripture. There was a Malchiah chief of a family in Israel. (1 Chron. xxiv. 9.) See also concerning others of this name 1 Chron. vi. 40. ix. 12. Ezra x. 25. Neh. iii. 11; xiv. 31. And the father of Pashur was a Malchiah; as he was also the worthless character whose name is rendered memorable, in infamy, for his cruelty to God's prophet. (See Jer. xxi. 1. and xxxviii. 6. &c.) The name but ill corresponded with the actions of those men. Malchiah is a compound of Melek, a king; and Jah, the Lord; therefore Malchiah means, "the Lord rules, or the Lord is king."

MALCHIEL

The son of Beriah. (Num. xxvi. 45.) God is my king. I cannot forbear remarking, that how ill soever some, yea, many of the Hebrews answered to their names, yet it was much to the honour of their fathers, to remind themselves and their children by those names, of the Lord God of Israel.

MALCHISUA

A son of Saul, who was slain with his father and brothers at mount Gilboa. (See 1 Sam. xxxi. 2.) compounded of Melek, king--and Jushah, Saviour.

MALCOM or MILCOM

One of the dunghill gods of the Ammonites. (1 Kings xi. 33.) See Abomination.

MALLCHUS

The servants, of the high priest, rendered memorable by the apostle Peter cutting off his ear in his zeal for Christ, and Jesus with his unequalled tenderness healing it; (see

John xviii. 10. with Luke xxii. 50, 51.) The name is derived from Melek.

MALEFACTOR

We meet with this word but upon one occasion in the Bible, namely, at the crucifixion of Christ, (Luke xxiii. 32.) and, therefore, for want of a stop at the word preceding it, we make a wrong application of it, and destroy the sense of the passage. The evangelist saith, "and there were two other malefactors led with him, (that is, the Lord Jesus) to be put to death." If we put a stop at the end of the word other, we express the true sense of the passage, and are in exact correspondence to the pure word of God. And there were two other-- which were malefactors. But without this detachment of the passage, we include him as a third, "who did no sin, neither was guile found in his mouth." Jesus indeed became sin and a curse for us, but when he did it, he was in the same moment "holy, harmless, undefiled, separate from sinners, and made higher than the heavens." (Heb. vii. 26.)

MALTA or MELITA

An island in the Mediterranean sea, rendered memorable in Scripture from Paul's landing there, (Acts xxviii. 1, &c.) so called from Mai, honey.

MAMMON

We meet with this word two or three times in the gospel, as used by our Lord Jesus Christ in a figurative manner. Jesus contrasts mammon to God. "Ye cannot serve God and mammon." (Matt. vi. 24,) "Make to yourselves friends of the mammon of unrighteousness." (Luke xvi. 9.) It is a Syriac word, and means, perhaps, generally speaking, not gain or riches only, but whatever is in opposition to the Lord. Every corruption of our nature may be called the mammon of unrighteousness, and as such is set forth by it as hostile to a state of grace.

MAMRE

The hallowed spot where the Lord appeared unto Abraham. (Gen. xviii. 1.) It is derived from Marah, bitter.

MANAEN

He was one of those with Barnabas and Saul at Antioch, when the Holy Ghost sent those servants out to the work of the ministry. (See Acts xiii. 1.)

MANASSEH

The eldest son of Joseph. (Gen. xli. 51.) His name was given him by his father, because, he said, God had made him forget all his toil, and all his father's house. The word in the margin of the Bible is forgetting, from Nahash, to forget. There was another Manasseh, son of Hezekiah, whose history we have, 2 Kings xx. xxi.

MANDRAKES

(Song vii. 13.) The original name is Dudaim, and is only mentioned in the instance of Reuben finding them in the field, and bringing them to his mother, (See Gen. xxx. 14-18.) and in this place of the Canticles. There doth not seem to be any determined fruit meant by those mandrakes; and some have concluded, that they were flowers, such as the jessamine or violet; and the language of the church in saying, that they gave a smell, seems to favour this opinion. Some authors, however, have described peculiar qualities to the mandrakes as fruits, not unlike, in their effects on our nature, to what is said of the flocks of Laban, (Gen. xxx. 37, &c.) and have concluded, that it was on this account that Rachel desired them. This, however, is but conjecture. The church describing them as fragrant, and perhaps having an allusion in that view to the fragrancy of higher objects, may be supposed to convey the idea of the sweet-smelling odour of Jesus, and the fruits and graces of his Spirit.

MANGER

We find this word no where in the Bible but when made use of in relation to the Lord Jesus Christ. Luke the evangelist tells us, that "when the days with Mary were accomplished that she should be delivered, she brought forth her first-born son, and wrapped him in swaddling clothes, and laid him in a manger, because there was no room for them in the inn," (Luke ii. 6, 7.) An English reader, unacquainted with the manners and customs of the East, from this relation, would be led to conclude, that from the fulness of the inn, and the poverty of the Virgin Mary, there was no other accommodation to be obtained for her. But travellers accustomed to the journies in Palestine, explain the circumstances connected with inns different to this nation. Every traveller takes with him, of some sort or other, accommodations for the way. There are, here and there, caravansaries, or inns, built for the accommodation of travellers, to shelter them from the inclemency of the weather; but sad must be the case of all travellers who carry nothing with them for their own comfort, when they take shelter in those hovels. It is to be hoped, that in Bethlehem, whose very name means the land of bread, there was sufficient provision of this kind for, the Lord of life and glory." But what other accommodations Mary had, we are left to conjecture. The humble circumstances in which Jesus appeared, in his first open manifestation in our nature, had a beautiful correspondence to the whole of his mission. The strongest expression we meet with in the word of God respecting the humiliation of Christ, is his emptying himself, or, as the apostle expresses it, making himself of "no reputation." (Phil. ii. 7.) The great object for which the Son of God became man, was to restore the divine glory, which, sin had obscured; so that it was not enough for the Lord Jesus Christ to give all glory to God in a way of obedience and death, but he will give away, for a time, his own glory, to make the satisfaction to God more abundant. An inn, therefore, without accommodation, a manger, not a sopha, became exactly suited for this humble Saviour to make his appearance in. And when we find the Son of God so debased, whose essential glory was, and is, equal to the Father, we behold an equivalent given for the debasement of God, the Father's glory by reason of man's sin. Hence, therefore, the Lord Jesus, in his coming to redeem our nature, will, from the manger to the cross, debase, humble, and empty himself, and make himself of no reputation, yea, become "sin and a curse for us, when he knew no sin, that we might be made the righteousness of God in him." It is very blessed thus to behold Jesus when entering our world, and to discover the causes wherefore there was no room for him in the inn!

MANNA

In the margin of the Bible it is called Man-hu, (Exod. xvi. 15.) meaning the bread with which the Lord fed. Israel in the wilderness. It was altogether miraculous: for this food began to fall from heaven from the time the Israelites arrived in the wilderness of Zin, which was the sixteenth day of the second month after their departure from Egypt, until that they came to Canaan, during the pilgrimage of forty years. And what rendered this daily mercy the more miraculous was, that on the Sabbath-days it never fell, during the whole of this eventful period. I beg the reader to read the interesting account of it, Exod. xvi. throughout: it will well reward his attention, The children of Israel called it Man-hu; that is, they asked the question, "What is this, far it is peculiar?" And hence Moses, (Deut. viii. 3.) reminds Israel of their surprize at first beholding it. "Who fed thee (said Moses) with that peculiar things which thou knewest not, neither did thy fathers know."

The miracle itself was designed to be a standing miracle, for Israel to remember and record in their generations for ever; hence an omer of it was to be reserved in a pot, and laid up before the Lord for a memorial. Here was a double proof of the miracle; for the manna itself was s perishable and delicate, that if only kept for day, it bred worms and stank; yet, to teach Israel to reverence the Sabbaths, that which we kept for the use of the Sabbath bred no worm nor stank; and the omer of it also which was laid up before the Lord, was preserved pure generation to generation.

It was also no less miraculous, the immense quantity which regularly fell every day in the supply. It gave supply to the whole camp Israel--six hundred thousand on foot that we men, besides children, and mixed multitude that went with Israel, came out of Egypt; therefore allowing for increase, we may safely put down near a million of souls, who were daily fed from the supply of manna. (See Exod. xii. 37, 38.) The manna had a remarkable quality, which, though not miraculous, is recorded as worthy our observation. Though it melted at the heat of the sun, yet when brought into the tent it became hard, so that the people ground it in mills, or beat it in a mortar. (See Num. xi. 7, 8. and Exod. xvi. 20, 21.) It may be proper to observe, that what is now called manna in the shop of the apothecary, hath no One resemblance or connection whatever with the manna of Scripture, but is the gum, or balsam, of certain trees. We are told indeed by historians, that in Arabia and in Calabria, and in other places, there is a dew on the ground still to be seen like manna. But that this cannot be similar to the manna of Israel is evident, for it is of medicinal quality, and affects the bowels. The Jews are so tenacious respecting the manna of their fathers, that they pronounce an anathema and execration on every one that would call in question the miraculous nature of it. And Christians ought not to be less earnest in defence of the same precious truth, since the manna of the Old Testament was but typical and figurative of the bread of life under the New. Jesus was all along thus represented to Israel; and was then, and is now, the living bread, by faith, with which the Lord feeds all the true Israel. (See John vi. 31-58. Rev. ii. 17.)

MANOAH

A name eminent in Scripture, from the manifestation that the Lord made to him in a time when visions of God were rare. (See Judg. xiii.) The name seems to be derived from Nuaeh, rest. When the reader hath turned to the chapter which relates this wonderful transaction, and read it, I beg him to pause over it, and consider the several interesting circumstances connected with it; and then let him judge for himself, who this person could be that appeared to the man and his wife but, the Lord Jesus Christ. It is certain, as far as we can judge, that both Manoah and his wife regarded their heavenly visitor but as a created angel, until that when in the flame of the sacrifice he ascended with it. But when they behold him thus go up in the flame, to give an acceptableness to their poor sacrifice, then they knew that it was that Glorious Holy One whom JEHOVAH had sworn into his office as High Priest for ever. The man knew by this that it was JEHOVAH the Son, and not a created angel; and as such, he said,"We shall surely die, because we have seen God," agreeably to the Lord's own declaration, "Thou canst not see my face and live? (Exod. xxxiii. 20.)

There is one beauty more in this transaction, and which serves to confirm this blessed doctrine, that this supposed angel was Christ; and that is, that when Manoah asked his name, the angel of the Lord said unto him, "Why askest thou my after name seeing it is secret?" In the margin of the Bible it is rendered, "seeing it is wonderful." And the name Wonderful is

MAON - MARRIAGE

Christ's well-known name (Isa. ix. 6.) Reader, what think you of the subject? Was it not Jesus, as if longing for the time of his coming to tabernacle openly with his people?

MAON

A city of Judah, (Josh. xv. 55.) The word means an habitation. (Exod. xv. 23-25,)

MARAH

A memorable spot, so rendered from the murmurings of Israel. The word signifies bitter or bitterness. No doubt, but that beside the history, there was much of a spiritual instruction in this event. All creature-comforts are in themselves disposed to produce bitterness: until Christ is seen and enjoyed in them, even our most common comforts will always prove unsatisfying, and never produce what they propose. But if Christ be in our appointments, whatever they are, like the tree the Lord shewed to Moses, which when cast into the waters of Marah made them sweet, then will all be sanctified and sweetened to our use, and the divine glory.

MARANATHA

We meet with this word joined to Anathema, 1 Cor. xvi. 22. See Anathema. In addition to what was then observed under this head, it may not be improper to remark yet farther, that when the apostle Paul useth this form of expression, which signifies, Let the offender that loves not the Lord Jesus Christ be punished when the Lord comes, he useth it not as a matter that was new, or a form that was never heard of before, but rather one well known. It should seem to be rather a proverbial method of saying, let a man that is guilty of such and such things be an Anathema Maranatha. It is as if the person so pronouncing the punishment meant thereby to say, it exceeds my power to express what ought to be the consequence of your crime, I therefore leave you to the Lord when he comes.

MARK

The evangelist. Probably the name is from the Greek, and means shining. There was another Mark, Acts xii. 12.

MARRIAGE

The Scriptures, both of the Old Testament and the New, have in a great variety of circumstances shew in what high esteem the holy estate of marriage was considered by holy men of old. And though in the Old Testament we read of many wives being joined to one husband, yet our Lord Jesus expressly said, that it was not so from the beginning. (Matt. xix. 3-9.) And there is reason to believe, that in numberless instances where we read of a man having more wives than one, all but one were rather as concubines than wives. Such, for example, as Abraham's Hagar and Ke-turah. And I think it very plain, from the New Testament doctrine upon this subject, that from the very first order of things, even from the creation, the spiritual marriage and unity between Christ and his church was all along respected by the marriage-state, and uniformly intended to be shadowed forth. In confirmation of this opinion, I beg the reader to consult 'the following Scriptures: Gen. ii. 18, to the end; Ephes. v. 22. to the end; Heb. xiii. 4. And when the readers hath fully considered the force of these Scriptures: let him turn to John's gospel, second chapter and there read how the Lord Jesus honouered the marriage both with his presence and first miracle that he wrought; than let him turn to the fifth chapter of Mathew's Gospel, and Luke the sixteenth and eighteenth, and mark how strongly the Lord attacheth adultery to the separation of men and their wives. From the whole of which taken together, I think it is very plain, not only of the original design from the beginning, that every woman should have her own husband, and, every husband his own wife, but also that the married state was intended, in the most dear and tender manner, to set forth and display Christ's union with his church. Perhaps it may not be improper under this article, to make another observation in the allusion to the customs of the East on the celebration of their marriages, and which may serve to illustrate and explain, in some measure, that circumstance respecting the man without a wedding garment, which our Lord speaks of in the marriage-feast the king made for his son. (See Matt. xxii. 1 to 14.)

We cannot need to be informed how splendid and costly the entertainments made for marriage feasts always were in the East, Their ordinary entertainments were great, and no expense was spared in them; but even the poorest of the people on bridal occasions exerted themselves to make the festivity as rich as possible. In the marriage therefore of the king's son, we may well suppose the display of magnificence must have been proportionably great. The circumstance of the wedding garment provided for the guests, was in exact conformity to the oriental custom. Certain rich vests, or caffans, were provided for every one, therefore, when the king came in to see the guests, and found a man without the wedding garment, the contempt he had shewn in refusing to put on what must have been provided for him, excited the king's displeasure, and rendered him a just object of the king's wrath. This explains the sense of the parable. But the spiritual meaning of the parable is still infinitely more important. The invitation of the gospel to the marriage of the Lord Jesus with our nature, runs in the same charter of grace. "Go ye into the highways, and as many as ye shall and bid to the marriage." So that wheresoever the sound of the gospel comes, it may be truly said, in the language of the parable, the invitation goeth forth, and there will be gathered together, all, as many as the servants find, both bad and good; and the wedding will be furnished with guests. The man therefore whom the king finds at his table without the wedding garment, is a type or representation of every one of the same description and character, who contumaciously refuses to be clothed with the robe of Christ's righteousness, but comes before the king with the filthy rags of his own righteousness; and as at the sight and remonstrance of the king that man was speechless, unable to speak a word by way of softening his guilt, so at the last day, when the Lord Jesus shall come to be glorified m his saints, and admired in all that believe, all that are found without the justifying garment of Jesus's salvation will be struck dumb, and overwhelmed with guilt and shame. The soul that is Christless now, will be speechless then. Such seems to be the evident scope and tendency of this beautiful parable of our Lord.

MARROW

The rich and delicious blessings of the gospel are figuratively set forth as marrow; hence David speaks of them as such to his soul. (Ps. lxiii. 5.) And the prophet Isaiah represents the salvation of the Lord Jesus Christ as "a feast of fat things, and full of marrow." (Isa. xxv. 6.)

MARSCHERAN

The eighth month, like October.

MARTHA

The sister of Lazarus and Mary. Her name is derived from Marar, bitter. We have her history, Luke x. 38-42. and John xii. This woman is rendered memorable in the church by reason of her pursuits, being so much engaged in earthly concerns while having conviction on her mind of the importance of heavenly objects. So that her name is become somewhat proverbial; and we call them the Marthas of the present day, who are careful and troubled about many things, and not so much in earnest for the one thing needful.

MARY

We meet with many of the name of Mary in the New Testament:
- The Virgin Mary.
- Mary, the mother of James and John.
- Mary, the mother of Mark.
- Mary, the wife of Cleophas.
- Mary, called also Salome.
- Mary, a pious woman whom the apostle Paul mentions. (Rom. xvi. 6.)

The word of God has recorded the names of those women as followers of the Lord Jesus, and from the interest they took in what concerned Christ; but with their history farther, excepting the Virgin Mary, and Mary Magdalene, we are not much acquainted. Concerning the Virgin Mary, we are most highly interested to have the clearest apprehension of her person and history, in that part which concerns the incarnation of the Lord Jesus; and therefore, in a work of this kind, I should consider it most highly deficient, if it were wholly passed over. I mean however, to be very brief upon, it, and only say enough to convey, to that class of readers for whom this Concordance is designed, clear apprehensions in what light the holy Scriptures explain to us the miraculous conception of Mary, and the incarnation of the Lord Jesus. I begin then from that part where the Lord Jesus begins to proclaim to the church, by the spirit of prophecy, the event of his coming. "Wherefore, when he cometh into the world, (Heb. x. 5, &c.) he saith, Sacrifice and offering thou wouldest not, but a body hast thou prepared me." Now here observe, Christ, by the spirit of prophecy, is speaking of the Father. Let this be marked down as first in the memorandum of this glorious mysterious subject. Then turn to the evangelist Luke, (chap. i. 35.) where we find, at the visit of the angel to Mary, to inform her of the miraculous conception, when Mary expressed her astonishment at the salutation, and modestly intimated the impossibility of the thing, the angel made this remarkable answer: "The Holy Ghost shall come upon thee, and the power of the Highest shall overshadow thee; therefore, also, that holy thing which shall be born of thee, shall be called the Son of God." Here let it be equally marked down, in strong memorandums of the heart, the part which God the Holy Ghost had in this stupendous work. We see then both the hand of God the Father, and God the Holy Ghost, in their personal offices and characters, engaged in the great undertaking; and that we might not overlook the part which Jesus himself had in it also, as God the Son, we are expressly told: that he took our nature upon him for the purpose of redemption, The words of the Holy Ghost on this point are very strong, and very particular. "Forasmuch then as the children are partakers of flesh and blood, he also himself likewise took part of the same." So again--, "For verily he took not on him the nature of angels, but he took on him the seed of Abraham." (See Heb. ii. 14. 16.) Let this also be put down in the mind, and then sum it up as a lesson in arithametic. All the persons of the GODHEAD, Father, Son, and Holy Ghost, had their almighty hand in the mysterious work of Christ's incarnation. This premised, we may now go farther, and observe that this body given by the Father, produced by the overshadowing power of the Holy Ghost, and taken by the Son, is to be of the same nature and quality as our nature, sin only excepted; for the more he is like to his redeemed in nature, the more suited he is to be our Mediator. Hence the Scripture saith, that "in all things it behoved him to be made like unto his brethren, that he might be a merciful and faithful High Priest in things pertaining to God, to make reconciliation for the sins of the people." (Heb. ii. 17.) It is plain then, that he must be man, bone of our bone, and flesh of our flesh. An angel's nature would not have suited the purpose of redemption: it was human nature that had sinned, and broken the divine law; it must be human nature that shall make amends, by obedience and death. The justice of God, though permitting a substitute and surety, will not permit that substitute and surety in any other nature than man. "The soul that sinneth it shall die." Hence, therefore, observe the beauty and the order in the divine government, for which the Lord Jesus took not on him the nature of angels but the seed of Abraham.

Let us advance a step farther. We see the blessedness and propriety that the Redeemer should be man, and not an angel;--the next enquiry is, how this manhood shall be united with the GODHEAD in the most suitable and becoming manner, agreeably to the purposes of the divine counsel and will, so as to answer all the great ends of redemption. Certainly the Son of God might have assumed a body such as ours, consisting both of flesh and spirit, and formed, as the first earthly man Adam was, of nothing; but then this would not have been what Scripture saith Christ must be, of "the seed of the woman," and what the promise declared. (See Gen. iii. 15.) And beside, the triumph of Christ over hell and the prince of darkness, would not have been as the promise declared it should be--"the seed of the woman to bruise the serpent's head." Hence, therefore, the Redeemer must be born of a woman, must be in all points like to his brethren, sin only excepted, both for the salvation of his people and the destruction of his enemies. But still it may be asked, could not all this have been done in Christ becoming man from the woman, as the woman originally was from the man. For we road that at the creation, the Lord God caused a deep sleep to fall upon Adam, and he slept; and he took one of his ribs and closed up the flesh instead thereof: and the rib, which the Lord God had taken from the man, made he a woman." (Gen. ii. 21-23.) No doubt the Lord God could have done this by the manhood of Christ; and in this case, it might have been said of the second Adam, as the first Adam said to Eve, "this is now bone of my bone, and flesh of my flesh." (Gen. ii. 22.) But neither could this have been called a birth, nor of the seed of the woman; neither would this have suited the purposes of redemption; for the Scripture saith, that "when the fulness of the time was come, God sent forth his Son, made of a woman, made under the law, to redeem them that were under the law, that we might receive the adoption of sons. (Gal. iv. 4, 5.) And elsewere it is said, "that both he that sanctifieth, and they who are sanctified, are all one, for which cause he is not ashamed to call them brethren." (Heb. ii. 11.) But had Christ, in his human nature, been produced from the rib of the woman, there would have been no such relationship as there now is; neither, as before remarked, would Christ have been of the seed of the woman, neither born under the law.

We find then, that for Christ to be of the seed of the woman, of the same flesh and blood with those he came to redeem, and to be born under the law, to redeem them that are under the law, he must still come nearer to our nature, and be born as the children are born, only with that distinguishing and vast difference, that though he partakes of our nature, yet it is the sinless infirmities of our nature only. He is, and must be, truly and properly man; as he is, and must be, truly and properly God; being "one with the Father, over all, God blessed for ever. Amen." But in assuming our nature, he will still be "holy, harmless, undefiled separate from sinners, and made higher than the heavens." (Heb. vii. 26.)

Now, in the accomplishment of this great and mysterious work, the formation of the body of Christ, it is blessed to see how very particular the sacred writers are to describe the (modus operandi) method of the divine working in this purpose. The original promise at the fall was, that Christ should be of the "seed of the woman;" and accordingly we find the prophet, in the after-ages, commissioned by the Holy Ghost to tell the church that "a virgin should conceive, and bear a son." (Isa. vii. 14.) Now observe the expression conceive: not a conception, as in the ordinary way of generation, in our fallen race; for this is by corrupt and sinful creatures; and therefore David very properly saith, "in sin did my mother conceive me." (Ps. li. 5.) But in the instance of the Virgin's conception, this was without the intervention of an human father, and consequently no sin in the conception; neither sin in the seed conceived, because this was by the miraculous impregnation and overshadowing power of the Holy Ghost. And here lie the holiness and blessedness, as well as the power and wisdom, of the almighty work. It was a conception of the Virgin, not a generation. Christ was conceived by the Virgin, not begotten; for it is said, he was made of a woman. And it is not the place or the womb that defiles, but the nature from whom it is begotten or conceived, as in our ordinary nature from Adam all along hath been done. But in the instance of the human nature Of Christ, begotten as it was by the overshadowing power of God the Holy Ghost, Christ is very properly, by way of distinction, called that holy thing, (not that holy person, but thing) to imply a conception without a generation. Here then we see in what view we are to consider the incarnation of the Lord Jesus, and of consequence the person and character of the Virgin Mary.

And it is a most blessed and soul-satisfying view, when opened to our understanding by the Holy Ghost, what the same Almighty Author of his sacred word hath taught us concerning it in the Scriptures of eternal truth. We now discover the suitability of our dear Redeemer for the great purposes of his mission, and plainly perceive how needful such a priest is for us, "who is holy, harmless, undefiled, separate from sinners, and made higher than the heavens. Well might the Lord Jesus, by the spirit of prophecy, declare, as he doth, (the hundred and thirty-ninth Psalm, which, I venture to believe, refers principally, if not wholly, to the Lord Jesus Christ) "I am fearfully and wonderfully made. My substance was not hid from thee when I was made in secret, and curiously wrought in the lowest paths of the earth." If, as we have before noticed, and from the authority of Scripture, Christ's body was the Father's gift, (Heb. x. 5.) and if the Holy Ghost, in his overshadowing power, was the almighty: worker in the dark place of the virgin's womb, here called "the lowest parts of the earth," what blessedness is given to the view of the subject amidst all the mysteriousness of it, and how are we taught to honour, reverence, love, and praise the whole united persons of the GODHEAD for those wonders of redemption by Jesus Christ. "Thanks be unto God, I would say, (will not the reader join my spirit in it?) for his unspeakable gift!" (2 Cor. ix. 15.)

MARY MAGDALENE

I cannot prevail upon myself to pass over this memorable name, without shortly noticing the distinguishing mercy of the Lord Jesus manifested to this poor sinner. She was the first, we are told, that had the honour and holy joy afforded her, lo have an interview with Christ after he arose from the dead, (Mark xvi. 9.) It was not Peter, nor James, nor John, no, nor any of the whole college of the apostles, to whom Jesus first shewed himself. A woman is marked out for this peculiar privilege, yea, and such a woman as one might hare supposed would have been not the first upon the occasion; for we are told, that Jesus had cast out of her seven devils. And what is more remarkable, the Holy Ghost is particular to tell the church this, in the same moment he speaks of the mercy; for so the sweet and gracious words run" Now when Jesus was risen early the first day of the week, he appeared first to Mary,

Magdalene, out of whom he cast seven devils;" Did the kind compassionate, Lord mean to say by this condescending act of grace, that there he will be most gracious where Satan hath been most, cruel? Did he thereby mean to intimate to all his disciples, that the poor lamb of his fold shall have, the softest lying down in his bosom, whom the prowling wolf hath most torn and worried with his claws? Oh! that every deeply-exercised follower of the Lord Jesus would frequently think of this; and, as often as this Magdalene riseth to their recollection, would behold the Lord Jesus in this unequalled act of mercy, that "where sin abounded, grace doth much more abound; that as sin hath reigned unto death, so might grace reign through righteousness unto eternal life, through Jesus Christ our Lord?" (Rom. v. 21.)

MASCHIL

We meet with this work out the head of several of the Psalms. The meaning certainly is, to instruct. But wherefore some Psalms should be thus prefixed with a title, and others not, is not so very plain, since the whole book may be justly said to be Psalms of instruction. Some have thought, therefore, that it hath reference to instruct in the music of the Psalm. See Musician.

MASH

We find this name, Gen. x. 23. Some suppose it to be the same as Mesheek, to take away,--from Mashash.

MASHAL

A city of Asher, 1 Chron. vi. 74. The name means a parable.

MASREKAH

A duke of Edom, Gen. xxxvi. 36. from Sharah, whistling.

MASSA

A memorable spot in the journeys of Israel, signifying temptation. See Gen. xvii. 2, &c.

MASTER

We use this term upon various occasions, and it is very commonly received among men, such as servants to their employers, children to their teachers, and the like; but strictly and properly speaking, it belongs to none but to the Lord Jesus Christ. So Christ himself enjoined: "Call no man your master, for one is your master, even Christ." (Matt. xxiii. 10.) There is certainly a somewhat of great softness in the expression in relation to Christ.

We should not give this title to the person of God the Father, or God the Holy Ghost; it seems too familiar. But eyeing Jesus in our own nature, the heart feels a nearness of affection, and the terms then of master, honoured Lord, seem expressive both of duty and love. Every thing in Jesus, and every office in Jesus, makes this title pleasant. You call me master, and Lord, (saith that gracious Redeemer to his disciples when upon earth) "and you say well, for so I am." (John xiii. 13.) I know not whether I shall offend, but I cannot forbear making a quotation from the writings of an eminently devout man of the sixteenth century upon the subject: I mean, George Herbert, who seemeth to have hung upon the name of Jesus his master, as the bee hangs upon the flower.

How sweetly doth *my master* sound, my master!
As ambergris leaves, a rich scent.
Unto the taster--.
So doth these words a sweet content,
An oriental fragrancy--*my master*!
My master! shall I speak? O that to thee
My servant were a little so,
As flesh might be,
That these two words might creep and grow
To some degree of spiciness to thee!
For when *my master*, which alone is sweet,
And ev'n my unworthiness pleasing,
Shall call and meet

MATRED - MEDES

My servant, as thee not displeasing,
That call is but the breathing of the sweet.
This breathing would with gains, by sweet'ning me,
(As sweet things traffic when they meet)
Return to thee:
And so this new commerce, and sweet,
Should all my life employ and busy me.

MATRED
The daughter of Mezahab, Gen. xxxvi. 39. The name signifies rod, from Mot, a rod--and Jarad, to descend.

MATRI
The chief of Saul's family, signifying rain. from Matar, 1 Sam. x. 21.

MATTAN
The father of Jacob in the genealogy of Christ. (See Matt. i. 15.) His name is from Nathan, gift. There was another of this name in Scripture, 2 Kings xi. 18.

MATTANAH
A place where Israel encamped, Num. xxi. 18. The name means a gift.

MATTANIAH
Or more properly Mattan-Jah--Gift of the Lord. A man's name, chief of the family of the Levites, 1 Chron. xxv. 16.

MATTHEW
The apostle and evangelist, or, as he himself in great humility writes, Matthew the publican, than, Matt. x. 3. His history we have in the gospel.

MATTHIAS
Or more property Mattath, gift—and Jah, the Lord. The disciple chosen in the room of the traitor Judas. (See Acts i. 23-26.)

MEARAH
(See Josh. xiii. 4.) It should seem to have been a cavern, or cave, as Mahar, a cavern.

MEASURE
Concerning the measures and weights of the Jews, they are all placed together at the end of the Bible in general, to which the reader may refer.

MEBUNNIA
The Heeshathite, one of David's worthies. (See 2 Sam. xxiii. 27.) His name signifies a son, from Ben or Banah, to build.

MEDAD
Medad and Eldad--we read of these men on whom the Spirit of the Lord came, Num. xi. 26, 27. If the former name be derived from Madad, it means he that measures; but more probably it is a compound word of Me, waters--and Duad, love. Eldad is a compound also of El, God; and Dod, love. A reference to the Scripture will give their history, which is but short.

MEDAN
The third son of Abraham by Keturah, Gen. xxv. 2. There is a place also called by this name and some have thought, that it is the same as is called in our Lord's time Magdala. Some suppose that the name means judgment; and others render it, the waters of Dan.

MEDEBA
A city beyond Jordan, Josh. xiii. 16. The name signifies the waters of trouble, from *Mi,* water--and Daab, trouble.

MEDES
We meet with the account of the Medes and Persians in the prophecy of Isaiah, and in the prophecy of Daniel. And as the Lord had appointed these nations for the destruction of Babylon when her time was come, so she was the Lord's scourge for Israel. The history of the Medes and

Persians, forms a subject of importance in. Scripture. If the reader wishes to possess the Scriptural account of those kingdoms, he must consult what, Isaiah and Daniel have declared concerning them. Isaiah begins the relation at his thirteenth chapter with the burden of Babylon, and the subject continues, in respect to Israel's deliverance from Babylon, through that add the following chapter. The prophet resumes the subject of Babylon's destruction at the twenty-first chapter; but the chief prophecy concerning the final ruin of Babylon, is in the forty-fifth and following chapters, where Cyrus the Persian, as the destroyer of Babylon, is called by his name, although this was near two hundred years before the events there predicted were intended to be fulfilled. Daniel takes up the subject at the period where the prophecy of Isaiah came to be accomplished, and in his fifth chapter relates to the church the downfall of Babylon, and the death of the impious gang Belshazzar. It may be proper to add under this article, that Darius the Mede, who conquered the kingdom with Cyrus the Persian, governed the Chaldean empire, and at his death Cyrus, who was his nephew, united the kingdom of the Medes and Persians into one. From this time Bablyon sunk to rise no more, and the Persian empire succeeded: so that from the close of Daniel's prophecy, if we prosecute the history of the church as an history, we must begin with the book of Ezra, the date of whose first chapter nearly corresponds with the close of Daniel's prophecy.

MEDIATOR

The very name of Mediator is precious. What, but for the Lord Jesus Christ becoming our Mediator, must have been the hopeless state of man to all eternity! Though under the article of Christ, (to which I refer the reader) so much hath been said concerning the person of Christ as God and man, and God-man united, the only possible suited Mediator for poor sinners, yet methinks the very name, at every renewed mention of it, calls up a thousand new endearments to prompt the heart to dwell upon it with unceasing rapture and delight. The apostle Paul felt this so forcibly, that whenever he speaks of his adorable Lord and master under this most precious character, he lays such an emphasis on his person as Mediator as serves to shew the high sense and feeling Paul had of the blessedness of looking up to the Lord Jesus in this point of view. Thus for example, in his Epistle to the Ephesians, the first chapter, and the tenth verse, where speaking, of the design of JEHOVAH in redemption, to bring and centre all things in Christ, and finally to make him the glorious end of creation, he saith, that "in the dispensation of the fulness of time, he might gather together in one all things in Christ, both which are in heaven, and which are in earth, even in him." Observe the strength of the expression with which the apostle closeth the account--even in him I so again, in his Epistle to the Colossians, the first chapter, and twentieth verse, the apostle, speaking of Christ "having made peace by the blood of his cross," makes the same emphasis on the person of Christ. "By him (saith Paul) to reconcile all things unto himself; by him, I say," (saith the apostle) repeating the lovely name as if, and which was truly the case, he found a double blessedness in it--" by him, I say; whether they be things in earth, or things in heaven."

And every one those heart is convinced of sin, and of the total inability in himself ever to come to God in any thing of his own, or by any way of acceptance in himself, how will he hail the Lord Jesus Christ in this most blessed and lovely and endearing of all characters, the only "Mediator between God and man, the man Christ Jesus!" If the reader be of the number of truly convinced sinners, the peculiar fitness of Christ, as God and man in one person, for this office, will strike him with full conviction. He must be qualified for the office, who, as God, is one with the Father, and as man, is one with us; and indeed so qualified as no other could be. The partaking of both natures gives this completeness of qualification; so that would I have my cause, (and a cause so infinitely important as that the happiness of eternity hangs upon the issue) would I have my cause in one that is able? here it is in the hands of Jesus; for he is God, mighty to save. And would I have it in the hands of one that is near to me? here also it is, for it is in the hands of Jesus, who is "bone of my bone, and flesh of my flesh;" one who can have "compassion on the ignorant, and on them that are out of the way; seeing that he himself (in the days of his flesh) was compassed with all our sinless infirmities." How blessedly the apostle follows up this Scriptural account of our Jesus! "Wherefore, saith the apostle, in all things it behoved him to be made like unto his brethren, that he might be a merciful and faithful High Priest in things pertaining to God, to make reconciliation for the sins of the people; for in that he himself hath suffered being tempted, he is able to succour them that are tempted." (Heb. ii. 17, 18.)

And if it will not be thought swelling this account too largely, I would beg to add, that over and above all our view and approbation of the Lord Jesus under this most precious and blessed of all offices, our God and Father's approbation of his dear Son, as such, tends to bring the Lord Jesus home still more if possible to our warmest affection. In the suitability of the Lord Jesus, and his personal fitness in this high character, (as such none but himself could ever be found) there is something so truly interesting when beheld as JEHOVAH'S appointment, as cannot fail to endear all the persons of the GODHEAD to the Lord's people. We discover hereby not only the wisdom of JEHOVAH in the choice, but the love of his heart in it also. The recovery of our nature from the fall, is the plan of infinite wisdom; and therefore he that accomplisheth this merciful purpose, shall be every way suited for it. But beside the wisdom displayed in the fitness of Christ, the love manifested in such an one as Christ performing it is most blessed: all the way along the heart of God the Father is seen in it. The Mediator to approach JEHOVAH, is his Elect, in whom his soul delighteth; in whom he beholds such unparalleled glory and beauty and loveliness, that the very heart of JEHOVAH is in all, and with all, Christ undertakes and is engaged in. There is something in this view of the mind of the Father, and the Son, and of the Holy Ghost, all taking part and becoming interested in the acts of the Mediator, that tends to make that office to his people yet more blessed, and readers him who is the person engaged in it, infinitely more endeared and endearing in every performance of it. Let the reader only turn to Isa. xlii. 1. and a few of the following verses, and then judge for himself of JEHOVAH'S great delight in beholding Christ in the character of Mediator. First he speaks of him, and calls upon the church to behold him: "Behold my servant whom I uphold, mine elect in whom my soul delighteth: I have put my Spirit upon him; he shall bring forth judgment to the Gentiles; he shall not cry, nor lift up, nor cause his voice to be heard in the street. A bruised reed shall he not break, and the smoking flax shall he not quench: he shall bring forth judgment unto truth; he shall not fail nor be discouraged till he have set judgment in the earth, and the isles shall wait for his law." He next speaks to him, and introduceth his address in the loftiest language of his Almightiness. "Thus saith God the Lord, he that created the heavens and stretched them out, he that spread forth the earth, and that which cometh out of it, he that giveth bread unto the people upon it, and spirit to them that walk therein, I the Lord have called thee in righteousness, and will hold thine hand, and will keep thee, and give thee for a covenant to the people, for a light to the Gentiles, to open the blind eyes, to bring out the prisoners from the prison,, and them that sit in darkness out of the prison house." And then, as if to put to silence the ignorance of foolish men, who allow Jesus Christ to be the Mediator, but deny him that GODHEAD by which alone the Lord Christ could be competent to this high office of Mediator, be adds "I am the Lord, that is my name, and my glory will I not give to another, neither my praise to graven images:" hereby plainly proving, that as this office of Mediator is carried on and exercised to the glory of JEHOVAH, so none but one in JEHOVAH could be competent to perform it. It would have been to have given the glory to another, if the Lord Jesus had not been one with the Father, ever all, God blessed for ever. Moreover, the glory of opening blind eyes, and the like, would have been unsuitable to any creature; and as JEHOVAH, in the very opening of his address to Christ, claims this as his distinguishing prerogative, would he mean to claim the crown of creation and yet put the crown of redemption on the head of a mere creature? Would not this have been to have given his glory to another? Oh, how plain, how very plain it is, that in the call and appointment of the Lord Jesus to this blessed office of Mediator, it is God's dear Son, in nature and essence one with the Father, and in office the God-man, Glory-man, Christ Jesus! Oh! that modern infidels, calling themselves Christians, but in name only so, and not in reality, would seriously lay this at heart. "Kiss the Son lest he be angry, and ye perish from the way, when his wrath is kindled but a little: blessed are all they that put their trust in him." (Ps. ii. 12.)

MEGIDDO

A city of Manasseh, rendered remarkable for the death of Josiah, (2 Kings xxiii. 29.) It seems derived from Magad, rich fruit. Probably it abounded with fruit; and this place abounded with celebrated waters. (See Judg. v. 19.)

MEGILLOTH

The children of Israel were used to call five books, namely, Ecclesiastes, Solomon's Song, Ruth, Esther, and the Lamentations of Jeremiah, by this name, which means a roll, or volume.

MEHETABEL

The son of Delaiah, Neh. vi. 10. It seems a compound of three words--Mah-to-bel, How good is God! Perhaps this name was given at a time of some remarkable providence, as we do not find the name any where else in Scripture for the name of a man; and this was at a time of peculiar exercises of Israel. It is further remarkable, that we have the same name for a woman, Gen. xxxvi. 39.

MEHOLATHITE

Adriel was of this place, 1 Sam. xviii. 19. Meholah signifies weakness or sickness.

MEHUJAEL

Son of Irad, Gen. iv. 18. If from Macha, the meaning is, blotted out, and the Lord God.

MELCHI

The son of Janna, Luke iii. 24. There is another of this name in the same genealogy, twenty-eighth verse, as Melek, king.

MELCHIZEDEC

A compound name of Melek, king; and Tzedec, justice; and a well-known name in Scripture, but little understood in person or character. There are several things said of Melchizedec, which must ever render it difficult to explain, so as to come at a perfect knowledge of him. He is said, in the first mention of his name, to be a priest of the Most High God, Gen. xiv. 18; and this was said at a time when the church had not been formed into a regular church, as it was afterwards in the wilderness, and, as far as the word of God teacheth, had neither temple, nor altar, nor sacrifice. Perhaps the bread and wine Melchizedec brought forth, as said in this Scripture, at the first meeting of Abraham, might not be given to the patriarch for the refreshment of the body, but sacramental--perhaps so, but by no means certain. The Holy Ghost, by his servant the apostle Paul, in his account of Melchizedec, Heb. vii. l, &c. saith, that he was king of righteousness. His name indeed saith as much, as hath been before noticed; and from the same authority we learn, that he was "without father without mother, without descent, having neither beginning of days, nor end of life." Had the apostle stopped here in his relation of Melchizedec, we should at once have concluded, that it was Christ himself; for we well know, that the Lord frequently made some sweet personal manifestations of himself, in the Old Testament days, long before his incarnation. His goings forth, we are told by the prophet, "have been from of old from everlasting, (Micah v. 2.) that is, goings forth, not JEHOVAH one with the Father, for in this sense the expression, I humbly conceive, would not have been correct; for in the essence of the GODHEAD there can be neither goings forth, nor withdrawings, consistent with that perfection of the divine nature, his immensity. But the account we have in Scripture of the Lord's appearing, in a visible from, sometimes as an angel, and sometimes as a man, must have been in the character of Mediator; as if to tell the church of the love he bore to his church, and these many manifestations were intended as so many proofs how much he longed for the time to come, when he would openly tabernacle with his people in the substance of our flesh.

Had the apostle therefore, when giving this account of Melchizedec, in describing the eternity of his nature, and the everlasting nature of his priesthood, stopped at this, we should have concluded that Melchizedec was Christ; but when the apostle proceeds farther to say, that Melchizedec is made like unto the Son of God, we pause over this conclusion, and know not how to pronounce sameness from what is said only to be a likeness.

But as the Holy Ghost hath left the subject in some obscurity, there it becomes us to leave it also, and undetermined. In reading what is said of Melchizedec, we are unavoidably led to contemplate what is revealed of the Lord Jesus; and if we are told of the one, that he was "without father, without mother, having neither beginning of days, nor end of life; we cannot overlook the other, concerning whom the prophet demands, "Who shall declare his generation?" (Isa. liii. 8.) No one that reads of the fatherless and motherless Melchizedec, can fail to recollect him that, like "the stone cut without hands, which became a mountain, and filled the earth," (Dan. ii. 34, 35.) was, as man, without a father, and as God, without a mother, and "a priest for ever, after the order of Melchizedec." (Ps. cx. 4.) Here then, if we desire not to be wise above what is written, we shall rest satisfied, blessing the Holy Ghost for what he hath revealed, rather than coveting to know what he hath not revealed. Jesus is our High Priest, and a priest upon his throne; (Zech. vi. 13,) this is our assurance. Here then we may always hail our great Melchizedec!

MELZAR

The government of the person of Daniel and his companions when captives in Babylon, (Dan. i. 16.) The word Melzar is of the Chaldean language, and signifies steward.

MEMPHIS

A city of Egypt, the residence of the ancient kings. The prophets often notice it. (Isa. xix. 13. Jer. xliv. 1; xlvi. 14. Hos. ix. 6.) It is derived from Moph, signifying by the mouth.

MEMUCAN

One of the seven princes of Persia, Esth. i. 14. The word means impoverished.

MENE

A Chaldean word, signifying, what Daniel interpreted it, together with the word Tekel, or Thechel, he was weighed. "Mene, Mene, Tekel Upharsin." (Dan. v. 25.) The whole taken together was the doom which, by a miraculous hand written upon the wall, was directed to the impious monarch Belshazzar, and explained by Daniel. There appears in the first reading of it some little difficulty. The hand-writing upon the wall was, as I have stated it, Mene, Merle, Tekel Upharsin--but Daniel renders it Mene, God hath numbered thy kingdom, and finished it--Tekel, thou art weighed in the balance, and found wanting. Upharsin, Daniel makes Peres; but the sense is the same. Parsin, or Upharsin, is Hebrew, and signifies the Persians--and Paresin, in the Chaldean language, signifies dividing. Daniel therefore takes both together, and renders it Peres, thy kingdom is divided. Solemn as this event was, and faithfully as Daniel's prediction was fulfilled, yet there is nothing uncommon in it. Doth not every day an hand-writing, even the solemn word of God, appear on the wall of every sinner's conscience? And are not the awful judgments threatened thereon fully executed? Who shall describe the trembling loins of sinners, and the paleness of soul, which seizeth them in the dying hour, on entering eternity?

MEPHIBOSHETH

Saul had a son of this name, and so had Jonathan his son, (2 Sam. iv. 4. and 2 Sam. xxi. 8, 9.) His name signifies reproach from the mouth, from Pe, a mouth--and Bosh, shame. It is thought by some, that the proper name of Jonathan's son was Merib-baal, (see I Chron. viii. 34.) and that his name was changed to Mephibosheth, because the Israelites were cautious of using the name of Baal. Idolatry was not then so much in fashion, as in the after days of the kings of Israel. But this point cannot be ascertained.

MERAB

Daughter of Saul, (1 Sam. xiv. 49.) Her name is taken from Rabah, mistress.

MERCY

Properly speaking, the name of Jesus. For David, speaking of grace, and pleading for it before the Lord, saith, as an argument and plea for receiving it, There is mercy (that is, there is Jesus) with thee. (Ps. cxxx. 4.) And when Zecharias prophesied, under the influence of God the Holy Ghost, at the coming of Christ, he said it was to perform the mercy promised. (Luke i. 72.) Jesus is the mercy promised.

MERCY-SEAT

Much is spoken of in the Old Testament Scripture concerning this sacred part of the temple, from whence the Lord promised to commune with his people. (Exod. xxv. 17, &c.) This, as a type of the Lord Jesus, is eminently to be regarded, since it serves to teach us, that by efficacy of redemption, the Old Testament saints, as well as New Testament believers, were alike included in the merits of "the Lamb slain from the foundation of the world." (Rev. xiii. 8.)

The form of the mercy-seat, or propitiatory, was that of an ark, covered with gold, at the two ends of which were placed the cherubim to cover over the mercy-seat, from whence JEHOVAH was supposed to speak. (Ps. lxxx. 1.) The apostle Paul gives a short description of the tabernacle, and the furniture in it, (Heb. ix. 1, &c.--and speaking of the cherubim of glory shadowing the mercy seat, he saith, "of which we cannot now speak particularly." The Hebrews called the mercy-seat Caphoreth, from the word

MERODACH-BALADAN - MESSENGER

Caphar, to expiate or pardon. And very probably the church had this in view when she said: "My beloved is unto me as a cluster of camphire (copher) in the vineyards of Engedi." (Song i. 14.) If, as it is believed, that it is Christ she is then praising, with an eye to his propitiation, when she thus expressed herself, it is very striking and beautiful. Jesus is indeed the true and only propitiatory and propitiation; and what a sweet addition to the blessed subject is it, that he is "the propitiation whom God the Father hath set forth through faith in his blood!" So that our faith finds a double warrant--first, in the completeness of the propitiation itself, and, secondly, in God's appointment of it. And how can a soul come short of salvation that acts faith upon the infinite merits of God the Son's righteousness, and the infinite faithfulness of God the Father's grace? See propitiation.

MERODACH-BALADAN

King of Babylon, Isa. xxxix, 1.--signifying sorrow.

MEROM

Josh. xi. 5. The word means waters.

MEROZ

A place near the brook Kishon. (See Judg. v. 23.) The word signifies secret. Perhaps in those times of trouble the inhabitants here secreted themselves.

MESHA

King of Moab, 2 Kings iii. 4. The name hath been thought to signify burden.

MESHACH

The name given by the Chaldeans to Mishael. See Abednego. Meshach, if derived from Mashac, means drawn by force.

MESHULLAM

There were several of this name in Scripture. (See 1 Chron. ix. 7, 8. 12. 2 Chron. xxxiv. 12. Neh. iii. 4. 6.) The name is derived from Shalam, peace.

MESOPOTAMIA

A province rendered remarkable for the first peopling of the earth after the deluge. The meaning of the word is, between two rivers--perhaps from Potamos, river.

MESSENGER

There would have required no notice of the office of a messenger, by way of explaining the nature of it, being perfectly well understood, and it not been that our Lord Jesus Christ, when becoming our Redeemer, condescended to submit to this office also; but as the Lord Jesus, in his unequalled humility, vouchsafed to be the servant and messenger of JEHOVAH, every motive of affection and duty demands our attention to behold Jesus in this most gracious character. The reader will have a better apprehension of the title when he is told that the same word translated messenger is also translated angel. This in Malachi, iii. 1. it might be read, the angel of the covenant. In like manner prophets, teachers, and ambassadors, are not unfrequently called messengers. (Mal. ii. 7. 2 Kings xvi. 7.) The infinite graciousness and condescension of the Lord Jesus in this character, serves therefore to recommend and endear him yet more to our heart; and blessedly Jesus speaks of it to his disciples. "Whosoever will be great among you, (saith that humble Lord) let him be your minister; and whosoever will be chief among you, let him be your servant; even as the Son of man came not to be ministered unto, but to minister, and to give his life a ransom for many." (Matt. x x. 27, 28.) And it is most blessed indeed, to behold the Lord of life and glory thus engaged in all offices, and filling all characters, relating to his mediatorship. He is the all in all of the whole covenant. At the call of his Father, he stood up from everlasting, the Head of his church and people, that he might fill all things. Hence *to* him the covenant of redemption was given; by him the whole covenant was fulfilled; in his almighty hand all the blessings resulting from the covenant are placed; and from him all must flow, in grace here, and glory hereafter, to his whole body the church. So that Jesus appears most lovely and engaging as JEHOVAH'S covenant in the full, and as the Surety of it, the Messenger of it, the Fulfiller of it, and the Administrator of it, both in time and to all eternity. Hail, almighty Messenger of thine own and thy Father's will to mankind, "thou Messenger and Interpreter, one among a thousand, to shew unto man JEHOVAH'S uprightness! Be thou all my salvation, and all my desire; for thou hast made and finished thine everlasting covenant, ordered in all things and sure."

MESSIAH

The Anointed. This term is peculiarly, and by way of eminency, applied to the Lord Jesus Christ, the Mashah or Meshiah of the Father, full of grace and truth. Hence, with pointed and personal distinction, God the Father is represented in the Scripture as saying: "I have laid help upon one that is mighty; I have exalted one chosen out of the people; I have found David my servant; with my holy oil have I anointed him. (Ps. lxxxix. 19, 20.) And no less God the Holy Ghost, in his divine office and character, in the economy of human redemption, is represented as ordaining and anointing Christ, as Christ, to the great work of salvation; for both Christ and his church came under this 'Cilia-act of God the Spirit. For as Christ could not have been Christ without the unction of the Holy Ghost, so neither could the church have been the church, the spouse of Christ, the Lamb's wife, without sovereign agency. And it is very blessed to behold in the Scriptures of truth the testimony of JEHOVAH to this grand doctrine of Christ the Messiah, as the Christ of God. Hence we find Christ speaking as Glory-man Mediator. (Isa. xlviii. 16, 17.) "Come ye near unto me, hear ye this: I have not spoken in secret; from the beginning, from the time that it was, thee am I; and now the Lord God and his Spirit hath sent me. Thus saith the Lord thy Redeemer, the Holy One of Israel). I am the Lord thy God, which teacheth thee, to profit, which leadeth thee by the way that thou shouldest go." In all these views, therefore, of Christ as Christ, we discover the work of the Father and the Holy Ghost. For one of the names of the Lord Jesus in the Old Testament is, the Messiah, that is the Anointed, as well as in the New; and as it is expressly said concerning him in the New Testament, when he appeared in the substance of our flesh, how God anointed Jesus of Nazareth: with the Holy Ghost, Acts x. 38.—so evidently was he called the Messiah, and consequently answer that name was, and is, from everlasting, the anointed of God by the Holy Ghost, before he openly manifested himself under that character in our flesh. Such then was and is the glorious Messiah, the Christ of God; and such we accept and receive him to his body the church.

I might detain the reader were it not for enlarging this work beyond the limits I must observe, with offering several most interesting reflections, which arise out of this view of our now risen and exalted Messiah as the Messiah, the Christ of God; but for brevity's sake, I shall only beg to offer this one observation, namely, how sweet and strengthening a testimony such views of Jesus give to the faith of the church, when receiving Christ as the anointed of the Father and the Holy Ghost, Recollect in that blessed portion, just now quoted what the Mediator saith as Mediator--"Come ye near unto me, hear ye this; I have not spoken in secret; from the beginning, from the time that it was, there am I; and now the Lord God and his Spirit hath sent me." Was there ever anything more full in point and in proof of this blessed doctrine concerning the Messiah? What could the Lord Jesus by the spirit of prophecy mean, but that he would have his church, when receiving him, read his credentials, and mark well his high warrant and authority. There should be no shyness, but his people should come near unto him; for this was not a new thing, a new doctrine, it was from the beginning, yea, before all worlds Jesus was spoken of, in his mediatorial character, as set up from everlasting; neither was it whispered in secret, but openly, in the first revelations, the man-nature of the seed of the woman, the anointed of the Father and the Holy Ghost, was all along declared, that *it was,* and that *I am,* saith Christ. Blessed view of Jesus this, and precious to the strengthening of the faith of God's people. Methinks I would cherish it with all the warmth of affection; I would carry it about with me wherever I go: and beg that God the Holy Ghost would cause it to be my complete unceasing encouragement in all approaches to the throne of grace, and in all ordinances of worship. This is the warrant of a poor sinner's hope and confidence. Christ, as Christ, as the anointed, as the Messiah, is the sure appointment and ordinance of heaven. In him we draw nigh by divine authority. Christ is not only suited to carry on all the purposes of our great High Priest, but acts in that blessed office by divine authority, and by the validity of an oath. "The Lord sware and will not repent, thou art a priest for ever, after the order of Melchizedec. (Ps. cx. 4.) Hence, therefore, the Lord Jesus, in effect, speaks to every poor sinner as he did to the woman of Samaria--"If thou knewest the gift of God, and who it is, and by what authority he saith to thee, Give me to drink, thou wouldest have asked of him, and he would have given thee living water." (John iv. 10.) Such is the blessedness of receiving Christ, and living upon Christ, as the Christ, the Messiah, of God.

METHUSALEH

Son of Enoch. (Gen. v, 21, 27.) This man attained the longest age ever recorded, even nine hundred and sixty-nine years. His name carries somewhat of an idea respecting it; one who demands his death, from Shelah, to demand; and Muth, death. Some derive Methusaleh from Sheol, grave. But the meaning in either sense is the same.

MICAH

There were many of this name in Scripture. (See 1 Chron. ix. 15. 2 Kings xxii. 12. 1 Chron. v. 5; xxiii. 20.) But the one of eminency to be particularly noticed in a work of this kind, is Micah the Morashite, that is, of Moresa, a village in the south of Judah. He is one of what is called the lesser prophets; and his prophecy forms a part of the sacred Canon of Scripture. His name is probably from Macac, poor, low, humble; though some read it Michaiha, and form it into a question, Who is like to JEHOVAH?

MICAIAH

The son of Imlah, whom Ahab hated, (1 Kings xxii. 8.) His name is the same in derivation as the former. We meet with another Micaiah or Michaiah, son of Gemariah, in the days of Jeremiah. (See Jer. xxxvi. 11, &c.)

MICHAEL

The name is a compound of Mi, who--Co, the same--and El, God--so that Michael means, one with God. We meet with this name only five times in Scripture: thrice in the prophecy of Daniel, chap. x 13. 21--xii. 1, once in Jude 9, and once in Rev. xii. 7. I beg the reader to look to each of those passages; and when the several portions where this person is spoken of are fully considered, I leave it to the reader's own determination, hoping God the Spirit will be his teacher, who it is that is meant by Michael. See Archangel.--Malachi.

MICHAL

Saul's daughter. (1 Sam. xviii. 20.) The name signifies, who is it all? from Mi and Col, the whole. Her history we have in the Scriptures of David.

MICHMASH

A place about nine miles from Jerusalem. (1 Sam. xiii. 5,) The name is supposed to be derived from Nacah, to strike.

MIDIAN

The chief city of the Midianites. (See Num. xxii.) The name is derived from Niddin, judgment There were several persons called Midian in Scripture. And it is thought by some, that the Midianites were descendants of Midian, Abraham's son. (Gen. xxv. 2.) Supposing this to be well founded, we may learn from hence, what evils spring out of illicit connections. Abraham's concubine, Keturah, brings forth, a son, whose descendants shall vex Abraham's lawful heirs to great afflictions. (See Num. xxv. 16-18.) And are not all the affections and lusts of our fallen nature, like illicit connections, continually harassing our spiritual joys!

MIGDAL-EL

We meet with mention of this place, Josh xix 38. The meaning of the name is very plain, from Migdol, tower--and El, God, the tower of God.

MIGDAL-GAD

A city of Judah. (Josh. xv. 37.)

MIGDOL

A tower remarkable in Israel's history, to which they arrived soon after their leaving Egypt. (Exod. xiv. 2.) Here it was Israel was commanded to encamp before the sea, where the Lord meant to display such a miracle in opening a way through it for Israel's safety, and the Egyptians, overthrow. And as this was at the very mouth of the sea, namely, Pihahiroth, which signifies the opening of the Foramen, and where Baalzephon, the dunghill god of Egypt, was supposed to watch to catch runaway servants, the Lord here made the triumph more conspicuous in sight of his enemies. (See the history, Exod. xiv. throughout.)

MIGRON

A village near Gibeah. (1 Sam. xiv. 2.) It means perhaps fear, from Magar.

MIKLOTH

There were two of this name, one the son of Abi Gibeon, (1 Cor. viii. 32.) and a Mikloth, one of David's worthies. (1 Chron. xxvii. 4.) If the name be derived from Makel, it signifies rods or staffs.

MILCAH

We meet with two of this name, one the daughter of Aram, (Gen. xi. 29.) and the other, the daughter of Zslophehad, (Num. vi. 26, 33.) The name is derived from Malkah, queen.

MILE

The Hebrews did not measure by the mile, but by the cubit. Our translators of the Bible have, however, very properly, rendered the measurement by the English standard; so that a mile, in our language, corresponds to two thousand cubits, and a furlong is the eighth part of a mile.

MILETUS

The place where Paul left Trophimus sick. (2 Tim. iv. 20.) It should seem that there was another place of this name near Ephesus. (See Acts xx. 17.)

MILK

It would have been unnecessary to have noticed this article, if information concerning what it is as food had been all that was intended from it; but as the term is figuratively made use of in Scripture to describe spiritual blessings, it may be proper to notice it in a work of this kind. The Holy Ghost was graciously pleased to point out some of the precious things in the person, work, and offices of Christ under this figure. The dying Jacob, speaking to his children in allusion to the times of the gospel, describes the spiritual Judah, among other distinguishing features of character, as having "his eyes red with wine, and his teeth white as milk." (Gen. xlix. 12.) And the church, as if giving testimony to the accomplishment of the patriarch's prophecy, compares her Beloved's eyes to "the eyes of doves, by the rivers of water, washed with milk." (Song v. 12.) Perhaps both images were meant to set forth the Redeemer, in that sweetness and loveliness of character, as blending the tender affections of his heart towards his people, like the softness of milk flowing in upon the souls of his redeemed, with a fulness of pity and compassion. And as the Holy Ghost thus drew the portrait of Jesus by the figure of the milk, so the same almighty Lord, in various parts of his holy word, hath described the church, and especially the younger babes in Christ, as nourished by, "the sincere milk of the word." (1 Pet. ii. 2.) Yea, Christ himself tells his church, that "her tips dropped as the honeycomb, and both honey and milk were under her tongue." (Song iv. 11.) There is a great beauty as well as tenderness in our Lord's expression. For in the eastern world, we are told by historians, that they had a certain food made of milk and honey, called by the Greeks Meligala; and it was the custom to give a portion of this to the new-married bride on entering her husband's house. As the Lord Jesus therefore is here speaking of his church, having betrothed her to himself under this character, his gracious salvation of her with these words is uncommonly beautiful and affectionate. And whenever the soul of a poor sinner is made glad in receiving the milk of the gospel, and Christ is apprehended in all his glory, suitableness, and all-sufficiency, no doubt, the droppings of the lips will be like honey and milk under the tongue, for "out of the abundance of the heart the mouth will speak."

I must not dismiss our attention to this article until that I have first yet farther remarked, that God's promise of Canaan to his people of, old was under the same type of bringing them into a land "which is the glory of all lands, a land flowing with milk and honey." (Exod. iii. 8.) And both the kingdom of grace, and the kingdom of glory, comprehending all sanctified temporal mercies, with all spiritual and eternal blessings, may well be represented under those rich figures. See Honey.

MILL

The use of the mill in the eastern world was very ancient, and peformed by the lowest of the people, So that when describing the different ranks whom the Lord would destroy in the general destruction of the firstborn in Egypt, the phrase is, "from the first-born of Pharoah that sitteth upon his throne, even unto the first born of the maid servant that is behind the mill." (Exod. xi. 5.) Hence when the Philistines had put out Samson's eyes, they bound him in fetters of brass, and compelled him "to grind in the prison-house." (See Judges xvi. 21.)

There is a very gracious precept in the law of Moses on the subject of grinding, which serves to shew the Lord's tender compassion over his people. "No man shall take the nether or the upper millstone to pledge, for he taketh a man's life to pledge." (Deut. xxiv. 6.) In what a very sweet and engaging point of view doth this represent the Lord! And when the precept is heightened in relation to spiritual bread, with what affection may the poor look unto

Jesus, the bread of life, concerning it!

MIRACLE

Miracles in Scripture are designed, for the most part, as so many, testimonies in proof of the doctrine delivered at the same time. Thus the Lord Jesus saith, "The works that I do in my Father's name, they bear witness of me." (John x. 25.) And when in concurrence with miracles, the word of God, and the works of God are joined together, these establish and seal the truth as it is in Jesus. There were certain particularities in the miracles of the Lord Jesus, which marked his divine nature in the performance of them in a way and manner different from all his servants. They performed all the miracles they wrought by the appointment and in the name of the Lord Jesus wrought his in his own name. It is true indeed, in the instance of the resurrection of Lazarus from the dead, the Lord Jesus first addressed his Father: but then he assigned the special reason for so doing; because "of them, said Jesus, that stood by, that they might know and believe that the Father had sent me." At the same time proclaiming himself as the resurrection and the life, and giving proof of it by becoming so to Lazarus. (See John xi. 23-44.) In addition to this, it should be farther remarked, that the miracles of the Lord Jesus were many of them of a personal kind, and not unfrequeuuy wrought without any immediate cause in confirmation of his doctrine, but to set forth his gracious character of Redeemer. In those acts of Christ in which he manifested forth the sovereignty of his power, he might be said to act in common with the other persons of the GODHEAD: and the Father, and the Holy Ghost, had a joint interest in these things with himself. But in those actions of the Lord Jesus peculiar to the Mediator as Mediator, and where, from having as Son of God abased himself for the purposes of salvation, he manifested forth the miracles he wrought, here the glory of the work became personal, and belonged wholly to Jesus as Mediator, I need not particularize instances, else I might observe, that the healed paralytic, the cleansed leper, the centurion's son, the water turned into wine; these and the tike are all of the personal kind. And perhaps it is not among the smallest instances of Christ's personal glory and grace, from the actions of miracles, that the Lord Jesus in all he wrought testified his personal love and mercy to his people. The evangelist John is careful to inform the church, that "the beginning of miracles in Cana of Galilee" was shewn in converting water into wine; as if to say, such are the blessings of the gospel, Our common mercies will be made rich mercies; and the nether springs in Jesus, if for his personal glory, shall become upper springs in Jesus. And this is still the more striking, because under the law the first miracle of his servant Moses was manifested in converting water into blood; but Jesus's first miracle shall be converting water into wine. Sweet thought to the believer! Jesus's person, and Jesus's grace, give a softening and a I converting blessing to all our states and circumstances. And what an argument of the most persuasive nature ariseth therefrom to look unto him under every exercise, and to wait his grace in every dispensation. Here it is, as in Cana of Galilee, Jesus manifesteth forth his glory, and his disciples believe on him. (John ii. 11 .)

MIRIAM

The sister of Moses and Aaron, and daughter of Amram. She was older than Moses, for she watched over him when placed in the ark on the river, and it is probable that she was older than Aaron. Her name is derived from Mara, which signifies bitterness. But if, as is more generally supposed, the name is derived from her father's, Amram signifies exalted. (See Exod. ii. 4, &c.)

MISHAEL

Him to whom the Chaldeans gave the name of Meshach. (See Dan. i. 7.) The meaning of Mishael is, one asked for of God. See Abednego.

MITE

A small Roman coin, so small, and of so little value, that we are told two of them made a farthing: (Luke xxi. 2.)--and yet the Lord Jesus declared, that this was a costly offering when thrown in by the poor widow into the treasury. Sweet thought to the truly charitable in Christ, teaching that it is not the largeness of the gift, but the largeness of the heart with which alms are given, that constitutes the value in the sight of God, and when given for his glory!

MITHCAH

An encampment of Israel. (Num. xxxiii. 28.) It should seem to be derived from Mathac, sweetness.

MITHREDATH

(See Ezra. iv. 7.) His name seems to be derived from Thur, law, and is meant to convey an idea of one studying the law.

MITYLENE

The place where Paul passed in his way from Corinth to Jerusalem. (See Acts xx. 14.) According to the Greek, the name means cleanliness.

MIZAR

A little hill. The Psalmist speaks feelingly of this, Ps. xlii. 6.

MIZPEH

A city of Judah. (Josh. xv. 38.) Perhaps the same that is spoken of by Samuel, where he set up, between Mizpeh and Shur, the Ebenezer. (See 1 Sam. vii. 5-7.) The name signifies a place of look-out, or enquiry.

Mizpeh and Tabor, in after-ages, were places which lay in the path from Samaria to Jerusalem; so that here the priests of the calves set spies, which Hosea the Prophet figuratively called nets, to catch the pure worshippers who ventured, in those dangerous times of idolatry, to go up to worship JEHOVAH at Jerusalem. (See Hos. v. 1.)

MOAB

The founder of the Moabites. Moab was the Son of Lot, by incest. An awful origin, and au awful progeny followed, in the sworn foes to God and his Israel! (See Gen. xix. 31-37.) The name signifies of his father.

MOLOCH

A king, the god of the Ammorites. (Acts vii. 43.) The Scriptures of God speak of Moloch upon several occasions in such a manner as make the subject very interesting to enquire into particulars concerning this horrid idol. The first account we meet with of this dunghill deity is in Leviticus, (chap. xviii. 21.) where the Lord prohibits Israel from allowing of any of his seed to pass through the rite to Moloch. It should seem, that the method in those acts was simply passing through the flame; and as this carried with it an idea of much personal bravery, it is likely that the children of Israel were much disposed to rival their neighbours in this supposed act of courage. Hence the Psalmist laments this degeneracy of Israel, in the one hundred and sixth Psalm, from the sixth verse almost to the end. Hence the prophet Amos, chap. v. 25. and following verses, laments it also, And Stephen, the first martyr, charged it upon the Sanhedrim. (Acts vii. 42, 43.) That this horrid custom prevailed to a great degree is plain, from the relation we have of it, through many generations. Solomon built an high place for Moloch, (1 Kings xi. 7.) and Manasseh a long time after caused his son to, pass through the fire in honour of him. (See 2 Kings xxi. l-6.) And in the valley of Tophet, the prophet Jeremiah speaks of those horrid transactions being carried on. (Jer. xix. 5, 6, &c.)

But beside the Scripture account, the corresponding history of the times furnish accounts which are truly distressing to read. The idol itself was made of brass, we are told, in the shape of a man, with his arms extended to embrace. The whole figure was hollow, and when any sacrifice was to be made to Moloch, they heated the statue until it was nearly red hot, and the wretched victim was then brought and put into the arms of Moloch, where it remained until consumed. To stifle the cries of the unhappy sufferer from being heard, instruments of music were made use of, which continued playing until the poor victim had expired.

An historian of veracity, in addition to this sad account of human superstition, arising from our fallen state, tells us, that upon some occation where human sacrifices of this kind had not been so frequent as they supposed necessary, and fearing their dunghill god was displeased by way of atonement, they chose out two hundred of the noblest of their children, and made at once a sacrifice of them publicly. It is truly distressing to observe yet farther, that even to the present hour the custom of the East but too much favours this horrid practice. "The feast of fire," so called, and indeed the general plan among the worshippers of idols in the vast territory of Hindostan, afford but sad instances of the savage custom of those who immolate their children in this way.

I have been more particular in noticing, under the article of Moloch, the general subject of human sacrifices, by way of calling the reader's attention to the happy state of the revealed word of God. Oh, how blessed is it to discover, from the relation of such things, the preciousness of that one sacrifice of the body of Jesus Christ once for all, whereby "he hath perfected for ever them that are sanctified."

MONTH

We meet with constant mention in the Bible concerning the months; but it is remarkable, that the Israelites had no particular names for their months until alter their connection, with Egypt. We read in Gen. vii. 11. of the second month, when the fountains of the great deep were broken up, and the ark rested on the seventh month upon the mountains of Ararat, (Gen. viii. 4.)--and the waters decreased continually until the tenth month. After the Exodus took place, and Israel went out of Egypt, we find names first began to be given by the Hebrews to their months, though still numbering them as before. Thus for example--"This day came ye out, in the month Abib." (Exod. xiii. 4.) And so again, (Deut. xvi. 1.) "Observe the month Abib, (Chodeseh Abib) the Lord thy God brought thee forth out of Egypt by night."But they did not lose sight of their numbering their months, and calling them by their numbers. The children of Israel came into the wilderness of Sin, which is between Elim and Sinai, on the fifteenth day of the second month, after their departing out of the land of Egypt. (Exod. xvi. 1. So again, Exod. xix. 1.) In the third month, when the children of Israel were gone forth out of the land of Egypt, the same day came they unto the wilderness of Sinai. And we find mention of months by numbering through all the Old Testament, and even in the New. (See Num. i. 1. Ezra iii. 8. Jer. xxxvi, 9. Ezek. xxxi. 1. Hag. i. 1. 15. Zech. viii. 19. Luke i. 26. 36.)

In Solomon's days we find names more particulary given to their months, yet still preserving the ancient method of speaking of their months after their numbers. Thus 1 Kings vi. 1, "And it came to pass, in the four hundred and eighteenth year, after the children of Israel were come out of the land of Egypt, in the fourth year of Solomon's reign over Israel, in the month Zif, which is the second month, that he began to build the house of the Lord." So again, thirty-seventh verse, "in the fourth year was the foundation of the house of the Lord laid, in the month Zif; and in the eleventh year, in the month Bul, which is the eighth month, was the house finished," ver. 38. So chap. viii. 2. Solomon held a feast in the month Ethanim, which is the seventh month. But it was only in the time of Solomon that the months were named, for we do not meet with the mention of the months by names, except that of Abib in Exodus and Deuteronomy, either before or after Solomon, until the Babylonish captivity. But whether the name Abib, which signifies green fruit, or ears of corn, and which was the spring answering to our March, was so particularly called in Egypt, and the Hebrews borrowed the name from thence, or Solomon learnt the names of Zif and Bul from the Phenicians When trading with them, is not easy to determine, neither perhaps is it important to know.

It is probable, however, that the Jews learnt in Babylon, the custom of the Chaldeans, to mark their months as they did by names, and from thence (or the Persians, under whom for a time they dwelt when the monarchy of Babylon was destroyed), they formed the following to all the months in the year.

The names of the months.
1. Nizan, which answers to March.
2. Jiar which answers to April.
3. Sivan which answers to May.
4. Thammuz which answers to June.
5. Ab which answers to July.
6. Elul which answers to August.
7. Tizri which answers to September.
8. Marschevan which answers to October.
9. Casleu which answers to November.
10. Thebet which answers to December.
11. Sebat .... which answers to January.
12. Adar. which answers to February.

The Hebrews observed a distinct order in the calculation of their time as it related to holy seasons and ordinary concerns. The holy year, as they termed it, began in the month Nizan, corresponding to our March, called in the Exodus Abib; no doubt, in obedience to that precept--"This mouth shall be unto you the beginning of months: it shall be the first month of the year unto you." (Exod. xii. 1, 2.) The ordinary year for civil concerns commenced with the Hebrews in the month Tizri, answering to our September.

MOON

The great luminary of the night, formed by JEHOVAH on the fourth day of creation, (Gen. i. 14-19.) Philosophers speaks much of this planet, in respect of its magnitude, form, phases, tides, &c.&c. But the great point in which we are taught to regard the moon, is from what the word of God saith concerning it. There we learn "that the Lord appointed the moon for certain seasons, and the sun knoweth his going down." (Ps. civ. 19,) Moses also beautifully speaks of the peerless majesty of this empress of the night ministering to her Maker's glory, when describing in the lot of Joseph's blessings the "precious fruits brought forth by the sun, and the precious things put forth by the moon." Probably the sacred writer, in allusion to those heavenly influences, meant to speak of yet far higher blessings in the sweet work of grace upon the soul, when Jesus, the Sun of righteousness, brings forth the fruits of his Holy Spirit, and causeth the soul from his influence, as the moon borrows from the sun, to put forth all precious things in him. Here is indeed the good will of him that dwelt in the bush. (Deut. xxxiii. 3.)

The moon is compared to the church, and considered a striking emblem of her; for as the whole of her light is derived from the sun, so the church wholly depends upon the Lord Jesus, and only shines in the glory she draws from him. And as the moon is subject to an eclipse, and hath her waxing and waning times, so the church knows how to be abased and how to abound. All her enjoyments, all her splendour, usefulness, services, depend wholly upon her Lord. When Jesus, the Sun of righteousness, causeth his rays of light to act upon the church, by their kind influences, the church then like the moon from the sun, ministers according to the divine appointment of her Lord; but if the earth comes between, that is, if earthly affections intervene between Christ and the soul, then, like the interposition in the planetary world, there will be an eclipse. Hence in a day of brightness, and light, and glory, the church is represented in the Revelations as "a woman clothed with the sun, and the moon under her feet." Every thing of earth and earthly affections will be under our feet, when our souls are clothed with the bright robes of Jesus's righteousness, and Christ himself "formed in the heart the hope of glory." (Rev. xii. 1. Col. i. 27.)

    We have a lovely description in the Canticles of such a view of the church, where Jesus himself is beholding her in this blessed state, and exclaiming with delight," Who is she that looketh forth as the morning, fair as the moon, clear as the sun, and terrible as an army with banners?" (Song vi. 10.) The whole church of Jesus, and every individual believer of the church, answers to this description. The morning in a day of grace, though small, has then the glimmerings of divine light in the soul; yet are they the sure harbingers of sun-rising, and "mark that path of the just which shineth more and more unto a perfect day." And the church is then fair as the moon in Jesus's eye, though, like the moon, when shining in her greatest brightness, spots may be seen upon her, and all the light she affords the earth is but what she first receives from the sun. In herself she is after all but an opaque body. What an exact resemblance to the church! She is fair and comely, but it is from the beauty and comeliness of her Lord; she hath nothing of her own, but all from him. But then she is still not only fair as the moon, but clear as the sun. Yes! I in Jesus the church is beheld, and in his righteousness she is righteousness; yea, the Lord himself commands her so to be called, after the name of her Lord and Husband, Jer. xxiii. 6. and xxxiii. 16. And how terrible as an army of banners must the church be, thus looking forth as the morning, fair as the moon, and clear as the sun, let the word of God decide. "The God of peace shall bruise Satan under your feet shortly." (Rom. xvi. 20.) 'See Queen of Heaven.

MORDECAI

A name rendered memorable in Scripture history, from the person so called being made an instrument in the Lord's hand for the deliverance of his people, and the destruction of his enemies. (See Esther chap. iii. and following.)

    The name of Mordecai seems to be derived from Marar, bitter: or, as some have supposed, from Mur, myrrh; and Duc, to bruise. We ought not to dismiss our record of Mordecai with his name only, since the Holy Ghost hath thought proper to give the church so large an account of his history, in the book of Esther, which is principally, if not wholly, recorded for this purpose, No doubt, that the almighty Spirit intended the relation of it for much usefulness to his people in all ages; and therefore it becomes both our duty and our wisdom to attend to it.

    The faithfulness of Mordecai exposed him to the anger and resentment of Haman the Hagagite. This poor despised Jew could not in conscience bow down and do homage to one of the spawn of Agag. Mordecai knew well that Haman was of that spawn; and what was yet infinitely higher and more important; he knew well, that the Lord had sworn to have war with Amalek, (now changed in name, but not in principle, to the Agagite) from generation to generation. Let the reader, for his information of the cause, consult Exodus xvii. 3, to the end, compared with 1 Sam. xv. Hence, therefore, the faithful Mordecai, zealous, like another Phineas, for God's cause and his people's welfare, would not, for he dared not, bow down to the sworn foe of the Lord and Israel. (See Num. xxv. 1-13.) Oh, for grace to be found faithful amidst all the Hamans and Agagites of the present day! Oh, that the Lord would raise up, in this sense, many faithful Mordecais from the midst of our British Israel!

Reader, let us not turn away from this history of Mordecai and Haman, until that we have taken one instruction more. Look at Haman. What, Haman! could not all the glory, all the riches, all the multitude of children, that you boasted, satisfy you? (See Esther v. 9. to the end.) What I had you your harem full of women for the riot of your lustful hours, concubines upon concubines, and the king's favour so great that none of the princes stood so high as yourself, and shall the sight of one poor miserable Jew, because he pays you no reverence, be enough to throw down all the props of this boasted grandeur? Must the blood of this man be shed before that Haman will acknowledge himself to be happy? yea, not this one poor. Jew only, but every Jew shall, die. for it, because Mordecai sat in he king's gate, and would not rise to give you reverence! (See Esther iii. 8, 9.) Is it indeed *so,* and is this the case? Ah, wretched, wretched Haman! what a representation you afford of the state of a heart of malignity! what a portrait of human life in all its highest characters void of grace! One baleful passion is enough, like the dye of crimson, or of scarlet, to tinge and give a colouring to the whole heart. Nothing can make the prosperous sinner truly happy so long as this spectre, like the Jew at the gate, riseth up and haunts the imagination. Precious Jesus! what everlasting blessedness hast thou introduced into the circumstances of our fallen state, when by thy visit to our world, and redemption of our nature in it, thou hast raised thy people from the ruins of the fall, and cleansed our hearts by thy blood from all those evil passions of our fallen nature.

MORIAH

A mountain, the name of which is well known to the readers of the Bible. Here Abraham was directed by the Lord for the offering up of his son. (See Gen. xxii. throughout.) The name itself is a compound of Mor and Jah, bitterness, or myrrh of the Lord. Here, in after-ages, the temple of Jerusalem was built by Solomon. (2 Chron. iii. 1.)

It will not be unpleasant to the reader if I add under this article, that Moriah, in the intended offering of Isaac, being typical of Christ and his Calvary, as well as Isaac himself, may serve at all times to furnish sweet subject of meditation, The myrrh or Moriah of the Lord becomes no unapt resemblance of Jesus, because Christ's suffering, like myrrh, had a bitter taste, though fragrant smell. "In the mount of the Lord it shall be seen." And the bruises of Jesus, when it pleased JEHOVAH to put him to grief, while they affect in contemplation the heart of the redeemed, yet, like sweet dropping myrrh, they distil all spiritual blessings in a fragrancy most refreshing and delightful, in pardon, mercy, peace, grace, faith and all the blessings of the covenant. Hence the church cries out, "All thy garments smell of myrth, aloes, and Cassia, out of the ivory palaces, whereby they have made thee glad." (Ps. xlv. 8.)

MORNING

There would have required no notice of this word in a work of this kind, had the mere sense of the meaning of the word morning been all that was intended; but the Scriptures of God have so often made use of the term in a figurative way, and yet more than that, have made so many beautiful allusions to Jesus under the metaphor of the morning, that I could not allow myself to pass it by without offering upon it a short observations It would be too extensive to notice all the places in both the sacred volumes where Christ is spoken of as the light of the morning, and the day-spring from on high, and the morning star, and the like; I shall only beg to select one passage, among the many, in proof of the similitude, and that from among the last words of David, (2 Sam. xxiii. 4.) where, speaking of Christ, he saith, "And he shall be as the light of the morning, when the sun ariseth, even a morning without clouds." There never surely was a more beautiful, a more just, more enlivening representation or figure of the Lord Jesus than what those words have given. In himself Jesus is all this, and infinitely more. One with the Father and the Holy Ghost, he is the first cause of life, light, and glory; incomprehensibly so, the fountain, source, and origin of all that constitutes these infinite and eternal perfections. And in his mediatorial character and office, he is essentially so, the light and life of his people. So that when, in the eternal council of peace, he arose, to enlighten the Gentiles, and to be the glory of his people Israel, he arose, as this Scripture represents him, as "the tight of the morning, when the sun ariseth, even a morning without clouds." For in himself he is a sun without a spot, a light in which there is no shade, a perfection of glory and beauty without alloy. A morning without clouds is a strong figure to denote Christ's person, and not more strong than just; for the glories of the Lord Jesus Christ are complete glories; nothing enters into them of an opposite quality. In the excellencies of creatures there are certain properties which enter, into their composition, and which prove their imperfection; indeed their very nature implies as much. The portrait, however beautiful, must have a shade. But not so with the Lord Jesus. He is a morning without a cloud. One of the old Puritan writers of the sixteenth century, calls him, a sea of sweetness, without one drop of gall."

And as Jesus is all this and infinitely more in himself, so is he in all that he is to his people. His love, his grace, his salvation, all are as "a morning without a cloud." There is nothing of mixture or imperfection in what he is to them, in what he hath done for them, and what he will be to them, and with them in glory to all eternity, His covenant is ordered in all things and sure; his salvation is an everlasting salvation. So that from the first dawn of grace in their hearts until that grace is consummated in glory, the Lord Jesus is a sun that no more goeth down, a morning without a cloud; for he not only giveth light, but is himself their light, and their God, their glory. Surely no figure comes up to our Lord Jesus with an exactness more full and complete than the beautiful one the Holy Ghost hath given by his servant David, "he shall be as the light of the morning when the sun riseth, eveen a morning without clouds!"

Think of Jesus under this sweet figure, I beseech you, reader; yea, never lose sight of him if possible. Jesus is a morning indeed without a cloud.

MOSERA or MOSEROTH

The name means binding, from Jasar, to bind. Deut. x, 6, it is called by the former name; and Num. xxxiii. 30, by the latter. This place was made memorable by the death and burial of Aaron. From hence this great high priest of the Levitical dispensation will arise at the last day. Here he rests in hope, who in his office was a type of our glorious High Priest after the order of Melchizedec. What a thought! If the ashes of Adam, or Aaron, or any, or all of the patriarchs were to arise this hour, their bodies would be all alike unconscious whether they had slept a single night, or several thousand years. "Blessed are the dead, said the voice from heaven, which die in the Lord"--in union with Christ, and a part of Christ.

MOSES

The name (as the margin of our Bibles states) means drawn out The illustrious history of Moses forms so large a page in the sacred volume of the Old Testament, that it supersedes the necessity of saying much about him here. He was a faithful servant in the house of the Lord: this is the character given of him by the Holy Ghost. (Heb. iii. 2.) And a blessed testimony it is! But the same testimony gives him no higher a character than a servant of Christ; and Moses himself thought this an honour high enough. He was a type himself of the law which he was commissioned to deliver; for as he was not permitted to enter into the promised land, so he thereby represented that the law could not bring God's people into Canaan, and consequently not into heaven, of which Canaan was a type. It is Jesus alone that can do this; "The law was given by Moses, but grace and truth came by Jesus Christ." (John i. 17.)

MOTHER

The name is too tender, too common, and too interesting to need much explanation; but though it is not necessary, in the ordinary acceptation of the word, to dwell upon it by way of explaining its meaning, yet it may not be amiss to remark the general application of it. As a woman who brings forth a child is by virtue of it immediately called a mother, so the church, which brings forth children to God in Christ is called "the Jerusalem which is above, who is the mother of us all." (Gal. iv. 26.) The name is applied to all that carry this kind of maternity. The synagogue is called the mother of the Jews. Where is the bill of your mother's divorcement, (saith JEHOVAH by the prophet) which I have put away?--here mother means the synagogue. (See Isa. 1:1.) Babylon is called the mother of harlots, Rev. xvii. 5. An holy matron is called a mother in Israel, 2 Sam. xx. 19, Judg. v. 7. Our grave is called by Job our mother's womb, Job i. 21.

MOUNT and MOUNT OF THE LORD

We find the church of Christ continually distinguished by this name in the Old Testament Scripture, and as such we cannot pass it over without some attention to the subject; otherwise the name itself is too familiar to every reader to require explanation. In allusion to the times of the gospel, the Holy Ghost, by his servants the prophets, pointed to the church under these figures.--"It shall come to pass in the last days, that the mountain of the Lord's house shall be established in the tops of the mountains, and shall be exalted above the hill,, and all nations shall flow unto it." So proclaimed both Isaiah and Micah, Isa. ii. 2. Micah iv. 1. So Zechariah viii. 3. "Jerusalem shall be called a city of truth, and the mountain of the Lord of hosts the holy mountain." And the gospel itself, with all its blessings, is described under the figurative language of a rich feast in the Lord's holy mountain." (Isa. xxv. 6, 7.)

The church, in allusion to the same, and looking forward to the coming of Christ, in a high and beautiful, strain of imagery, saith, "Until the day break, and the shadows flee away, I will get me to the mountains of myrrh, and to the hill of frankincense." The mountain of myrrh can mean no other than the Lord's house, the church of Jesus. And the expression of myrrh is beautifully adopted to denote Christ's sufferings on the mount, when his sacred body was bruised, and the fragrance of his merits became like the rich perfume of myrrh and frankincense which grew there. And if, as some think, that both these figures of the mountain of myrrh, and hill of frankincense, have peculiar reference to the mount Moriah, where Isaac was intentionally offered up a type of Christ, the figure is striking and just indeed. And what it is to the church at large, such is it to every child of God during the dark shades of night, until the day of the renewed life breaks in upon the soul at conversion.

Oh, that the Lord may graciously

enable every one of this description to say with the church, Until the day of grace break, and the shadows flee away, I will get me to the mountain, the church, there the myrrh of Christ's fragrancy in sufferings will refresh me, until the day of glory and the everlasting light, unmixed with the shades of night, shall break in upon my soul, and I shall then dwell in the everlasting mountain of the house of God for ever! Amen.

Perhaps the reader will be pleased to behold the several most remarkable mountains of Scripture brought into, one point of view. I shall not arrange them according to the order in which they stand in the Bible, but, for the better apprehension and memory, in alphabetical order, together with references to the Scriptures where the account of them may be seen.

MOUNT AMALEK

So called from Am, people--Lacac, to lick up, or take away. It is probable that this mountain took its name from Amalek, the grandson of Esau. (See Gen. xxxvi. 12.) It was situated in Arabia Petraea, between the Dead Sea and the 'Red Sea, or more properly speaking, between Havilah and Shur. (1 Sam. xv. 7.) And this Amalek, who gave name to this mountain, or derived his name from it, was father to the race of Amalekites, which were the deadly foes of Israel from Israel's first departure from Egypt. And this was the nation concerning whom the Lord sware, that he would utterly put out their name from under heaven, and have war with from generation to generation. (See Exod. xvii. 8. to the end.)

Behold, reader, in the history of Esau's race, and their bitter enmity against the seed of Jacob, the type of that unceasing and everlasting war which takes place between nature and grace, between the children of the bondwoman and the children of the free. It is blessed when, from well-founded evidences, we can say with the apostle, So then, brethren, we are not children of the bondwoman, but of the free." (Gal. iv. 31.)

MOUNT AMANA

A mountain beyond Jordan, in the tribe of Manasseh. It was situated near Cilicia, and which divided it from Syria. Some suppose that the river Abana, which is at the foot of it, took its name from it. (See 2 Kings v. 12.) In the Ketib it is written Abana, but in the Keri it is read Amana; and so the margin of the Bible hath it. It was from hence Christ called his Spouse the church--"Come with me from Lebanon, (my spouse) with me from Lebanon: look from the top of Amana, from the top of Shenir and Hermon, from the lions' den, from the mountains of the leopards;" (Song iv. 8.) meaning from the fellowship of the evil, which is like the ferocity of beasts, to the sweet communion of Jesus, in his love, and grace, and favour.

MOUNT CALVARY

See Calvary--Gethsemane--and Golgotha.

MOUNT *CARMEL*

This was a mountain in the land of Judea, near the Mediterranean sea. It took its name from the fruitfulness of it, being covered with vines and corn-fields. (See Isa. xxxv. 2. Amos i. 2,) Hence Christ, when describing his church's beauty, saith, "Thine head upon thee is like Carmel:" (Song vii. 5.) meaning, no doubt, himself; for Christ is "the Head of his body the church, the fulness which filleth all in all." (Eph. i. 2'2, 23.) Here it was the prophet Elijah did such wonders by faith, to the glory of God. (See 1 Kings xviii.)

Mount *Ebal*. So called from Balah, old age. Probably an ancient heap mouldering to decay, and unfruitful. It was situated in Ephraim, near Shechem, over against Gerizim. (See Deut. xi. 29, 30.) See Gerizim.

MOUNT ENGEDI - MOUNT HERMON

MOUNT ENGEDI

The same as Hazzazon Tamar, (2 Chron. xx. 2.) near the Dead Sea; a place remarkable for rich vines. Hence Christ is compared by the church "to a cluster of camphire in the vineyards of Engedi." (Song i. 14.) See Cluster.

MOUNT GAASH

This was the memorable sepulchre of Joshua, in Tinmath Serah, in mount Ephraim. (See Josh. xxiv. 30.) It should be observed, that the mountains of Ephraim were several detached portions of rising ground, here and there, dispersed through the land belonging to that tribe.

MOUNT GILBOA

So called from Gal, to change--and Bahah, on enquiry. This mountain will always be remembered by the readers of the Bible, on account of the death of Saul and Jonathan, and the beautiful elegy of David composed on that occasion. It lay southward of Jerusalem. (See 2 Sam. i. throughout.)

MOUNT GILEAD

Here it was Laban overtook Jacob in his flight. (See Gen. xxxi. 33.) In after-ages the place became memorable, and was formed into a kingdom. (2 Sam. ii. 9.) The plains below were well calculated for cattle; and hence the Reubenites and Gadites desired to possess it in the general distribution of Canaan. (See Num. xxxi. 1.) And we find the Lord Jesus, when praising his church for the comeliness he had put upon her, compares her to the flocks beheld from this mount. "Behold, thou art fair, my love, behold thou art fair; thou hast dove's eyes within thy locks, thy hair is as a flock of goats that appear from mount Gilead." (Song iv. 1.) It is, no doubt, lovely sight, from an eminence of rising ground to behold the plains below covered with the fleecy inhabitants grazing in their pastures. But how much more lovely to behold the Lord's flock, from the mountain of the Lord's house, feeding in the pasture of his word and ordinances, and by the still waters beside which "the great Shepherd of Israel leads his flock at noon." (Song i. 7, 8. Ps. ii. 3.)

MOUNT GERIZIRN

This mount lay on the other side Jordan towards the way of the going down of the sun in Canaan. And here it was that Moses commanded Israel, from this mountain, to pronounce blessings upon the people. (Deut. xi. 29, 30.) There should seem to have been a special design in this appointment of the Lord by Moses; for here it was, beside the plains of Moreh, that Abraham first came, at the call of God, when he left Haran. (See Gen. xii. 1-6) So that though Moses himself had never been there, nor ever would, yet here blessings should immediately, on their arrival, be pronounced, to Israel's fidelity, in the very spot where, in ages before, the Lord had first revealed himself to their father Abraham. There is a great sweetness in the connexion in proof of covenant love; and I hope the reader, as oft as he calls to mind mount Gerizim, will call to recollection this view of it. The reader may find farther account of the blessings which the Lord appointed to be pronounced on mount Gerizim, Deut. xxvii. 11. and xxviii. 1-14. and the confirmation of the whole, as fulfilled by Joshua after Israel had passed over Jordan, taken Jericho and Ai, Josh. viii. 33. to the end.

MOUNT *HEBRON*

So called from forming society. It was situated in the land of Canaan. Here Sarah died. (Gen. xxiii. 2.) This place became a kingdom in after-ages, for David reigned there. (2 Sam. ii. 11.)

MOUNT HERMON

This was called by the Sidonians Sirion, and

the Amorites calked it Shenir, (Deut. iii. 9.) Its height was very great, and always covered with snow. The faithful in the Old Testament celebrated the beauties of Hermon in their songs. It was situated so near the temple, that it formed a part of it; indeed Zion is called Hermon. (Deut. iv. 28.) See Hermon.

MOUNT *HOR*

This place was rendered memorable by the death of Aaron. (See Num. xxi. 23. to the end.) Hor was situated on the confines of Idumea. The name is taken from somewhat that conceives or shews.

MOUNT HOREB

The name means desert, a poor dry place. Horeb was situated so near mount Sinai, that it appears to be but one and the same place, only that Sinai is east and Horeb west. This mountain will always be memorable in Scripture; because here it was the Lord appeared to Moses. (Exod. iii. 1. &c.) Here the Lord seemed to stand, as if to intimate that the law was given by Moses, "but grace and truth came by Jesus Christ." (See also I Kings xix. 8.

MOUNT LEBANON

See Lebanon.

MOUNT *MORIAH.*

See Moriah.

MOUNT *NEBO*

The memorable mount where Moses died. It was situated beyond Jordan. The name is derived from a root which signifies to prophecy: whether in allusion to the death of this great man, so called, I presume not to determine. But certain it is, that his death on this mount, and by the express appointment of the Lord, is very singular and striking. The Pisgah view which Moses had of the land of Canaan from this mount, must have been from special assistance from the Lord. We are told that he saw from thence all the land of Gilead unto Dan, and all the land of Naphtali and Ephraim and Manasseh, and all the land of Judah unto the uttermost sea, together with the south and the plain of the valley of Jericho, the city of palm trees, unto Zoar. (Deut. xxxi. 1-3.) So that the extremity on one view could not be well less than three-score miles and on the other more than double that; a thing next to an impossibility had not the Lord, for the purpose, supernaturally assisted him. And is it not so with all the objects of faith? Jesus himself, when beheld by faith, is made lovely indeed to the eye of grace; but to the carnal "there is no beauty that we should desire him."

I cannot dismiss this view of Nebo, and the man of God's privileges upon it, without observing, that all he saw was but a type and shadow of the reality which believers in Christ by faith now enjoy of a better country, which Jesus is gone before to take possession of in their name. Old Testament saints were far less blessed in this particular than New Testament believers. They saw Christ's day afar off, they rejoiced, and were glad. We have seen that day accomplished, and brought nigh, and by faith enter now upon the possession of it in the promises. Oh! for grace then in lively exercise in views more bright and clear than the Pisgah sights from mount Nebo, to set the Lord always before us, and daily to walk by faith in the closest communion and fellowship with the Father and with his Son Jesus Christ, till the Lord shall take us home to himself in everlasting fruition, that "where he is, there we may be also." Amen.

MOUNT OLIVET

Sweet and sacred spot from whence the Lord Jesus ascended, when having finished redemption-work, he returned to glory! and where, according to the voice both of prophets and angels, his feet shall again stand, when the mountains shall cleave in the midst, and Jesus shall come to reign before his ancients gloriously. (See in confirmation Isa. xxiv. 23. Zech. xiv. 4. to the end; Acts i. 9-12.) This hallowed mount is situated at the east of Jerusalem, being separated only by the brook Kedron, and the valley of Jehoshaphat. Here it was that David (typically of Christ) went up barefoot and weeping, when he fled from Absalom, as the Lord Jesus went by it when he entered Gethsemane, and passed over the same brook of Kedron. (See 2 Sam. xv. 22-30. John xviii. 1. Matt. xxvi. 30-46.) The reader, if not much acquainted with the sacred history will be surprized to find that the spot rendered so memorable to David by sorrow should be prophaned by Solomon his son. But so it was, when king Solomon loved many strange wives, those illicit connexions led him into idolatry; hence we read that Solomon built an high place for Chemosh, the abomination of Moab, in the hill that is before Jerusalem, and for Moloch, the abomination of the children of Ammon. (1 Kings xi. 1-7.) Hence, in the after-reign of the good king Josiah, when the king, removed those idols, so much prophaned had been this mount, that it had acquired the name of the mount of corruption. (See 2 Kings xxiii. 13.) Blessed be the Lord for taking away the corruption, and making the spot infinitely more hallowed than it had ever been before, by the presence and ascension of the Lord Jesus from it, when he had finished the sacred purposes of his redemption.

Here would my soul, methinks, frequently wander in sacred meditation, that glory which shall be revealed. Here, I would say, from hence Jesus ascended when he went up on high, and led captivity captive, and received gifts for men; yea, when he received gifts for men in the manhood of Christ Jesus. And here my contemplating soul would listen to the angel's words who graced the Lord Jesus's triumph, and still hear, in the ear of faith, their blessed tidings vibrating in the sweetest sound on my ravished senses--"Ye men of Galilee, why stand ye gazing up into heaven? this same Jesus which is taken up from you into heaven, shall so come, in like manner as ye have seen him go into heaven." (Acts i. I 1.)

MOUNT PARAN

We find mention made of this mountain by the name of El-paran. (Gen. xiv. 6.) And it was here that Moses, when rehearsing the mercies of God to Israel, delivered those blessed sermons which are recorded in the book of Deuteronomy. (See Deut. i. 1.) The prophet Habakkuk also, in that beautiful chapter of his, begins his relation of the glories of the Lord from this place. "God (saith he) came from Teman, and the Holy One from mount Paran." Habak. iii. 3.)

This mount formed a part of the desert of Arabia Petrsea, and lay south of the land of promise. The name is derived from the Hebrew word pear, signifying beauty. The place is rendered memorable from events which are recorded concerning it in the several providences of God. Here it was that Hagar, the handmaid of Sarah, fled from her mistress, and here the angel of the Lord visited her. (Gen. xxi. 14.-21.) Here Israel, after leaving mount Sinai, arrived and encamped, being so directed by the resting of the cloud. (See Num. x. 12.) Here David found a refuge, in after-ages from the persecution of Saul. (I Sam. xxv. 1.) So that Paran hath proved an asylum to the distressed on many occasions, as recorded in the Scriptures; and in how many more that are not recorded in public memorials, who shall say! It is blessed when souls under exercise find the Lord in the wilderness dispensations, who have missed such discoveries in the peopled city. Hagar and David, and thousands besides, have experienced a Paran when and where they least expected it; and wilderness straits have sometimes brought forth such freedoms, as to make the wilderness blossom as the rose. Wheresoever Jesus is, as he was to Hagar, and as he was to David, when he speaks, and when he opens the eyes to see his grace, we find near to us the well of water "springing up to everlasting life." So may my soul find many a Paran in the present wilderness, and Jesus will sweeten and soften all straits by the gracious enlargements of his love.

MOUNT PISGAH

This is the same as Nebo, for the word Pisgah only means hill or top, from Pasag; so that Nebo, Pisgah, and Abarim, are one and the same, near mount Peor, over against Jericho, in the country of Moab. (See Num. xxi. 20. Deut. xxxiv. 1.) See Mount Nebo.

MOUNT SAMARIA

This mount, spoken of in the Old Testament, became memorable, in after-ages, in the New, for the worship of the Samaritans. Hence, in the conversation the woman at Jacob's well had with Christ, she seemed anxious to know whether they were right. (See John iv. 20.) She referred, no doubt, to what the Lord had said by Moses concerning Jerusalem, Deut xv, 5. The mount of Samaria formed a part only of Samaria; for Omri, king of Israel, built Samaria, and bought the hill of Shemer, from whence Samaria took its name. (See 1 Kings xvi. 23, 24.) We have reason to bless the Lord whenever we hear or read of Samaria, from that most interesting discourse, recorded by the Evangelist, which took place here between Jesus and the poor adulteress. What unnumbered discoveries of grace have distressed sinners found in those encouraging words of Jesus! The constraint upon the Lord Jesus to go there to seek and save this sinner, the unprepared, unconscious state of her mind at the time, the tender waitings of Jesus to the hour of her arrival at the well, for he was first there, the tenderness and compassion in all that he said and manifested towards her, his condescension in abiding with the Samaritans two whole days, and the effects wrought upon the hearts of many of the people, as well as this poor woman; these, with numberless other incidents which are found in Christ's visit to Samaria, must always make the very name interesting to the heart of a believer, and especially when the same saving grace which wrought upon this woman's mind hath taken place in ours, so that we can hold out the invitation concerning Christ to others, which she did to her countrymen: "Come, see a man which told me all things that ever I did; is not this the Christ!" (Read the whole relation, John iv. 1-42.)

MOUNT SEIR

This mountain (or rather mountains) is at the south and east of the Dead Sea, near Moab. The name should seem to have been taken from Shahar, which means hairy: probably the mount had a rough appearance. The mount itself is rendered memorable from the patriarchal history. The Horites originally possessed it, as we read Gen. xiv. 6. But in process of time the descendants of Esau. Moses relates that the children of Esau destroyed the Horims, and took possession of Seir. (Deut. ii. 12.) But what makes Seir an interesting subject to the Lord's people is, that here it was Jacob, in his return from Mesopotamia, had those soul-exercises which we read of Gen. xxxii. 3-20. And here, soon after, we find those gracious manifestations which the Lord vouchsafed to him, to strengthen his faith, and to prepare him for the interview with his brother Esau. Read the close of the chapter, and to the end of the sixteenth verse of the thirty-third chapter.

MOUNT SINAI

So called from Senah, bush. This place will be always memorable, from the law having been delivered from it accompanied with thunderings and lightnings, and all the other awful demonstrations of the divine presence. Horeb, and Sinai, are not exactly one and the same, for they are evidently two

MOUNT TABOR - MOUNT ZION

distinct mountains. And as Sinai is at the east, and Horeb lies west, at sunrise (we are told by travellers) the right is very magnificent. Sinai is all shining, from the sun's beams, and yet forming a shade on Horeb; so that the one is bright, and the other dark. Mount Sinai hath been always considered figurative of the blackness, and darkness, and terror of that dispensation which issued from it. And what the apostle, by commission from the Holy Ghost, said of it, Heb. vii. 18-21, plainly sets forth the cause. It was a mount, Paul saith, that "burned, with fire, and blackness, and darkness, and tempest f intimating the dread which must ever fill the soul at the delivery of the law, when the soul is filled with a conscious sense of having broken that law, and stands under the conviction of it, as yet unconscious of Christ. Moses himself tells us, that he exceedingly feared and quaked. There can be no enduring that which was commanded. Hence the apostle Paul (to the Galatian church, who seemed ignorant of this trembling of soul, who seemed ignorant from not having been sufficiently humbled under a sense of sin; and were running back to a covenant of works for justification,) cries out, "Tell me, ye that desire to be under the law, do ye not hear the law?" (Gal. iv. 21.) As if he had said, do ye not hear the awful threatenings to disobedience, and the total impossibility of being justified by the law? Such was, and is, and ever must be, mount Sinai in the church. What a blessedness that we are not come to it; but delivered from it, by the offering of the body of Jesus Christ once for all!"

MOUNT TABOR

In Galilee. The name, in Hebrew, signifies a rising; and as it was centered in the midst of a wide country, it hath been called the Navel of Jezreel, similar to the holy land being called the midst of the earth, as the margin of the Bible renders it, the Navel of the earth. (See Ezek. xxxviii. 12.) The mount of Tabor is spoken of, as beautifully covered with trees and herbage, and always affording a rich verdure. Hence, we find the Lord himself referring to mount Tabor as eminent among the mountains; "As I live, saith the King, whose name is the Lord of hosts; surely as Tabor is among the mountains, and as Carmel by the sea, so shall he come." (Jer. xlvi. 18.) And the Psalmist celebrates this mountain as rejoicing with Hermon in the Lord. (Ps. lxxxix. 12.) Some have thought that it was in mount Tabor the Lord Jesus was transfigured. And if so, the Psalmist, by the spirit of prophecy ages before, might well speak of the honour given to this mount, for JEHOVAH'S voice was then heard in it, when he said of Christ, "This is my beloved Son, hear him.", (Luke ix. 12.)

MOUNT ZION

The last mountain to; be noticed in this work, according to the order of the alphabet; but the first in point of excellency and glory? We may well cry out with the Psalmist our every account, while we contemplate this holy mount, "Beautiful for situation, the joy of the whole earth, is mount Zion I Glorious things are spoken of thee, thou city of God." (Ps. xlviii. 2. Ps. lxxxvii, 3.) The name is derived Tzun, a monument raised up. And considered as the church of Jesus, it is indeed a monument of grace here, and glory hereafter, raised up to all eternity! Here David built his city of David, a type of the city of God in Christ. Here Solomon built the temple, a type also of Christ's body. So that when in other Scriptures (numberless as they are) we read that "the Lord hath founded Zion, and the poor of his people shall trust in it." (Isa. xiv. 32.) When we hear JEHOVAH saying, "Behold, I lay in Zion, for a foundation, a stone, a tried stone, a precious corner-stone." (Isa. xxviii.. 16.) And the Holy Ghost commissioning an apostle to tell the church, that this is Christ. (1 Pet. ii. 6-8.) When, with the eye of faith, like John, we behold "the Lamb standing on mount Zion, surrounded with his redeemed." (Rev. xiv. 1.) Who but must exclaim, in the language of inspiration, "Praise waiteth for thee, O Lord, in Zion: and unto thee shall the vow be performed!" (Ps. lxv. 1.) Reader! what are your views, in contemplating this mountain of the Lord's house, which he hath established "in the top of the mountains, and of which he hath said all nations shall flow unto it?" (Isa. ii. 2. Micah iv. 1. &c.) Are you come spiritually so, and by faith, "to mount Zion: the city of the living God, the heavenly Jerusalem: to an innumerable company of angels; to the general assembly and church of the first-born, whose names are written in heaven: and to God the judge of all, and to the spirits of just men made perfect; and to Jesus the Mediator of the New Covenant; and to the blood of sprinkling that speaketh better things than that of Abel?" (Heb. xii. 22-24.)

Pause over the solemn and most interesting question? Souls that are come, know their privilege, and are conscious of their high calling; and having found peace in the blood of the cross, have constant access to a mercy-seat, and enjoy the sweet Bethel visits, of daily communion with the Father, and with his Son Jesus Christ. The prophets, with one voice, have described their privileges. "The ransomed of the Lord (saith one of them) shall return and come to Zion with songs, and everlasting joy upon their heads." (See Isa. xxxv. 10.) "They shall come (saith another) and sing in the height of Zion, and shall flow together to the goodness of the Lord, for wheat, and for wine, and for oil, and for the young of the flock, and of the herd: and their soul shall be as a watered garden, and they shall not sorrow any more at all." (Jer. xxxi. 12.) And all the prophets in like manner, describe this blessedness of the gospel church in Zion. (Joel ii. 32. Obad. xxi. Zech. viii. 3.) Reader! see to it, that these privileges and these blessing are yours.

MOURNING

We find in the early ages of the church, great lamentation observed at the death of their friends

The funeral of Sarah is set forth in this view. And still more, in that of the patriarch Jacob, Seven days the funeral halted at the threshing-floor of Atad. And the astonishment of the inhabitants of the land was so great, that they gave a name to it, and called it Abel-mizraim; that is, the mourning of the Egyptians, (Gen. 1:7-11. We find that the Israelites themselves called all places of their mourning by one name, Bochim, that is weepers. (See Judges ii. 1-5.)

MULBERRY-TREE

There is somewhat sacred in the mulberry-tree, and holy Scripture seems to have pointed this out very strikingly, when directing the movement of the Lord's army to be, when the people heard the sound of a going m the mulberry-trees; for thereby they should know that the Lord went out before them. (2 Sam. v. 24.) The Psalmist speaks of the church passing through the valley of Baca (that is the mulberry-trees), meaning soul exercises with the sweet fruit of divine love. For when the Lord calls to trial, he gives to his people a grace suited to support. (Ps. lxxxiv. 4-6.)

MUPPIM

The son of Benjamin. (Gen. xlvi. 21.) The word signifies the mouth.

MURDER

Every sinner is a soul-murderer. Hence the prophet saith, "O Israel, thou hast destroyed thyself; but in me is thine help." (Hos. xiii. 9.)

MUSIC

Of the music of the Old Testament Scripture it is no easy matter to form a right apprehension. That the Hebrews were fond

MUSICIAN - MUSICIAN

of music is readily admitted. And that they excelled in the art, can as readily be allowed; since we find upon record, strong testimonies of the power and effect upon the mind, both from the strength and charm of the melody, and the skill of the performer. David's harp quieted the disturbed state of Sauls mind. (1 Sam. xvi. 14. to the end.) And in like manner, we find other testimonies of the influence of music. When Saul sent messengers to seize David, the melody of the prophets so affected their minds that they joined the chorus. And when other messengers were sent, the same effect followed. Yea, Saul himself felt the contagion, and for the moment his passion of anger subsided. (See 1 Sam. xix. 19. to the end.)

But, while all possible allowance is made to this view of the music of the Hebrews, we cannot conceive that all that is said of musical instruments in the Old Testament Scriptures means literally so to be received. The antiquity of music, no doubt, gave birth, very early, to the invention. Jubal, before the deluge, is said to have been "the father of all that play on the (kinnor) harp, and (hugab) organ." (Gen. iv. 21.) Indeed, the very sound of the human voice is musical, and must have given rise very early in the world to the invention. But after all, it is not to be supposed, that every instrument of flute, harp, sackbut, psaltry, and dulcimer, literally mean those things which we take them for. In numberless instances we may conclude, that they rather mean stringed instruments of the heart. See the hundred and fiftieth Psalm and the like. Hence the great variety of the names we meet with at the head of numberless Psalms, can never be supposed to refer to such things. Whether we comprehend their meaning or not, common sense might suppose that somewhat higher is intended.

MUSICIAN

We meet with an address, or dedication, at the opening of very many of the psalms: "To the chief Musician." And not a few have been led to suppose, that it means no more than a superscription to the master or chaunter who presided over the temple service; as if the Holy Ghost was mole attentive to have the Psalm played or sung well with the instrument or voice, than to have the blessed contents of the Psalm itself impressed upon the heart. We do not know that there was such an office over the choir as chief musician; certain it is, that neither the Chaldee paraphrase, nor any of the other versions, say any thing about this chief musician. Besides, if it be supposed that David had such a character in his band as chief musician, what authority is there to suppose that the prophet Habakkuk knew of any such a character; and yet he also addresseth his hymn to the chief sinner. (See Hab. iii. 19.) I find an author of no small authority observe, that the word which (1 Sam. xv. 29.) is rendered strength, and is a well known title of Christ, is not dissimilar to the word in the Psalms rendered chief musician. See Parkhurst's Lexicon, 410 and 496. And in confirmation of this, it is well worthy of remark that Habakkuk saith, (chap. iii. 19.) "The Lord God is my strength." In this sense, the close of Habakkuk's prophecy will be rendered thus: "The Lord God is my strength, and he will make my feet like harts' feet; and the Giver of victory, or my stringed instruments, will cause me to tread on my high places."

It should be observed, moreover, that the word Lamenetz is rendered by the Seventy to the end. And what end, but the end of Christ's triumphs by virtue of his sacrifice? And as Christ is the end of the law for righteousness to every one that believeth," may not those numberless sweet Psalms which so plainly refer to him, be supposed to be addressed to him as the end? So we find the title of the sixth Psalm, and the twelfth Psalm, to be addressed to the chief musician upon Sheminith. And every one cannot but know that these Psalms are both of them spoken prophetically of the person of Christ, the God-man-Mediator; and therefore, as such, surely it is doing no violence to the word Sheminith, joined with Lamenetz, to suppose that it forms an address to Christ, as the strength of Israel in his Sheminith or abundant riches, suited to his high character as the chief end of salvation to his people. But as I have elsewhere said, in similar observations in my "Poor Man's Commentary on the Psalms," so I beg to add here, I do not decide on the enquiry. I have thought it worth while to give the views I have of it to the reader, and here with humble requests to the Lord to pardon every unintentional error, I leave the subject.

MYRRH

This aromatic gum is from a tree common in Arabia. The Hebrews called it Mur. It formed a principal ingredient in the holy ointment for anointing the tabernacle and the vessels of the sanctuary, and also Aaron and his sons; and the Lord forbade the use of it in common, or any composition by way of imitating it, on pain of being cut off from his people. Was not this a striking type of the Holy Ghost in his divine offices, and the awful consequence of attempting any thing which bore a resemblance to the holy unction of the Spirit? (See Exod. xxx. 22-33.)

The Holy Ghost hath been pleased to mark out so many things concerning the Lord Jesus under the figure and type of myrrh, that we ought not to pass over a short consideration of some of them at least. Jesus himself is the sweet scented myrrh of his gospel; hence the church saith of him, that he is "a bundle of myrrh," (Song i. 13.) meaning, no doubt, that he is a cluster, a fulness, of all divine and human excellences. Every thing in Christ, and from Christ, is most grateful and full of odour to his church and people; hence his garments are said "to smell of myrrh, aloes and cassia"--all temporal, all spiritual, and eternal blessings are in him for his spouse, his fair one, his redeemed. "I will get me (saith the church) to the mountains of myrrh, and to the hill of frankincense, until the day break, and the shadows flee away." (Song iv. 6.)

Myrrh is not only figuratively made use of to denote the sweetness and rich odour of Jesus, in his person, grace, and fulness, but the blessed Spirit uses the figure of myrrh to speak of his sufferings also; yea, the offered myrrh mingled with wine to Jesus on the cross, and which was among the predictions concerning the Lord in that solemn season, plainly testified the bitterness of Christ's sufferings. And the double quality of this Arabian gum, its fragrancy, and its bitterness, formed a striking union to shew forth how precious a sacrifice of a sweet smelling savour was that very death, which to Jesus was gall and bitterness, indeed, in the extreme. (Mark xv. 23.) And may we not suppose that the Lord Jesus had an eye both to his own sufferings, and to the sufferings of his faithful ones, who had followed him to glory through persecution and not unfrequently death, when he said: "I have gathered my myrrh with my spice?" for in his own person he trod the wine-press of the wrath of God alone, and may be said to gather the fruits of the labour and travail of his soul when beholding the blessed effects of it in the everlasting salvation of his people. And in their lesser conflicts and exercises, the bitterness of their sorrows Jesus takes notice of and gathers, when owning them for his own, and bringing them home to his Father's house, he brings them to himself, that where he is there they may be also. Blessed Lord Jesus! come as thou hast said to my house, to my heart, while thine hands are dropping with myrrh, and thy fingers with sweet-smelling myrrh, and be thou "like a young roe or an hart upon the mountains of spices!" (Song v. 1.5; viii. 14.)

MYSIA - MYSTERY

MYSIA

A province of Asia Minor. Here Paul preached. (Acts xvi. 7, 8.)

MYSTERY

Oh, what a mystery is the gospel of salvation, and the blessed contents of it! What a mystery is that great and fundamental truth, "God in Christ, and Christ in God!" (2 Cor. v. 19. Collos. iii. 3.) What a mystery that Three sacred persons should be in One, and yet the same eternal, undivided, JEHOVAH! (1 John v. 7.) What a mystery Jesus speaks of when addressing the Father, and speaking of himself and church--"I in them, and thou in me!" (John xvii. 23.) What a mystery, yea, what a great mystery, is godliness: "God manifest in the flesh, justified in the Spirit, seen of angels preached unto the Gentiles, believed on in the world, received up into glory!" (1 Tim. iii. 16.) And is there not another mystery, to every truly regenerated believer, as great, yea, if possible, greater than any, namely, that I should believe in Jesus, and Christ be formed in my heart the hope of glory, when thousands neither know the Lord, nor believe the record God hath given of his dear Son!

N

NAAM
The son of Caleb. (1 Chron. iv. 15.) His name signifies beautiful, from Nahom.

NAAMAH
There are two of this name in Scripture. Naamah, the daughter of Lamech, (Gen. iv. 22.) and Naamah the wife of Solomon, an Ammonitess, (1 Kings xiv. 21.) The same signification as Naaon, beautiful.

NAAMAH
A city of Judah. (Josh. xv. 41.)

NAAMAN
There are several of this name in the Bible. Benjamin had a son of this name, Gen. xlvi. 41; and a grandson, 1 Chron. viii. 4. And Naaman, the Syrian, well known from the history of his leprosy, and the cure of it by Elisha the prophet, 2 Kings v. 1, &c. The name is the same in meaning as Naam or Naamah, amd from the same root; and signifies beautiful or pretty.

The subject of Naaman's leprosy, and the wonderful cure by the prophet Elisha, in the name of the Lord, hath afforded large scope for the most improving meditation. I refer the reader to the article Leper, for farther remarks on the nature of the disease itself, and shall only add on that subject, that if such was the power of the servant of the prophet in his Master's name, instantly to cure this Syrian, what may we suppose, is the sovereign power and grace of the Lord God of the prophets, to heal all the leprosies of the souls of his people! Would to God (I would say in the words of the poor captive to her mistress) every poor sinner convinced by the Holy Ghost of his leprous state of sin, were with the Lord Jesus Christ, the Almighty prophet of his church and people, for He would recover him of his leprosy! (See 2 Kings v. throughout.)

There is one circumstance more, well worthy of being noticed in this history of the cure of this Syrian. It appears from this man's narrative, that he was smitten with conviction, that the God of Israel was the true God; and therefore, he resolved from henceforth, he would serve no other. But recollecting the idolatry of his master, and knowing that on his return he should, as before, be called to go with the king to this idol worship, he thought now to compromise the matter, and therefore begged the prophet to indulge him in this with his pardon. "The Lord pardon thy servant (said he) in this thing." And it should seem the two mules' burden of earth, he begged permission to take home with him to Syria, were intended after each renewed instance of bowing in the house of Rimmon, to be used by way of cleansing from their sin. I do not decide upon the subject, but as we know from historians that the sprinkling of earth where no water was immediately at hand, was occasionally used in the Eastern countries, in their religious services in the stead of water, it is probable, this might be the object Naaman had in view, in craving the indulgence of carrying home two mules' burden with him. The Syrian had found the efficacy of Israel's sacred stream of Jordan, and he concluded that the earth of Canaan was as sacred also. As therefore, he could not take the river with him, he desired a portion of the earth, which he supposed would prove equally salutary to the cleansing from sin.

But whether such were the views or not, with which Naaman's mind was influenced, when he desired the earth of Israel; it may, at least, serve to teach us a lesson from this Syrian's faith, how to appreciate all our mercies in the Lord God of Israel. How doth the faith of this man, and so immediately wrought as it was in the mind of this poor idolater, reproach the supposed followers of the Lord Jesus

NAAMATHITE - NAHBI

Christ, who, after all the miracles, and evidences, and testimonies, with which the truth, as it is in Jesus, is brought home and confirmed to the heart, can hardly keep alive, from day to day, a suitable dependence upon Him! May we not take up the words of the Lord Jesus upon this occasion, and say, as he did: "Nevertheless, when the Son of man cometh, shall he find faith on the earth?" (Luke xviii. 8.)

NAAMATHITE

We read of Zophar the Naamathite, Job ii. 11. The word is derived from the same root as Naaman, and of the same meaning, beautiful. And perhaps he came from Naamah, a city of Judah. (See Josh. xv. 41.) But there is no authority to form this conclusion.

NAARAT

One of David's valiant men. (1 Chron. xi. 37.) The meaning of this name is, my young children, from Nahar, youth.

NAARATH

A city of Ephraim. (Josh. xvi. 7.) From Nahar, youth or child.

NAASHON or NAASSON

The son of Aminadab, in the genealogy of the Lord Jesus Christ. (Matt. i. 4.) The name is derived from Nichesh, and signifies a foretelling. Some derive it from Nechash, serpent.

NABAL

The Carmelite. We have his history, 1 Sam. xxv. His name is very expressive, and signifies fool.

NABOTH

We have his history, 1 Kings xxi. Same name in meaning as Nebajoth, son of Ishmael.

NACHON

Mention is made of this man but once in the Scripture; namely, 2 Sam, vi. His name signifies prepared, from Cum .

NADAB

The son of Aaron. His awful death is related to us, Lev. x. 1, 2, with the cause of it. His name signifies princely, from Nadab. We meet with others of this name, Nadab, son of Jeroboam, 1 Kings xv. 25. And Nadab, son of Shammai, 1 Chron. ii. 30.

NAGGE

Son of Maath. (Luke iii. 25, 26.) His name signifies brightness, from Nagah. This man is in the genealogy of Christ.

NAHALAL

A city of Zebulon. (Josh. xix. 15.) The meaning of this name is strength, from Hallal.

NAHALIEL

A place where Israel encamped in the wilderness, and is compounded of Nahal, brook--and El, God. (Num. xxi. 19.)

NAHASH

There are several of this name in Scripture. Two kings of the Ammorites. (See 1 Sam. xi. 1. and 2 Sam. xvii. 27.) And there was a third, Nahash, father of Abigail, (2 Sam. xvii. 25.) it is somewhat singular to find persons of this name, for it is derived from Nachash, serpent. And so the serpent is called, Gen. iii. 1.

NAHATH

Son of Ruel. (Gen. xxxvi. 13.) From Nuach, rest.

NAHBI

One of the spies sent to search out the promised land. (Num. xiii. 14.) Probably derived from Chadab, well beloved.

NAHOR

Father of Terah, and grandfather to Abraham. (Gen. xi. 24.) Probably derived from Charor, choked. Abraham had a brother also of this name. (Gen. xi. 26.)

NAHASSON

See Nasshon.

NAHUM

One of the lesser prophets. He was a native of Elkoshai, a village in Galilee. His name signifies comforter. See his prophecy.

NAIL

It is worth while to consider the Scripture sense and meaning of the word Nail; seeing God the Holy Ghost hath thought proper to describe the Lord Jesus by this figure. Ezra had an eye to Christ, no doubt, when he said, "The Lord God had given the church a nail in his holy place!' (Ezra ix. 8.) And. the prophet Isaiah was commissioned to tell the church, that JEHOVAH would fasten him "as a nail in a sure place," when describing Jesus under the type of Eliakim, the son of Hilkiah. That all that is here said of Eliakim hath respect to Christ is evident, because Jesus himself so explains a portion of it, Rev. iii. 7. And Ezra, who lived after the prophet Isaiah between two and three hundred years, evidently had an eye to what Isaiah had said in respect to Christ, in this beautiful description. (See Isa. xxii. 20. to the end.)

It is a delightful view of the Lord Jesus. He is a nail in a sure place, so that neither the nail, nor the place can give way. And it is JEHOVAH that hath fastened him. In his person, in his work, in his offices, characters, relations, what he is in the eye of God the Father; what he is in himself; what he is to his people in all things, and for all causes in time and in eternity; for all purposes, temporal, spiritual, and eternal; Christ is fixed to be the nail on which shall hang both his people's safety and welfare, "and all the glory of his Father's house." And what tends to endear this view of Christ still more is, that not only all, and every thing relating to the kingdoms of nature, providence, grace, and glory to the church at large, is so, but to every individual of that church, "the vessels of small quantity," meaning the lowest, the humblest, the least, and most inconsiderable of his people, all shall hang upon Jesus alike, "from the vessel of cups, even to all the vessels of flagons." Sweet thought to the humble timid believer!

But the prophet, in the close of this relation, saith, "that in that day, saith the Lord of hosts, shall the nail that is fastened in a sure place be removed, and be cut down and fall." What is here meant? Not, surely, that what is fastened in a sure place shall lose his hold-fast, or the vessels that are hanging upon him lose their safety; but, on the contrary, "by the removal and the cutting down," secure the everlasting safety of all that hang upon him. For it should be observed, that there is nothing said of the vessels hanging upon this nail in a sure place being separated from the nail, or being injured by the nail's removal and the nail's being cut off, for the prophet adds," that the burden that was upon it shall be cut off;" and what is this burden but the sins of Christ's people, "which he bore in his own body on the tree when he died, the just for the unjust, to bring us to God!" (1 Pet. iii. 18.) "He was wounded for their transgressions, and was cut off out of the land of the living; for the transgressions of my people (saith the Holy Ghost by this same prophet) was he stricken." (Isa. liii. 8.)

I hope the reader will be enabled to make a nice and just distinction in what is here said, and he will then discover that so far is the close of this chapter, in the removal of this nail in a sure place, and the cutting of it down, any objection to this doctrine, that it tends to confirm it still more. Jesus is the nail on which his people hang their all, their persons, life, and salvation; so that between him and them there never can be a separation, for he saith himself: "Because I live, ye shall live also." (John xiv. 19.) But while their persons, and their present and eternal all are secured in him, he is himself cut off and removed when bearing their sins, and consequently their sins are cut off never more to arise against them; "for the mouth of the Lord hath spoken it;" while he himself riseth again as the nail fastened in a sure place, that he may appear with all his people, whose sins he hath borne, whose persons he hath redeemed, and who are enabled by his grace to hang all their high hopes of mercy and salvation upon him as the Lord their righteousness.

NAIN

A city of Palestine, rendered memorable from the Lord Jesus raising the widow's son from death at the gate of this city. (See Luke vii. 11.) The word is derived from Naham, beauty.

NAIOTH

The place where David fled from Saul. (1 Sam. xix. 22.) It is in the plural number, and means beauties, from the same root.

NAKED and NAKEDNESS

In Scripture language, these terms mean somewhat more than the mere uncovering of the body; they have peculiar respect to the soul. Thus Adam and his wife in the state of innocency were naked, but not ashamed. (Gen. ii. 25.) Whereas, when the soul is without grace, unwashed in the blood of Christ, and unclothed with the robe of Jesus's righteousness, this is a state of spiritual nakedness; hence Christ describes the church of Laodicea in this awful state, and yet unconscious of it. "Because thou sayest, (saith Christ) I am rich, and increased with goods, and have need of nothing, and knowest not that thou art wretched, and miserable, and poor, and blind, and naked." (Rev. iii. 17.) So that nakedness implies, in the scriptural and spiritual sense of the word, a soul that is destitute of all covering before God. A sinner unawakened, unregenerated, hath nothing to clothe him against the calamities of the rain, and storm, and tempest of divine wrath; hence the whole of their corruption must appear; and how then, independent of every other consideration, can such an one enter the kingdom of God? "Here shall in no wise enter into it" (saith the decided language of the word of God when describing the glories of heaven, and the characters that dwell there) "any thing that defileth, neither whatsoever worketh abomination, or maketh a lie." (Rev. xxi. 27.) Hence sweetly doth Jesus admonish to take of him the suitable covering. "I counsel thee (saith Christ) to buy of me gold tried in the fire, that thou mayest be rich; and white raiment, that thou mayest be clothed, and that the shame of thy nakedness do not appear." (Rev. iii. 18.)

It was not perhaps without reference to something of the same kind, though not so explained and brought to light as it is now by the gospel, that the easterns went without sandals into the temple. Moses at the bush was commanded by the Lord to put off his shoes from off his feet, for the place whereon he stood was holy ground. (Exod. iii. 5.) Hence perhaps arose the custom of the priests ministering in the temple with their feet uncovered; and the frequent washings appointed in the Jewish ordinances had a gospel significancy, to intimate both the uncleanness and nakedness of our poor fallen nature, and both needing the cleansing by Christ's blood, and the clothing in Christ's righteousness, with which to appear before God. What a blessed thing is it that Jesus, when finding his church in this state of spiritual nakedness, and cast out as the child in the open field of nature, to perish, passed by and bid us live; yea, washed us, clothed us, and made us beautiful in his comeliness put upon us, that our renown went forth among the heathen for our beauty. (Ezek. xvi. 1-14.) Surely, every child of God may well say, "I was a stranger, and Jesus took me in; naked, and he clothed me." (Matt. xxv. 35, 36.)

NAME

By the name is meant in Scripture, the person of any one. Thus we read in Rev. iii. 4. "Thou hast a few names in Sardis"--the meaning is, thou hast a few persons there. So it is said, "they that know thy name will put their trust in thee." (Ps. ix. 10.)--The sense is, that the right knowledge of the Lord can only induce a right dependance upon him: and in this sense, what a blessedness is there in the name of JEHOVAH! Hence Moses, towards the close of his ministry, admonisheth Israel to this proper apprehension concerning JEHOVAH. "That thou mayest fear (said Moses) this glorious and fearful name, THE LORD THY GOD." (Deut. xxviii. 58.) And what an infinite fulness is contained in this glorious and fearful name! Observe, not only The Lord, that is JEHOVAH in his threefold character of person, Father, Son, and Holy Ghost, but Thy God, that is, God in covenant; so that in this view of the name of JEHOVAH, is included both his essence, nature, attributes, perfections, counsel, will, and purpose. All his gracious revelations in the person of his dear Son, his grace, love, wisdom, mercy, and the whole constellation of glories manifested in Christ and by Christ; and so running through the whole kingdoms of nature, and providence, and grace, and glory; so much, and infinitely more, is included in this one view of the glorious and fearful name of The Lord Thy God.

And this may serve to explain, in some measure, the awfulness of taking this glorious and fearful name in vain--a sin but little considered, but yet most tremendously heinous. The Jews were so tenacious of it, that they never made use of it in their ordinary discourse, even when intending to speak with reverence; but always substituted some other expression, to intimate their meaning without using the very name. See JEHOVAH under this particular.

And we find the Lord himself helping his people, as it were, in this sacred regard which they desired to have to his honour, by commanding them to avoid all temptations to it, in prohibiting their use of the names of the dunghill gods around them; knowing that the familiar use of the one, might insensibly lead to the use of the other. "And in all things that I have said unto you, (saith the Lord) be circumspect: and make no mention of the name of other gods, neither let it be heard out of thy mouth." (Exod. xxiii. 13.) And hence we find, in after-ages of the church, the Lord again interposing with his grace on this occasion, and saying: "And it shall be at that day, saith the Lord, that thou shalt call me Ishi, and shalt call me no more Baali; for I will take away the names of Baalim out of her mouth." (Hos. ii. 16, 17.) The Israelites were not only in danger from using the same name of Baali, which signifies Lord, as their idolatrous neighbours did, when speaking of their gods, but they had been upon numberless occasions infected also with their idolatry. Hence the Lord graciously promised, in this sweet and condescending Scripture, to remove the temptation to this sin, by taking the names of Baal and Baalim out of their mouths. As if the Lord had said, by being called Ishi, my man, the Lord would came home nearer to their affections.

I must not dismiss this view of the glorious and fearful name of JEHOVAH, of which we are so repeatedly told, in the word of God, the Lord is jealous, without first begging the reader to remark with me the very tender intimations the Lord gives of this name, in the person, work, and righteousness of the Lord Jesus Christ. Hence the church sings," Because of the savour of thy good ointments, thy name is as ointment poured forth." (Song i. 3.) And when a poor sinner, sensible of the loathsomeness of his own person, hath found Jesus, and what is contained for all the purposes of salvation in the person and glory of Christ, then is the name of Jesus more fragrant than all the costly perfume of the sanctuary. The soul then enters into tile enjoyment of all those names of Jesus which the prophet hath described him by, in one full constellation: "His name (saith he) shall be called Wonderful, Counsellor, the Mighty God, the Everlasting Father, the Prince of Peace!" (Isa. ix. 6.)

NAOMI

The wife of Elimelech. Her history, and a most interesting history it is, we have in the book of Ruth. Her name signifies beautiful or pleasant.

NAPHISH

Son of Ishmael, Gen. xxv. 15,--derived from Naphish, soul.

NAPHTALI

Son of Jacob by Bilhah. (Gen. xxx. 8.) The name signifies struggling. The margin of our Bible saith, that Rachel called him thus, "my wrestlings." The patriarch when dying gave a particular blessing to Naphtali, and said "Naphtali is a hind let loose: he giveth goodly words." (Gen. xlix. 21.) This prophetical blessing of Jacob hath not been regarded in terms equal to its importance, according to my apprehension; and yet the Holy Ghost seems to have called up the attention of the church to it, upon various occasions, in his holy word. I would ask, are not many of the dying patriarch's benedictions to his children considered more with reference to Christ, than to the twelve patriarchs? Do we not consider the blessing of Judah, as one whom his brethren shall praise, and as one from whom the sceptre shall not depart, as having respect principally, if not altogether, to the person of Christ? And are not the several blessings prophesied of Joseph, on the dying bed of his father, spoken directly with an eye to Joseph's Lord? And if so, why may we not with equal safety, in the blessing of Naphtali discover Christ also? Is Naphtali an hind let loose? And can we overlook that hind of the morning, even Jesus, whom the hunters pursued, and the dogs of Bashan compassed around? (See Psalm xxii. in the title of it, and throughout the Psalm.) And when we read what the church saith of her Lord, as a roe or a hind upon the mountains of spices, and thus frequently through the book of the Songs, surely it can be no difficult matter to behold Jesus in the type, and regard him who giveth goodly words.

I am the more inclined to those discoveries of Jesus, in the view of Naphtali, because in my apprehension of the subject, Moses, the man of God, in his dying benediction concerning Naphtali, confirmed what Jacob in his dying moments had before said concerning him. (See Deut. xxxiii. 23.) "O Naphtali! (said Moses) satisfied with favour, and full with the blessing of the Lord, possess thou the west and the south." And to whom are we to look for any, or for all the tribes of Israel in the possession of the divine favour, and so satisfied with it? Of whom, among the sons of Jacob, can it be said with truth, "that they are full of the blessing of the Lord," unless we first behold him in whom it hath "pleased the Father that all fulness should dwell," and from him, and in him, and by him, all the seed of Israel "are justified and shall glory?" Surely it is blessed first to eye Christ as possessing and being the cause of the true Naphtali's portion, and then, by virtue of an union with him, and interest in him, to behold those blessings flowing in upon his inheritance. It is Jesus alone who hath satisfied for sin, and with whom alone JEHOVAH is satisfied; and therefore Jesus, as the Head of his body the church, is satisfied with favour, and full of the blessings of the Lord. Both the west and the south are his for a possession; yea, his dominion shall be from sea to sea, and from the river unto the ends of earth, men shall be blessed in him, and all nations shall call him blessed." (Ps. lxxii, throughout.) See Hind.

NAPHTUHIM

The son of Mizriam. (.Gen. x. 13.) His name means openings.

NARCISSUS

In the Greek, the word means surprise. He is spoken of Rom. xvi. 11.

NATHAN

There were many of this name in the Bible. The first we meet with is the faithful prophet in the days of David, 2 Sam. xii. The name signifies who gives. (See also 2 Sam. xii. 14.) Another Nathan is recorded, 2 Sam. xxiii. 36; another, 1 Kings, iv. 5; another, Ezra viii. 16.

NATHANIEL

Compounded of Nathan, gift--and El, God. We have many of this name, Num. i. 8. 1 Chron. ii. 14; xv. 24; xxiv. 6. 2 Chron. xvii. 7; xxxv. 9. Ezra x. 22. And the eminent Nathaniel, so highly spoken of by the Lord Jesus Christ, John i.47. See Bartholomew.

NATHAN-MELECH

An officer in the court of Manasseh, king of Judah, 2 Kings xxiii. 11. His name is compounded of Nathan, gift--and Melech, king.

NAVEL

In the margin of the Bible, Ezek. xxxviii. 12. "The midst of the land" is more strikingly marked by this term, Navel, to intimate the centre or middle of the earth; for as the navel of the human body is the centre of the body, so the holy land of Palestine is the Mediterranean of the world.

There is something very particular in this, and worth regarding. Christ comes upon earth for the redemption of his people.--But where shall he make his appearance? Surely as near the centre as possible. It is so then, Jesus shall appear, to fulfil all righteousness, in that part which is the solid globe of the earth, that here to this centre all the ends of the earth may have their views directed. Hence the Psalmist speaking of it, saith, "for God is my king of old, working salvation in the midst of the earth." (Ps. lxxiv. 12.) And hence the Lord Jesus is represented by the Holy Ghost as calling from his throne, in the centre of it, to his redeemed, saying, "Look unto me, and be ye saved, all the ends of the earth, for I am God, and there is none else." (Isa. xlv. 22.) And hence, at the last day, the redeemed "in their return to Zion with songs of everlasting joy upon their heads, are represented as coming from the east, and from the west, and from the north, and from the south, to sit down in the kingdom of God." (Luke xiii. 29.)

Now it is blessed to observe what the Holy Ghost hath said in his records of truth concerning those things. "His foundation (saith the Lord, by the Psalmist) is in the holy mountain." (Ps. lxxxvii. 1.) Christ himself indeed is the foundation JEHOVAH laid in Zion. (Isa. xxviii. 16.) But here the Holy Ghost is speaking of the church of Christ founded in himself; and this foundation of the Lord Jesus is in this holy mountain, the navel, or centre of the earth. Here the Lord Christ founded it; here the Lord of his temple came suddenly to it, Mal. iii. 1. where Jesus, as had been prophesied of him, filled it by his presence with glory, and thereby made" the glory of the latter temple greater than the glory of the former." And here it was the Lord gave peace. (See Hag. ii. 7. 9.)

And is there not yet an higher view of the subject, considered as to the glorious persons who are the united source and cause of our salvation? If salvation is wrought out for the church in the middle of the earth, is not the Son of God, by whom it was wrought, the middle person of the GODHEAD? And not only so, the middle person of the Holy Three in One who bear record in heaven, but the middle person, the Mediator, between God and man, as the man Christ Jesus? (1 John v. 7. 1 Tim. ii. 5.) And can the imagination conceive any thing more blessed and suited for the glory and happiness of the church, than that he who is the centre in all these views, should be the centre towards whom all things should move, and in whom all should centre? And hence we read, that when John saw heaven open, he saw Christ as a lamb in the midst of the throne. (Rev. vii. 17.) Nay, we are told by the Holy Ghost, through the ministry of his servant Paul, (Eph. i. 10) that the great purpose of redemption is, "that in the dispensation of the fulness of time, he might gather together in one all things in Christ, both which are in heaven, and which are on earth, even in him." So that not only shall all the redeemed of the Lord ultimately centre in him, but the enemies of the Lord shall be given up into his almighty hands, and here, as to one centre, shall they all meet for destruction; all evil things, sin, Satan, death, and hell to be put under his feet, when the Lord Jesus Christ shall come "to root out of his kingdom all things that offend." So that as in him and from him, and by him, all the blessings of grace now flow, as from a centre, to his redeemed upon earth, and all glory to his redeemed now and for ever in heaven; so all the enemies of God and his Christ will meet their final overthrow and everlasting destruction from him that is in the midst of the throne, when the Lord of hosts shall "reign in mount Zion, and in Jerusalem, and before his ancients gloriously." (Isa. xxiv. 23.)

NAZARENE

As this name was given to our Lord Jesus Christ, and we are told by the evangelist, that his residence in Nazareth was on this account, that he might be so called, it will certainly merit particular attention.

The word Nazarene or Nazarite, (for it is one and the same) is derived from Nezar, and means separated; so that a Nazarite is one separated and given up to God from the womb. The Jews, out of contempt to the person of Christ, called him the Nazarite or Nazarene; and certainly they meant no other by it but, as we mean, an inhabitant of a place, when we say, one of Plymouth, or the like. And as Nazareth itself was but a small city of Zebulun, they had yet greater contempt for Christ's person, for springing, as they supposed, from thence. "Can there any good thing come out of Nazareth?' (John i. 46.) But we shall find that this title, Jesus Christ of Nazareth, was all along designed of God, as of the highest import, and among the strongest testimonies to this peculiarity of character, as the one, yea, the only one great Nazarite of God.

As the proper apprehension of this point is, in my view, of infinite value in the faith of a believer, I beg the reader's indulgence to state the whole subject very particularly.

And first, then, I request to remark on the expression of the evangelist Matthew, (chap. ii. 23.) "And he came and dwelt in a city called Nazareth, that it might be fulfilled which was spoken by the prophets--he should be called a Nazarene?

The question is, what prophets are there who so spake concerning Christ? To which I answer, all the writers of the Old Testament are generally called prophets, because many of their sayings are really and truly prophesies. Thus Jacob when dying called his sons and said, "Gather yourselves together, that I may tell you that which shall befall you in the last days." (Gen. xlix. 1.) Eminently Jacob was a prophet in what he here predicted of his sons, and the glorious events he then delivered, since fulfilled, proves it. And the apostle Peter denominates the whole of the Old Testament "a word of prophecy;" for speaking of it he saith, "we have a more sure word of prophecy, whereunto ye do well that ye take heed. (2 Pet. i. 19.) So that not only the immediate writings of the prophets whose titles are expressly so spoken of as prophetical, but the scope of the whole body of Scripture, and especially such as are looking into gospel times, and speaking of events then to be accomplished, may be truly and justly called prophecies, and the writers of them prophets.

The next enquiry is, which of the sacred writers is it that thus predicted Christ should be called a Nazarene? To which I answer, in type and figure, Jacob and Moses both represented this great truth in their dying testimonies concerning Joseph, the typical Nazarite of the Lord Jesus Christ. Jacob's prophecy concerning Joseph in this particular runs thus: (Gen. xlix. 26.) "The blessings of thy father have prevailed above the blessings of my progenitors, unto the utmost bound of the everlasting hills: they shall be on the head of Joseph, and on the crown of the head of him that was separate from his brethren." In the original the word separate is Nezer, that is, a Nazarite among his brethren. And this is the same word, used in Gen. xlix. 26. as is used, Judges xiii. 5. for Nazarite. Strong testimonies these to the point in question. Moses, in like manner, makes use of the same allusion, when delivering his dying prediction concerning Joseph as typical of Christ. For the good will of him, (said he) my dweller in the bush, (referring to his first views of God incarnate, Exod. iii. 2. compared with Acts vii. 30.) "Let the blessing come upon the head of Joseph, and upon the top of the head of him that was separate from his brethren." In the original the very same word for separate is used as Gen. xlix. 26.--so that Moses as well as Jacob, declared by the type Joseph, that the great Antitype should be the Nazarite or separate from among his brethren.

The third step to which I beg the reader to follow me, in this most interesting subject concerning our glorious Nazarite, and justly called so, is in the writings of the evangelist St. Luke; where I hope we shall discover, under the teaching of God the Holy Ghost, that Jesus, though born at Bethlehem to fulfil another prophecy, was literally and truly conceived at Nazareth, and as such became a real Nazarene.

Thus the Holy Ghost, by the evangelist, states the circumstances of the conception, of Christ, (Luke i. 26, &c.) "And in the sixth month, the angel Gabriel was sent from God, unto a city of Galilee named Nazareth, to a virgin espoused to a man, whose name was Joseph, of the house of David, and the virgin's name was Mary. And the angel came in unto her, and said, Hail! thou that are highly favoured, the Lord is with thee, blessed art thou among women. And the angel said unto her, Fear not, Mary, for thou hast found favour with God; and behold thou shalt conceive in thy womb, and bring forth a son, and shall call his name Jesus." From hence we date the conception. The miraculous power of the Holy Ghost is no sooner announced, and Mary's consent obtained, than the impregnation takes place; so that "that Holy thing," or the man of the unction, as Christ is declared by the angel to be, is immediately conceived, and the Nazarite from the womb is formed in the city of Nazareth, as the prophet had foretold. (See Isa. vii. 14.) This, in my view of the subject, is most blessed indeed!

Under a fourth particular, the reader will find this great event most strikingly shadowed out in the instance of Samson, the type of Christ, and especially in this feature of character as a Nazarite. Here indeed we find many wonderful things to shew the correspondence between the type and the antitype. The birth of Samson was announced precisely in the same manner, by the ministry of an angel. The wife of Manoah, Samson's mother, was barren at the time, as if to shew that the birth of this child, though not miraculous, yet was extraordinary. The message the angel brought to Manoah's wife, and to the Virgin Mary, were (as far as the similarity of circumstances would admit) so much alike, that one might be led to conclude that the messenger was the same, and the one ministered but to the other. And lastly, and above all, as the angel concerning Samson declared, that he should be a Nazarite to God from the womb, and should begin to deliver Israel out of the hand of the Philistines, so eminently did the angel announce to the Virgin Mary concerning the Lord Jesus Christ, that he should be that Holy Thing, and be called the Son of the Highest, and should deliver "his people from their sins." (Compare Judges xiii. 2-7. with Luke i. 26, &c. and Matt, i. 20, 21.) I do not think it necessary to insert in this place, at large, the law concerning Nazarites to God. The reader will find it, Num. vi. 2-5. But from the particular precepts concerning it, and the case of Samson, seen with an eye to Christ, "as the end of the law for righteousness to every one that believeth," I humbly conceive that the point is thus strikingly illustrated.

I have only one thing more to add, in order to shew that this our glorious Nazarite was the one, and the only one, to whom all that went before were mere types and shadows, and only ministered in this character to him; and also that the law concerning Nazarites had an eye wholly to him, and in him alone was completed. I say I have only to add, in confirmation of it, that when we find so many different characters all directly overruled to call Jesus by this name, and thus decidedly stamping his character as the Nazarite of God, however many of them meant not so, neither did they intend it, nothing surely can more plainly prove that the whole must have originated in the divine mind, and that JEHOVAH adopted all these methods to shew that Christ, and Christ only, is the One Holy and glorious Nazarite to God.

The first we meet with in the gospel who called our Lord Jesus of Nazareth, or the Nazarite, was Satan, when he said, "Let us alone; what, have we to do with thee, thou Jesus of Nazareth? Art thou come to destroy us? I know thee who thou art, the Holy One of God." (Mark i. 24.) Next we find the apostles giving in their testimony to the same blessed truth, John i. 45. "We have found him (saith Philip) of whom Moses in the law and the prophets did write, Jesus of Nazareth, the son of Joseph." When the band of men and officers from the chief priests came to apprehend Christ in the garden, they enquired after the Lord under the same name, Jesus of Nazareth, (John xviii. 5.) The servant maid in the hall of Pilate spoke of our Lord by the same name; for charging Peter as an accomplice, she said, "And this fellow also was with Jesus of Galilee." (Matt. xxvi.71.) And yet more, the Roman governor, as if constrained by an overruling power, in giving a testimony to Christ the very reverse of the ignominy he meant to put upon him, both subscribed to his regal authority, at the same time he proclaimed him the Nazarite to God; and wrote a superscription in three different languages, and put it on the cross, "Jesus of Nazareth, the King of the Jews." (John xix. 19.) Still farther, the angels which attended the Lord's sepulchre, when he arose from the dead, announced to the pious women the resurrection of Christ by the same name, "Ye seek Jesus of Nazareth, which was crucified; he is risen, he is not here; behold the place where the Lord lay." (Mark xvi. 6.) In like manner, the apostles, after our Lord's ascension to glory, continually dwelt upon this name. Jesus Christ of Nazareth, said Peter, in his sermon on the day of Pentecost, a man approved of God among you; as if to insist upon this glorious feature of the man, the Nazarite. (Acts ii. 22.) So again, when he healed the cripple at the gate of the temple, the blessed words he used were, "In the name of Jesus of Nazareth." (Acts iii. 6.) So again Acts iv. 10. And lastly, to mention no more, the Lord Jesus himself, when calling to Paul from heaven, called himself by this name, "I am Jesus of Nazareth," or, as it might be rendered, I am Jesus *the* Nazarite, not *a* Nazarite, but *the* Nazarite, *the very identical, yea, the only one.* (Acts xxii. 8.)

From the whole then, I hope the reader will think with me, that God the Holy Ghost had all along a design, from the first dawn of revelation, with an eye to the Lord Jesus in this most important character; and to this end and purpose directed his servants' minds, Jacob and Moses, to point to this great Nazarite, by type and figure, in the separation of Joseph from his brethren. And I trust that the reader will also see with me from the Lord's own teaching, that the law of the Nazarites, (Num. vi.) and especially the striking typical representation in the case of Samson, had no other meaning but to set forth the feature of the Lord Jesus Christ.

It is not enough, in my view, to allow these things to be typical of Christ, if at the same time we allow them to have any secondary and subordinate reference to themselves. They only spake of Jesus; they only ministered to him. Any sanctity or supposed sanctity in themselves, or any Nazarites under the law, is foreign to the very spirit of the Gospel of Christ. The word of God not only insists upon it, that there is salvation in no other but Jesus, but it includes all other under sin. "The imagination, yea, every imagination of the thoughts of man's heart is only evil, and that continually," (Gen. vi. 5.) consequently there could be no real Nazarite to God but this one. Every thing that we read of concerning holy vows and dedications, as far as they were true, were all typical of Christ. And by this exclusive personal right in our Jesus to this Nazarite of God, we plainly discover this sweet feature of character in our Lord, which endears him to his people, and shews the solemn dedication of himself for them to God. Hail, thou precious blessed Lord Jesus Christ of Nazareth! Blessings for ever be on the head of him that was separated from his brethren! Verily, "thy father's children shall bow down before thee:" here, and to all eternity, thou shalt be called the Nazarite of God!

NAZARENES

Some of the early Christians, in contempt, were branded with this name; hence Paul is called a ringleader of the sect, every where spoken against. (Acts xxviii. 22.)

NAZARITES

-- Or Nazarim, from Nezer or Nazar, separated

All were called by this name who voluntarily made themselves Nazarites, by their dedicating themselves to God. We have the law at large concerning Nazarites, (Num. vi.) to which I refer. I only beg to observe concerning Nazarites, that it is evident the design and good pleasure of God the Holy Ghost, in disposing the minds of his people to the vow of the Nazarite, and forming laws so particular as this chapter contains, had all along an eye to Christ, the one great and only true Nazarite. As if the Holy Ghost in this order would keep up in Israel the constant thought of this sanctification and separation towards God, until "he came who for their sakes sanctified himself," is made of God to them sanctification and redemption. (John xvii. 19. and 1 Cor. i. 30.)

We find in the most degenerate state of the church, there were still persons of this order. The prophet Jeremiah speaks of them in his Book of Lamentations in a very affecting manner: "Her Nazarites (saith he) were purer than snow, they were whiter than milk, they were more ruddy in body than rubies, their polishing was of sapphire, their visage is blacker than a coal, they are not not known in the streets." (Lam. iv. 7,

8.) So the prophet Amos: "I raised up of your sons for prophets, and of your young men for Nazarites. Is it not even thus, O ye children Of Israel? saith the Lord. But ye gave the Nazarites wine to drink; and commanded the prophets, saying, Prophesy not." (Amos ii. 11, 12.) Nothing can be more plain than that this order was altogether typical, when we consider the wretched condition of Israel in both those periods when Jeremiah and Amos exercised their ministry. The whole of both those men's preaching is reproof; and therefore, if at such a time the order of the Nazarites was preserved, and as the Lord himself saith, it was of his raising up, surely it proves to a demonstration, that God the Holy Ghost intended from it, like all the sacrifices under the law, to be continued only until he came in whom all types, shadows, sacrifices, and ordinances centered, and in whom all had their completion, and were done away.

NEAH

A city of Zebulun. (Josh. xix. 13.) The word Neah or Noch, means a city.

NEAPOLIS

We read of this place, Acts xvi. 11. perhaps so called from being then newly formed meaning a new city.

NEARIAH

One of the sons of Shechaneah (1 Chron. iii. 22.) From Naarah, youth or child.

NEBAJOTH

Ishmael's eldest son. (Gen. xxv. 13.) The name signifies fruits, if from Nubai, fruits.

NEBALLAT

A city of Benjamin. (Neh. xi. 34.)

NEBAT

The father of Jeroboam, (1 Kings xi. 26.) from Nubai, that beholds.

NEBO

We meet with this name for three different places. There was a city of the Reubenites called Nebo, (Num. xxxii. 38.)--and according to Jeremiah, in his days the Moabites had it in possession. (Jer. xlviii.) There was also a city of Judah of this name in the days of Ezra and Nehemiah. (Ezra ii. 29. Neh. vii. 33.) And the famous mountain on which Moses died was called Nebo. (Deut. xxxiv. 1.5.) One of the idols of Babylon bore the name of Nebo. (Isa. xlvi. 1.) The root of the name seems to be much the same as that of Nebat.

NEBUCHADNEZZAR

King of Babylon. We have much said in Scripture concerning this monarch, in the book of Daniel. His name is formed from several words not of Hebrew, but of the Chaldean. The idol name of Nebo forms apart in it, for the Babylonians were much disposed to this. Various have been the opinions of men concerning the wonderful change wrought upon Nebuchadnezzar, as related Dan. iv. 28.33; but, after all that hath been said on this subject, the matter stands just where the Scriptures have left it. And those who do not desire to be wise above what is written, will do well to accept of this and all the other parts of sacred Scripture in the Lord's own way, referring all into his sovereign decree, "who worketh all things according to the purpose of his own will. My counsel (saith he) shall stand, and I will do all my pleasure. (Isa. xlvi. 10.) Let the reader read the close of the forty-fourth chapter of Isaiah, and form his conclusions accordingly.

NEBUSHASBAN

One of those princes who was sent from Babylon at the taking of Jerusalem. (Jer. xxxix. 13.) A compound word, principally having a regard to the idol of Babylon, Nebo.

NEBUZARADAN

Captain of the guard of Nebuchadnezzar's army. (See Jer. xxxix, and xl.)

NECHO

We read of Pharaoh Neeho, king of Egypt, 2 Kings xxiii. 29. Probably the name of Necho was added to that of Pharaoh on account of some lameness, as Necho means lame.

NECROMANCER

We meet with this name but once in Scripture, (Deut. xviii. 11.) but that once is enough to shew, that from the earliest days there have been characters of such awfulness. The word is derived from Nekros, Greek, and signifies one who pretends to discourse with the dead. By the law, all that exercised this art were condemned to punishment; yea, the Lord said, "I will even set my face against that soul, and will cut him off from among his people." (Lev. xx. 6.) The woman at Endor practised this art, and made Saul in his horrors of mind, a dupe to her delusion. (1 Sam. xxviii. 5, &c.) The prophet Isaiah hath described the character of such, Isa. xxix. 4. Is it not astonishing that in the days of the gospel any should be found daring enough to exercise such an art, and still more that any should be found so foolish as to give credit to such persons?

NEDABIAH

Son of Jaconiah. (1Chron. iii. 18.) This man's name is compounded of Nadab, gift-- and Jah, Lord.

NEGINOTH

A title to many of the Psalms. See Musician.

NEHELAMITE

Perhaps a Nehelamite was a native or inhabitant of Nahallal, which is spoken of Josh. xix. 15. Nehalmi, signifies dreamer; so that it is probable that Shemaiah, the Nehelamite, spoken of by Jeremiah, might mean the dreamer. (Jer. xxix. 24.)

NEHEMIAH

The Tirshatha or Governor under the Persian king; a well known faithful character in the church after the return of the people from Babylon. (See the Book of Nehemiah.) His name if derived from Nacham, signifies the comfort of the Lord. Nacham, or Nehem, and Jah.

NEHILOTH

See Musician.

NEHUSTAN

The name which Hezekiah gave to the brazen serpent which Moses had lifted up in the wilderness. (See 2 Kings xviii. 4.) It should seem very plain, from what is said in this Scripture, that what Moses in his days had lifted up at the command of God, and for the most blessed purposes, the Israelites in after-ages had perverted into an idol. We find, by what is said of Hezekiah's destroying it, that the Israelites had preserved it, and brought it with them into Canaan. But what a sad delusion must they have fallen into in setting it up for an object of worship, and burning incense to it! (See Num. xxi. 6. compared with John iii. 14.) The name Nehushtan is from Nachash, serpent; so that by Hezekiah calling it not Nachash, but Nehushtan, he meant to shew by the alteration his contempt of it as an idol. It is a sort of play upon the word, somewhat like that we meet with Isa. lxi. 3. where the prophet, speaking of the exchange to be made of beauty for ashes, useth two words in sound much alike, but very different in their meaning--Pheer, beauty, for Epher, ashes. In our English language we have numberless instances of the kind.

NEIL

A city of Ashur. (Josh. xix. 27.) From Nuah, shaking--and El, God.

NEKEB

A city of Naphtali. (Josh. xix. 33.) Nekeb, that bores, or makes a penetration.

NEMUEL

There are two of this name in Scripture, one the son of Eliab, (Num. xxvi. 9.) and another the son of Simeon, (Num. xx. 12.) It is compounded of Nun, sleep--and El, God—the sleep which God gives. (Ps. cxxvii. 2.)

NEPHEG

One of David's sons. (2 Sam. v. 15.) The name means weak or faint, from Phug.

NEPHTOAH

We read of the water of Nephtoah, which went towards mount Ephron, Josh. xv. 9. Perhaps the name means opening, if from Pathac.

NER

Father to Abner, captain of the host to Saul. (1 Sam. xiv. 5.) His name is light or lamp.

NEREUS

A friend of Paul's, (Rom. xvi. 15.) derived from Ner.

NERGAL

An idol of the men of Cuth, (2 Kings xvii. 30.) compounded of Ner and Gal, light discovered.

NERGAL SHAREZER

Captain of Nebuchadnezzar's army, (Jer. xxxix. 3.) A compound name, Ner, light—Shar, prince—Abzar, treasure.

NERIAH or NERI

We meet with two of this name. The father of Baruch, Jer. xxxii. 12. and the son of Melchi, Luke iii. 27. Light of the Lord, or the Lord is my light.

NETHANIAH

The father of Ishmael. (2 Kings xxv. 23.) And there is a Levite of this name, I Chron. xxv. 2. Nathan, gift--and Jah, Lord.

NETHINIMS

We read of the Nethinims in the first book of the Chronicles, ix. 2. and in Ezra ii. 43. 58, &c. and Nehemiah iii. 26, &c. but no where else in Scripture. Perhaps the name is derived from Nathan, gift; and it is probable, that as we are told, (Ezra viii. 20.) David had appointed them for service to the Lecvites, who were of the lower order of those who ministered in the temple. But we know nothing more concerning them. Many will be found at the last day, it is to be hoped, among those who, when upon earth, were but "as hewers of wood, and drawers of water, to the sanctuary," whom Jesus will own for his Nethinims, the gift of the Father to the Son, who lived and died unnoticed, and, for the most part, unknown to men, like some sweet fragrant flower of the mountain, but in everlasting remembrance in the sight of God.

NETOPHAH

We read Ezra ii. 22. of this place; and some have thought that it was a city between Benjamin and the pleasant village of Anathoth, where Jeremiah dwelt. (Jer. i. 1.) The name is derived from Nataph, gum or spice; probably so called from the precious gums produced there.

NEW MOON

The Hebrews were very earnest in observing the first day of the new moon, not in any idolatrous manner it is to be hoped, but probably more for the calculation of time. We read much of their feasts and friendly meetings with each other. Moses appointed a burnt offering at the opening of each month. (Num. xxviii. 11.) But this was accompanied with no precept for any particular day, neither any service with it; and the new moon festival, it should seem to have been rather in the view of a pious sanctification of families, when meeting together as Job did, (Job i. 5.) than any immediate religious service towards the Lord. Hence we read of David being expected at the king's table on the first day of the new moon, and being particularly missed because it was that day. (See 1 Sam. xx. 5, 6. 24. 27.) So we find the husband of the Shunamite making particular observations upon his wife's wishing to go to the prophet, when it was neither sabbath nor new moon. (See 2 Kings iv. 23.) We read also of the new moon festivals in other parts of Scripture. (See 1 Chron. xxiii. 31. 2 Chron. viii. 13. Isa. i. 13, 14. Ezek. xlv. 17.) I believe even in very late times, and perhaps with some even now, the Jews are attached to friendly visits with each other, more particularly in the new moon.

NEW WINE
See Bottle--Wine.

NEZIAH
We read of the children of this man, Ezra ii. 54. His name is a compound of Ne and Jab, from Netzac, victorious.

NEZIB
A city or village spoken of Josh. xv. 43. Strength, from Netzib.

NIBHAZ
The idol which the Avites made. (See 2 Kings xvii. 31.) If from Nub, to be fruitful, it means one that makes fruitful.

NIBSHAN
A city of Judah, (Josh. xv. 62.) If from Shanah, it means to change.

NICANOR
One of the seven first deacons in the church of Christ after the descent of the Holy Ghost. (Acts vi. 5.) The name is taken from the Greek, and means to conquer.

NICODEMUS
A well known name in the gospel, compounded, it should seem, of Nake, innocent--and Dam, blood. We have abundant reason to bless the Holy Ghost, in causing to be recorded that memorable conversation, as well as the character of Nicodemus manifested in it, that took place between the Lord Jesus and Nicodemus, as given at large John iii. How blessed the light thereby thrown upon that most important doctrine of regeneration, and which Jesus declares to be indispensably necessary for an entrance into the kingdom of God. And it is blessed to trace the effects of this glorious work of God the Holy Ghost upon the heart of Nicodemus himself. When he first came to Christ it was by night. Some impressions, no doubt, of the Spirit had been wrought upon his mind, or he would not have sought after Jesus; but his views were so dark and indistinct, that when Jesus opened to him the doctrine of regeneration, he thought it an impossible thing. The next account we have of him is John vii. 50. where he ventures in open daylight to stand up for Christ before the whole council, and got himself no small contempt upon the occasion. By the time the Lord Jesus had finished his redemption-work on the cross, we find Nicodemus so advanced in the divine life and his love to Christ, that, in company with Joseph of Arimathea, he went boldly unto Pilate and begged the body of Jesus. (See Luke xxiii. 51, 52. with John xix. 38, 39.) It is very blessed thus to trace the progress of grace, and to prove the truth of that sweet Scripture, "the path of the just is as the shining light, that shineth more and more unto a perfect day." (Rev.

iv. 18.)

NICOLAS

One of the seven deacons. (Acts vi. 5.) Some have supposed that he was the head and leader of the sect called the Nicolaitaines; but there are no authorities in Scripture for this. Our Lord saith, (Rev. ii. 6.) that he hated the deeds of the Nicolaitaines, but he doth not say that Nicolas the deacon was the founder of that sect.

NICOPOLIS

From hence Paul wrote to Titus. (See Tit. iii. 12.) It was a province in Macedonia.

NIGER

We have the name of this man Acts xiii. 1. He is there called a prophet, but we have no account of his ministry, or any of his writings.

NIGHT

I only pause at this word just to remark, that the Hebrews reckoned their hours different from modern custom. They always began at six in the evening to count their hours; so that what we call three in the afternoon was to them the ninth hour of the day. And so by a. parity of calculation, of all the rest. Hence when Peter and John, as we read Acts iii. 1. went up to the temple at the hour of prayer, being the ninth hour, this would have been with us three in the afternoon. I need not stay to remark, for I presume the sense of the expression is generally understood, that night in Scripture language is sometimes figuratively used for darkness in divine things. Thus God's people are called children of the day, and not of the night; meaning their conduct is according to light, and not darkness. (1 Thes. v. 5.)

NIMRAH

A city of Gad and Reuben. (Num. xxxii. 3.) If derived from Namer, it signifies leopard; if from Marah, as some have supposed, bitterness.

NIMROD

The son of Cush. (Gen. x. 8, 9.) The character given of this man is that of a mighty hunter before the Lord.

NIMSHI

The father of Jehu, (1 Kings xvi.) If derived from Mashah, it signifies saved from danger.

NINEVEH

A city, and the capital of Assyria. Derived from Naah, handsome. We have a very interesting account in the book of Jonah concerning the Ninevites, and the number of souls it then contained, when the prophet was sent to exercise his ministry there: to which I therefore refer. Historians give wonderful accounts of Nineveh. They make it the most ancient as well as the most populous and powerful city of the world. The founder of it certainly was Nimrod. (See Gen. x. 10-12.) It stood on the banks of the Tigris, supposed to be seven leagues long; for Jonah relates that it was three days journey to go through it. And where is it now? Where is Nineveh and Babylon, and the seven churches of proconsular Asia? Alas! not a vestige of either remains. Let the reader turn to the thirteenth chapter of Isaiah's prophecy, and read from the nineteenth verse to the end, to see a picture of God's desolation upon sinful nations and kingdoms. Thus do all monarchies fade and die away, while the kingdom of God and his Christ shall endure for ever. How sweetly Paul speaks on the subject. (Heb. xii. 28.)

NISAN

One of the months of the Hebrews, answering to our March. Perhaps derived from Nus, meaning flight.

NISROCH

An idol of the Assyrians--derived from the same root as Nisan, but not an Hebrew derivation. (2 Kings xix. 37.)

NO

We read in the prophet Nahum of populous No. (Nahum iii. 8.) And Jeremiah and Ezekiel both speak of this city. (Jer. xlvi. 25. Ezek. xxx. 14, &c.) But we know very little about it.

NOADIAH

A false prophetess. (See Neh. vi. 14.) The name is a compound of Nuach, rest--and Jah, the Lord.

NOAH

His name signifies rest or repose, from Nuach. Some derive it from Nacham, consolation. The Holy Ghost hath given the character of this patriarch when calling him a preacher of righteousness. (2 Pet. ii. 5.) We have his history, Gen. v. 28. to the end; vi. 8. to the end; and vii. viii. and ix. throughout. We have the Holy Ghost's own comments upon Noah's history and character. (Heb. xi. 7.) To those Scriptures I refer.

NOB

A city of priests, so called, 1 Sam. xxi. 1. from Nabach, talk.

NOBAH

This man gave name to the city Nobah. (Num. xxxii. 42.)

NOD

The land of Nod, the country where Cain withdrew after slaying Abel. (Gen. iv. 16.) It should seem that this wretch going thither gave this name to the place, for it means vagabond or wanderer. See Vagabond.

NODAB

We read of this place 1 Chron. v. 19. Probably the name is derived from Nadab, prince or chief.

NOGAH

One of the sons of David. (1 Chron. iii. 7.) The name is brightness.

NOHAH

A son of Benjamin. (1 Chron. viii. 2.) From Nuah, rest.

NOPHAH

A city of Israel, originally belonging to the Moabites. (Num. xxi. 30.) From Naphak, that breathes.

NOPHET

A province in Zebulun and Manasseh. From Naph, that drops.

NOSE

The church is compared by our Lord to various things in nature beautiful and lovely, and her several features Jesus draws a resemblance between them and the most engaging objects around. Among the rest he saith, "her nose is as the tower of Lebanon, which looketh towards Damascus." (Song vii. 4.) It is a beautiful metaphor, intimating the quickness of discernment by smell of all that is fragrant in Jesus, and his redemption in mount Lebanon, his gospel church. And not only the discoveries, by the smell of his garments, of righteousness, like the myrrh, and aloes, and cassia, but the looking towards Damascus, implying the extent of that longing for Christ which, like the tower, or an high mountain, may be seen from afar off; so the church is always on the look-out for Jesus, when coming over the mountains of spices and hills of frankincense.

NUMBERS - NYMPHAS

NUMBERS

The third Book of Moses, so called from containing the numbers of the Israelites after coming out of Egypt.

NUN

Son of Elishama, and father of Joshua. (Josh. i. 1.)

NUTS

Christ is represented as going down into the garden of nuts. (Song vi. 11.) The word rendered nuts in this passage is never used elsewhere in the Bible. Some suppose it means pruned gardens, from the word pruning. But the great point intended from it is, to denote the grace and condescension in Christ, to visit his churches, and to take notice of the graces he himself hath planted in them.

NYMPHAS

The person whom Paul salutes in his Epistle to the Colossians, chap. iv. 15. The name is supposed to have been a woman's name, being feminine, and in the original Greek signifying spouse; but the church is said to be in his house, and therefore Nymphas is of the brethren.

O

OGADIAH

We meet with many of this name in Scripture. The name is evidently derived from Habad, a slave, or labourer; and the Jah being connected with it, renders the name Obad-jah, the Lord's servant, or slave or labourer. In a gospel-sense this is very blessed; for as slaves were purchased, so believers are said "to be bought with a price," and therefore, above all men, are called upon to "glorify God in their body and in their spirit, which are God's." (1 Cor. vi. 20.) But Peter, the apostle, makes a beautiful contrast between the purchase of the slaves of men, and the purchased of the Lord. "Forasmuch (saith he) as ye know that ye were not redeemed with corruptible things, as silver and gold, but with the precious blood of Christ, as of a lamb without blemish and without spot." (1 Pet. i. 18, 19.)

We have no less than five men of the name of Obadiah in the first book of Chronicles, chap. iii. 21; vii. 3; viii. 38; ix. 16; and xii. 9;--and one in the second book of the Chronicles, chap. xvii. 7. There is another of this name, Neh. x. 5; and a principal man he was in signing the covenant. And we must not forget in this enumeration, the faithful Obadiah in the days of Ehjah. (See 1 Kings xviii.) But the most important to us among the Obadiahs of the Scripture, is the one whom God the Holy Ghost raised up for a prophet and hath given to the church, even to this hour, this man's labours. See the prophecy of Obadiah. I do not presume to say as much, but I humbly would ask, whether the close of his man's vision hath not respect to the latter day glory, in a blessed event yet to be fulfilled. (See seventeenth verse to the end.)

OBAL

Son of Joktan. (Gen. x. 20.) Derived from Balah, old age.

OBED

We meet with two of this name in Scripture, Obed the father of Jesse, Ruth iv. 17.--and Obed the father of Jehu, 1 Chron. ii. 37. The name is Hebrew, and means servant.

OBED-EDOM

We have the honourable testimony which God the Holy Ghost gave of this man, 2 Sam. vi. 9-12; and again recorded, 1 Chron. xiii. 13, 14. And his numerous family, 1 Chron. xxvi. 4, 5. His name is compounded of Obed, slave--and Edom, or the Idumean. But as Obed-jah, the prophet, was called the slave or labourer of the Lord, so Obed-edom, the slave of the Adam or Edom, the earth or earthy, was eminently the Lord's chosen for that peculiar service of receiving the ark, when David himself trembled on the occasion.

But I hope the reader, in beholding the blessing of the Lord upon Obed-edom and his house, for the ark of God's sake, will not overlook the cause. That ark was a type of the ever-blessed Jesus. In receiving the ark into his house, into his family, and among his people, he did, to all intents and purposes, receive Christ into his heart, and like the faithful descendant of the faithful Abraham, "saw the day of Christ afar off, rejoiced, and was glad."

Obed-edom was no stranger to the dreadful consequences which had fallen on the Philistines for their daring impiety, in taking the ark of God, and detaining it. He could be no stranger to the awful death of Uzzah, for touching it presumptuously; for, no doubt, it was in every one's mouth. Nay, he could not but know that the reason wherefore David wished Obed-edom to take the ark into his house was, because he was afraid to take it into his own. What was it then, that prompted the mind of this pious faithful Gittite to receive the ark of God under such alarming circumstances? What was it, but thy grace almighty Lord, that taught him to rejoice in thee and thy favour, while others were trembling under thy judgments? Oh! the blessedness of distinguishing grace, which makes that to thy people "a savour of life unto life," whilst to others it becomes" a savour of death unto death." Three whole months was Obed-edom favoured with the abode of the ark. No doubt, the tokens of the divine presence were so visibly bestowed upon this man and his household, that the whole neighborhood, yea, the whole kingdom, could not but take notice of it; for it is said, "that it was told king David, saying, the Lord hath blessed the house of Obed-edom, and all that pertained to him, because of the ark of God," ver. 12.

Hear this ye parents, masters of families, and guardians of houses, interested in your own present and everlasting welfare, and that of your young ones of the rising generation. Behold the blessedness in Obed-edom, and all that pertained to him, for receiving the ark of God into his house. And observe the special time when this was done. It was when others trembled, he was made hold with an holy boldness. When none ventured to serve the interest of God, and to receive his ark, he was faithful.

And what is it now? If that ark was a type of Christ, who are they that may be said to be faithful in the midst of the present perverse and crooked generation, but they who receive Christ Jesus the Lord into their hearts, and houses, and families, whilst others despise him! Who are the Obed-edoms of the present day, but such as receive Christ Jesus the Lord, and walk in him, and live to him, and rejoice in him, as the Lord our Righteousness! And if there ever was a day of peculiar blessedness, for the manifesting this distinguishing love to Jesus and his cause, surely the present is the one. Oh! for grace, therefore, that while the ark of God, the Christ of God, is shut out of such numberless houses in this adulterous and sinful generation, many an Obed-edom may yet be found in our British Israel to welcome the Lord Jesus to their hearts, and he, and he alone, be formed there the hope of glory. Hail Obed-edom, thou faithful servant of thy Lord! Ever will thy memory be blessed in the church; and when the temple of God is opened again in heaven, as it was to the beloved apostle (Rev. xi. 19.) and the ark of the Testament is beheld by the whole church, still will it be held in everlasting remembrance how the Lord blessed the house of Obed-edom upon earth, for the ark of God's sake.

OBIL

The Ishmaelite. (1 Chron. xxvii. 30.) Aubil the Hebrews pronounced this name, from Abal that weeps.

OBLATION

See Sacrifice.

OBOTH

All encampment, so called, in the wilderness, after leaving Panon. (Num. xxi. 10.) If from Ob, skin, Oboth means skins, or bottles of skins.

OCRAN

The father of Pagiel. (Num. i. 13.) If from Hucar, trouble. Ocran, it should seem, might mean one that troubles.

ODED

The father of Azariah. (2 Chron. xv. 1.) And there was another of this name, a prophet of the Lord. (2 Chron. xxviii. 9.) The name is taken from Hoded, to lift up.

OFFERINGS

The old church formed in the wilderness abounded in offerings of various kinds, both civil and religious. The general term for offerings was Corban. (See Corban.) But the temple service offerings were all denominated Mincha. Those offerings of Mincha consisted of flour made into cakes, all unleavened, probably to prefigure Christ. (See 1 Cor. v. 7, 8.) And besides the burnt offerings, and peace offerings, and sin offerings, under the law, were many, and scrupulously regarded by the Jews, being so strictly enjoined by the Lord. How blessed is it for us to observe under every one of them direct references to the person and offering of the body of Jesus Christ once for all, whereby "he hath perfected for ever them that are sanctified!" Without him the whole was an unmeaning service; but considered as typical of Jesus, how infinitely important doth that all-sufficient sacrifice of Christ on the cross appear, when we behold it introduced with such vast solemnity and expense through so many ages to the coming of Christ.

OG

King of Bashan. (Deut. iii. 11.) We have an account of this wonderful man; and his size must have been enormous, if we judge of it by his bedstead of iron. Nine cubits long, by four wide, makes in English measure, fifteen feet four inches long, and six feet ten in breadth. But what is length or strength in man, when opposed to those who fight in the strength of the Lord? Og proves to be in such a case, as his name is, "a cake baked in ashes." (See Num. xxi. 33.)

OHAD

One of the sons Simeon, (Gen. xlvi. 10.) The name signifies praise, from Judah, to praise.

OHEL

Son of Zerubbabel (1 Chron. iii. 20.) If derived from Hillul, it means brightness.

OIL

It is very generally understood by oil what is meant in the common use of it in life; but the holy oil for the sanctuary is of a very different nature, and merits particular attention. When we consider that the whole office of the Holy Ghost in that feature of his sovereign character, namely, the unction of the Spirit, is described by anointing, and this not only of the persons of the members of Christ's mystical body, but Christ, the glorious Head himself; when we consider Christ, really and truly so called, and literally becoming Christ, from this anointing of God the Holy Ghost, the subject of the holy oil, as typical of these blessed things, riseth in importance to our view, and demands the closest attention of every truly awakened heart. If the reader desires Scriptural information on this interesting subject, he should diligently read the Lord's directions concerning the holy oil, Exod xxx. 22, to the end.

Concerning the office of God the Holy Ghost in his anointing character, as set forth by the holy oil of the temple, it would far exceed the limits of a work of this kind to go through the whole of the blessed Spirit's agency, in the description of it, under the various manifestations. It will be sufficient to say in general, that to this one glorious office of the Holy Ghost all the anointings we read of in the Old Testament, and the uses to which the the holy oil was appropriated, evidently pointed. It is God the Holy Ghost who is uniformly represented, in his divine influences and gifts, by the figure and emblem of the holy oil and the ointment; for as oil hath numberless operations to soften, to take off rust, to counteract poison, to give cheerfulness to the countenance, and to facilitate actions in the limbs when benumbed and grown hard; so the blessed influences of the Holy Ghost, by his divine anointings, soften our hearts, take off the rust of ignorance in our minds, expel the poison of sin and corruption, and not only raiseth up the drooping spirits, by administering to our hearts the oil of joy and gladness, but causeth us "to run the way of God's commandments when the Lord hath set our heart at liberty."

And what a blessed thought it is, that as the holy oil was poured on the head of Aaron, the great high priest of the Jewish dispensation, which ran down to the skirts of his clothing, so God the Holy Ghost anointed Jesus, our great and almighty High Priest, to whom Aaron was but the shadow, with "the oil of joy and gladness above and for his fellows;" yea, the Spirit was not given "by measure unto him, for in him all fulness dwelleth? And Christ and his church being one and the same, he the glorious Head, and they his members, of "his fulness do we all receive, and grace or grace." (See Anointing. See Holy Ghost. See these Scriptures, Ps. xlv. 7; cxxxiii; John i. 16; ; iii. 34.)

OLIVE TREE

The church is compared to an olive tree upon many occasions, (Jer. xi. 16. Ps. Iii. 8.)--and the young converts in Zion to olive branches. (Ps. cxxviii. 3.) And Paul in a beautiful figure, represents the state of conversion from nature to grace by the change from the olive tree which is wild, by nature, to that of a true olive tree, which is planted by grace. (Rom. xi. 17, to the end.)

I must not dismiss this subject without first remarking the allusions made by men in general to the olive branch, as an emblem of peace. It is more than probable that this took its rise from the circumstance of Noah's dove in the ark, when from being sent forth to discover whether the waters of the flood had subsided at length returned with the olive-branch in her mouth. The raven he dismissed found means of subsistence in going to and fro, probably from the carcases of those drowned; but the dove found no rest for the sole of her foot until returning to the ark. It is so with God's people; hence they are said to come as "doves to their windows." And it is remarkable, that when the Psalmist saith, (Ps. cxvi. 7.) "Return unto thy rest, O my soul!" the original is, Return unto thy Noah, thy Christ; for he is the rest wherewith the Lord causeth the weary to rest. The olive branch in the mouth of the dove is a token of peace. God will no more destroy the earth by a flood. The ark is a type of Jesus, through whom and in whom God is at peace, in the blood of his cross. (See Isa. xxviii. 12. Matt. xxviii. 29, 30.)

OLIVET

See Mount Olivet.

OLYMPAS

A believer in Christ of this name. (Rom. xvi. 15.)

OMAR

Son of Eliphaz, (Gen. xxxvi. 11.) from Aumai, he that speaks.

OMRI

There were several of this name in Scripture. 1 Kings xvi. 23. there was a king of this name; and a son of Becher, 1 Chron. vii. 8; and an Omri the son of Michael, 1 Chron. xxvii. 18. The name seems to mean, my words, or my discourses.

ON

Son of Peleth, (Num. xvi. 1.) The word means pain.

ONAN

Son of Judah. If the name be derived from Anoh, it signifies trouble. We have this man's short history, Gen. xxxviii. 8-10. and short as it is, it is awful. From this man's sin arose the name of Onanism to that particular offence which he was guilty of, and for which the Lord slew him. Who shall say the numbers which since his days have fallen into it? And who shall calculate the army which by Onanism have hastened the termination of a life of sin, and hurried themselves into eternity! Into how many streams of evil, diffusing themselves into all the parts of our poor fallen nature, hath that one deadly poison the old serpent put into Adam manifested itself through all our passions! Blessed Lord Jesus! what, but for thy gracious recovery of our nature, could have saved the wretched race of Adam from the wrath to come.

ONESIMUS

A name well known in the New Testament, whose history is exceedingly interesting. His name, it should seem, is derived from the Greek, and means useful. And very useful hath the relation which is given of his conversion proved to the church in all ages ever since.

It appears from the short Epistle of Paul to Philemon, (which see) that Onesimus was originally the slave or servant to Philemon. And though it is not expressly said in so many words that he robbed his master, yet from some expressions in Paul's letter, there seems great probability of it. Be this however as it may, certain it is that he ran from his master, and thereby manifested much worthlessness of conduct. In his wanderings he came to Rome, when Paul was there imprisoned the first time; and knowing the apostle while in his master's service, he visited the apostle in the prison. The Lord, who by his providence brought Onesimus to Paul, made this interview prosperous by his grace; and those visits ended, by the Lord's blessing, in the epistle Paul sent by him to his master Philemon relates those interesting circumstances. And as we find the Epistle to the church of the Colossians was sent from Rome by Onesimus, there is reason to conclude that Philemon sent him back to Paul to minister to him in the prison.

The epistle of Paul to Philemon is a master-piece for elegance and simplicity of style. Methinks it were devoutly to be wished, that all the followers of the Lord Jesus would form their letter-writing by this model. How truly blessed doth the epistle open, after subscribing himself as the prisoner of the Lord, in praying that grace and peace to Philemon might flow from God the Father and the Lord Jesus Christ! And how blessedly doth the apostle close his letter, in a similar prayer, that the grace of the Lord Jesus Christ might be with his spirit! Amen. And as the epistle opens and closeth in so sweet and gracious a spirit, so all the parts of it breathe every thing that is truly lovely and becoming the blessed Gospel of Christ.

But while I thus venture to recommend to myself and to others this style of writing. I beg yet more to remark the abundant grace of God the Holy Ghost, in causing such a blessed fragment of his sacred word to have been recorded and handed down in his church. Was it thought an object of everlasting moment thus to preserve in the book of God the history of a poor fugitive, and to let the church know that, in the instance of this slave, the Lord's grace outruns even all our undeservings? Was it indeed meant to shew in this, as well as in a thousand and ten thousand other instances, that "where sin aboundeth grace doth much more abound?"

What a precious example is held forth in this epistle to ministers of the word of God, to parents, masters of families, and all that are interested in the care and government of incautious youth, to feel what Paul felt, and to take an earnest concern in the recovery of transgression of every description and character! Did Paul count this runaway servant a brother, yea, his son, and speak of him as his own bowels, with what affection ought the ties of the minister and his people, the parent and his children, the master and his servant, to be felt and acknowledged in all the circumstances of life! How tenderly the same great apostle elsewhere recommends those gracious principles as the common actions of the christian! "Put on therefore (saith the apostle) as the elect of God, holy and beloved, bowels of mercies, kindness, humbleness of mind, meekness, long-suffering, forbearing one another, and forgiving one another; if any man have a quarrel against any, even as Christ forgave you, so also do ye." (Col. iii. 12, 13.)

It is hardly possible, while thus naming the name of Jesus, and in this endearing character of his forgiveness, it is hardly possible to overlook how eminently the Lord himself stands forth in his high office of Intercessor for every Onisemus of his people, who, like this poor fugitive, have all run away from our Lord and master, and wandered from his service. If Paul found Onesimus, how much more hath Jesus found us in our lost estate, "for his mercy endureth for ever!" And if Paul's intercession was so prevalent with Philemon, what must the Lord Jesus's be with the Father!

ONESIPHORUS

This person is spoken of by the apostle Paul with honorable testimony, 2 Tim. i. 16. His name is a compound from the Greek, and means to bring usefulness.

ONO

A city of Benjamin, (1 Chron. viii. 12.) If from On, strength, there was also a man of this name Ezra. ii. 33.

ONYX

A precious stone: it formed a part in the high priest's breastplate. (Exod. xxviii. 20.)

OPHEL

The name of a wall in the house of the Lord.(2 Chron xxvii. 3.)

OPHIR

We read much in Scripture of the gold of Opher, 1 Kings ix. 28. The word is perhaps derived from Aupher or Epher, which means ashes; probably from the dust to which gold in the process of melting is brought. But be this as it may, certain it is that the gold of Ophir, supposed to be the purest of all gold, is after all but ashes; and the very name serves to set forth its emptiness and vanity. Was it not with this view (I do but ask the question, and not determine it) the Holy Ghost by the prophet said, "I will make a man (or more properly, the man Christ Jesus) more precious than fine gold, even a man, than the golden wedge of Ophir?" (Isa. xiii. 12.)

OPHNI

A city of Benjamin, (Josh. xviii. 24.) perhaps from Gophni, weary.

OPHRAH

A city of Benjamin, (Josh. xviii. 23.) from Haphar, dust.

ORACLE

We find mention made (2 Sam. xvi. 23.) of the oracle of God; but we are at a loss to understand so as to speak with certainty concerning the meaning. In the building of Solomon's temple we are told, that there was "a part for the oracle, even for the most holy place." (1 Kings vi. 16.) By which it should seem, that the mercy-seat or propitiatory, was intended by the word oracle. And the Psalmist seems to throw a farther light upon the term, considered in this point of view, when he saith, (Ps. xxviii. 2.) "Hear the voice of my supplications when I cry unto thee, when I lift up my hands towards thy holy oracle." For where should a soul lift up his hands and his heart, but to the mercy seat, God in Christ speaking from between the cherubim? The word Dabir, which is the word used for oracle, 1 Kings vi. 16, properly signifies oracle. But the word Caphoreth (from Capher or Copher, to expiate or pardon) is used for the mercy seat, Exod. xxv. 18. But in either sense, or in both, by oracle must imply the answers of the Lord to his people. And what is said, of the answers by Urim and Thummim, by visions of the night, by prophecy, and the like, all is one and the same, when the Lord makes known the sacred purposes of his will. Hence the apostle, speaking of those who ministered in holy things, enjoined this precept, "If any man speak, let him speak as the oracles of God;" that is, the truths of God. (1 Pet. iv. 11. See Gen. xxvii. 5, 6. Num. xiii. 6-8.)

OREB

One of the princes of Midian. (Judges vii. 25.) If from Harab, it means raven.

ORLON

One of the rich constellations in the south. (Job. ix. 9.)

ORPAH

Wife of Chillon, son of Elimelech. (Ruth i. 4.) If from Sarah, the name means nakedness.

OSTRICH

This very extraordinary bird is so spoken of in the Scripture, that it would be wrong in a work of this kind not to notice it, especially as the Lord himself, from the whirlwind, condescended to call the attention of the man of Uz to it. (Job xxxix. 13, &c.) "Gavest thou (saith the Lord) the goodly wings unto the peacocks, or wings and feathers unto the ostrich, which leaveth her eggs in the earth, and warmeth them in dust, and forgetteth that the foot may crush them, or that the wild beast may break them? She is hardened against her young ones, as though they were not hers: her labour is in vain without fear; because God hath deprived her of wisdom; neither hath he imparted to her understanding. What time she lifteth up herself on high, she scorneth the horse and his rider."

Such a relation concerning the ostrich, and given by the Lord himself in his blessed word, certainly merits our attention.

But we must be indebted to the account of travellers who have visited the countries where the ostriches are, in order to enter into the beauties which are contained in the Lord's description of this wonderful bird.

Dr. Shaw, in his travels into Arabia, had opportunity of making many curious observations concerning the ostrich, and he hath very largely described the properties of the ostrich in the Supplement to his book of Travels, folio edition, page 66, &c. The doctor's account of the ostrich becomes very explanatory of the several circumstances related concerning this bird in the book of Job. The wings and feathers of the ostrich are so formed, as to be expanded at ease, that they form a kind of sail, not only from motion, but from the air, to hasten the flight; so that at any time if when feeding in the valley, or behind some rocky or sandy eminence in the deserts they are surprised, they stay not to be curiously viewed or examined, neither are the Arabs ever dexterous enough to overtake them, though mounted upon their jinse, or horses. As the Lord hath described the ostrich, so it is found, "what time she lifteth up herself on high, she scorneth the horse and his rider." "Nothing certainly (saith this writer) can be more beautiful and entertaining than the sight. The wings of the ostrich, by their repeated though unwearied vibrations, equally serving them for sails and oars, whilst their feet no less assist them when conveying them out of sight, and no less insensible of fatigue." The circumstance of "leaving her eggs in the earth, and being hardened against her young," forms another remarkable feature in the nature and character of the ostrich. This bird lays very many eggs, from thirty to fifty, and sometimes more in number; probably so appointed by the Great Author of nature, to make suitable provision for those very circumstances: not, as it appears for the brood only, but for food for herself and young. For here is another singularity in the ostrich,--she is exceedingly fond of her own eggs: in which the wisdom of the ostrich's Creator becomes striking. For those parts of the Sahara which these birds chiefly frequent, are destitute of all manner of food and herbage, except some few tufts of coarse grass, so that by this means there is always a supply of food to answer the demands of hunger.

Her want of feeling to her young is so great that there seems to be no instance of natural affection in the ostrich, nothing of that storge which marks the tenderness of the hen, and others of the winged race. She forsakes her nest upon the most trifling occasion, and never returns to it again. The Arabs will sometimes meet with whole nests of the ostrich eggs undisturbed, and sometimes young ostriches straggling and moaning about half starved, like so many distressed orphans, bewailing the loss of their mother. What a beautiful light this throws upon that passage in the prophet, "The daughter of my people is become cruel, like the ostriches in the wilderness? (Lam. iv. 3.)

And so senseless is this bird in respect to caution in food, that she swallows indiscriminately every thing that comes in her way, whether it be rags, leather, wood, stone, or iron. "I saw (saith Dr. Shaw) one of these birds at Oran that swallowed, without any seeming inconvenience, several leaden bullets, as they were thrown upon the floor scorching hot from the mold."

But such are the powers of digestion in the ostrich, as, by their strong friction, to wear even iron itself, that evidently no injury is induced by this inattention. It should seem indeed as if their organs of smell or taste were totally different from all other creatures; for the ostrich is fond of her own dung, and will greedily eat it as soon as voided. All which particularities serve to illustrate what is said concerning her, "because God hath deprived her of wisdom, neither hath he imparted to her understanding."

I would only add under this article, that in Scripture sometimes the owl is put for the ostrich, but corrected in the margin. Jaanah and Rinonem are the names by which, in the Scripture, the ostrich is known; the latter name from Onah and Ronah, meaning noise: for by night their cry is hideous. Dr. Shaw saith, "I have often heard them groan, as if in the greatest agonies." The prophet beautifully makes allusion to it when he saith, "I will make a wailing like the dragon, and mourning as the ostrich." (Micah i. 8. See Isa. xiii. 21, in the margin; and xxxiv. 13, in the margin; and xlii. 20, in the margin.)

OTHNI

Son of Shemaiah. (1Chron. xxvi. 7.) From Let, time, and the addition, my.

OTHNIEL

Son of Kenaz. (Josh. xv. 17.) From Leth, time--and El, God.

OUTCASTS

We several times in Scripture meet with this expression. It is spoken not only concerning the several nations of the earth, but of Israel also. Thus by the prophet Isaiah, chap. lvi. 8. "The Lord God, which gathereth the outcasts of Israel, saith, Yet will I gather others to him besides those which are gathered to him." So that it should seem, that there is a peculiar meaning in the term outcasts, as if the outcasts of other nations had a reference to that part of the Gentile church which is to be brought into one fold, under one shepherd, Jesus Christ the Lord. And concerning the outcasts of Israel, in several parts of Scripture we find the Lord is expressing more than ordinary attention to them. "They called thee an outcast, saith the Lord, by Jeremiah, (chap. xxx. 17.) saying, This is Zion whom no man seeketh after. The Lord will gather them; (for he saith, Ps. cxlvii. 2) "The Lord doth build up Jerusalem, he gathered together the outcasts of Israel." And during their state of being outcasts, the Lord watcheth over them for good, yea, he makes provision for them even in the midst of their enemies. There is a beautiful passage to this effect, (Isa. xvi. 4.) "Let mine outcasts dwell with thee, Moab; be thou a covert to them from the face of the spoiler." Rather than God's children shall go without food, they shall be fed from their enemies table. Even Moab, the sworn foe of Israel, shall take them in when they are turned out, If the Lord hath corrected them, they are still his children; if the Lord for a time hath cast them out, he hath not cast them off. Outcasts they are, but still they are the Lord's outcasts; the Lord still owns them as such. "Let mine outcasts dwell with thee, Moab; and do thou defend them, shelter them, feed them, and take them in as inmates for a time. In due season the Lord will take them home; for the Lord will set up an ensign for the nations, and assemble the outcasts of Israel, and gather together the dispersed of Judah from the four corners of the earth." (Isa. xi. 12.)

What a blessed consideration ariseth out of this view of the outcasts both of the Jewish and the Gentile church. Jesus speaks of both when he saith, (John x. 16.) "And other sheep I have which are not of this fold, them also I must bring, and they shall hear my voice; and there shall be one fold and one shepherd." And agreeably to this, the prophet Isaiah was commissioned to tell the church that in that day, meaning the gospel-day, "five cities in Egypt should speak the language of Canaan. And in that day there shall be an altar to the Lord in the midst of the land of Egypt; and the Lord shall be known to Egypt, and the Egyptians shall know the Lord in that day." And after many blessings of grace that the Lord promiseth shall be shown to Egypt in smiting and healing, it is added, "whom the Lord of hosts will bless, saying, Blessed be Egypt my people, and Assyria the work of mine hands, and Israel mine inheritance." (See Isa. xix. 18, to the end.)

OWL

Moses places the owl among the unclean birds; but whether all, or of what species, as there are several, is not said. (Lev. xi. 17. Deut. xiv. 17.) The loneliness of the owl gave occasion to the Psalmist to describe thereby his solitary state of affliction. (Ps. cii. 7.)

OZEM

One of the sons of Jesse. (1 Chron. ii. 15.) And there is another called by this name, the son of Jerahmeel. (1 Chron. ii. 25.) Derived from Tzam, to fast.

OZNI

Son of Gad, of the family of the Oznites. (Num. xxvi. 16.) The meaning of the name seems to be my balances.

P

PAARAI

The Arbite. (See 2 Sam. xxiii. 35.) Wherefore so called is not so easy to determine, unless from being born in Arbe, called afterwards Hebron. The founder of Arbe or Hebron was Arbe, as it is probable the city was first possessed by the Anaks, afterwards it was given to Judah in the lot of Caleb. There was a tradition among the Rabbins, as it is related by Jerome in his questions on Genesis, that Arbe, the original name of Hebron, was so called because it means four, and Adam, Abraham, Isaac, and Jacob were buried there. It is remarkable that Paraac, in 1 Chron. xi. 37, is called Naarai.

PADAN ARAM

A remarkable place in Jacob's history. (See Gen. xxviii. 6.) From Padan, of the field-- and Aram, Syria.

PADON

One of the Nethenims. (Ezra ii. 44.) Her name is probably derived from Padah, to redeem. See Nethinims.

PAGIEL

Son of Ocran. (Num. vii. 72.) His name comes from Pagah, to pray--perhaps so called from being the child of prayer to God. (See 1 Sam. i. 20. margin of the Bible.)

PAHATH MOAB

Place so called in Moab. Pahath is probably derived from Pacah, prince. (Ezra ii. 6.)

PALAL

The son of Uzai. (Neh. iii. 25.) So called from Pillel, to beseech.

PALESTINE

See Canaan.

PALM TREE

This beautiful tree is spoken of in Scripture with so much commendation, that it merits our attention; and the more so because the Lord Jesus, when describing the loveliness of his church, compares her stature to it, and speaks with a degree of fervour and delight while professing his determination to take hold of her. "I said I will go up to the palm tree, I will take hold of the boughs thereof: now also thy breasts shall be as the clusters of the vine, and the smell of thy nose like apples." (Song vii. 7, 8.)

So very highly esteemed in the eastern world was the palm tree, that Jericho, where they chiefly grew, was called by the name, "The city of palm trees." (Deut. xxxiv. 3.) Engedi was also called Hazazon Tamar, or the village of palm trees, from the number of palm trees which grew there. The Jews called the palm tree Tamar. And not only in Judea, but in all places of the east where palms are found, the branches of it have always been celebrated as the tokens of triumph and victory; hence when the Lord Jesus entered Jerusalem, the multitude, as if overruled by a divine power, "took branches of palm trees, and went forth to meet him, and cried, Hosanna, blessed is the King of Israel, that cometh in the name of the Lord." (John xii. 12, 13.) And hence also, as if to shew the same glorious testimony to the Lord Jesus, the redeemed in heaven are represented as "standing before the throne, and before the Lamb, clothed with white robes, and palms their hands." (Rev. vii. 9.) I defy any man upon earth to shew the shadow of a reason wherefore the correspondence between Christ's appearance upon earth, in the day of his unequalled humility, and the day of his supreme power and glory, should have been thus set forth, but from the one certain and unquestionable truth of his almighty power and GODHEAD, and the divinity of his mission. What could have induced the whole multitude to have honoured Christ with those palm trees in the days of his flesh, when in the garb of a poor Jew, but the power of God overruling the whole mind of the people as the mind of one man? And wherefore the same display made in heaven, but to testify the approbation of God?

I cannot prevail upon myself to dismiss our attention to the palm tree before that I have first remarked some of the properties of it, by way of illustrating the beauty of our Lord's comparing his church to it. The Psalmist hath said, (Ps. xcii. 12.) that "the righteous shall flourish like the palm tree; he shall grow like a cedar in Lebanon." And there will appear a striking allusion between the believer in Jesus and the palm tree of Engedi, if we consider a few of the leading particulars. The growth of the palm is very upright and tall; and, as we are told by naturalists, is to old age always in this state of progression. And surely the church of Jesus, and every individual of the church, is in constant tendency upward. Trees of the Lord's "right hand planting are trees of righteousness," always supposed to be looking upward to Jesus, and their branches extending in every direction according to the exercise of his grace in them, by living wholly upon him in his person, blood, and righteousness.

Moreover, the palm tree is very fruitful, and the fruit is both lovely to the eye and delicious to the taste. And such are the followers of the Lord Jesus. What more lovely than to behold a truly regenerated believer in Christ Jesus? and who more blessed in his day and generation? Like the lofty and luxuriant palm tree of Engedi, which forms both a shade to the traveller to protect him from the heat, and fruit to refresh him as he passeth by, so the church of Jesus becomes a blessedness in her Lord to every spiritual traveller, and affords shelter, and nourishment, and every delight.

There is one property yet, if possible, more striking in the palm tree, which serves to open to a spiritual. Improvement, in allusion to Christ and his church, of a very singular nature, and peculiar, as far as I have learned, to the palm; namely, that the chief source of life in this tree is in its top; or, as it is physically called, the brain of the tree. We are told by those who are acquainted with the nature of palm trees, that if by any means this top be cut off, the tree is for ever after barren. Now here the reader will instantly perceive the striking resemblance between the palm tree and the child of God. To be wholly in Jesus is found the source of life and fruitfulness; and were it possible for a believer to be separated from Christ, yea, but for a moment, everlasting barrenness would follow. How blessedly hath Jesus spoken to this point when he said, "From me is thy fruit found." (Hos. xiv. 8.) And so again, (John xv. 4.) "Abide in me, and I in you; as the branch cannot bear fruit of itself, except it abide in the vine, no more can ye, except ye abide in me?

We are told that the palm tree is all evergreen. On the top of the tree is a kind of tuft or coronet, which never falls off, but is continually the same in verdure. A beautiful representation this of the church in Jesus. Many parts of Scripture correspond in speaking of the real disciple of Christ as one whose "leaf shall never fade nor fall;" and certainly, in the unceasing spring and summer of his glorious head, into whom he is ingrafted, there are no wintery dispensations or change.

One property more merits regard in the resemblance of the palm tree to the Christian, namely, the great duration and continuance of the palm. Dr. Shaw, in his travels, relates that the commonly-received opinion of the inhabitants of those countries where palm trees mostly abound is, that for seventy or eighty years the palm will live, bearing fruit to a great extent, even of 300 lb. weight of dates every year. It need not be noticed, by way of shewing the striking

PALSY - PARABLE

similarity to our nature, that the Psalmist represents the age of man as three-score years and ten, and (saith the Psalmist) "by reason of strength sometimes to four-score years." (Ps. xc. 10.) What a lovely palm tree then is the real follower of the Lord Jesus, if thus living to extreme old age he still brings forth fruit to the praise of the Lord's grace, "some thirty fold, some sixty fold, some au hundred fold!" So speaks the Holy Ghost concerning the faithful: "Those that be planted in the house of the Lord shall flourish in the courts of our God; they shall still bring forth fruit in old age, they shall be fat and flourishing; to shew that the Lord is upright: he is my rock, and there is no unrighteousness in him." (Ps. xcii. 13-15.)

PALSY

A particular malady of body inducing a deadness in the part affected. We read, (Mark ii. 1-13.) of an interesting cure the Lord Jesus wrought on a poor man labouring under this disease; and the complaint of this cripple in body gave occasion to our Lord to manifest thereby his sovereign and almighty power in healing the crippled state of the souls of his people. The palsy is one of the most striking emblems of the dead and helpless state of our fallen nature. Every sinner, until healed by Christ, is palsied in all his faculties; so that in all the instances of palsy we behold in the present day, we see living evidences before our eyes of the effects both of original and actual sin. The sinner is no more able in himself to give health and activity to his soul, than the man of palsy to rise up and use the limbs which are benumbed. Oh! that a sense of this most unquestionable truth were but fully incorporated in our nature, that the Lord Jesus, beholding the faith which he alone can give, might say to the paralytic in soul as to this sick of the palsy in body, "Son, be of good cheer, thy sins are forgiven thee."

PALTI

The son of Raphee. (See Num. xiii. 9.) He was one of those sent by Moses to spy the land of promise. His name, if derived from Palat, signifies deliverance. It should seem by 2 Sam. xxiii. 26, that there must have been a place called Palat, for Helez one of David's worthies, is said to be the Paltite or Pelonite. (See 1 Chron. xi. 27.)

PALTIEL

Son of Azzan, a prince in the tribe of Issachar. (Num. xxxiv. 26.) His name is compounded of Palat, deliverance--and El, God.

PAMPHYLIA

A province of Asia. Here Paul came in his travels. (Acts xiii. 13; xiv. 24.) The name is taken from the Greek, and signifies altogether amiable or lovely.

PAPHOS

A city in the island of Cyprus, where the apostle Paul struck Elymas the sorcerer with blindness
(Acts xiii. 6-12.)

PARABLE

A mode of speaking, in order to illustrate and make familiar to our apprehension divine and spiritual things, by human and natural figures of expression. It was a method of teaching common in the eastern part of the world, and hence all the sacred writers and servants of the Lord adopted it. Yea; the Lord Jesus himself condescended to the same; and indeed so much so that at one time we are told, "without a parable spake he not unto them." (Matt. xiii. 34.)

There is another sense of the word parable, in which it is sometimes used in Scripture when spoken in a way of reproach; hence Moses, when charging Israel to faithfulness, declares that if the people of God apostatize from him, and set up idols in the land, the Lord would scatter them among all nations, "and thou shalt become (saith Moses) an astonishment, a proverb, (or parable) and a by-word, among all nations whither the Lord shall lead thee." (Deut. xxviii. 37.) See Types.

PARADISE

We find this word three times in the New Testament, (Luke xxiii. 43. 2 Cor. xii. 4. Rev. ii. 7.) but the word is not used in the Old. But as the word itself is derived from the Hebrew or Chaldee, it signifies forest or garden of trees; and the same meaning is annexed to what Nehemiah useth for the king's forest, Neh. ii. 8; and what Solomon saith, Eccles. ii. 5, about his gardens and orchards; and of the church it has the same meaning when Jesus commending her saith, "Thy plants are an orchard of pomegranates"--that is, a very paradise.

We are apt to confine our ideas of the word paradise to the garden of Eden, as being so during our first parents' innocence; and this being lost, we now look forward to the possession of a better paradise in the kingdom of glory. What the Lord Jesus said to the dying thief upon the cross, (Luke xxiii. 43.) and to the church of Ephesus, (Rev. ii. 7.) have tended much to establish this opinion. It is sufficient however for all the purposes of knowledge concerning the word itself, that it means a place of unspeakable happiness and delight; and our Lord's promise to the dying thief decidedly settles the point. I would only beg to observe upon that sweet promise of Jesus, in what he plainly shewed, and by his own words, in the manner of expression, that the blessedness of paradise consisted. The happiness of the poor pardoned sinner was not in the place, not simply as paradise, for this he might have been, and in the company of angels also, and yet not blessed. This was not the chief blessing spoken of by the Lord Jesus; but the felicity of which paradise was made up, and which formed the sum and substance of all joy, was Christ. Verily, (said Jesus) "I say unto thee, this day shalt thou be with me in paradise."

Shall I be indulged with subjoining one thought more on the subject of paradise in general, and the ease of this highly-favoured pardoned sinner in particular, just to remark that this promise of Jesus to him, that that very day he should be with Christ in paradise, carries with it a conviction of the truth of that doctrine, that the souls of the redeemed pass instantly to glory on their separation from the body. The voice John heard from heaven, commanding him to write "Blessed are the dead which die in the Lord; from henceforth," that is, immediately, instantly, the bodies rest from their labours, until the resurrection of the just, and then the solemn events Jesus speaks of will take place. (John v. 28, 29.) But to be to-day with Jesus in paradise, carries with it a palpable demonstration of immediate consciousness and unspeakable felicity. I beg the reader to connect with this what the Holy Ghost hath said by the prophet of the consciousness of the opposite character entering eternity. (Isa. xiv. 9, 10.) In the person of the impious king of Babylon, the sacred writer thus addresseth him: "Hell from beneath is moved for thee to meet thee at thy coming; it stirreth up the dead for thee, even all the chief ones of the earth; it hath raised up from their thrones all the kings of the nations. All they shall speak, and say unto thee, Art thou also become weak as we? art thou become like unto us?' Now here we see not only a state of living consciousness described, but the miserable already departed speaking to the miserable now come among them, and giving them the horrible gratulation of partnership in endless woe. Let the reader compare both descriptions; that which Jesus said to the penitent thief, and that which is here described by the prophet; and let him then form his own judgment whether the happiness and misery of the eternal world to the different characters is not immediate on death.

PARMENAS

One of the seven deacons. (Acts vi. 5, 6.) His name is derived from the Greek word, to abide.

PARNACH

Father of Elizaphan. (Num. xxxiv. 25.) If from Parah, to produce; and Nachah, spice, it should seem that his name meant grateful odour or smell.

PAROSH

We read of the tribe of Parosh, Ezra ii. 3. Perhaps his name is derived from Parah, to produce; and Hash, moth; and if so, the meaning might be, life is but vanity.

PARSHANDOTHA

One of the sons of Haman, destroyed with his father. (Esther ix. 7.) A Persian name, supposed to signify exposed to trouble.

PARTHIANS

We read of them Acts ii. 9. Supposed to be the same as the ancient Persians.

PARUAH

The father of Jehoshaphat. (See 1 Kings iv. 17.) From Parah, to flourish.

PASHUR

The son of Immer; a deadly foe to the church. His name is derived from Pashah, to spread; but from his enmity to the people of God while governor in the land, and his cruelty upon the person of the prophet Jeremiah, the prophet called him Magor-missabib, which the margin of the Bible renders fear round about. (See Jer. xx. 1-6.) I pause over the name and character of this man just to remark the blessedness of all times in the church, when the Lord is pleased to give to his exercised people precious testimonies to his truth over and above the grace he manifests to their own hearts. Though, as Asaph saith, apparently the way of the wicked prospereth to outward view, yet to inward feelings they are total strangers to any good; and who shall take upon them to say what sorrows fill their minds? "There is no peace, saith my God, to the wicked." (Isa. lvii. 21.) When the Lord's people therefore hear of such characters, or behold them in their own neighbourhood, (and they are to be found in every place) and observe in the midst of much outside appearances of gaiety, that they are like so many Pashur Magor-missabibs in themselves, surely a voice from every parish steeple where they dwell could not more loudly testify to the truths of God! I would recommend the reader, at any time, when at a loss to explain what he beholds of the prosperity of the wicked and the adversity of the Lord's exercised family, to read what Asaph, taught by the Holy Ghost, hath said, Ps. lxxiii. throughout; and if he adds to Asaph's observations what the man of Uz hath said on the same subject, he will find both profitable. (Job xxi. 7-13.) Moses also, the man of God, hath left upon record the portrait of the inward terrors of the haunted mind. (Deut. xxviii. 65-67.)

PASSING THROUGH THE FIRE

We read concerning Manasseh, (2 Chron. xxxiii. 6.) that "he caused his children to pass through the fire in the valley of the son of Hinnom." And it should seem, from the positive precept which the Lord gave by Moses to Israel to refrain from such horrid customs, that the thing itself was very common in the east, and of great antiquity. (See Lev. xviii. 21.) Indeed, even to the present hour, if we may give credit to modern historians, the funeral burnings which many make of themselves in honour to the dead, serve to shew that the minds of men are not by nature better than from the first.

We are told that there is still a custom observed in the east, where at an annual feast, called the Feast of Fire, many voluntarily engage to walk barefoot over a vivid fire of burning embers, and of great length. This horrid custom, at this dreadful fair, is kept for near three weeks, during which time the wretched creatures which engage to this service pass through the element when stirred up and quickened to burn more lively; and they who walk with the slowest pace are thought the highest of. When the carnival is finished, those who survive are crowned with flowers.

Oh, thou blessed Jesus! what unspeakable mercies hast thou bestowed upon thy people in bringing life and immortality to light by thy gospel! To what a deplorable state is our nature universally reduced by the fall; and how great are our privileges in the Lord in having raised up our poor nature from such gross ignorance and sin! See Moloch.

PASSION

We find mention made of our Lord's passion in the Acts of the Apostles: (chap. i. 3.) and indeed the whole tendency of the Scriptures is to bring the church acquainted with this one great event, in the sufferings and death of Jesus. The reader will do well to have this always in remembrance in all his researches and enquiries concerning Christ.

PASSOVER

While we have the comment which God the Holy Ghost hath given us by his servant Paul, (1 Cor. v. 7.) concerning the Passover, in expressly calling Christ by that name, we must be convinced that it is our highest interest and most bounden duty to study the subject with the closest apprehension, in order to obtain the clearest sense of that the important subject of the Passover means. The reader, therefore, I trust, will bear with me if I call his attention somewhat more particularly to this point.

The Jews called the Passover Paschah or Pesach, and the original meaning is flight or passage--perhaps in allusion to the flight or hasty departure of Israel from Egypt. We have a very circumstantial account of the Passover, Exod. xii. to which I refer. The Israelites, no doubt, had higher views in the institution itself than to suppose it merely referred as a memorial of their deliverance from Egypt. They considered it typical; and the ordination of it being of perpetual standing in the church, must have led them to this conclusion. And may we not add, that, since all the leading features of the redemption by the Lord Jesus, in his person, work, offices, and character, are more or less exhibited in shadow and figure in the Passover, surely the Lord the Spirit gave to many a true Israelite grace and faith to eye, in the paschal lamb, the type of the "Lamb slain from the foundation of the world." (Rev. xiii. 8.)

If the lamb appointed in the Jewish Passover was to be a male of the first year without blemish and without spot; such was Christ. If the lamb was set apart four days before the Passover--so was Christ, not only in the original purpose, and council, and foreknowledge of God before all worlds, but also in four days' entrance into Jerusalem, as it is remarkable Christ did before his sufferings and death. And if the Jewish lamb was roasted whole with fire, and not a bone of him broken, who but must see in this a type of him who, in the accomplishment of salvation sustained all the fire of divine wrath against sin in his sacrifice, and whose bones, it is expressly said, were not broken, that this Scripture might be fulfilled? (John xix. 36.)

Various are the accounts given by various writers of the manner in which the Jews of modern times observe the Passover. They all make it a very high festival. Eight days, for the most part they continue this festivity, during which time they would not for the world knowingly have any leaven within their houses. Nothing would hurt the mind of a Jew more than the discovery of any thing disposed to fermentation, or to make leaven. And on the fourteenth day of

Nisan the Passover begins. And the ceremony generally commenceth in every family by the first-born observing fasting, by way of reference to the destruction of the first-born in Egypt. When this is over, and the time of the evening service being come, all the household enter on prayer, which when finished they proceed to the feast of unleavened bread, with some portion of a lamb, and bitter herbs. During the service they hold wine in their hands, and recount the history of their fathers in Egypt, and the Lord's deliverance of them. The close of their devotions is generally with some of the Psalms, such as from the one hundred and twelfth Psalm, to the one hundred and eighteenth, always beginning with Hallelujah. When the devotional part is all over, they sit down to eat and drink, generally break up their meeting with praying for the health and prosperity of the prince in whose dominions they dwelt, agreeably to the advice of Jeremiah, chap. xxix. 7. So much concerning the method of the observance of the Passover by the children of Israel. I cannot dismiss this part of the subject without first remarking, that as far as decency and seriousness are observed by them in their seasons of worship, it were to be wished that many Christians would follow their example.

It appears from the relation given by the several evangelists, that the Lord Jesus observed this feast of the Passover four times during his ministry, which was but about three years and a half; but by our Lord's entering upon his ministry sometime before the first of the four Passovers he kept, the annual period came round the fourth time before his crucifixion, and therefore we count four in the life of Jesus.

The first public Passover Christ observed is related to us by John, chap. ii. 13, to the end.

The second Passover which Christ graced with his presence is recorded John v. 1, &c. when he healed the cripple at the pool of Bethesda

The third public Passover where we find the Lord Jesus also present is recorded John vi. 4. The feast we read of John vii. 37. was the feast of tabernacles. (See John vii. 2, &c.)

The fourth and last Passover the Lord Jesus honoured in the observance was, as is recorded by all the evangelists, when in the midst of it he summed up and finished the whole shadow of types and ordinances in that one offering of himself upon the cross, whereby "he hath perfected for ever them that are sanctified." (See the relation of this Passover at large, Matt. xxvi. Mark xiv. Luke xxii. John xii. and xiii.)

I would only make one observation upon the whole in this place, namely, if the Lord Jesus never once during his ministry omitted his attendance on the Passover, how hath he thereby endeared to his redeemed his holy Supper, instituted and appointed as it was by himself to take place in his church in the room of the Jewish Passover! Surely by this Jesus might be supposed to intimate his holy pleasure, that his people should be always present at the celebration of it. Methinks by this constant attendance of the Lord, he meant to say that not one of his little ones should be absent at his Supper. And his servant, the apostle, seems to have had the same views of his Master's gracious design in this particular when he saith, "For as often as ye eat this bread and drink this cup, ye do shew the Lord's death till he comes." (1 Cor. xi. 26.)

PASTOR or SHEPHERD

A well-known office of the Lord Jesus Christ. The Holy Ghost delights to set forth Jesus under this lovely character in all his word. Sometimes he represents him as the Great Shepherd, (Heb. xiii. 20.)--and sometimes he calls him the Good Shepherd, which giveth his life for the sheep, (John x. 11.)--and by his servant the prophet Zechariah, he calls him JEHOVAH'S Shepherd, (Zech. xiii. 7.)--and by Peter, the Chief Shepherd, holding him forth to the under pastors of his flock as a glorious pattern for them to follow, assuring them that when the Chief Shepherd shall appear "they shall receive a crown of glory that fadeth not away." (1 Pet. v. 4.) And to distinguish him from every other, and as the only Shepherd of JEHOVAH, to whom the flock is given, and who alone was, and is, able to purchase it with his blood, and to preserve it by his power, by his servant the prophet Ezekiel, he is expressly called the one Shepherd; "I will set up one Shepherd over them, and he shall feed them." (Ezek. xxxiv. 23.)

The Holy Ghost hath not only thus delighted to mark the sweet features of his character, but hath given the several features also of his office. "He shall feed his flock (saith the Lord, by the prophet Isaiah, chap. xl. 11.) like a shepherd." And how is that? Surely, from a knowledge of their persons, their wants, their desires, their abilities, Jesus graciously makes suitable provision for every one, and for all. It is his flock the church, both from the Father's gift, his own purchase, the conquests of his grace, and the voluntary willingness of his people in the day of his power. "He calleth his own sheep by name: they shall all pass (saith the Holy Ghost, by the prophet Jeremiah, chap. xxxiii. 13.) under the hands of him that telleth them." Hence, from a knowledge of their number, their persons, their wants, and necessities, it is impossible that one can be overlooked, forgotten, neglected, or lost. He saith himself, "My sheep shall never perish, neither shall any pluck them out of my hand." Oh, the precious office and character of the Lord Jesus as the Pastor and Shepherd of his people! He feeds, he protects, he heals, he watches over, restores when wandering, and gathers them out from all places whither they have wandered in the cloudy and dark day, and leads them in the paths of righteousness, for his name's sake.

Jesus hath his under pastors also, by whom he feeds and directs his flock; hence the Lord, by Jeremiah, promised," I will give you pastors according to mine heart, which, shall feed you with knowledge and understanding." (Jer. iii. 15.) And a whole chapter is spent by the prophet Ezekiel, the thirty-fourth, in reproving the evil pastors who abused their office, and fed themselves of the flock, and not their people. Sometimes princes and governors are called pastors; thus David is said to have been taken from the sheepfold to be ruler over the Lord's people Israel. (2 Sam. vii. 8.)

PATARA

A sea-port of Lycia. It was here Paul the apostle found a ship bound for Phœnicia, into which he entered. (Acts xxi. 1.)

PATMOS

An island in the Ægean Sea, where the beloved apostle John was banished. (Rev. i. 9.)

PATHROS

A city of Egypt. (Isa. xi. 11. Jer. xliv. 1.) Perhaps derived from Path, mouth,--and Raphos, water.

PATHRUSIM

Inhabitants of Pathros.

PATRIARCHS

This name is not of the Hebrew, but Greek language. The title is chiefly confined to the heads of families before the law; for when we speak of the patriarchs without particularizing by name it is generally understood of those before the flood, and afterwards confined to the persons and families of Abraham, Issac, Jacob, and their tribe. The Hebrews rather call them princes than patriarchs, and distinguish all of this description by the general appellation Roshe Aboth. As to the name of patriarch given to the Greek church in modern times, this is altogether fanciful, and not derived from any authority in Scripture.

PATROBAS

A companion of the apostle Paul. (Rom. xvi. 14.) His name hath an allusion to somewhat that is fatherly.

PAU

The name of a city. (Gen. xxxvi. 39.) Perhaps derived from Pahah, to cry.

PAUL

The apostle. His name at the first was Saul; but, as is generally supposed, after his being made an instrument in the hand of God for the conversion of Sergius Paulus, the deputy of Paphos, (see Acts xiii. 7.) he was called Paul. Some have indeed supposed that the change of name was made at his own conversion; but this doth not seem likely, as so long a space had taken place between that period and the time of Sergius Paulus's conversion, during all which the Holy Ghost still called him Saul. His own conversion was about the year of our Lord God 35; whereas the conversion of the deputy of Paphos did not happen until the year 45. See particularly Acts xiii. 2; where God the Holy Ghost called our apostle by name, Saul; and the manner of expression in which the name of Paul is first spoken of in the Scriptures, seems to imply that it was then only given to him, for afterwards we hear no more of the name of Saul. (See Acts xiii. 9.) And some have gone so far as to say, that the Deputy himself called Paul by this name, as giving him one of his own names in token of his love for him, as Vespasian the emperor, it is well known, called Josephus Flavius, his own name, out of regard.

Concerning this great apostle of the Lord Jesus Christ, it would form a place more suited for the separate volume of an history, than as an article of a mere explanatory memorandum in a Concordance, to enter into a detail of Paul's life and ministry. Pleasing as the subject in itself would be, I must suppress the gratification. Indeed a reference to the sacred word of God is much more suited for the obtaining information of Paul's history, because while attending to the memoirs of the apostle we may also gather instruction from his doctrine. It will answer all the purpose to be wished for, by way of information, concerning Paul, in a work of this kind, just to observe that from his conversion to his martyrdom we find in the apostle's history one uniform invariable course of faith and practice in the path of the gospel. And those fourteen blessed Epistles which God the Holy Ghost hath given to the church by him, will render his memory blessed to the latest ages. It should seem, from calculating the periods of Paul's life and ministry, that he was born about two years before Christ's incarnation, and suffered martyrdom under, the emperor Nero in the year 66.

PEACE

It would have been perfectly unnecessary to have noticed this word, in order to have explained its general sense and meaning in reference to the use of it among men, had that been all. The peace and war of nations, or among houses or families, or kingdoms, are terms with which every one is familiar. But the Scripture sense of the word peace, and more especially the gospel signification of it, in respect to that peace believers have with God in Christ makes it well worth attention in a work of this kind.

It may not perhaps have struck an ordinary reader, that the word peace carries with it the idea that the breach then said to be made up presupposes that there had been a state of amity existing before the breach came in to interrupt it; and this is indeed the blessedness of the gospel. Hence it is called the "ministry of reconciliation." (2 Cor. v. 18.) So that to reconcile God and man in Christ, which is the grand object of the gospel, is to bring together again those who had before been friends, but were then at enmity; and hence is clearly proved, what the word of God all along is setting forth, that the present state is not the first, neither will it be the final state of man: it is but intermediate and preparatory. There was a period in the annals of eternity when God and man, in the person of the Glory-man, set up before all worlds, were in perfect amity and friendship. And there is another period to come when, from the reconciliation now made between God and man in the blood of the cross, this amity and friendship will continue uninterrupted and unbroken to all eternity. And there is another sweet thought connected with the gospel meaning of the word peace, namely, that all the overtures for a reconciliation began on the part of God, the injured party; and all the peace that follows becomes the sole result of his divine operation. JEHOVAH it is that first publisheth his royal intentions of being reconciled to his offending creature man. It is JEHOVAH that points out and provides the means, and accomplisheth the end, in the attainment of it. Nothing on the part of the sinner could be found even helpful towards it; yea, so totally incapable of putting forth the least aiding hand upon this business is the transgressor, that when proposed to him he must be made willing to accept it; and before proposed to him, he is unconscious of the want of it. Blessedly therefore is it said by the apostle, under the authority of the Holy Ghost, (2 Cor. v. 19.) that "God was in Christ, reconciling the world unto himself." And blessedly doth he open his commission, when acting as the servant of his royal master, he adds, "Now then we are ambassadors for Christ, as though God did beseech you by us we pray you in Christ's stead, be ye reconciled to God."

Such then is the Scripture sense of that peace of God and peace with God, in the blood and righteousness of God's dear Son, "which passeth all understanding, keeping the heart and mind, in Jesus Christ." (Phil. iv. 7.) And so truly great and glorious was the first promulgation of it, when the news broke out in heaven, that the holy angels delighted to be the first preachers of it upon earth. The multitude of them that came flying, down to the Jewish shepherds at Bethlehem in the morning of Christ's nativity, hailed them with this joyful sound. "Glory to God in the highest, and on earth peace and good-will toward men." (Luke ii. 13, 14.) And the prophet in ages before, looking into gospel times, was so struck with the contemplation of the work in the exercise of the ministry of reconciliation, that he declared the very feet of them that preached it became beautiful to the view of broken-hearted sinners. "How beautiful (said Isaiah) upon the mountains are the feet of him that bringeth good tidings, that publisheth peace, that bringeth good tidings of good, that publisheth salvation, that saith unto Zion. Thy God reigneth!" (Isa. lii. 7.)

PEARL

The pearl of great price, mentioned, (Matt. xiii. 46.) being a figurative expression to denote the preciousness of Jesus and his salvation, may serve, to explain wherefore it is that the glories of Christ's person, and the beauty of his church in him, are so often set forth in Scripture under the similitude of pearls, and rubies, and precious stones. The Hebrews called pearls peninim, (Job xxviii. 18. and Prov. lii. 15.) the same word is translated rubies. Some have considered them therefore as one and the same; but certainly they are very distinct things; however, the spiritual sense in that which relates to Christ and his church may be called both. Hence the description of the New Jerusalem. (Rev. xxi.21.) And indeed it is very blessed to eye Jesus under all the loveliness of everything we meet with in the whole compass of creation, both in the kingdoms of nature, providence, grace, and glory. All that is

PEDAHZUR - PELICAN

lovely, or beautiful, or useful, or ornamental, all derive their exellency from him. Jesus and his salvation surpasseth the gold of Ophir, the topaz of Æthiopia, and all the pearls and rubies of the world. So Jesus hath said, and so all his redeemed know it to be true: "Riches and honour are with me; (saith Christ) yea, durable riches and righteousness. My fruit is better than gold, yea, than fine gold; and my revenue than choice silver." (Prov. viii. 18, 19.)

PEDAHZUR

The father of Gamaliel. (Num. i. 10.) The stone of redemption is the meaning of this remarkable name, if, as is reasonable to suppose, the derivation is from Padah, to save,--and Tzar; stone. .

PEDAH-EL

The son of Ammiud. (Num. xxxiv. 28.) Saved of God, from Padah, to save--and El, God.

PEDAH-IAH

The father of Zebudah. (2 Kings xxiii. 36.) We have several of this name in the Scripture: the son of Jeconiah, 1 Chron. iii. 18.--the son of Parosh, Neh. iii. 25, Saved of the Lord, from Padah and Jah.

PEKAH

Son of Remaliah. (2 Kings xv. 25.) He that opens, from Pacah.

PEKAHI-JAH

Son of Menahim. (2 Kings xv. 22.) The Lord opens, from Pacah, to open--and Jah, the Lord.

PELAIAH

A Levite. (See Neh. viii. 7.) A thing secret, from Pelah, to hide.

PELALIAH

Son of Amzi. (Neh. xi. 12.) Compounded of Pillel, to meditate or pray--and Jah, the Lord.

PELATIAH

Son of Hananiah. (1 Chron. iv. 42.) There was another of this name in the days of Ezekiel, chap. xi. 1. Derived from Palat, to deliver--and Jah, the Lord.

PELEG

Son of Eher. (Gen. xi. 16.) So called from Pillig, to cut or divide.

PELET

One in David's army. From Palat, to deliver.

PELETH

Son of Pallu. (Num. xvi. 1.) From Palal, to judge.

PELETHITES

So called from Peleth, meaning judges. The Pelethites and Cherithites (or Cherim, more properly speaking) were much spoken of in the days of David. (1 Sam. xxx. 14. and 2 Sam. viii. 18.) It should seem to have been an office in the inferior courts for judging the people; hence the Pelethites and Cherithites were judges. The word Cherim means excommunication: and there were three degrees of it observed. The first was a simple separating, called Niddui; the second Cherim, somewhat like what the apostle calls Anathema Maranatha; and the third implied death, and was called Shammathah.

PELICAN

The pelican is classed by Moses among the unclean fowls. (Lev. xi. 18.) Notwithstanding the Psalmist seems to have had much respect to the solitary pursuit of this bird, when describing his loneliness of soul under this figure--"I am like a pelican of the wilderness." And if this psalm be considered (as I confess I feel much inclined to believe) to have more of David's Lord in it than David, there is something very stalking in the similitude of the pelican. I refer the reader to my Poor Man's Commentary, on the-one hundred and second Psalm, for my thoughts concerning Jesus as the glorious person to whom the principal characters in that psalm have respect. The Hebrews distinguished the pelican by the name Kaath. It hath been a generally-received opinion, and some of the early fathers have given countenance to it, such as St. Austin, and Isidore, that the pelican feeds her young with her blood, and by sprinkling it on her young also contributes to their life. Be the fact so or not, yet certain it is that our heavenly Pelican both feed§ and sprinkles his young with his blood, and is their life and their portion for ever. He saith himself, "Except ye eat the flesh of the Son of Man, and drink his blood, ye have no life in you. And whoso eateth my flesh, and drinketh my: blood, hath eternal life; and I will raise him up at the last day." (John vi. 53, 54.) These are sweet views of Jesus! Blessed are the souls who are daily living thus upon him. Surely the pelican in this point of view becomes no unapt resemblance of Christ.

PELONITE

An inhabitant of this city in Judea. (1 Chron. xi. 36.) The name is taken from Pala, somewhat concealed.

PENIEL

A spot remarkable in Scripture from the vision of Jacob. The patriarch called it by this name on this account; for he said, "I have seen God face to face, and my life is preserved." (See Gen. xxxii. 30.) The word is a compound, from Pana, to see--and El, God. And who was it Jacob saw, and with whom did he wrestle? If JEHOVAH, in his threefold character of person, Father, Son, and Holy Ghost, how could this be, who is said to be invisible? If "no man hath seen God at any time," if, as JEHOVAH declared to Moses, (Exod. xxxiii. 20.) "There shall no man see me and live," who could this be whom the patriarch Jacob saw, conversed and wrestled with; but the Lord Jesus? Him whom though no man hath seen God at any time, yet "the only begotten Son, which is in the bosom of the Father, he hath declared him." (John i. 18.) Let the reader read the whole passage concerning this Peniel, this hallowed ground, as it is recorded through the whole chapter, (Gen. xxxii.) and let him then compare what is there said with what the prophet Hosea, about a thousand years after, said concerning this vision; and let him then, looking up for the teaching of God the Holy Ghost, determine for himself. "He took his brother by the heel (said Hosea, speaking of Jacob) in the womb, and by his strength he had power with God; yea, he had power over the angel, and prevailed. He wept and made supplication unto him. He found him in Bethel, and there he spake with us, even the Lord God of host: the Lord is his memorial." (Hos. xii. 3.5.)

The history of Jacob, in this very interesting transaction, I am not at present engaged in: it is Jacob's Lord that we are now seeking after. And when the reader hath duly attended to the several striking particularities here recorded, and compared them with other Scriptures, I venture to believe that his conclusions will correspond with mine, that this, and indeed all the representations of the Old Testament concerning the Lord's appearance and manifestation to his people, are directly spoken of in reference to the person of the Lord Jesus Christ.

Let the reader first remark that the patriarch called the place Peniel on this account, that "he had seen God's face, and his life was preserved." And yet we are told, (ver. 24.) that it was a man which wrestled with Jacob until the breaking of the day. Now it is remarkable, that he whom the prophet Hosea, in the passage just quoted, in one verse calls the angel, in another he calls "the Lord God of hosts," and saith that "the Lord is his memorial." And observe the prophet doth not say an angel, but the angel, thus particularizing and defining one identical person; and we well know that Christ is often called the "angel of the covenant," (Mal. iii. 1. Acts vii. 30, 31.) Indeed the patriarch Jacob himself, in another period of his life, called him by this name. (See Gen. xlviii. 15, 16.) And if we add to these striking particulars what is said of the Lord, and by the Lord, under the character of human feelings, in other parts of the Old Testament, I cannot but conclude that the whole is abundantly confirmed, that it is the Lord Jesus, and him only, in his mediatorial character, who is all along to be understood as the visible JEHOVAH. Thus it is said, that "his soul was grieved for the misery of Israel." (Judges x. 16.) A beautiful and most interesting portrait of Jesus if beheld as picturing him, but inexplicable in any other point of view. So again the Lord is represented as saying: "I will rejoice over my people to do them good; and I will plant them in this land assuredly with my whole heart, and with my whole soul." (Jer. xxxii. 41.) Here again, supposing it is Jesus-Mediator which thus speaks, nothing can be more plain and nothing more blessed, for we know that his whole heart and soul is his people's; but concerning the Lord JEHOVAH, in his threefold character of person, Father, Son, and Holy Ghost, we dare not, because we are not authorized in any part of Scripture thus to speak of him as possessing parts or passions. He is, as the Holy Ghost himself by the apostle describes him, "the king eternal, immortal, invisible." (1 Tim. i. 17.) Hence, When the read in the word of God that the eyes of the Lord are over the righteous, and his ears open to their prayers, and that he openeth his hand and satisfieth the desire of every living thing, these expressions are literally true, as well as blessedly refreshing, considered as spoken of Him in whom it hath pleased the Father that "all fulness should dwell," and who is the Head of all principality and power; but cannot be said of JEHOVAH in his absolute nature and GODHEAD, "dwelling in the light which no man can approach unto, whom no man hath seen or can see." (1 Tim. vi. 16.)

I shall find cause to bless God if these observations on Peniel, and the thoughts arising out of the same, be directed of the Lord to throw the least light on a subject so highly interesting, and enable any precious lover of Jesus to form clearer views of him, whom truly to know is life eternal. (John xvii. 2, 3.) Surely nothing can be more blessed than to discover Jesus thus refreshing Old Testament saints with such precious manifestations of himself, as if to shew what love he had to his church and people, and how much he longed for the time appointed when he would openly manifest himself as our glorious Head, and Surety, and Saviour. Precious Jesus! methinks I would say for myself and reader, grant many Peniel visits to thy redeemed now, and make all the manifestations of the full GODHEAD in glory to thy redeemed in heaven tenfold more sweet and blessed, by the communications in thee, and through thee, to flow in upon the souls of thy whole church in eternal happiness for ever. Amen.

PENINNAH

The second wife of Elkanah. (1 Sam. i. 2.) Her name signifies, precious stone, or jewel, from Paninim.

PENTECOST

The day of Pentecost was so first called after our Lord's ascension. Before that period the church called it "the feast of weeks," (Exod. xxxiv. 22.) and it was one of those three great feasts in which all the males were require to appear before the Lord. The word Pentecost means the fiftieth, being fifty days from the Passover. The feast itself was appointed perhaps with a double view; first, to commemorate the giving of the law on mount Sinai, which was on the fiftieth day after the children of Israel had left Egypt; and, secondly, and for which it was enjoined as a feast, to testify that Israel's Lord was the rightful owner of all Israel's property, and they as tenants holding those possessions during the pleasure of their almighty landlord, and thus they were called upon cheerfully to pay their high rent in offering to him the first fruits of all their increase.

This festival in the ancient church was very highly celebrated, as we may plainly perceive from the multitude that came from all parts, to trade on those occasions, on the day of Pentecost, as we read in the Acts of the Apostles, chap. ii. How far religious duties occupied the minds of the children of Israel, in those dark ages, is not very easy to determine.

The modern Jews of the present hour, holding by tradition the festival as chiefly referring to the giving of the law on mount Sinai, of which they are very tenacious, and not knowing that it is the ministration of condemnation, they celebrate this festival for two days with great attention. They adorn both the synagogue and their own houses with flowers, and make it altogether a time of festivity. In the religious parts of their services on those occasions, it is said that they read in the Scriptures of Moses what relates to the feast of weeks, and conclude their ceremonies in mutual good wishes for the prosperity of each other and their nation.

What a vast superiority hath the true believer in Jesus in celebrating our Pentecost! This blessed festival in the church of Christ is wholly spiritual. Contemplating the first open descent of God the Holy Ghost as the first fruits of the Lord Jesus's gifts to his people in his return to glory, when he had finished redemption-work upon earth, we are taught to hail the coming of the Holy Ghost as the most blessed of all evidences, concerning the truth as it is in Jesus. And when the soul of a real believer in Christ is truly regenerated, and enabled by divine teaching to enter into a real heartfelt enjoyment of what is contained in the doctrine of the descent of God the Holy Ghost upon the church, then this only festival becomes to every individual believer a renewed Pentecost indeed.

As the proper apprehension of this subject is truly interesting, I shall beg permission from the reader to dwell yet somewhat more particularly upon it.

If we attend to what the word of God hath graciously revealed in, reference to the sacred purposes of JEHOVAH in redemption, we may discover that as all the three divine persons of the GODHEAD have been and are engaged in the accomplishment of the work, so the Scriptures point out the special office of each. In the Old Testament we find God the Father proclaiming to the church the coming of his dear Son. In the New Testament we have that promise realized, and God the Son accomplishing the whole purposes, of salvation. And after his ascension and return to glory we have the visible manifestation of God the Holy Ghost on the day of Pentecost, to carry on and render effectual the great purposes of redemption in the hearts of the people by his almighty grace and power. So that there is a beautiful order in the design and execution of the work itself, as well as grace and mercy in the dispensation.

The day of Pentecost therefore opens with the manifestation of the Holy Ghost in his sevenfold gifts and graces. Hitherto the kingdom of grace had been supplied with the occasional effusions of the Spirit on the church, as the sacred purposes of JEHOVAH'S will required. "The Holy Ghost, it is said, was not yet given, because that Jesus was not yet glorified." (John vii. 39.) But now that the Son of God hath finished the whole of his ministry upon earth, and is returned to glory, the Holy Ghost comes down in a fulness of blessings, and to him is committed the whole efficiency of the work, as the Almighty Minister in the church, to render the whole effectual; and to this agree the words of the prophets: Isa. xliv. 3-5. Joel ii. 28, &c. Acts ii. 14-34.

I beg to add one observation more on this view of our Christian Pentecost, namely, what a confirmation it gives to all the interesting doctrines of our most holy faith. The promise of God the Father in the Old Testament, and the promise of God the Son in the New Testament, both taught the church to be on the look-out for the coming of the Holy Ghost. And as the glorious period drew nigh when this Almighty Spirit would come and dwell in the hearts of his redeemed, the promises concerning him became more clear and pointed. The Lord Jesus, in his farewell sermon, when instituting his holy Supper as the standing memorial of his death, most particularly described his person, character, and offices. (See John chap. xiv. xv. and xvi.) And again, in the very moment of his departure, he reminded his disciples of the near approach of this blessed guest. "Behold (said Jesus) I send the promise of my Father upon you; but tarry ye in the city of Jerusalem until ye be endued with power from on high." (Luke xxiv. 49.) And still farther he added at the same parting interview, "John (said Jesus) truly baptized with water; but ye shall be baptized with the Holy Ghost not many days hence." (Acts i. 5.) And agreeably to this promise, the Holy Ghost actually came down ten days after, on the day of Pentecost when those events took place which are recorded in the second chapter of the Acts of the Apostles.

Now from hence the following just and evident conclusion is unavoidable, and must follow: If Christ had not been God, how could he have had power and authority to have sent the Holy Ghost? If Christ had not completed salvation, and finished the work the Father gave him to do, how would his promise have been fulfilled in the gift of the Spirit? If Christ had not ascended, how would the Holy Ghost have descended in exact conformity to what he had said? Can any thing upon earth be more palpable and plain in confirmation of all the great truths of our holy faith, that when the Holy Ghost came down, Jesus was gone up, and God the Father confirmed the perfect approbation he had several times from heaven by a voice given of his dear Son, that he was well pleased in him, by sending down, according to Christ's promise, the Holy Ghost? The Lord Jesus had told his disciples before his departure, that it was expedient for them he should go away. "For (said Jesus) if I go not away, the Comforter will not come; but if I depart, I will send him unto you." (John xvi. 7.) He did depart, and the Holy Ghost came. What an evidence to all the other glorious testimonies of his mission! And I must contend for it, as for one of the plainest matters of fact the world was ever called to judge upon, that in the descent of the Holy Ghost on the day of Pentecost, we have as palpable a seal to the truth of the gospel as we have to any one of the most common events in the circumstances of human life; yea, the subject will warrant my going farther, and to say, that in the heart of every individual sinner whom "the Lord hath made willing in the day of his power," that soul is a living evidence of the descent of the Holy Ghost. And surely it is by these evidences now, in the present awful day of infidelity, and a Christ-despising generation, the Lord is bringing forth proofs to the doctrine of his dear Son. The Lord speaks in every one of them in terms similar to the words by the prophet: "Ye are my witnesses, saith the Lord, and my servant whom I have chosen." (Isa. xliii. 10.)

I have greatly swollen this article beyond my first intention, yet I cannot take leave of it without adding a short observation, just to remark how needful it must be in every follower of the ever-blessed Jesus to examine in his own heart for the evidence of his Pentecost mercy, whether that holy Spirit hath witnessed in his spirit to "the truth as it is in Jesus?" Blessed is the man that can testify to the Spirit's work in his own heart in all the offices, characters, and gifts of God the Holy Ghost. When we know him as Jesus described him, the Spirit of truth to guide into all truth; the Witness to our spirits that we are the children of God; the Glorifier of Jesus; the Comforter of the soul; the Spirit of grace, of supplication, and prayer; the Helper of our infirmities; the Spirit of wisdom and knowledge in the revelation of Christ Jesus in a word, the great and sovereign minister in the church and heart of all his people, from the first quickenings of grace, until grace be consummated in eternal glory. Oh, for the blessed earnest of the Holy Ghost thus to testify to his own impressions on the soul, whereby believers are "sealed unto the day of redemption!" (Eph. iv. 30.)

PENUEL

This is the same word as Pentel, which see. There are two persons of this name in Scripture, namely, the son of Hur, (1 Chron. iv. 4.) and Penuel, the son of Shashak, (1 Chron. viii. 25.)

PEOPLE

This, though a word of general import as referring to nations, or the persons of particular kingdoms, yet in respect to the Lord's people, hath a special designation. The redeemed of Christ are called a peculiar people, (1 Pet. ii. 9.)--a "people that dwell alone, and are not reckoned among the nations." (Num. xxiii. 9.) Hence God the Father, speaking of them to his dear Son, saith, "Thy people shall be willing in the day of thy power." (Ps. cx.) And elsewhere the Lord saith, "Thou art an holy people to the Lord thy God; the Lord, thy God hath chosen thee to be a special people unto himself, above all people that are upon the face of the earth." (Deut. vii. 6.) And it is wonderful to observe how distinguishing the grace of God is manifested towards them. They are given of the Father to the Son, and set apart in the counsel and purpose of God from all eternity; they are the object of Jesus's love before all worlds; and they are brought; under the anointings of God the Holy Ghost, with pepeculiar marks of his love during the whole of their eventful pilgrimage-state, from the first dawnings of grace unto the fulness of glory. Such are the characters of the redeemed of the Lord. "Oh! bless, our God, ye people, and make the voice -of his praise to be heard." (Ps. lxvi. 8.)

PEER

The word means opening, from Pahar. See Baal-peer.

PERGAMOS

One, of the seven churches in Asia, The account we have, Rev. ii. 12-17.

PERIZZITES

The word is derived from Peras, or Pherazoth. Such as dwell in villages: or perhaps, as villages are scattered buildings different from cities, the Perizzites might mean the scattered enemies of Israel, whom the Lord would drive out before them. (Exod. xxxiii. 2.)

PERSIA

A kingdom in Asia. This was the kingdom, in the government of the world, which succeeded the Babylonish, when Cyrus, king of Persia, had destroyed the Chaldean powers. (See Isaiah xlv. and Daniel v. 30, 31.)

PETER

The apostle. We have a very circumstantial account of this man in the New Testament, so that it supersedes the necessity of any observations here. His name was altered to

Cephas, a Syriac word for rock. We must not however totally pass by our improvements on the apostle's life and character, though we do not think it necessary to go over the history of this great man. Certainly the Holy Ghost intended, that the very interesting particulars in the life of Peter should have their due operation in the church through all ages; and it must be both the duty and the privilege of the faithful to follow up the will of God the Spirit in this particular, and to regard, the striking features which mark his character. As a faithful servant of Jesus how very eminent Peter stands forth to observation; for who among the apostles so zealous, so attached to his Lord, as Peter? And that such an one should fall from his integrity, even to the denial of his Lord, what caution doth it teach to the highest servants of Jesus! But when we have paid all due attention to those striking particularities in the life of Peter, the most blessed and most important instruction the life of this apostle exhibits, is in the display of that sovereign grace of Jesus manifested in Peter's recovery. Oh, how blessedly hath the Holy Ghost taught, in this man's instance, the vast superiority of God's grace over man's undeservings! However great our unworthiness, the Lord's mercies are greater. Divine love riseth above the highest tide of human transgression. "Where sin aboundeth, grace doth much more abound; that as sin hath reigned unto death, so might grace reign through righteousness unto eternal life, through Jesus Christ our Lord." (Rom. v.21.)

I cannot close my observations on the character of Peter without first expressing my surprize that the apostle did not adopt the name of Cephas from the first moment Jesus called him so. (John i. 42.) Paul indeed did call Peter by this name, Gal. ii. 9; but it doth not seem to have been in general use among the brethren. And yet we find, in the instance of Abraham and Jacob, the Lord when he changed their names seemed to express his pleasure in calling them by those names. I would ask, is not this change of name among the Lord's people now a part of their high calling and character? Did not the Lord so promise the church when he said, "And thou shalt be called by a new name, which the mouth of the Lord shall name?" (Isa. lxii. 2.) And did not Jesus confirm this when he said, "Him that overcometh will I make a pillar in the temple of my God; and I will write upon him my new name." (Rev. iii. 12.) Reader, is not this done now as much as in the instance of Old Testament saints, and New Testament believers in the ages past? Let us cherish the thought.

PETHAHIAH

He was the head of a family. (1 Chron. xxiv. 16.) His name means gate of the Lord, from Pathac, gate--and Jah, Lord.

PETHOR

The city of Baalam. (Num. xxii. 5.)

PETHUEL

The father of the prophet Joel. His name signifies mouth of God, from Path, mouth-- and El, God; or if from Pathah, to persuade, it will be persuasion of God.

PEULTHAI

One of the Levites, (1 Chron. xxvi. 5.) from Pahal, work--and the pronoun I, my work.

PHALLU

Son of Reuben. (Gen. xlvi. 9.) From Phala, to hide.

PHALTI

Son of Laish, (1 Sam. xxv. 44.) husband of Michal, Saul's daughter. From Palat, flight.

PHANUEL

Of the tribe of Asher. This man's name is rendered memorable in being the father of

Anna. (See Luke ii. 36.) His name is derived from Pana, to see--and El, God.

PHARAOH

King of Egypt. It should seem that Pharaoh was the common name of the kings of Egypt, since we find that both he that knew Joseph, and he that knew him not, were both called Pharaoh. Indeed we find a Pharaoh in the days of Abraham. (Gen. xii. 10-15.) The name of Pharaoh implies a destroyer, derived from Parah. But some have thought that the name is a title, and not unsimilar to those used in modern times of royal, and highness, and the like. But it is of little importance what the name meant, or how used. The Pharaoh, the tyrant of Egypt, we know most of in Scripture, was a type of the devil; and as such the Lord's people should read his history, with the Lord's striking observation upon him. (Exod. ix. 16.)

PHAREZ

Son of Judah, by Tamar, (Gen. xxxviii. 29.) The word is translated in the margin of the Bible a breach. The same word as David afterwards used from the breach made at Uzzah's touching the ark. (2 Sam. vi. 8.)

PHARISEE

A sect in the days of our Lord, remarkable for their scrupulous exactness to certain points, while relaxed in the higher principles of real vital godliness. The name Pharisee is derived from a root signifying separation, and suited to them, from their being very singular in their order. For the character of the Pharisee I refer to Matt. xxiii. throughout. The modern Pharisee of the present hour is he that prides himself upon the rectitude of his own heart, and ventures his everlasting welfare upon the merit of his good works before God; or, in a less degree, takes to himself the consolation of being part his own Saviour, and hoping that Christ will make up the deficiency. The portrait of such an one we have, Luke xviii. 9-14.

PHARKAR

A river of Damascus, rendered memorable from the circumstance of Naaman's leprosy. (2 Kings v. 12.)

PHEBE

A pious woman noticed by Paul. (Rom. xvi. 1.)

PHENICE

A place where the apostle Paul anchored (Acts xxvii. 12.)

PHICOL

Captain of Abimelech's army. (Gen. xxi. 22.) His name, it should seem, is taken from Pe, a mouth; and Calab, to complete.

PHILADELPHIA

One of the seven churches. (Rev. iii. 7.) The name is taken from the Greek, and is compounded of Philo, to love; and Adelphos, a brother.

PHILEMON

The master of Onesimus. See Epistle to Philemon. See Onesimus.

PHILETUS

One that erred from the faith. (2 Tim. ii. 17, 18.)

PHILIP

The apostle. (See John i. 43, 44.) There was also a Philip who was ore of the seven deacons. (Acts vi. 5.)

PHILIPPI

A city of Macedon, rendered memorable from Paul the apostle having preached the gospel to the people there by the direction of a vision, and having sent that blessed Epistle there which we have still preserved in the New Testament, and made so truly blessed to the church. See the Epistle to the Philippians.

PHILISTINES

A race well known to the church; the sworn foes to God and his people. The name is not derived from the Hebrew, but is a common name for dwellers in villages.

PHILOSOPHY

The meaning of the word is a rover of wisdom, but most wretchedly applied, when spoken of in reference to the wisdom of this world. See proofs, of it, Rom. i. 21, &c.

PHINEHAS

Son of Eleazar the priest. He was the third high priest, from the first order of the priesthood. Aaron, Eleazar and Phinehas. The name seems to have been derived Panah, to shine, See an honorable testimony given by the Lord himself to this man. (Num. xxv. 6-13.) There was another Phinehas in Scripture, but of a very different character, namely, Phineas the son of Eli. (See 1 Sam. it. 27. to the end.)

PHLEGON

A friend of the apostle Paul. (Rom. xvi. 14.) His name is taken from a Greek word signifying burning.

PHURAH

The steward of Gideon, (Judg. vii. 10,11.) derived from Parah, to bear.

PHUT

One of the sons of Ham, (Gen. x. 6.) The word means fat.

PHYGELLUS

Paul complains of this man. (2 Tim. i. 15.) The word is derived from the Greek, and means a fugitive.

PHYLACTERIES

We meet with this word but once in the whole Bible, namely, Matt. xxiii. 5. Our blessed Lord condemned the Jews for making broad their phylacteries. It should seem that the Jews had a superstition, that by wearing certain amulets or borders with words of Scripture upon them, they would act like so many charms, and preserve them from danger. The word phylacteries, which is derived from the Greek, means to preserve. The Jews, it is said by some, justified this from what was commanded in Scripture. "And it shall be for a sign unto thee, upon thine head, and for a memorial between thine eyes, that the Lord's law may be in their mouth." (Exod. xxxiii. 3.) But had the Jews observed the pure sense of this precept, it was their wonderful deliverance from Egypt that was to be the memorial, and not the preservation from future dangers to which this command had respect. It should rather seem, therefore, that that natural proneness the children of Israel had to imitate their idolatrous neighbours, tempted them to do as the heathen did, whose superstition is well known to have been of this kind; though Israel in the midst of their using charms like them, still had respect to words of Scripture. That this was the case, seems highly probable, in that the Lord Jesus reproved them for it. See Frontlets.

PIHAHIROTH

The memorable spot where the Lord displayed his grace to Israel. (Exod. xiv. 2.) The word is compounded of Pe, mouth, Kirath, a noramen or opening. And it was the opening, of the Red Sea. At this place the Egyptians had a migdol or tower, and one of their dunghill gods, called Baal-Zephon, had a temple here, as if to watch that no runaway servant or slave might escape from Egypt; at least, it was intended to act as a bugbear to deliver the fugitive. What a contempt did the Lord throw upon the idols of Egypt, in making this the memorable spot to deliver Israel. See Baal-Zephon.

PILATE

A name of everlasting infamy, well known to every reader of the Bible, and as universally detested as known. So unjust in his judgment, while acting as the Governor of Judea, that in the very moment he pronounced sentence of death upon the Lord Jesus Christ, he solemnly declared his innocency; and in confirmation of our Lord's holiness and his own guilt, took water nod washed his hands before the people in token of the deed. He was Governor of Judea, under the Emperor Tiberius. His name was Pontius as well as Pilate, perhaps, he might be of Pontus. With what horrors will he arise at the tremendous day of God, when every eye must see Jesus, and they also that pierced him! when that sacred head he crowned with thorns will appear in the fulness of glory, and before whose presence heaven and earth will pildash flee away! (Rev. i. 7.)

PILDASH

Son of Nahor and Milcah, (Gen. xxiii. 22.) If from Palah, ruin, it should seem that the name means somewhat ruinous.

PILEHA

One of the chief priests in the days of Nehemiah, (See Neh. x. 24.) The name is probably from Palach, to divide.

PILLAR

The pillar of cloud, and the pillar of fire in the wilderness, which went before and followed Israel, were among the symbols of the divine presence. I do not presume to say as much, or to decide upon a subject of such infinite importance; but, when we take into one mass of particulars, all that we read of the Lord Jesus Christ in those early ages of the church, methinks I cannot hesitate to believe, that it was Christ that they went before, and that thus surrounded his people during their whole eventful history. Jacob at Bethel, and Moses at the bush, had real views of JEHOVAH'S glory and fulness in Christ. The manifestation made on both occasions as the God of Abraham, Isaac and Jacob, plainly shows that the covenant of redemption, in the seed of the woman, was the great and leading cause of all. And as the Holy Ghost hath graciously been pleased in so many words to tell the church, that the Rock which followed Israel was Christ; (1 Cor. x. 4.) it should seem as if this was intended by the blessed Spirit, to act as a key for opening; similar manifestation to the church in those other tokens of divine, love, which appear in their wonderful history. Nothing can be more blessed in confirmation of the Redeemer's love to his church and people, than thus beholding him in the "pillar of cloud by day, and the pillar of are by night," conducting and guarding them through all their journey: And as then, so now, every manifestation, under all the various forms of it, was intended to show the church the love he bore to them, and to lead his people into the most endearing views of love and good will. And hence; the sacred writers, through the several parts of sacred Scriptures, keep up the remembrance of those manifestations in the wilderness, as so many proofs of the Lord's presence with his people. We are told that "when Moses went out unto the tabernacle, all the people rose up, and stood every man at, his tent door, and looked after Moses, until he was gone into the tabernacle. And it came to pass, as Moses entered into the tabernacle, the cloudy pillar descended, and stood at the door of the tabernacle, and the Lord talked with Moses." (Exod. xxxiii. 8, 9.) So again the Psalmist saith, that "he spake unto them in the cloudy pillar." (Ps. xcix. 7.) Who was it spake unto them but, God in Christ? Surely all that we hear from God is received in him, and by him, and through him, who is the only Mediator, the Glory-man Christ

Jesus. For the Holy Ghost, by John the apostle, tells the church that no man hath seen God at any time; but he graciously adds, that "the only-begotten Son, which is in the bosom of the Father, he hath declared him." (John i. 18.) And what then can be more plain and evident in proof that Christ is the visible JEHOVAH, and by whom alone all revelations are made? I need not add what endearing representations all those things made of his person and his love to his church, when taken into one mass of particulars, which we read of Christ under such a vast variety of manifestations which he hath made of himself.

The word pillar is sometimes used in the language of Scripture to denote the church of the Lord Jesus, Thus the Holy Ghost, by Paul, calls the church "the pillar and ground of truth." (1 Tim. iii. 15.) And it is not a violence to the expression to consider this as in allusion to her Lord, who is the Head of his body the church. For if Jesus be the pillar of cloud, and the pillar of fire; and if, as it is said, "the Lord will create upon every dwelling place of mount Zion, and upon her assemblies, a cloud and smoke by day, and the shining of a flaming fire by night," (Isa. iv. 5.)--surely there is a great propriety that his church should be called after the name of her Lord, He is the pillar of cloud and of fire; and she by him is made the pillar and ground of truth; and hence his servants who minister in his name shall be called pillars in his temple. "Him that overcometh, saith Jesus, will I make a pillar in the temple of my God." (Rev. iii. 11. See Prov. ix. 1.) Hence the Lord saith to Jeremiah, (chap. i. 18.) "Behold, I have made thee this day a defenced city, and an iron pillar." (See Gal. ii. 9.) And very blessed it is to see, that while Christ is the foundation stone JEHOVAH hath laid in Zion, all his redeemed ones are built upon this foundation, and are lively stones and pillars in this spiritual house, "to offer up spiritual sacrifices, acceptable to God, through Jesus Christ." (1 Pet. ii. 5.)

PINE TREE

This tree is spoken of in Scripture by the Lord himself, as one of the trees which the Lord would take to beautify his sanctuary, (Isa. lx. 13.) No doubt, it is figuratively spoken in allusion to believers. See Cedar Tree.

PINNACLE OF THE TEMPLE

We are told that here it was, on the pinnacle of the temple, the devil, in his temptations of Christ, set the Redeemer. (Matt. iv. 5.) An ordinary reader might here from be led to conclude, that if the pinnacle of the temple was like the present towers of our churches, it was hardly possible to have stood upon them. But he should be told that the pinnacles were on square roofs, like terrace walks, with galleries, so that they formed a platform to walk upon. One of the Jewish historians relates, that the roof of the temple had spikes of gold on it, to hinder the birds from resting there, that they might not defile it. The pinnacle of the temple, therefore, though high and elevated, yet formed a sufficient spot for walking upon. Probably here, like the galleries the church speaks of persons retired for conversation. See Gallery and Galleries.

PIRAM

King of Jarmuth. One of the Kings destroyed by Joshua. (Josh. x. 3, &c.) If the name is derived from Para, it means the wild ass. Am is mother.

PIRATHON

A city of Ephraim: hence the inhabitants were called Pirathonites. (Judg. xii. 13.) From Parah.

PISGAH

A mountain over against Jericho. This place is rendered memorable from Moses. (Deut. xxxiv. 1.) The name means hill or mountain, from Pasag.

PISIDIA

A province in Asia. Here Paul preached the gospel. (See Acts xiii. 14.) The word is Greek, meaning pitch.

PISON

One of the four great rivers which watered Eden. (Gen. ii. 11.) Compounded of Pe, mouth, and Shanah, to change.--A river changing.

PITHOM

One of the cities which the children of Israel built for Pharaoh during their captivity in Egypt. Perhaps the name is derived from Pe, the mouth--and Sham, which signifies to finish;--but there is no authority for it. A much more important consideration is it to remark the diligence of Israel in their captivity, thus building houses for their masters. Though the Egyptians oppressed them, and made their lives bitter by reason of the task-masters set over them, ye we do not find that the poor captives gave over their duty because of their enemies' cruelty. The Holy Ghost compels the foes of the church thus to give testimony, however unwillingly, to the dutiful and honourable deportment of the people. "And they built for Pharaoh treasure cities, Pithom and Ramases. But the more they afflicted them, the more they multiplied and grew. And they were grieved because of the children of Israel." (Exod. i. 11, 12.) I beg the reader to observe how every thing turned out the reverse of their tyrants' intention. Egypt wished to lesson Israel by cruelty: Israel thrived and multiplied the more. Egypt intended to make their lives bitter to them; whereas the bitterness recoiled on themselves. Thus the Lord carries on the gracious purposes of his government in the minds of men in all ages! We have another striking testimony of a like kind to the good conduct of the Lord's people upon a similar occasion, when the people were again brought into bondage. I mean when Jobin, king of Canaan, ruled with an iron rod over Israel. (See Judg, chap. iv. and v.) The mother of Sisera gave this unintentional testimony to the good housewifery of our mothers in Israel, when, looking out at a window to watch for the coming of her son in triumph, she cried out," Have they not divided the preys to every man a damsel or two; to Sisera a prey of divers colours, a prey of divers colours of needlework, of divers colours of needlework on both sides, meet for the necks of them that take the spoil?" (Judg. v. 30.) Here we see that the daughters of Israel, as their fathers before them, ate not the bread of idleness, for their divers colours of needlework manifested their industry. But what an awful character must this mother of Sisera have been, to take pleasure in the lusts of her son! Forgetting the chastity of her sex, she seemed to rest in the very thought that the daughters of Israel would serve for the savage sports of her son and his army, and a damsel or two fall to the lot of every man. We see here, in striking features, a mind indeed ripe for hell. We behold sin become so exceedingly sinful, that the sinner enjoys in idea what in reality he doth not partake of. This is the state which the apostle Paul describes of sinners, "who knowing the judgment of God, that they who commit such things are worthy of death, not only do the same, but take pleasure in them that do them." (Rom. i. 32.) The imagination can form no picture out of hell of equal malignity of mind. Such are full ripe for hell; the next step brings them into it. They are like a vessel brim full, one drop more, and they sink to the bottom.

PLAGUES OF EGYPT

It may not be unacceptable to the readers of this work to have brought before them in one short view the account of the plagues of Egypt, in order to take into a comprehensive manner the judgment of God over the Egyptians, while manifesting grace to his

PLAGUES OF EGYPT - PLAGUES OF EGYPT

Israel.

There were ten different sorts of plagues which the Lord brought upon Egypt, all succeeding one another, with only the intermission of a few days; and each rising in succession with more tremendous judgments, until in the last of them the Egyptians began to discover that if the Lord persisted in the infliction, all Egypt was destroyed.

The first was that of turning the waters of their famous river the Nile into blood. It is worthy remark that the first miracle wrought by Moses was this of turning water into blood; but the first miracle of the Lord Jesus Christ was that of turning water into wine. (John ii. 11.) And was it not in both instances figurative of the different dispensations of the law and the gospel? Every thing under the law, like the full flowing streams of the Nile turned into blood, is made a source of condemnation: it is called indeed the ministration of death, (2 Cor. iii. 7.) Every thing under the gospel brings with it life and liberty. Jesus puts a blessing into our most common comforts, and the whole is sanctified.

The second plague of Egypt was that of the frogs. (Exo. viii. 1, 14.) There was somewhat particularly striking in this progression of Egypt's torments. The first was remote and distant, confined to the rivers and water; but this second is brought nearer home, and comes near their persons, in their houses, and their chambers, "Their land, (saith the Psalmist,) brought forth frogs in abundance in the chambers of their kings." (Ps. cv. 30.) When one affliction loseth its effect, a second and a greater shall follow. If distant corrections are not heard, the stroke shall be both seen and felt within our houses. This progressive punishment of the Lord, even upon his own people, is set forth in the most finished representation. (See Lev. xxvi. 3. to the end.)

In the third plague, that of lice, the punishment is heightened. Now the Lord is come home indeed by his afflictions on the person of the Egyptians. Before, the judgment was confined to the river and to the land; but here the Lord made a marked distinction from the former, so as to compel the magicians of Egypt to acknowledge in it the finger of God. (See Exod. viii. 16-19.)

The plague of flies was the fourth judgment with which the Lord smote Egypt. And here I beg the reader to remark how every visitation became more and more distressing, rising, as it did, in circumstances heightened with misery. The plague of lice was great, but this of flies abundantly more. Even in our own climate, in hot summer-seasons, when passing through narrow lanes and hedges in the country not much frequented, where insects of the winged kind increase unmolested, the horse and his rider sometimes feel their sting, and are almost made mad. But in hot countries the swarms of those creatures are at times destructive indeed. And what must the plague of flies in Egypt have been when purposely armed and sent by the Lord. We may form some conjecture of the dreadful effect that this plague wrought on Pharaoh and his people, for he called for Moses, and in his fright consented to the Israelites' departure. I beg the reader to consult the account of this plague, as recorded in Scripture. (Exod. viii. 20. to the end.) And I beg him also to observe how the Lord, concerning this plague, called upon both the Egyptians and the Israelites to observe the tokens of his discriminating grace over his people; for we are told that the Lord marked the land of Goshen, where Israel dwelt, that no swarm of flies should be there. Let the reader pause over this account; and let him say, what must Israel have felt in this marked distinction. Oh, what an evident token of the Lord's love! And is it not so now, and hath been through all ages of the church? Yea, are we not told that thus we are "to return, and discern between the righteous and the wicked, between him that serveth God and him that serveth him not?' (Mal. iii. 18.) I beg the reader to turn to the article Flies for a farther illustration of this subject.

The fifth plague of Egypt, rising still in terror, was that of the pestilence and mortality among all the cattle of the Egyptians; in which, as a continuance of the same discrimination as had been shewn before in the plague of the flies, while all the cattle of Egypt died, there was not one of the cattle of the Israelites dead. (See Exod. ix. 1-7.) Beside the very tremendous judgment on Egypt as a nation by this plague, we may remark somewhat leading to the gospel dispensation in this appointment. "The whole creation (we are told) groaneth and travaileth in pain together." (Rom. viii. 22.) The earth bore part in the curse for man's disobedience; hence therefore in man's redemption, of which the bringing Israel out of Egyptian bondage is a type, the inferior creatures are made to bear part in punishment. It is more than probable also, that some among the cattle that were destroyed were included in the idols of Egypt; for certain it is, that from the Egyptians the Israelites learnt the worship of the calf, which afterwards they set up in the wilderness. (See Exod. xxxii. 1-6.) What contempt, therefore, by the destruction of cattle, was thrown upon the idols of Egypt!

In the view of the sixth plague of Egypt, "the boils breaking forth with blains upon man and upon beast," we behold the hand of the Lord falling heavier than ever. The persons of Pharaoh and his people in those boils and ulcers were most dreadfully beset. It should seem to have been not only one universal epidemic malady, but a malady hitherto unknown--bodies covered with running sores. When Moses afterwards in the wilderness was admonishing Israel to be cautious of offending the Lord, and threatening punishment to their rebellion, he adverts to those boils as among the most dreadful of divine visitations. "The Lord will smite thee with the botch of Egypt, and with the emerods, and with the scab, and with the itch, whereof thou canst not be healed." (Deut. xxviii. 27.) The imagination cannot form to itself, in bodily afflictions any thing more grievous; and when to the sore of body, the corroding ulcer of soul is joined, and both beheld as coming from the Lord, surely nothing this side hell can be wanting to give the most finished state of misery! (See Exod. ix. 8-12.) And if the reader will read also Moses's account of a corrosive mind, he will behold the awful state of having God for our enemy. (Deut. xxviii. 15. to the end.)

The seventh plague of Egypt was the "thunder, lightning, rain, and hail." (Exod. ix. 13, to the end.) This tremendous storm was ushered in with a solemn message from the Lord to Pharaoh, that there should be a succession of plagues until that the Lord had cut him off from the face of the earth; and that the Lord had indeed raised him up for this very purpose, to shew in him the Lord's power, and that the Lord's name should be declared throughout all the earth. But what I particularly beg the reader to remark in these plagues of Egypt is, the progressive order from bad to worse, leading on to the most finished and full state of misery.

In this we mark also distinguishing grace to some of the servants of Pharaoh. We are told that they, among them that feared the word of the Lord, called home their servants and their cattle to places of shelter before the storm came. And as when Israel went up afterwards with an high hand out of Egypt, a mixed multitude went with them, were not these such as grace had marked for the Lord's own? May we not consider them as types of the Gentile church given to the Lord Jesus, as well as the Jewish church? (Isa. xlix. 6.)

The eighth plague is introduced by the Lord with bidding Moses, the man of God, to remark to Israel that the Lord had hardened the heart of Pharaoh purposely, that he might set forth his love to Israel in shewing these signs and wonders before them. The Lord delights in distinguishing grace, and the Lord delights that his people should know the proofs of it also. "That thou mayest tell it, (saith the Lord) in the ears of thy son, and of thy son's son, what things I have wrought in Egypt, and my signs which I have done among them, that ye may know how that I am the Lord." The plague of locusts succeeded that of thunder, lightning, rain and hail. (Exod. x. i.) This was so grievous that the very earth was covered with them, and the whole land was darkened. (See Locusts.) We read these transactions, and form an idea that the suffering of the people must have been great: but all apprehension must fall short of what was the reality of the evil. (See Exod. 1-20.)

The ninth plague was that of "darkness covering Egypt," while Goshen, the habitation of Israel, had light. (Exod. x. 21.) And this both in duration and extent exceeds all that was ever heard of in the history of the world. Three days it continued in Egypt, so that they saw not one another, neither did any arise from his place; and to aggravate the horrid gloom, it was a darkness which reached to feeling also, though through mercy we know not what that means. Such perhaps as the torments of the damned. Every misery is increased, be it what it may, when the hand of an angry God is felt in it.

The tenth and last plague which the Lord inflicted upon Egypt, preparatory to Israel's departure, was that of the destruction of the first-born both of man and beast; and so universal was it, that it reached from the first-born of Pharaoh that sat upon his throne, to the first-born of the maid servant which ground at the mill. And to aggravate this finishing stroke of misery, the Lord appointed it at midnight. The imagination, can hardly conceive with what horrors the Egyptians arose to the death of their first-born when the midnight cry was so great, because there was not an house where there was not one dead. (Exod. xii. 29, 30.) I must refer the reader to the sacred Scriptures for the wonderful account of this tremendous judgment, for it would too largely swell the pages of this work, to enter into the relation of it here. But I beg the reader, when he hath read the Holy Scriptures on this subject, as contained in the eleventh and twelfth chapters of Exodus, to pause over the history, and to remark with me whether there is not somewhat typical in the destruction of Egypt's first-born, and the salvation of Israel. The lamb the Israelites were commanded to have slain, and which was called by the Lord himself the Lord's Passover was typical of Christ. The sprinkling of the blood on their houses was also typical, and the eating of it was typical; in short, the whole of this service, and appointed in such a moment, while Egypt was destroying, was wholly typical of Christ, and Israel's alone salvation by him. And though in our present twilight of knowledge our greatest researches go but a little way, yet certain it is, the destruction of Egypt, the hardening of Pharaoh's heart, and the heart of his people, and the delivery of Israel, all pointedly preached the same solemn truth, as it is the whole, tenor of revelation to declare, that the distinguishing grace of God is the sole cause wherefore Israel is saved and the Egyptians destroyed. The apostle Paul, commenting on this history, and taught by the Holy Ghost, hath said all that can be said in confirmation of the doctrine itself, and all that can be said by the most unbelieving mind against it, in one of his chapters to the Romans. But the issue of Paul's reasoning finisheth the subject in the most decided manner, by referring the whole to the sovereignty and good pleasure of God. I cannot better close the subject on the history of the plagues of Egypt, than by referring the reader to the apostle's divine conclusions on the same, and very earnestly begging the reader to go over, with suitable diligence and attention, and with prayer to God the Holy Ghost attention, and with prayer to God the Holy Ghost to bless him in the perusal, the ninth chapter of the Epistle to the Romans.

PLANE TREE

The Hebrews were very partial to trees; and it is not to be wondered at, for those trees which formed shades, by their long growing and wide spreading branches, must have been highly grateful in sheltering them from the heat. The plane tree is supposed to have been the chesnut spoken of Gen. xxx. 37. The word Harmon, or Ormon, is so rendered in that Scripture. We have a lofty description of Pharaoh, king of Egypt, under the similitude of those elegant tress of the forest. (Ezek. xxxi. 8.) But when the reader hath pondered over these beauties of nature, I beg him to observe how, in a yet far higher degree, the Holy Ghost is pleased to make use of them in setting forth the glories of grace, when describing the Lord Jesus under the similitude of the wide spreading branches of the trees of the wood, to represent the shelter he affords to his people. Hence the church sings of sitting under "his shadow with great delight, and his fruit becoming sweet to her taste." (Song ii. 3.) Hence the prophet describes Jesus as "a strength to the poor, a strength to the needy in distress, a refuge from the storm, a shadow from the heat, when the blast of the terrible ones is as a storm against the wall." (Isa. xxv. 4.) And in many other parts of Scripture the same figures are beautifully chosen by way of representing the Lord Jesus as both a protecting power from every danger, and a source of refreshment in all good. Jesus is all this, and infinitely more; for like the wide spreading branches of some rich and fruitful tree of the desert, he forms every thing that is lovely to our view, and both shelters from the heat, and refresheth our thirst by his fruit in this desert of our nature, when from under his shadow "we revive as the corn, and grow as the vine, and his scent is more fragrant than the wine of Lebanon." (Hos. xiv. 7.)

PLAY

We should not have needed any attention to this word, had the general acceptation of it in Scripture been similar to the received opinion of it among men. By play we understand pastime, or sport, or diversions; but this is not always the case in Scripture language. The word Zachach, which is rendered play, means also to mock, or insult, or fight. Thus we read, (2 Sam. ii. 14.) "Abner said to Joab, let the young men now arise and play before us." But the Scripture shews that this play was fighting; for we are told that "they caught every one his fellow by the head, and thrust his sword into his fellow's side, so they fell down together; wherefore that place was called Helkath-hazzarim"--which the margin of the Bible renders the field of strong men." And there was a very sore battle that day. So again we read, (Exod. xxxii. 6.) that when the people had sat down to eat and drink at their sacrifices, they rose up to play. But the history itself, as well as the New Testament explanation of it, (1 Cor. x. 7.) shews that this play was the mockery of the Lord by the grossest idolatry. Hence, therefore, it is necessary that in our reading Scripture, we should have a right apprehension of the terms and words made use of, that we may not confound things. By play is not only meant an idle frivolity, and "jesting and foolish talking," as the apostle speaks, and which he condemns, (Eph. v. 4.) but sometimes, as we have seen, yet much worse. Indeed play, and what the world calls amusements, even of the least offensive kind, are unsuited to dying creatures, and therefore ought not to be once mentioned among Christians professing godliness. The apostle's direction on these grounds is absolute and unaccommodating; and every truly regenerated heart wishes to adopt the same, though there had been no precept for it. (Eph. v. 1-31. 2 Cor. vi. 17, 18.)

PLEDGE

"Take his garment (saith the wise man) that is surety for a stranger: and take a pledge of him for a strange woman." (Prov. xx. 16.) This was indeed done in the person of the strangers' best and truest friend, when the Lord Jesus came from his heavenly home to be a Surety for more than strangers, yea, enemies to God by wicked works. Nevertheless, in the common circumstances of human life between man and man, the tender mercies of God over Israel, commanded that they should be very cautious how they took pledges and retained them. The law of pledges seems to have been, that in cases where the word or assurance of the borrower might be doubted, some valuable article should be left with the lender by way of assuring payment. But it is really blessed to observe how tenderly the Lord himself interposed, that usury and unkindness might not creep in among his people. "No man shall take the nether or the upper millstone to pledge, for he taketh a man's life to pledge." (Deut. xxiv. 6.) By these the man grinds his daily bread, and therefore he will starve if the implements for providing his food be taken from him. And in a spiritual sense how much higher the argument runs! Take not away the means and ordinances of worship, by the use of which, under the blessing of God, the bread of life is administered to him.

So again: The Lord prohibited the lender from entering the borrower's house to take his pledge. (Deut. xxiv. 10.) Every man's house is his castle; to enter it therefore is a violation of all right, and especially to enter it in order to oppress. And the law of pledges went farther. If a poor man through necessity had compelled him to pawn his garment, the law enjoined that the lender should not sleep with his pledge. "In any case, saith the Lord, thou shalt deliver him the pledge again when the sun goeth down, that he may sleep in his own raiment, and bless thee." And as an additional motive to the exercise of this mercy, the Lord declared that such regard to a poor brother the Lord would consider as done to himself. "It shall be, (said the Lord,) righteousness unto thee before the Lord thy God." (Deut. xxiv. 10-13.) Precious Jesus! I would say as I read those sweet Scriptures of mercy, I have pledged to thee all I have, and all I am; and do I not see in this blessed command of thine thy gracious tenderness of heart to give me all my justly forfeited pledges, that the sun may not go down and I be found naked, but sleep secure in thy garment of salvation, that my soul may bless thee! This is indeed the Lord's righteousness, which is upon all, and unto all, that believe. Oh, that the usurers of the present day would read those Scriptures, and be no longer so, but like Job, "drive not away the ass of the father less, and taken of the widow's ox for pledge!" (Job xxiv. 3.)

PLEIADES

We find twice mention made in the book of Job of the heavenly constellations. (Job ix. 9. and xxxviii. 31.) The sacred writer enumerates but some of them, Arcturus, Orion, the Pleiades, and Mazzaroth; but we may suppose the whole are equally included as those whose influences we cannot bring forth nor bind. "He calleth them all by their names." (Ps. cxlvii. 4.) And we read that there was a time when the stars in their courses fought in the Lord's course. (Judg. v. 20.) There is an uncommon degree of beauty as well as sublimity in this relation of the heavenly bodies. The Pleiades are those stars which form a cluster, vulgarly called the seven stars, though even with a naked eye, in a clear night, more can be seen in the ring. Perhaps this is the smallest of the heavenly constellations with which we are acquainted; very beautiful they are to every beholder; and small as they are, yet we find they have "their sweet influences." The bands of Orion are also spoken of as perfectly uncontrollable; and this forms that very large constellation, perhaps none larger in the chambers of the south. Arcturus is among the northern of the heavenly bodies, alike independent of man's government, or man's guidance. But what a refreshing thought it is to the true believer in Jesus, the sinner's Saviour is the Maker of them all; and to whatsoever purpose else they are formed to minister, their alt by his appointment serve to his glory, and his people's welfare!

POMEGRANATE

This was a fruit of Palestine, beautiful in its appearance, and very pleasant in its taste; and therefore Christ, in celebrating the loveliness of the church, compares her temples to "a piece of pomegranate within her locks." (Song iv. 3.) And the church, speaking of the glories of her Husband, saith, "I would lead thee, and bring thee into my mother's house; I would cause thee to drink of spiced wine of the juice of my pomegranate." (Song viii. 2.) The sense is, the church would treat Jesus with her best fare. And as every thing she had and was came from her Lord, surely her Lord should have the best of his own gifts and graces. In a spiritual sense, believers may be said to entertain Christ when, in their exercises of faith in any of the gracious, or providential dispensations of the Lord, our sorrows are so sweetly tinged with the presence and sanctifying blessings of the Lord, that they are like to spiced wine in which is infused the juice of the pomegranate. Jesus sweetens all, as the bitter waters at Marah were sweetened by the tree cast into them. (Exod. xv. 23-25.)

PONTIUS

See Pilate.

POOR

There are various terms of signification annexed to the word poor. By the character of poor is generally meant persons in indigent circumstances of body; but the Scripture meaning of the word poor, is the poverty of soul in respect to our lost and ruined estate by nature. And there is a third sense of the term, namely, the poor in spirit, of whom our Lord saith, "Theirs is the kingdom of heaven." (Matt. v. 3.) It is proper to keep alive the proper distinction of these different views of natural and spiritual poverty when reading the word of God.

PORATHA

Son of Haman. (Esth. ix. 8.) The term is Persian, and signifies fruitful.

PORTERS

See Levi, and Levites.

PORTIUS FESTUS

He succeeded Felix in the government of Judea. His name is only rendered memorable in Scripture from the history of the apostle Paul.

POSSESSED OF THE DEVIL

We meet with many instances of this in the days of our Lord. Indeed, as the Son of God was manifested that he might destroy the works of the devil, it should seem that at that time the great enemy of souls had permission exert a more than usual power, that in his being cast out the Lord Jesus might be manifested thereby. But that the influence of the evil spirit is not now wholly restrained, is too evident to be denied. The general term made use of in our courts of justice in the indictment of criminals, is plain in proof for the running phrase is, that such an one, not having the fear of God before his eyes, and being moved by the instigation of the devil, did such and such things. But while the fact itself is undeniable, it is a blessed relief to the minds of God's people to know that the influence of the devil is not according to his wishes, but according to the Lord's permission; not whom he will, but whom he may. And it is still more blessed, the conviction that all his temptations, however differently intended by him, must produce good in the result to the people of God. From the first moment the arch fiend entered the garden of Eden, through all the exercises of the faithful, he is only accomplishing the gracious purposes of God. Never would he have been allowed to bruise the heel of the Lord's chosen, but that finally the Lord might bruise his head. The whole powers of darkness in their exercises of possessions, plots, contrivances, imprisonments, temptations, and the like, over the Lord's Israel, are only hastening on the ruin of their own kingdom. "The God of peace will bruise Satan under the feet of his people shortly." (Rom. xvi. 20.)

POTIPHAR

An officer in the court of Pharaoh--master to the patriarch Joseph. (Gen. xxxvii. 36.) His name is derived, as it should seem to be, from Parah, which means to scatter.

POTTER'S FIELD

See Aceldama.

PREDESTINATE

The apostle Paul in his Epistle to the Romans, (chap. viii. 29.) speaking of God, saith, "For whom he did foreknow, he also did predestinate to be conformed to the image of his Son." And elsewhere the same apostle, speaking of the church in Christ, saith, "that he hath predestinated them to the adoption of children by Jesus Christ to himself, according to the good pleasure of his will." (Eph. i. 5.) Hence it will follow, that all the purposes of God in Christ concerning redemption are first formed in the Lord Jesus, and then the church in him; and hence the church is represented as saying: with one voice, (2 Tim. i. 9.) "Who hath saved us, and called us with an holy calling, not according to our works, but according to his own purpose and grace, which was given us in Christ Jesus before the world began."

PREPARATION

The preparation of the heart is the great subject of enquiry in a work of this kind, and to which therefore I would particularly direct the attention. To prepare any person or thing may be easily understood in fitting and qualifying, in disposing or making ready; but in Scripture language the whole of the work, both in fitting and qualifying, in disposing or making ready, is of the Lord. So Solomon was commissioned to teach the church; and so every individual of the church is made sensible. (Prov. xvi. 1.) The word preparation seems to be taken from military maxims; and as soldiers are put in order under arms, and made ready for their service, so the Lord disposeth the frames and motions of his people's hearts for his service. And it is very blessed when a child of God feels this predisposing grace, and is conscious of being led on and carried through every duty. From the first awakenings of grace until grace is consummated in glory, the whole preparations of the heart, and the answer of the tongue, is from the Lord. And when the soul of a poor sinner hath been first prepared of the Lord, by regenerating, illuminating, convincing, and converting grace, and is thus brought into an union with Christ, all the subsequent acts of grace, in the goings forth of the soul upon the person, blood and righteousness of Christ, sweet preparing and disposing work of God the Holy Ghost. It is most blessed to know this, and to enjoy it. The daily access to the throne of God in Christ is by the Spirit. (Eph. ii. 18.) It is that blessed, holy and eternal Spirit, in his own office-work, which prepares the soul, by calling off the mind from every object, and fixing the affections on the person of Jesus. It is he which awakens desire, creates a longing in the soul, points to the Lord Jesus as alone able to supply and satisfy the desires of the soul, and opens a communication between Christ and the soul. He that "searcheth all things, yea, the deep things of God," searcheth both the heart, and prepareth the heart for enjoyment. He spreads the rich table, and prepares both the spiritual food and the spiritual appetite to receive and enjoy it. In a word, it is the Holy Ghost that is the great Author and Giver of all that life and joy and peace in believing, when the souls of the redeemed are made to abound "in hope, through the power of the Holy Ghost." Hence, therefore, to him alone should believers be always looking for the preparations of the heart; for in this sweet office of the Spirit, God's Christ and the redeemed soul are brought together; and the Lord the Spirit doth more in one moment to prepare our unprepared hearts than, without his influence, could be accomplished in ten thousand years by all our labours in prayers and tears. How blessedly the church sings to this note of praise, for the preparing and disposing grace of the Spirit, when she cried out: "Or ever I was aware, my soul made me like the chariots of Amminadib!" (Song vi. 12.) As if she had said, before I had the least apprehension of the mercy, my Lord my Husband made me willing, by the swift manifestations of his love, and the awakenings of his grace in my heart, as rapid as the chariot wheels of a princely people.

PRESENTS

We read in Scripture of presents upon various occasions; and it should seem to have been intended as not only important on account of the value of what was given, but also more so as a testimony of some particular meaning. Thus the king of Assyria desired the people to make an agreement with him by a present. (2 Kings xviii. 31.) And it is marked with peculiar emphasis's in the slights put upon Saul at his election, that they brought him no presents. (1 Sam. x. 27.) But there is reason to believe that the circumstance is borrowed from a matter of greater moment, and hath a spiritual reference. Thus we read from the first, that Cain and Abel brought their mincha, their offerings, unto the Lord. (Gen. iv. 3, 4.) The after-age presents were to the same amount; for the mincha of the temple was simply an offering of meal or fine flour, and carried with it the idea of a mincha of peace. Thus Jacob's present to appease his brother, for he said, "I will appease him with the present, and afterwards I will see his face." (Gen. xxxii. 20.) It should seem, therefore, that in all those presents, which evidently were presents of conciliation, there was an eye, however darkly and indistinctly understood, to the great doctrine of propitiation: and in confirmation of this, it is remarkable that Malachi uses the very word mincha, a present, or offering, when speaking of the offerings that in the days of the gospel should be offered unto the Lord. "For from the rising of the sun, even unto the going down of the same, my name shall be great among the Gentiles; and in every place incense shall be offered unto my name, and a pure offering." (Mal. i. 11.)

PRIEST

Strictly and properly speaking, there is but one priest of JEHOVAH, and he the great High Priest of his church, the Lord Jesus Christ. Every other priest, even Aaron himself, acted no higher than as the type of JEHOVAH'S High Priest. For the High Priest of JEHOVAH must be as JEHOVAH himself, a Priest for ever; whereas, (as the Holy Ghost blessedly speaks by Paul, Heb. vii. 23, 24.) those priests were not suffered to continue, by reason of death; but this man, because he continueth ever, hath an unchangeable priesthood. And how graciously the Lord adds, "Wherefore he is able also to save them to the uttermost that come unto God by him, seeing he ever liveth to make intercession for them." (Heb. vii. 25.)

In our view of the Lord Jesus as

PRIEST - PRIEST

Priest, it will be necessary to consider the several features, of this high character, in order to have a proper conception of it. Nothing can be more interesting to know, in the whole offices of Jesus to his church and people, and therefore I beg the reader that he will indulge me with being somewhat more particular upon it.

And first, the office and character of the priest should be considered, in order that we may discover the personal fitness and suitability for Christ in this office; and by the performance of which the Lord Jesus proves that he, and he only, became the proper High Priest for his church and. people. The Priest of JEHOVAH must be one consecrated and set apart specially and personally to this office, and this by JEHOVAH himself. And his office comprehends the offering of sacrifice, praying, and interceding for the people, and also blessing the people in JEHOVAH'S name and by his authority. He must be suited in sovereignty and power to act, by virtue of his high office, as a proper Priest and Mediator of his high office, as a proper Priest and Mediator between Him before whom and to whom the offerings are made, and the persons for whom they are made. And he must be suited in personal feeling and interest, to take part with them, and for him in whose suit he acts; so that neither party between whom he acts, as Priest and Mediator, may suffer wrong, but both parties have right and justice shewn them by his priestly administration.

From this view of the office of the priesthood, it is evident that the person undertaking and acting in this high capacity must be both God and man. It is expedient that he should be God to give merit and efficacy to his offerings, to give energy and power in the act of offering, to carry on the purposes of his priestly offices in the unceasing agency of his intercession, to become the object of faith, love, hope, adoration, and trust, to all his people, and to preserve for and give unto the objects for whom he undertook this priestly employment all the blessings purchased for his church and people by this great undertaking. And it became equally expedient that he who engaged to be JEHOVAH'S High Priest, in the purposes of redemption, should be man as well as God. Had he not been man he could not have been the suited. Surety for the representation of his people, he could not have fulfilled the law, answered the demands of justice, proved himself to be the seed of the woman, redeemed the mortgaged inheritance of his poor brother, by death overcome death, and by rising to life again become the resurrection and the life, and been suited to be the Head of his body the church, "the fulness that filleth all in all." So that in every point of view, and upon every consideration, the absolute expediency is manifested that JEHOVAH'S Priest must be both God and man. None else could suit the office, or be competent to the discharge of this high character. And such was the Lord Jesus, and him only. Indeed, so peculiarly suited was Christ as God and man in one person, for this office, that if it could be supposed any other had been, or could have been, found competent to it, it would by so much have lessened the Lord Jesus in this character. But it is the blessed consideration to the church, that the personal and peculiar fitness of the Lord Jesus, and the fulness of fitness in him, and in him only, is what endears him both to JEHOVAH and to his people in this express office of character.

So much then for the office itself, and the peculiar suitability of the Lord Jesus to it. Let us next consider the authority by which he acts, and the glory he hath displayed, and still is displaying, in the unceasing and everlasting exercise of it.

The Scriptures are full of information on this most blessed point. Set up from everlasting in the council of peace, we are told that he was regularly called, consecrated and sworn into his office by virtue of the oath of JEHOVAH before all worlds. For thus the charter of grace runs; "The Lord hath sworn and will not repent, thou art a Priest for ever, after the order of Melchizedec." (Ps. cx. 4.) And this authority of JEHOVAH was indispensibly necessary to give efficacy and validity to all the acts of his priesthood; for it is not only the suitability of Christ which renders his priesthood so dear to his people, but it is the authority and appointment of JEHOVAH which gives a warrant for faith to act upon concerning him. Hence the Holy Ghost particularly caused it to be recorded for the church's confidence and joy in this particular, that Christ "glorified not himself to be made an High Priest, but was called of God, as was Aaron. For he that said unto him, "Thou art my Son, this day have I begotten thee, said also in another place, Thou art a Priest for ever after the order of Melchizedec. (Heb. v. 4-6.)

Thus called, consecrated, and sworn into his office, by the oath of the almighty appointer, it is most blessed to behold how the Lord Jesus, in every point of view, comes up to this high character, and by the union of both natures carries on and perfects the gracious office of our High Priest and Intercessor. The sacrifice he once offered being of infinite value, by virtue of his infinite nature, he hath, "by that one offering of himself once offered perfected for ever them that are sanctified." (Heb. x. 14.) And as the offering itself is a fulness of perfection, so the divine nature on which he offered it became the golden altar of presentation to JEHOVAH The incense Jesus presents is his own merits, and presented also from off the golden censer of his divine nature. (See Rev. viii. 3, 4.) So that the Lord Jesus is in one and the same moment every thing in himself which constitutes both priest and priesthood; for he is the Sacrifice, the Sacrificer, and the Altar on which alone all presentations are or can be made, and the only medium by which all can be offered. Hail! thou glorious, gracious, great High Priest of JEHOVAH and thy people! Be thou my New Testament altar, my sacrifice, my offering, and do thou, Lord, graciously carry on thy high priestly office still in heaven for all thy church and people, until thou hast brought home thy redeemed, "that where thou art, there they may be also!"

Having thus taken a short view of the Lord Jesus as JEHOVAH'S High Priest, and a Priest upon his throne, it may not be amiss to offer a short observation concerning the priesthood taken from among men. It will be always profitable to read the Scriptures of God concerning earthly priests, while we keep in remembrance that all and every one of them appointed by the Lord were never considered higher in all their ministry than as types of the ever-blessed Jesus. The law, with all its costly services, we have authority from the Holy Ghost to say, was but a shadow of good things to come, the body was Christ. (Heb. x. 1, &c.)

Now from the earliest ages of the church, and before the law, the patriarchs and holy men of God ministered as priests in their families. Abel, Noah, Abraham, and the fathers, offered their sacrifices, and as such acted as priests. But that the church might not err in their explanation of those things it is worthy our closest regard, that God the Holy Ghost hath expressly taught us that all these were by faith. Let the reader read the account of Abel's offering, Gen. iv. 4; Noah's, Gen. viii. 20, 21; and Abraham's, Gen. xv. 17, 18; xxii; and then turn to Heb. xi. 3.7. 17; and mark the sweet truth opened and explained, as it is, by God the Holy Ghost. These holy men of old offered all their offerings by faith; faith in whom but the Lord Jesus Christ, that Lamb of God slain before the foundation of the world? (Rev. xiii. 8.) Hence, therefore, every priest typified and represented Christ. Every lamb slain, every sacrifice offered, every propitiation set forth, all shadowed forth the person, work, blood-shedding, and righteousness of the Lord Jesus Christ. He, and he only, is, and was, and ever will be, JEHOVAH'S Priest. All other priests, whether Aaron or his sons, Levitical or Christian, are no otherwise priests than as they act in the Lord Jesus's name, are ordained by his authority, and minister for his glory. He is the fountain of all order in his church; and all true believers in Christ are expressly said to be made by him both kings and priests unto God and the Father, agreeably to JEHOVAH'S ancient, promise to the true Israel: "Ye shall be unto a kingdom of priests, and an holy nation." (Exod. xix. 6. Rev. i. 5. I Pet.ii. 9.)

PRINCE

This is one of the titles of the Lord Jesus. The prophet Ezekiel, in the close of his prophecy, dwells much upon the character of the Lord Jesus under the title of prince. I refer the reader to the forty-fourth, forty-fifth, and forty-sixth chapters of Ezekiel. I shall not think it necessary to enlarge in our views of our adorable Lord as our Prince and Saviour, for every act of his manifests his royal princely sovereignty and power as the glorious Head of his body the church. All his reigns in nature, providence, grace, and glory, set him forth as the Prince of Peace, the universal Lord and emperor in heaven and in earth. Hail, thou almighty Lord! do thou reign and rule in me and my poor heart now and for ever. Amen. It may not be amiss to observe, in a world of this kind, that the Scripture attaches the title of prince to various characters among men. We read of the Dukes of Edom and other places in the first ages of the world. (Gen. xxxvi. 15, &c.) And the heads of families were called Cohen, prince, and Cohenim, princes, by way of distinction. Indeed the word is sometimes rendered priest also, as in thee case of Jethro, priest or prince of Midian. (Exod. ii. 16.) So the word is sometimes rendered Governor. (2 Chron. xviii. 25.) And even Satan is called the prince of this world, and the prince of the power of the air; (John xii. 31. Ephes. ii. 2.) The general acceptation, therefore, of the term implies somewhat of power and dominion.

PRISCILLA

One of Whom Paul the apostle speaks highly, Rom. xvi. 3-5. It is probable that this is the same person spoken of by the same apostle, 2 Tim. iv. 19. It should seem tint she and her husband Aquila, had offered their house for worship. What a lovely view of saints of God!

PRISON

In the common acceptation of the word, we generally understand by a prison a place of confinement for the body; but in Scripture language there is added to this view of a prison a state of captivity to the soul. Hence the Lord Jesus is said to be come to open the prison doors, and to bring sinners from the captivity of sin and Satan. Believers are sometimes said to be in prison-frames when, from looking off from Jesus, they get into a dark and comfortless state, and are in bondage to their own unbelieving hearts. And when at any time the soul of a poor buffeted child of God is again delivered by some renewed manifestation of the Lord Jesus, when he is brought out of the prison house, he is constrained to cry out," O Lord, truly I am thy servant; I am thy servant, and the son of thine handmaid; thou hast loosed my bonds." (Ps. cxvi. 16.)

PROCHORUS

One of the first seven deacons. (Acts vi. 5.) The name is taken from the Greek, and means one that is head of the choir.

PROFANE

In the general sense of this word we readily understand that by doing any act contrary to God's holy law, such as breaking the Sabbath, touching holy things with polluted or defiled hands, and the like, we profane them. But while these things are plain enough, and cannot well be mistaken, there are some other cases where the word to profane is used in Scripture, that may not be so generally apprehended.

In the law of Moses we find this precept, Deut. xx. 6. "And what man is he that hath planted a vineyard, and hath not yet eaten of it? let him go and return unto his house, lest he die in the battle, and another man eat of it." In the margin of the Bible the word is rendered, instead of eaten, hath not made it common, that is, profaned it. And agreeably to this we find the general precept concerning the fruit of the vineyard, Lev. xix. 23-25. "And when ye shall come into the land, and shall have planted all manner of trees for food, then ye shall count the fruit thereof as uncircumcised: three years shall it be as uncircumcised unto you: it shall not be eaten of. But in the fourth year all the fruit thereof shall be holy to praise the Lord withal. And in the fifth year shall ye eat of the fruit thereof, that it may yield unto you the increase thereof; I am the Lord your God." It should seem very evidently by these Scriptures, that things were considered uncircumcised and unclean in the first product of them; but after the time limited they were no longer unclean, but were now brought into common use, and were profane; that is, were to be considered fit for common use. So that the word profane means common. Hence the prophet Jeremiah was, commissioned to tell the people, that when the Lord returned again the captivity of his people, "they should yet plant vines upon the mountains of Samaria, and that the planters should plant and eat them as common things." In the margin of the Bible it is, shall profane them. (Jer. xxxi. 4, 5.) The sense is, that they should enjoy them in common as privileged things.

Let us add one Scripture more in proof. Our blessed Lord, in the days of his flesh, walking through the cornfields, and his disciples eating of the ears of corn on the Sabbath-day, were reproved by the pharisees for it. The Lord made this answer: "Have ye not read in the law, how that on the Sabbath days the priests in the temple profane the Sabbath, and are blameless?" (Matt. xii. 5.) Now it doth not appear from what we meet with in the law, that the priests did any thing particularly on the Sabbath-day of defilement; therefore the profaning Christ speaks of cannot mean what, in the common acceptation of the word, we should call profaneness. But if we interpret this expression of our Lord concerning profaning the temple by the analogy of Scripture, and not our ordinary sense of the word, it would follow that the priests were considered blameless in the temple in using the Lord's blessings, of what kind soever they were, to the Lord's glory, when the three years of their uncircumcised state had passed as appointed by the Lord. Then those things were, as the prophet Jeremiah had observed, to be eaten as common or profane things.

If these observations serve to throw a light on the Scriptural word profane, they also serve to give a clear apprehension of our Lord's meaning concerning the profaneness of the priests in the temple, and remaining blameless. In this sense the whole is clear; but without it there is a great difficulty in accepting the word profane in the ordinary way of somewhat that is defiled, and the priests defiling the temple, and yet being free from blame.

The sense of the name given to Esau is upon this ground plain and intelligible. He is called a profane person, who for one morsel of meat sold his birthright. (Heb. xii. 16.) The expression of profane person doth not simply mean a defiled person, for in this sense all the Jacobs of God are unclean and defiled as well as the Esaus; but the profaneness means, the low esteem which Esau had to the birthright of the promise in Christ, which he despised, and to shew his contempt of it sold it for a morsel of present

PROMISES - PROPHET, and PROPHECY

food. He regarded not Christ.

Will the reader indulge me with humbly offering one thought more on this subject? We find by the law that the fruits of the trees in Canaan were prohibited for three years, and the reason given was, that they were uncircumcised; but that then in the fourth year, after a circumcision had taken place, all the "fruit was declared holy unto the Lord; and the fifth year the fruits were deemed profane for use. I do not presume to speak decidedly upon the subject--I rather write humbly to enquire than to decide; but I would venture to ask, whether these things were not typical of the Lord Jesus Christ and his salvation? When, by the three years of Christ's ministry and death, redemption-work was completed, and believers by the circumcision of the Spirit are brought into a state of regeneration and justification before God, all the fruits of the Spirit are like the plants upon Samaria; they shall then profane them as common things; they shall do as the priests did, and be blameless; they shall enter into the full enjoyment of them as common things. "To the pure all things are pure." What God hath cleansed we are commanded not to call common or unclean. (Tit. i. 15. Acts x. 15.)

PROMISES

We have a most extensive sense to the word promise, since every thing in the Bible, yea, the Bible itself, is the word of promise. The word includes every thing that hath respect to the life that now is, and of that which is to come. All the persons of the GODHEAD form the subject and substance of the promise. God the Father is the promise, and the matter of every promise. The great and comprehensive promise is, "I will be their God, and they shall be my people"---in which the Lord gives himself, and a property in himself, and all his divine perfections. Christ is also, in his person, fulness, suitableness, and all-sufficiency, the promise of the Scriptures; and God the Holy Ghost, in his sevenfold gifts and graces, the promise to the church and people; and every thing of blessings, temporal, spiritual, and eternal, in and with the Holy Three in One, form the promise of JEHOVAH. To particularize would be endless. The highest concern is, to enquire our interest in the whole, and whether we are the children of promise. "If we are Christ's, saith the Holy Ghost, by the apostle, "then are we Abraham's seed, and heirs according to the promise." (Gal. iii. 29.)

PROPHET, and PROPHECY

Christ is the great prophet of his church. John calls him, and very properly so, the Lord God of the prophets, (Rev. xxii. 6.) And the apostle Paul draws a line of everlasting distinction between him and all his servants when, in the opening of his Epistle to the Hebrews, he saith, "God, who at sundry times, and in divers manners, spake in time past unto the fathers by the prophets, hath in these last days spoken unto us by his Son, whom he hath appointed heir of all things, and by whom he made the world?' (Heb. i. 1, 2.)

Concerning the Spirit of prophecy, the Holy Ghost hath taught the church that prophecy came not in old time by the will of man, but "holy men of God spake as they were moved by the Holy Ghost." (2 Pet. i. 21.) A plain proof of the agency of the Holy Ghost in the old church, as hath been manifested in a more open display, since the ascension of Christ, under the new. But between Jesus and his servants an everlasting difference marks their different characters as prophets. The servants of the Lord who ministered to the church in his name as prophets, had the gifts and anointings of the Holy Ghost; but this, it should seem, not always, but as occasion required. Hence we read that the Spirit of the Lord came upon them; to every one was given grace according to the measure of the gift of Christ. But to Christ himself the anointings were always. "He, saith John,

PROPHET, and PROPHECY - PROPHET, and PROPHECY

whom God hath sent, speaketh the words of God, for God giveth not to the Spirit by measure unto him: in him dwelt all the fulness of the GODHEAD bodily." The influences of the Holy Ghost were never in any mere man, yea, even the highest prophet, but as water in a vessel; but in Christ, he himself was the fountain, in whom was all fulness. So that between the highest servant and the master there was this everlasting and essential difference. Moses, the man of God, of whom we are told, "there arose not a prophet since in Israel like unto Moses, whom JEHOVAH knew face to face," (Deut. xxxiv. 10.) yet of this great man the Holy Ghost tells the church by Paul, though "he was faithful in all the Lord's house as a servant"--yet of Christ he bears witness that he was "as a Son over his own house." (Heb. iii. 1-6.) And so again of John the Baptist, who came in the Spirit and power of Elias, and by the lip of truth itself was declared to be "the greatest prophet born among women;" yet when compared to Christ, his Lord, he was but a voice, which witnessed to Jesus and then died away, the "very latchet of whose shoes he was not worthy to stoop down and unloose." (Matt. xi. 11. John i. 23--27.)

Concerning the prophets of the Old Testament, they were sometimes called seers; but before the drays of Samuel we do not meet with the name. (See 1 Sam. ix. 9.) Hence afterwards we read of Gad, David's seer, 1 Chron. xxi. 9. So again Heman, the king's seer, 1 Chron. xxv. 5. The difference, it should seem, between the prophet and the seer lay in this, the prophets were inspired persons, to predict to the church the will of JEHOVAH either by word of mouth, or writing; the seer committed to writing the records of the church. Hence we read concerning the acts of Manasseh, that they were written among the sayings of the Seers, (2 Chron. xxxiii. 19.)

It were unnecessary to remark, what every reader of the Bible is supposed to know, that we have recorded, from the grace of God the Holy Spirit, the writings of four of what, by way of distinction, are called the greater prophets, Isaiah, Jeremiah, Ezekiel, and Daniel; and the Writings of the twelve of lesser prophets, as they are named, Hoses, Joel, Amos, Obadiah, Jonah, Micah, Nahum, Habakkuk, Zephaniah, Haggai, Zechariah, and Malachi. I do not apprehend that these distinctions of greater and lesser prophets is given to them from the most distant idea that the writings of the lesser prophets are less important than those of the greater, but wholly on account of their bulk. All are alike given by inspiration of God, and all alike give witness to Jesus; for "the testimony of Jesus is the Spirit of prophecy." (Rev. xix. 10.)

I have elsewhere, in my Poor Man's Commentary on the Bible, when giving a statement of the order of the books of Scripture, marked down (and I hope with tolerable accuracy.) the particular date in which each of those holy men of old ministered in the church. I rather, therefore, refer to that statement, which the reader will find immediately after the title-page and preface, than swell the balk of these sheets with reciting it again. It will be sufficient in this place to observe, that all these servants of God ministered in their day and generation to one and the same cause, namely, to bring forward the church's attention to the coming of Christ; and when the Holy Ghost was pleased to suspend their ministry, it was only done by way of causing the minds of the faithful to pause over their sacred records, and to wait by faith and hope to behold the fulfilment of their prophecies in the advent of Jesus. From the close of Malachi's prophecy to the opening of the mouth of Zacharias, (Luke i. 67.) there passed an intervening period of near three hundred and fifty years; but this dark season only indicated a brighter day that was coming on. The evening of the prophets only testified the approach of the morning of the evangelists. The day-dawn and the day-star were hastening to arise, when Jesus the Son of Righteousness, should appear, to go down no more, but to be the everlasting light of his people, their God, and their glory!

PROPITIATION

We meet with this word but twice in the Bible, namely, Rom. iii. 25; and 1 John ii. 2; but it is most blessed and precious in both. The Septuagint reader it Ilasmos; and the propitiatory, or mercy-seat, they call Ilasterion. The plain and evident sense of propitiation is, that of conciliating favour and reconciling persons which before were at variance. To propitiate, therefore, is to restore that amity and friendship which had subsisted before the quarrel took place, and thus make friends again. Such, in a very high degree, is the propitiation accomplished by Christ Jesus for his people; and hence, by way of special emphasis, Christ is himself called the propitiation. For when sin had made a dreadful breach between God and man, Christ stood forth the propitiation, and made "peace by the blood of his cross? This doctrine was beautifully shadowed forth in the Old Testament, and accomplished under the New. (See Exod. xxv. 17-27.)

As the subject itself is of all others the most late resting, and the just and proper apprehension of it highly important, I persuade myself that I shall have the reader's indulgence if I enter into the consideration of it a little more fully.

The two great features in the doctrine of propitiation, are the greatness of the act itself by the Lord Jesus Christ, and the authority and approbation of God the Father in the appointment. And Scripture is express in explaining both; for speaking of Christ as a propitiation, the apostle saith, that "having made peace by the blood of his cross, by him to reconcile all things to himself; by him, I say, (saith the apostle) whether they be things in earth, or things in heaven." (Col. i. 20.) The apostle lays the greatest stress upon the personal glory of Christ in this act, and repeats his expression by him, I say, as if to shew, and which is indeed the chief glory of it, how much depended upon the infinite dignity of Christ's person, and the infinite merit of his work. And no less to shew the momentous consequence that the hand of JEHOVAH should also be found to concur in this great design, the same apostle was commissioned to tell the church that it was God "which set him forth as a propitiation, through faith in his blood." (Rom. iii. 25.) Yea, so much was the heart of JEHOVAH in every part of this gracious undertaking, that God was in Christ reconciling the world unto himself, not imputing their trespasses unto them." (2 Cor. v. 19.) Oh, precious consideration of a precious God in Christ!

Reader, what saith your experience of these things? What views have you of Christ, the propitiation with the Father, and set forth by the Father? Are you daily, hourly, looking to this for the only acceptation of your person and your offering? Depend upon it, it is to this propitiation of his dear Son alone that God hath respect. The very sight of Christ, the lamb slain, in the midst of the throne, becomes the cause of God the Father being propitious to the sinner. To Jesus, as to the rainbow round the throne, JEHOVAH looks, and remembers his everlasting covenant. And what a sweet thought! Jesus not only thus appears in the presence of God for us, but his blood pleads for us too. It is indeed a speaking blood, for it speaks to God of Jesus's preciousness, and it speaks from God of the Father's faithfulness; and by both to confirm the blood of the covenant. Jesus I my full, my glorious, my complete, and all-sufficient Saviour! be thou my daily object of unceasing delight, my mercy-seat, propitiation, high priest, altar, sacrifice, and sacrificer; yea, my all in all: I need no more in time, and to all eternity! See Mercy Seat.

PROSELYTE

The Hebrews called a proselyte Ger, or Necher, which signifies a stranger. And as a proselyte, meant a proselyte of the gate, one converted from heathenism to the truth, and admitted into what was called the court of the Gentiles, no doubt the name was very proper. Such was the honest centurion, Cornelius. (Acts x.)

PROVERBS

The general sense of the word, accordding to Scripture, means somewhat that is instructive. The Eastern method of teaching by similitudes, and figures, and parables, was the most general: hence Solomon's whole book is to this amount. The Hebrews called proverbs Mishle. Our blessed Lord was pleased to follow this popular mode of instruction, for which we are indebted for those numberless beauties in the gospel. So much so was this plan adopted by Christ, that we are told that at one time without a parable spake he not unto them. (Matt. xiii. 14.) But such was the grace of Jesus to his disciples, that when he was alone he expounded and explained all things unto them. When we read, therefore, the parables, or indeed any other of the blessed sayings which dropped from Christ's mouth, when we are alone with Jesus we should ask the indulgent Lord to do the same by us, and make the word doubly sweet and blessed by unfolding and explaining all things to us himself.

PROVIDENCE

We meet with this word (as far as I recollect) but once in the Bible, and that is in the famous speech of the orator Tertullus. (Acts xxiv. 2.) If the consult the Scripture, he will reader will find the occasion upon which it was used, I should not have thought it necessary to have given it a place in this work, but with the hope of correcting the improper application of it which is but too common in life. I have noticed upon numberless occasions this error, yea, even among truly pious persons, from whom one might have expected better things; and therefore I hope I shall not offend in my observations upon it. The word providence is somewhat similar to that of dispensation, or ordination, and hath a general reference to the appointments of God. Hence when we speak of the Lord's government, either in the kingdoms of nature or grace, we say, the Lord by his providence hath ordered all things in heaven and in earth. It is he that provideth for the raven his food. (Job xxxviii. 41.) So again, speaking of the Lord's care over his people, it is said, "thou preparest them corn when thou hast so provided for it." (Ps. lxv. 9:) From all which it appears, that providence or providing are acts of the Lord, and not the Lord himself. Therefore when it is said, (as it is too frequently said) I hope providence will do this or that, I trust to providence, providence hath been very good, and the like, this is ascribing to the deed what belongs only to the Lord, the doer of that deed; and however unintentional on the part of the speaker, it becomes a great error. We should never give any glory to the creatures of God which belongs only to God himself; and to ascribe to providence what belongs only to the God of his providences, is certainly doing so. Both providence and grace are creatures of God; and however the Lord is carrying on his merciful purposes of redemption by both to his church and people, yet to give glory to either, instead of glorifying the Author of either, is to overlook the loveliness of the Lord in the loveliness of his creatures, and to place secondary things in the stead of the first. Whereas we ought to say, to use somewhat like the form of the apostle James, "If the Lord will, we shall live by his providence and grace." (Jam. iv. 15.)

PSALMS

The book of Psalms is called by the Jews Sepher Tihillim, which more particularly signifies, the book of psalms, or hymns of praise. But there are two other names given by the Hebrews to the psalms, Zemer and Sher. The former is taken from, a root in Hebrew signifying to prune; and the latter from a word signifying power. And hence some have thought, that as the chief scope and tendency of the psalms is to lead to Christ, the former implies his humiliation, and the latter his glory. And it is remarkable, (but whether it may be considered as confirming this opinion I do not presume to say) that when the Lord Jesus was expounding to the two disciples, in his way to Emmaus, on the morning of his resurrection, the things concerning himself, he made use of those very arguments as proofs in his humiliation, and glory of his divine mission. "Ought not Christ (said he) to have suffered these things, and to enter into his glory." (Luke xxiv. 26.)

The Psalms have been generally divided into five heads, but it doth not appear that the Holy Ghost hath given any authority for this division. Taken as one grand whole, they form a complete epitome of the gospel; and from those which plainly point to Christ, and can refer to no other, we may venture to conclude that those which do not in our apprehension, the obscurity ariseth from our dulness, and not from any want of allusion to him. As to Jesus give all the prophets witness, and as the Psalms many of them are prophetical, evidently they are included. It is best in the perusal of every one of them to be on the look-out for Jesus, for precious are the things contained in the Psalms concerning him.

On those fifteen psalms entitled A song of degrees, from the one hundred and twentieth to the one hundred and thirty-fourth included, I can offer no one observation to form the least conjecture what the title means. As the Holy Ghost hath not thought proper to explain the cause for which they are so called, it should seem to be the safest plan to avoid all unprofitable enquiries, than attempt to be wise above what is written. The Psalms themselves are full of Jesus, and therefore in the discovery and enjoyment of him it will be our highest wisdom to direct our researches, praying that as often as the Holy Ghost opens any part of this precious volume to our meditation, he that hath the key of David may open our heart to the right apprehension of them, to make us wise unto salvation, through the faith that is in Christ Jesus.

PUA

There were two of this name--Pua, son of Issachar, Gen. xlvi. 13; and Pua, the father of Tola, Judg. x. 1.

PUAH

One of the midwives of Egypt. The name is derived from Pahah, meaning to groan or cry. The honourable testimony given of this woman, as well as Shiphrah, see Exod. i. 15. to the end; and the houses said to be built for them is rather to be taken figuratively, that the Lord built up their households. And as they had endeavoured, in defiance of the king's command, to save Israel's children, the Lord saved to them theirs.

PUBLICAN

It were to be wished that the term publican was well understood when reading the New Testament, since to the want of it many errors may occur. In modern times we all perfectly consider by the name of publican, one who keeps a public house or tavern. Very different from this was the character of the publican in Scripture. Among the Romans they had tax-gatherers, who were called publicans; and as the office was odious to all Jews being under the government of the Roman power, and as the office itself was invidious, so was the person collecting. Hence they were considered as the most worthless of men, and always classed with the refuse of the people. It became proverbial to join publicans and sinners together; and especially if a Jew, for the sake of gain, hired himself out to gather the taxes for the Romans, and thereby exacted it from his brethren, his name and character became altogether detestable. And hence when the Lord Jesus was pointing out to his disciples a man of more than ordinary worthlessness, he said, "Let him be unto thee as an heathen man, and a publican." (Matt. xviii. 17.)

It is very blessed and encouraging to discover that with all this odiousness of character, we find a Matthew and a Zaccheus eminently distingushed as partakers of the grace in Christ Jesus. Such indeed are the proper grace, Lord seems to delight in giving tokens of its distinguishing power. "Publicians and harlots, said Jesus, to the proud self-righteous pharisees, go into the kingdom of God before you." (Matt xxi. 31.) The reader will find a beautiful and interesting portrait of an humble publican contrasted to a proud pharisee, Luke xviii. 9. And the reader will find a yet more lovely and interesting portrait of Jesus receiving poor publicans, and being encircled with them, Luke xv. 1, &c.

PUBLIUS

The chief man of the island at Malta when Paul landed there. (Acts xxviii. 7-9.)

PUDENS

One of whom Paul makes honourable mention, 2 Tim. iv. 21.

PUHITES

They are mentioned 1 Chron, ii. 53. but what they were, or their office, is not known. Some derive their name from Pathah, to seduce.

PUB

King of Assyria. The name is not Hebrew, but rather Assyrian, from Phol, which some read Bean.

PUNISHMENTS

There were many kinds of these among the Hebrews, according to the crimes committed--scourging, stoning, imprisonment, hanging, and many others. But it is observable that in all cases, excepting high crimes against God, tenderness was mingled with their punishments. So much of the mercy of the gospel was even then shadowed out in Christ Jesus!

PUNON

A place were Israel pitched in the wilderness, between Petra and Segor, Some have thought that it was here Moses set up the brazen serpent, Num. xxi. 7. and Num. xxxiii. 42. The name Punon means precious stone.

PUR and PURIM

Feasts of the Jews, so called, Esth. iii. 7. The word means Lot. So that Purlin (or Lots in the plural) were those seasons when they celebrated their triumph over Haman and his house; and which festivals are kept even to this hour.

PUTEOLI

A city rendered memorable from the apostle Paul residing there a week in his way to Rome. (Acts. xxviii. 13.)

PUTIEL

Father to the wife of Eleazar. (Exod. vi. 25.) The name seems to be a compound of Phut, fulness and I-el, my God. God is my fulness.

Q

QUAILS

We read of the Lord's giving Israel those birds for food upon two occasions. First, soon after they left Egypt in the wilderness of Zin, (Exod. xvi.) and the second time when they were encamped at Ribroth-hattaavah, which the margin of the Bible renders the graves of lusts. (Num. xi. 34.) And upon both occasions this food was given to them in consequences of their rebellion; hence therefore it was in correction, and not in favour.

Various have been the opinions of men concerning the nature and kind of the quail. Moses called it Shalor. It is said to have been a small birth off great delicacy. The supply was so great the second time, that they victualled a camp of more than a million of persons for a whole month; so that they must have been like the shoals of pilchards on the western coast, every day covering the ground in multitudes.

I would refer the reader to those portions in the word of God for the history of those events, Exod. xvi. and Num. vi. 11. And I would beg of him, when he hath diligently read those Scriptures, to consider what solemn lessons such views hold forth of God's people running counter to God's government. The Psalmist hath made a beautiful observation upon this self-will of Israel, and the lawful consequence of it, when saying, "they lusted exceedingly, or as the words are, they lusted a lust in the wilderness, and tempted God in the desert. And he gave them their request, but sent leanness into their soul." (Ps. cvi. 14, 15,), It is an awful thing to be gratified in the creature, when such gratifications tend to rebellion against the Creator. "Give me children (said Rachel to Jacob) or else I die." (Gen. xxx. 1.) She had her desire, but she died in child-bearing. The child was a Benoni; that is, as she herself called him, (and is rendered in the margin of our Bibles) the son of my sorrow. (Gen. xxxv. 18.) Jonah's gourd was very refreshing to the prophet, but the disappointment, ended in sin. It is a blessed thing to let God choose forms, and this will be always right, but if we will ride restive, like Jeshurun, a fall must be the consequences. Children never carve for themselves but they cut their fingers. See Kibroth-hataawah.

QUARTUS

A brother, Paul calls him (Rom. xvi. 23.) No doubt, he meant a brother beloved in Christ. (See Phil. xvi.)

QUEEN OF HEAVEN

There can be but little doubt but by the phrase we meet with Jer. vii. 18. queen of heaven, was meant the moon; and such was the apostacy of Israel in the days of Jeremiah, that as the prophet tells them, the "children gather wood, and the fathers kindle the fire, and the women knead their dough to make cakes to the queen of heaven."

There had been always in Israel from their intercourse with other nations, a proneness to idolatry; and hence Moses cautioned them against being infected therewith. I beg the reader to turn to the fourth chapter of Deuteronomy, and observe, from beginning to end, with what tenderness and affection the man of God admonished Israel on this point.

Concerning the disposition to pay adoration to the heavenly bodies, we find this, more or less, pervading the human mind untaught of God among all nations. And as the greater light, the sun which JEHOVAH made to rule the day, was called Baal Shemim, lord of heaven, so the lesser light, the moon, which governed the night, was naturally called Malkah Shemem, queen of heaven; and from the influence of both they naturally became idle. While we behold such things, what cause of thankfulness ought it to call forth towards

God, who by the coming of the Lord Jesus Christ, hath opened to us the knowledge of himself, that "we might turn from idols to serve the living and true God!" Beautifully hath Moses pointed out to us, in his dying benediction to Israel, the blessedness of the Israel of God beyond the precious fruits brought forth by the sun, and the precious things put forth by the moon, "in the good will of him that dwelt in the bush." (Deut. xxxiii. 14. 16.)

QUICKEN

The Scripture sense and meaning of quickening is very great, and meaning of quickening is very great, and includes some very precious properties, with which every child of God is supposed to be acquainted in his own person and circumstances. It runs indeed through the whole of the divine life of God in the soul, from the first quickening the sinner, which is by nature clad in trespasses and sins, through all the after-ages of the renewed life, until that grace is finished in everlasting glory.

And what tends to endear this divine favour to all the happy receivers of it, the Scriptures graciously declare that all the persons of the GODHEAD are engaged in this merciful work, and every individual soul carries about with him, from day to day, evidences in his own heart of the united love, and grace, and favour, which is upon him, form the quickening operations of the Father, Son and Holy Ghost. I beg the reader to attend to what holy Scripture saith on this point, and then look into his own heart for the blessed testimonies to be found there corresponding to the word of God.

Concerning God the Father's quickening grace upon the soul, we read, (Rom. iv. 17.) that "God quickeneth the dead, and calleth those things which be not as though they were." And agreeably to this, the apostle Paul tells the Ephesians (chap. ii. 4, 5.) that them he had quickened, "who were dead in trespasses and sins. God (said he) who is rich in mercy, for his great love wherewith he loved us, even when we were dead in sins, hath quickened as together with Christ."

And, we know from the same authority, that one of the divine characters of our Lord, given of him by the Holy Ghost, is that of a quickening Spirit "The last Adam (was made) a quickening Spirit." (1 Cor. xv. 45.) And this is in perfect agreement to what the Lord Jesus himself said: "For as the Father raiseth up the dead, and quickeneth them, even so the Son quickeneth whom he will." (John v. 21.)

And with equal clearness of truth, the same blessed things are spoken in Scripture of the quickening power of God the Holy Ghost. "It is the Spirit that quickeneth: (saith the Lord Jesus) the flesh profiteth nothing. The words that I speak unto you, they are spirit, and they are life." And the apostle Peter was directed to tell the church, that even the human nature of Christ, as the Head of his body the church, when put to death in the flesh, was quickened by the Spirit. (1 Pet.iii. 18.)

What a blessed contemplation do such views open to the souls of the redeemed, when made conscious of their own personal interest therein! Jesus as the Head of his body the church, unites all his individual members to himself. By virture of this headship, and their union in him, he becomes the source, and fountain, and spring of all spiritual life. For by virtue of that union, of what he is in himself as their head, he communicates to them perpetual supplies in a life-giving, soul-quickening, soul-renewing, strengthening, refreshing power, from day to day; and like some rich, overflowing, and ever-flowing fountain, diffuseth life, grace, strength, and joy to all his members. "Because I live, (he saith himself) ye shall live also and hence his servant the apostle saith, "your life is hid with Christ in God." Such are the blessed privileges to which all true believers in Christ are begotten! By those quickening influences of the GODHEAD, they are first

QUIVER - QUIVER

brought into a new and spiritual life from the death of sin, from which they are awakened. They are carried on from day to day, in the renewed acts of grace they receive from the same source of mercy; under all spiritual decays, arising from their own helplessness and frailty, they are raised up by the continual streams of "that river which maketh glad the city of God;" and the same almighty power which first brings forth into life the renewed soul, preserves from all future decays, dissolution, and death, the spiritual frame, until brought home to everlasting glory. Hence David, sensible of the source from whence all the energies of grace were derived, cried out no less than nine times in one Psalm for the quickening influences of the Lord's Spirit, (Ps. cxix. 25. 37. 40. 88. 107. 149. 154. 156. 159.)

QUIVER

We meet with this word in reference to the Lord and to his people. The Lord Jesus, speaking of JEHOVAH'S eternal purpose and covenant respecting himself, saith: "The Lord hath called me from the womb; from the bowels of my mother hath he made mention of my name. And he hath made my mouth like a sharp sword; in the shadow of his hand hath he hid me; and made me a polished shaft; in his quiver hath he hid me." (Isa. xlix. 1, 2.) No doubt, from the womb of eternity, in the council of peace, and before all worlds, was Jesus in his mediatorial character set up, as well as his name declared to be Jesus by the angel before he was conceived in the womb of the Virgin Mary. The quiver, or, God is a fine expression, both to express the power and secrecy in which the person and purposes of God in Christ were concealed. So that the whole plan and determined end of redemption, were in JEHOVAH'S quiver concerning Christ not only; before his incarnation, or even as the promised seed; "but while as yet he had not made the earth, nor the fields, nor the highest part of the dust of the world." (Prov. viii. 26.) What a blessed consideration to the souls of the redeemed!

The Holy Ghost is pleased to make use of the term quiver in reference to the Lord's people. The arrows of a mighty man are said to be striking figures of children and a blessedness is declared to be the portion of that man that hath his quiver full of them. (Ps. cxxvii. 4, 5.) Children of grace are indeed blessed portions in a gracious man's quiver. Such in the great day of the Lord will be subjects of real joy; and the Lord, who hath given them, will give holy boldness with them, that there will be no shame when standing before their enemies in the gate.

R

RAAMAH

One of the sons of Gush (Gen. x. 7.) There was a Raam-jah also among them that returned from Babylon (Neh. vii. 7.) And as Raam, or Raamah is derived from Rabam, thunder, Raam-jah, means thunder of the Lord.

RAAMSES

One of the cities built by the children of Israel in Egypt for Pharaoh. (Exod. i. 11.) The word is derived from the same root, Raham.

RABBI or RABBONI

This name is variously pronounced, but all mean one and the same, namely, my master. The Rab of an house, or family, means the head of it; hence Daniel speaking of Ashpenaz, the master of the eunuchs, calls him Rab Sarism. And if there were more than one person dignified with the name of master, doctor or Lord, instead of Rabbi, my master, they were called Rabbim, masters. There were different degrees, we are told, in those titles. The head of a school or college was called Chocham. And those titles were not sought for, or studied for, by any rules or laws; but when the people discovered any to be eminently blessed with superior learning to others, he was as by general consent, called Rabbi, my master, or Chocham, wise.

  Rabbim of schools sat upon places raised above their pupils; hence Paul declares; that his was brought up at the feet of Gamaliel. (Acts xxii. 3.) How sweetly Christ taught humbleness concerning these names of honour! and who so suited to teach it as that humble Saviour? (Matt. xxiii. 8.) See Master.

RABBAH

This city, with Kirjath-baal, or Kinjath-gearim, was among those which Joshua divided by lot to Israel. (Josh. xv. 60.)

RABBAH, or RABBATH AMMON

The City of waters. (See 2 Sam. xii. 26, 27.)

RABBA-MOAB

The same as Kirheres.(Jer. xlviii. 31.)

RAB-MAG

A general in the king of Babylon's army. (Jer. xxxix. 3.) The word is compounded of Rab and Magi--the chief of the magi, or wise men.

RAB-SHAKEH, or RAB-SACES

A compound of words--Rab, master--Shakeh, cupbearer (2 Kings xviii. 17.)

RAB-SARIS, or SARIM

Master of the eunuchs. A title of office. (Jer. xxxix. 3.)

RACA

A Syriac word, signifying somewhat very opprobious, such as sorry fellow, villain, and the like; so that it is a term of the utmost contempt, and seldom used unless accompanied with spitting. See Spitting. Our blessed Lord hath defined three several degrees of guilt in the use of improper anger and names. (Matt. v. 22.) "I say unto you (saith Jesus) that whosoever is angry with his brother without a cause, shall be in danger of the judgment; and whosoever shall say to his brother, Raca, shall be in danger of the council; but whosoever shall say, Thou fool, shall be in danger of hell fire." It was a law of the Sanhedrim, founded upon the law of God, that no one should cherish anger against another, much less bring a railing accusation. He that did so was justly exposed to the judgment of God; but if he went farther than mental anger, and called his brother Raca, should be brought before the council, that judgment might be speedily obtained. But, if still prosecuting his malignity, and said, Thou fool, that is, thou child of hell, and this to a brother who is a child of God, Such an one was in danger of hell fire. The Jews had three different sorts of punishment. Beheading was commanded by judgment; stoning by the order of the Sanhedrim, or council; and burning in Gehenna, the valley of the son of Hinnom. (See Jer. vii. 31, 32.) Joshiah, the good king, in order to pollute this place, and render it everlastingly, hateful to Israel, commanded all the filth he could rake together, and dead men's bones, to be thrown into it. (2 Kings xxiii.) There is somewhat of difficulty at first view in this passage of our Lord. To say to another Raca, subjects the offender to the curse and condemnation of the council; but to say thou fool, makes the offender in danger of hell-fire. Whereas we find the apostle, Paul using the very phrase in his discourse on the resurrection. (1 Cor. xv. 36.) And our blessed Lord him self, when reproving the dullness of his disciples, said, "O fools, and slow of heart, to believe all that the prophets have spoken." (Luke xxiv. 26.) But the difficulty vanisheth when the passages are compared together. In the instance of the apostle, and his master, the term fool is but a gentle reproof, and meant in a tender way to correct a dullness of understanding. In the case to which Jesus refers, the utmost anger and malice is sup posed; so that when the offender calls his bro ther, fool, he means one that is a child of hell, and under the curse of God. Oh, for grace to be kept from sins of such heinousness and malignity!

RACHEL

A well-known and interesting name in the Bible, the beloved wife of the patriarch Jacob, and daughter of Laban. The name itself means sheep. And from being engaged in keeping flocks, in these early days of patriarchal simplicity, it is probable the name was taken on that account. Her history we have, Gen. xxix. 30, &c. It may be observed, that we have a city in the tribe of Judah called Rachal, or Rachel; probably in honour of this mother in Israel. (1 Sam. xxx. 29.)

RADDAI

One of the sons of Jesse, and brother of David. (1 Chron. ii. 14.). The name is probably borrowed from Radad, to stretch.

RAHAB

The memorable woman of the city of Jericho, of whose faith the Holy Ghost hath given such honourable testimony, Heb. xi. 31. Her name is derived from Raah, and signifies proud. And if there be aught upon earth to make sinful dust and ashes proud, surely the faith this woman possessed formed the strongest temptation to it; when we consider who she was, what she was; where she lived, and how she acted in the cause of the Lord. Her history is as great and striking, in the illustrious actings of her faith, as any in the records of truth.

She was one of the inhabitants of Canaan, a Gentile, an alien, and by nature an enemy to the commonwealth of Israel, "without hope, and without God in the world." Moreover, she was, as we say, a publican, and an harlot, not only kept an inn, exposed to numberless temptations, but a woman of ill-fame, notoriously known for such a character. She lived also in the accursed city of Jericho, a city devoted to destruction before the Lord, and of peculiar malignity of evil in the Lord's sight. And yet with all those disadvantages, this Rahab, this harlot, was a believer in the Lord God of Israel! Oh, the wonders of distinguishing grace! And what tends yet more to raise our views of the Lord's peculiar manifestation and love to this poor· harlot, is the consideration that from the stock of this woman, after the flesh, the Lord appointed the future advent of his dear Son. By her marriage to Salmon; from whom sprang Boaz; and by the marriage of Boaz with Ruth, sprang Obed; and from Obed, Jesse; and from Jesse, David; and from David, after twice fourteen generations after the flesh, sprang Christ. (See Matt. i. 1-17.) What subjects of wonder the glorious redemption by the Lord Jesus Christ involves in it! Here, as in a thou sand instances beside, we learn that the Lord's ways are not our ways, nor his thoughts as our thoughts!" I pray the reader to give a diligent attention to her history, Josh. ii. throughout.

We meet with the mention of another Rahab, Ps. lxxxvii. 4. And in Ps. lxxxix. 10, Rahab is said to be broken in pieces: by which is meant most probably, Pharaoh and his host. We find, and not unfrequently, names figuratively used to denote the Lord's enemies. Thus the Psalmist elsewhere saith, Thou brakest the heads of Leviathan in pieces, and gavest him to be meat to the people inhabiting the wilderness." (Ps. lxxiv. 13, 14.) Here is an evident allusion to the destruction of Pharaoh; and his host in the Red Sea; and afterwords causing the people, when at any time in their wilderness-state, to meet with difficulties, that the recollection of this mighty deliverance might become food to their faith, to help them through any present trouble.

RAHAM

Son of Shema, (1 Chron. ii. 44.) The word Raham, or Racham, is bowels.

RAIN

Every one knows what rain is, and all are sensible of the importance of this blessing on the earth. No doubt it is produced by the exhalation of the sun, forming vapours from the earth and sea, which return in showers, to carry on the merciful purpose of the Lord in his blessings on nature. And the same in the moral and spiritual world, all comes from the same course in the Lord's own sovereignty and goodness; for as the sun the natural world is the first and predisposing cause, so in the moral and spiritual world it is the Sun of righteousness, from his divine operation on the hearts of his people, which brings forth the showers of grace, and induceth all the blessed effects which follow in their lives and conversation. The prophet Hosea beautifully expresseth this truth in one of his chapters. He represents a time of drought by the bottles of heaven being stopped, and the earth languishing for thirst; and under these circumstances he brings in the heavens and the earth as sending forth their cries for the needed mercy, and the goodness of the Lord in answering them. "And it shall come to pass in that day, I will hear, saith the Lord, I will hear the heavens, and they shall hear the earth; and the earth shall hear the corn, and the wine, and the oil; and they shall hear Jezreel. And I will sow her unto me in the earth; and I will have mercy upon her that had not obtained mercy; and I will say to them which were not my people, Thou art my people, and they shall say, Thou art my God." (Hos. ii. 21-23.) It is in vain for the men of Jezreel to expect the corn, and oil, and fruits of the earth, if the Lord restrain the clouds of heaven and the rain, that they withhold their fatness. It is in vain for the earth to cry to the heavens to send the rain, if the Lord of heaven gives not his commands to the clouds to answer the wants of nature. But if the Lord puts the cry in the heavens above, and in the hearts of his re deemed below, and he that puts the cry comes forth to answer it in mercy, then all these blessed effects follow each other as the prophet hath described. And as in nature, so in grace, the Lord sends showers of grace upon his inheritance when they are weary, from the blessed cause he here assigns: I will say to them, Thou art my people; and they shall say, Thou art my God?

We hear often mention made in the Scriptures concerning the first rain, and the

RAIN - RAIN

latter rain, in their season, (Deut. xi. 14,)--and, no doubt, there was somewhat particularly suited and seasonable in both. The Hebrews called those rains by different names. The first, or former rain, they called Jorah, which in the autumn, because in their calculation the Jews began their year at that season. The latter rain was in the spring of the year, and this they called Malkush, which is supposed to be the peculiar and special refreshment for the dry earth. Moses, the man of God, prepared the ;minds of the people for those blessings in Canaan, as to kens of divine favour, by putting the people in mind of their past labour in Egypt. For though the river Nile, which the Egyptians prided themselves so much upon, did indeed overflow the banks of it at certain seasons, yet the higher and remote ground from it could not be benefited thereby; and therefore the inhabitants were obliged occasionally to water their ground, in order to render it fruitful. Moses prepares Israel, therefore, for the Lord's special blessing over them in this particular when they get into Canaan. "For the land (saith Moses) whither thou goest in to possess it, is act the land of Egypt from whence ye came out, where thou sowedst thy seed, and wateredst it with thy foot, as a garden of herbs. But the land whither ye go to possess it, is a land of hills and vallies, and drinketh water of the rain of heaven; a land which the Lord thy God careth for: the eyes of the Lord thy God are alway upon it, from the beginning of the year even unto the end of the year? (Deut. xi. 10-12.)

I cannot dismiss this view of the former and latter rain without first calling upon the reader to notice a passage in the writings of Hosea, where, if I mistake not, the Holy Ghost, by his servant the prophet, hath blessedly made those springs and autumns of the rain beautifully descriptive of the person and visits of Jesus. "Then shall we know, if we follow on to know the Lord, his going forth is prepared as the morning; and he shall come unto us as the rain, as the latter and former rain unto the earth." (Hos. vi. 3.). If the reader will consult the Bible, from whence these words are taken, he will discover, what the whole context proves, that what is here said is spoken of the Lord Jesus Christ. Indeed it could be said of no other. And he will discover also, that that little word if is in italics, to intimate that it is not in the original; and therefore the coming of the Lord as the morning, is not made to depend upon our ifs, but is the sole result or, his own free grace. And surely no thing can be more beautiful and lovely in the promise of Jesus coming to his people, both in the early and latter manifestations of his grace, than in the resemblance here made of it to the genial influences of the early and the latter rain. His goings forth are prepared as the morning of eternity, and in the morning of time, his first manifestations in grace, and in all the after seasons of his love, when visiting his people. Who shall describe the sweet and silent droppings of the rain, the dew from the Lord, and the showers upon the grass, that tarrieth "not for man, nor waiteth for the sons of men!" Who shall calculate their number, their richness, their refreshing influence, coming from him who "from the womb of the morning hath the dew of his youth!" Who shall mark down the times and the seasons in the unobserved, unnoticed, unknown visits to all but to the souls of his redeemed, to whom he imparts his blessings in secret, when carrying on the sacred purposes of his "kingdom which cometh not by observation." Surely every redeemed soul that knoweth what these things mean must be constrained to say with David: "He is as the light of the morning when the sun ariseth, even a morning without clouds; as the tender grass springing out of the earth, by clear shining after other beauties in the Scriptures concerning divine things, which are described under the similitude of rain; but I must not enlarge, and therefore can only make reference to the Scriptures themselves. (See Deut. xxxii. 2. Job xx. 22, 23. Ps lxv.10; lxviii. 9; lxxii. 6; cxlvii. 8. Isa. xxx. 23; lv. 10. Hos. x. 2. Acts xiv. 17.)

I cannot however refrain from making one observation more upon the subject of rain, though differing in quality from the ordinary rain to which in this country we are accustomed. In that solemn chapter in the book of Deuteronomy where Moses, the man of God, is denouncing threatenings to Israel's disobedience, we find this remarkable expression: "The Lord shall make the rain of thy land powder and dust; from heaven shall it come down upon thee until thou be destroyed." (Deut. xxviii. 24.) The thing would not be so striking if it referred to the hurricanes which sometimes take place on the deserts of the East, where whole caravans have been known to be covered over and destroyed. But the particularity in this account of Moses is, that the storm of powder and dust "shall come down from heaven upon thee." I confess the expression by a figure may be said to be from heaven, even when the whirlwind is made by the winds on the sand of the earth, because it is the Lord's judgment: yet, I humbly conceive, somewhat more is meant by this rain of powder and dust than the raising it from the earth. But in either sense, or in both, the circumstance is alarming. We see that the Lord can convert our very blessings into curses; and make those showers of rain, which are essential and necessary to the very existence as well as the comfort of man, become showers of powder and dust to destroy.

And here, reader, I beg again to point to the Lord. Jesus Christ, who is as blessed to us against this calamity as he is blessed to us in the showers of rain, when he cometh to us as the "latter rain and as the former rain upon the earth." The prophet was commissioned by the Holy Ghost to point him out under the beautiful similitude of a shelter to his people, when he said: "And a man (or the man Christ Jesus) shall be as an hiding place from the storm, and a covert from the tempest; as rivers of water in a dry place, and as the shadow of a great rock in a weary land." (Isa. xxxii.) Jesus is all this and infinitely more when the storm of sin raiseth up the powder and dust of our corrupt nature, and threatens to swallow us up in everlasting destruction. And while he protects from wrath, he comforts with his refreshments of grace; and is not only a covert from the wind, but like rivers of water to the soul, which satisfy the thirsty desires, as travellers in a desert when they find a sweet spring in the way. See Dew.

RAINBOW

I know not how it is, but so it is, as if by natural instinct, as often as I see that beautiful arch in the heavens called the rainbow, I call to mind what JEHOVAH once said after the deluge: "I do set my bow in the cloud, and it shall be for a token of a covenant between me and the earth and it shall come to pass, when I bring a cloud over the earth, that the bow shall be seen in the cloud. And I will remember my covenant which is between me and you, and every living creature of all flesh: and the waters shall no more become a flood to destroy all flesh. And the bow shall be in the cloud; and I will look upon it, that I may remember the everlasting covenant between God and every living creature of all flesh that is upon the earth." (Gen. ix. 13-16.) As oft therefore as I behold the rain bow, I consider the graciousness of the Lord's renewed token of this covenant; and I consider also the high privilege in looking in one and the same moment to the same object to which my God is looking. There is somewhat in this peculiarly blessed. And moreover, when I call to mind, what the beloved apostle John saw when heaven was opened to his view, "the rainbow round about the throne," (Rev. iv. 3.) and also that mighty, angel whom he saw with a "rainbow upon his head," (Rev. x. 1.) I confess I feel great delight. For I cannot but conclude, that the bow JEHOVAH set in the cloud after the deluge, and the rainbow John saw in heaven round about the throne, and encircling or covering the head of the mighty angel, were all to the same purport, and all representing Christ. For surely Jesus is himself the covenant JEHOVAH hath made with our nature in the person of his dear Son. Notwithstanding, therefore, what some men tell us of the physical causes by which the rainbow, they say, is produced, yet still I desire to look at it as the result of higher purposes in grace, and to behold it in every renewed view as the sweet and glorious token JEHOVAH hangs out in the heavens of JEHOVAH'S covenant in Christ. Men who study nature may see God in the works of nature; and they who study providences may see God in the works of his providences; but they who study the works of grace; when taught of God, will discover Christ in the whole of those great designs, and behold the light of the knowledge of the glory of God in the face of Jesus Christ!

RAKEM

Son of Shiresh. (1 Chron. vii. 16.) If derived from Rakah, the name means empty or vain.

RAKKATH

A city of Naphtali. (Josh. xix. 35.) From Rakah empty.

RAKKON

A city of Dan. (Josh. xix. 49.)

RAM

Son of Hezron. (1 Chron. ii. 9.) There was another Ram, from whom sprung Elihu. (Job xxxii. 2.) Perhaps from Ramah, lifted up.

RAMAH

There was a Ramah, a city of Benjamin, near Bethel. (Josh. xviii. 25.) And there was a Ramah, called Ramathaim-Zophim, in mount Ephraim, where Elkanah and Hannah, Samuel the prophet's parents, lived. (See 1 Sam. i. 19.) And yet it is very possible, that both these might be but one and the same Ramah; for the frontiers of Benjamin and Ephraim joined each other. And as Ramah means a hill, and Zophim is the plural of Zoph, to behold, it is possible the place of Samuel's dwelling might be called Ramathaim-Zophim, the two hills of beholding.

RAMIAH

--Or more properly Ram-jah

One who returned from Babylon, (Ezra x. 25.) The compound makes the name, raised up of the Lord.

RAMOTH GILEAD

A city in the mountain of Gilead. In Josh. xv. 26, it is called Ramoth-mizpeh; that is, the watchtower. This was one of the cities of refuge. (Deut. iv. 43.) It became the subject and occasion of much war in the after-days of the kings. (1 Kings xxiii. 2 Kings, chap. viii. and ix.) There was a son of Bani called Ramoth. (Ezra x. 29.)

RAMS-HORNS

We read of rams-horns made use of by Joshua's army, at the command of the Lord, in the destruction of Jericho. (Josh. vi. 4, 5.) An English reader, in the perusal of this Scripture, will unavoidably connect in his ideas the ordinary horns of the ram with which he is acquainted. But this would be erroneous. No doubt, we have borrowed the word Ram from the original Hebrew; but have very differently applied it. The word Ram, in the Hebrew, signifies somewhat that is raised up, elevated, or exalted. Probably the horns made use of at the siege of Jericho were the wild bull's, from his height and size; and if not the bull's, it might be of the beef kind. But be this as it may, no doubt there was a sweet and gracious instruction intended from the use of such feeble instruments, to teach the church in all ages, that as there was no comparison between the weapon and the work, the church should be always looking off from themselves, in order to be always eyeing the Lord. His is the work, and his the glory. But over and above this very obvious instruction, I venture to think that in the appointment of those horns there was somewhat in allusion to the Lord Jesus. I hope the Lord will pardon me if I err. But when we consider what an eminent type of Christ Joshua was, we may expect every thing connected with his ministry may be supposed to bear some reference to him. Moses, as a type of the law he was the minister of, could not bring the children of God into Canaan. The law never did; it never was designed for that purpose, for it is the ministration of death. This was reserved for Joshua, whose very name is the same with Jesus. And if we find Joshua entering on his ministry with the instruments of rams-horns, may we not, yea, must we not connect with it what is said of Jesus as the horn of salvation to his people, which JEHOVAH promised to raise up? Luke i. 69. Let the reader connect with this view what Moses, in his dying moments, when the spirit of prophecy was upon him, spake of Joseph typical of the Lord Jesus Christ: "His glory (said he) is like the firstling of his bullock, and his horns are like the horns of unicorns with them he shall push the people together to the ends of the earth; and they are the ten thousands of Ephraim, and the thousands of Manasseh." (Deut. xxxiii. 17.) And Habakkuk, under the same spirit of prophecy, speaks of the Lord Jesus Christ, (chap. iii. 4.) as having horns coming out of his hand, and there was the hiding of his power. I would not speak pre sumptuously on this or any other subject connected with matters of such infinite moment; but as the Lord Jesus Christ is the visible JEHOVAH in our nature for all the purposes of redemption, and as every part of the Bible testifies that the grand design of all revelation is to exalt him, I humbly conceive that it is of Jesus wholly the Holy Ghost is continually speaking in all the great events connected with his church and people.

RANSOM

This word is used several times in Scripture to denote the immense price the Lord Jesus gave for the purchase of his people. He saith him self, (Matt. xx. 28.) "The son of man came to give his life a ransom for many." And his servant the apostle saith, (1 Tim. ii. 6.) "Who gave himself a ransom for all to be testified in due time." And to heighten the subject, beyond all possible conception, of the greatness of the value, Peter was commissioned to tell the church that "they were not redeemed with corruptible things, as silver and gold, but with the precious blood of Christ, as a lamb without blemish and without spot." (1 Pet. i. 18, 19.) And the Psalmist brings in his testimony to the same amount, (Ps. xlix. 7, 8.) "None can by any means redeem his brother, nor give to God a ransom for him: for the redemption of his soul is precious, and it ceaseth for ever." But to shew, at the same time, that what the Lord Jesus gave was fully equal, yea, more than equal to the vast purchase, 'the Holy Ghost, in the book of Job, introduceth JEHOVAH as speaking concerning the redeemed sinner, "Deliver him from going down to the pit, I have found a ransom." (Job xxxiii. 24.) And hence, in proof that this one offering of the body of Jesus Christ, once for all, hath perfected for ever them that are sanctified, the prophet Isaiah is appointed to describe the happy effects of redemption in the everlasting salvation of all Christ's people. "The ransomed of the Lord (saith he) shall return, and come to Zion with songs and everlasting joy upon their heads; they shall obtain joy and gladness, and sorrow and sighing shall flee away." (Isa. xxxv. 10.)

I hope the reader will indulge me

with one short observation on the subject of Jesus giving himself a ransom for his people. Never in all the annals of mankind was there ever heard of such unparalleled love. Suppose some generous prince, out of compassion to any of his captive subjects, were to abridge his pleasures, and give large sums of money to bring them out of captivity--how would the deed be applauded, and his name be idolized to all gene rations! But supposing this generous prince was to give himself for them, and exchange their persons in slavery by voluntarily surrendering up himself to such a state--what would be said of this? And yet the Lord Jesus hath done this, and infinitely more, not for friends, but enemies, not for those who loved him, but those who hated him; and not only by slavery, but by death. He hath died for them, washed them in his blood, brought them out of slavery and the shadow of death, and hath broke their bonds asunder, and purchased for them an endless state of happiness, and is gone before to take possession of it in their name, and will come again to receive them to himself, that where he is there they may be also. "Wonder, O heavens, and be astonished, O earth, for the Lord hath done it!"

RAPHA

Benjamin's fifth son was called by this name, I Chron. viii. 2---And Binea had a son called Rapha, 1 Chron. viii. 37. The name means medicine or healing.

RAPHAEL or REPHAEL

Son of Shemaiah, (1 Chron. xxvi. 7.) The name is a compound of Rapha and El, medicine, or remedy of God.

RAPHAIMS

(Gen. xiv. 5.) Those were probably the same as Moses takes notice of Deut. ii. 10, 11, there called Emims, a people great and tall, which in times past, it is said, were called giants, as the Anakims; but the Moabites called them Emims. Rapha means giant, consequently Raphaim makes it plural giants. In the margin of the Bible, (2 Sam. xxi. 18, 20.) to the name of giant in each verse Rapha is preserved.

RAVEN

The raven is classed among the unclean by the law, (Lev. xi. 15.) Notwithstanding, we have an account in Scripture of the ministry of this bird upon two remarkable occasions. The former from the ark of Noah, (Gen. viii. 7.) and the other feeding the prophet Elijah at the brook Cherith. (1 Kings xvii. 4-6.) Some have supposed that the word Orebim, which our translators render ravens, means the inhabitants of Oreb, near to Bethshan. But in this case the prophet would not have been hid; and this was the reason wherefore the Lord bid him go to Cherith. Besides, if any human beings brought the prophet bread and flesh, so they might also water. But the Scriptures have uniformly held forth this history of Elijah as miraculous, which would not have been the case but in the supposition of his being fed by ravens. The church sets forth the headship and beauties of her husband Christ under the similitude of the fine lustre of the gold, and the rich black shining gloss of the raven. "His head is as the most fine gold; his locks are bushy and black as a raven." (Song v. 11.) And to those who know Christ, and eye him as the Head of his body the church, he is all this, and infinitely more.

REAJAH

Son of Shobel. (1 Chron. iv. 2.) There was another of this name, the son of Micah. (1 Chron. v. 5.) Compounded of Rea, or Raah, to see--and Jah, Lord.

REBA

One of the five kings of Midian slain by Israel. (See Num. xxxi. 8.) His name is from Rub to quarrel.

REBEKAH

Daughter of Bethuel, and the wife of Isaac. (Gen. xxiv.) Her history we have at large in Genesis. Her name, if from Rabah, means fat.

REBEL and REBELS

I beg the reader's indulgence while giving to him my sense and apprehension of the Scriptural meaning of rebel and rebels. If I err, I pray the Lord to forgive me, and to preserve the reader from following my opinion.

I humbly conceive that by the term, in the language of Scripture, is meant reprobate; and therefore is never used in application to any of God's children, in confirmation of this opinion, I beg the reader to consult all the places in Scripture where the word occurs; and these, as far as I recollect, are only five, namely, Num. xvii. 10; xx. 10. Jer. 1. 21--in the margin of the Bible, Ezek. ii. 6; and xx. 38. Now the reader will discover, that in every one of those instances, excepting one, namely, Num. xx. 10. (and that one, as I shall hereafter endeavour to shew, becomes the greatest instance in confirmation of my opinion) the term is invariably made use of in reference to reprobates.

It should seem by the term rebels, in those passages of Scripture, the Holy Ghost intended to mark the children of the wicked one, by way of distinction, from the children of the kingdom: hence the word is similar to that of traitor. And we read of no traitor in the word of God but the traitor Judas, who is said to have fallen by transgression, that he might go to his own place, (Acts i. 25.) his own proper place, his birth-right. So Balaam said of himself: "I go, said he to Balak, unto my people." And what that place and that people implied, the Scriptures, in other parts, explain. Christ speaking of this very traitor Judas, saith of him, "It had been good for that man if he had not been born." (Matt. xxvi. 24.) And Jude, speaking of all such, calls them ungodly men," who were before of old ordained to this condemnation." (Jude iv.) And Paul speaks of similar characters under the general term of traitors, (2 Tim. iii. 4.) So that Judas and his company, the reprobate, are the only traitors we meet with in the word of God; and in this sense rebels and traitors are one and the same.

It will be said perhaps in answer to this statement, that the Lord frequently calls his children rebellious children, and pronounceth a woe against them. (See Isa. xxx. 1, &c. To which I answer, Yes; the Lord most certainly doth so; but there is a vast distinction between rebellious children and rebels. A child may be, and God's children all are by nature, rebellious; and even when in grace too frequently rebellious again; but still, though rebellious, they are children, and not rebels. Rebels they never were, nor of the seed of the serpent. The Holy Ghost himself hath made this precious distinction when, by his servant John, he points out in the instances of Cain and Abel the mighty difference. "Not as Cain, (saith he) who was of that wicked one, and slew his brother." (1 John iii. 12.) And hence when the Lord promiseth to separate his people from among the reprobate, he expresseth himself by those striking words: "And I will purge out from among you the rebels, and them that transgress against me; I will bring them forth out of the country where they sojourn, and they shall not enter into the land of Israel, and ye shall know that I am the Lord." (Ezek. xx. 38.)

And with respect to the woe the Lord pronounceth against his rebellious children, everyone who reads his Bible with attention, under the Holy Ghost's teaching, will discover that this woe is all of a temporal nature, and hath respect only to chastisements. In confirmation, I beg the reader to consult the thirtieth chapter of Isaiah, where this woe is spoken of most particularly. The prosecution of that chapter is the fullest proof of it; for after the Lord had said that the woe of his people should be, to find their punishment in the very things from which they sought protection and help, the Lord declares that he still waits to be gracious, and that his people should be blessed. And from the eighteenth verse to the close of the chapter, the Lord shews his graciousness to his people, by favour to them, and destruction to their enemies.

Though I have largely trespassed under this article, yet I must still detain the reader with one observation more to fulfil my promise, by shewing, as I proposed, that the one only place in Scripture where the Lord's children are called rebels was misapplied, and in that misapplication of the name, and the Lord's displeasure in consequence on this occasion, becomes in my view the highest confirmation of the whole. The case I refer to is Num. xx. 10. I beg the reader to turn to the chapter, and read the whole passage from the first to the thirteenth verse. When the reader hath made his own observations upon it, let him turn to the one hundred and sixth Psalm, and hear what God the Holy Ghost saith upon it, ver. 32, 33. Let him then ask, (for I presume not to determine upon it,) what was the particular sin of Moses on this occasion? Perhaps the unhallowed manner of joining himself with the Lord, when he said, must we fetch water out of this rock? Perhaps the smiting the rock twice, when but once on the former occasion, at the Lord's command, was done, Exod. xvii. 6. But might there not be an offence also in calling the Lord's heritage rebels? Let the reader remember I do but ask the question, and not decide. But when we recollect how jealous the Lord is of his glory, how dearly he prizeth his people, calling them his portion, his jewels, his treasure, surely it is but reasonable to suppose that Moses herein offended also. If, as our Lord Jesus in after-ages taught, that whosoever should say to his brother Raca, or fool, (Matt. v. 22.)a term implying a child of hell, should be in danger of hell-fire, we may conclude that when Moses called God's children rebels, or children of hell, there was great sin in it. Reader, pause! If this opinion be at all founded in right, think, how precious the Lord's people are in his sight!

RECHAB

There are several of this name in Scripture; but he that is most recommended to our attention by the Holy Ghost, is he who by his rules to his family gave an honourable testimony to the house of the Rechabites; and which is handed down to us of this house.

RECHAH

We have an account of the men of Rechah, 1 Chron. iv. 12. But how employed, or to what service the house of Rechah was engaged, is not said.

REDEEMER

One of the blessed names of our Lord Jesus Christ: and sweetly doth the Holy Ghost bear witness to it--"For thy Maker is thine husband, the Lord of hosts is his name: and thy Redeemer the Holy One of Israel; the God of the whole earth shall he be called." (Isa. liv. 5.)

In considering the peculiarity of this character of Christ, so as to endear him to the heart of his people, it will be sufficient to observe that what constitutes redemption, in the entire accomplishment of it, could be wrought by none but Christ himself. It is the personal and peculiar fitness of the Lord Jesus to the office of Redeemer, that forms the special greatness and importance of the work itself; for if it could be shewn, or ever supposed, that any other beside Christ had been competent, it, would have lessened the dignity, the personal dignity, and glory of the Son of God, and reduced the infinite value of redemption itself. But as none but the Son of God could perform it, so in that performance the value and efficacy of it is heightened beyond all the conceptions the imagination can form of it.

We shall set this in a clear point of view, if we consider what forms the great and leading characters of redemption, in the contemplation of which the glory of Christ will appear abundantly striking as the great Redeemer.

And first, the very idea of redemption is to buy out, or deliver, what was lost or forfeited, and this by giving a full and equivalent value for it. Thus when Abraham made a purchase of a burying-place from the sons of Heth, it is said that he weighed and gave "four hundred shekels of silver, current money of the merchant." (Gen. xxiii. 16.) Now such was the redemption by the Lord Jesus Christ of our nature. He gave what might be called current money, that is a full and rich equivalent: yea, more than an equivalent, when for the sins and transgressions of his people he paid for it with the price of his blood. (See 1 Pet. i. 18, 19.)

But the great work of redemption did not rest here. Jesus by his merciful undertaking not only re deemed us from sin, in buying out our mortgaged and forfeited inheritance, but he redeemed our long lost privileges. We were not only justly exposed by nature, and by practice, to the wrath and displeasure of Almighty God, but our whole nature was under the dominion and influence of sin; and none short of Christ could buy us out. The Son of God, therefore, by price and by power accomplished both those purposes of salvation; and not only delivered us from the wrath to come, but brought us into the privileges of a purchased inheritance. Yea, he induced in us a new nature, in taking away the natural enmity of our hearts, and making us "willing in the day of his power."

And lastly, having delivered us from all evil, and brought us into all good, he hath accomplished the whole purposes of redemption, so as to obtain favour and peace with God, through Jesus Christ our Lord.

Such are the outlines of redemption, and such the wonderful work which the Son of God hath in our nature accomplished by his blood! And what tends to endear the Lord Jesus Christ yet infinitely more under his character of Redeemer is, that in the whole of this immense transaction all he hath accomplished is in our nature. It is the man whose name is the Branch, it is Jesus, who in his human nature is bone of our bone and flesh of our flesh, that hath wrought out salvation. So that both redemption itself, and the glorious person by whom it is brought, gives a double relish to all the purposes of it, and lifts the heart to all the acts of adoration and praise to the great Author of our felicity. Hail! I would say, thou great and Almighty Redeemer and benefactor of mankind!

REDEMPTION OF THE FIRST-BORN

See this subject largely treated under the article First Born.

RED HEIFER

Among all the laws of the Levitical priesthood concerning sacrifices, there is hardly one more striking in all the particulars of it: as referring to the Lord Jesus Christ; and yet there is not one so generally little understood, or attended to. I beg the reader's attention to it as a subject highly interesting. He will find the account of it set forth at large, Num. xix. from the first verse to the tenth. Moses was commanded to speak unto the children of Israel to bring a red heifer without spot, wherein was no blemish, and upon which never came yoke. Eleazer the priest was to bring her forth without the camp, and one was to slay her before his face. Eleazer was then to take of her blood with his finger, and sprinkle of her blood directly before the tabernacle of the congregation seven times.

RED HEIFER - RED HEIFER

One was then to burn the heifer in his sight; her skin; her flesh, and her blood, with her dung, all was to be burnt. Then the priest was to take cedar wood, and hyssop, and scarlet, and cast it into the midst of the burning of the heifer. Then the priest was to wash his clothes, and to bathe his flesh in water, and afterward he was to come into the camp, and be unclean until the even. And he that burned the heifer was to wash his clothes in water, and bathe his flesh in water, and be unclean until the even. And a man that was clean was to gather the ashes of the heifer and lay them up without the camp in a clean place, to be kept for the congregation of the children of Israel for a water of separation: it is a purification for sin. And this was to be both to the children of Israel, and the stranger that sojourned among them, for a statute for ever.

Such are the interesting particulars in the Lord's appointment of the sacrifice of the red heifer. I would now beg to call the reader's attention to the service itself, in order to remark the prominent features of the ordinance, as typical of the person and offering of the Lord Jesus Christ,

And first, the heifer was to be red. A most un likely thing to obtain, as if to prefigure the singularity of the person of Jesus; for none but the Lord Christ could be suited for our salvation: and the personal fitness of Jesus, in the singularity of his person and character, is that which endears him so highly to his people. Perhaps the reader may not know, or if he doth, he may not immediately re collect, that Adam was called Adam, or Adamah, on account of the red earth or dust from whence he was taken. Pure virgin earth is naturally red. Now the Lord Jesus is also called the last Adam. (1Cor. xv. 45.) And it is said of him, with peculiar reference to his human nature, that "forasmuch as the children are partakers of flesh and blood, he also himself likewise took part of the same." (Heb. ii. 14.) And hence the church sings of him in the joy of her heart, "My beloved (said she) is white and ruddy, the chiefest among, ten thousand. (Song v. 10.)

Secondly, this red heifer was to be without spot, and wherein there was no blemish. What could more strikingly depicture the features of him "who with out spot offered himself to God!" He was indeed, as the Holy Ghost hath drawn him, "holy, harmless, undefiled, separate from sinners, and made higher than the heavens." (Heb. vii. 26.) We are told that the Jews were so very tenacious that this heifer should be exactly corresponding to the ordinance in those particulars, that if the animal had but a spot of different colour from the red, yea, but in a single hair, it was rejected. Surely nothing could be more in reference to the "lamb of God who was without blemish and without spot." (1 Pet. i. 19.)

Thirdly, that particularity of the red heifer in the Jewish church, that it should be one upon which there never came yoke, is of all others the most striking, as typical of Christ; and the more so, be cause, among all the sacrifices under the law, it is the only one we ever meet with of such an appoint ment. There was no yoke, no obligation, upon Christ, but his own freewill, for which he became a sacrifice for his people. For although he glorified not himself to be either an high priest, or sacrifice, uncalled and unsent of God, yet equally certain it is, that without his own voluntary offering he could not have suited the purpose of our redemption. Hence he saith himself, (John x. 17, 18.) "Therefore doth my Father love me because I lay down my life, that I might take it again. No man taketh it from me, but I lay it down of myself; I have power to lay it down, and I have power to take it again. This commandment have I received of my Father."

Fourthly, the heifer, to signify uncleanness, was "slain without the camp."

And Jesus, that he "might sanctify the people with his own blood, suffered without the gate," The apostle makes a most beautiful persuasive and unanswerable appeal to the church, in this view of Jesus, when he saith, "Let us go forth therefore unto him without the camp, bearing his reproach;" (Heb. xiii. 12, 13.)

Fifthly, when the heifer had been slain, the blood was to be sprinkled directly before the tabernacle seven times. And it forms an express doctrine of the cross, the blood of sprinkling. As the tabernacle represented the whole church of Jesus, so all his people are supposed to be brought under the cleansing by the blood of Christ. Believers are said to have received the atonement. (Rom. v. 11.) Hence Paul, speaking of the privilege of the church, saith, "Ye are come to the blood of sprinkling." The blood of the heifer shed was not sufficient; it must be sprinkled. The blood of Christ is not only shed, but sprinkled, speaking peace from God to the sinner, and speaking of covenant faithfulness to God, in the infinite fulness of Christ's merits. Seven times performing the sprinkling of the blood of the heifer may probably mean, as Scripture numbers sometimes do, an indefinite number for a definite, by way of shewing the importance of it. The number seven is certainly used in Scripture with peculiar honour. The seven days of creation, the seventh day for the Sabbath, the seven times seven for the Sabbatical or Jubilee year, and the seventh day becoming an emblem of the everlasting Sabbath of heaven; all these are very high evidences of the peculiar honour conferred on the number. But no special reason otherwise that I know of is given in the word of God for the consecration of seven to sacred things.

Sixthly, the heifer was to be wholly burnt, no part nor portion exempted. So Christ is a whole Saviour. They that are looking to him for salvation must wholly look. "Is Christ divided?" saith the apostle. The completeness of acceptance in Jesus renders it essentially necessary that his people should look only to him, for the everlasting acceptance of their persons in him. "If righteousness come by the law, then Christ is dead in vain." (Gal. ii. 21.)

Seventhly, the whole congregation are said to be alike interested in this heifer, both in providing it, and in the enjoyment of the privileges of it. So the Lord Jesus is said "to have given himself a ransom for all, to be testified in due time." (1 Tim. ii. 6.) And as we do not read in any other part of this ordinance being appointed to be observed but once, so nothing could more blessedly point out the everlasting efficacy of that "one offering of the body of Jesus Christ once offered, whereby he hath perfected for ever them that are sanctified." (Heb. x. 14.)

The Jews have a tradition, that this one heifer, with the ashes of the water of purification, lasted for near a thousand years, until the time of the captivity. But of this we have no Scriptural authority. It is sufficient for Christians to behold Christ both preached to the ear, and set forth to the eye, in type and figure, under the law. And it is doubly blessed, under the gospel, to behold the whole fulfilled in the person, blood, and righteousness of the Lord Jesus Christ. The Lord give his people grace, while beholding the law as having "a shadow of good things to come," to know that Christ is the substance, and that Christ is indeed "the end of the law for righteousness to every one that believeth!"

REED

We read of Ezekiel's reed, Ezek. xl. 3. which was six cubits and three inches; that is, about three yards and a little more of our English measure. But the word is not unfrequently used in Scripture figuratively. Thus Egypt, an account of her inability to Israel, is called a reed. (2 Kings xviii. 21.) Humble believers in Christ are called bruised reeds; concerning which it is blessedly spoken of the Lord Jesus, "that he will not break the braised reed, nor quench the smoking flax"--meaning, that the tender and frail mind in the first awakenings of grace, though it be unable of itself to stand no more than the bruised reed Jesus will not break, but support; and the warmth of affection in the regenerated soul, though it hath no flame, and only sends forth the risings like the smoke of burning flax, Jesus will not suffer to be put out. It is in both a day of small things; but it is a day Jesus will not despise. He will raise the bruised reed to a great tree, like the cedar of Lebanon, and he will kindle a flame in the smoking flax, that by his perpetual quickening shall burn with great power and brightness for ever. (See Isa. xlii. Matt. xii. 18-20.) We read of a reed put into our Lord's hand, in the hall of Pilate, by way of mock royalty; but this it should seem to have been of the rod kind. (Matt. xxvii. 29.) How little, did they think that both the crown of thorns and the reed, were emblems of the Lord Jesus's character as the Messiah. Never was there any but Jesus crowned with thorns; for though all his people feel the briars and the thorns, yet it was he, and he only, on whom and in whom the sentence at the fall was to be completely fulfilled. "Thorns also and thistles shall it bring forth to thee." (Gen. iii. 18.) And little did they think that when they had crowned him with thorns, and put the reed in "his right hand, JEHOVAH had that day set him for his king upon his holy hill of Zion. What a beautiful observation the apostles made upon the whole of these events, Acts iv. 24-31.

REELAIAH

One of the priests which returned to Jerusalem from the captivity of Babylon, Ezra ii. 2. Probably the name is derived from Rahal; astonishment-and Jah, the Lord.

REFUGE

This word is of very plain and obvious signification; and it is blessed to see in the Scriptures of truth how sweetly accommodating all the persons of the GODHEAD are brought home to the believer's heart under the figurative language of refuge. Hence in allusion to God the Father, Moses was commissioned to tell the church this grand and all-supporting truth--"The eternal God is thy refuge; and underneath are the everlasting arms: and he shall thrust out the enemy before thee, and shall say, Destroy them." (Deut. xxxiii. 27.) And the Lord Jesus Christ is the immediate refuge of his people, for he is said to be their hiding place and their covert from the storm and tempest. And how truly blessed is it to discover, that in his person, blood, and righteousness, as the glorious Head and Mediator of his redeemed, they are secretly and securely hid with Christ in God; so that neither law nor justice, sin nor Satan, death nor hell, the world nor the grave, can come to injure them. (Ps. xxxii. 7. Isa. xxxii. 2.) And no less so is God the eternal Spirit, in his own sovereign power and GODHEAD; for he by his gracious influences stamps the whole authority of redemption on the hearts of his people, gives them his earnest of the promised possession, and effectually seals their souls unto the day of redemption. (2 Cor. v. 5. Eph. l. 13.)

Under this article of refuge, it will be proper to notice those cities of refuge, which the Lord appointed under the Old Testament dispensation, as a shelter for the manslayer who unintentionally killed another, and hated him not in times past. If the reader will consult the Scriptures which relate to those cities of refuge he will find a very ample account Num. xxxv. 9. to the end; Deut. xix 1, --13. Josh. xx. throughout. And when he hath read the several particulars there recorded, he will discover that those cities of refuge were wholly intended to screen the unintentional murderer. And so exact was the law to be regarded, that on the poor fugitive's arrival at the suburbs of either of those cities, the congregation was to proceed on the subject of enquiry; and if any malice pretense was found in the mind towards the person he had murdered, the law enjoined that he should be taken even from the altar, and put to death.

And this security, even to the unintentional murderer, continued only while he remained in the city of refuge; for if he was found without the suburbs, the avenger of blood might by law kill him.

We are informed that the Israelites were so much interested in following up the divine commands concerning those cities of refuge, that the magistrates once in every year made a point to examine the roads leading to those cities from every direction, and to have them put in perfect repair, that no obstruction might be found to stop the fugitive in his flight from the avenger of blood pursuing him. And it is said, that at every opening there was placed a direction-post with the word Miklat upon it, (meaning refuge) as if to say, this is the way to the city of refuge. A beautiful type of the ministers of our God, who are supposed to be always as watchmen upon the walls of Zion crying aloud to sinners, murderers of their own souls, "to flee unto Christ as a refuge to lay hold of, and as an anchor to the soul both sure and stedfast within the vail." (Heb. vi. 18, 19.)

There was somewhat very significant in the names of those cities, and it is not fanciful to remark their allusion to the purpose for which they were appointed. They are called Kedesh, Shechem, Kirjotharba, or Hebron. These were on this side Jordan. And on the other side, by Jericho eastward, there was Bezer in the wilderness of Ramoth in Gilead, and Golan in Bashan.

If, as we cannot but conclude from all the other parts of Scripture, that as every thing under the law typified the Lord Jesus Christ, so these cities of refuge had an eye to him, as the only shelter for soul-murderers, then we shall find somewhat remarkable in the names of those cities. Kedesh which signifies holy, was a beautiful memorandum of him concerning whom the Holy Ghost saith, by the apostle, Heb. vii. 26. "Such an High Priest became us, who is holy, harmless, undefiled, separate from sinners, and made higher than the heavens. Shechem is the Hebrew for shoulder, or of one consent." And it is so translated in the margin of the Bible in Zeph. iii. 9. which see. And it is no violence to the expression to make application of this word to him whose government was declared to be upon his shoulder, Isa. ix. 6. line of the old writers, Raphelius, makes a very striking observation concerning this expression of the government being said to be upon Christ's shoulder; because said he we carry burdens on our shoulders, therefore Christ is said to carry his. And this he did when he became the Almighty burden-bearer of the sins of his people. The third name of those cities of refuge, Kirjath-arba, which is Hebron. (Kirjath-arba means the city of four, from Arba, four) Hebron signifies unity, fellowship, concord, or the like. And when sinners are brought into an union with Jesus, they are said to "have fellowship with the Father, and with his Son Jesus Christ." (1 John i. 3.)

And the names of the three cities on the other side of Jordan were not less striking in allusion to Christ. Bezer or Bazar was used for a market place among the Eastern nations in after-ages; and Betzer meant an inclosure: so that in either sense the word is striking. As the man-slayer found in this city of refuge a blessed exchange, and a safe inclosure, both under one, so soul-murderers, when taking shelter in Christ, barter their sins for his righteousness, and find peace and safety in the blood of his cross. So Ramoth and Golan both read with an eye to Jesus, as they express exaltation and joy, may be supposed to imply the raising up of the depressed spirits of a sinner when fleeing to Christ for refuge, and finding him all he

REGEM - REGENERATION

stands in need of, as well as that "joy and peace in belie ving, when abounding in hope through the power of the Holy Ghost."

It is very blessed in reading the Old Testament Scripture, to discover in every part of it so much of the New. And when we are enabled, by the sweet teaching of the Holy Ghost, to discern Christ thus preached to our fathers in type and figure, what an infinite importance do such views tend to convey, when we find both in law and prophets every minute circumstance pointing to him who is "the end of the law for righteousness to every one that believeth."

REGEM

The son of Jahdai, 1 Chron. ii. 47. If derived from Ragam, the name means he that stones."

REGEM-MELECH

One of the men sent to the house of God to enquire about the days of the fast, Zech. vii. 2. Who this man was doth not seem clear: not an Israelite, I should think, for the name is of the Chaldeans, and means to stone the king. Melek, king--and Regem, to stone.

REGENERATION

This is the word, and the doc trine connected with it, which hath been, and ever will be, a stumbling-block to the whole world of mere natural men, who receive not the things of the "Spirit of God, for they are foolishness unto them, neither can they know them, because they are spiritually discerned." (1 Cor. ii. 14.)

The carnal mind, in every age of the church, hath been disposed to receive the doctrine of re generation as a mere figure of speech. They are unable to explain it upon any principles of their own, and therefore wish of all things to class it under the character of metaphor or parable. But it will be found to all the unawakened and unregenerated in eternity an awful reality to them. I well remember to have heard it said concerning a prelate of the highest rank in the establishment, who in the close of life expressed himself on this subject in these very solemn words: "I have read (said he) much on the doctrine of regeneration, and I have heard much upon it; should hope, it is after all, but a mere figure of speech; but if it be a real truth, I can only say, that I known nothing of it in my own experience." What a dreadful confession this for a man in his dying hours!

Our blessed Lord, who brought life and immortality to light by his Gospel, brought this doctrine of regeneration also, as a fundamental part of that Gospel, to the full and complete testimony of it in his conversation with Nicodemus the Jew. (John iii. 1-21.) I beg the reader to pay a close attention to this blessed Scripture, looking up to God the Holy Ghost to render it plain and intelligible; and, under his divine teaching, the doctrine itself cannot fail to appear in its true light.

The holy Scriptures, with one voice, declare, that man by the fall of Adam lost all apprehension of the divine nature; he became virtually dead in trespasses and sins: so that the recovery from hence could only be effected by the quickening influences of the Holy Ghost. Hence every son and daughter of Adam is born, as to spiritual faculties, in a state of spiritual death, and is as incapable, until an act of regeneration hath passed in quickening to a new and spiritual life, of any act of spiritual apprehension, as a dead body is to any act of animal life.

Scripture describes the different degrees of death in a clear and distinct manner. The death of the body is the separation of soul and body, so that the soul, which is the life of the body, if fled, leaves the body lifeless, and without any longer principle of consciousness. "The body (saith an apostle) without the spirit is dead." (Jam. ii. 26.)

Spiritual death is the death of sin, by reason of the want of the quickening Spirit of God in the soul; so that as Christ is the life of the soul, every Christ-less soul is a dead soul. Eternal death is the separation both of soul and body from God for ever: and this is the state of the unreclaimed and unregenerate wicked.

Now then, as in the first instance, while the soul actuates the body that body is alive, but without; the soul so actuating, the body would be dead; so in the second, unless Christ, who is the life of the soul, actuates the soul by regeneration, that soul continues dead as by original transgression was induced. And in the third, if living and dying without the blessed influence of regeneration, that soul and body must remain in a state of eternal death, and separation from God for ever.

Now, from this Scriptural statement of spiritual death, it will be easy to gather what is meant and implied by the doctrine of regeneration. It is, to all intents and purposes, in the spiritual faculties creating a new life, a new birth, a new nature: hence the Scriptures describe the recovery from sin under the strongest expressions. "You, (saith the apostle, speaking to the regenerated Ephesians, chap. ii. 1.) hath he quickened, who were dead in trespasses and sins." So again, ver. 5. "Even when we were dead in sins, hath he quickened us together with Christ." So again--"If any man be in Christ, he is a new creature." (2 Cor. v. 17.) And hence the apostle elsewhere saith, that our recovery to a state of grace, and the new life, is "not by works of righteousness which we have done, but by the washing of regeneration, and renewing of the Holy Ghost, shed on us abundantly through Jesus Christ our Lord." (Tit. iii. 5, 6.) I only add an humble prayer to God to grant to all his renewed members the sweetest testimony in their own experience to this most blessed truth, that they may know that they are born again, "not of corruptible seed, but of incorruptible, by the word of our God, which liveth and abideth for ever." (1 Pet. i. 23.)

REHABIAH

One of the Levites, 1 Chron. xxiii. 17. His name seems to be derived from Rachab, breadth, or extent--and therefore joined to Jah, it may be supposed to mean an enlargement in my Lord.

REHOB

King of Zobah in Syria, 2 Sam. viii. 3. It should seem that the name is derived from Rachab, breadth. There was also a Rehob among the captives of Israel which returned from Babylon, Neh. x. 11. And there was a city of Asher called Rehob, bordering upon Syria, on the road to Hamath. See Josh. xix. 28. Num. xiii. 11. The Syrians called it Bethrohob. See 2 Sam. x. 6.

REHOBOAM

Son of Solomon, and successor to his kingdom. His name seems to be a compound of Rehob and Am, the people-- probably derived from Rachab, and if so, it will be the enlargement of the people. We have his history at large from 1 Kings xi. 43, where it begins, to the rebellion against him by Jeroboam, where it ends in his death, 1 Kings xiv. 31.

REHOBOTH

We read of a river of this name Gen. xxxvi. 37; where one Saul, a descendant of Esau, resided on the borders of it. If the word be taken from Rachab, it means enlargement or extent.

RHESA

The son of Zorahabel in the ancestry of Christ, Luke iii. 27. Probably derived from Ratzah, will.

REHUM - REMPHAN

REHUM

We meet with two of this name in Scripture, one a Levite, son of Beri, who returned from Babylon with the captives, Ezra ii. 2.--and another Rehum, the chancellor. See Ezra iv. 9. The name is Syriac, and means friendly or merciful.

REI

A person of some eminency in the house of David. (See 1 Kings i. 8.) If derived from Raha, friend, Rei. will mean my friend.

REKEM

There were two of this name, Rekem, one of the five kings of Median, slain by Israel, Num. xxxi. 8. and Rekem the son of Hebron, 1 Chron. ii. 43. If from Racah, it means pain. There was a city of this name also, Josh. xviii. 27.

REMALIAH

Father of Pekah, king of Israel, (2 Kings xv. 25.) If the word be a compound, and derived from Ram-am, it means exalted of the Lord. If otherwise, from Ramah, with the preposition Lamed, it may mean the reverse, namely, rejected of the Lord.

REMEMBERANCER--Or Recorder

We find this officer, in the court of David, in the person of Jehoshaphat. (2 Sam. viii. 16.) See also the margin in this verse. I pause over the title and office purposely to notice an infinitely higher in the same department, in the court and church of the spiritual David. I mean in the person, office, and work of God the Holy Ghost. He is the Remembrancer indeed, in the sweet and most blessed sense of the word, for so the Lord Jesus testified of him. "The Comforter, (said Jesus) which is the Holy Ghost, whom the Father will send in my name, he shall teach you all things, and bring all things to your remembrance, whatsoever I have said unto you, (John xiv. 26.)

It will be the reader's wisdom, when at any time he feels his soul refreshed with the remembrance of past mercies, in the reviving, upholding, quickening, comforting, and strengthening manifestations of divine love in Jesus, to call this blessed office of the Holy Ghost into recollection, and to ascribe the whole of his joys and refreshments to this gracious source. And what a gratifying thought is it to the true believer in Christ, to consider that from the indwelling residence of the Spirit in the hearts of the Lord's people, there is not a blessing or mercy they enjoy in Jesus but the Holy Ghost gives the relish to the soul in the moment of enjoyment, and makes the after recollection of it again blessed to the soul by the exercise of this divine office. For as the person of God the Holy Ghost is infinite, he dwells in the whole body of Christ's mystical members, and carries on in the hearts of each and of all every office, to teach, to lead, to guide, into all truth, and to bring all things to their remembrance what soever Jesus hath told them. Blessed and almighty Spirit, I would say, fill my heart, my house, the church, and every member of Jesus with thyself, and glorify the Lord Christ in all sweet remembrances! Amen.

REMETH

A city so called. There are two cities of this name, one a city of Simeon, in the south, and another of Issachar. (See Josh. xix. 8. 21.) The word is the same as Ramoth, signifying high or lofty.

REMMON

A city, Josh. xix. 7. And there was a Rammon a village, about fifteen miles north from Jerusalem.

REMPHAN

We nowhere meet with the name of this idol in the sacred Scriptures but in one place, and that is in Stephen's address before the

Sanhedrim. (Acts vii. 43.) And in this very passage which Stephen is quoting, it is from the writings of the prophet Amos, v. 25, 26.--but it is remarkable that Stephen doth not quote it as the original is, or even the translation, but in the place of Chiun substitutes Remphan. However it is very evident, from the name of Moloch, and the days of Amos's ministry what species of idolatry it was to which the whole referred. If the reader will look at a passage much about the same period, 2 Kings xvii. 29, 30, he will find that the fashion of the day respecting idolatry was at the height. "Every nation, (we are told,) made gods of their own." The men of Babylon made Succoth-benoth; and the men of Cush made Nergal; and the men of Hamath made Ashima; and the Avites made Nibhaz and Tartak; and the Sepharvites burnt their children in the fire to Adrammelech, and Anammalach, the gods of Sepharvaim. It is probable that Adram, and Anam, or On, were the ancient idols of Egypt: Potipherah was the priest of the latter. (Gen. xli. 45.) What an awful portrait of human depravity doth the whole afford! See Succoth-Benoth. See Moloch.

RENEW and RENEWING

I pause at these words purposely to drop an observation or two on a point of so much consequence, in the Christian life, as the blessed effects of these divine operations in the heart, by God the Holy Ghost. His is the gracious work to renew the mind of every sinner, when by his grace he makes willing in the day of his power. He opens the eye to see, and the heart to feel, the dreadful consequences of sin, and the infinite importance of salvation. His is the blessed act to bring the heart savingly acquainted with the person, offices, characters, and relations of the Lord Jesus Christ. His is the delightful ministry to bring the distressed soul under the comforting influences of his supporting love, and to shew the heart, under desponding circumstances, that there is more in Jesus's blood and righteousness to save, than in all our sins to destroy. And by bringing home these soul-strengthening, soul-refreshing views of Christ, and applying them with sovereign power to the heart, "he fills the heart with joy unspeakable and full of glory." I hope the reader hath not now for the first time to learn acquaintance with this divine office of the Holy Ghost, but can say with the apostle, "the Lord, according to his mercy, hath saved us, by the washing of regeneration, and renewing of the Holy Ghost, which he hath shed on us abundantly through Jesus Christ our Saviour." (Tit. iii. 5, 6.)

REPENTANCE

This, in idea, is supposed to be perfectly understood by every one; but in reality very few have a true scriptural apprehension of it. Re pentance, like faith, is the sole gift of God. The act itself is so impossible to be assumed or taken up by any, that it is equally easy to alter the colour of the hair, or the features of the countenance, as to change the heart. Jesus, it is said, (Acts v. 31.) "Is exalted a Prince and a Saviour, for to give repentance to Israel and forgiveness of sins." What therefore Christ gives cannot be the work or the merit of man. There may be, and there often is, a false repentance, which men of no religion may possess, but which is as distinguishable from true repentance as darkness from light, when the principles of both are analyzed. False repentance is that which springs from a sorrow for the consequences, not the causes of sin. True repentance is that which flows from the consciousness of the sin itself. The man of godly sorrow sorrows for having offended God. The man of worldly sorrow sorrows that his sin hath brought punishment. The one is the effect of fear; the other of love. The repentance for the consequence of sin goes no further than as it dreads the punishment: the repentance for the cause of sin becomes the continued gracious sorrow of the heart. These

REPHAH

observations may be sufficient to mark the very different features of both, and under grace enable any one to understand the vast distinction.

REPHAH

Of the family of Benjamin. (1 Chron. vii. 25.) The name seems to be derived from Rapha, medicine, or healer.

REPHAIM

See Raphaim.

REPHIDIM

An encampment of Israel in the wilderness, Exod. xvii. 1. remarkable for the murmurings of the people grace in giving them water. See Rock. The word is derived from Raphad, rest--hence in the plural, Rephidim, rests.

REPROACH

The Scriptural sense of reproach is not so generally understood. It means, in the fullest sense of the word, reproach for God or God's cause. Thus Joshua, when circumcising Israel at Gilgal, is said to have taken away their reproach. The Lord God said, This day I have rolled away the reproach of Egypt from off you." (Josh. v. 9.) Hence the place was called Gilgal, rolling away. Similar passages we have Gen. xxx. 23. Isa. iv. 1. Isa. liv. 4.) In a gospel sense, the reproach for Christ's name is when a believer is content to be considered vile, rather than relinquish his christian calling. The Holy Ghost, by Peter, pronounceth peculiar happiness on such as are "reproached for the sake of Christ." (1 Pet. iv. 14.)

REPROBATE

The apostle to the Romans, (chap. i. 28.) hath this awful expression, "God gave them over to a reprobate mind," The doctrine of reprobation is of all others the most solemn. The expression of the apostle of God giving them over to it doth not convey that the Lord makes them reprobate, but leaves them in it. It is they that have gone on to harden their heart, and they are left in that hardness of heart; for God doth not give grace to bring them out of it, therefore they are given over, or given up, in being left alone to this state of reprobation.

It should seem that the word is equivalent to that of rejection; such as in the case of Cain, Gen. iv. 5; such as Esau, Heb. xii. 16, 17. Hence the prophet, speaking of all such, saith, "reprobate silver shall men call them, because the Lord hath rejected them." (Jer. vi. 30.) Awful doctrine! (See Jude 4-13. Tit. i. 16. See vagabond.)

RESPECT

By respect to persons or things, in Scripture language, is meant the preferring one to another. It means therefore distinguishing grace; hence it is said, "the Lord had respect unto Abel and his offering; but unto Cain and his offering he had no respect? (Gen. iv. 4, 5.) We are told elsewhere the cause, in that Abel offered his offering by faith in Christ, Cain did not. (Heb. xi. 14.) Hence it was in Christ, and for his sake only, the difference of respect was shewn. So again, it is said, God is no respecter of persons, (Acts x. 34.) Certainly not: for it is not the person of the believer, but the Lord Jesus Christ in that believer, or by virtue of JEHOVAH beholding the person of Christ in that believer, that is the sole cause of acceptation. This is a sweet thought! Though personally considered JEHOVAH hath no respect to the person of the poor believer, yet beholding and for his sake respects him in the Lord and blesseth him in Jesus.

REST

Every one knows what it is to rest from labour, from weariness of body and mind. And every one who is acquainted with the Bible cannot but know that there is a rest promised to the people of God. (Heb. iv. 9.)

But the sweetest of all thoughts to a poor, distressed, weather-beaten sinner, is to behold Christ himself this rest for him to lie down upon for ever. The Holy Ghost, by Isaiah, gave account of this rest in Jesus when he said, "This is the rest wherewith ye may cause the weary to rest, and this is the refreshing." (Isa. xxviii. 12. See also Ps. cxvi. 7. Matt. xi. 28, 29.)

RESTORE

The Scriptural sense of restoration is to give back to its rightful owner whatsoever had been taken away. And nothing can more fully come up to this standard, than when Christ made restoration to God for his people of all that they had taken away, or injured God in. Our nature by sin and transgression, had robbed God of his glory and man of his happiness. The glory of God was robbed in the injury, and dishonour done to his attributes, to his law, and to his justice. When therefore Jesus restored that he took not away, as he saith himself, by the spirit of prophecy, (Ps. lxix. 6.)--he restored glory to the attributes of God, he restored more than an equivalent to the law of God by his personal obedience, and to the justice of God by his personal sufferings and death. And in as much as the obedience and death of the Lord Jesus, from the dignity of his person, and the infinite worth and merit of his obedience and sacrifice, became infinitely more valuable than the everlasting obedience and death of all the creation of God would have been had both been so offered, God was more glorified by those personal acts of the Lord Jesus Christ, than he had ever been dishonored by man's disobedience and rebellion.

And as the Lord Jesus thus restored to God his glory and honor, so he restored to man thereby his happiness. Man had been robbed of God's favour, God's images God's blessing. All these were fully, completely, and most satisfactorily restored, by the person and redemption-work of the Lord Jesus. God's favour is procured, God's image is restored, and God's everlasting blessing is obtained, by the blood of the cross. And what endears the whole is, that it is so obtained as that it can be lost no more. Such is the Scriptural sense of restoration by the Lord Jesus!

RESURRECTION

Here is a word of words! The doctrine of which, and the eventful consequence of which, involves in it all our high hopes and expectations of happiness for the life that now is, and that which is to come. The resurrection is the key-stone in the arch of the Christian faith: so that as the apostle Paul strongly and unanswerably reasons, "if there be no resurrection of the dead, then is Christ not risen; and if Christ be not risen, then is our preaching vain, and our faith is also vain." Yea, saith the apostle, (as if he had said, and that is not the worst consequence if the doctrine be not true, for then) "we are found false witnesses of God, because we have testified of God that he raised up Christ whom he raised not up, if so be that the dead rise not; for if the dead rise not, then is Christ not raised; and if Christ be not raised your faith is vain, ye are yet in your sins; and then all they that are fallen asleep in Christ are perished." (1 Cor. xv. 14.-18.)

The subject therefore, is infinitely important and the apostle hath placed the doctrine in the clearest light possible. It is reduced to this single point--if Christ be not risen, then there is no resurrection of the dead; but if Christ be himself risen, then is he become "the first-fruits of them that slept." For by his own resurrection he gives full proof to all the doctrines he taught; and as he declared himself to be the resurrection and the life, and promised that whosoever lived and believed in him he would raise up at the last day, and in confirmation of it arose himself; hence it must undeniably follow that our resurrection is involved and secured in his. He said himself, "because I live, ye shall live also." (See John xi. 25.

26, &c; v. 21.-29; xiv. 19.)

Concerning the fact itself of our Lord's resurrection I do not think it necessary to enlarge. The New Testament is so full of the interesting: particulars, and the truth of it is so strongly confirmed by the in numerable witnesses both of the living and the dead, yea, God himself giving his testimony to the truth of it, that in a work of this kind I consider it a superfluous service to bring forward any proof. I rather assume it as a thing granted, and set it down as one of the plainest matters of fact the world ever knew, that Christ is risen from the dead. I shall therefore only subjoin under this article the observations which naturally arise out of this glorious truth, in proof also that as Christ is indeed risen from the dead, he arose not as a private per son, but the public Head of his church, which is his body, and thereby became the first fruits of them that slept.

The first view of Christ's resurrection, as connecting our resurrection with it, is the full assurance it brought with it that the debt of sin Christ under took, as our Surety, to pay, was discharged. For never surely would the prison-doors of the grave have been thrown open, and Christ let out, had not the law of God, and the justice of God both been satisfied. In that glorious moment when Christ arose from the dead, he proved the whole truth of what he had taught. "Destroy this tem ple; (he said, and he spake of the temple of his body) and in three days I will raise it up." (See John ii. 18-22.) And hence God the Father on this occasion is called the God of peace, who brought again from the dead our Lord Jesus Christ," because by the blood of the everlasting covenant he had now fulfilled the contract on his part and God now fulfilled it in his, and in confirmation is here called the God of peace. (Heb. xiii. 20)

The next view of Christ's resurrection, as including in it ours, is that as the man Christ Jesus arose, so assuredly must the bodies of all his redeemed. And as it was said by Moses to Pharaoh concerning Israel's deliverance from Egypt, "not an hoof shall be left behind," (Exod. x. 26,) so it may be said of Israel's seed, not an hair of their head shall perish, much less the humblest and least of Christ's mystical body shall be lost in the ruins of the world, which at the resurrection is then to be burnt. And this resurrection of the bodies of Christ's members is secured by virtue of their union and oneness with their glorious Head; for so the character of the covenant runs--"If the Spirit of him that raised up Jesus from the dead dwell in you, he that raised up Christ from the dead shall also quicken your mortal bodies by his spirit that dwelleth in you." (Rom. viii. 11.) Sweet thought to the believer! He may truly say, I shall arise, not simply by the sovereign power of that voice that raiseth the dead, but by his Spirit which unites me to himself now, and will then quicken me to the new life in him forever. And this is the meaning of that blessed promise of God the Father to the Son--"Thy dead men shall live;" yea, saith the Lord Jesus, in answer as it were, and in a way of confirmation, "together with my dead body shall they arise." And then comes the call-- "Awake and sing ye that dwell in the dust, for thy dew [the warm, reanimating, life-giving dew of Jesus in resurrection power to glory, as in regenerating power first in grace from the womb of the morning, in which Christ had the dew from his youth; Ps. cx. 3.] is as the dew of herbs, and the earth shall cast out her dead." (Isa. xxvi. 19.) Beautiful figure! the dew of herbs revives those plants which appear through the winter like dry sticks, and not the least view of herbage remains. Son of man! can these sticks live? Such will be Christ's dew to the bodies of his people. Oh, precious, precious Jesus!

One thought more on this subject of Christ's resurrection, and of his church so highly interested in it, and that is, that as Jesus's resurrection is the cause of ours, and he himself accomplisheth ours by his Spirit as a germ dwelling in us, so the blessedness of our resurrection is, that as Christ's identical body arose, so shall ours. "He will change our vile body, that it may be fashioned like unto his glorious body." Changed it will be from what it was sown in weakness, because it will be raised in power but its identity, consciousness, reality, will be the same. Here again we feel constrained to cry out, Oh, precious, precious Lord Jesus! and to say with Job, "I know that my Redeemer (or, as the words are, my kinsman Redeemer) liveth, and that he shall stand at the latter day upon the earth. And though after my skin worms destroy this body, yet in my flesh shall I see God, whom I shall see for myself, and mine eyes shall behold, (for myself) and not another for me." (Job xix. 25-27.)

So much for the doctrine of the resurrection, and the unanswerable testimonies on which it is founded. The Lord strengthen all his people in the faith of it, seeing that by the resurrection of their Lord they are begotten "to this lively hope in Jesus, to an inheritance incorruptible, and undefiled, and that fadeth not away, reserved in heaven for them who are kept by the power of God through faith unto salvation." (1 Pet. i. 3-5.)

REUBEN

Eldest son of Jacob by Leah. We have his history from (Gen. xxix. 32.) through the relation of the patriarchs. His name is derived from Rahah, to see--and Ben, son; so that the compound may be, the son of vision.

REUEL

Son of Esau, (Gen. xxxvi. 4.) The name is from Reuah, friend--and El, God.

REUMAH

Concubine to Nahor. (Gen. xxii. 24.) If from Ramam, the name means lofty or high.

REZEPH

A city of Syria. (2 Kings xix. 12.)

REZIN

King of Syria. (2 Kings xv. 37.) Probably derived from Ratza, meaning a freedom, or some what voluntary.

RHEGIUM

A city of Italy mentioned in Paul's travels. (Acts xxviii. 13.)

RHODA

A name ever-memorable from Peter's history, in the angel delivering him from prison. The name in the original means rose. (Acts xii. 13, 14.)

RIBAI

Father of Ittai, one of David's worthies. (2 Sam. xxiii. 29.) If from Rebah, that multiplies.

RIBLAH

A city of Syria where judgment was given on Zedekiah, and where his eyes were put out. (2 Kings xxv. 6. Jer. lii. 9.) If from Rub, it means quarrel.

RIGHTEOUS and RIGHTEOUSNESS

It is very highly important and interesting to have clear apprehensions of the Scriptural meaning of the term righteous. What notions we annex to it is of little consequence if the word of God decides other wise. Certain it is, that in the world's dictionary the term righteous is very freely and commonly bestowed, and upon characters that call in question many of the Lord's declarations concerning sin, and the sinfulness of our fallen nature. It is highly important therefore to hear what the word of God saith on this point, and not lean upon the human opinion of vain men.

Now the Scriptures with one voice, and in the most unqualified and unaccommodating manner, declare that when the Lord looked "down from heaven upon the children of men, to see if there were any that did understand and seek after God," the result of that enquiry was, that "they were all gone aside, and altogether become filthy, that there was none that did good, no not one." (Ps. xiv. 2, 3.) And the apostle Paul quotes this passage, and confirms it by enlargement. (See Rom. iii. 1-19.)

It is in vain for any man to make an appeal against this decision. No comparative statement can, in the least, alter the case. No man, not a single man of the whole race of men sprung from Adam, can be an exception to this universal decree of God.

What then is the righteousness of the Scripture, and who is the righteous man before God? The answer is direct. None but the Lord Jesus Christ. He, and he only, is set forth under this title; and he alone is the Righteousness of his people. It is high treason to talk of any other; and it is equally high treason to talk of any comparative statement between man and man concerning righteousness. The account from heaven is, "All have sinned, and come short of God's glory. The whole world is become guilty before God. And by the deeds of the law can no flesh be justified before God." Hence, therefore, it undeniably follows that Christ is the only righteousness of his people; and he is what Scripture declares his name is, and shall be, JEHOVAH our Righteousness. (Jer. xxiii. 6.)

Now then the conclusion from this statement of Scripture is evidently this--if Jesus be the only righteousness of his people, either this is my right eousness, or I have none at all. Wholly sinful in myself, and wholly righteous in him I must be; or I have no part nor lot in this matter. If there be not in me a total renunciation of every thing the mistaken calculation of men calls righteousness, yea, more than this, if there be not a full and unreserved confession of universal sin and unworthiness in me, I cannot be wholly looking for acceptance to, and living wholly upon, the Lord Jesus Christ as the Lord my Righteousness. And the gospel knows no mixture, no mingling the righteousness of the sinner with the righteousness of the Saviour. "A little leaven leaveneth the whole lump." Blessed and happy souls who, from a deep conviction of the total corruption and depravity of their own nature, are resting all their high hopes of acceptance and justification before God in the perfect and complete righteousness of the Lord Jesus Christ; who behold him, and accept the authority of JEHOVAH for this well-grounded confidence of beholding him, and rest with full assurance of faith in him, as the Lord their righteousness; and to whose spirits the Holy Ghost bears witness that "he is made of God to them wisdom, righteousness, sanctification, and redemption, that, according as it is writ ten, he that glorieth let him glory in the Lord." (1 Cor. i. 30, 31.)

RIMMON

We meet with this word frequently in the Scripture. A City of Zebulun was called by this name, (1 Chron. vi. 77.) Also a rock to which the Benjamites retreated, (Judg. xx. 45.) And there was an idol of the Syrians so called. (See 2 Kings v. 18.) The name signifies somewhat great or greatness, from Ramam.

RIMMON PAREZ

A place where Israel encamped. (See Num. xxxix. 10.)

RING or RINGS

See Signet.

RINNAH

Son of Shimon, 1 Chron. iv. 20. If from Ranan, the name signifies song.

RIPHATH

Son of Gomer, Gen. x. 3. If from Raphah, the name means remedy.

RISSAH

A place of encampment to Israel, (Num. xxxiii. 21.) If from Rasah, it means watering as the dew.

RITHMAH

A place of encampment where Israel rested in the wilderness, (Num. xxxiii. 18.) Probably the place abounded with juniper trees, since the name signifies juniper.

RIVER

We read of the several rivers in Scripture, even from the garden of Eden. And as in those hot countries nothing was so highly valued, it is no wonder that the sacred writers made use of them so often figuratively. Hence we read of "the river of life, and the river of pleasures," and the like. But the most striking are those expressions in which all the persons of the GODHEAD are described under this metaphor. "There is a river, (saith the psalmist) the streams thereof make glad the city of God." (Ps. xlvi. 4.) God the Father is thus described, Jer. ii. 13. Ps. lxv. 9; God the Son is thus described, Song iv. 15, Zech. xiii. 1; and God the Holy Ghost, John vii. 38. and John iv. 14.

RIZPAH

Daughter of Aiah, Saul's concubine. (2 Sam. xxi. 10.) Perhaps the name is taken from Ratzpa heat or fire.

ROCK

This name is familiar to every one who is conversant with the things of nature. And in Scripture we meet with the continual mention of rocks by particular names, such as the rock of Horeb, the rock of Adullam, the rock of divisions, called Selahammah lekoth. See the margin of the Bible, 1 Sam. xxiii. But it would have been unnecessary in a work of this kind to have noticed the word had it not been for the special application of the term, in a figurative way and manner, to the person of the Lord Jesus Christ as the visible JEHOVAH He is, if I mistake not, the glorious person all along spoken of in the Old Testament Scripture, and explained most clearly in the New "as the rock whose work is perfect? Beautifully to this purpose doth Moses, the man of God, speak of him under this figure, "He is the rock, (saith Moses) his work is perfect; for all his ways are judgment: a God of truth, and without iniquity, just and right is he? And speaking of the defects of Israel, and his departure from the Lord, he saith, "he forsook God which made him, and lightly esteemed the rock of his salvation. Of the rock that begat thee, thou art unmindful, and hast forgotten God that formed thee." And then tracing the sad effects of their being brought into captivity by their enemies, to the cause of having forsaken their confidence in the Lord, Moses adds, "how should one chase a thousand, and two put ten thousand to flight, except their rock had sold them, and the Lord had shut them up? For their rock is not as our rock, even our enemies themselves being judges;" (Deut. xxxii. 4. 15. 18. 30, 31.)

But the most striking and particular use of the term rock, as a figure applied to Christ, is that we read in the eventful history of Israel, beginning at Horeb, (Exod. xvii. 6) where we find the Lord speaking unto Moses in those remarkable words; "Behold, I will stand before thee upon the rock in Horeb, and thou shalt smite the rock and there shall come water out of it, that the people may drink" Now it never would have been known to any farther extent concerning this miracle of grace, but that the Lord did here, as upon many other occasions, work a miracle to supply the pressing occasions and wants of his people, had not the Holy Ghost in his love and condescension to the church, thought fit to explain this transaction, and not only declared that it was Christ which wrought this miracle, but that this rock was Christ himself, If the reader will turn to the tenth chapter of Paul's First Epistle to the Corinthians, and first and following verses, he will behold the gracious comment of the Holy Ghost upon it. "Moreover brethren, (saith the apostle) I would not that ye should be ignorant how that all our fathers were under the cloud, and all passed through the sea, and were all baptized unto Moses in the cloud and in the sea, and did all eat the same spiritual meat, and did all drink the same spiritual drink; for they drank of that spiritual rock that followed them, and that rock was Christ." The margin of the Bible is stronger, for it saith that this rock went with them.

Now I beg the reader's close attention to this most interesting of all subjects. It is what intimately concerns true believers in Christ to have just and right apprehensions of what the Holy Ghost hath so graciously explained.

Nothing can be more certain than that the Gospel was preached to the church in type and figure to Israel then, as much and as fully as it is now to the true Israel in sum and substance. For so the Holy Ghost declares by Paul, (Heb. iv. 2.)--so that Christ was the one great ordinance and design of the whole. And whether he was preached as the rock, or the paschal lamb, or the manna, or the brazen serpent, all pointed to Jesus, and in him all had their completion.

But what I more particularly beg the reader to observe is, the manifestation that is made by the rock, and the streams flowing from it of God in Christ. The proclamation of the Lord was on this occasion,, "Behold, I will stand before thee upon the rock in Horeb;" intimating, as plain as words can shew, when opened to us by the Holy Ghost, that the whole dispensation is God in Christ. For as God in Christ was, and is, the foundation of all reconciliation, so is it God in Christ which was, and is, the source of all the blessings of redemption flowing there from. Hence the several manifestations of JEHOVAH in both Testaments of Scripture are all to this effect.

And as these several dispensations pointed all to Christ as the only possible supply for the church, so the church is uniformly considered under every estate, both in the Old Testament and New, as living by faith upon Jesus, and deriving all supplies from him. We are told that "they did all eat the same spiritual meat, and did all drink the same spiritual drink." There was no difference in the supply, neither in the privilege of the receivers, for all was Christ. Hence it proves that from the beginning all the grace the church would stand in need of through the whole period of time in every individual instance of it, this glorious Head of his body the church had in him; and whether it was the manna or the rook, he, and he alone, was the sum and substance of all. Sweet consideration to my soul! Hence, with one of old, I would say, "when my heart is overwhelmed, lead me to the rock that is higher than I." (Ps. lxi. 2.)

ROD

The holy Scriptures have a variety of meanings concerning this word. We perfectly well understand the sense if taken naturally. A rod may be formed from all the various trees of the wood. But when it is used figuratively, the meaning is not so clear. Thus the Lord Jesus himself is called a rod out of the stem of Jesse. (Isa. xi. 1.) And his church is called the rod of his inheritance. (Ps. lxxiv. 2. Jer. x. 16.) Sometimes the expression is made use of to denote the exercise of the Lord's power. Thus speaking of his enemies he saith, "Thou shalt break them with a rod of iron." (Ps. ii. 9.) And by the exercise of it for his people, he shall make them willing in the day of his power." (Ps. cx. 3.) And the

Psalmist comforts himself in the Lord's exercise of it over him when he saith "thy rod and thy staff they comfort me." (Ps. xxiii. 4.) I refer to the Scripture for the general account of the rod "of Moses and Aaron's rod that budded," and the like. (Exod. iii. &c. Num. xvii, 17.)

ROGELIM

A place in Gilead, the residence of Barzillai (See 2 Sam. xvii. 27.) Probably the same as Enrogel, the fountain of Rogel.

ROHGAH

Son of Shamer, (1 Chron. vii. 34.) If from Ravah, to drink-and Hagah, to speak, the name, it should seem, means drunk, or filled with a fulness for discourse.

ROLL

A sort of skin for making records upon. Before the art of printing, this was the method of forming registers, and making memorandums. Hence we are told that the prophet Jeremiah was commanded to take the roll of a book, and write all the words which the Lord had said unto him concerning Israel and Judah; and that Baruch wrote upon a roll, from the mouth of Jeremiah, all the words of the Lord. (Jer. xxxvi. 1, &c.) So Ezekiel's visions were written in a roll, and the Lord caused him to eat it; intimating, no doubt figuratively, the durable impression the words of the Lord made upon his mind. (See Ezek. chap. ii. iii. Rev. x. 9. See also Jer. xv. 16.)

ROSH

One of the sons of Benjamin, (Gen. xlvi. 21.) Rosh means head. Probably, therefore, this son of Benjamin became the head of a family.

RUHAMAH

See Ammi.

RUTH

A well-known name in Scripture. In the original it signifies, one that is filled or elevated. She was by birth of Moab. And when Elimelech, with his wife Naomi, and his two sons, Mahlon and Chillon, left the land of Bethlehem-judah, and went down into Moab, there Chilion married Ruth. And at the death of Elimelech, and Mahlon, and Chilion, Naomi and Ruth left Moab for Bethlehem-judah; where, after a time, Ruth was married to Boaz, from which union sprang Obed; and from hence, in a direct line, sprang Christ after the flesh. So that Ruth becomes an interesting character, because her history doth not lead to endless genealogies, but leads directly to the Lord Jesus Christ; and not only is Ruth meriting this attention from being found among the ancestors of Christ, but also we behold in it a sweet type, in her recovery from Moab to Bethlehem, of the call of the Gentile church, and the union of both Jew and Gentile in Christ.

The Book of Ruth, which the Holy Ghost hath been pleased to give the church in her name, is a blessed portion, though short, of divine truths; and beside the historical part it bears in the events of the church it forms a beautiful allegory of divine and spiritual things. The Jews have never disputed that it is of the canon of Scripture; but in their Bibles they place it different from ours. We subjoin it to the book of Judges, and very properly so, because what took place in the house of Elimelech, as is recorded, happened in the days of the Judges; but the Jews have thought proper to call it one of the five Migilloth, or volumes--that is, as they place and number them," Solomon's Songs, Ruth, Lamentations of Jeremiah, Ecclesiastes, and Esther." It is more than likely that the Prophet Samuel was the writer of the book of Ruth. There is a similarity in style and manner, and in a few passages in the phrases. (See Ruth i. 17. with I Sam, iii. 17. xiv. 44.-xx. 43. See also 2 Sam. iii. 9. 35.)

RUTH - RUTH

I cannot close this account of Ruth without begging the reader, whenever he peruseth this precious portion of the word of God, to be on the lookout for the Lord Jesus. The book begins with an ac count of a famine in the land of Bethlehem-judah, which means the land of bread, and which inclines the family of this certain man Elimelech, whose name signifies my God a king, to go down, into Moab. We know that a certain man, even our first father Adam, did so, when by transgression he lost Eden; and all the children of Adam, like Mahlon and Chilion, whose names signify sickness and consumption, prove the sick and consumptive stock from whence they sprung. Nothing but union with Christ can bring us back to the Bethlehem of our almighty Judah; and nothing but salvation by Christ can restore to us our justly forfeited privileges. Some sweet views of Jesus the book of Ruth presents to us on these points. May the Lord bless it to the reader!

S

SABACHTHANI

See Eli Eli.

SABAOTH

We meet with this word twice in the New testament. (Rom. ix. 29. and Jam. v. 4.) Perhaps the word might be more properly read Zabaoth, armies, from Tzaba, army, (Jer. xi. 20.) And when joined to the incommunicable name of JEHOVAH, it forms together that glorious title The Lord of hosts, or armies. And when we call to mind that the whole creation of God are his armies, what a sense of greatness and glory do such ideas awaken in the mind! It may serve in some measure to teach us the reverence Moses, the man of God, endeavoured to impress the children of Israel with when he proclaimed JEHOVAH under these characters--"that thou mayest fear (said Moses) this glorious and fearful name, the Lord thy God." (Deut. xxviii. 58.)

SABBATH

This was the original name first used by the Hebrews for the Lord's day. It is indeed an Hebrew word, and signifies repose or rest; and hence Christ, "who is the rest wherewith JEHOVAH causeth the weary to rest, and who is their refreshing." (Isa. xxviii. 12.) is the very Sabbath of the soul. See Christ's invitation under this character. (Matt. xi. 28 30.) It is worthy remark that Noah, a type of Christ in the ark, is so called, from Nuach, which signifies rest. Some indeed derive his name from Nacham, consolation. But in either sense, or in both, it is blessed to eye Christ in the type. Hence the psalmist saith, (Ps. cxvi. 7.) "Return unto thy rest, O my soul, for the Lord hath dwelt bountifully with thee." In the original it is, return to thy Noah. And surely JEHOVAH hath dealt bountifully with the souls of all his. redeemed, when like the dove returning to the ark whom she found no rest out of the ark for the sole of her foot, we return to the Lord Jesus, the only rest for the soul, and our salvation for ever. (Gen. viii. 9.)

The Sabbath was instituted, from the first dawn of the creation; for when JEHOVAH had called into existence the several works of his almighty hand, which his sovereign will and pleasure gave being to "he is said to have rested from his works which he had made;" and reviewing with complacency what his hands had wrought, beholding their number and order in the several ranks and disposals of his design, he sanctified the day of his rest, and commanded every seventh day to be hallowed for his more immediate worship, adoration love, and praise, by all his intelligent creatures. The Apostle to the Hebrews makes a short but beautiful observation on the spiritual tendency of the Sabbath when with an eye to Jesus he represents the believing soul resting in Christ as the rest for the people of God. "For he (saith the apostle) that is entered into his rest, he also hath ceased from his own works, as God did from his." (Heb. iv. 10.)

Since the resurrection of the Lord Jesus Christ from the dead, the name of Sabbath hath been less used, and that of the Lord's day substituted more generally in its place; and the authority for so doing is derived from the apostles. Thus John, when speaking of those revelations made to him by the Lord Jesus in the Isle of Patmos, saith that he was in the Spirit on the Lord's day. (Rev. i. 10.) And it is no small confirmation of the Lord's approval of the first day being appointed for the ordinance of the Sabbath, that not only the Lord Jesus arose on that day from the dead, but God the Holy Ghost made his first public descent, agreeably to Christ's promise, on that day. Hence divine honour is given in the observance of the Lord's day on the first day of the week to all the persons of the

GODHEAD, for creation, redemption, and sanctification. It hath been said that the Jews at the giving of the law lost the true reckoning of the seventh day. It were devoutly to be desired that believers in the Lord Jesus, in their ordinary conversation, would distinguish the Sabbath by its proper name, and call it what the apostle called it, the Lord's day. Sunday is a name without meaning, unless indeed it he connected with its derivation, and then it becomes still more improper! for if it be supposed, as some have said, that it took its rise during the time of the Saxon Heptarchy, and had reference to the sun, and therefore called Sun-day, it savours of idolatry. We know that the sun hath been in all ages the great idol of the eastern world. (See Deut. iv. 15. 19. 2 Kings xxiii. 11. Job xxxi. 26-28. Ezek. viii. 16.) It is strange, therefore, that the name should be retained when the Holy Scriptures have never once mentioned such a name, and the apostle's example so sweetly recommends what ought to be so dear when we speak with reverence of the Sabbath, that we call it the Lord's day.

We meet with several expressions connected with the Lord's day in the New Testament, such as "a Sabbath day's journey, the second Sabbath after the first." These are not explained to us in Scripture, and therefore we are left to conjecture concerning their meaning. It is said that among the Jews there was a tradition not to walk more than six Stadia, or seven hundred and fifty paces, on the Sabbath day--that is, somewhat less than one of our miles. And perhaps in allusion to this it might be that our Lord, speaking of the destruction of Jerusalem, enjoined his disciples to pray that their flight might not be in the winter, neither on the Sabbath day. (Matt. xxiv. 20.)

Concerning the second Sabbath after the first, which we read of Luke vi. 1; the meaning of it is not so clear as to determine exactly. But it hath been conjectured that the Jews particularly numbered their Sabbaths from the Passover, and that the second Sabbath was intended to mean from the Passover. But others have concluded that the second Sabbath meant the Pentecost, and the first the Passover.

It is astonishing to behold with what veneration the ancient Jews esteemed their Sabbaths. They considered the appointment of it by the Lord so peculiar a mercy, in that it distinguished them from all others nations, that they took the greatest delight in it, calling it their spouse. It is to be feared that in modern times their descendants have lost this reverence, as well as the true knowledge of their own Scriptures. Oh, that the Lord would hasten the time when "the Deliverer shall arise out of Zion, to turn away ungodliness from Jacob? (Rom. xi. 26. Hos. iii. 4, 5.)

SABEANS

The Scriptures in various parts speak of those men. We meet with them Job i. 15. And it is very probable that by the men of Sheba is meant the same. (Ps. lxxii. 10. 1 Kings x. 1, 2.) In the writings of Isaiah they are spoken of as men of stature. (Isa. xlv. 14.) But who they are, or to what purpose designed, there is no mention. It is a blessed thought however, what is said, Ps. lxxii. throughout, concerning the ultimate extension and prosperity of the Redeemer's kingdom "when the kings of Sheba and of Seba shall offer gifts; yea, when all kings shall fall down before him, all nations shall serve him." (Ps, lxxii. 10. 11.) Oh, what wonders will by and by break out in the earth, when from the rising of the sun even unto the going down of the same Jesus's name shall be great among the Gentiles, and in every place incense shall be offered unto his name and a pure offering! (Mal. i. 11.)

SABTAH

One of the sons of Cush. (Gen. x. 7.) And there is another son of Cush named Sabtecha--both derived from the same word, Sabah, to surround.

SACAR

One of David's worthies. (1 Chron. ii. 35.) If his name be derived from Shakar, it should seem to mean somewhat alluding to drunkenness.

SACKBUT

This was an instrument of music known in the court of the Chaldeans; but we do not find mention of it elsewhere. (Dan. iii.) The Hebrews had a variety of stringed and wind instruments as well as a kind of tympanum or drum. The Hebrews called it Taph. But certain it is that very little hath ever been understood, even among the Jews themselves, after their return from Babylon, concerning the instruments to which their fathers had been so partial. See Music.

SACKCLOTH

We read much of the sackcloth with which the prophets and mourners in Zion clad themselves upon occasions of sorrow. Rending the garment, and putting on sackcloth, are terms every where to be met with in the Old Testament. And at any time when a reverse of circumstances took place, they rent the sackcloth from their loins: hence David is represented as saying, "Thou hast turned for me my mourning into dancing; thou hast put off my sackcloth, and girded me with gladness." (Ps. xxx. 11.) I refer the reader to the word of God for accounts of this apparel. (Gen. xxxvii. 34. Ps. xxxv. 13. Isa. xx. 2.) There is a prophecy in the book of the Revelations which some think yet remains to be fulfilled, where it is said that the Lord's "two witnesses shall prophecy a thousand, two hundred, and three-score days, clothed in sackcloth? (Rev. xi. 3,) Others suppose the event hath been already accomplished.

SACRIFICE

The sacrifices under the Old Testament dispensation were all shadowy representations and types of that one great and all-sufficient sacrifice of the offering of the body of Jesus Christ once for all, whereby "he hath perfected for ever them that are sanctified."

It is proper to observe that though the sacrifices under the law were all typical of Christ, yet sacrifices did not first come in under the law. In the garden of Eden we find their observance. And as a still farther confirmation that every sacrifice, both under the law, and before the law, was typical, we are expressly told by the Holy Ghost that by faith they were offered--that is, faith in the promised seed. "By faith Abel offered unto God a more excellent sacrifice than Cain. By faith Abraham when he was tried offered up Isaac." And what could this faith be in but Christ? (See Heb. xi. 4. 17.)

The sacrifices under the law were of different kinds, but all signified the same thing. To Jesus Christ, "the Lamb slain from the foundation of the world," they all referred, and in him the whole had their accomplishment. Whether the sacrifice was what was called the burnt offering, or Holocaust, the sacrifice for sin, or expiation, or the peace-offering, or sacrifice of thanksgiving, Christ was the great object set forth in every one. For neither could the blood of bulls, and of goats, and the ashes of an heifer, "sprinkling the unclean, sanctify to the purifying of the flesh, but Jesus, by his own blood, and by entering once into the holy place, having obtained eternal redemption for us." (Heb. ix. 12, 13.)

It may be proper to observe under this particular of sacrifice, wherein it differed from oblation. In the former there was somewhat done as well as presented. The offering, of whatever sort it was, whether a burnt offering, or a sacrifice for sin, underwent a change; it was either in part or in whole consumed: whereas an oblation simply consisted in the presentation or dedication of it. See Passover.

SADDUCEES

These were a sect among the Jews, but possessing nothing of the principles of Abraham, but rather a class of Epicureans: They were rigid to a degree for the law, because, denying any future state of reward or punishment, angel or spirit, they made the chief good to consist in an attention to the observance of order in this life.

It is worthy remark, and indeed it is the only reason for noticing characters of this kind at all in a work of this nature, how our blessed Lord was opposed off the one hand and on the other by those fashionable sects which abounded in his day. The "Scribes and Pharisees, the Sadducees and Samaritans," all arose in opposition to the cross. This should be remembered by the faithful and humble follower of the Lord Jesus in the present day, when at any time the privileges of his faith and conversation in Jesus is opposed or called in question. Sweetly the Holy Ghost persuades to this when he saith, "Consider him that endured such contradiction of sinners against himself, lest ye be wearied and faint in your minds." (Heb. xii. 3.)

SAINT and SAINTS

If I apprehend right, those titles are used in Scripture with different meanings. Thus when spoken of angels, or beings of higher intellect than man, there is a peculiar degree of holiness annexed to the word saint in those instances. Thus Moses, describing the descent of the Lord upon mount Sinai, saith, "He came with ten thousands of saints." (Deut. xxxiii. 2.) But when the same word is made use of in application to men, whether the apostles and first servants in the church, or ordinary believers, I apprehend it means no more than sinners regenerated, and made saints in Christ Jesus. Thus Paul the apostle, addressing his first Epistle to the Corinthians, useth these remarkable words--"Unto the church of God which is at Corinth, to them that are sanctified in Christ Jesus, called robe saints." (1 Cor. i. 2.) I do not presume to point out the difference,--I only state it as it is. Probably there is no real difference in sanctity, because all holiness in every creature can be but a derived holiness. The high and Holy One who inhabiteth eternity, strictly and properly speaking, is the only Holy One. Every thing, therefore, of holiness is just so far so, and no more, as hath been received from him. And with respect to the holiness of men or angels it is possible, yea more than possible, even highly probable, that when a sinner is washed from all his sins in Christ's blood, he is holier than an angel which never sinned; and eminently on this account--the holiness of the sinner in his renewed nature is the holiness of God our Saviour, from a life received from Jesus and union with Jesus: whereas the holiness of the angel is but the holiness of the creature, a created holiness, and not derived from any life-union with Christ. If this be true, let the reader contemplate, if he can, the personal glory of the Lord Jesus Christ in this holiness of his nature, and his redeemed in him, Such honour have all his saints! And when he hath duly pondered this most blessed of all subjects, let him add this to it, namely, that it is an holiness that never can be lost, sullied, or lessened. "Such an High Priest (saith Paul) became us, who is holy, harmless, undefiled, separate from sinners, and made higher than the heavens? (Heb. vii. 26.) As the holiness of Christ in his human nature, deriving every thing of sanctity as it must from the union with the GODHEAD, gives a completeness both of durableness and excellency to that sanctity, so must it ensure the same in all his members. The holy angels are said by JEHOVAH (Job. iv. 18.) to have no trust put in them, yea, "he chargeth them with folly, or weakness--that is, with a possibility of falling. For though they are free from sin, yet not secure from the possibility of sinning. Angels have fallen, and therefore angels may fall. But believers united to Jesus are everlastingly secure in him. He saith himself, "Because I live ye shall live also." (John xiv. 19.) What an unspeakable felicity this to the church of God in Christ Jesus called to be saints!

SALAH

Son of Arphaxad. (Gen. xi. 12.) If derived from Shalach, the name means branches,

SALAMIS

A city in the island of Cyprus. (Acts xiii. 5.) Here the apostle Paul in his travels preached the word of God, being sent forth with Barnabas by God the Holy Ghost for that purpose. We have a most interesting record concerning the apostles' success in this island, in being instrumental to the conversion of the deputy governor, and the opposition they met with from Elymas the sorcerer. I refer the reader to the relation as it is recorded in the above-mentioned chapter.

SALATHIEL

There are several of this name in Scripture: one among the sons of Jeconiah, (1Chron. iii. 17.) and another mentioned by Ezra chap. iii. 2.--but here it is spelt according to the Hebrew, Shealtiel, but both is the same name, and derived from the same root, Sheal, a loan. So that it should seem the father of the first Salathiel called his son by this name, as Hannah did her Samuel, because it was a loan or gift asked of God. (See 1 Sam. i. 20.)--in the margin also of the Bible. We meet with another Salathiel (Matt. i. 12.) and another, (Luke iii. 27.) though some have thought that this was one and the same person, the branches here uniting in this genealogy of Christ.

SALCHAH

A city belonging to Bashan beyond Jordan. (Deut. iii. 10.) If from Salah, perhaps the name means treading down.

SALEM

There are various places called by this name. The first we meet with in Scripture is where Melchizedek is said to be king of Salem. (Gen. xiv. 18.) Jerusalem and Salem in Scripture are one. In Salem, saith the Psalmist, speaking of JEHOVAH, is his tabernacle, and his dwelling in Zion. (Ps. lxxvi. 2.) There was a Shalem also in the country of the Shechemites, were Jacob in his travels came. (Gen. xxxiii. 18.) And it is more than probable that the Salim where John baptised was a distinct place known by this name. The name itself is Shalam, peace. Hence when Gideon was visited by the angel under the oak at Ophrah, at the close of the interview he built an altar unto the Lord, and called it Jehovah Shalom--that is, as the margin of the Bible renders it, the Lord send peace. (Judg. vi, 24.)

SALISSA or SHALISHA

A city north of Jerusalem. Mention is made of it, 1 Sam. ix. 4--and probably it is the same place which is called Baal Shalisha, 2 Kings iv. 42. If from Shalosh, it means third.

SALLAI

One of the priests returned in the captivity. The name means my rising. (Neh. xii. 20.)

SALLU

The son of Meshullam. (1 Chron. ix. 7.) If from Salal, the name means basket.

SALMA or SALMON

(See Ruth iv. 19, compared with 1 Chron. ii. 11.) If from Shalom, the name means peace.

SALMONE

A sea-sport in the island of Crete. See Paul's travels, Acts xxvii. 7. Derived from Shalom.

SALOME

The wife of Zebedee. Honorable mention is

made of this woman in her attendance on the Lord Jesus, Mark xv. 40; xvi. 1.

SALT

We meet with so many portions of Scripture where this word is used, and in senses so very different from each other, that it merits our more particular attention. The Israelites called it Melach--and probably from the sovereign properties with which it is endued.

I shall beg to set before the reader some of the Scriptures where we meet with it, in order that we may have a better apprehension of the design of God the Holy Ghost in the use of it. I shall begin with those which speak of its destructive quality.

The first account we read of salt is Gen. xiv. 3; where mention is made of the Salt Sea in the vale of Siddim; and this is probably what elsewhere is called the Dead Sea, forming the spot where once stood Sodom and Gomorrah, and the cities of the plain, which the Lord destroyed by fire, and over which Jordan in the seasons of its overflowing pours itself. It is said even to the present hour to send up such steams of a sulphureous nature, as to kill every bird attempting to fly over it.

The next account of salt is in the instance of Lot's wife made a pillar of salt. (Gen. xix. 26.) We read in the prophecy of Ezekiel also concerning the miry places, and the marshy places, which were never to be healed, but to be given to salt. (Ezek. xlvii. 11.) And the prophets Jeremiah and Zephaniah have much the same expressions concerning the perpetual barrenness of lands given to salt, (Jer. xvii. 6. Zeph. ii. 9.) The psalmist saith, (Ps. cvii. 34.) that the Lord turneth a fruitful land into saltness, (so the margin renders it) for the wickedness of them that dwell therein.

Those instances may be sufficient, in the view of the Scripture, concerning salt, where its use is marked in a way of destruction. Let us now look into the holy volume again for passages where an opposite quality is described, as resulting from the appointment of it.

The first account we meet with where salt is directed to be used in the way of a blessing is in Leviticus, chap. ii. 13. "And every oblation of thy meat-offering shalt thou season with salt; neither shalt thou suffer the salt of the covenant of thy God to be lacking from thy meat-offerings; with all thine offerings thou shalt offer salt." So again when the prophet Elisha sweetened the waters of Jericho, he did it by casting a cruse of salt into them; and this was done by commission from the Lord, for the prophet added, "Thus saith the Lord, I have healed these waters; there shall not be from thence any more death or barren and." (2 Kings ii. 21.) And that salt was considered in the light of a blessing it is said, (2 Chron. xiii. 5.) "that the Lord God of Israel gave the kingdom over Israel to David for ever, even to him, and to his sons by a covenant of salt." Hence we find also that Jesus called his disciples the salt of the earth, as if to intimate that his grace in them preserved the earth from universal putrefaction. (Matt. v. 13.) And elsewhere the Lord said, "have salt in yourselves, and have peace one with another." (Mark ix. 50.) And his servant Paul figuratively recommended the church that their speech should be always with grace seasoned with salt. (Col. iv. 6.)

From both those views of salt, according to the holy Scripture, in being appointed as a figure of evil and of good, it becomes a very interesting enquiry to know yet somewhat more particularly the mind of God the Holy Ghost respecting the use of it. And if I do not greatly err, that service in the church concerning the salt of the oblation, throws a great light upon the whole. We there read that every oblation of the meat-offering was to be seasoned with salt. The salt was never to be wanting; with all offerings the salt was to be offered. And what gives a strong leading feature to the whole was this, that this was called "the salt of the covenant of JEHOVAH." (Lev. ii. 13.)

Now if we first consider the property of salt, that it is to save from corruption, we discover that the salt, which was never to be omitted in the offering, was the grand object the Lord had regard to in the whole. It is expressly called "the salt of the covenant of thy God." Supposing then that this figuratively sets forth the Lord Jesus Christ, we instantly perceive that such is the importance that his person, blood, and righteousness, should be in and with all our offerings, that there can be no coming to the Father but by him. Where Christ is not, there is no savour; it is his blood which gives a fragrancy and a perfume to our most holy things, And if Jesus be the salt of the covenant of our God, and with all our offerings he be first and last presented, both the Alpha and Omega, in our view, as he is in the view of God our Father, then is that Scripture blessedly fulfilled which the Lord delivered by the prophet: "For in mine holy mountain in the mountain of the height of Israel, saith the Lord God, there shall all the house of Israel, all of them in the land, serve me. There will I accept them, and there will I require your offerings, and the first fruits of your oblations, with all your holy things. I will accept you with your sweet savour; and ye shall know that I am the Lord." (Ezek. xx. 40-42.) Observe, your sweet savour! and the Holy Ghost by Paul, calls Christ's sacrifice a sweet-smelling savour. (Ephes. v. 2.)

There is another consideration in the view of the subject which serves to confirm the doctrine yet farther, namely, the universal use of salt. It is essential to all the purposes of food. It not only ministers to give a taste to the several articles of meat, but to preserve animal life from leprosy, and similar diseases. What is called curing of meat, that is, salting it, hath much signification of a spiritual nature in it. I do not presume to say as much so as to decide upon it, but I venture to believe that the term of "curing of meat by salt" took its rise from the circumstance of the divine cure of our nature by the salt of the covenant. Job saith, "Can that which is unsavory be eaten without salt'?" (Job vi. 6.) Much more may it be said, Can our poor nature be accepted but in Christ? Can our nature be cured and preserved from everlasting corruption but by the Lord Jesus?

Once more--salt is of the Lord's own providing: it is among the natural productions of the earth. There is indeed a process of art now used for refining salt, and making it minister to various ways of usefulness; but the rock salt in its own pure nature is not of human production nor contrivance; like the earth itself, it is of JEHOVAH'S forming. "The earth is the Lord's and the fulness thereof." (1 Cor. x. 26.) Such then is Christ, JEHOVAH'S own providing for curing the souls of his people. So that in the salt of the covenant we offer nothing of our own for acceptance, but what God hath first given to us. JEHOVAH is very jealous of his honour. "An altar of earth shall thou make unto me: and if thou wilt make me an altar of stone, thou shall not build it of hewn stone, for if thou lift up thy tool upon it thou hast polluted it." (Exod. xx. 24, 25.)

Fourthly, if the reader will consult the context concerning this meat-offering with the salt of the covenant, he will find that it was an offering also made by fire unto the Lord. (See Lev. ii. 13-16.) Hence the salt of the covenant was not simply to cleanse and render pure for acceptance, but it was to sprinkle the offering made by fire. Hence therefore, when the offering was offered with the salt of the covenant, and the Lord gave token of his acceptance by consuming the sacrifice with fire, this formed a confirmation of the divine favour. This is beautifully explained, Lev. ix. 24. "And there came a fire out from before the Lord, and consumed upon the altar the burnt offering and the fat, which when all the people saw they shouted and fell on their

SALU - SALVATION

faces." Here was both God's acceptance of the salted offering, and testimony at the same time given that the consumption of the sacrifice became the salvation of the people. The fire that consumed the one would, but for the acceptance of the salted sacrifice, have consumed the other. Well might the redeemed shout for joy while they fell on their faces with the lowest reverence.

Now if the reader will pause over the subject, and by looking back take a retrospective view of the whole, he will perceive that salt in the church of God had a twofold dispensation: and, like Him whom it evidently prefigured, it became "the savor of life unto life, or of death unto death? (2 Cor. ii. 16.) Jesus was set for "the fall and rising again of many in Israel, and for a sign which shall be spoken against." (Luke ii. 34.) Where Jesus is like the salt of the covenant, he will preserve from putrefaction, "That little leaven shall leaven the whole lump." (1 Cor. v. 6.) Like the tree of Marah, Jesus makes the waters sweet. (Exod. xv. 25.) Like the cruse of salt at Jericho, though salt in its own nature will make sweet water brackish, Jesus will heal the spring, and make it wholesome. In short, where Jesus is there is the salt of the covenant--"Destroy it not, there is a blessing in it." (Isa. lxv. 8.)

On the other hand, "if the gospel be hid it is hid to them that are lost." (2 Cor. iv. 3.) Where Christ, the salt of the covenant, is rejected, that land, that people, that family, is given up to perpetual, barenness: it never can be healed. Oh, for grace to know our mercies, and truly to value them! For he that now saves from corruption, will one day be the everlasting condemnation of those that reject him. "For (he saith himself) every one shall be salted with fire, and every sacrifice shall be salted with salt. Salt is good, but if the salt have lost his saltness," (if Jesus be not the savour of life unto life) "wherewith will ye season it?" (who can then give acceptance to the sinner?) Christ "becomes the savour of death unto death"--graciously therefore he adds, "have salt in yourselves, and have peace one with another." (Mark. ix. 40, 50.)

Very largely as I have trespassed on this article, I cannot forbear, by way of confirmation to the whole, to add the relation given by a traveller concerning the usage in the eastern nations of making solemn engagements with salt. He tells us, that one of those people, willing to assure him of the seriousness of his promise to him, and that he would certainly fulfil it, called to a servant to bring him bread and salt; as soon as it was brought, he took a little of the salt between his fingers, and looking very gravely, he put it on a morsel of the bread and ate it, assuring me that now I might rely on his promise. Baron Du Tott. Is it not possible that this might have been a custom received by tradition, however ill understood, and worse applied, of the offering made with salt in the Scripture?

SALU

The father of a rebellious son called Zimri, a prince in the house of the Simeonites. (See Num. xxv. 14.) His name seems to be borrowed from Salah, signifying basket.

SALVATION

A blessed word of a most blessed doctrine founded in the Lord Jesus Christ, who is JEHOVAH'S salvation to the ends of the earth. (Isa. xlix. 6.) I refer the reader to the article Redeemer for the several features of salvation. And in addition to what is there said, I would just beg to observe that the thing itself meets poor lost souls so many ways, and answereth to their wants in such a variety of purposes, that it is always blessed to meditate upon it.

The term salvation implies somewhat more than a state of recovery from a state in which before the sinner was lost, but it includes every thing that is blessed in that state of recovery. The lost soul is not only brought out of bondage and the shadow of death, but brought into the liberty of the sons of God. So that in salvation is meant a release from all evil, and an introduction into all that is good. A right and interest in all temporal, spiritual and eternal blessings, is the sure consequence. Everlasting life, with all its preliminaries, for it hath the promise of "the life that now is, and of that which is to come."

And what endears salvation yet more, is the consideration of the almighty and all-loving author of it, and by whom it was accomplished. What he is in himself, in the glories of his person, his greatness, fitness, suitability, and all-sufficiency; what he is in his work, and what he hath done for his redeemed, the salvation he hath wrought beyond all conception of value in its completeness, and beyond all reach of extent in its efficacy, being like himself, everlasting and eternal; and what he is in his relations to his people, being their everlasting Father, Brother, Husband, Friend all these things, included as they all are in salvation, give the happy partakers of it "a joy unspeakable and full of glory; so that every individual finds cause to join in the hymn of the church, and say: "I will greatly rejoice in the Lord, I will joy in the God of my salvation: he is a rock, his work is perfect, just and right is he." (Isa. lxi. 10.)

SALUTATION

The Lord Jesus takes notice of the salutations of the Scribes in the market-place, and their delight to be called of men Rabbi. (Matt. xxiii. 7.) Contrary to this when the Lord sent out his disciples to teach and to preach, he commanded them to "salute no man by the way." (Luke x. 4.) To an ordinary reader unacquainted with eastern customs, these things appear strange. We are so much in the habit of familiar conversation as we pass persons we know, that the salutation Good morning, or Good day, or the like, seems but common courtesy. But in the manners of the orientals, these things would make constant confusion. Numberless transactions, and that of the highest kind, are carried on with them by the mere bend of the body or the motion of the head, without speaking a word. A modern historian relates, that even upon their public days of transacting business, and where a multitude of concerns is carried on, so much of the whole is done by sign and gesture, that if a blind person were present, he would be unconscious of any company when perhaps some hundreds were assembled. What would those eastern people think of the clamour of voices in our Royal Exchange? In families, among the servants with their masters, a thousand commands are issued and executed, and not a voice heard. This may serve to shew a new beauty on that sweet Psalm of David, the one hundred and twenty third, were the soul of a believer in the Lord is described as waiting in silent adoration and obedience to receive the Lord's commands, "as the eyes of servants look unto the hand of their masters, and as the eyes of a maiden unto the hand of her mistress.

SAMARIA

The chief city in the kingdom, of the ten tribes. It was built by Omri, as we read 1 Kings xvi. 24. It seems to have taken its name from Shamar, and hence called Shomeron by the Israelites: so that his Shamar might mean his prison or his guard. Samaria formes an interesting history to the church, both in the Old Testament and the New. From 1 Kings chap. xvi. to the end of the Second Book of the Kings, and in the Gospel the woman of Samaria, John iv., and numberless other occasions render it memorable.

SAMARITANS

Those were the inhabitants of Samaria. We have a most interesting account of the conversion of many of this people to the faith of Christ in consequence of the woman's bringing them to Jesus, and hearing our Lord themselves. (See John iv.

SAMLAH - SAMUEL

28-42.)

SAMLAH

We know nothing more of this man than that he was king of Masrekah, (Gen. xxxvi. 36.) The name is Hebrew, and signifies raiment.

SAMOS

Here the apostle Paul in his voyage landed; (see Acts xx 15.) It was an island of the Archipelago.

SAMOTHRACIA

Here the apostle Paul arrived after his departing from Troas, (Acts xvi. 11.) It was an island in the Ægean Sea.

SAMSON

A well-known character in the Old Testament: in one grand instance, as a Nazarite, a type of the Lord Jesus Christ. (See Judg. xiii. &c.) His name is derived from Shemesh, sun. I refer to his life as is recorded in the book of the Judges; and shall only make one observation upon it, namely that the Holy Ghost hath made honourable mention of him by enrolling his name among those worthies, so eminent for their faith, who are said to be such of whom "the world was not worthy." (Heb. xi. 32.) See Nazarene.

SAMUEL

A well-known and eminent prophet of the Lord. His name is derived from Shael, a loan, or gift; hence Shem and Urel of God. It would form a separate history to enter into all the interesting particulars which relate to the life and ministry of Samuel. I must beg the reader to gather it for himself out of the Bible, under those writings which bear his name. But the call of Samuel when a child to the knowledge of the Lord is so truly interesting, and forms a point of decline so intimately connected with the gospel of Christ, that I cannot wholly pass it by without begging the reader's permission to offer a short observation upon it.

The Bible account of this event is given in the most beautiful simplicity of representation, 1 Sam. iii. 1. &c. "And the child Samuel ministered unto the Lord before Eli. And the word of the Lord was precious in those days; there was no open vision. And ere the lamp of God went out in the temple of the Lord where the ark of God was, and Samuel was laid down to sleep, that the Lord called Samuel, and he answered, Here am I.

There are a great number of very interesting things in this relation that I must not stay to dwell upon. The preciousness of the Lord's words, in this period of the church, when open visions were for a time suspended; the special grace shewn to Samuel in a season of general depravity, and when even the sons of Eli, who were priests of the Lord, were given up to a state of daring impiety end uncleanness; the childhood of Samuel, so particularly noted in the history, as if to encourage the youthful part of the Lord's people to be found waiting on the Lord in ordinances; all these, and more to the same purport, which this relation of the call of Samuel brings forward, would furnish much observation for improvement. But I must passover the consideration of these things, however interesting, to notice with more special marks of attention the call of Samuel, and the manner of it. Nothing can be more evident, from the history of this transaction, than that at the time when Samuel lay down to sleep, he was perfectly unconscious of all divine revelations, and totally ignorant of their meaning. Indeed, ye are told, in the seventh verse that, "Samuel did not yet know the Lord, neither was the word of the Lord revealed unto him." So that in Samuel's instance, as in every other, of the real conversion of the heart to God, the gracious act begins on the part of God. If we love him, it is because he first loved us, It was the Lord first called Samuel, yea, repeated that call, or Samuel never world have called upon the Lord. This is what the Scriptures call preventing grace; hence David, in a degree of holy rapture, cries out, The God of my mercy shall prevent me; that is, shall be before hand with me in all my need. (Ps. lix. 10.)

The next beautiful representation this call of Samuel furnisheth, is the secret, silent, and personal nature of it. Eli heard it not, though the priest of God; it was Samuel only and this by name. Had thousands been present like Eli, it was a voice they would not have heard, and in which they had no concern. It was directed to Samuel, and to him in secret, and what the Lord said related to him personally. Such are the marks of distinguishing grace in all ages of the church. Jesus saith, "My sheep hear my voice, and he calleth them all by name, and leadeth them forth. Who can mark the properties of distinguishing grace in their own case and circumstances without having the heart melted into the fullest sense of affection? "Lord "Lord how is it (said the astonished disciple) that thou wilt manifest thyself unto us and not unto the world." (John xiv.)

One thought more on the call of Samuel. The mercy that was thus preventing, unexpected, unlooked for, and secret, silent, and personal, became also powerful, effectual, and sure, to all the gracious purposes. He that called the child called not in vain. A marvellous light shined with the voice in the heart, and a commanding power accompanied it within. Samuel never lost sight of it, I venture to believe, through all the after-stages of his life. Both the time and place, the manner and effect, no doubt became like Bethel to Jacob, so that he could say with the patriarch, "Surely the Lord is in this place, and I knew it not. How dreadful is this place! this is none other but the house of God and this is the gate of heaven." (Gen. xxviii. 11.17.)

I cannot prevail upon myself to dismiss our view of Samuel before that I have first requested the reader to remark with me some features in the portrait of this great prophet, which bear resemblance, however faint, to the person and offices of the Lord God of the prophets, Jesus Christ. Samuel, we are told, was so called to shew that he was asked of God. And how earnestly was the Lord Jesus asked by the Old Testament saints before his coming! How blessedly did JEHOVAH, in the opening of Samuel's life, point to the Lord Jesus as the faithful Priest he would raise up, who should do according to all that was in his heart! (2 Sam. ii. 35.) And what a delightful view doth the prophet Samuel exhibit, as typical of the Lord Christ, under the several offices he sustained, not only as prophet, as Priest and as Judge in Israel!

SANBALLAT

The great enemy to Israel after their return from the captivity of Babylon: (see Neh. ii. 10.19. and ch. vi.) The name is not strictly derived from the Hebrew: it hath been thought that as Sene means bush, and Lut, to hide, the union of those words forming a suitable name for the enemies of God's people, Sanballat was so called to imply an enemy in secret.

SANCTIFICATION

Very much hath been said in the christian church respecting sanctification some making it the work of the creature, as if a man that is a polluted creature could sanctify himself; and others referring the whole work into the sovereignty and grace of the Lord. It may not be improper in a work of this kind to examine the doctrine by the standard of Scripture, which, is the only unerring standard, in order to form a right judgment upon a point of such infinite consequence.

It will be a sure plan in forming just conceptions of sanctification, if we bring all that is said of it in Scripture under these two distinct branches, namely, the

SANCTIFICATION - SANCTIFICATION

sanctification which means setting apart, consecrating, or appointing to solemn and holy purposes--and the sanctification which means making that holy which before was polluted and defiled. I venture to believe that under one or other of these distinct particulars every thing in Scripture relating to sanctification may be included.

Concerning the first mentioned, the sanctification which means to set apart, to consecrate, or appropriate, to solemn and holy purposes, we meet with expressions in Scripture leading to this in both Testaments. Thus it is said that when JEHOVAH had finished the works of creation, he blessed the seventh day, and sanctified it--that is, set it apart for his more immediate honor. (Gen. ii. 3.) So again, holy places were set apart and sanctified in their separation from ordinary things: thus the tabernacle, and all the vessels of the ministry under the law were sanctified. In like manner the first-born were all set apart as the Lord's right-- "The Lord spake unto Moses, saying, Sanctify unto me all the first-born, whatsoever openeth the womb, among the children of Israel both of man and beast, it is mine," (Exod. xiii. 1, 2.) When the Lord thus claims it for his own, and saith, it is mine, it means not that this sanctifying it to the Lord's use made the first-born holy, but that it set it apart for his service. In like manner, when the Lord Jesus Christ saith, "for their sakes I sanctity myself," (John xvii. 19.) surely he did not mean to say that he made himself more holy, for that was impossible, but that for the sake of his church and people he set himself apart in dedicating himself to God as their Surety and Saviour. Thus much may serve to explain the former sense of sanctification of persons and things dedicated to God

The other sense of sanctification in making that holy which before was polluted and defiled, is by much the most general sense of the term sanctifying, in Scripture. Thus the church of the Corinthians, when regenerated and brought into fellowship with Christ's mystical body, are said to have been cleansed and purified thereby: And such, saith the apostle, (speaking to characters notoriously known to have been once in the filth and under the dominion of sin, but now brought nigh by the blood of Christ) "and such were some of you; but ye are washed, but ye are sanctified, but ye are justified, in the name of the Lord Jesus, and by the spirit of our God," (1 Cor. vi. 11.)

But the most essential point, in sanctification is to enquire concerning the source and fountain of it, not being founded in creature-power, or creature-holiness, but wholly in the Lord; and this will very fully appear from what the Scripture saith concerning it. All the persons of the GODHEAD, concur and co-operate in the work. That God the Father is the author and giver of it, is plain from what the apostles Paul and Jude have said. The former in his First Epistle to the Thessalonians, prays that the God of peace may sanctify them wholly; (1 Thes. v. 23.)--and the latter expressly addresseth his Epistle to them that are sanctified by God the Father. (Jude 1.) And that God the Son is no less the author of sanctification is evident, because the very purpose for which he gave himself for his church was that he might sactify and cleanse it. (Ephes. v. 23.) And concerning God the Holy Ghost it is said, by the apostle to the Thessalonians, that we are bound to give thanks always to God, because from the beginning the church is chosen to salvation through sanctification of the Spirit. (2 Thess. ii. 13.)

It is most blessed and refreshing to a soul thus to trace the doctrine to its source, and behold all the glorious persons, of the GODHEAD as the united authors of it; and while we are justified freely by the redemption that is in Christ Jesus, to see also that all our sanctification is of him, and that "he is made of God to us wisdom and righteousness, sanctification and redemption, that he that glorieth may glory in the Lord. (1 Cor. i. 30, 31.)

And were it not for trespassing too largely in this article, it would be blessed to trace sanctification through all its branches, and to discover the Lord's hand in every one. The beginning of it is of the Lord. "He saith Paul, that hath begun the good work in you, will perform it unto the day of Jesus Christ." (Phil. i. 6.) The keeping it alive in the soul is of the Lord, for he saith, "The path of the just is as a shining light, that shineth more and more unto the perfect day." (Prov. iv. 18.) The restoration of it when at any time under decaying circumstances is of the Lord. "They shall revive (saith the Lord) as the corn, and grow as the vine. (Hos. xiv. 7.) "Because I live, ye shall live also." (John xiv. 19.) The final perseverance of it is of the Lord; for in the covenant of grace the charter runs thus-- "I will not turn away from them to do them good, but I will put my fear in their hearts, that they shall not depart from me." (Jer. xxxii. 40.) Most blessedly, therefore, and graciously the Lord undertakes for both--I will not, saith God, and they shall not. Glorious Security! And finally to add no more--as the commencement of all grace and sanctification is in God, so the consummation of all glory is in him also. Jesus, who justifies and sanctifies his people freely, hath engaged to complete the whole for JEHOVAH'S glory and his people's happiness. It is said that the whole purport of redemption is that he might finally and fully, and completely, present his church to himself "a glorious church not having spot, or wrinkle, or any such thing, but that it should be holy and without blemish." Oh, the unspeakable felicity of being clothed in his garments of righteousness, and presented by Jesus, and to Jesus, in that day before JEHOVAH and a congregated world, holy, and sanctified in his holiness and sanctity, and made so for ever!

SANCTUARY

The Scriptures have several distinct meanings for this word, according as the word itself is made use of. The apostle to the Hebrews describes the sanctuary how it was appointed, (chap. ix. 1-5.) No doubt the sanctuary was a type of JEHOVAH'S throne in heaven; hence (Ps. cii. 19.) the Lord is represented as "looking down from the height of his sanctuary, from heaven did the Lord behold the earth? The church of Christ is represented as the Lord's sanctuary under the type of the holy land. (Exod. xv. 17, 18.) And there is another very sweet and precious figure of the Lord's sanctuary, when his people are considered in this light. The psalmist celebrates this in one of the loftiest strains of sacred poetry: (Ps. cxiv.) "When Israel came out of Egypt, the house of Jacob from a people of strange language, Judah was his sanctuary, and Israel his dominion. The sea saw it and fled, Jordan was driven back.

SANDALS

We meet with this word but twice in the Scripture, Mark vi. 9. Acts xii. 8. They formed the covering for the feet. In the eastern part of the world the going barefoot was considered as a token of respect in the presence of a superior; hence, when the Lord called to Moses from the bush, he commanded him to put off his shoes from his feet, for the ground was holy on which he stood, being made so by the divine presence. (Exod. iii. 5.) Hence Soloman also, in after-ages, admonished to keep the foot when going to the house of God. (Eccles. v. 1.)

SANSANNAH

A city of Judah, (Josh. xv. 31.) If Senah, a bush, it should seem to mean "the bush of the bush."

SAPH

Of the race of the giants. (2 Sam. xxi. 18.) His name signifies rushes.

SARAH - SATAN

SARAH

A memorable name in Scripture well known to all lovers of the Bible. The wife of Abraham. Various have been the interpretations given to her name, according to the root from whence various commentators on the Bible have supposed it to have been derived. The most general opinion hath been, that it is taken from Shar, prince; and if so Sharah or Sarah will be princess. It would be to give an abridgement of that part of the word of God which contains the history of Sarah to amplify observations in this place on her character. The reader will do well to turn to the relation given of her in the book of Genesis, and in summing up her character to recollect what honorable testimony the Holy Ghost hath given of Sarah in giving her a place among those illustrious persons-who all died, as they had lived, in faith, "not having received the promises, but having seen them afar off, and were persuaded of them, and embraced them. It is but a short inscription over Sarah's portrait in those lively pictures of the faithful, but it is a very blessed one, "She judged him faithful who had promised." (Heb. xi. 11-13.)

Though I think it unnecessary to swell the pages of this Concordance with the history of Sarah, because we have it already most blessedly set forth in the holy Scriptures, yet I cannot shut up this article without making a short observation on that beautiful allegory which the Holy Ghost hath given us in Paul's Epistle to the Galatians, fourth chapter, and twenty-second and following verses. Under the history of Sarah and Hagar, the Holy Ghost there teacheth the church that he hath represented the two covenants of the gospel and the law. No man upon earth, untaught of God the Holy Ghost, would ever have had the most distant idea of those things being shadowed forth in Sarah and Hagar's history, had not the Lord the Spirit so taught. But being there so beautifully and strikingly explained, it becomes a subject of sweet consolation and instruction, and gives to all true believers in Christ new occasion to bless God when discovering their relationship in Jesus, that they "as Isaac was, are the children of promise." It is indeed most blessed to discover that "we are not children of the bondwoman, but of the free."

SARDIS

A city of Asia. One of the seven churches to whom the Lord Jesus Christ sent the solemn message in the second and third chapters of the book of the Revelations. If it be derived from the word Sharar, it means to rule, or of authority.

SATAN

One of the names of the devil; and as all the names of this apostate spirit have special signification beside that of identifying his person, we may consider this of Satan as implying that horrid part of his character, the adversary and accuser of the brethren. Thus he is particularly called Satan as the accuser, Job i. and Zech. iii. 1, &c.

It would form subject sufficient for a volume more than a Concordance to enter into the particulars the Holy Bible hath given us concerning this old serpent, the devil, and Satan which deceiveth the whole world. Nevertheless, in a work of this kind, I cannot prevail upon myself to pass it wholly by, without offering a few brief observations concerning the Scripture account which is given us of one, to whose infernal malice we owe all the miseries, sorrows, and evils of the present life.

Now the Scriptures of God relate to us that the devil, under the appearance of a serpent, beguiled our first parents in the garden of Eden, prompted them to break the divine commands, and by so doing introduced death into the circumstrances of them and all their posterity.

The Scriptures farther teach concerning Satan, that having thus by the introduction of sin brought in all the consequent effects of sorrow and misery, he hath set up a kingdom in the hearts of men and is "the ruler of the darkness of this world," and carries on a despotic government over all men, yea even the Lord's own children while remaining in their unregenerate and unawakened state. Hence he enticeth them to sin, as he did Ahab, when he became a lying spirit in the mouth of all his prophets. (1 Kings xxii. 22.) And the same in the instance of Ananias and Sapphira, when he filled their hearts to lie unto the Holy Ghost. (Acts v. 3, &c.) So in the case of Hannah while going childless, he is said to have made her fret. (1 Sam. i. 6.) In like manner the traitor Judas, concerning whom it is expressly said, "Satan, entered into him." (John xiii. 27.)

Hence, therefore, when the Lord Jesus Christ is spoken of in the holy Scriptures as coming for the redemption of his people, this great feature of character is intimately linked with it; "for this purpose was the Son of God manifested, that he might destroy the works of the devil. (1 John iii. 8.) So again the apostle Paul, in his Epistle to the Hebrews, was commissioned to tell the church that forasmuch "as the children were partakers of flesh and blood, he, that is, Christ, also himself likewise took part of the same, that through death he might destroy him that had the power of death, that is, the devil, and deliver them who through fear of death were all their life-time subject to bondage. (Heb. ii. 14, 15.)

I stay not to remark, what hath not indeed in so many plain words Scripture authority, positively saying so, but what hath been the received opinion of learned and studious minds in all ages pondering over the word of God on this subject, that the devil's enmity began not with our nature, but with the Son of God for assuming our nature. Personally first with Christ, and then with all mankind in Christ, that so he might persecute and render miserable the seed of Christ. I must not go so far into the subject as to bring in all that the Scripture seems to intimate of the quarrel of the devil being first levelled against Christ for becoming the Head of his body the church. This would lead too far. The war, said to be in heaven between Michael and his angels, and the Dragon and his angels, (Rev. xii. 7.) hath been thought by some very able and learned divines to say as much. But I do not speak decidedly on the subject, though I had not even mentioned it, if I had not inclined to the same opinion. But be this as it may, very certain it is, that among the grand purposes for which the Son of God became incarnate this was eminently one, that he should conquer the devil and all the powers of hell, and "root out of his kingdom all things that offend." This formed as great a part in the plan of JEHOVAH for the glory of Christ, as the salvation of men for his glory. "

In this view of the subject, if we take a comprehensive survey of what the Scriptures have said on the matter, we shall find that the kingdom Satan hath attempted to set up in the earth is personally directed against the kingdom of God and of his Christ: hence our Lord, speaking of Satan, calleth his empire a kingdom. Thus, when the Jews charged the Lord Jesus with casting out devils through Beelzebub, the prince of the devils, Christ made this answer, "If Satan cast out Satan he is divided against himself: how shall then his kingdom stand?" (Matt. xii. 26.) So that the struggle of life and glory, hath been from first to last directed against Christ's kingdom, and to establish the kingdom of Satan through the earth.

When therefore we behold the Lord Jesus going forth for the salvation of his people, we behold him, as he is represented through all the Scriptures, as first conquering Satan in his own person and then destroying his dominion in the hearts of his people. The first he did when through death, as the Scripture speaks, he destroyed him that had the power of death;

and the second conquest was, and is, in every individual instance of his people, when by his regenerating grace in the sinner's heart he converts him from sin to salvation, and the sinner is translated out of "the kingdom of darkness into the kingdom of God's dear Son." (Col. i. 13.)

And there is another and a open display of victory: which the Lord Jesus Christ will obtain over Satan, before a whole congregated world, when he will set up a visible kingdom upon earth before the final judgment, during which period the Scriptures tell us Satan will be shut up, and his power restrained from tempting any of Christ's church, as he now is permitted to do, neither will he during that period be allowed to deceive the world and make the ungodly harrass and afflict Christ's people any more. The beloved apostle John, in one of the chapters of the Revelations, hath most sublimely stated those great truths, (chap. xx. 1, &c.) "And I saw an angel come down from heaven having the key of the bottomless pit, and a great chain in his hand; and he laid hold of the dragon, that old serpent, which is the Devil and Satan, and bound him a thousand years, and cast him into the bottomless pit, and shut him up, and set a seal upon him, that he should deceive the nations no more till the thousand years should be fulfilled; and after that he must be loosed a little season." To this account succeeds the relation of Christ's kingdom upon the earth. "And I saw thrones, and they sat upon them, and judgment was given unto them. And I saw the souls of them that were beheaded for the witness of Jesus, and for the word of God, and which had not worshipped the beast, neither his image neither had received his mark upon their foreheads or in their hands, and they lived and reigned with Christ a thousand years."

To this succeeds the accounts of the final and everlasting triumph, of the Lord Jesus Christ over Satan, when bringing this infernal spirit to open trial before the whole world of angels and of men at the last day, the day of judgment. At the close of which follows the everlasting and eternal, destraction of the devil and his angels in hell forever.

I must not farther enlarge. Let what hath been said suffice to comfort every, child of God under all the exercises he is called to go through, from the subtilty of Satan still working upon, and with the remains of indwelling corruption in our poor fallen nature. Blessed be our triumphant Jesus, his devices are but for a season, for Christ hath conquered him for us, and he will conquer him in us; the victory is not doubtful, for it is already won, and, "the God of peace will bruise Satan under our feet shortly." (Rom. xvi. 20.) In the meantime let us join that song of heaven, for we truly bear a part in it--"Now is come salvation and strength, and the kingdom of our God, and the power of his Christ, for the accuser of our brethren is cast down, which accused them before our God day and night. And they overcame him by the blood of the Lamb, and by the word of their testimony, and they loved not their lives unto the death." (Rev. xii. 10, 11.)

SAVIOUR

The peculiar name and character of our Lord Jesus Christ, including most evidently both natures, God and man, and thereby forming one Christ. Had he not been God, how should he have been able to save, for who less than God can save? And had he not been man, there would not have been a suitability in the Lord Jesus Christ for such an office, justice so requiring that the same nature which sinned, and broke the divine law, should atone and make ample restoration. So that in the character of the Saviour we behold Christ, and Christ alone, the suited Saviour for his people. Hence we find him assuming to himself this distinction of character--"I, even I, am the Lord, and beside me there is no Saviour." (Isa. xliii. 11. So again, Isa. xliv. 21, 22.)

"There is no God else beside me, a just God, and a Saviour; there is none beside me, Look unto me, and be ye saved, all the ends of the earth, for I am God, and there is none else."

In this view of the Lord Jesus Christ as a Saviour, it is blessed to behold not only the ability, in perfection of character and completeness of work, in the person of the Lord Jesus, but also the authority by which he came and accomplished the glorious office of a Saviour. God the Father declared that he sent him as a Saviour and a great one, and he should deliver his people, and his name should be called Jesus: (see Isa; xix. 20. Matt. i. 21.) Hence the believer in Christ finds a just warrant for faith to rest upon, not only in the completeness of what Christ hath wrought, but also in the appointment and approbation of God the Father: so that here the preciousness of the Saviour, and the preciousness of the salvation, come home endeared to the heart.

SAUL

King of Israel. His name is as remarkable as his history, if it be derived, as some have thought, from Sheol, or Shaal, hell, or sepulchre. His history we have at large in the first book of Samuel. The great apostle Paul, whose name was originally Saul may, it is probable, have had his name changed at his conversion on this account: but this, the reader will recollect, is only conjecture.

SCEPTRE

This word in Scripture language seems to be intended for much more than is generally annexed to the term in ordinary speech. By sceptre we connect with the idea some insignia, or staff of office; but as the same word is used in Scripture in a very different sense as well, it certainly merits our attention, may not confine it to the one meaning take it in both. It is well known that the word Shebeth, which is translated sceptre in the memorable prophecy of the dying patriarch Jacob when declaring that the sceptre should not depart, from Judah, nor a lawgiver from between his feet, until the Shiloh should come," (Gen. xlix. 10.) is also translated, Judg. v. 14, pen. The whole passage is. "Out of Zebulun they that handle the pen (Shebeth) of the writer." So that the word, it should seem, is equally to be used for sceptre or pen.

Now if I mistake not (and if I do, may the Lord pardon the unintentional error), there is an uncommon beauty in the word, as used in both places, in reference to the Lord Jesus. Why may not both his regal office, and his prophetical office, be supposed as implied? The sceptre of Judah, and the pen of Zebulun, both might bear part in reference to Christ. The prophet Isaiah was commissioned to tell the church, "that the dimness should not be such as was in her vexation when at the first he lightly afflicted the land of Zebulun, and the land of Naphtali." But at the coming of him whom the prophet was about to speak of, "the people that walked in darkness have seen a great light, and they that dwell in the land of the shadow of death upon them hath the light shined. (Isa. ix. 1, &c.) And whosoever compares what Isaiah hath said in this chapter with Matt. iv. 13-16, will I think conclude that the Shebeth of Judah, and the Shebeth of Zebulun, are only beautiful duplicates, under different views of office, both pointing to the Lord Jesus, and only applicable to him. I beg the reader to observe that I do not speak decidedly upon the subject--I only venture to offer what hath been said by way of conjecture. Of one thing I am very sure: the Old Testament well as the New, is full of Christ; and it is blessed to catch a glimpse of him in places where we least expected. See Shiloh.

SCORPION

When we consider the wilderness state through which the Lord brought the church after coming out of Egypt, and hear what the Lord saith to his people concerning his care over them there, it is very blessed to trace a subject so abundantly interesting. "Who led thee (saith the Lord) through that great and terrible wilderness, wherein were fiery serpents, and scorpions, and drought, where there was no water." (Deut. viii. 15) There is somewhat so very gracious in this, especially when we consider what naturalists tell us of the venomous quality of those reptiles. Though the scorpion is not a large animal, yet its bite, unless restrained by the Lord, was sure death. The creature had a bladder full of poison, which he conveyed with his bite into the wound. And as the scorpion had two eyes at each extremity, and one species of scorpions possessed wings like the locusts, what could be more formidable to the traveller through the hot, sultry, unwatered wilderness!

What a sweet thought is it to the church of Christ, that as this as a figure of the present life, it is Jesus that now speaks to his people in the same gracious language, while they are going home through their eventful pilgrimage! What scorpions, what fiery flying serpents, do they meet with in every part of their warfare! "Behold, (saith the Lord Jesus) I give unto you power to tread on serpents and scorpions, and over all the power of the enemy, and nothing shall by any means hurt you." (Luke x. 19.) And they find the truth of this promise every step they take. "No weapon formed against them can prosper; and every tongue that shall rise against them in judgment the Lord will condemn. This is the heritage of the servants of the Lord; and their righteousness is of me, saith the Lord." (Isa. liv. 17.)

SCRIBE

We read in the Old Testament Scripture of this office in the time of the Kings, and it should seem at that time that it was an employment of great power. Thus when the king of Assyria sent to Hezekiah a blasphemous message and letter, we are told that then came out to the messengers Eleakim, which was over the household, and Shebna the scribe, and Josh the recorder. (2 Kings xviii. 18.) And the name in the Hebrew for scribe, Sepher, seems to intimate a person of learning. In the days of our Lord the scribes were among the leading men of the nation. One thing however appears striking, and worthy our notice, namely learned as they might be in the law, they were ignorant of the spiritual sense of it. And what an awful string of woes hath the Lord Jesus caused to be recorded concerning then! (Matt. xxiii. 13; to the end.)

SCRIPTURES

By Scriptures are specially and particularly meant the holy Scriptures, which are able to make us wise unto salvation, through the faith which is in Christ Jesus." In the strict sense of the word, Scriptures no doubt mean writings, generally speaking, for all writings are Scriptures; but long use hath long fixed to the term the Holy Scriptures, and them only, including the two books of the Old and New Testament. The Apocrypha is no more implied in the term Scriptures than any other uninspired writings of fallible men. But the blessed Book of God, comprized as it is in the two sacred canons of the Old and New Testament, form the Holy Scriptures, concerning which, as the Lord Jesus saith of the breasts of his spouse, they are like two young roes that are twins. (Song iv. 5.)

And it is most blessed to see what a beautiful harmony there is between them. Doth the Old Testament shadow forth by type and figure the person work, character, and relation of the Lord Jesus Christ? And what is the New Testament record but the sum and substance of the same? Doth the Old Testament relate the prophecies, hold forth the promises, and insist upon the doctrines, which were to be revealed openly, and completed in the person of Jesus? And is not Jesus, in the testimony given of him in the New Testament, the spirit of prophecy, the yea and amen of all the promises, and the pardon and remission of sins, the glorious doctrine in his blood and righteousness fully proclaimed and confirmed to his church and people? In short, the former prefigured, and the latter realized, the immense event of salvation, and all in Christ. Nothing do we find predicted of Jesus in the Old Testament but what the New brought forth the accomplishment of; and nothing that we hear of or meet with concerning the person and glory of Christ in the New Testament, but what the Old had foretold. So that when reading the one fulfilled in the other, we may say; in language similar to what the disciples did after Jesus was glorified--"These things they understood not at the first but when Jesus was glorified, then remembered they that these things, were written of him, and that they had done these things unto him." (John xii. 16.)

Such then is the meaning of the word Scriptures. And it is the most blessed of all employments to be everlastingly studying those precious oracles of divine truth, which the Lord Jesus so strongly enjoined in relation to the Old Testament, and which all his believing people find more refreshing than their necessary food, both in the Old and New. "Search the Scriptures, (said that dear Lord) for in them ye think ye have eternal life; and they are they which testify of me." (John v. 38.) "Thy words were found, (said one of the prophets) and I did eat them, and they were unto me the joy and rejoicing of my heart." (Jer. xv. 16.) "Oh, how I love thy law (said another) it is my meditation all the day! The law of thy mouth is dearer unto me than thousands of gold and silver." (Ps. cxix. 97. 72.)

SEA

The Hebrews called the ocean Jam, and they called also the lakes and rivers, and even large pools, by the same name. They distinguished the different seas with which they were acquainted with different names, as the Red Sea, the Salt Sea, the Great Sea, the Dead Sea, and the like; and the entrance is sometimes called the tongue of the sea. (Isa. xi. 15.)

It is worthy remark, however, that Jerusalem, which the Lord chose for his people had no sea or navigable river near it. There was no river of any consequence belonging to it but the sacred river Jordan, so that Jerusalem had not, as most cities, a garrison, or rocks, or water, to defend it, neither of maritime resources to open commerce and trade with other powers. But what the holy city wanted in those supplies of nature and art the Lord abundantly, compensated in his presence to protect, and in the supply of his manifold gifts, to bless. The prophet beautifully speaks of this in his usual style of devotion and elegance--"Thou shall not see (saith he, speaking of the glory of all lands) a fierce people, a people of a deeper speech than thou canst perceive, of a stammering tongue that thou canst not understand. Look upon Zion, the city of our solemnities; thine eyes shall see Jerusalem a quiet habitation, a tabernacle that shall not be taken down, not one of the stakes thereof shall ever be removed, neither shall any of the cords thereof be broken: but there the glorious Lord will be unto us a place of broad rivers and streams, wherein shall go no galley with oars, neither shall gallant ship pass thereby." (Isa. xxxiii. 19-21.)

SEAL

We find the use of seals of great antiquity, and they are so spoken of through the whole book of God. Judah gave Tamor the seal, or signet and pledge, as a token. (Gen. xxxviii. 17, 18.) And the custom was uniform among all the persons of the east. (1 Kings xxi. 8. Esther iii. 12.) But what I have thought particularly worth our notice under this article is, that the Lord himself condescends to make use of this custom in relation to divine things. Hence the work of the Holy Ghost upon the heart is called the seal of the Spirit. (Ephes. i. 13.) Yea Christ

SEED - SELAH

himself is said to be sealed by the Father. (John vi. 27.) And very sweetly the church, under the consciousness of these precious things being sealed, cries out in an earnestness to her Beloved, "Set me as a seal upon thine heart, as a seal upon thine arm; for love is strong as death jealousy is cruel as the grave, the coals thereof are coals of fire, which hath a most vehement flame." (Song viii. 6.) Some have thought that this is the desire of Christ, to be set as a seal upon the arm and in the heart of the church, and for the same reasons. And it is possible it may be so; indeed I see no reason why we may not make application of them to both. But be this as it may the Scripture sense of sealing is the same; Christ desires his church, and his church desires her Christ, that there may be such a nearness, and connection, and union, and intimacy between them as is formed between those where the arm is always lifted up to protect and help, and the heart hath an everlasting impression in love abiding, so that the person and interest is never taken off from the mind. Abide in me, said Jesus to his disciples, and I in you. (John xv. 4.) One in heart, in mind, in all!

SEED

This word is differently used in Scripture--sometimes in figure, and at others literally. It is used in a way of figure when spoken of the word of God; thus Christ compares his word to "seed cast into the ground." (Luke viii. 5.) Peter calls it the "incorruptible seed which liveth and abideth for ever." (1 Pet. i. 23.) But it is used in a literal sense also when referring to the increase of men or beasts. (Jer. xxxi. 27.) And it is used in a spiritual sense when the faithful in Christ Jesus are called the seed of Abraham, (Gal. iii. 29.) And yet in a still more peculiar, personal, and eminent manner when considered in relation to our union with Christ; "I will pour my Spirit (saith JEHOVAH to Christ) upon thy seed, and my blessing upon thine offspring." (Isa. xliv. 3. lix. 21.)

SEER

We read in the First Book of Samuel that he "who was then called a prophet was before time called a seer." (1 Sam. ix. 9.) I think it is very remarkable, however, that there is this striking difference between the two names, in that we find the word seer made use of as being the king's seer, but when the name of prophet is used, it is said "the prophet of the Lord." Thus of Samuel it is said that "all Israel, from Dan even to Beersheba, knew that Samuel was established to be a prophet of the Lord." (1 Sam. iii. 20.) But concerning the name of seer, we find frequent mention made of this character, not as the Lord's seer, but the king's; thus Gad is called the prophet Gad, but expressly said to be David's seer; (see 2 Sam. xxiv. 11.) So Heman is called the king's seer, though he is not said to have been a prophet of the Lord. (1 Chron. xxv. 5.) I do not presume to explain the circumstances wherein the difference lies. Some have thought that a seer was only a recorder of the events of the king's reign. A prophet was one who acted in the Lords name, and by the Lord's authority. The offices in this ease no doubt differed, but, as in the instance of Gad, reign, be performed by one and the same person. But I add no farther observations on the subject.

SEIR

See Mount Seir.

SELAH

This is a pure Hebrew word, and written exactly as it is here. The translators of the Bible have thought proper to preserve, entire as they found it. We find it scattered up and down in the book of the Psalms no less than seventy times; sometimes several times in one Psalm, and in many of the Psalms not at all. It is three times also in this third chapter of Habakkuk, and no where else that I remember in all the Scripture.

It would furnish matter for a separate treatise to bring into one view all that hath been said upon this word Selah; and after all we should be still left to conjecture. Some ancient writers have considered it as a word of particular observation, as if Selah meant to tell the reader to pause, said consider what went before. But this opinion is liable to great objection; for in this case David and Habakkuk are the only writers that thus impress consideration on their Readers, and they that always, neither at what we should consider the most striking parts of their writings: and if this were indeed the sense of Selah, how comes it that not one of the Lord's servants have ever used?

Others, and that a great majority of writers on Scripture, have concluded that the word Selah had reference to the music in the temple-service, and was a note of the ancient psalmody, but which now and for a long time, hath lost its use. This opinion doth not seem more satisfactory than the former; for supposing this to be the case, it were unaccountable that the Holy Ghost should have uniformly watched the word so as to preserve it with equal care as the Scriptures themselves with which the word is connected.

One class more have concluded that the word Selah means an end, not unlike the Amen. And though there might seem an objection to this, in that the word is more frequently found in the middle part of the psalm or hymn, and not at the last verse, yet, say they, the sense of that part ends there. I humbly conceive that this explanation, though in part it may be right, yet is not wholly so. If the word Selah means the end, perhaps it may be found not to mean the end of the Psalm where it stands, but to a higher end, even pointing to him who is "the end of the law for righteousness to every one that believeth," and to whom the law of Moses, and the prophets, and the Psalms, all refer as the end. (Luke xxiv. 44.) He is the great end, no doubt, as well as the beginning, in his mediatorial character, of all the creation of God, the Amen, and the faithful witness of heaven. (Rev. iii. 14.) But here I leave the subject. I am persuaded the word Selah is important; and I am inclined to thin, like some other words preserved to us in the Psalms that it refers to Christ. If the reader wishes to look at theses other words, let him turn to the word Musician.

SENNACHERIB

A well-known enemy of the Church of the living God, We have his history, as far as relates to the church, 2 Kings xviii. 13. His name it should seem is a compound of Sennah, the sword; and Charab, to destroy.

Though I should not have thought it worth the record of even inserting this man's name in a work of this kind, neither would his name have been remembered in history, had it not been for being connected with the church's history, yet as that part of his history which relates to the church opens a beautiful lesson, for instruction, I hope the Reader will indulge me with adding a few lines more before that we dismiss the recollection of the impious character of Sennacherib.

We are told that in the Lord's delivering the church from the threatenings and slaughter of this man, the "angel of the Lord went out that night, and smote in the camp of the Assyrians an hundred, fourscore, and five thousand; and when they arose in the morning, behold they were all dead corpses." (2 Kings xix. 35.) By the angel of the Lord we may suppose is meant the messenger of the Lord, for so the word is. It is not necessary to connect the meaning of the passage, as if it was one of those beings of light which are called angels. Some have thought that this visitation from the Lord was by pestilence, or one of those fatal winds which are known to visit those climates, which, wheresoever they come they sweep off with the besom of destruction. And they who have construed the passage in this sense have observed that it is said by the Lord, before the judgment took place. "Behold, I will send a blast upon him." See the parallel history, Isa. xxxvii. And as it was by night, and the Assyrian camp unprepared for so unexpected a judgment, this blast, like a devouring, fire, entered the camp, commissioned by the Lord, and destroyed them. One circumstance is related which seems very striking--in the morning they were all dead corpses. Those who have witnessed the injury done by this pestilential meteor, or fiery wind, or blast, relate that the bodies so destroyed are quickly after reduced to ashes as if calcined or burnt in an oven. When we consider what is said of the Siroc winds of the warm though milder climates than Africa, I mean Sicily and Malta, we may easily conceive how fatal the Semyel, or Simoon as they are called, of those pestilential climates may be, especially when commissioned by the Lord. And the slaughter of such an army in one night carried with it the fullest and most decided testimony that it was indeed effected by the messenger, the angel of the Lord.

    I have introduced this observation of the Lord's judgment on Sennacherib's army by way of introducing another; namely, what safety are the people of the Lord brought into when all the creation of God waits as ministering servants to execute the divine judgments on their enemies! "Winds and storms fulfilling his word," sickness and the word, angels and messengers, all wait to execute the Lord's commands. "Are they not all (saith the Scripture) ministering spirits, seat forth to minister for them who shall be heirs of salvation? (Heb. i. 14.) Hence with an eye to Christ, and to his people secured in him, the Lord's promise runs--"He shall cover thee with his feathers, and under his wings shalt thou trust his truth shall be thy shield and buckler. Thou shalt not be afraid for the terror by night, nor for the arrow that flieth by day, nor for the pestilence that walketh in darkness nor for the destruction that wasteth at noon day. A thousand shall fall at thy side, and ten thousand at thy right hand, but it shall not come nigh thee." (Ps. xci. throughout.) First spoken to Christ, and then to all the seed of Christ everlastingly secured in him.

SEPHARVAIM

We read (Gen. x. 30.) of an antient mount in the east called Sephar--and it is probable that the Sepharvaims were of this land; but from whence the name is, it is difficult to say. Sepher means book, or scribe; but we know of no writings or books before Moses. When Shalmeneser, king of Assyria, had besieged Samaria, and carried away the children of Israel captive, we are told that he brought men from Sepharvaim and other places, and put them in Samaria. (See 2 Kings xvii. 24.) But what is most worthy our notice is, that in the Lord's displeasure with Israel he should not only cause his people to be led into captivity, but Samaria to be inhabited by idolaters. Those Sepharvites, We are told, burnt their children in the fire to their dunghill idol. (See 2 Kings xvii. from 24. to the end, which is an interesting record.)

    I hope the reader will, make a suitable application from this affecting account. The Lord hath promised that his church, which is founded upon a rock, shall never be removed, neither shall the gates of hell prevail against it; but he hath no where promised that that church shall be confined to any nation or kingdom. The golden candlestick is a moveable furniture in the Lord's house; and the Lord hath said to a sinful land that he will "come unto it quickly, and remove their candlestick out of his place." The Lord Jesus said this to the once flourishing church of Ephesus; and the Lord fulfilled the awful threatening. For where is now that church? yea, where are now the seven flourishing, churches of

Asia? Alas! there is not a vestige of either remaining. And they are now the huts of a few miserable fishermen the ignorant followers of Mahometan superstition. (Rev. ii. and iii. throughout.) Oh, that the Lord may raise up a praying seed to wrestle with him night and day for our sinful land!

SEPULCHRE

I should not have noticed this word in our Concordance by way of explanation of the term, for that is unnecessary--every one knows that it means a burial place, or grave; but the reason I have paused over this word, and for which I presume that the reader will desire to pause too, is in respect to that memorable one in which the holy body of the Lord Jesus for a space lay. Here the mind will find subject for unceasing meditation.

The sepulchre of the Lord Jesus, no doubt, became a sacred spot, dear to every beholder, as soon as the eastern world became subject to the christian faith. But the thorough change which took place at the overthrow of Jerusalem, which our Lord predicted, and which was literally fulfilled when "not one stone was left upon another that was not thrown down," totally altered the face of this sepulchre, as well as the whole of the holy city. They who have made again of relics, and got money by shewing spots and places, do, no doubt to this hour, pretend to shew the tomb where Jesus lay, and numberless circumstances connected with the history. But these things are impossible; hence in proof we know that Jesus suffered without the gate. (Heb. xiii. 12)--consequently Mount Calvary was without the gate; whereas now Calvary is almost in the centre of Jerusalem. So also Mount Zion, which in our Lord's days, and before, was on a hill, and the most beautiful eminence of the old Jerusalem, but is now excluded from the city, and the ditches around the base of it are filled in. So that it may with truth be said, that there are scarce any remains of the city as it was in the days of the Lord Jesus Christ.

"Yet" saith Dr. Shaw in his Travels, (page 334. folio edition) "notwithstanding these changes and revolutions, it is highly probable that a faithful traditon hath always been preserved of the several places that were consecrated, as it were, by some remarkable transaction relating to our Saviour and his apostles. For it cannot be doubted but that, among others, Mount Calvary, and the cave where our Saviour was buried were well known to his disciples and followers."

Indeed as a confirmation to this, it is well known that the emperor Adrian, the bitter enemy of Christianity, in contempt to Christ, caused an image of heathenish idolatry to be erected in those hallowed spots where Jesus was born, and another where he was crucified, and a third at his speulchre. And all these continued to the days of Constantine, when the whole empire becoming professors of christianity, the images were then removed, and churches built in their place.

But while it remains an impossibility in the present hour to ascertain the very spot of Christ's sepulchre, the sepulchre itself opens the same sacred subject of devout meditation. Here the faith of the believer may frequently take wing, and still hear by faith the angels invitation-- "Come, see the place where the Lord lay." From hence it was the first clear views were made of the invisible world; and from hence all the faithful are taught to follow, in sure and certain hope, their risen and ascended Saviour to the everlasting mansions of the blessed. That pure and holy corn of heavenly wheat which then fell into the ground did not abide alone, but by dying hath given life in his life to all his seed, and become thereby the first fruits of them that sleep. (John xii. 24.)

SERAIAH

There were several of this name in the Old Testament. (2 Sam. viii. 17. 1 Chron. iv. 14.

35. Jer. lii. 21.) The name seems to be compound-of Sera, or Shera, to govern--and Jah: hence, it means the Lord is my governor.

SERAPHIM

The name is one with cherubim. See Cherub. It is derived from Sharaph, or Seraph, to burn. Hence the burning serpents were called Seraphim. (Num. xxi. 6.)

SERPENT

The interesting circumstance as related in the very opening of the Bible concerning the subtlety of the serpent, and the direct application of it to the devil, renders it a subject of peculiar importance in a work of this kind that it should be noticed.

I do not mean, however, by what I have said, to enter into all the wonderful relations which we meet with in sacred record concerning the serpent. It will be sufficient to all the purposes I mean to offer upon the subject, to observe that the Great and Almighty Author of Scripture hath in many places plainly declared that by the serpent is intended the devil, yea, the devil is expressly called the old serpent. (Rev. xii, 9.) I beg that this may be fully understood. And it were to be much wished that the sense of it was as fully impressed upon the mind of every reader. (See Job xxvi. 13. Isa. xxvii. 1.)

The whole tenor of Scripture, therefore being directed to set forth the devil under this image and figure of the serpent, there appears a beautiful analogy between the brazen serpent lifted, up in the wilderness at the command of God, and the Lord Jesus lifted up on the cross for the salvation of his people by the same authority--and for this plain reason, because none but the serpent of all the creatures in the creation of God was cursed; and therefore none but the serpent among the creatures of God could be the suitable type or figure to represent Christ when redeeming, his people from the curse of the law, "being made a curse for them." And as the simple act of faith in the Israelite in the wilderness, when beholding the brazen serpent as typical of Christ, became the sole means of recovery when dying under the effects of the serpent's poison in the old dispensation, so the simple act of faith in the Lord Jesus Christ becomes the sole cause of salvation when dying under the consequences of sin and Satan under the New. Indeed so Christ himself explained it and so the faithful in all ages have understood it; and, no doubt, thousands who are now in glory, while they were upon earth, accepted this beautiful illustration of the subject, and lived and died in the most firm conviction of the truth of it, to the Lord's glory, and their souls' happiness.

I have thought it worth while to be the more particular on this point, not because there is the least question to be made of our Lord's own illustration of this subject, but because some doubts have arisen whether it was truly a serpent which beguiled Eve, or some other creature. But while the uniform testimony of Scripture is with this subject, and the devil is continually called by the name of serpent through the whole of the Bible, and while the faithful in all ages have, without a single instance of departure, received no other idea, it should seem the safest method to accept the good old way of translation, assured that if the fact had not been so, God the Holy Ghost would have taught the church accordingly.

The objection arising from the Serpent's being endowed with speech and reined in conversing with our first mother, and persuading her by argument, is no more in reality an objection than that of the ass possessing both in the instance of Balaam's history. Both were miraculous; both induced by the sovereign power of God for the accomplishment of the Lord's purposes. And of the two examples of the kind, surely, the great event of man's apostacy became a much more important occasion for such a miracle than the condemnation of a single character like Balaam.

I cannot help making a farther remark, that the Hebrew name for serpent (Nechash) is the general name used throughout the whole Scripture. And it is not only an ingenious but a beautiful thought of Mr. Parkhurst in his Lexicon, page 390, that the reason for which Moses in the wilderness when commanded to make the figure of a fiery serpent, made it of brass or copper, was not only because it was the nearest in resemblance to the colour of the serpent, but also from the noxious qualities of poison in it. For, saith Mr. P. "as man, no doubt, was acquainted with animals long before he had any knowledge of minerals and their qualities, it seems highly probable that the primeval language might in some instances, and where there was a similarity of qualified, describe the latter by names deduced from those which were at first given to the former. And in the present case it is observable that copper is not only of a serpentine colour, but resembles those noxious animals in its destructive properties, being in all its preparations accounted poisonous." All this is strikingly just upon the presumption that the word (Nechash) he rendered, as it hath uniformly been rendered, serpent, by all the translators of the Bible for centuries; but, if another beast of the field be substituted the beauty in the resemblance, is lost.

It is worthy of farther remark, in confirmation, that the church all along considered the word (Nechash,) which is rendered in our translation serpent, to have been uniformly connected with the idea of this beast; for we find, in the days of Hezekiah, that in his removing the brazen serpent which Moses had made, and calling it not immediately (Nechash,) but Nehushtan, thus playing upon the word, but still preserving the idea of the thing itself the good old king plainly, proved what the judgement of the church concerning it was in his day. Hezekiah saw that Israel had idolized the type, and forgotten the thing signified, therefore in removing it, and calling it Nehushtan, he aimed to direct the minds of the people from the type and shadow to him it was intended to prefigure. (See 2 Kings xviii. 4. See Nehushtan.)

SERVANT

I should not have, stopped at this word, had the general sense of it been the object I had in view to have noticed. Every one is perfectly at home in his apprehension of the term servant, throughout the same time it may be remarked, that perhaps there are but few, even in the common acceptation of the word servant, who are aware how very general, in the extensive sense of the term, it is, as observed in the circumstances among men.

In relation to the character of servant, as it refers to the service the whole creation owe the Lord, we may take up the language of the Psalmist, and say, all things continue, according to JEHOVAH'S ordinance: for all things serve thee. (Ps. cix. 91.) "The deceiver and the deceived are his." (Job xii. 26.) Wicked men, and devils, as well as the faithful servants of JEHOVAH, may be said to minister to the Lord's will and pleasure; and though not by their intentions, yet by the overruling and sovereign power of God, do carry on his administrations in his almighty government. This doctrine, if it were capable of being opened and explained if all the multiform instances of it, would unfold such a display of wisdom, and of glory, as would call up the everlasting and increasing admiration, love, and praise, of all the intelligent creatures of God to all eternity.

And in relation to the word servant, in the mutual services men owe, and are in fact exercising, of receipt towards one another; here also, the subject is almost boundless. No state, no condition of rank in life, is altogether exempt from it. The King and the beggar have both their respective provinces in life; and as Solomon saith, "the

SERVANT - SERVANT

profit of the earth is for all the King himself is served by the field." (Eccles. v. 9.)

But I should not have introduced the word servant in my Poor Man's Concordance, had it been merely to have noticed these things. I have another, and as I hope, a higher object for its introduction; I mean in relation to the person, work, and offices of the Lord Jesus Christ, as JEHOVAH'S servant, and the servant of his people, as set forth in these unequalled words of humility and tenderness, and which are Jesus own, when he said. "The son of man came not to be ministered, unto, but to minister, and to give his life a ransom for many." (Matt. xx. 28.)

This view of the Lord Jesus, as JEHOVAH'S Servant, in the great work of redemption, and the servant of his people, opens to our contemplation, one of the most endearing and most affectionate in all the office-characters of our Lord Jesus Christ. Hence we find God the Father speaking of him as such, when calling him by this name. "Behold my Servant, whom I uphold: mine Elect in whom my soul delighteth!" Observe here the Father is speaking to the church of him, and bids the church to accept him, and receive him in this sweet character. And immediately after he speaks to him--"I the Lord have called thee in righteousness, and will hold thine hand, and will keep thee, and give thee for a Covenant of the people? (Isaiah xlii. 1-8.)

In a following chapter, (Isaiah xlix. 1-6.) we find the Lord Jesus calling to the church, in consequence of this covenant and commission, to accept and receive him in this character. "Listen O isles unto me; and harken ye people from far! the Lord hath called me, from the bowels of my mother hath he made mention of my name; and said unto me, Thou art my Servant, O Israel, in whom I will be glorified?

Such then being plainly and evidently the case, that the Lord Jesus Christ is JEHOVAH'S Servant, it will be highly proper and important that every follower of the Lord Jesus Christ should have a just and right conception of the sense in which this is meant in Scripture.

Now it is plain, that as God, and God alone, unconnected with the manhood, the sense of Servant cannot be meant. For he is "one with the Father over all, God blessed for ever." In this equality of nature and of essence, he is not JEHOVAH'S Servant, for he is JEHOVAH'S Fellow. (Zech. xiii. 7.) But when in the council of peace, before all worlds, in that covenant transaction which took place for the redemption of our nature between the glorious persons of the GODHEAD, the Son of God undertook to become man, that he might be the Surety and Sponsor of his church and people; here by this infinite condescension, we discover how Christ, as God and man united in one person, might, as he really and truly did, become the servant of JEHOVAH.

And so far was this act of humiliation from lessening the infinite dignity of the Lord Jesus Christ, or in a single circumstance departing from his own essential power and GODHEAD, that had he not been God as well as man, he could not have been a suited person of JEHOVAH'S Servant. And although he did veil the glories of the GODHEAD, during the time of his tabernacling in substance of our flesh here below, yet was it utterly impossible to be a moment void of it; and oftentimes he caused it to burst forth in wonderful display of sovereign glory and power. He, and he only, as God and man in the person, could be the competent Servant, of JEHOVAH to obey and fulfil all righteousness; to cancel and take away all sins by his blood; and as JEHOVAH'S righteous servant, to justify many, and to be "his salvation to the ends of the earth.;

I hope the reader will be able from this short relation of the person of the Lord Jesus Christ, as the Christ of God, God and man united, to form full and just ideas of the sense in which it is, that our dear

Redeemer is JEHOVAH'S Servant. Indeed this character is so peculiarly and personally his own, and his alone, that it is impossible any other should be. And he is so fully and so completely JEHOVAH'S Servant, out of zeal to his Father's glory, and out of pure free unpurchased love to his church, his Spouse, that the proper knowledge of the Lord Jesus Christ in his character, among all his other offices and characters, is life eternal. (See John xvii. 3.)

And now reader, if the Lord, the Holy Ghost, whose office it is to take of the things of Jesus, and to shew to the people, hath graciously shewn Christ to you in this lovely and endearing character; what a sweetness must your soul find, as often as you hear God the Father calling upon you in that sweet Scripture, to behold his Servant, your Surety, whom JEHOVAH upholds, and in whom his soul delighteth! And how blessed must you be to behold your Lord Jesus as JEHOVAH'S Servant and your Surety, entering, as the Scriptures have set him forth, the service of his Father, magnifying his holy law, and fulfilling all righteousness; yea, more than repairing all the breaches our sins had made, and purchasing for his redeemed a greater abundance of glory and happiness by his righteousness and blood shedding, than a whole eternity will be able to recompence! Oh, what endless glories, even now by faith, break in upon the soul, while contemplating the Father's grace, and Jesus' love, in this great salvation! "Haste, haste my beloved, and until the day break, and the shadows flee away, be thou like a roe or a young hart upon the mountains of Bether." (Song ii. 17.)

SETH

Sea of Adam, and father of Enos. (Gen. v. 3.) His name is taken from Sheith, to put.

SEVENTY

We read of our Lord's appointing seventy persons of a rank inferior, it should seem, to the apostles, and sending them out by two and two, before his face, with authority to teach and to preach in the cities
(Luke x. 1, &c,) Some have thought that this was in honour of the seventy called the Septuagint, who were the first that translated the original Hebrew into Greek, in the time of Eleazin the High Priest, about 240 years before the manifestation of Christ in the flesh. But this is wholly conjectural. It is true that the church of God, by the Lord's appointment, is highly indebted to their ministry on this occasion, It is said to have been undertaken at the request of Ptolomeus Philodelphus, then King of Egypt. How truly blessed is it to minister in the Lord's service, in any and in every employment; yea, how truly honourable! A great and powerful King declared that he would rather be a doorkeeper in the house, of God, than to dwell in the richest tents of wickedness. (Ps. lxxxiv. 10.) And to be a hewer of wood, and a drawer of water, for the Lord's sanctuary, when appointed thereto by the great Master of the household is more honourable than the seats of the earth.

SHAALABLIN

A city of Dan. (Joshua xix. 42.) The name seems to be taken from Shual, fox--and Bun, understanding. Perhaps hidden like foxes.

SHAARAIM

A city of Simdon. (1 Chron, iv. 31.) Probably the same as formerly belonged to Judah. (Joshua xv. 36.) From Shahar Shaddai. This is the Hebrew name for Almighty. Sometime, it is joined, with El; as Gen. xvii. 1, and then rendered God Almighty. But frequently it is alone, as Num. xxiv. 4, 16. Job. vi 4. Indeed if I mistake not, it is used in the book of Job not less than thirty times. Some derive this word from Shadad, which signifies to destroy; but others render it very differently, to make all sufficient; El

SHADOW - SHADOW

Shaddai, of many paps, or breasts to suck at. But perhaps Shaddai means both; for he thus is all sufficient to open thousands of paps to his people, can open as many vials of wrath to pour on his enemies. If the reader would keep both the senses in view; as oft as he meets with El Shaddai, God Almighty, he will find constant paps of consolation to suck for his own comfort, and the comfort of the church in all ages; and as constant consolation for support in the sure destruction of all his, and the church's enemies

SHADOW

I should not have paused at this word by way of explaining the word itself, had that been all. Every one knows what it means, and the Scriptures frequently use it. We meet with life, represented under the figure of a shadow; and we read of the shadow of death, and the like. But I rather fear that when the word shadow is used in reference to the things of the law, when it is said, "the law was a shadow of good things to come, but the body is of Christ," (Coloss. ii. 17.) the full sense is not so generally understood as it were to be wished. I beg therefore to offer a short observation upon the subject.

Now it is and must be, very plain to common sense, that before there can be formed a shadow, there must be a body that is somewhat of substance to form that shadow. Let that shadow be what it may, suppose the shadow of a man, or of a tree, or of a house, plain it is, that the man, tree, or house, must have been before the shadow; it could not be formed before the substance which gave birth to the shadow was formed; that would be impossible. A shadow, strictly and properly speaking, is formed from some substance, no matter what, standing between the shadow formed and light of any kind forming that shadow, by shining upon the substance. If I stand between the light of the sun, or the light of the moon, or any lesser light than either, and the earth which is behind me, my shadow will be formed upon the earth in consequence of that shining. If there be no substance between, or if there be no light shining upon that substance, there will be no shadow. All this is so abundantly plain that it can need no farther proof.

To apply this then to the shadow of the law, the law is said to be a shadow, but the body or substance is Christ. And consequently Christ the substance was before that shadow, yea, formed that shadow, when as the, lamb slain before the foundation of the world," Christ stood up at the call of JEHOVAH from everlasting. (Rev. xiii. 8.) But how stood up? Surely not openly revealed to men, but openly to and before JEHOVAH, when in the council of peace he was the Man, the Branch; and that in the ancient settlements, of redemption before all worlds. (Zech. vi. 11, 12.) Hence, Moses was admonished of God "when he was about to make the tabernacle: for see, saith he, that thou make all things according to the pattern shewed to thee in the Mount." (Heb. viii. 5. Exod. xxv. 40.) So then, the pattern or substance in the Mount preceded all the shadows that followed in the tabernacle service. And if Christ be indeed, as the Holy Ghost by Paul saith he is, the body, while all the services of the tabernacle were but shadows, (Coloss. ii. 17.) is it not plain that, however, not openly to the church, yet openly to God, the substance of the pattern must somehow have been before the shadow? Never could these shadows have had even the shadow of a being, had not the substance been before, and formed them. If we could go farther, and demand how these things could be, the only answer proper to be given is read to us by the prophet: "If it be marvelous in the eyes of the remnant of this people in these days, should it also be marvelous in mine eyes, saith the Lord of hosts?" (Zech. viii. 6.)

I will only detain the reader with a short observation upon the whole, namely, to say that it must be very blessed and very precious to the soul of the believer to discover in this instance, as in every other, that Jesus, as Christ, God, man, and mediator, was as the apostle saith he was, and is, "before all things, and by him all things consist." It was essentially necessary that he should be so, and the Holy Ghost bears witness by his servant Paul to it, that "in all things he might have the preeminence." (Coloss. i. 15. &c.) Hail! thou glorious Alpha, and Omega, of thy church's glory! Thou art indeed the substantially all of thy people's persons, safety, security, happiness, as well in grace as glory. All but thee are but as shadows, for thou alone art the body, and as thou hast said, "I will cause them that love me to inherit substance, and I will fill their treasures." (Prov. vii. 21.)

SHADRACH

This was the Chaldean name given to Hannaniah. (Dan. i. 7.) Perhaps from Shadah, field--and Racach, tender.--See Abednigo.

SHALISHA

See Baal Shalisha.

SHALLUM

This is a very common name in the Old Testament, and frequently given by the Hebrews to their children: and is not to be wondered at, for it is derived from Shalem, peace.

SHALMANEZER

King of Assyria, whose name would, most probably never have reached the present day, but from his connection with Scripture history. (See 2 Kings xvii.) If the name be compounded of Shalem, peace,--and Azar, to fasten; the meaning of it is easily put together.

SHAME

Every one knows what shame means, it implies somewhat that is disgraceful, somewhat connected with sin. Hence, where sin is not, there is not properly speaking, shame. So that our first parents in the garden, before sin entered into the world, knew nothing of shame. For it is expressly said, "And they were both naked, the man and his wife, and were not ashamed." (Gen. ii. 25.) But after the fall, instantly a conscious sense of sin made them attempt to hide themselves from the presence of the Lord, amidst the trees of the garden. (Gen. iii, 7, 8.) What a sweet thought is it, that as a sense of sin induceth shame, so a consciousness that sin is done away in Christ takes away that shame, and induceth holy boldness. Hence John saith, when speaking of Christ, "And now, little children, abide in him, that when he shall appear we may have confidence, and not be ashamed before him at his coming." (1 John ii. 28.)

SHAMGAR

Son of Anath: he was: one of the Judges in Israel. (Judges iii. 31.) His name seems to be derived from Shem, name--and Ger, stranger.

SHAMMAH

See Jehovah Shammah.

SHARON

There were several places called by this name in Palestine. Indeed there might be more elsewhere, for the name itself signifies a plain, or a place of fruitfulness. Hence the prophet celebrates it so much. (Isa. xxxv. 2. lxv. 10.)

SHEAF

The sheaf of the first fruits to be offered unto the Lord had much of Christ in it. (Lev. xxiii. 10-12.) Christ is the first in every thing. But as the first fruits of the harvest, Christ was eminently so here, for by his resurrection from the dead, we are

SHEALTIEL - SHEMAIAH

told that he thereby became the first fruits of them that slept. (1 Cor. xv. 20.) The sheaf was to be waved before the Lord, not only to acknowledge him as the Lord, proprietor of all the earth, but also to have an eye to the Lord in Christ, as sanctifying and blessing all our enjoyments. Hence, the Priest was to receive the first fruits of the sheaf, and to wave it before the Lord: and then and not before, the people had liberty to use it. Sweetly teaching us that Christ is first to be eyed in the blessing and then he will be enjoyed in the blessing; so that both law and gospel hold forth the same blessed teaching; "Honour the Lord with thy substance, and with the first fruits of all thine increase; so shall thy barns be filled with plenty, and thy presses shall burst out with new wine." (Prov. iii. 9, 10.)

SHEALTIEL

The father of Zerrubabel. (Ezra iii. 2.) The name is derived from Sheal, to ask—and El, God.

SHEBA

The memorable queen of Sheba renders this name familiar to the lover of the Bible. See her history, (1 Kings x. 1, &c.) Our Lord's honourable mention of her we have, Matt. xii. 42. Sheba signifies captivity, from Shaba.

SHEBNA

The scribe. He was in the court of Hezekiah. (2 Kings xviii. 18.)

SHECHINEH

See Signs.

SHEEP. See Lambs.

SHEKEL

A weight used among the Israelites; supposed in silver to be worth somewhat about two shillings and three-pence farthing current coin of our English money. If of gold it was about eighteen shillings. The name seems to be derived from Shakel, to weigh.

SHELAH

Son of Judah. (Gen. xxxviii. 11.) The name means to break.

SHELEMIAH

There were several of this name (Ezra x. 41. Neb. xiii. 13.)The Lord is my peace, is the meaning of this name, from Jab, the Lord--and Shalem, peace.

SHELOMITH

This woman's name is rendered memorable in Scripture, from having a son who blasphemed the Lord. See the history, (Lev. xxiv. 10.) to the end, Her name seems to have been derived from Shalem, peace--but her unhappy commerce with an Egyptian brought forth in this son both disorder and unhappiness. Alas! what can such events produce but evil? "Lust (saith the Holy Ghost by the apostle) when it hath conceived bringeth forth sin, and sin when it is finished bringeth forth death." (Jam. i. 15.) It is somewhat remarkable that this name of Shelemoth, though it is evidently of a feminine termination, was used for several of the sons of the Hebrews. (1 Chron. xxiii. 9. 18, xxvi. 26.)

SHEM

Son of Noah. (Gen. vi. 10.) The genealogy of Shem on account of the promised seed, is more particularly recorded than the other sons of Noah in the Bible. The name of Shem means emineney or renown.

SHEMAIAH

A prophet of the Lord. His history we have, 2 Chron xi. His name means, that hears the Lord, from Thamah that hears--and Jah, the Lord. There are many of this name in the Old Testament. (1 Chron. iv. 37. Ezra viii. 16. Neh. vi. 10. Jer. xxix. 24, 25. xxxvi. 12.)

SHEMARIAH

(See 1 Chron. xii. 5. Ezra x. 32.) From Shimar, a guard--and Jah, the Lord. The Lord is my guard.

SHEMER

From this man's name Samaria derived its name. (See 1 Kings xvi. 24.): The name itself should seem to be taken from Shamar, thorn; but is reported to have been a very lovely mountain.

SHEMINITH

We find this word before two of the Psalms, the sixth and twelfth! and it is used 1 Chron. xv. 21. And in the margin of our old Bibles, in this chapter of the Chronicles where it is said on the Sheminith to excel, it is rendered on the eighth to oversee. Hence some have supposed that it meaneth an instrument of eight strings. But this is by no means satisfactory; it is too trifling to suppose that the blessed and precious truths of the Psalms were composed for the purpose of mere musical instruments. Those Psalms beyond all doubt have an eye to Christ, and express sweet leading features of his office-character as Messiah. If therefore we suppose (and which I venture to think may be done without violence) that the blessed things contained in them refer to Christ, may we not suppose also that the Psalm itself is therefore dedicated to him? If the reader wishes to see yet farther the foundation of such probable conclusions, I refer him to Parkhurst's Lexicon, page 696, or Fenwick on Titles of the Psalms, page 18. See Musician.

SHEN

A place near Mizpah. The name means a rock or stone. See Ebenezer.

SHEPHATIAH

There were several of this name in Scripturae. (2 Sam. iii. 4. 1 Chron. iv. 8. vii, 5. 2 Chron. xxi. 2. Jer. xxxviii. 1.) The name is a compound of Shaphat, judgment—and Jah, Lord.

SHEPHERD

I should not have paused at this word, being in itself so very well understood, but only to remark the very great blessedness and tenderness of it as assumed by the Lord Jesus Christ. He saith himself, "I am the good Shepherd; the good Shepherd giveth his life for the sheep." (John x. 11.) And God the Father also sweetly holds forth the Lord Jesus, in his mediatorial character, under this endearing point of view, as the Shepherd of his church and people.

It would form the subject of a volume, rather than an article in a Concordance, to enter upon the character and office of a Shepherd as peculiarly suited and carried on by Christ; I cannot therefore propose such an undertaking. But while I refer to the Scriptural account of our Lord Jesus under this character, and which is more or less scattered over the whole Bible, I cannot content myself, without just observing how very blessed it must be for all the sheep of Christ and the lambs of his fold to know Jesus, and to make use of Jesus as God the Father evidently intended he should be used, as their Shepherd.

As Jesus is the Shepherd, so they are the flock; the one character implies the other; and the church made up of sheep and lambs are his property. He received them as the gift of his Father, and he hath purchased them with his blood; so that every tye of nature, interest, property, and grace, endears them to Christ. And hence he saith himself, "I give unto my sheep eternal life, and they shall never perish, neither shall any pluck them out, of my hand. My Father which gave them me is greater than all, and none is able to pluck them out of my Fathers hand. I and my Father are one." (John x. 28-30.)

I must not enlarge on this point, how sweet soever and interesting it is; but I do beg the reader who is conscious of being one of Christ's fold, and especially, the lambs of that fold, never to lose sight of Jesus under this pastoral office. Jesus knows all sheep, he calleth them all by name, his eye is always upon them, and his heart full of love towards them; he knows how helpless, poor, and prone to wandering they are; and he hath a suited grace for every one and for all. He saith himself that he will search and seek them out in every place whither they are scattered in the cloudy and dark day. His love, and not their deserts, is the cause of his care over them. He will feed them, protect them, help them, heal them, refresh them, restore them, and carry them through, the whole of this wilderness state, until he brings them all home to his fold in heaven. And all this and ten thousand things more, because he is their Shepherd, because he is, and ever must be, Jesus. "Hail, O thou almighty Shepherd of Israel, thou that leadest Joseph like a flock, thou that dwellest between the cherubim, shine forth!" (Ps. lxxx. 1, &c. See Pastor.)

SHEPHERDS

I notice the character of shepherds in order to offer a short observation on what is said concerning the abomination the Egyptians had to shepherds, which may not perhaps so immediately strike the reader. It appears by the history of Joseph that the patriarch used this policy when bringing his father and his brethren before Pharaoh, in order that they might be separated from the Egyptians, and have the land of Goshen assigned them. (See Gen. xlvi. 31. to the end, and following chapter.)

It hath been supposed by some that this abomination of the Egyptians to shepherds arose from their employment, because while the Egyptians worshipped animals the shepherds killed them occasionally for food. There might perhaps be somewhat in this for which the hatred arose; but then had this been the sole motive in the mind of Joseph, his plan of separation must have had respect still farther--the hatred would not have subsided by the mere separation, in putting his family in Goshen.

I rather think, (though I speak not in the most distant way decidedly upon the subject) that the mind of the patriarch Joseph had an eye to Christ and aimed, upon this and every other occasion, to keep up the gracious distinction of character of the seed of Abraham, whose first and most decisive feature all along was of "the people that dwell alone, and that were not to be reckoned among the nations." The character of shepherds, simply as shepherds, would not have been so odious to the Egyptians, for we read of the flock and cattle of Egypt, as well as those of Israel, and therefore they must have had shepherds also. But circumcised shepherds, and sacrificing shepherds, to the God of Abraham, when the cause of covenant grace and mercy was discovered, would have done then as it hath ever since done in the church of Jesus, stirred up the natural hatred of the heart against the chosen seed.

Reader, the offence of the cross is not yet ceased, and blessed is it for Christ's people it never will. The Egyptians of the present hour have their abomination still. It is the felicity of the Lord's people to dwell in Goshen--that is, to be separated from men of the world. They dwell alone in the purpose, council, will, and love of God the Father, the grace and favour of Christ, and the anointings quickenings, and fellowship of God the Holy Ghost.

SHESHBAZZAR

A prince of Judah. (Ezra, i. 8.) The name seems to be compounded of Shush, joy--Beth, the preposition in—and Tzarar, tribulation; perhaps alluding to the faithful in Babylon still rejoicing in the Lord in the midst of tribulation.

SHETHAR-BOZNAI

One of the king of Persia's princes who

accused the Jews. (Ezra v. 6.) It is a Persian name, and hath been supposed to mean one that despiseth.

SHEW BREAD

The shew bread was placed on the golden table of the sanctuary every Sabbath. They were twelve loaves in number, meaning one for every tribe, to be presented before the Lord. (See Lev. xxiv. 5-7. with Exod. xxv. 30.). Those twelve loaves were carried in by the priests hot before the Lord, and the twelve which had been there from the Sabbath before were then taken away. Generally there was upon those occasions all offering of frankincense and salt. The Hebrews called them Lechem Panahim, the bread of faces: probably from being thus presented before the face of the Lord.

Surely the believer may discern strong pointings to Christ in this service. And the call of the church as strongly referred to him, when the united prayer of the congregation went up, "Behold, O God, our shield, and look upon the face of thine anointed. (Ps. lxxxiv. 9.)

SHIBBOLETH

We meet with this word Judges xii. 6; and the history connected with it concerning the men of Ephraim is not a little singular. Wherefore they could not pronounce it, is not easily explained. They used the Samech instead of the Shin. It is blessed for us that our gospel privileges are given to us upon very different terms--when we cannot speak of them, yet looking to Christ we are blessed in them.

SHIELD

The Lord is frequently pleased to call himself the shield of his people. (Gen. xv. 1. Ps. v. 12. Ps. lxxxiv. 11.) And most blessedly, with an eye to Christ, do the sacred writers speak in this language. (Ps. xviii. 1, 2.) And where Christ is indeed the shield, what weapon formed against his people can prosper? (Isa. liv. 16, 17.)

SHIGGAION

We meet with this word (Habakkuk iii. 1.) and in the title of the seventh Psalm. Some read it Shigionoth, which makes it plural; the word is the same. Some suppose it means a Song of David. But as both prophets, David and Habakkuk, are celebrating things of higher moment than what relates to themselves, I cannot but be led to believe the word itself hath a reference, and the Scriptures connected with this title, to the Lord Jesus Christ. See Musician.

SHILOH

One of the names of the Messiah, given by the dying patriarch Jacob under the spirit of prophecy, and to which both Jew and Gentile agree; though in the application of the name to the person of Christ they differ. (Gen. xlix. 10.) It is worthy remark, however, that unless it be applied to the Lord Jesus Christ, it can be applied to no other. The dying patriarch said that the sceptre should not depart from Judah, nor a lawgiver from between his feet, until the Shiloh come. Now the lawgiver is departed, and the sceptre also; for they have no law, nor king, nor governor. But both they boasted of unto the coming of Christ. We have a law, said they to Pilate, when they demanded the death of Christ. (John xix. 7.) But now Christ was come, however unconscious of it, they said, "We have no king but Cæsar." (John xix. 15.)

I cannot dismiss this article without first observing that Shiloh is rendered the more remarkable, because as the name of the Messiah, nor indeed as any other name of a person, we no where meet with it but in this place. (Gen. xlix. 10.) And I beg yet farther to observe that it merits our attention the more, because it is the third blessed promise JEHOVAH gave, in his holy word, in the covenant of grace concerning redemption. The first was all gospel, and all of Christ: (Gen. iii. 15.) "The seed of the woman shall bruise the serpent's head." The second was all gospel, and all of Christ: and this was given to Abraham, (Gen. xxii. 18.) "In thy seed shall all the nations of the earth be blessed." And God the Holy Ghost, by his servant Paul, directly applies this to Christ, Gal. iii. 16. And the third was this blessed promise of Shiloh, which comprehends in its bosom the former two, and confirms and explains them. They both promised Christ. This saith when and how to be known. Do you enquire then, Is Shiloh come? I answer; Is the sceptre departed from Judah, and the lawgiver from between his feet? Then is Shiloh come. Precious Lord Jesus, I would say, Art thou come indeed, to my heart, to my house, to my family? Lord, when shall the full gathering of thy people be? Haste, haste, my Beloved, and arise out of Zion, "to turn away ungodliness from Jacob; Be thou as a roe, or a young hart, upon the mountains of spices!" (See Sceptre.)

SHILOH

A city of Ephraim, (Josh. xviii. 10.) This place was rendered memorable in the history of Israel, (Josh. xix. 51. 1 Sam. iv. 4. 1 Kings xiv. 2. Jer. vii. 12, &c.)

SHIMEI

There were several of this name in the Old Testament. (2 Sam. xvi. 5, &c. 1 Kings i. 8. 1 Chron. iv. 27, &c.) The name seems to be derived from Shamaah, fame--and the postfix pronoun makes it, my fame.

SHINAR

Rendered remarkable for the tower of Babel being built there. (Gen. xi. 2, &c.) The word Chaldean.

SHIP

It was among the prophecies of the dying patriarch Jacob, (Gen. xlix. 13.) that Zebulun should dwell in "the haven of the sea, and be an haven for ships." And how distant soever this allusion may appear to some concerning the days of Christ, and the eventual dispersion of the gospel to the Gentile islands of the sea, yet from subsequent prophecies to the same amount, when illustrated by each other, I confess that I am inclined to believe that some great maritime power, such as our own, may be fairly referred to in the several prophecies to this amount. I beg the reader before he goes farther to consult Num. xxiv. 24. Isa. ix. 107. Matt. iv. 13-16. Ezek. chap. xxvii. And xxviii. And Dan. iv. 13-6. Ezek. chap. xxvii, and xxviii, and Dan. xi. 30. No doubt, The Tyrus spoken of is mystical as well as other places mentioned in those prophecies. The limits to be observed in this Poor Man's Concordance will not allow me to enlarge.

I cannot however dismiss the subject without first observing that, however partial we may be to our own country as to fancy the great maritime power alluded to means our British Zion, the present æra is highly unfavourable to the character of faithful worshippers. Whoever takes a fair and impartial statement between the purity of our faith and practice, and the period after the Reformation, will be struck with astonishment in the sad change. I was much pleased with the perusal of a paper which lately fell into my hands, entitled the Bill of Lading for a Ship. From the beautiful simplicity of style, as well as the evident marks of grace in which it is written, I take for granted that it was first in use in that glorious period, when the pure doctrines of the gospel were as much known and valued as they are now forgotten or despised. I mean from about the year 1560. I shall venture to believe the reader, if he hath never seen a Bill of Lading for a Ship, will thank me for inserting it under this article. It is in my esteem a precious fragment of the devotion of our Navy, as well as our fathers at that time in this kingdom engaged in commerce.

"Shipped by he grace of God, in good order, and well conditioned, in and upon the good Ship called the ...... whereof is master, under God, for this present voyage, A. B. and now riding at anchor in the river Thames, and by God's grace bound for ...... such and such goods. And which said goods are to be delivered in the like good order, at the said port (the act of God, the king's enemies, fire, and all and every other dangers and accidents of the seas, rivers, and navigation, of whatever nature and kind soever, excepted.) And so God send the good ship to her desired port in safety. Amen."

SHITTIM

The sacred wood which was much used in the tabernacle, of which moderns know but little.

SHOSHANNIM

This is used as a title to several of the psalms. Some have supposed that the word hath a reference to some musical instruments. But whoever reads the forty-fifth psalm, where it is used, and with the additional title, A song of loves, will, I conceive, be inclined to think with me that somewhat higher is intended by it. If the whole psalm be of Christ, is it not likely that the title should be? See Musician.

SHUAH

This name was common in Israel to both sons and daughters. We meet with a Shuah, the brother of Chelub, or Caleb, 1 Chron. iv. 11.--and Shuah, sister to Japhlet, 1 Chron. vii. 32. The name is from a similar word, to cry. It is probably that the Shuhites were from this stock. Abraham's son Shuah, or Shuach, might be the founder of the Shuhites, or Shuchites. (Gen. xxv. 2. Job ii. 11.)

SHULAMITE

This name is given to the church in the Songs of Solomon. (Song vi. 13) It hath been variously accounted for. Some have supposed that it is in consequence of her marriage with Solomon, and bearing therefore his name; for Shulamite is the feminine, as Solomon is the masculine, both being derived from Shalem peace. And if so there is a great beauty in it as it relates to Christ and his church; for if Jesus be the Shalem, the peace of his people, his spouse hath peace in him and his blood and righteousness. We have a beautiful instance of the same kind, and from the authority of the Holy Ghost, Jer. xxiii. 6. with xxxiii. I 16; where, in the first of these chapters, Jesus is called by JEHOVAH'S appointment the Lord our righteousness, and in the second the church, by the same authority, as one bearing the name of her husband, is called the same.

But beside these considerations there is a great propriety in calling the church Shulamite, for Shulem or Salem is the same as Jerusalem; and this is the mother of the church, (Gal. iv. 26.) Hence Melchizedec is said to have been king of Salem, king of peace. (Heb. vii. 2.) What a sweet thought! Our Jesus, our Melchizedec, is king of Salem, and all his people are in this sense "Shulamites;" for they are "fellow-citizens with the saints, and of the household of God." (Ephes. ii. 19, &c.)

And it is very blessed yet farther to trace the propriety of the name in reference to the church's connection and interest with her Lord; for she is a Shulamite indeed in the peace and perfection of beauty put upon her by the comliness and perfection of Jesus. Hence when the daughters of Jerusalem, smitten with a view of her loveliness in Christ, call upon her, it is to return, that they may look upon her beauty. "Retrun, return, O Shulamite! return, return, that we may look upon thee." So struck were they with her righteousness in Jesus. (Song vi. 4.)

SHUNEM - SIGHT

SHUNEM

--Or Shunamite, is the same with the former, only by a corrupt reading Shunem for Shalem

One of David's wives, and the generous woman to the prophet Elisha, were each called by this name. (l Kings i. 2, &c. 2 Kings iv. 12, &c.)

SHUR

A wilderness so called. Here it was that, Hagar found a sweet Bethel: see Gen. xvi. throughout, well worth regarding. And how many of God's dear children have found the same wilderness dispensations laying a foundation for rich enjoyments! I verily believe that the family of Jesus would have lost some of their most precious seasons, had they lost some of their wilderness exercises. It was not without an eye to this that the Lord said, "Therefore, behold, I will allure her, and bring her into the wilderness, and speak comfortably to her." (Hos. ii. 14.) Indeed, the very word Shur, a wall, carries with it this idea. Reader, do not forget it if at any time Jesus brings you into Shur. He who brings you there will not leave you there, but will manifest himself to you there. Oh, how precious the faith that enables a soul to say, under all wilderness straits and difficulties, Thou God seest me! Oh, for all the family of Jesus to call such wildernesses Beer-lahai-roi--namely, the well of him that liveth and seeth me!"

SHUSHAN

The captial city or palace of Persia. (Dan. viii. 2.) It is a word also used for Shushan, or Susanna, a lilly. Jesus calls his church by this name, Song ii. 2. Indeed he calls himself so. And what is the sense of both, bearing the same name, but a confirmation of all the precious truths contained in the charter and covenant of grace! They are the same in name, in likeness, in pursuits, desires, affections; but then let it never be forgotten it is wholly on Christ's account. What Jesus is, he is in himself, underived. What she is, she is from him. "Christ is the rose of Sharon, and the lily of the valley." His church is the lily among thorns, because Jesus hath made her so. Thou art comely, he saith, "from the comeliness which I have put upon thee." (Ezek. xvi. 14.)

SICHAR or SYCHAR

A city of Samaria. It is supposed that this is the same with Sechem, and only changed, as it is said, by the Jews, out of reproach to the Samaritans, whom they did not love nor deal with. Sichar means drunkenness. (John iv. 5.)

SIDON or ZIDON

A fishing town made memorable from our Lord's occasional visits there. Some derive it from the word Tzada, to fish. It was an antient place. (See Josh. xi. 8. Matt. xv. 21.)

SIGHT

The recovery of sight to the blind was predicted to be among the events which should mark the person and acts of the Messiah. (See Isa. lxi. 1, &c. compared with Luke iv. 16-21.) But the greatness of the miracle hath not perhaps been considered but by few, equal to its importance, both in its relation to bodily and spiritual blindness. I am free to confess that I did not discover the whole loveliness of it until reading somewhat of the manners and customs among eastern nations.

In many cases of the blind there is not only a loss of vision but a loss of the eyeballs. And in eastern countries, where for capital punishment the eyes are literally scooped from their sockets, it is not simply a restoration to give sight to such miserable eyeless creatures, but it is a new creation. We meet with numberless instances, in the Old Testament Scripture, where such cruel punishments were inflicted. The case of Samson, Judg. xvi. 21; the case of Zedekiah, Jer. lii. 11. In the margin of the

Bible in the former instance it is, the Philistines bored out his eyes. Now in all such cases there is not only the loss of sight, but the loss of eyes. I beg the reader to connect this idea all along with what is said concerning this feature of character in the Lord Jesus Christ giving sight to the blind, for, it is literally giving eyes also, and consequently a new creation.

Now look at the prediction in this point of view concerning Christ, and it must instantly strike the mind with the fullest conviction that such acts to the bodies of men demonstrated his GODHEAD; for he not only gave vision, but he created eyes. And in respect to the souls of his people, which those miracles to the bodies were intended to set forth, surely here was exhibited the new creation in the most striking manner. Unawakened sinners are represented as "dead in trespasses and sins;" Jesus came to give them life. Jesus came to bind up the broken in heart; and a broken heart is a dead heart. Jesus came to give sight to the blind whose eye-sockets had no eyes, being put out for the capital punishment of high treason, even sin against God. And hence the charter of grace runs in those soul-reviving words: "A new heart will I give you, and a right spirit will I put within you; ye shall be my people, and I will be your God." (Ezek. xxxvi. 26, &c.)

SIGN

I should not have paused at this word had it not been with a view to have noticed the five signs of the Jews, which they regarded as so highly important in the first temple, and which they confessed the second temple was destitute of.
- First, The Urim and Thummim, by which the High Priest was miraculously instructed in the will of God.
- Second, The ark of the covenant from whence the Jews observed JEHOVAH gave answers by revelation.
- Third, The fire upon the altar, which was always burning.
- Fourth, The Shechinah, or manifestation of glory, to intimate the divine presence.
- Fifth, The spirit of prophesy.

Now as these five symbols or signs of the Lord's favour to his church and people were in the first temple, but not in the second, what a blessed prophecy and promise was that of the Lord by Haggai, that the glory of the latter house should be greater than the former! (Hag. ii. 9.) A circumstance only to be explained by the actual presence of the Lord himself in the temple, which those five signs typified and represented. And what a blessed accomplishment of both prophecy and promise was it, when the Lord Jesus himself came suddenly to his temple in substance of our flesh! (Mal. iii. 2.) In him all the signs and symbols, shadows, types, and figures, had their whole meaning realized. Oh, the felicity to behold in him "all the fulness of the GODHEAD bodily!" (Col. ii. 9.)

SIHON

King of the Amorites: his history we have, Num. xxi. 21, &c. If the word be, as is supposed, its own root; it means rooting out.

SILENCE

There is a great and extensive meaning in this word as used by the Hebrews. It doth not simply mean where nothing is spoken, but a certain complacency and delight. Thus the Lord himself is said by the prophet to rest in his love, or as the margin of the Bible renders it, he will be silent in his love. (Zeph. iii. 17.) In relation to the ordinary silence of the Hebrews, I refer to the word Salutation.

SILOAM

This was a pool under the walls of Jerusalem, between the city and the brook Cedron. The prophet Isaiah speaks of it as the waters of Shiloah. (Isa. viii. 6.) The name is derived from Shiloah, meaning sent. (See John ix. throughout.)

SIMEON
Son of Jacob, by Leah. (Gen. xxix. 33.) It is derived from Shamah, to hear. We meet with this name often in Scripture. Indeed it is a common name, Simeon, or Simon.

SIN
The Hebrews had in use several words by way of expressing the nature of sin; in the diversities of it. But the truth is, that sin doth not consist in this, or in that act of it, for the acts of sin are but the branches; the root is within: so that strictly and properly speaking, in the fallen and corrupt nature of man, sin itself is alike in every son and daughter of Adam. And that it doth not break out alike in all is not from any difference in the nature of man, but in the power of the divine restraints. If this doctrine, which is wholly Scriptural, were but thoroughly and fully understood by all men, what humbling views would it induce in all, and how endeared to all would be the person, blood, and righteousness of the Lord Jesus Christ! I beg to leave this on the reader's mind.

SINAI
See Mount Sinai.

SION
--Or Shion, or Zion. See Mount Zion

SISERA
The captain of Jabin's army. (Judges iv-v.) Some derive his name from Susraah, to see an horse.

SODOM
A city ever-memorable in Scripture, and now most probably the very spot of the Dead Sea. The name is properly Sodomah, and signifies their secret, from Sodom, and Ah. For the history of this city, and its overthrow, see Gen. xiii.--xix.

SOLOMON
Son of David, king of Israel: his name is derived from Shalem, peaceable. His history we have at large in the first book of the Kings. But the greatest improvement we can make of the view of Solomon, is to consider him in those features of his character which were typical of the Lord Jesus Christ. I shall beg to detain the reader for a few moments on this account respecting Solomon, as it is striking.

As Solomon was the son of David after the flesh, so Christ in his human nature is expressly, marked for the comfort of the faithful, as of the same stock. "Remember (saint Paul to Timothy) that Jesus Christ, of the seed of David, was raised from the dead according to my gospel." (2 Tim. ii. 8.) Hence when Christ "whose son he was, they answered, the son of David." (Matt. xxii. 42.) And it is remarkable that the Lord should have sent by the hand of Nathan, at the birth of Solomon, and called him Jedidiah, that is, beloved of the Lord. (2 Sam. xii. 24, 25.) And we need not be told how the Lord, by a voice from heaven, proclaimed Christ to be his "beloved Son in whom he was well pleased." Add to these, Solomon king of Israel typified Christ as a king and as a preacher in Jerusalem; and also in his wisdom, in the riches, magnitude; peaceableness, and glory of his kingdom, and in the building of the temple, which was a beautiful type of the Lord Jesus; who is not only the builder of the temple, which is his church, but the foundation of it, the substance, and the glory of it; for he and he alone, as the Lord said by the prophet, was the only one fit to build the temple of the Lord, and he alone "could only bear the glory." (Zech. vi. 13.)

But when we have looked at Solomon, king of Israel, as in those and the like instances, as becoming a lively type of the ever-blessed Jesus, and see in our Lord

Jesus Christ a greater than Solomon in every one, I would request the reader to detach from the person and character of David's son all that belongs not to him in those Scriptures, and particularly in the book of the Psalms, which are as if directed to him and spoken of him, but certainly with him have nothing to do. I mean such as the twentieth and twenty-first psalms, and the seventy-second psalm. I know that some commentators have supposed that what is there said is said first of Solomon, king of Israel, and secondly in an higher sense of the Lord Jesus Christ. But oh, what a degradation of the subject is it thus to suppose! Oh, what indignity is thereby offered to the Lord Jesus Christ! I have said so much on this point in my Poor Man's Commentary on the Book of the Psalms, that I think it unnecessary in this place to enlarge; but I could not suffer the subject even in this little work, while speaking of Solomon, to pass by without remarking the great perversion of the Scripture to suppose that there is in those things the least reference to Solomon, king of Israel.

SPARROW

The Holy Ghost hath taken such notice of this little bird, and thereby rendered the term so familiar to our ears, by his frequent mention of it in Scripture, that I could not altogether find in my heart to pass it by unnoticed. Moreover, it is one of the clean birds: (see Lev. xi.) not that I suppose that the sparrow, so called in Scripture, is of the same genus or tribe as our English sparrows of the barn; though this much despised bird is in my esteem a very sweet, interesting, and domestic bird; but certainly the sparrow, or the Tzipher, as the Hebrews called it, of the Scriptures, must have been of gentle and familiar manners. I do not doubt, at the same time, but that the name Tzipher was used for certain small birds beside the one so particularly noticed.

But let the reader pause over the thought of the sparrow making a nest for herself, and where in safety she might lay her young, high on the altar of the Lord's house, far out of the reach of the malice of all robbers of her nest, or murderers of herself and her young; and then let him contemplate the beauty of the similitude, when a child of God flies to the New Testament altar of his security, even to Jesus, and finds a rest in him, far above the reach of all disturbers of his repose, by resting in him, and resting to him, yea, making Jesus himself his rest, and his portion for ever! (See Ps. lxxxiv. 1-4.)

SPIKENARD

So called from Narred or Nard. We meet with this word not very frequently in Scripture. The spouse in the Canticles speaks of it. (Song i. 14.)--And the woman who anointed the head of Jesus before his sufferings, is said to have done it with the ointment of spikenard. (Mark xiv. 3.) Certainly in both it was figurative. The spikenard itself is a small uninteresting shrub, not likely to attract the attention of any which are fond of plants, for there is no beauty in it; yet the smell and fragrancy of it is said by some to be unequalled. So that in whatever point of view we esteem the figure or similitude, whether in allusion to Christ, or his church, or his gospel, the resemblance is striking. What so humble, low, despised, and overlooked as Jesus, though the plant of renown? (Ezek. xxxiv. 29.) "There was no beauty that we should desire him"--and yet what fragrancy, like the sweet incense of his blood and righteousness, to perfume the persons and offerings of his people? So his church; what more contemptible in the eyes of the great ones of the earth?--or his gospel, what more despised and set at nought? Yet how lovely, and how fragrant, in the view of Jesus! Hear what Jesus saith, "How fair is thy love, my sister, my spouse; how much better is thy love than wine, and the smell of thine ointments than all spices!" (Song iv. 10.) Oh, for grace to echo back to such

SPIRIT - SPITTING

matchless grace--While the king sitteth at his table--while his grace and the influences of his Holy Spirit, are calling forth into lively exercise those blessed principles he himself hath planted in my heart--"my spikenard sendeth forth the smell thereof." Yea, Jesus himself is the spikenard of my soul; his person, his blood, and righteousness, are an everlasting frangrancy to come up before my God as a sweet-smelling savour.

SPIRIT

See Holy Ghost.

SPITTING

We meet with so much in the holy Scriptures on the subject of spitting, and the being spitted upon, and in the eastern world, among the customs and manners of the people, the thing itself was considered a matter of such great reproach, that I have thought it worth while to consider it somewhat particularly. And I am the more inclined to this, from the treatment shewn to our blessed and adorable Redeemer in this way, concerning whom it is said, with peculiar emphasis, "he hid not his face from shame and spitting." (Isa. 1. 6.)

In order to have the better apprehension of the subject, we must look as far back as the Levitical law, where we find that even the spittle of an unclean person, though not accompanied with any anger, get if falling by accident upon another, was considered a defilement; and the person so spit upon was unclean until the even. (See Lev. xv. 8.) But when this was done by design, and accompanied with anger, the uncleanness and the disgrace were considered more flagrant. Thus in the case of a father's spitting in his child's face it should seem that this was tantamount to the leprosy, for the same law, and by the Lord's own appointment, took place in both cases--the child was shut out of the camp for seven days. (Compare Num. xii. 14, with Lev. xiii. 50.)

We may farther remark, that the action of spitting was made a matter of shewing the most sovereign contempt in the eastern world, in some of the most important circumstances of life. Thus the woman who was refused by her brother's husband, was to testify her utter abhorrence of him by spitting in his race; and this together with the loosening the shoe from his foot, was considered as the greatest of all possible reproaches. So that from henceforth his name was called in Israel, "The house of him that hath his shoe loosed." (See Deut xxv. 5-10.)

These circumstances may serve to explain in some measure with what abhorrence the action of spitting upon another was considered in the manners of the east. When it was done in anger, it was looked upon as the greatest of all outrages: and even when done unintentionally no affront in common life was equal to it. A French writer (Niebuhr) in giving his history of the Arabs, saith, "I remember to have seen in a caravan one of the company spitting from it sideways, and the spittle by accident fell upon the beard of another standing by. The offender instantly not only begged pardon for what every one saw was unintentional, but kissed his beard in token of respect. This had the desired effect, and seemed to pacify; and perhaps nothing but the kiss would have repaired the wrong."

I have introduced these observations merely by way of offering another, which I humbly conceive is of infinitely greater importance; I mean in respect to the personal indignities shewn to the Lord Jesus Christ in the article of spitting upon him. Few writers which I have met with take notice in terms equal to its importance, according to my view of the subject, of those indignities manifested to Christ. And yet it should seem that the Holy Ghost hath laid great stress upon them; yea Jesus himself referred to them by the spirit of prophecy ages before his incarnation. He speaks of it as a thing done even then, so much was it upon his holy mind--"I gave my back (said Jesus) to the smiters, and my cheeks to them that plucked off the hair; I hid not my face from shame and spitting." (Isa; 1. 6.) And it is expressly said by his servant the apostle, that for the glory which was set before him, he endured the cross, and despised the shame. (Heb. xii. 2.)

I do not presume to speak decidedly upon a subject so infinitely great, and wrapped up as it is in mystery; but I confess that I am inclined to think that no small part of the glory of Christ's work in redemption consisted in the humiliation of the Son of God in the accomplishment of it. If he who knew no sin became sin, and he who had incurred no penalty became a curse, well may it be supposed that he who knew no shame should be exposed to the greatest shame, to do away both the sin, curse and the shame, which Adam's transgression had brought upon the whole church when he had made the whole earth naked to their shame.

Let the reader pause over the solemn and affecting subject; let his faith take wing, and flee to the solemn spot of Gethsemane, Pilate's hall, and Mount Calvary; let him in imagination behold the meek and unoffending lamb of God in the midst of the bulls of Bashan, and view him giving his back to the smiters, and his cheeks to them that plucked off his hair, and hiding not his face from shame and spitting; let him behold the crown of thorns, and the reed for a sceptre, and the gorgeous robe, the bowing of the knee in mockery, and the wagging of the head in derision, spitting in his face, blindfolding him, and striking him with the palms of their hands; let him behold all these forming a horrid mixture of cruelties, and the whole will serve, in some measure though faintly, to represent the Redeemer's sufferings in this particular.

And amidst all these instances of mockery and shame, so cruelly and wantonly poured upon the sacred person of Jesus, there was one to heighten all, which I believe never before was heard of in the annals of mankind, in the vilest malefactor which ever suffered death for his crimes; I mean when the rabble mocked at the dying prayers of Jesus, and endeavoured to turn them into ridicule. It was said by Jesus ages before this great event took place, when speaking by the spirit of prophecy in allusion to his Father's hiding his face, "Thou hast known my reproach, and my shame, and my dishonor: mine adversaries are all before thee: reproach hath broken my heart." (Ps. lxix. 19, 20.) When therefore, under the pressure of a broken heart, Jesus cried out, "Eli, Eli, why hast thou forsaken me?" instantly they perverted the cry of Jesus, and jeered him, as if instead of calling as he did, upon his God and Father, he had called for one that was no helper, in Elias, and cruelly insulted him with adding, "Let be, let us see whether Elias will come to save him!"

Reader, I would only add, amidst the glories of Jesus, in the hall of Pilate, and on the cross, do not overlook the glory of the Son of God in the voluntary shame he endured. If Adam hath made us by original sin naked, and we all by actual transgression have done the same--behold Jesus. Stripped and made shame for us, as well as sin and a curse, that we might be made the righteousness of God in him. Think often of him who hid not his face from shame and spitting; and in the moment of such views of his unequalled shame and ignominy, recollect that when JEHOVAH brought in this first-begotten into the world, he said, "Let all the angels of God worship him." Precious Lord Jesus! the hour is hastening when that sacred head once crowned with thorns, and that glorious face so blasphemously spit upon, shall be seen with holy joy by all thy redeemed, when "every knee shall bow before thee, and every tongue confess that Jesus Christ is Lord, to the glory of God the Father. Amen."

SPRINKLE and SPRINKLING

The Scripture sense of those acts being very interesting, renders it necessary that we should have a proper idea thereof; and therefore I have thought it not improper to detain the Reader with a short observation.

The first account we meet with in the Bible concerning sprinkling as a religious ordinance, is at the institution of the Passover, when Moses, at the command of the Lord, enjoined the children of Israel to take of the blood of the lamb appointed to be slain, and strike the two side posts and on the upper door post of the houses, where they eat the Passover. And hence, in allusion to this, we find the Holy Ghost, by his servant the apostle, telling the church in after-ages that they were come to the blood of sprinkling. (Compare Exod. xii. 7. with Heb. xii. 24.) So that we cannot err in making application from the type to the thing signified; and as the Holy Ghost in so many words calls Christ our Passover, (1 Cor. v. 7.) hence the blood of sprinkling must mean the application of the whole benefits of Christ's sacrifice and death to the souls of his redeemed. And hence, when the Holy Ghost is recording the faith of Moses, in his view, of the Lord Jesus Christ, the blessed Spirit expresseth the whole of Moses's dependance upon Christ by this one act of the ordinance appointed--"Through faith he kept the passover, and the sprinkling of blood, lest he that destroyed the first born should touch them." (Heb. xi. 28.) We find the same blessed allusion to Christ and his blood in other acts of the Jewish law. (See Lev. vii. 14. Num. xix. 18, &c.) And the apostle Peter expresseth the whole of the fulness of Christ's salvation, and the two grand branches of it, the obedience and the sprinkling of the blood of Jesus Christ. That is, his active and his passive obedience. (1 Pet. i. 2.)

It may not be amiss to add that such was the custom in the eastern world in the article of sprinkling, that great part of their salutations and welcomes were manifested by this ceremony. One of our own countrymen in his travels saith that he was sprinkled with the water of orange flour, as a grateful refreshment. And a French author relates the same thing as a custom of the eastern manners, in courtesy and affection. I do not take upon me to determine the matter, but I would ask, is it not probable the custom was taken from Scripture? and is it not probable also that the meaning of it had an allusion to the precious doctrine of the application and sprinkling of the blood of Christ? It is worthy of farther remark, as an additional reason to this probability, that one of the prophets when speaking of Christ, said that he should sprinkle many nations. (Isaiah lii. 15.) And another prophet was commissioned to teach the church that their recovery from sin and from all uncleanness should be accomplished by the Lord's sprinkling the people with the clean water of his covenant, even the blood of Christ. "Then will I sprinkle clean water upon you, and ye shall be clean from all your filthiness, and from all your idols will I cleanse you." (Zech. xxxvi. 25.)

STAR

I should not have paused over this word which we meet with in the bible, had it not been that among the numberless names, by which the Lord Jesus is distinguished in Scripture, he condescended to be called the bright and morning Star. It is always profitable to eye the Lord Jesus Christ under any, and every name, by which the Holy Ghost reveals him. And there is somewhat very gracious and interesting in this similitude of a star, and particularly in that of the bright and morning star. The Hebrews called the Star Chocab. And that memorable prophecy the Holy Ghost extorted from the mouth of Balaam, no doubt had an allusion to Jesus the bright and morning star. And so again in the instance of Caiaphas. Let the reader compare Num. xxiv. 17. with John x. 49.-52. Those united views of Balaam and Caiaphas will shew how the Holy Ghost, by his sovereign power, overrules the minds of men to say and predict sometimes the very reverse of what they intend, and makes them the unwilling instruments of proclaiming his precious truths.

It is very blessed to behold how the Lord Jesus is distinguished in Scripture by his different names, and offices, and characters. And it is doubly blessed to behold how JEHOVAH delights to hold him forth to his church's view under every sweet and endearing manifestation, by which he may be brought home to the warmest affections of the heart of his redeemed, and formed in them the hope of glory. All, and every name, and perfection and grace, ascribed to the person of the Lord Jesus, shews that JEHOVAH'S great intention hath been from everlasting to exalt and glorify his dear Lord. And if the reader, as he reads his Bible, would remark it, he would discover that whenever the Lord speaks of any thing of eminency, or greatness, or glory, it is by way of introducing the Lord Jesus. Hence, he speaks of himself as the light and the life of men, the light of the world, the sun of righteousness, the bright and morning star. Hail! I would say for myself and readers, hail the blessed brightness of thy Father's glory, and the express image of his person! Do thou in mercy arise, morning by morning, upon my soul, to chase away all the remaining darkness of my poor wintry, cold, and cheerless heart, and give me grace to be hold thee, and accept thee, as the sure pledge of that everlasting day, whose sun shall no more go down, but the Lord himself will be "my everlasting light, and my God, my glory." (Isaiah lx. 19.)

STATUTES
See Testimonies.

STOICKS
We meet with this word but once, as I remember, in the whole Bible, namely (Acts xvii. 18.) But it may not be improper, though but once met with in the word of God, to observe upon it that it refers to a Sect which in every age hath been numerous and decided enemies to the truths of God. The Sect took their name from a Greek word, signifying a Porch; because it is said that Zeno, a Philosopher of these ages of darkness, taught his pupils in a porch, in the city of Athens. Indifferency to all feeling, human pride, in the strength of human reason, being sufficient to bear a man up against all the trials and afflictions of life. These were among the distinguishing doctrines of the Stoicks. How utterly contradictory to the word of God, and to the experience of all mankind. From such false doctrines and mistaken pride of the unhumbled heart, may the Lord deliver all his people!

SUN
The Hebrew called the Sun Shemesh from being the great luminary of the heavens. And from its beneficial use and influence, as appointed by the great Creator, it is no wonder that men in the darkened state of a fallen nature, made it the idol of worship. It is only from Revelation, that we learn that the Sun in all his brightness, is but the creature of God. And hence, under diving teaching, Job could and did say, that he dared to kiss his hand in token of adoration when he saw the Sun shining, in his strength, or the Moon walking in her brightness. (Job xxxi. 26-28.)

The Holy Ghost hath been pleased to teach the church to consider the Sun as the servant of the Lord Jesus, and as becoming a faint emblem of his glorious shining. The prophet Malachi to this purpose was "commissioned to say, that to them that feared the name of the Lord, the sun of righteousness should arise with healing in his wings." (Mal. iv. 2.) And indeed when we consider that the Sun, as the creature of God, becomes the source and fountain of light and life to the whole world, of animal and vegetable life; there is certainly a great beauty in the allusion to him, the Sun of righteousness, from whom the whole of the spiritual as well as the natural world, derive their very being, their upholding, and prosperity. Who shall describe the wonderful, unbounded, and endless influence of the Lord Jesus, in calling into life, continuing and carrying, on that life, and warning, referring, healing, and in short imparting all the properties of the sun of righteousness in his blessed and everlasting influence on the souls of his people. But the emblem of the Sun of this lower world, considered as referring to Christ the Sun of righteousness, falls far short in a thousand instances where Jesus becomes most precious to his people. The planet of the day reacheth but to the day, and leaves a long wintry night wholly destitute of his power. Not so with Jesus, his is a Sun that goes not down, but frequently in the darkest shades of sorrow, makes his rays most bright and glorious.

Very blessedly therefore the Holy Ghost caused it to be recorded by one of the prophets, that when the Lord Jesus shall come to be glorified by his saints, and admired in all that believe that his superoior lustre shall make his creature the sun to blush and not shine before him. "Then shall the moon be confounded, and the sun ashamed, when the Lord of hosts shall reign in mount Zion, and in Jerusalem, and before his antients gloriously." (Isaiah. xxiv. 23.)

SURETY

This is a very important term to be perfectly understood, from being the very character of our Lord Jesus Christ, who became the Surety for his church and people. It was an antient custom among the Hebrews to admit of a surety or sponsor for each other. Thus, if a man became bound for another, he was called his surety. And it should seem to have been the method upon all these occasions, that when one became responsible for another, he struck hands with the creditor. We find Judah pledging himself as a surety to his Father for his brother Benjamin. (Gen. xiii. 37.) And Job and, Solomon both take notice of the same, under the article of suretyship. (See Job xvii. 3. Prov. vi. l, 2.) But I should not have thought it necessary to have introduced the subject in this place, had it not been with a view to have brought the reader into a more intimate acquaintance with the nature of a surety as it concerns the person of our Lord Jesus Christ. Here the matter becomes so abundantly interesting, that it merits the closest regard of his people.

The Holy Ghost by his servant the apostle Paul, hath informed the church that Jesus "was made surety of a better testament," that is the testament or covenant of redemption by Christ's blood. (Heb. vii. 22.) By which we understand that in the antient settlement of eternity, the Lord Jesus Christ stood up at the call of his Father, the covenant Head and Surety of his people, to answer both for their debt and their duty. So that he stood in their law, room, and stead, in all he did and suffered, and it was covenanted and agreed upon by the Almighty Covenanters, that all Jesus did and suffered should be put to their account. This is the idea of a surety, and Christ was precisely this. So that when he had fulfilled all righteousness, and by his spotless sacrifice had done away all the penal effects of sin, his people were to all eternity and purposes, righteous in his righteousness, and free from all sin in his blood. Such is the idea of a surety considered with an eye to Christ. Blessed are they who are interested in it, and who no longer seek for justification but in him who is made the Surety of a better testament than the old covenant of a man's own works. All of this description find the blessedness of being accepted in the Suretyship of the Lord

Jesus, and can join the prophet's declaration: "Surely shall one say, In the Lord have I righteousness and strength: even to him shall men come, and all that are incensed against him shall be ashamed. In the Lord shall all the seed of Israel be justified, and shall glory." (Isaiah xlv. 24, 25.)

SUSANNA

A name well known in Scripture; probably derived from Shoshan, a lily, or rose. And some have thought on this account that the church calls herself Shoshan, when in the Canticles she saith, "I am the rose of Sharon and the lily of the vallies." And if so, it is worthy remark that Jesus confining this name to his church, when immediately after he adds, "as the lily among thorns, so is my love among the daughters." (See Song ii. 1, 2.) But whether so or not, certain it is that the church in Christ's esteem is, as Shoshan, their is both the rose and the lily, for grace, loveliness, and fragrancy. Let any one behold the church made white, or the lily in her Redeemer's righteousness, or red as the rose, being washed in his blood; let the fragrancy of the graces of faith and love, when going forth in the lively exercise upon the person of her Lord, be considered; let the fruitfulness of the once wilderness state of the heart, now blossoming like the rose, be marked: and when like the rose the odour is called forth and exhaled by the sun's beams shining upon her, and let every one then say, what can be more beautifully descriptive of the church than such emblems.

SYRIA

The principal city of Damascus: made memorable from the frequent wars with Israel.

T

TAANACH

A province in Canaan. In the division made by Joshua, it was given to Manasseh in the portion of Issachar and Asher. (See Joshua xvii. 11.) But in Deborah's song of victory, she describes the battle of Sisera as near these borders. (Judges v. 19.) Perhaps the name itself is derived from Hanah, to humble.

TABBATH

A place to which the Midianites fled in the battle of Gideon. (Judge vii. 22.) The word means goodness from Job, good.

TABERAH

In the encampment of Israel. So called from the burning there. (See Numb. xi. 3. in the margin of the Bible.)

TABERNACLE

Various are the significations of this word in Scripture. Sometimes it is intended to mean the place of worship the Israelites had in the wilderness. At others, is meant no more than a common dwelling place. Thus, Eliphas adviseth Job to put away iniquity from his tabernacles. (Job xxii. 23.) But in a much higher sense than every other, Christ's human nature is said to be the true tabernacle which "the Lord pitched, and not man." (Heb. viii. 2.) And as this view of the word tabernacle throws aside the consideration of every other; so doth the contemplation of this furnish a subject of everlasting pleasure and delight.

The Holy Ghost by the apostle informs the church, that this tabernacle of the human nature of Christ was the dwelling place of JEHOVAH. "In him dwelleth all the fulness of the GODHEAD bodily." (Coloss. ii. 9.) Not as the Holy Ghost dwelleth in the bodies of his people which are said to be his Temple, (1 Cor. vi. 19.) but substantially, personally, permanently, and for ever. So the GODHEAD fills the human nature of Christ. For that nature being filled with the divine, receives the same effect as iron heated in the fire is made fiery, like the fire which is filled by it. So the GODHEAD dwells bodily in the manhood of Christ. What a blessed soul-refreshing view of the Lord Jesus as JEHOVAH'S Tabernacle, is this!

And what endears it yet more is, that the Holy Ghost immediately adds in the following Scripture, concerning the church's interest and completeness in him, "And ye are complete in him." (Coloss. ii. 10.) Founded in his marvellous person, the church hath her Tabernacle in Christ Jesus, her resting place, her sure portion for grace here, and glory for ever.

Pause, I beseech you, reader, over the soul-transporting subject. Behold Jesus, (yea thy Jesus, if so be united to him by the Holy Ghost) in his mediatorial fulness as the Tabernacle of JEHOVAH. Here to this one glorious individual person, the Christ of God, JEHOVAH communicates his personality, his subsistence, or to use the words of Scripture: "in him dwelleth all the fulness of the GODHEAD bodily." And by virtue of Christ's human nature, to which his whole body, the church, is united; all, and every individual member, the weakest and humblest, as well as the strongest and the highest, have their completeness in the justifying righteousness of his person to bear them up, and bring them on before JEHOVAH, in grace here, and to bear them home, and bring them in before JEHOVAH in his three-fold character of person, Father, Son, and Holy Ghost, in glory for evermore. Oh, the blessedness of that tabernacle, "which the Lord pitched, and not man!"

TABITHA

It should seem that this is rather a Syriac than a Hebrew word, meaning clear-sighted, as some think. We find an honourable widow called by it in the Acts of the apostles, whose death gave occasion for the Holy Ghost by the ministry of the apostle Peter, to manifest his almighty power in raising her again. (See her history, Acts ix. 36, &c.)

TABLE

We meet with this word in the Holy Scriptures for various and very different purposes. The Table of the Lord, the Table of Shew-bread, the Tables of the Law given to Moses on Mount Sinai, are all of them very different to each other, both in their office and design. I must refer the reader to the sacred word itself, for the several explanations of each. (See Exod. xxxii. throughout. Num. iv. &c.) But I detain the reader to make a short remark on the method constantly used in the old church, in providing such rich and costly provisions for the Lord's table in the Temple. (See Exod. xl. 4, &c.) Surely, these things were emblematical of the Lord's table under the New Testament dispensation. The bread and the wine, and the salt of the Covenant, (See Levit. ii. 13.) and this constantly burning, and the perfumes always shedding forth their fragrancy: what could be more expressive of the Lord Jesus, and his rich and costly salvation? He is himself the living bread, and not only the salt of the covenant, but the whole of the covenant. (See Isaiah xlii. 6.) The sum and substance of it, the Messenger, the Surety, the Fulfiller, the Administrator, the All in all. And at his table every view of his endearing character is set forth in his body represented as broken, and his blood shed, with the enlightenings of his holy Spirit, and all the graces he sheds abroad in the hearts of his redeemed guests, as the costly perfumes of his incense and sacrifice. Lord grant that when thy people sit at thy table, they may have to say, "the cup of blessing which we bless, is it not the communion of the blood of Christ? the bread which we break, is it not the communion of the body of Christ?" (1 Cor. x. 16.)

TABOR

See Mount Tabor.

TABRIMON

The father of Benhadad, King of Syria, made memorable from his wars with Israel. (1 Kings xv. 18.) His name is compounded of Job, good--and Rimmon, the fruit pomegranate.

TAHAPENES

A city of Egypt. It is spoken of by the prophet Jeremiah. It is an Egyptian word, but supposed to be derived from a root, which signifies hidden. Tradition will have it, that Jeremiah was buried there. We know that he was carried thither. (See Jer. xliii. throughout.)

TALENT

Called in Hebrew Chiquar. In gold, it was worth 54,752l. and in silver 342l. or thereabouts.

TALITHA CUMI

Perhaps the former of these words is Syrac and means young women; and the latter is Hebrew Cumic, arise. (See Mark v. 41.)

TALMUD

Although we do not meet with this word in the Bible, yet as the Jews are very tenacious of what they called their Talmud, I thought it might not be amiss just to notice it in a short way. The word Talmud or Thalmud, means to teach. And the Talmud contains the substance of the Jews' doctrine and traditions in religion and morality. They have the Talmud of Jerusalem, and the Talmud of Babylon, according to the different periods in which they were compiled. As may be supposed, it consists in a multitude of unfounded histories: in many it is to be feared act unlike the

TAMAR - TARES

Apocrypha. Since the invention of printing, there have been copies of them from the press.

TAMAR

A character remarkable in Scripture. We have her history in Gen. xxxviii. throughout. Her name signifies palm-tree. There are some circumstances in the history of this woman which strike the mind with astonishment. We read them, we ponder them, and when this is done we commonly say, the "Lord's thoughts are not our thoughts, neither our ways his ways." (Isaiah lv. 8) It is a very remarkable circumstance also, that in the genealogy given by the Evangelist Matthew, under the inspiration of the Holy Ghost, of our Lord Jesus Christ, in the first chapter of his gospel, no mention is made of any women but of this Thamar, verse 3; of Rachab or Rahab the harlot, verse 5; Ruth the poor Moabitess, verse 5; and Bathsheba the wife of Uriah, verse 6. Was this intentional to set forth the grace of JEHOVAH and the unparralleled condescension of the Lord Jesus? Who shall answer the question? Who shall explain the subject? One thing is certain; as every thing in redemption is mysterious, so in our exercises on mysteries the lowest humbleness of opinion becomes the highly-favoured objects of such unheard of mercy Lord! I would say for myself and reader, "thy way is in the sea: and thy path in the great waters, and thy footsteps are not known." (Ps. lxxvii. 19.)

TAMMUZ

Perhaps this might be taken from the word Ammuz, which means somewhat concealed. We no where meet with the word but Ezek. viii. 14. And the Holy Ghost, by his servant the prophet, hath thought proper to say so little upon it, that we can only form conjectures from the Scriptures connected with it. As this was an age when Israel were gone far into idolatry, it should seem that this was an idol particularly worshipped by the women, as the sun was the idol of the men. And from the connected circumstances with the idolatry of the neighboring nations, there is reason to believe that acts of obscenity and lewdness accompanied this horrid species of Israel's transgressions. One of the old writers, David Kimchi, hath gone so far as to explain according to his views, and perhaps from tradition, that this figure of Tammuz was made of hollow brass, the eyes of the figure filled with a composition that when melted from the heat of a fire made within, seemed to drop like tears; and that upon those occasions the women at their festivals presented themselves before the idol as weeping before it. Oh, what an awful state is our nature reduced to by the fall! (See Moloch.)

TARES

Our blessed Lord having been graciously pleased to speak of the mysteries of his kingdom under the similitude of good seed, as in opposition to tares, the subject becomes exceedingly interesting, that we may obtain a just and proper notion concerning the tares.

I do not presume to speak decidedly on any subject but such as God the Holy Ghost hath been pleased most clearly to reveal; and therefore what the eastern writers have said on the article of tares, I only venture to relate, as the matter appears in their account, leaving the reader to his own conclusions under the grace of God. But if what they have said concerning tares be true, it serves to throw a more beautiful light on our Lord's parable concerning them than is generally understood.

They describe the tares, as in form and colour, so much alike to the pure grain, that to a common eye the difference is not discernable. In the blossoming season the resemblance is said not to be so striking then as in the earlier appearance; but from that time to the fruit forming and advancing to ripeness, the discovery becomes more and more discernable. Hence, the reader will remember the caution given by the householder, not to gather up the tares until the time of harvest, test in plucking up the tares the servants should gather up the true seed with them.

But what makes the parable of Christ so truly striking on the subject is, that while the tares are said to have carried with them so strong a resemblance to the pure seed, the tares differed so very highly from it in quality as to be little short of being poisonous. They possessed the power of intoxicating, and formed a very heavy load on the stomach of those, who by accident, gathered them mingled with their corn.

The parable of our Lord of the wheat and tares contains in its first, plain and obvious sense many delightful instructions; but under this view which eastern writers give, that tares are not simply weeds, that by springing up with good seed check the growth, but are destructive and poisonous, the parable becomes infinitely more pointed. Our Lord indeed, when speaking of the tares, and explaining to his disciples in private the parable, expressly calls them "the children of the wicked one, and the enemy that sowed them the devil." (See Matt. xiii. 38. 39.) But this view of them, as in their nature poisonous, however in appearance like to the good seed, is certainly a striking beauty in the parable.

I would only beg to add a short observation upon the subject, and just to say, under this view, how mistaken must be the notion of those, who fancy that when our Lord said, Let both grow together until the harvest, that this was meant to say, perhaps the tares if continued under the means of grace might become good corn. Surely the Lord Jesus meant no such thing. Never can the children of the kingdom become devils, however too often found in such company, and doing Satan's service, and wearing his livery. Neither can the children of the wicked one become heirs of the kingdom, however like tares in the midst of the good seed they may grow up in the same field, and bear an outward resemblance for a while to the true corn. They are all along defined whose they are, and to whom they belong; and to his all-seeing and discriminating eye they are well known, and their different characters, with their final issue, appointed and determined from everlasting. "In the time of harvest, (saith the Lord Jesus) I will say to the reapers, Gather ye together first the tares, and bind therein bundles to burn them, but gather the wheat into my barn." (Matt. xiii. 30.)

TARGUM

This word is not in the Bible, but as the Jews very much prize their Targum, it may not be amiss, just in a cursory way to notice it. The name itself signifies explanation. Sometimes the word is found in the plural number, Targumim, meaning that more than one subject is explained. No doubt, the Targum, took its rise from the Chaldee Paraphrase of the books of the Old Testament. And it is more than probable that this Targum was read to the people at the reading of the Scriptures after their return from Babylon; for it is said that when they read in the book of the law, "they gave the sense, and caused them to understand the reading.'" (Neh. viii. 8.)

The Jews speak with great confidence of the Targum. They have what is called the Targum of Jonathan, and the Targum of Onkelos. Jonathan was about 30 years before the coming of our Lord, and Onkelos somewhat later. They are said to be but short; the former chiefly on the prophecies, and the latter on the five books of Moses.

TARSHISH

The sea-port where Solomon's fleets were. (1 Kings x. 22.)

TEKEL - TEMPTATION

TEKEL
Part of the hand writing on the wall of Belshazzar's palace. (Dan. v. 25.) The word means weight, from Thechel, to weigh.

TEKOA
A city of Judah. (2 Chron. xi. 6.) So called from Thakah.

TEMPLE
This word in Scripture, though generally made use of to express one and the same thing, namely, the house of God, hath various references in relation to the divine glory. There was no building in the church of God called the temple, until the one built by Solomon. Before those days the house appropriated for the worship of the Lord was called the tabernacle, or sanctuary. But when the Lord bad instructed his people by his servant Nathan the prophet, (see 2 Sam. vii.) concerning the temple, we find Solomon, by the Lord's appointment, building this first temple on Mount Moriah. And independent of every other consideration, how blessedly did the very spot typify Christ, the true temple for the glory of JEHOVAH to be manifested in. This temple was begun somewhat about a thousand years before Christ, and took nine years in building. The desolation of Jerusalem by the king of Babylon at the captivity, brought on the desolation also of the temple, until it was totally destroyed in the eleventh year of Zedikiah, after it had stood amidst many ravages and injuries, from the plunder of the enemies of Israel, somewhat more than four hundred years.

During the captivity of Babylon the temple remained in ruins; but in the first year of Cyrus at Babylon, the Jews were permitted to return to Jerusalem, and to rebuild the temple of the Lord. And amidst much persecution and many interruptions, the people accomplished the purpose, and the second temple was completed at a period of somewhat more than five hundred years before the coming of Christ. I refer the reader to the prophecies of Haggai and Zechariah, and to the books of Ezra and Nehemiah, for the Scriptural account of this great event.

This second temple continued until the manifestation of the Lord Jesus Christ in substance of our flesh, thereby confirming and fulfilling the prophecy of Haggai ii. 9, "The glory of this latter house shall be greater than of the former, saith the Lord of hosts." And this was literally the case from the presence of Jesus, notwithstanding it had none of the five signs which Solomon's temple had, namely--1. The Urim and Thummim; 2. the ark of the covenant; 3. the fire upon the altar, which never went out; 4. the Shechinah, or manifestation of the Lord's presence: 5. the spirit of prophecy. When Jesus entered the temple, his presence became the sum and substance which all these signs did but faintly resemble and minister unto; and therefore confirmed JEHOVAH'S promise of the greater glory of the second, than of the first temple.

But the great object, the temple itself in both, and indeed in all other instances represented, was the person of Christ in his human nature; "for in him dwelleth all the fulness of the GODHEAD bodily." (Col. ii. 9.) Hence, therefore, as in the tabernacle in the wilderness, and in the temple at Jerusalem, the glory of the Lord was graciously manifested to the people to intimate the divine presence, so in the person of Christ Jesus, all that is visible it JEHOVAH did appear. See those sweet Scriptures in confirmation. (John ii. 19-21. Ephes. ii. 20-22.) See Tabernacle.

TEMPTATION
This word is perfectly understood in relation to the act itself as exercised by the devil, or bad men, upon the hearts of the Lord's people. It invariably means exciting them to sin. But when the word is made use of in respect to the Lord's exercises of his

people, it invariably means the reverse. I beg the reader to turn to the memorable instance of Abraham, and consider the result of that interesting transaction, Gen. xxii. throughout; and read also what the apostle James hath said concerning temptation; and I venture to hope, under the Holy Ghost's teaching, the truth will appear very plain and obvious. (James i. 2-15.)

In addition to these precious things from Scripture I would beg to subjoin an observation, and from the same authority, that the exercises of the Lord's people ought not to be considered in the light of probation, as some affect to call the present life, but as so many proofs of divine love. "As many as I love I rebuke and chasten, said Jesus to the church of Laodicea." (Rev. iii. 19.) But this is not as if to see how those whom Jesus loves will improve the trials and temptations by which he is exercising their gifts and graces; for if this were the case it would be to make the event of his grace to depend upon their use or abuse of the mercies given them, and instead of a covenant of his grace, render their final hope dependent upon a covenant of their good works. Not so the grace of God which bringeth salvation. Jesus by his death hath purchased redemption for his people; and God the Father hath engaged to bestow all the blessings of it in his covenant. The Lord therefore may, and the Lord will, bring his people as he himself was led up before them into the wilderness of temptation to try their spirits, and to prove his faithfulness: but the issue is not doubtful. The covenant stands firm as the ark did in the waters of Jordan, amidst all the beating waves, until the people are all clean gone over. And that sweet promise which belongs to the covenant, and is a part of it, never hath failed, neither can fail to every one of the people--"There hath no temptation taken you but such as is common to man, but God is faithful, who will not suffer yon to be tempted above that ye are able, but will with the temptation also make a way to escape, that ye may be able to bear it." (1 Cor. x. 10.)

TERAPHIM

We meet with this word, Judges xvii. 5. The translators of the Bible have retained the word as it is in the original, in this place, and also Hosea iii. 4; but the same word, Gen. xxxi. 19, they have rendered images, though they still have preserved the word Teraphim in the margin at that verse. It is attended with no small difficulty to apprehend what these Teraphim were. It would be easy to suppose, and indeed at once conclude, that they were idols for worship, were it not that the Lord by the prophet Hosea seems to speak in the Scripture referred to, that the children of Israel in their desolations should be without them, which, if idols, would have been their mercy, and not their misery. Nevertheless, as in the case of Rachel there seems a pretty clear testimony that her Teraphim were idols for worship, it is more than probable the whole we meet with in Scripture were to the same purpose. (See Gen. xxxv. 2-4.)

TERTIUS

This man hath honourable mention made of him in Scripture, from his services to the Apostle Paul. (Rom. xvi. 22.)

TERTULLUS

The famous orator before Felix, Acts xxiv. 1-9. It is somewhat singular that his name should be so very suited to his character, for it is a Greek derivation from Terata logos, and means a teller of lies.

TESTAMENT

This word is very familiar to the reader of the Bible. Every one knows what is meant by the New Testament; but perhaps the peculiar blessedness of the name, seen with an eye to Christ, is not so richly and so fully enjoyed as it ought even by real believers. There is indeed a most precious savour in the word, when we have respect to it, as Jesus had to the symbols of his supper, when he called the sacred service "the New Testament in his blood."

A testament, in the common acceptation of the term, implies the last act and will of a person in disposing of his effects. So the apostle called it, Heb. ix. 15-17. Such therefore was the blessed act of Christ; and the gospel was called so because it contained the legacies and testamentary effects Jesus bequeathed to his church and people.

In respect to the term, New Testament, that was not added as if the contents of it differed from the Old; for in fact it became a fulfilment and confirmation of all that went before: every thing in the Old Testament was the shadow and type of the New. But the peculiar cause for calling it New was, as being newly accomplished and sealed by the blood of its almighty Author; and when first so called the Lord Jesus had but just shed his blood at Jerusalem.

I cannot dismiss the subject, after thus explaining the meaning of the term itself, without calling upon the reader to remark with me how very precious the very name of the New Testament ought to be to every lover of the Lord Jesus, who by the regenerating influence of the Holy Ghost is conscious that he is interested in the contents of it. Reader! pause over the name--"The New Testament in Christ's blood," Surely, I would say, Jesus by his death hath confirmed it, and made all the blessed legacies in it secure and payable. For as the Holy Ghost saith by Paul, "A Testament is of force after men are dead, otherwise it is of no strength at all while the testator liveth." (Heb. ix. 17.) Shall we not enquire then what Jesus hath left, and to whom he hath left, his vast property? We know that all power is his in heaven and in earth; all blessings are his, temporal, spiritual, and eternal. And surely, it is worth enquiry after such durable treasure!

Now Jesus, before his departure, expressed himself to his disciples on this subject when he said, "Peace I leave with you; my peace I give unto you; not as the world giveth, give I unto you." (John xiv. 27.) Hence therefore the legacies of Jesus are to his people, his disciples, his children. As men before they die make their wills, and give their property to their relations and friends, so the Lord Jesus did his. It is his church, his spouse, his offspring, which are by name mentioned in his will, and who alone are interested in it. Oh, for grace then to prove the Lord's will in it. Oh, for to lay claim to all the legacies contained in it! Am I married to the Lord, and hath Jesus bethrothed me to him for ever? Am I gathered out of nature's darkness, and become a child of God by adoption and by grace? It is said, If any man be in Christ, he is a new creature. Am I a new creature, renewed by the Holy Ghost; and hath the Lord given me a new heart and a new mind, so that old things are passed away, and all things are become new? Oh! for the blessed discovery of these sure marks of a relationship to Christ, and in Christ; for then sure I am, that I have an interest in Christ's will, and he that gave himself for me, hath given all blessings to me. And as he died to make his Testament valid, so he ever liveth to be the executor and administrator of his Testament, and to see the whole blessings of his will faithfully given to his whole Church and people. Hail thou glorious Testator of the New Testament in thy blood!

TESTIMONY and TESTIMONIES

These words would need no explanation in their simple sense and meaning, whether as they relate to the Lord's testimony or to man's. Every one cannot but know, that the direct tendency of a testimony is to witness to some certain truth. Thus the whole Bible is a testimony of JEHOVAH'S sovereign will; and the Gospel a special testimony of the riches of his grace in Christ Jesus to the church and people.

But we meet with the word testimonies in the book of the Psalms, in a sense so peculiarly sweet and blessed, that I could not prevail upon myself to pass it by, without calling the reader's attention to it.

If the reader will turn to the one hundred-nineteenth psalm he will find the word testimonies, together with nine other words there evidently placed for the same meaning, which mutually serve to throw a light upon each other. The ten words are-- testimonies, way, law, commandments, precepts, word, judgments, truth, (or faithfulness) statutes, and righteousness. And what is very remarkable, one or other of these ten words is in every verse of that Psalm, except one, (as far as my memory helpeth me) namely, verse 122.

I beg the reader first to inform himself of his very striking circumstance, and then to consider, from the manner and occasion in which the words are applied, what is their obvious sense and meaning. If, for example, we consider the common and general acceptation of the word law, surely the Psalmist David could never be supposed to say, that the law of Moses as a covenant of works was his delight and joy, as he saith the law was in this Psalm, verses 72, 97, &c. Had he been looking to his own personal performance of the law of God, the conviction of his manifold breaches of the law would have made him rather tremble. But if the law spoken of in this Psalm be considered with an eye to what the Holy Ghost saith by his servant the apostle, "that Christ is the end of the law for righteousness to every one that believeth, (Rom. x. 4.)--and if Christ himself be the speaker represented by his servant the Psalmist, the whole then is abundantly clear and evident. Jesus might well say, and Jesus alone could say it, "I delight to do thy will O my God, yea thy law is within my heart "--or as the margin renders it, "in the midst of my bowels," (Ps. xl. 8.)--meaning that it was wrapt up, yea forming his very nature, from the entire holiness of that nature. (See Heb. vii. 26.)

In like manner the word testimonies, these had evidently a reference to the table of testimony in the Jewish church. It was before this testimony the omer of manna was placed. (See Exod. xvi. 33, 34.) Now, as the whole of this service plainly typified Christ, we cannot be at a loss to discover what is meant under the term of testimonies in this Psalm, when we hear the blessed speaker saying, "Thy testimonies have I taken as mine heritage for ever, for they are the rejoicing of my heart." (ver. 111.)

Similar observations might be offered on each of the other words in this Psalm, but these are enough in point. I only desire to add, what may be considered as a key to the whole, that one verse in the middle of the Psalm determines at once to whom the whole refers, and who is the speaker; and the evangelist's application of the words to the person of the Lord Jesus Christ very fully confirms it: "My zeal hath consumed me, because mine enemies have forgotten thy words," (verse 139. Psalm lxix. 9. John ii. 17.)

TEXT

This word is generally used to express the body of Scripture. Thus the Bible itself is said to be faithfully translated out of the original tongues, that is, the text: in opposition to what may be called human composition. And hence, the translation becomes a faithful one, being taken from the original text. The translation we have in English is among the first, if not the very first work ever accomplished by man, and demands the daily tribute of praise for it to Almighty God.

THADDEUS

One of the Apostles of Christ, this was his surname, for Lebbeus was his former name. (See Matt. x.3.) If his name was derived from Jaduh or Thaduh, it signifies praise.

THEOPHILUS

The person to whom the Evangelist Luke sent his gospel and the Acts of the Apostles. His name is a compound of two Greek words, meaning together, "a lover of God." (Luke i. Acts i.)

THESSALONIA

This city was in ancient times the metropolis of Macedonia. Here Paul preached the gospel, being called to it by a vision. (See Acts xvi. 9, 10.) And having first preached at Philippi, he afterwards visited Thessalonica, (Acts xvii. 1, &c.) It was to the church of the Thessalonians he sent those two blessed Epistles, which through grace are in all the churches. It is probable that the first of those Epistles was the earliest in point of date, of all the apostle's writings, being sent to the church about the year of our Lord God 51.

THIGH

I pause at this word in order to notice the very remarkable custom, and of the highest antiquity, observed by the patriarchs, and which it is said is observed even now by some of the descendants of Abraham after the flesh, of swearing with the hand under the thigh. Thus we find Abraham desired his servant Eliezer to swear, concerning the taking a wife for his son. (Gen. xxiv. 2.) So in like manner Jacob caused his son Joseph to swear concerning burying him not in Egypt. (Gen. xlvii. 29. &c.) It is remarkable however, that we do not, after these striking instances, meet with a like ceremony among the Israelites, of swearing by putting the hand under the thigh, though there is smiting, in token of shame and sorrow. (See Jer. xxxi. 19. Zech. xxi. 12.)

Various have been the opinions of writers as to the intention and design of it. Some have supposed that the oath was to remind the person taking it, that he and the person demanding it, were both circumcised: so that it was pledging himself by the covenant relationship between them. Others carry the matter farther, and while supposing, as the former, that the oath had respect to this fraternity and relationship in one common covenant, they add to it a reference to the person, and the expectation of the Messiah as the head and substance of the covenant; and in confirmation of this opinion they refer to that passage, Gen. xlvi. 26. where it is said that "all the souls which cause with Jacob into Egypt, came out of his loins," or, as the margin renders it, his thigh. By which I humbly conceive is meant, as still with an eye to the covenant, an interest in the Messiah. And if this should have been the allusion, what a blessed testimony doth it hold forth of the patriarch's esteem of the salvation by Jesus Christ, and of their faith and assurance concerning it! And why may we not suppose that that early song of the royal nuptial feast of Christ with his church, which was sung by the psalmist a thousand years before Christ's incarnation, had an eye to the same, when Jesus was called upon to gird himself with his sword upon his thigh? (Ps. lxv. 3.) We lose numberless beauties of the holy Scriptures, in our ignorance of the customs and manners of the East. But if the loins and thigh in relation to Israel's seed were the same as we have seen, Gen. xlvi. 26, surely the girding of Christ and the clothing of Christ may without violence he considered not unsimilar. And why may not the Lord be invocated as the most mighty, with his glory and majesty to gird himself upon the seed of his loins or thigh, as God the Father be heard claring concerning the whole seed of Christ, that he shall be clothed with them? "As I live, saith the Lord," speaking to his dear Son as Mediator, "thou shalt surely clothe thee with them all as with an ornament, and bind them on thee as a bride doth? (Isaiah xlix. 19.) But I add no more, the Lord pardon what I have already sold if I err.

THOMAS

One of the apostles of Christ. His history we have in the gospel. His other name Didymus signifies a twin. And it is remarkable that the Hebrew for twin is Tham.

THREE

I pause over this number to make a short observation concerning what we read of the sacred Three in one described by the Apostle John, and which bears a beautiful and glorious correspondence to all the testimonies of the holy writers in the Bible. "For there are three that bear record in Heaven, the Father, the Son and Holy Ghost, and these three are one." (1 John v. 7.) It is somewhat remarkable that the word Trinity is never used by any of the sacred writers: that is to say, by the translators of the Bible into our mother tongue, while they are so express in numberless instances, giving the sum and substance of it. Evidently many of the old Rabbi gave distinct names to each glorious person of the GODHEAD, as their writings testify. They called the Father, JEHOVAH, and the Son, the Word or Memur: and the Holy Ghost, Ruach. And they expressed the union of those Three Glorious persons by the word Shalithith, which is "as near as possible the word Trinity. It must be confessed, (for it maybe be very safely allowed without the smallest injury to the true faith,) that there are numbers among the Jews of modern times, who from the ignorance of their mind and blinded understanding, are looking for the Messiah in the simple humanity of the man, and know nothing of JEHOVAH in his threefold personality of character. But these do by no means invalidate the true faith, any more than Socinians and Arians, by their denial of the GODHEAD of Christ. The ancient descendants of Abraham, and it is to be hoped the modern stock of Israel, though overlooking the time, have lost not sight of his Almighty person. They know what the prophet said to be true concerning the Messiah, and expected him in that character. "Behold, your God shall come and save you." (Isaiah xxxv. 4.)

THUMMIM

See Urim.

THYATIRA

A city of the lesser Asia. Here was one of the seven churches to whom the Lord Jesus sent his epistles. (See Rev. ii. 18.)

TIMOTHY

A name well known in the New Testament. The church hath reason to bless the Lord for the conversion of this man, since the Holy Ghost hath been pleased to give the church those two sweet Epistles, addressed to him by Paul.

TIRZAH

A city in the land of Judaea, belonging to Ephraim, and from the days of Jeroboam, King of Israel, to the reign of Omri, Tirzah was the royal city and the King's residence.

It is said to have been a beautiful, spot, and the name Tirzah, which, comes from a root, signifying somewhat grateful, evidently seems, to say so, Jesus compares his church to it. "Thou art beautiful, O my love, as "Tirzah, said the Redeemer, "comely as Jerusalem and terrible as an army with banners," (Song vi. 4.) And is not the church all this when beautiful, in his salvation and comely in the comeliness which he hath put upon her? And what an awe do Jesus's little ones strike even now upon the ungodly, when they behold them living in his faith, and fear and love? And who, will dare to oppose them, by and by, when they shall see the Lord Jesus come to be "glorified in his saints, and admired in all them that believe?"

TITUS

The friend and companion of Paul. We have

a precious epistle addressed to this man, by the Apostle, for which we have great cause to bless the Holy Ghost. (See Epistle to Titus.)

TOWEL

I have thought it worth the reader's attention to pause at this word, in order from the customs of the East to be enabled to form a better apprehension concerning the towel with which the Lord Jesus girded himself when he washed his disciples' feet. John the Evangelist, with his usual simplicity of narration, describes the Redeemer as arising from supper and laying aside his garments, taking a towel and girding himself. And then with that unequalled humility which distinguished the Lord of life and glory, washing his disciples' feet and wiping them with the towel wherewith he was girded. (John xiii. 3, &c.)

We shall have a more lively idea of this most interesting scene, as well as the wonderful grace and condescension of the Almighty Redeemer in this act of his, if we attend to what was the custom of the dress among those eastern people in the days of our Lord. "Dr. Shaw, in his Observations on the customs and manners of the East," hath very largely entered into the subject, page 292 of his folio edition. He saith that it was the custom to wear underneath their hykes (the hyke was a large woollen blanket) a close bodied frock or tunic, not unlike the Roman tunic." So that when the Lord Jesus laid aside his garments he threw off this hyke, and was then in this close-bodied tunic only. Such was always the method observed for labour of all kinds. Similar was the act of Peter on the sea of Tiberias, when it is said "he girt his fisher's coat unto him, for he was naked." (John xxi. 7.) It doth not mean absolutely without the least covering, for this close-bodied tunic was always upon them. But it means he had not the hyke girt about him. In like manner when Peter was in prison, (Acts xii. 8.) the angel commanded him to cast his garments (that is this hyke) about him, for he was with his tunic only before.

Dr. Shaw therefore observes, that the hyke and burnoose (which was also a cloak or upper garment) being probably at that time the proper dress or clothing of the Eastern Nations, as they continue to be at this day of the Kabyles and Arabs, the laying them aside, or appearing without them, might according to the eastern manner of expression, be other words only for being naked of their hyke. If these remarks in allusion to the dress of the Orientalsbe properly attended to, they will serve to throw a light upon many similar passages in holy writ which we meet with that require some explanation properly to apprehend.

I cannot dismiss this view of Jesus girded with the towel, and washing the feet of poor fishermen, without calling upon the reader once more, yea, evermore, to behold in this endearment of character the Lord of life and glory. Was there ever an instance of humility like this? and at a time, it should be remembered, also, Jesus knew that "all things were given into his hand as Mediator, the Sovereign of heaven and earth." (See John xiii. 3.) Let the soul of all his redeemed take encouragement to come to him from such displays of unequalled grace and love. Did Jesus, I would, methinks, have every poor sinner say, did Jesus not think it unbecoming of him then to wash poor fishermen's feet? And will he reject the humble cries of poor sinners now? Yea, will he not delight to receive them? Is he not become more glorious to our view, from becoming so gracious to our need? Precious Lord, I would say for myself and reader, give each of us grace to be everlastingly beholding thee into his most lovely portrait girded with thy towel; and the lower thou comest down to suit the wants of our souls, be thou the higher exalted in our hearts, and live and reign there for ever!

TOWER

We meet with an account of many towers in the word of God. The tower of Babel. (Gen. xi. 9.) The tower of Edar. (Gen. xxxv. 21.) The Migdol at Pihahiroth. (Exod. xiv. 2.) The tower of Shechem, (Judges ix. 46.) and the like. And we meet with the word tower sometimes made use of by way of figure, such as the tower of the flock, and God is my high tower, &c. The Hebrews called every tower by the general name of Migdol. The church is beautifully compared by Christ to a tower in one of the Songs, Chap. iv. 4. "Thy neck (said Jesus) is like the tower of David, builded for an armoury; whereon there hang a thousand bucklers, all shields of mighty men." What a gracious act in the Lord Jesus was it thus to speak of his church under such a comparison! The tower of David, it is well known, was the strong hold of Zion which he took from the Jebusites, which anciently possessed what was not their right, Jerusalem. Now then as David here typified Christ driving out the strong man armed, who possessed the Lord's Zion not by right, but by deceit; so when the church was put in possession by her conquering Lord, her neck, by which may be considered all her members united to the head, even the Lord Jesus, becomes like a tower, impregnable, and which Christ, the true David, builded for an armoury (for it is Christ that builds all, and supports and gives life and strength, to all). Here then on him and his building they hang all their bucklers and shields, even to a thousand and ten thousand; for all is founded in him, and to him, and by him; on him himself they hang all the glory of his Father's house? And what endears the whole is, that the humblest and east, as well as the highest and the best, are like this neck, like the tower of David, united to the head. For in this gospel day to which the whole refers; "he that is feeble among them at that day shall be as David, and the house of David shall be as God, as the Angel of the Lord before them, (Isaiah xxii. 22, to the end, Zech. xii. 8.) It is very blessed to behold Jesus using such strong and beautiful figures to shew his people's union and oneness with him, and their everlasting safety and security in him.

TRADITION

Among the Jews, they had certain sayings and opinions supposed to be received from the earliest fathers, and handed down from one generation to another, which they called traditions. And in some instances! they were more tenacious to hold and regard them than even the word of God. Our adorable Lord was constant in reproof concerning them, and hence we find in many parts of the gospel his just condemnation of them, (See Matt. xv. Mark vii. &c.) It were to be devoutly wished that the weakness, and in some instances the wickedness, of traditions had ceased with Jews and Christians. But the trumpery of legends and reliques; and the like; which some have held with equal veneration to the Scriptures, plainly prove that those things, are in common from the folly and corruption of poor fallen nature, both of Jew and Gentile.

TRAITOR

See Rebel and Rebels.

TRANSFIGURATION

This relates to that glorious scene recorded by three of the Evangelists, in which the glory of Christ's person broke out in the presence of the disciples in Mount Tabor. All description of it fails, I can only therefore refer the reader to the Scripture account of it, as the Holy Ghost hath recorded it, Matt. xvii. Mark ix. Luke ix.

TRANSLATION

The translation of the Holy Scriptures into our English language is among the highest instances of divine mercy. And the work itself may be considered as among the most blessed monuments of the church. The memory of the authors of it under the grace of the Holy Ghost is truly blessed, and proves that Scripture, "the righteous shall be in everlasting remembrance." (Ps. cxii. 6.)

TREASURE

The Hebrews had one general name for treasure, and called it Ozer. The sweetest of all thoughts is, that Jesus is the treasure of his people. JEHOVAH promised the church by Moses, that he would command the blessing upon Israel in his storehouses, and in all that he would set his hand unto. And when the Holy Ghost explains this to the soul of the redeemed, and he sees that this is emphatically the blessing; then, and not before, he enters into an apprehension of the sense of the covenant promise. Hence, Jesus speaking under the character of Wisdom-Mediator, saith: "That I may cause those that love me to inherit substance, and I will fill their treasures." Where Jesus is, there is treasure, yea durable riches and righteousness. But where Jesus is not, nothing, be it what it may, can be called treasure. (See Deut. xxviii. 1. 14. Proverbs viii. 18-21.)

TREE

We meet with the names of a great variety of trees in Scripture, but if we may give credit to ancient writers, there was nothing in the Hebrew language less determined than the special names of trees. The sacred writers, however, have very largely and very beautifully classed them under their respective names. I do not take upon me to say that in numberless instances the names and trees are not figurative, for I rather think they are. It has been thought so by some writers, and there is reason for the opinion; and when we consider how God the Holy Ghost, from the description of the garden of Eden, in the very opening of the Bible, to the closing the canon of Scripture, in the description of the Paradise of God, makes use of the several names of "the tree of life, and the tree of knowledge of good and evil," which were evidently symbolical and sacramental, I cannot but pause over the several elegantly and highly finished representations which the whole Book of God abounds with, more or less, from beginning to end, and accept them as such. Hence, in this point of view, are the "trees of the garden and of the forest, the trees of righteousness, and of the Lord's right hand planting;" but chiefly and above all in beholding that most striking and lovely representation of Jesus, under the similitude of the tree of life. (Rev. xxii. 2.) Amidst a thousand beauties included in this lovely figure, how blessed is it to see that in his person, the life, the fruit, the healing, the shadow of his branches, the everlasting root, the verdure of his leaves, all, and every one, are beautifully described as figurative of temporal, spiritual, and eternal blessings in Jesus. And it is not the least of the beauty of this similitude, that this tree of life is said to be in the midst of the street, and on either side of the river. For as the church of Jesus, though but one, and the only one of her mother, (Song vi. 9.) is in both worlds, the river of Jordan only separating in place, but not in union; Jesus is equally the life of both, and gives blessedness to the body below as well as happiness to the society above. Hail! thou everlasting and eternal tree of life! Cause me to sit down under thy shadow with great delight this side the river, until thou shalt bring me home to the everlasting rest and enjoyment of thy fulness, in the paradise of God above. Amen.

TRUMPET

We read much of the use of trumpets in the old church in the wilderness. And as they were formed by the express command of the Lord no doubt their signification was important. (See Numb. x. 1, &c.) I do not stay to enter into particulars, for the limits I must observe necessarily compel me to be very short on each subject. It maybe proper however to remark on this particular, that there were four distinct uses for the service of the trumpet in the church of Israel. They had the trumpet to call the people to their religious service; the fast trumpet, the feast trumpet, and the war trumpet, beside the Jubilee trumpet, which was heard but once in nine and forty years; and though it was never heard but on that day, yet so particular was the sound of it that no captive in Israel could mistake its meaning. See Jubilee.

TRUTH

If I detain the reader at this word, it is not simply to explain what is not plain as to require no comment, as the word is in itself, but it is to remind the reader how sweetly and graciously the Lord Jesus hath applied it to himself, and determined that this is one of his precious names, which, for fragrancy, is as ointment poured forth, (See John xiv. 6.) And this is what the Holy Ghost by the wise man meant, when he recommended the church "to buy the truth, and sell it not." (Prov. xxiii. 23.)

Who can contemplate the Lord Jesus Christ under this most blessed character, without joining the apostle in his expressive account of Jesus-- "This is the true God and eternal life." (1 John v. 20.) For surely Jesus is the whole sum and substance of all the truths of God; in his divine nature the true God, and eternal life; in his human nature the true man, whom it behoved to be made like unto his brethren in all things; and in the union of both, the true glory-man, and only Mediator between God and man, the man, Christ Jesus, Hail, blessed Lord! I would say, thou art indeed "the way, and the truth, and the life. No man cometh to the Father but by thee: all that the Father giveth thee shall come to thee: and none that cometh unto thee, wilt thou in any wise cast out." (John vi. 37.) See Testimony.

TRYPHENA

A devout follower, of the Lord, spoken of by Paul. (Rom. xvi. 12.) The word is truly feminine, meaning somewhat tender.

TRYPHOSA

This was another of the devout Christian women whom Paul makes honourable mention of, (Rom. xvi. 12.) and her name is to the same purport, somewhat tender, delicate.

TUBAL

The son of Japheth. (Gen. x. 2.) His name is probably taken from Thebal, earth. And there was a Tubal-Cain, son of Lamech. It hath been thought by some that as Cain is derived from Canah, this junction seems to imply that this man had much earthly possession, or perhaps figuratively so called from being the first instructor, or as the margin of the Bible renders it, the whetter of the metals of the earth. (See Gen. iv. 22.)

TURTLE

The Holy Ghost hath been pleased to say so much concerning this bird in his sacred word, that I think it a duty, as well as a pleasure, to enquire somewhat concerning a bird so particularly recommended to our notice.

In the law, we find many offerings appointed of the turtle; and before the law, Abraham was directed to the use of, the turtle in sacrifice, by the Lord himself. (See Gen. xv. 9.) But what I would yet more particularly desire the reader to regard concerning the turtle, is the application of it in a figurative way to several characters in Scripture. The church calls herself, the Lord's turtle dove, (Ps. lxxiv. 1.9.) and begs the Lord as such to keep her from her enemies; and Jesus calls the church his dove, (Song ii. 14.) as if in answer to this cry, and bids her see her security, for that she is in the cliffs of the rock--perhaps, meaning the secret decrees of JEHOVAH, or, in Christ, the rock of ages, or probably both.

But some have supposed that by the turtle is meant God the Holy Ghost, whose voice is said, (Song ii. 12.) after the long winter of the Jewish dispensation, to be heard in our land. And no doubt the voice of the Holy Ghost might truly be said to be heard, when by the preaching of the gospel salvation was proclaimed in the name, and by the blood and righteousness of Jesus Christ.

While speaking on this subject, I hope I shall be pardoned when I add, that all representation off God the Holy Ghost by the pictures and paintings of a dove are improper, and disgrace the subject they are intended to honour: neither are they Scriptural, nor founded in any one authority of the Lord.

I am not to be told that the custom hath arisen from the subject of our Lord's baptism, where it is said that "when Jesus went up straightway out of the water, lo, the heavens were opened unto him, and he saw the Spirit of God descending like a dove, and lighting upon him." (Matt. iii. 16.) But this by no means becomes the least authority for the representing the Holy Ghost as a dove; for the passage expressly saith, that the Spirit of God was seen by Jesus descending as a dove descends, that is, hovering over a thing, and at length resting upon it: so the Holy Ghost descended, and rested upon Christ. But if the passage had meant to say, that the Holy Ghost descended in the shape and form of adore, the words would have been very different. Every one, that knows the original, knows that the words are (osei peristeran), which is, as the words are rendered in our Testament, like a dove; but if it had been meant to say, that the Holy Ghost came down in the shape and form of a dove, the words ought to have been, osei peristeras. There is a most essential difference between the two.

In the descent of the Holy Ghost at the day of Pentecost, we find the representation very much to the same purport, and if compared with this of St. Matthew, will serve to throw great light upon it. "And there appeared unto them cloven tongues like as of fire, and it sat upon each of them." (Acts ii. 3.) Now here the words are, like as of fire, (osei puros) not really fire, but like as of fire. So in the former instance, like a dove; not really a dove, but like it; for it was indeed, and in truth, the Holy Ghost that hovered over the person of the Lord Jesus, and rested upon him, as a dove when descending hovers over a thing, and at length resteth upon it. This plain illustration of the passage, will fully prove the meaning of the evangelists, and, of consequence, shew how unscriptural, irreverent, and improper, it must be to paint the invisible and eternal Spirit in the figure of a dove.

And I beg the reader before he dismisseth the subject, that he will take with him the consideration what a blessed, full, and unanswerable testimony this passage, concerning Christ's baptism, affords to the glorious doctrine of our holy faith. "There are three which heart record in heaven, the Father, the Word, and the Holy Ghost, and these three are one." (1 John v. 7.) Here was Jesus in the act of being baptized; here was the Holy Ghost descending like a dove, and lighting upon him; and here was the voice of God the Father from heaven saying, "This is my beloved Son, in whom I am well pleased." (Matt. iii. 16, 17.) Reader, I beseech you to carry this precious testimony about with you wherever you go, as among the sweetest credentials of your holy religion. It will serve, under the Lord, to act as an antidote against the poisonous and pestilential vapours of the present adulterous and sinful generation.

TYCHICUS

A friend and companion of Paul. (Ephes. vi. 21.)

TYPES

We meet with this word, as far as I remember, but once in the whole Bible, and even there it is only in the margin, namely, (1 Cor. x. 11.)--but the sense of it is too important not to be known and well regarded. By types, we mean the figure or shadow of matters they represent. "Thus the brazen serpent, the scape goat, the lamb of the morning, and the lamb of the evening, were all types of the Lord Jesus Christ." Indeed the whole law was but a type or shadow of "good things to come, the body was, and is, Christ." And we never can be sufficiently thankful to God the Holy Ghost for his gracious condescension in this particular, by thus mercifully attending to our weakness of apprehension, in the use of types and figures to represent divine things by. The Lord cause them to minister to this end, in our improvement, and to the divine glory. Amen. See Parable.

U

ULAI

The memorable river near the city of Shushan, from the banks of which Daniel heard the man's voice. (Dan. viii. 16.) When we consider what is said of the voice of the Lord God, walking in the garden in the cool of the day, Gen. iii. 8; when we mark the same grace manifested upon many occasions during the Old Testament dispensation, 1 Sam. iii. 4; 1 Kings xix. 9; and when we call to mind, the numberless sweet and gracious tokens of the Lord Jesus, manifested to his servants in the early ages, before he openly tabernacled in substance of our flesh: may we not venture to suppose this voice to have been Him, who in after ages openly tabernacled among us? I only humbly propose the question. I by no means presume to decide upon it. Some have called this river Ubal, Ulai; because Ubal is the name of the river itself, and Ulai defines the particular one by name.

UNBELIEF

It should seem that amidst the deadly poison infused into our nature by the great enemy of souls, this of unbelief was his master-piece, of contrivance. And to say the truth, it is of all others, the most diabolical and ruinous. For it denies the sovereignty of divine mercy: it sets at nought, the infinite merit and value of Christ's blood and righteousness. It is said concerning the Lord Jesus in the days of his flesh, "that he did not many mighty works there, because of their unbelief." (Matt. xiii. 58.) Yea, the Lord declares the sin of unbelief to be unpardonable: "He that believeth not shall be damned." (Mark xvi. 16.), And his servant, the beloved apostle, confirms the awful account, when in the close of the canon of Scripture, he saith that "the fearful and unbelieving shall have their part in the lake which burneth with fire and brimstone; which is the second death." (Rev. xxi. 8.) How solemnly the apostle to the Hebrews sums up the history of those whose carcases fell in the wilderness, when he saith, "So we see that they could not enter in because of unbelief." (Heb. iii. 19.)

UNCTION

It is not to be wondered at that the Israelites had such frequent use of anointings, when we consider that the very order of their institution as a church and people, was to be looking for the coming of the Messiah, that is, the anointed One. Hence their kings, priests, vessels, and all things consecrated, had the unction. (See Exod. xxx. 23.)

How holy and blessed is it to the church of Jesus now, to discover that in this unction, thus figuratively set forth in the old church, all the outlines of the Lord Jesus anointing by the Holy Ghost, and the church also in him were displayed. Now, as Christ the Messiah could not have been Christ, that is, anointed, but by the Holy Ghost's anointing, so neither could the church have been his church, his spouse, his beloved, and the only one, of her mother, (Song vi. 9.) but by the anointing also of God the Holy Ghost. Hence then it should be considered, (and I beg the pious reader to consider it, and keep it in remembrance proportioned to its infinite importance) as Christ is called Messiah, that is Christ, as the anointed of God, before he openly appeared at his incarnation, so the church of Christ is called his church; and for which, in salvation-work, Christ was made Christ, before he was made flesh, and dwelt among us; nor, as the Son of God, had it not been for his church's sake, ever would have been sent by the Father, neither would have taken our nature into the GODHEAD, neither have been anointed by the Holy Ghost. So by his becoming the anointed for this express purpose, proves the original anointing of the church in him, and for him; and sets forth the everlasting love of all the persons of the GODHEAD to the church of

Christ in all ages.

UNPERFECT

Though we meet with this word but once in the whole Bible, namely, Psa. cxxxix. 16, yet, as in the two translations we have of the Psalms, the word in the one is rendered imperfect, which in the other is rendered unperfect, and as the difference is very striking when properly considered, I think it an object of no small moment in a work of this kind, to guard the reader against an error into which he may be apt to fall for want of due attention in this particular.

I am well aware that with the generality of readers, the words imperfect, and unperfect, are considered the same. But this is a mistake. For not to remark that though a thing may be said to be unperfect, because unfinished, which when finished would be no longer unperfect; yet imperfect may not simply mean because unfinished, for when finished, it may be imperfect still. So that the words themselves are, in their original sense and meaning, not the same; and can by no rule be used synonimously. But in the instance before us in this Psalm, by the substituting one for the other we are led to a very dangerous conclusion.

Let the reader remember, that Christ, under the Spirit of prophecy, is speaking in this Psalm of his substance, his body, and which in another Scripture, he is introduced as saying to his Father "A body hast thou prepared me," (Heb. x. 5.) compared with Psalm xl. 6.) Now in this Psalm also Christ is speaking to the Father, and saith: "Thine eyes did see my substance, yet being unperfect: and in this book all my members were written, which in continuance were fashioned, (or as the margin of the Bible renders it what days, they should be fashioned,) when as yet there was none of them."

In whatever sense therefore the expressions are taken with respect to this substance, this body of Christ, whether personally of Christ himself, or of his members; the church, whose names are elsewhere said to be written in the book of life, or of both Christ and his church; in either case, and in all, the sense must be the same as to the perfection of this substance. It never could be said to be imperfect. It might be, and indeed it was unperfect, because unfinished: that is, as it was to be finished in the full manifestation of Christ in substance of our flesh in what is called in Scripture language, the fulness of time. (Gal. iv. 4.) But in point of perfection, it was always perfect to his comprehensive view, before whom, past, present, and to come, forms but one and the same object. And in this one, complete whole of perfection in JEHOVAH'S esteem, hath Christ and his members been beheld from all eternity! Hence, therefore, to read the passage as it now stands in our reading Psalms, imperfect, is an error, and of the greatest kind.

And the word which the Septuagints have made use of in this Psalm, (as the learned cannot but know) implies no more when rendered unperfect than of a substance which though perfect in itself in point of perfection in all its component parts, yet waits the perfection of being all brought into one and compounded together. (A katergaston, from Katergazomai.)

It may not be generally known perhaps by the readers of this Poor Man's Concordance, that the reading Psalms as they are called, and which are used in our churches, are taken from Cranmer's Bible, first published in Henry the Eighth's time, 1539. Whereas the Psalms in our Bibles are from the translation in James the First's days, 1605.

I cannot close this article without expressing my wish that the faithful of the Lord's people may always use the word unperfect, instead of imperfect, when reading this most blessed verse, in this most blessed Psalm. Every thing is perfect in Him who is himself the perfection of beauty, and the praise of all his saints. And oh, for grace to see the church's perfection in him who is the Lord our righteousness, and "who is made of God to us wisdom and righteousness, sanctification and redemption: that, according as it is written, he that glorieth, let him glory in the Lord." (1 Cor. i. 30.)

UPHAZ

We read of the gold of Upham, perhaps the same as Opher: the certain man, Daniel) saw in a vision, had his loins apparently girded with it. (Dan. x. 5.) The church speaks of her Lord's head, as of this gold. (Song v. 11.) And John's account of the Lord Jesus Christ is much to the same amount. (Rev. i. 13, &c.) What sublime descriptions they all are of the glories of his person. But how infinitely short of what Christ really is!

UR

The memorable spot from whence the Lord called Abraham when an idolater. Sweet thought to the believer! It is JEHOVAH'S grace, and not man's deserts, even in the instance of an Abraham, that is the sole cause of salvation. Some make Ur to mean light or fire, from Aor. (Gen. xi. 28.)

URIAH

A name memorable in the history of David. (2 Sam. xi. 5, 6.) His name is a compound of Ur, light; and jah, the Lord. Hence Uriah means, the Lord is my light.

URIM

The Urim and Thummim are supposed to have been the precious stones worn by the high priest upon his breast-plate, when going into the temple, and before the mercy seat. The meaning is supposed to be lights and perfections. But farther than these explanations, the multitude of commentators have not advanced. It is the happiness of the church in Jesus, however, to look to all the shadows of the law, through the medium of the gospel, and to discover every thing is the former as ministering but to the latter. So that when Aaron was thus adorned and went in before the propitiatory, he represented our Almighty Aaron, who was, and is himself, both the light and the life, the perfection, and the glory of all his redeemed. Hence when Moses in his dying prediction of the children of Israel, declared that JEHOVAH'S Urim and Thummim should be with his Holy One, none could be alluded to but the Lord Jesus Christ, and in him, the whole tendency of both, had their accomplishment.

UZ

This was the land made memorable by the dwelling of Job. The name seems to be taken from Hetz, counsel.

UZZAH

We have the short but striking history of this man, in 2 Sam vi. 3-8. His name, if it be as is supposed, derived from Hazaz, means strength. In consequence of his sudden death, David called the place where the Lord smote Uzzah, Perez-Uzzah, that is, as the margin of the Bible renders it, The breach of Uzzah. I refer the reader to the passage for the account of it.

It hath been a subject of much enquiry with some, what there was so highly offensive in Uzzah's conduct to bring forth so awful a judgment. But the answer is not far. It appears that the ark was exposed to view, whereas it ought to have been concealed. For upon a former occasion the Lord made a great slaughter among the men of Bethshe-mesh, for looking into the ark. (See 1 Sam. vi. 19.) This Uzzah, as a Levite, should have prevented. And certainly the carrying the ark on a cart, and causing it to be drawn by oxen, was a violation of the law; for the Lord provided how the sons of Aaron were to prepare for the covering of the ark, and how the sons of Kohath, were to bear it on their shoulders.

(See Num. iv. 5-15. and vii. 9.) Add to these, the hasty and irreverent touch of Uzzah might have been done in such a way as incurred the just judgment of the Lord. We may at least learn from hence with what reverence and godly fear the Lord is to be approached in ordinances. And we ought to learn moreover the blessedness of our privileges, in having such an High Priest as the Lord Jesus, in whom, and through whom, we have access to a mercy seat, "to obtain mercy and find grace to help in all time of need."

V

VAGABOND

This name was given to Cain by the Lord himself; and it should seem that he, on whom the Lord pronounced the sentence, whatever it might in its fullest sense mean, felt the awfulness of it; for he mentions it with peculiar distress when declaring "his punishment to be greater than he could bear." (See Gen. iv. 21,13, 14.) I am inclined to think that the word contains more in it than is generally supposed. In the sentence on Cain, it is joined with the word fugitive; so that while, according to our ideas; a vagabond implies a state of restlessness and of wandering, a fugitive carries with it the notion of flight. So that in both, the person was without rest, and always on flight, like Pashur, whose name was Magor-missabib; that is, as the margin of the Bible renders it, fear round about. (Jer. xx. 3.) Even in this point of view the case was truly awful.

I cannot but think, however, that there was much more in Cain's sentence concerning these terms of a fugitive and a vagabond, than what is here supposed. The reader will remember that I do not speak decidedly upon the subject, but only propose my views of the passage. I would humbly enquire, doth not the term mean an everlasting unsettledness and fear, when it is considered on whom the sentence was pronounced, and the cause for which it was passed? Cain had not only murdered his brother, but had rejected, by his offering without a sacrifice, the salvation by Christ: yea, the very murder of his brother was induced from this cause, "because the Lord had respect to Abel and to his offering, but unto Cain and to his offering he had not." The Holy Ghost explains the cause-- Abel offered by faith. (Heb. xi. 4.) Cain did not. Abel had an eye, by his sacrifice, to Christ, and as such, confessed himself a sinner, who stood in need of salvation. Cain trusted to his own righteousness and was rejected: and hence the Lord said, "If thou doest well--that is, if thou offerest a pure, unblemished, perfect obedience; shalt thou not be accepted?" As if the Lord had said, whosoever seeks acceptance in himself and his own well-doing, it must be wholly and completely so: a failure in a single point is a failure in all. Cain failed, and hence, became a fugitive and a vagabond; and that for ever. "So that the term can with it, an exclusion from that rest which remain for the people of God." (Heb. iv. 9. Isa. xxviii. Matt. xi. 28-30. Ps. cxvi. 7.)

I beg once more to be understood, while speaking upon the subject, that I do not speak decidedly. I only conceive that the word vagabond hath somewhat in it of a reprobate state; and I am the more confirmed in this opinion from what Satan said of himself, Job i. 7. He describes himself in the same state of a vagabond. And it is remarkable that the Holy Ghost, by his servant John, declares Cain to be of that wicked one, when speaking of the children of the devil; (see 1 John iii. 10,-12.) And I would ask whether those vagabond Jews spoken of, Acts xix. 13. were not of the same race? Jeremiah speaks to the same purport, if I mistake not, chap. vi. 30, under the figure of reprobate silver.

Whether the conjecture be, or be not well founded, certain it is that in Scripture language a vagabond carries with it a high degree of odium, and ought not to be brought into use in common life, as it is too often is done to describe the persons of wandering poor. Many a child of God, it is to be hoped, are among those poor who are removed from parish to parish, and whose poverty is their only reproach. To call such vagabonds, if the Scripture sense of the word be as I have before stated, is unsuitable in man, and offensive to God.

VAIL or VEIL

I think it right to stop at this word, because we meet with it very often in the Scripture, though it is to be lamented that our little acquaintance with the customs of the people of the East, makes us lose numberless beauties in the sacred volume, when we meet with expressions of a local nature, for want of being acquainted with their manners and customs.

The vails worn by the women, were chiefly, no doubt, intended for the concealment of their persons. Female children were no vails, we are told by the historians of those countries, until they had arrived at seven or eight years of age; after that, if a woman was seen uncovered, it became the mark of a woman of ill-fame. Hence Rebekah put on the vail on her approach to Isaac. (Gen. xxiv. 65.) And Tamar disguised herself with her vail. (Gen. xxxviii. 14.) Indeed, so much the use of vails was observed in the eastern world, that the married women, it is said, were never seen, even in their families, without the Radid, as they called the married vail.

These things, will, in some measure, serve to explain those passages in the apostle Paul's writings to the Corinthians of the women praying or prophecying uncovered, that is, unvailed, because it implied the want of chastity. And this one circumstance alone leads us into a proper apprehension of the apostle's whole discourse. (See 1 Cor. xi. 3-15.)

There is a great beauty in that passage of the Songs respecting the church, which, if explained to us in allusion to the custom of vails, becomes very sweet and interesting. "The watchmen (said she) that went about the city found me, they smote me, they wounded me: the keepers of the walls took away my vail from me." (Song v. 7.) If the reader enters into the full apprehension of the custom of the vail, he will consider the spouse of Christ as here clothed with her Radid, her marriage vail, shewing who she was, and that she was in subjection to her own husband, (Ephes. v. 23, 24.) seeking him in the ordinances, which are here called the streets of the city, were she ought to seek him; and the watchmen, the ministers of the gospel, found her in this enquiry, but instead comforting her with some new and sweet view of her Lord, speaking to her in her then dispirit case and circumstances, in shewing her the safety of a soul justified in Christ's blood and righteousness, however dark and uncomfortable in herself; instead of this, time keepers took away her vail, her covering in Christ, treated her as if a strumpet, as though she was not married to Jesus, and had no right to the Radid, or marriage vail.

I pause over this view of the subject to ask my own heart, while I desire the reader to consult his own also, whether this treatment may not in the present hour be too often shewn to the church, the spouse of Christ, in numberless instances of the individual members of his mystical body, when ministers, watchmen, and keepers of the walls of Zion, instead of strengthening seeking souls in the Lord Jesus's blood and righteousness, are taking away their confidence in him, to direct them in seeking somewhat in themselves. Oh, how little do the best-taught ministers of Christ know of their people's sorrows, and of Jesus's all-suitableness and all-sufficiency! But to take away the believer's Radid, her marriage vail, her wedding garment, her nuptial band, in Christ, oh! what a wounding, what smiting, of a poor sin-sick soul must this be! And it is possible yea, more than possible, that Christ own ministers may but too often fall into this error, when, instead of making Christ what God the Father had made him, the Alpha and Omega of his church, they are directing their people to somewhat besides Jesus for comfort and consolation. The general direction to what is called experience, by way of confidence, is a sad instance of this kind.

While speaking of vails, I must not forget to notice the vail of the temple, which was appointed by the Lord to separate the outer place where the daily service was performed from the holy of holies, into which the high priest entered once in a year, on the great day of atonement. We have the account of it, Exod. xxvi, &c. Lev. xvi.--and these Scriptures are again blessedly explained to the church by the Holy Ghost, Heb. ix. 1-12.

That this vail was figurative and typical, need not be insisted upon. The most superficial attention to Scripture very fully shews this. The human nature of the Lord Jesus was no doubt represented by the temple itself; hence Jesus spake of the temple of his body. (John ii. 9-22.) And the vail of the temple, forming a separation, and none but the high priest passing within it, and that only once in a year, and even not without blood, those were too striking particularities not to he understood as pointing to him who hath entered with his own blood into "heaven itself, there to appear in the presence of God for us."

But the fullest and most delightful explanation of the vail of the temple, was given in the moment of our Lord's death on the cross; for when the Lord Jesus bowed his sacred head, and gave up the ghost, instantly, we are told, the vail of the temple was rent in twain, by some invisible hand, from the top to the bottom; thus signifying that now, from the highest heaven to the lowest earth, Jesus had opened a new and living way by his blood, and was now not only entered himself within the vail, but as our forerunner, and that we should assuredly follow him, that "where he is there we might be also."

And as Jesus had now opened a new and living way of his people, so he had broken down all the vails of separation between himself and his redeemed The Jew and the Gentile were now brought into one fold, the vail of mysteries, of ordinances, of darkness, of ignorance, of blindness, in short the vail of all obstructions was now no more. Jesus had now, agreeably to his prophecy, destroyed in his holy mountain the church "the face of the covering cast over all people, and the vail that was spread over all nations." (Isa. xxv. 7.)

And it is a sweet addition to all those precious views of the Lord Jesus removing every vail in his church, when he hath in the heart of his redeemed also taken away the vail of unbelief, and opened, to the soul's comfort, sweet and soul-ravishing views of his own person and glory. Reader, think what a glorious object will that day, that wonderful day, open to the soul, when Jesus, removing the last vail of death, shall appear in all his beauty to take home his redeemed to himself, and when they, awakening up after his likeness, shall be fully and eternally satisfied with his presence for ever.

VALLEY

We meet with an account of numberless values and vales in the Scripture. There is the valley of Achor, for a door of hope. (Hos. ii. 15.) The valley of Baca, a place of Bochim, or weeping. (Judges. ii. 1.) The valley of Eshcol, or grapes. (Num. xxxii. 9.) In short they are too numerous to be all noticed in this little work. But by valley the scriptural and figurative sense is, this lower world. Hence Ezekiel's vision in the valley of the dry bones. (See Ezek. xxxvii. 1-14.) I would only beg to call the reader's attention to a beautiful instance in point, where Jesus, speaking of visiting his church, useth this figure, "I went down (said Christ) into the garden of nuts, to see the fruits of the valley; and to see whether the vine flourished, and the pomegranate budded." (Song vi. 11.) What an endearing representation this is of Jesus, coming down into time valley of our world, and taking notice of his own graces given by himself to his own people. Sweet thought to comfort every poor fearful believer

VINE and VINEYARD

The holy Scriptures abound with the most lovely representations of Christ and his church under these similitude's; and it is not to be wondered at. The hill-country of Judea abounded with the richest and most luxurious vines. Therefore when the church would speak of her beloved, she called him, "a cluster of cypress in the vineyards of Engedi." (Song i. 14.) And evidently on this account, because Jesus is not one blessing, but every one and all. In his person, blood, and righteousness, the church finds an Eshcol, a cluster of all divine perfections, all suited grace, all glory. Hence some read the words of the church in this lovely song, Esh col copher, that is, the man that hath atoned, and is all things of blessing.

And as the church, taught by the Holy Ghost, sings her Epithalamium, or nuptial song, to the praise of Jesus, under the similitude, the Lord Jesus sings his love-song to the same figure: "I am the vine, saith Jesus, and ye are the branches." (John xv. 1, &c.) But I must not enlarge on those topics, how sweet soever they are. The reader will find numberless clusters of them in the sacred word. (Gen. xlix. 11. Ps. lxxx. 1, &c. Song vii. 8-12, &c.)

VIPER

The Hebrews called the viper Peten, Ephee. It is frequently spoken of in Scripture, and not unfrequently in allusion to the great enemy of souls. (Job xx. 16. Isa. xxx. 6.) And the Lord Jesus in the gospel called the children of the evil one a generation of vipers. (Matt. xii. 34; xxiii. 33.)

VIRGIN

The Jews had certainly a distinction in the meaning of this word. When they spoke of a young woman simply as such, they contented themselves with the expression of youth; but when they meant to speak of a virgin, they called her Almah, and generally subjoined, as in the instance of Rebekah, "neither had any man known her," (Gen. xxiv. 16.) and the Hebrew word Almah, at once expresseth this, for it means concealed. Hence the Virgin Mary, by way of distinction is thus spoken of, implying that she was after, as well as before, the birth of Christ, the Almah. See Mary.

VISION

This word hath several significations in Scripture. In the first ages of the world the Lord was pleased to manifest himself to the children of God by vision; sometimes by open revelations, at other times by dreams in the night. (Gen. xv. 1, &c; xlvi. 2.) Beside these, the books of the prophets are called visions. (Isa. i. 1.) And even in the after-ages, when Jesus had finished his redemption work, and was returned to glory, the Apostle Paul speaks of visions. (2 Cor. xii. 1, &c.)

VOW

We meet with numberless circumstances in the Old Testament Scripture respecting vows. It is our happiness, however, under the New Testament dispensation, that we are brought under no particular ordinance concerning them. The dedication of the heart to the Lord doth not come under the article of a vow, because, in a believer, the offering the soul to God in Christ is in the Lord's strength. A vow in man savours of human strength too strongly to come under the character of the gospel dispensation.

WALL

This word is used in Scripture, not unfrequently figuratively. Sometimes the Lord speaks of himself as "a wall of fire round about his people." (Zech. ii. 5.) And as a fence of safety in his salvation, which are Israel's walls and bulwarks. (Isaiah xxvi. 1.) And the church describes Jesus as standing behind our wall and looking forth at the windows, when representing the wall of our mortal flesh, obscuring the otherwise glorious views the soul would have of his beauty, and which the soul will have when the spirit shall be disembodied. (Song ii. 9.)

WALKING

In the language of Scripture, this is frequently made use of to denote the state of the soul before God. Thus the Lord commanded Abraham: "I am the Almighty God, walk before me, and be thou perfect." (Gen. xvii. 1.) Where it is blessed to observe that the Lord in the precept gives the ability to perform, and gives his glorious name as the security for Abraham's doing it. He that is God Almighty (the El Shaddai), wills the patriarch into the perfection he is to walk in. We have a similar passage. (John xv. 4.) On the contrary, to walk in darkness, implies the state of darkness of the mind. (1 John i. 47.)

WASHING

In Scripture language the act of washing carries with it an interest in the service for which it is observed. Thus, Jesus washes his disciples' feet. (John xiii. 3-12.) Hence the apostle speaking of the truly regenerated in Christ saith, "Now ye are washed, ye are sanctified, ye are justified in the name of the Lord Jesus, and by the Spirit of our God." (1 Cor. vi. 11.) And the redeemed in glory, are represented as having "washed their robes, and made them white in the blood of the Lamb." (Rev. vii. 14.)

We are so little acquainted with the customs of the East that it is next to an impossibility to have a full and clear apprehension of the signification of washing as expressed in the Scriptures. It will be enough for all our purposes however to consider in general, that it had in spiritual concerns a blessed intimation in those that were washed of being partakers in the pardoning and sanctifying blood of the Lord Jesus Christ. (Psa. li. 2. Acts xxii. Rev. i. 5.)

WATER

In the language of Scripture, this word hath numberless applications made of it, but in a peculiar manner is principally made use of in relation to the person, work, and offices of God the Holy Ghost. For as water is essentially necessary to animal life, so is the blessed Spirit to spiritual life. But it would form a subject in itself, and fill a volume, to shew how many and how various the ways by which the Holy Ghost is represented in the Bible under this sweet figure, as supplying the church with living water. Hence he is called the "water of life, a well of water springing up in the soul to everlasting life." And he is described as quickening the marshy ground; cleansing, refreshing, comforting, cooling, and strengthening the souls of his people, by the continued streams of his grace. "There is a river (said the Psalmist) the streams whereof do make glad the city of God? (Psa. xlvi. 4.) It should not be overlooked or forgotten also, that each and all of the persons of the GODHEAD are so described in the word of God, and which by the way, let it be observed, becomes a decided proof of the unity of the GODHEAD, while it no less shews the distinction of person. Hence, God the Father is set forth by the prophet as a fountain. (Jer. ii. 13.) God the Son as a fountain. (Zech. xiii. 1. Song iv. 15.) And God the Holy Ghost as a fountain, filling the hearts of the redeemed, and causing them to overflow in the day of Christ. (John

vii. 38.)

WEDDING GARMENT

The custom of the East at their marriage feasts, can only explain that expression of our Lord in his parable, (Matt. xxii. 11.) of the man that had not on a wedding garment. The uniform custom at all marriages, even among the poorer sort, was to make presents of clothing to the persons invited. And for the king's son in his marriage, which the parable represents, the presents must have been splendid indeed. An Eastern writer, describing a nuptial feast in the year 1612, speaks of a retinue of mules laden with tapestry, cloth of gold, of velvet, and satin, and other riches which were to be used upon this occasion. Therefore for the king on coming in to see his guests, to find there a man without the wedding garment, implied such a contempt to his person, and to his son's marriage, as might well justify the anger shewn.

And as the parable of Jesus on this subject was wholly figurative, and with an eye to the gracious marriage of the Son of God with our nature, nothing could have been more happily chosen to have shewn the awful consequence of the unbeliever, in his appearing now at ordinances, and finally at the last day, at judgment; unclothed with the righteousness of Christ, and standing naked and defenceless in his own sinful nature, when the King shall come in to the marriage supper of the Lamb in heaven! It would be well if every man who is looking for acceptance, either wholly or in part from any garment of his own, would pause over the awful subject of such contumacy and self-righteousness!

WEIGHING

I should not have thought it needful to have called the reader's attention to this article of weighing, but for a particular circumstance, and which I am inclined to think serves to elucidate to an English reader, a very interesting passage in Scripture.

It is too well known to need my pointing out that in the article of money among the Hebrews, their estimate of gold and silver, was by weight and not by any standard of coin. Thus Abraham when he bought ground of the sons of Heth, weighed the money agreed upon, four hundred shekels of silver," current money with the merchant." (Gen. xxiii. 16.) In like manner, when at the appointment of the Lord, Jeremiah bought the field of his uncle's son, he weighed him the money, even seventeen shekels of silver. (Jer. xxxii. 8, 9.)

From hence it appears that the real value of money was ascertained by weighing. And this gives a beautiful explanation concerning the Lord's declaration of Belshazzar, by the hand writing on the wall, "Thou art weighed in the balances, and found wanting." (Dan. v. 27.) With us in our English customs, base coin becomes for the most part the cause of its not passing. But the want of weight with the eastern manners was the sad prevention, and it serves to shew the solemn doctrine of rejection most strikingly.

I shall be forgiven I hope, if on the credit of one of the eastern writers, I relate that it is the custom with them to weigh their monarch once in every year, and generally on his birth-day. It should seem to be more than probable that the custom, however it was derived, was taken from Daniel's history of Belshazzar. But, that the eastern prince of those modern days might never come into the condemnation, or even the apprehension of such an event as took place to the Chaldean monarch, the eastern prince is put into one of the scales for trial, and his weight is made out by sliver in the other, which afterwards is distributed to the poor. What a sweet thought is it to the believer in Jesus that he is weighed only in person of his Lord, where can be found no lightness or deficiency! Jesus's righteousness is indeed "current money with the merchant." (Song. iii. 6.)

WELLS, or SPRINGS, of WATER

The Hebrews prized their wells or springs as the chiefest of all their treasure. Hence their contests about them. (See Gen. xxvi. 18-22.) The general name they gave a well or spring was beer. Hence Hagar called the well where she had found the Lord's presence eminently blessed, Beer lahai-roi, that is, as the margin of the Bible renders it, "the well of him that liveth and seeth me? (Gen. xvi. 14.) And hence also we find the name of Beer, a well; joined to words denoting places, such as Beersheba, &c. There is a well eminently spoken of, Numb. xxi. 16-18. Perhaps the reader may be led by the Holy Ghost to discover much of Christ in this song of Israel.

WINE

Wine in Scripture is frequently put for some choice thing. Thus when Jesus wrought his first miracle in Cana of Galilee, in turning the water into wine; as this set forth the glories of his person and righteousness, it might be truly said the gospel then preached, compared to all former revelations, was keeping the best wine to the last; (John ii. 11, 12.) and hence the gospel itself is called wine on the lees well refined. (Isaiah xxv. 6.) But the sweetest commendation of Jesus and his gospel, is that which under the similitude of wine is given by the spouse, (Song i. 2.) where she desires to be kissed with the kisses of Jesus's mouth, for, said she, thy love is better than wine. And for this self-evident reason. Wine no doubt is a delightful cordial, and properly used will tend, under the devine blessing, to revive a poor sick and sorrowful heart. But never was it known to do what Christ's love hath done, to raise a sinner dead in trespasses and sins. Oh, precious love of a most precious Saviour! Surely here every one must allow that Jesus's love is better than wine. Here the largest draughts can never injure as the juice of the grape; but as Jesus gives, so may souls receive the largest portions, not only unhurt, but more blessed. His language is: "Eat, O friends: drink, yea, drink abundantly, O beloved!" (Song v. 1.)

WISDOM

This is one of the names of the Son of God, as Mediator; Christ the wisdom of God. That is by covenant engagement in the ancient settlements of eternity. (See Prov. viii. throughout 1 Cor. i. 24.)

Wisdom is also used as a term in Scripture to denote somewhat supernatural, and in opposition to carnal blindness. (James iii. 14, 15.) The Hebrews called it Cachemah.

WITNESS

The Holy Ghost is said by the Lord Jesus to be his witness, and to testify of him, John xv. 26. And the apostle Paul saith, (Rom. viii. 26.) that this Almighty person, in his office-character, witnesseth to the Lord's family that they are the child of God. And it is most blessed to every child of God at one time or the other to receive this testimony of the Holy Ghost, witnessing to their adoption character. He it is that convinceth the heart of sin, and proves in the conscience the absolute necessity of Christ. He it is that causeth the glory, the beauty, the suitableness, and all-sufficiency of the Lord Jesus Christ, to appear to the soul what Jesus is, and at the same time persuades the soul into the love of him. And he it is that both gives a conviction to the heart of the firmness and security of all the promises of God in Christ Jesus, add witnesseth to the safety of every believer's gracious estate in Christ Jesus, in testifying that all the promises of God in him are Yea, and in him Amen. Blessed Spirit of all truth, do thou witness to my personal safety in Christ Jesus, as being the earnest of the promised inheritance!

WOMB

I should not have stopped at this word, but

from a wish to offer a word on the subject as it concerns the virgin's womb. I humbly conceive that the womb of the virgin was altogether passive, (except in the simple act of consenting to the dead) in the conception of Jesus in the womb. For when the angel announced to the Virgin Mary the miraculous incarnation, and when to the seeming impossibilities of the thing itself, as it appeared to her, the angel explained how it should be accomplished by the miraculous impregnation of the Holy Ghost, Mary at once consented to the deed--Be it unto me according to thy word--and immediately the work was wrought· (Luke i. 31, &c,) And to this agrees the prophecy of the psalmist, (Ps. cxxxix. 13.) "Thou hast covered me in my mother's womb." See all that follows to this amount in the succeeding verses of that glorious psalm, until Jesus comes to speak by was same spirit of prophecy in it, to the writing of all the names of his members, meaning every individual of his body the church, in the book of life. And hence the Lord Jesus, in another prophecy, had ages before said, "The Lord hath called me from the womb." (Isa. xlix. 1.) So that from hence we see the willingness of the Virgin, and the consent of Christ, at the call of his Father, and both together serving to illustrate and explain, as far as the nature of the mysterious subject can be explained, the wonderful transaction.

WORD

In Scripture this is used for the uncreated word, which John calls Christ by, in relation to his eternal power and GODHEAD, (John i. 1,) &c.--and also the written word, the word of God, which the Hebrews called Dabar. See Christ.

WORLD

The Scriptures not only mean by this word to describe the heavens and the earth, but not unfrequently it is put for the people. Hence the apostle saith, "the world (that is, mankind) by wisdom knew not God." (1 Cor. i. 21.) The term by which the Hebrews marked the universe, was Thebel.

WORM

This is sometimes figuratively used. The Lord Jesus calls himself a worm and no man, (Ps. xxii. 6.) to intimate the unparalleled humility of his person. Hence, JEHOVAH speaking to Christ, under the character of Jacob, saith, Fear not, thou worm Jacob! (Isa. xli. 14.) Sometimes the word is also used by way of figure, to represent the torments of the damned. "Their worm, (said Jesus,) dieth not, and the fire is not quenched," Mark ix. 44.-48. Some of the old writers have contended, however, that this worm, here spoken of by Christ, is not in figure, but in reality. Of this opinion was Austin.

Y

YEA

I detain the reader at this word in order to mark the peculiar sweetness of it. Our gracious Lord in recommending it to his disciples, evidently shewed that there was somewhat interesting in it. "Let your communication (said Jesus) be Yea, yea, Nay, nay; for whatsoever is more than these, cometh of evil." (Matt. v. 37.) I would not be understood, as speaking decidedly on any point where God the Holy Ghost hath not done it; but I venture to ask, did not our gracious Lord, mean by this recommendation to shew that the Yea, yea, of his people, should be in contemplating the verily, verily, of himself? And if with an eye to him, our yea had a frequent use, would there not be a peculiar sweetness derived from it?

YEAR

The Jewish year differed much in point of time, before, and after their sojourning in Egypt; and unless we could (which now is impossible) ascertain with more clearness whether their calculations were made by what is called the solar year, or the lunar year, that is, by the revolution of sun, or moon--it is not possible to determine with accuracy the point. But all difficulties vanish in respect to the different periods of calculation, by whatever mode they are calculated, if we only are careful to consider the different dates from whence they take their calculation. As for example--in the promise the Lord made to Abram, (Gen. xv. 13.) concerning the affliction of his seed in a strange land, and their deliverance from it, the Lord marked the period, four hundred years; but in counting up the time when that deliverance took place, Moses makes it "four hundred and thirty years." But the period of both, is precisely the same, when the difference is allowed from the different dates of the commencement, or time, the account began. When it is said, as in Gen. xv. 13, "four hundred years," it is connected with the birth of Isaac, which was thirty years after Abraham left Chaldea, and consequently, this period must be added to the account; and thus it will be found, by a parity of calculation in the several statements the Jewish year at different times give. See Hour.

YESTERDAY

In Scripture language this expression doth not simply mean the day which preceded the present, but sometimes refers to the eternity of ages past. Thus, the Lord Jesus Christ is said to be the same "yesterday, and to-day, and, for ever." (Heb. xii. 8.) That is, the yesterday, before creation; to-day, meaning the whole period of time from the creation, to the consummation of all things; and for ever, including the whole eternity to come, when time shall be no more. Sweet thought to the believer in Jesus, both as it concerns the nature and essence of Christ, and as it refers to the everlasting sameness and unceasing efficacy of his redemption and love to his church and people! Amen.

Z

ZACCHEUS

I stop to note a circumstance in the history of the conversion of Zaccheus, which deserves attention. The Lord Jesus observed, when speaking of the salvation that was then to come to his house, "for so much as he also is a son of Abraham." (Luke xix. 1-10.) Now if Zaccheus was, as is Generally supposed, a Gentile by birth, this sonship in Abraham must have been as Paul speaks of it, spiritually. "If ye be Christ, then are ye Abraham's seed, and heirs according to the promise." (Gal. iii. 29.) I do not speak positively upon the subject; but the office of a Publican or Taxgatherer among the Romans was so invidious an employment that few of the Jews would engage in it. So that it is probable, Zaccheus might have been a gentile. And hence, by the way, a sweet testimony to that blessed truth, that Christ was given both for a light to lighten the Gentiles, and to be the glory of his people Israel. (Isaiah xlix. 6.) (Luke ii. 32.) If Zaccheus derived his name, as is supposed, from Zacac, of the Syriac, meaning just, or justified; the name was truly applicable to the person, justified freely as he was in the salvation of Christ.

ZECHARIAH

We meet with many of this name in Scripture, and it is not to be wondered at, when we consider the sense of it, and the general desire which the Hebrews all had, to carry somewhat in name, which referred to the Lord. Zachar means memory, and Jah the Lord. Zechariah therefore, seemed to intimate the hope, that the person so called should be remembered of the Lord.

ZADOK

A memorable name in the history of David. See both the books of Samuel. His name is derived from a root, signifying just.

ZEAL

We can have no lively idea of this word, but as it is made use of by the Lord Jesus Christ. But when we hear that blessed Holy One, by the spirit of prophecy, crying out, "the zeal of thine house hath eaten me up." (Ps. lxix. 9.) And when we behold in confirmation of it, such a miracle as scourging from the temple the multitude of those who performed it--a miracle, properly considered, almost as great as any Christ performed on earth; such a view of Jesus may, but nothing else can, give a lively idea of zeal! (John ii. 13-17.)

ZEBEDEE

He was the father of two apostles, James, and John. His name seems to have been derived from Zabad, portion. Hence also, Zebadiah, portion of the Lord. (Matt. iv. 21.)

ZEBOIM

One of the cities of the plain. (Gen. xiv. 2.) The word appears to be plural, and probably the place abounded with deer and goats, as the word means.

ZEBULUN, or ZEBULON

A place in Capernaum. (Matt. iv. 13.) One of Jacob's sons was called by this name, to whom a blessed promise was given. (Gen. xxx. 20. Deut. xxxiii. 18. compared with Gen. xlix. 13.) Perhaps, the root of this name is Zabad, to endow, or finish.

ZEDEKIAH

There are several of this name in Scripture; and it is no wonder, being a compound of Zedek, justice--and Jah, Lord. The Lord is my judge. And how very blessed is such a name, considered with an eye to Christ, the justifier of his redeemed!

ZEPHANIAH - ZOAR

ZEPHANIAH

An eminent prophet, though his writings are small. His name is a compound, from Tzaphan, secret--and Jah, the Lord. And very suited was this name to the prophet; for much of the Lord Jesus is in his prophecy, when opened and explained by God the Holy Ghost. Hence, that Scripture, "the secret of the Lord is with them that fear him, and he will shew them his covenant." (Ps. xxv. 14.)

ZERUBBABEL, or ZOROBABEL

A man much engaged in building the second temple. (Zech. iv. 6, 7.) The name seems to have been derived from Zer, stranger--and Babel, confusion.

ZERUIAH

Well known in David's history. Perhaps from Tsarar, chains.

ZION

See Mount Zion.

ZOAR

The city of Lot's refuge. The very name signifies little. (Gen. xix. 22.)

Other Related Titles

In addition to *The Poor Man's Concordance & Dictionary* that you now possess, Solid Ground Christian Books is delighted to announce our completion of the following titles by Robert Hawker:

Hawker's Poor Man's Old Testament Commentary in six wonderful volumes. This set contains more than 4,200 pages of exposition and reflection by the man who loved Christ and delighted to make Him known to others. The volumes are as follows:

> Volume One: Genesis – Numbers
> Volume Two: Deuteronomy – 2 Samuel
> Volume Three: 1st Kings – Esther
> Volume Four: Job – Psalms
> Volume Five: Proverbs – Lamentations
> Volume Six: Ezekiel – Malachi

Hawker's Poor Man's New Testament Commentary in three wonderful volumes. The volumes are as follows:

> Volume One: Matthew – John
> Volume Two: Acts – Ephesians
> Volume Three: Philippians – Revelation

Hawker's Poor Man's Morning and Evening Portions which is a daily devotional work of more than 900 pages. In the words of Don Fortner:

> "*Robert Hawker's* **Poor Man's Daily Portions** *is, in my opinion, the very best book of daily devotional readings I have yet read. My wife and I have used it for many years, always with great profit to our souls. Why is it such a blessing? It is full of Christ and full of grace. Every reading leaves the reader looking to, resting in, and rejoicing in our all-glorious Savior.*"

Solid Ground Christian Books
2090 Columbiana Rd, Suite 2000
Birmingham AL 35266
(205) 443-0311
sgcb@charter.net
http://solid-ground-books.com

Ric Ergenbright Titles

The beautiful photograph that graces the cover of these volumes of Robert Hawker was taken by Ric Ergenbright, a man who rejoices in the sovereign grace of God. He has published several volumes that combine the beauty of God's creation with the glory of His Word. We are delighted to offer the following for sale:

The Art of God
This is the award winning volume that has been useful all over the world in spreading the glory of God's saving grace. Ric gives the story of God's grace in his life which is the backdrop of this breathtaking volume.

Think About These Things
This is the second volume in the *Art of God* trilogy, and in the words of John Piper, *"Here you will find (as always with Ric Ergenbright) the art of God wrapped in the Word of God."* Another splendid, God-honoring book.

The Image of God
This is the third and final volume of the *Art of God* trilogy. This time Ric turns his camera to people, created in the image of God. People from all over the world are portrayed here with Scripture illuminating each photo.

Reflections
This is a devotional book unlike any you have seen. It takes Scripture, hymns and beautiful photography and leads you to see God, His world and His Word in a new way. There is room given for you to write down the things that you have learned that can be passed down to your posterity.

The Mercy of God and the Misery of Job
Ric joins his unique gift with John Piper to bring home the message of Job in a new and creative way. This book not only contains the words of Piper and the photos of Ergenbright, but it also has a cd of the book read by John Piper as well. This book will help you understand both the mercy of God and the misery of Job in new and profound ways.

Please visit Ric's website at **http://ricergenbright.com** and see the magnificent work that he has been doing in service of the King of kings.

Order from us toll free at **1-877-666-9469**
E-mail us at **sgcb@charter.net**
Visit our web site at **http://solid-ground-books.com**

Other SGCB Classic Reprints

Solid Ground Christian Books is honored to present the following titles, many for the first time in more than a century:

COLLECTED WORKS of James Henley Thornwell (4 vols.)
CALVINISM IN HISTORY by *Nathaniel S. McFetridge*
OPENING SCRIPTURE: *Hermeneutical Manual* by *Patrick Fairbairn*
THE ASSURANCE OF FAITH by *Louis Berkhof*
THE PASTOR IN THE SICK ROOM by *John D. Wells*
THE BUNYAN OF BROOKLYN: *Life & Sermons of I.S. Spencer*
THE NATIONAL PREACHER: *Sermons from 2nd Great Awakening*
FIRST THINGS: First Lessons God Taught Mankind *Gardiner Spring*
BIBLICAL & THEOLOGICAL STUDIES by *1912 Faculty of Princeton*
THE POWER OF GOD UNTO SALVATION by *B.B. Warfield*
THE LORD OF GLORY by *B.B. Warfield*
A GENTLEMAN & A SCHOLAR: *Memoir of J.P. Boyce* by *J. Broadus*
SERMONS TO THE NATURAL MAN by *W.G.T. Shedd*
SERMONS TO THE SPIRITUAL MAN by *W.G.T. Shedd*
HOMILETICS AND PASTORAL THEOLOGY by *W.G.T. Shedd*
A PASTOR'S SKETCHES 1 & 2 by *Ichabod S. Spencer*
THE PREACHER AND HIS MODELS by *James Stalker*
IMAGO CHRISTI by *James Stalker*
A HISTORY OF PREACHING by *Edwin C. Dargan*
LECTURES ON THE HISTORY OF PREACHING by *J. A. Broadus*
THE SCOTTISH PULPIT by *William Taylor*
THE SHORTER CATECHISM ILLUSTRATED by *John Whitecross*
THE CHURCH MEMBER'S GUIDE by *John Angell James*
THE SUNDAY SCHOOL TEACHER'S GUIDE by *John A. James*
CHRIST IN SONG: *Hymns of Immanuel from All Ages* by *Philip Schaff*
COME YE APART: *Daily Words from the Four Gospels* by *J.R. Miller*
DEVOTIONAL LIFE OF THE S.S. TEACHER by *J.R. Miller*

Call us Toll Free at 1-877-666-9469
Send us an e-mail at sgcb@charter.net
Visit us on line at solid-ground-books.com

Uncovering Buried Treasure to the Glory of God

LaVergne, TN USA
19 November 2010

205621LV00006B/29/A